FEDERAL TAXATION PRACTICE and PROCEDURE

Tenth Edition

Robert J. Misey, Jr.

William T. Lundeen

Michael G. Goller

®CCH

a Wolters Kluwer business

Editorial Staff

Production . . . . Christopher Zwirek

The content of this book is the opinion of the writers and does not necessarily represent the positions of the Internal Revenue Service.

This publication is designed to provide accurate and authoritative information in regard to the subject matter covered. It is sold with the understanding that the publisher is not engaged in rendering legal, accounting, or other professional service and that the author is not offering such advice in this publication. If legal advice or other expert assistance is required, the services of a competent professional person should be sought.

ISBN: 978-0-8080-2686-0

Printed in the United States of America

Certified Chain of Custody
SUSTAINABLE FORESTRY INITIATIVE
Promoting Sustainable Forestry
www.sfiprogram.org
SFI-01268

SFI label applies to the text stock

About the Authors

ROBERT J. MISEY, JR., J.D., M.B.A., LL.M., is a shareholder with the law firm of Reinhart Boerner Van Deuren s.c. in Milwaukee, Wisconsin. Mr. Misey concentrates his practice in the areas of tax controversies and international taxation. He previously worked as an attorney with the IRS Chief Counsel (International) in Washington, D.C. and as a large-case attorney in the Western and Southeast Regions. He has tried 23 cases before the U.S. Tax Court.

Mr. Misey received his Master of Laws degree, with high distinction, from Georgetown University, where he was the graduate student editor of *The Tax Lawyer*, and received his Juris Doctor and Master of Business Administration degrees from Vanderbilt University. He is a member of the Tax Section of the District of Columbia, California, and Wisconsin bars and a former member of the Inn of Court at the U.S. Tax Court in Washington, D.C.

Mr. Misey often speaks on taxation at continuing education programs and has written numerous articles. He also teaches in the Master of Taxation program in the University of Wisconsin system. He is a co-author of a *Practical Guide to U.S. Taxation of International Transactions*, which is published by CCH, a Wolters Kluwer business.

WILLIAM T. LUNDEEN, C.P.A., J.D., LL.M., has served in tax positions in all three branches of the federal government as well as in the private sector and in state government.

While on the staff of a Senate Finance Committee member, Mr. Lundeen worked on matters related to the Economic Recovery Tax Act of 1981. After graduating from the University of Virginia School of Law in 1984, where he served as an Articles Editor of *The Virginia Tax Review*, he practiced tax law in New York City with a Wall Street boutique firm, Everett, Johnson & Breckinridge. There, he worked on matters such as corporate reorganizations and Eurobond financing. Upon graduation from New York University School of Law with an LL.M. in Taxation in 1988, Mr. Lundeen was appointed an Attorney-Advisor at the United States Tax Court where he served for two years. Thereafter, Mr. Lundeen served from 1990 to 1995 as an attorney within the Office of Associate Chief Counsel (International) where, first, he worked extensively on Subpart F matters and, then, on foreign currency issues including a win in a case of first impression involving IRC Sec. 988. In his last assignment within the Chief Counsel's Office, Mr. Lundeen led teams that negotiated Advance Pricing Agreements with financial institutions that engaged in continual global trading of derivatives.

From the Internal Revenue Service, Mr. Lundeen accepted an appointment as the General Counsel of the State of Illinois Department of Revenue. From 1995 to 1999 he was responsible for the all legal aspects of the Department's mission. Mr. Lundeen re-entered the private sector in 1999 and served as a partner in a regional and then in a Big Four accounting firm where he led the Midwestern tax controversy and risk management services practice. Currently, Mr. Lundeen serves as a Competent Authority Analyst in the Internal Revenue Service's Office of Tax Treaty. Mr. Lundeen authored his contributions to the *10th Edition of Federal Tax Practice and Procedure* prior to assuming his current role with the IRS.

MICHAEL G. GOLLER, J.D., is the Department Chair of Reinhart Boerner Van Deuren's federal Tax Controversy Department. He focuses on tax controversy and tax litigation as well as tax planning. His clients range from large public corporations to mid sized, privately-held businesses and their owners. Michael works on behalf of his clients in disputes with the Internal Revenue Service, Department of Justice and various other taxing authorities. He represents his clients before the United States Tax Court, various Federal District courts, the United States Court of Federal Claims and the Seventh Circuit Court of Appeals.

An experienced tax attorney and tax litigator, Michael helps his clients navigate the challenges of complex federal and state tax audits, disputes, administrative appeals, trials, and subsequent appeals. He has an impressive track record of both trying cases and negotiating favorable settlements for his clients before trial.

Michael regularly shares and deepens his expertise as a tax litigator through professional speaking and writing. He frequently speaks to professional and business audiences and organizations on issues of tax controversy, tax litigation and tax planning. He is listed in the Best Lawyers in America and Milwaukee Super Lawyers.

Michael is a faculty member at the University of Wisconsin Milwaukee's School of Business where he teaches Tax Practice and Procedure in the Graduate Tax Program. He is consistently evaluated by his students as one of the Business School's top teachers.

Michael received his undergraduate degree in accounting and his law degree, cum laude, from Marquette University.

Acknowledgments

I would like to acknowledge the assistance of my father and mentor, Robert J. Misey, Sr., Esq., who provided organizational and, as always, motivational input with respect to various aspects of this work. I would also like to acknowledge the assistance of my legal secretary, the incomparable Donna Simon. Finally, I would like to acknowledge the professional support and encouragement of my managers at various offices of the IRS Chief Counsel—Barbara M. Leonard, George M. Sellinger, and Robert A. Nadler—your retirements are truly a loss to the tax bar!

Robert J. Misey, Jr.

I would like to acknowledge the invaluable support, assistance and guidance given to me by my legal secretary, Jacki Serrano.

Michael G. Goller

Preface

As a practitioner, it is extremely important to have an understanding of the workings of the Internal Revenue Service and the authority of its various employees. The current administration has proposed an agenda of increased taxes and an increase in the number of personnel to enforce those tax laws. The Internal Revenue Service has also created an issue-oriented system that focuses on the severity of tax compliance with respect to an issue and those issues are categorized as either Tier I, Tier II, or Tier III. This text addresses the fundamentals of dealing with the Internal Revenue Service in its current state.

Robert J. Misey, Jr.
William T. Lundeen
Michael G. Goller

October 2011

TABLE OF CONTENTS

Chapter 15: Claims for Refund

Chapter 16: Private Letter Rulings and Determination Letters

Paragraph

Chapter 17: International Tax Practice and Procedure

Chapter 18: Criminal Tax Procedure

Chapter 19: Indirect Methods of Proving Income

CHAPTER 1
ORGANIZATION OF THE INTERNAL REVENUE SERVICE

¶101 INTRODUCTION

All tax practitioners must possess an understanding of the organizational structure of the Internal Revenue Service (IRS). This should include an awareness of the responsibilities, power and authority granted to the various representatives of the IRS. The IRS is part of the Treasury Department. It is headed by the Commissioner of Internal Revenue, who serves under the direction of the Secretary of the Treasury. The Commissioner is appointed by the President for a five-year term.

¶102 THE RESTRUCTURED INTERNAL REVENUE SERVICE

In accordance with the IRS Restructuring and Reform Act of 1998 (the Act),[1] the IRS modified its entire structure. In response to the Act, the IRS set out to make five fundamental changes:

1. Redefine its business practices;

2. Rebuild its organizational structure;

3. Establish management roles with clear responsibility;

4. Create a balanced set of performance measures; and

5. Implement new and revamped technology to support the changes mentioned above.

The IRS's restructuring primarily focused on changes number two and three. The restructuring improved customer service, encouraged voluntary compliance and streamlined collection efforts.

The fundamental nature of the IRS's restructuring is reflected in the way its mission statement changed. Its old mission statement provided as follows:

> The purpose of the Internal Revenue Service is to collect the proper amount of tax revenue at the least cost; serve the public by continually improving the quality of our products and services; and perform in a manner warranting the highest degree of public confidence in our integrity, efficiency, and fairness.[2]

The IRS's new mission is to:

> Provide America's taxpayers top quality service by helping them understand and meet their tax responsibilities and by applying the tax law with integrity and fairness to all.[3]

---

[1] P.L. 105-206.
[2] IRB 1998-01.

[3] See the IRS website (www.irs.gov/irs/article/0,,id=98141,00.html).

The IRS's new structure is vastly different from the old, pyramid-type organization. Under the old structure, the IRS was comprised of a National Office, four Regional Offices, 33 District Offices and 10 Service Centers. Each District Office and Service Center was charged with the responsibility of administering the entire tax law for every type of taxpayer within a defined geographic area (see Exhibit 1-1 at ¶108). The restructuring—while maintaining much of the National Office structure—eliminated Regional and District offices and in their place created operating divisions (see Exhibit 1-2 at ¶109).

National Office. The Act resulted in the most comprehensive restructuring of the IRS in half a century. The IRS reorganized itself principally around a service delivery model focused on populations of similar taxpayers. While much of the National Office organization remained the same, significant changes did take place.

The Commissioner.[4] The IRS continues to be led by a Commissioner appointed directly by the President of the United States with the advice and consent of the U.S. Senate. However, now the Commissioner's term is for five years.

Principal Offices That Report to the Commissioner. In addition to the Chief of Staff to the Commissioner, several IRS functions report directly to the Commissioner. Those include: The Office of Chief Counsel; the Office of Appeals; the National Taxpayer Advocate; Equal Employment Opportunity and Diversity; Research Analysis and Statistics; and Communication and Liaison. We discuss a few key features of several of these offices next.

Office of Chief Counsel.

The Chief Counsel of the IRS is appointed by the President to provide legal services to the IRS through the Office of Chief Counsel. There are three major areas of the Office of Chief Counsel.

Technical. The Chief Counsel Technical organization is located in the National Office and its role is to provide authoritative legal interpretations of the tax law. This responsibility involves issuing regulations, revenue rulings, private letter rulings, technical advice and advance pricing agreements.

Division Counsel. Within the Office of Chief Counsel there is an Operating Division Counsel for each operating division. This Operating Division Counsel provides legal advice and representation and participates in the plans and activities of the operating division management. Each Operating Division Counsel serves as a counterpart to the General Manager of each of the four operating divisions. The Operating Division Counsel and staff are physically located on site at each of the four operating division headquarters. Counsel's geographic co-location is important for maintaining a close working relationship with the General Manager of each operating division.[5]

The main focus of the Operating Division Counsel is to provide legal services to the operating divisions, to take part in planning the strategic use of litigation resources, and to assist the operating divisions in developing compliance approaches and new taxpayer service initiatives.

---

[4] Today's IRS Organization, www.irs.gov.

[5] *IRS Watch* by David Blattner and Kristen Starling, and *Tax Practice and Procedure,* June/July 1999 edition, page 11.

It is hoped that by physically locating the Operating Division Counsels at the operating division locations, taxpayers' needs will be more clearly understood, legal issues will be identified and resolved earlier, and better coordination and communication with the operating divisions will result. However, due to the close proximity of counsel with the operating divisions, it may be more difficult to retain impartiality, consistency and uniformity. To counter this possibility, the National Office Subject Matter Experts are organized by Internal Revenue Code section matter and report to the Chief Counsel, as opposed to the Operating Division Counsel. In addition, the Operating Division Counsel reports to the Chief Counsel rather than the Operating Division General Manager to ensure independence.

Field Counsel. Prior to 2000, the Office of Chief Counsel organized its field legal operation on a geographic basis. In 2000, the Office of Chief Counsel reorganized its field legal operations based upon taxpayer classification in order to align themselves with the new IRS operating divisions. This reorganization caused difficulty in some field legal offices due to workload imbalances and the limitation in the range of experiences available to individual attorneys. In 2006, the Chief Counsel reorganized its field operations using a "matrix management" structure that is an attempt to combine certain features of the old geographic structure with certain features of the new taxpayer classification structure. There are now 49 managing counsel, six area teams and one national field leadership team. A key feature for practitioners is that there will be a single legal managing counsel in charge of each office.

Office of Appeals.

The Appeals Office is headquartered in Washington, D.C. but maintains the geographic location of current offices. Historically, Appeals has had a geographically-based structure but as part of the restructuring of the IRS it moved to a functionally-based system with Appeals officers assigned to work on cases from a particular operating division. This realignment proved difficult to maintain in the smaller offices and led to workload disparity and morale problems. After a reassessment of Appeals in 2002, it was decided to change back to a geographically-based structure. Currently, the field operations of Appeals are divided into nine areas under an Area Director. Each Area Director reports to the Director, Field Operations West or the Director, Field Operations East. Local offices are under the direction of Appeals Team Managers, who report to the Area Directors. We discuss the Office of Appeals in more detail in Chapter 12.

Taxpayer Advocate Service.[6]

The National Taxpayer Advocate was designed to help taxpayers who have problems with the IRS that have not been resolved through the normal administrative process. The National Taxpayer Advocate is organized around two major functions: (1) the casework function, and (2) the systemic analysis and the advocacy function. The purpose of the first function is resolving all individual taxpayer problems with the IRS. The systemic analysis and advocacy function is responsible for working with the operating divisions to identify systemic problems, analyze root causes, implement solutions to mitigate such problems and proactively identify potential problems with new systems and procedures.

The National Taxpayer Advocate is physically located in geographic locations so as to allow contact with local taxpayers. A National Taxpayer Advocate

---

[6] Taxpayer Advocate Service At-A-Glance. www.irs.gov.

within each operating division helps to identify systemic problems in the division.

As part of their ongoing effort to help taxpayers, the National Taxpayer Advocate established the Citizens Advocacy Panel (CAP) pilot program in 1998, which was expanded nationwide in 2002 and renamed the Taxpayer Advocacy Panel.

Communications & Liaison.

The mission of Communications & Liaison is to communicate a consistent message to internal and external stakeholders, i.e., those affected by the mission of the IRS such as the general public, Congress, the media, and taxpayers. Communications & Liaison delivers on its mission through three primary offices: Office of Communications & Liaison, Office of Legislative Affairs, and the Office of National Public Liaison.

Deputy Commissioners. One of the significant changes brought by the Act was the creation of an additional Deputy Commissioner. Consider for example the expansion of the old Deputy Commissioner in Exhibit 1-1 at ¶108 into that of two Deputy Commissioners in Exhibit 1-2 at ¶109. Under the new National Officer structure there are two Deputy Commissioners, each of whom reports directly to the Commissioner, one for Operations and Support and a second for Services and Enforcement.

Deputy Commissioner for Operations Support. This Deputy Commissioner oversees the integrated internal IRS support functions, with the goal of facilitating economies of scale and instilling better business practices. These functions include: Chief Technology Officer, Agency-Wide Shared Services, Human Capital Officer, Chief Financial Officer, and the Office of Privacy, Information Protection and Data Security. We focus briefly on one of these functions, the Office of Privacy, Information Protection and Data Security.

Office of Privacy, Information Protection and Data Security (PIPDS). This office was formed in July of 2007 to provide a centralized privacy program for the IRS that combines responsibility for all of the major privacy programs within the IRS. PIPDS mission is to protect taxpayers' personally indentifiable information, such as Social Security numbers and to ensure IRS integrity regarding the use of that information.

Deputy Commissioner for Services and Enforcement. This Deputy Commissioner oversees the five primary operating divisions of the restructured IRS along with other mission-critical service and enforcement functions. These operating divisions and functions include: the Wage and Investment Operating Division; the Small Business/Self Employed Operating Division; The Tax Exempt and Government Entities Division; the Large Business & International Operating Division; Global High Wealth Operating Division; Criminal Investigations; Office of Professional Responsibility; and the Whistleblower Office. We discuss each of the later three functions next.

Criminal Investigation. Under the IRS's restructuring plan, Criminal Investigation (CI) reports directly to the IRS Commissioner and Deputy Commissioner. It operates as a nationwide unit with 35 Special Agents in Charge, reporting to six area directors. CI closely coordinates its activities with the operating divisions and is supported by specific attorneys within the Chief Counsel's office.

¶102

CI's mission is to serve the American public by investigating potential criminal violations of the Internal Revenue Code and related financial crimes. CI has been modernized in order to create the structures, systems and processes necessary to comply with its mission. The new CI focuses more on tax administration issues and less on nontax crimes (e.g., drug cases). It provides a streamlined investigative review process and a geographic alignment that is more consistent with the location of the various United States Attorney's Offices. Agents working for CI will obtain more training in basic tax law. Further, IRS counsel will be consulted throughout the investigative process.

Office of Professional Responsibility. The mission of the Office of Professional Responsibility (OPR) is to establish and enforce consistent professional standards for tax professionals, and other individuals and groups subject to IRS Circular 230 entitled, "Rules of Practice Before the IRS". We will discuss the professional standards of Circular 230 as well as the way in which OPR operates in Chatper 2.

Whistleblower Office. Established by the Tax Relief and Health Care Act of 2006, the office processes tips received from individuals who report tax problems in their place of employment, in their everyday lives, or anywhere else where tax problems may be encountered. An award worth between 15 and 30 percent of the total proceeds that the IRS collects may be paid to whistleblowers provided that the IRS acts on the information they receive and provided that the amount identified by the whisteblower meets certain criteria. The Whistleblower Office takes in the reports, assesses them and then credible reports are assigned throughout the IRS for further investigation and follow-up.

Each of the above functions, whether positioned within the IRS at the Commissioner level or at a Deputy Commissioner level, are necessary for the IRS to serve taxpayers and to enforce the internal revenue laws. Howerver, it is important to note that the formation of the four "operating divisions" constitute the most fundamental change brought by the Act.

¶103 THE OPERATING DIVISIONS

The starting point to understanding the restructured IRS is the five major operating divisions.

The Wage and Investment Income Division (W & I).[7] W & I covers individual taxpayers, including those who file jointly, who receive wage and/or investment income. W & I is comprised of an estimated 120 million filers. Most of these taxpayers deal with the IRS once a year when filing their income tax returns. Further, due to over-withholding, most of these taxpayers receive refunds. Compliance matters are focused on a limited range of issues such as dependency exemptions, credits, filing status and deductions.

Within the W & I group there are four operating units:

1. Customer Assistance, Research and Education (CARE)—this unit's primary role is education;

---

[7] W & I Division At-A-Glance, www.irs.gov.

2. Customer Account Services (CAS)—this unit's role is to process returns submitted by taxpayers and validate that the proper taxes have been paid; and

3. Compliance—the role of this unit is to address the limited compliance and collection issues that may arise with respect to this group of taxpayers.

4. Electronic Tax Administration and Refundable Credits—the role of this unit is to oversee all aspects of electronic information exchanged between the IRS and individual taxpayers, businesses and practitioners.

Most of the income earned by W & I taxpayers is reported by third parties (e.g., employers, banks, brokerage firms). Furthermore, almost all of the tax on this income is collected through third party withholding. Accordingly, this group is highly compliant.

Small Business and Self-Employed Division (SB/SE).[8] SB/SE covers self-employed individuals and small businesses. This division includes corporations and partnerships with assets less than or equal to $10 million. Further, estate and gift taxpayers, fiduciary returns and all individuals who file international returns are under the jurisdiction of this group. SB/SE includes approximately 57 million filers, 41 million self-employed persons, 9 million small businesses with assets less than 10 million, and 7 million employment, excise, estate and gift tax returns.

The typical SB/SE taxpayer interacts with the IRS four to 60 times per year. Tax obligations of these taxpayers include personal and corporate income taxes, employment taxes, excise taxes and tax withheld from employees. Because of the wide variety of complex tax issues involved, the probability of errors that result in collection and compliance problems is higher with respect to this group than groups of taxpayers in the other divisions.

SB/SE is organized around five major organizations:

1. Collection;

2. Compliance Services Campus Operations;

3. Examination;

4. Specialty Taxes: and

5. Communication, Liaison and Disclosure.

The mission of the Compliance unit is to provide prompt, professional and helpful service to taxpayers. The goal is to increase overall compliance and the fairness of the compliance programs.

Tax-Exempt Organizations and Governmental Entities Division (TE/GE).[9] TE/GE covers pension plans, exempt organizations and the governmental entities. This group is comprised of about 3 million filers. These entities generally pay no income tax; however, this group pays over $220 billion in employment taxes and income tax withholding and controls about $8.2 trillion in assets. There are also three other large groups served by TE/GE. First, private and public

---

[8] SB/SE Division At-A-Glance, www.irs.gov.   [9] TE/GE Division At-A-Glance, www.irs.gov.

retirement plans with some 4 trillion in assets. Second, approximately 1.6 million exempt organizations, of which 400,000 are religious organizations, with approximately $2.4 trillion in assets. Third government entities with approximately $1.8 trillion in outstanding exempt bonds and other federal, estate, local and Indian tribe government entities.

Large Businesses & International Operating Division (LB&I).[10] LB&I includes businesses with assets over $10 million (i.e., about 210,000 filers). This group pays hundreds of billions in taxes (i.e., income, employment, excise and withholding) each year. Collection issues are rare; however, many complex matters such as tax law interpretation, accounting and regulation issues are common. The largest taxpayers in this group deal with the IRS on a continuous basis.

The LB&I is aligned by industry groupings, as opposed to a geographical alignment. These groups are as follows:

1. Financial Services;

2. Natural Resources and Construction;

3. Heavy Manufacturing and Transportation;

4. Communications, Technology and Media;

5. Retailers, Food, Pharmaceuticals, and Healthcare; and

6. Global High Wealth

We will discuss LB&I and its functions in more detail in chapter 5.

¶104 IRS OVERSIGHT BOARD

In addition to making internal changes to the IRS, the Act also created or enhanced certain external stakeholders. One external body that the Act created is the IRS Oversight Board. The Oversight Board is a nine-member independent body comprised of seven members appointed by the President of the United States with the advice and consent of the U.S. Senate and two others: The Secretary of the Treasury and the Commissioner of Internal Revenue. The Oversight Board is charged to oversee the IRS as the IRS administers the internal revenue laws.

The Oversight Board lends its experience, independence, and stability to the IRS so that the IRS can stay focused in meeting its short term and long term goals. For example, in the 2005 Annual Report of the Oversight Board, Chairman Raymond T. Wagner kept pressure on the IRS to stay focused on service channels that met *both* IRS and taxpayer needs, not just the IRS needs:

> "It is understandable in light of budget reductions that the IRS is looking to funnel taxpayers to the channels that are least expensive for the IRS to operate. However, taxpayer needs and preferences must also be taken into account. . . . The IRS should perform more research . . . [that] could help the IRS decide which functions were most effectively performed by each service

---

[10] LB&I Division At-A-Glance, www.irs.gov.

channel—telephone, internet, e-mail, and in-person—and how to influence taxpayers to use the most appropriate channel for each circumstance."

¶105 TREASURY INSPECTOR GENERAL FOR TAX ADMINISTRATION

Another external stakeholder established by the Act was the Treasury Inspector General for Tax Administration (TIGTA). The purpose of TIGTA is to provide independent oversight of internal IRS activities. In this way TIGTA makes two valuable contributions to federal tax administration. First, TIGTA promotes efficiency and effectiveness of tax administration by its internal inspections and reports on tax administration programs. Second, TIGTA prevents and detects fraud, waste and abuse within the IRS by its internal investigations of IRS personnel.

¶106 GOVERNMENT ACCOUNTABILITY OFFICE

Although the Government Accountability Office (GAO) has been in existence long before the Act, the GAO periodically studies how well the IRS is performing its responsibility to administer our internal revenue laws. For example, in a 2005 report entitled, "Continued Progress Requires Addressing Resource Management Challenges" the GAO found that while the IRS was making progress in delivering better service since the passage of the Act, GAO also found that the IRS was experiencing troubling declines in enforcement staffing.

¶107 CONCLUSION

In the wake of the Act, the profile and authority of a number of IRS stakeholders, both internal and external to the IRS, has increased. Throughout, the intent has remained to keep the IRS focused on effective taxpayer service and efficient tax administration and enforcement. In this chapter we have considered the role of the Commissioner, the Deputy Commissioners, the operating divisions, the National Taxpayer Advocate, The IRS Oversight Board, TIGTA, and GAO in ensuring that taxpayers are educated concerning the existence and meaning of our internal revenue laws and that taxpayers respect those laws and pay their fair share of taxes.

¶108 Exhibit 1-1

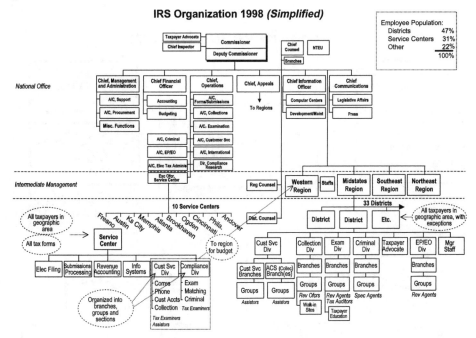

IRS Organization 1998 *(Simplified)*

¶109 Exhibit 1-2

U.S Department of Treasury

Internal Revenue Service

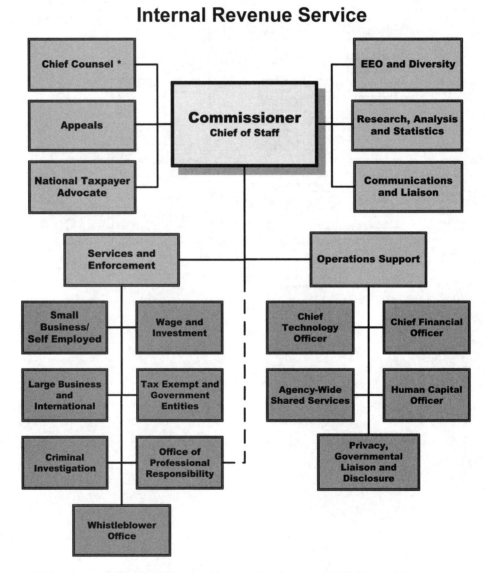

* With respect to tax litigation and the legal interpretation of tax law, the Chief Counsel also reports to the General Counsel of the Treasury Department. On matters solely related to tax policy, the Chief Counsel reports to the Treasury General Counsel.

¶110 Exhibit 1-3

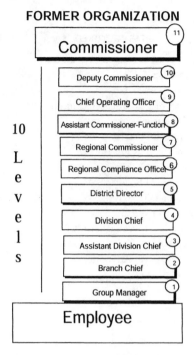

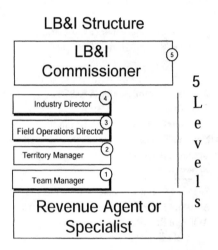

¶111 Exhibit 1-4

Partial List of IRS Job Titles

OLD	RESTRUCTURED
National Office	*National Office*
Commissioner	Commissioner
Chief Counsel	Chief Counsel
Associate Chief Counsels (Technical)	Associate Chief Counsels (Technical)
	Division Counsels
Assistant Commissioner (Examination)	Eliminated
Assistant Commissioner (Collections)	Eliminated
	Commissioner SB/SE
	Commissioner LB&I
Assistant Commissioner (EP/EO)	Commissioner TE/GE
Chief Operations	Commissioner W&I
Assistant Commissioner (Criminal)	Chief Criminal Investigations (CI)
National Director of Appeals	Chief Appeals
Taxpayer Advocate	National Taxpayer Advocate
Regional Offices	*Area/Industry Offices*
Regional Commissioners	Eliminated
Assistant Regional Commissioner (Exam)	Eliminated
Assistant Regional Commissioner (Collections)	Eliminated
	LB&I Industry Directors
	SB/SE Area* Directors
Assistant Regional Commissioner (CI)	CI Area Directors
Regional Counsel	LB&I Industry Counsels
	SB/SE Area Counsels
	TE/GE Area Counsels
	CI Area Counsels
Regional Director of Appeals	LB&I Area Directors
	SB/SE Area Directors
Regional Problem Resolution Officer	National Advocate Area Director
Assistant Regional Commissioner (EP/EO)	EP Area Directors
	EO Area Directors
District Offices	*Field (Local) Offices*
District Director	Eliminated**
Chief Examination Division	Eliminated
Chief Collection Division	Eliminated
	LB&I Industry Territory Managers
	SB/SE Territory Managers
Chief Criminal Investigation	Special Agent in Charge
Chief Appeals	LB&I Team Managers
	SB/SE Team Managers
Chief Problem Resolution	National Advocate Local Manager
Examination Case Managers	LB&I Team Managers

District Offices	*Field (Local) Offices*
Examination Group Managers	SB/SE Group Managers
Collection Group Managers	SB/SE Group Managers
Revenue Agents	Revenue Agents
Revenue Officers	Revenue Officers
Tax Auditors	Tax Compliance Officers
Special Agents	Special Agents
Appeals Officers	Appeals Officers
Counsel Attorneys	Counsel Attorneys

* Areas differ geographically from prior Regions and differ geographically within the various functions.

** A manager in each office is designated "Senior Commissioner's Representative" and has responsibility for various internal administrative duties.

¶112 DISCUSSION QUESTIONS

1. The directory for the IRS at the Federal Building, 1234 West Main Street, Anywhereville, USA, contains the following listing:

Room 101—Appeals Officer

Room 102—Special Agent

Room 103—Revenue Agent SB/SE

Room 104—Team Member LB&I

Room 105—Local Taxpayer Advocate

Room 106—Tax Auditor/Tax Compliance Officer

Room 107—Reviewer

Room 108—Inspector

Room 109—Revenue Officer

Room 110—Customer Service Representative

Room 111—Chief Counsel

Room 112—Group Manager SB/SE

Room 113—Team Manager LB&I

Room 114—Territory Manager Financial Services LB&I

Situation A

Mary Mutual, a life insurance sales agent, receives a notice from the IRS that her return has been selected for audit. It asks her to bring her books and records for a conference at the Federal Building.

To which room should Mary Mutual go?

Situation B

Billy Bankrupt has received a bill for additional tax due in the amount of $5,000. At the moment Bankrupt cannot pay the entire amount, and he wishes to pay it off in installments.

To which room should Billy Bankrupt go?

Situation C

Ingrid Informer, who is employed as a nurse in Dr. Deceptive's office, is very upset at Deceptive because he cut her salary. She wishes to inform the IRS that Deceptive has been running a duplicate set of books and has been omitting a substantial portion of his gross receipts from his tax returns for the past five years. She has also read that as an informant she can receive a fee of up to 10% of the tax collected as the result of the information that she brings to the IRS.

To which office should she go?

Situation D

You recently accepted a job as tax manager for IBN Corporation. Your first day on the job you receive a letter from the IRS which is signed by "Harry Hawk, Group 6969." Later that day, while attending a luncheon seminar with other tax professionals, one of your colleagues tells you that Group 6969 is the "LB&I" group.

Which office is occupied by Harry Hawk?

Situation E

Friendly Fast Food LLC, owned and operated by Frank Friendly, is a small "family type" restaurant. On February 10, 2009, he received a notice that the restaurant's 2003, 2004 and 2005 tax returns are being examined by the IRS. He is notified that the IRS would like to begin the audit at the place of business on March 15, 2007. Frank would like to postpone the audit.

To whom would he address his request?

2. C-Ment Industries, Inc. is in the business of designing, manufacturing and selling concrete equipment vehicles. In 2009, C-Ment designed and manufactured a line of concrete pumping vehicles to transfer concrete from cement mixers to specific points within a construction site. The pumping equipment is mounted on a specially modified truck chassis.

Situation A

C-Ment wishes to ensure that the concrete pumping vehicles are not subject to excise tax under Internal Revenue Code Sec. 4051.

(1) With what *level* of the IRS will Wheeler have to deal?

(2) With which office?

Situation B

Assume that C-Ment goes ahead with the sales of the concrete pumping vehicles without seeking assurance as to the excise tax consequences from the IRS. Two years later its excise tax returns are reviewed at one of the IRS campuses.

(1) Who determines if the return should be audited?

(2) To what level of the IRS are C-Ment's returns sent if it is determined that it will be necessary to contact the corporation during the audit process?

Situation C

In discussing this case with the IRS representative, C-Ment has tried to convince the revenue agent that the concrete pumping vehicles are not subject to excise tax. Because the agent will not concede the issue, C-Ment now seeks to get a higher level of the IRS to advise the agent that "as a matter of law" the vehicles are not subject to excise tax under Code Sec. 4051.

(1) What *level* of the IRS, if any, would make such a determination?

(2) How would C-Ment go about requesting IRS participation?

Situation D

Assume that eventually the IRS determines that there is additional excise tax due as a result of C-Ment's improper accounting for the concrete pumping vehicles. C-Ment wishes to seek review of this determination within the IRS.

(1) With what level of the IRS must Wheeler deal for such formal review?

(2) What formalities must Wheeler follow?

Situation E

Assume that eventually the IRS determination is upheld throughout the formal review and that C-Ment is sent a bill for the tax due resulting from the deficiency.

(1) What level of the IRS sends the bill to C-Ment?

(2) Where can C-Ment make payment of the amount of the bill?

Situation F

Because of financial difficulties, C-Ment is not in a position to pay this bill in full.

(1) With what level or levels of the IRS will C-Ment deal in attempting to resolve the unpaid bill?

(2) If personal contact with C-Ment is required to resolve the problem, who will make the contact?

CHAPTER 2
PRACTICE BEFORE THE INTERNAL REVENUE SERVICE

¶201 INTRODUCTION

What is Practice Before the Internal Revenue Service?

Taxpayers can have various dealings with the Internal Revenue Service (IRS): (1) a return may be selected for audit and the taxpayer invited to attend a conference with the examiner, (2) the collection function may request an interview to determine whether the taxpayer is in a financial position to pay a delinquency, or (3) the taxpayer may seek an advance determination as to the tax consequences of a proposed transaction. In each of these instances, a taxpayer can appear personally to deal with the IRS, or he or she can authorize another person to act on behalf of the taxpayer as a representative. Such representation may constitute "practice before the Internal Revenue Service."

The rule that defines what practice before the Internal Revenue Service means is found in a document published by the Treasury Department and is commonly referred to as "Circular 230," located at Title 31, Part 10, Code of Federal Regulations. In general, Section 10.2 of Circular 230 provides that practice before the IRS encompasses any presentation of information to the IRS with respect to a taxpayer's rights, privileges or liabilities. It includes, but is not limited to, the preparation and filing of documents, communication with IRS personnel and the representation of a client at Conferences, hearings or meetings.[1]

Significantly, Section 10.2(a)(4) of Circular 230 was amended in 2011 to provide explicitly that "preparing documents" and "filing documents" constitutes practice before the Internal Revenue Service.[2] This amendment is intended to make clear that preparing tax returns and any other documents for presentation to the Internal Revenue Service falls within the scope of activities that are regulated by Circular 230.

Who May Practice Before the Internal Revenue Service?

A federal statute allows two groups of professionals to represent others before the IRS without further qualification. Public Law 89-332[3] (the Act) provides that any attorney (defined as a member in good standing of the bar of the highest court of any state or the District of Columbia) can represent others before any agency of the federal government (except the Patent Office) upon filing a written

---

[1] Treasury Department Circular 230, § 10.2(a)(4).
[2] Circular 230, § 10.2(a)(4).
[3] Act of November 8, 1965, 79 Stat. 1282 § 1(a).

declaration that he or she is qualified as an attorney and is authorized by his or her client. The Act further entitles any person duly qualified to practice as a certified public accountant in any state or the District of Columbia to represent others before the IRS, upon filing a declaration.[4]

In particular, Section 10.3 of Circular 230 authorizes professionals in addition to attorneys and certified public accountants to practice before the Internal Revenue Service. Specifically Circular 230 authorizes enrolled agents, enrolled actuaries, enrolled retirement plan agents, and certain others to practice before the Internal Revenue Service. Generally these practitioners must satisfy the particular qualification requirements promulgated by the Treasury Department before they may practice.

After undertaking an extensive study in 2010,[5] the Treasury Department articulated the goal of registering and regulating tax return preparers as part of an effort to upgrade the oversight and quality of practice before the Internal Revenue Service. Accordingly, more individuals have been made "practitioners" under Circular 230 which results in them being regulated under Circular 230.

Of particular significance, Circular 230 creates a new category of practitioner, the "registered tax return preparer." Section 10.2(a)(8) of Circular 230 defines a "tax return preparer" as an individual within the meaning of Code section 7701(a)(36) and regulation section 26 CFR 301.7701-15. Accordingly, a tax return preparer includes anyone who for compensation prepared all or substantially all of a tax return even if he or she does not sign the return.

In order for a tax return preparer to become a "registered" tax return preparer, Section 10.5 of Circular 230 requires that the person apply to become "registered" by using prescribed forms and following required procedures set forth by the Internal Revenue Service. In addition the applicant must pay the prescribed fee and may have to undergo an examination. The Internal Revenue Service is authorized to perform a federal tax compliance check to check that the applicant has filed all returns and paid all taxes. And the Internal Revenue Service is further authorized to conduct a suitability check to determine whether the applicant engaged in activity as of the date the application is submitted that would justify suspension or disbarment including disreputable conduct as defined in section 10.51 of Circular 230.

Section 10.3(f)(2) limits the scope of practice of a registered tax return preparer to preparing and signing certain tax returns and claims for refunds, along with other documents submitted to the Internal Revenue Service. The Internal Revenue Service will publish guidance on which forms a registered tax return preparer may prepare and file. A registered tax return preparer is limited in representing a taxpayer in an examination before revenue agents and similar officials to situations in which he or she signed the return and claim. Unless the Internal Revenue Service provides guidance otherwise, a registered tax return preparer may not represent a taxpayer before appeals officers, revenue officers,

---

[4] P.L. 89-332, Act § 1(b).

[5] Publication 4832, Return Preparer Review Report.

Counsel or similar officers. Finally, registered tax return preparers are fully subject to the provisions of Circular 230 in the same manner as other practitioners.

✳ **Example 2-1:** Roger, a registered tax return preparer, received a phone call from Clarie Client informing Roger that the tax return he prepared for Clarie has been selected for examination. Since Roger prepared the return, Circular 230 allows Roger to represent Clarie before the Revenue Agent and others in the examination division. This examination ends up unagreed on all issues. Unless the IRS publisheds permission otherwise, Roger is not authorized to represent claims before IRS Appeals.

Preparer Tax Identification Number

The second major aspect of the Treasury Department's decision to register and regulated tax return preparers is found in Circular 230 Section 10.8 "Return preparation and application of rules to other individuals." Section 10.8 provides that anyone who prepares or assists in preparing all or substantially all of a tax return or a claim for refund must obtain a "preparer tax identification number" or "PTIN." In order to obtain a PTIN a person must be an attorney, certified public accountant, enrolled agent, or registered tax return preparer, unless otherwise provided by regulatory guidance. Finally, anyone required to obtain a PTIN is also subject to the requirements of Circular 230 subpart B relating to practice and is subject to the sanctions in subpart C for violating any regulations.

¶202 ATTORNEYS, CPAs, ENROLLED AGENTS, ENROLLED ACTUARIES, RETIREMENTS PLAN AGENTS AND REGISTERED TAX RETURN PREPARERS

As noted above, the rules governing the right of attorneys, certified public accountants, enrolled agents, enrolled actuaries, enrolled retirement plan agents and registered tax return preparers to practice before the IRS are contained Circular 230. Set forth below is the current text of relevant portions of Subpart A of Circular 230, Rules of Practice Before the IRS (31 C.F.R., Part 10, Subpart A, §§ 10.1-10.9).

PART 10—PRACTICE BEFORE THE INTERNAL REVENUE SERVICE

* * * * *

Subpart A—Rules Governing Authority to Practice

§ 10.1. Offices. (a) *Establishment of office(s).* The Commissioner shall establish the Office of Professional Responsibility and any other office(s) within the Internal Revenue Service necessary to administer and enforce this part. The Commissioner shall appoint the Director of the Office of Professional Responsibility and any other Internal Revenue official(s) to manage and direct any office(s) established to administer or enforce this part. Offices established under this part include, but are not limited to:

[1] The Office of Professional Responsibility, which shall generally have responsibility for matters related to practitioner conduct and discipline, including disciplinary proceedings and sanctions; and

[2] An office with responsibility for matters related to authority to practice before the Internal Revenue Service, including acting on applications for enrollment to practice before the Internal Revenue Service and administering competency testing and continuing education.

(b) Officers and employees within any office established under this part may perform acts necessary or appropriate to carry out the responsibilities of their office(s) under this part or as otherwise prescribed by the Commissioner.

(c) *Acting.* The Commissioner will designate an officer or employee of the Internal Revenue Service to perform the duties of an individual appointed under paragraph (a) of this section in the absence of that officer or employee or during a vacancy in that office.

§ 10.2. Definitions. (a) As used in this part, except where the text provides otherwise—

(1) *Attorney* means any person who is a member in good standing of the bar of the highest court of any state, territory, or possession of the United States, including a Commonwealth, or the District of Columbia.

(2) *Certified public accountant* means any person who is duly qualified to practice as a certified public accountant in any state, territory, or possession of the United States, including a Commonwealth, or the District of Columbia.

(3) *Commissioner* refers to the Commissioner of Internal Revenue.

(4) *Practice before the Internal Revenue Service* comprehends all matters connected with a presentation to the Internal Revenue Service or any of its officers or employees relating to a taxpayer's rights, privileges, or liabilities under laws or regulations administered by the Internal Revenue Service. Such presentations include, but are not limited to, preparing documents; filing documents; corresponding and communicating with the Internal Revenue Service; rendering written advice with respect to any entity, transaction, plan or arrangement, or other plan or arrangement having a potential for tax avoidance or evasion; and representing a client at conferences, hearings, and meetings.

(5) *Practitioner* means any individual described in paragraphs (a), (b), (c), (d), (e), or (f) of § 10.3.

(6) *A tax return* includes an amended tax return and a claim for refund.

(7) *Service* means the Internal Revenue Service.

(8) *Tax return preparer* means any individual within the meaning of section 7701(a)(36) and 26 CFR 301.7701-15.

§ 10.3. Who may practice. (a) *Attorneys.* Any attorney who is not currently under suspension or disbarment from practice before the Internal Revenue Service may practice before the Internal Revenue Service by filing with the Internal Revenue Service a written declaration that the attorney is currently qualified as an attorney and is authorized to represent the party or parties. Notwithstanding the preceding sentence, attorneys who are not currently under suspension or disbarment from practice before the Internal Revenue Service are not required to file a written declaration with the IRS before rendering written advice covered under § 10.35 or § 10.37, but their rendering of this advice is practice before the Internal Revenue Service.

(b) *Certified public accountants.* Any certified public accountant who is not currently under suspension or disbarment from practice before the Internal Revenue Service may practice before the Internal Revenue Service by filing with the Internal Revenue Service a written declaration that the certified public accountant is currently qualified as a certified public accountant and is authorized to represent the party or parties. Notwithstanding the preceding sentence, certified public accountants who are not currently under suspension or disbarment from practice before the Internal Revenue Service are not required to file a written declaration with the IRS before rendering written advice covered under § 10.35 or § 10.37, but their rendering of this advice is practice before the Internal Revenue Service.

(c) *Enrolled agents.* Any individual enrolled as an agent pursuant to this part who is not currently under suspension or disbarment from practice before the Internal Revenue Service may practice before the Internal Revenue Service.

(d) *Enrolled actuaries.* (1) Any individual who is enrolled as an actuary by the Joint Board for the Enrollment of Actuaries pursuant to 29 U.S.C. 1242 who is not currently under suspension or disbarment from practice before the Internal Revenue Service may practice before the Internal Revenue Service by filing with the Internal Revenue Service a written declaration stating that he or she is currently qualified as an enrolled actuary and is authorized to represent the party or parties on whose behalf he or she acts.

(2) Practice as an enrolled actuary is limited to representation with respect to issues involving the following statutory provisions in title 26 of the United States Code: sections 401 (relating to qualification of employee plans), 403(a) (relating to whether an annuity plan meets the require-ments of section 404(a)(2)), 404 (relating to deductibility of employer contributions), 405 (relating to qualification of bond purchase plans), 412 (relating to funding requirements for certain employee plans), 413 (relating to application of qualification requirements to collectively bargained plans and to plans maintained by more than one employer), 414 (relating to definitions and special rules with respect to the employee plan area), 419 (relating to treatment of funded welfare benefits), 419A (relating to qualified asset accounts), 420 (relating to transfers of excess pension assets to retiree health accounts), 4971 (relating to excise taxes payable as a result of an accumulated funding deficiency under section 412), 4972 (relating to tax on nondeductible contributions to qualified employer plans), 4976 (relating to taxes with respect to funded welfare benefit plans), 4980 (relating to tax on reversion of qualified plan assets to employer), 6057 (relating to annual registration of plans), 6058 (relating to information required in connection with certain plans of deferred compensation), 6059 (relating to periodic report of actuary), 6652(e) (relating to the failure to file annual registration and other notifications by pension plan), 6652(f) (relating to the failure to file information required in connection with certain plans of deferred compensation), 6692 (relating to the failure to file actuarial report), 7805(b) (relating to the extent to which an Internal Revenue Service ruling or determination letter coming under the statutory provisions listed here will be applied without retroactive effect); and 29 U.S.C. 1083 (relating to the waiver of funding for nonqualified plans).

(3) An individual who practices before the Internal Revenue Service pursuant to paragraph (d)(1) of this section is subject to the provisions of this part in the same manner as attorneys, certified public accountants, enrolled agents, enrolled retirement plan agents, and registered tax return preparers.

(e) *Enrolled retirement plan agents.* (1) Any individual enrolled as a retirement plan agent pursuant to this part who is not currently under suspension or disbarment from practice before the Internal Revenue Service may practice before the Internal Revenue Service.

(2) Practice as an enrolled retirement plan agent is limited to representation with respect to issues involving the following programs: Employee Plans Determination Letter program; Employee Plans Compliance Resolution System; and Employee Plans Master and Prototype and Volume Submitter program. In addition, enrolled retirement plan agents are generally permitted to represent taxpayers with respect to IRS forms under the 5300 and 5500 series which are filed by retirement plans and plan sponsors, but not with respect to actuarial forms or schedules.

(3) An individual who practices before the Internal Revenue Service pursuant to paragraph (e)(1) of this section is subject to the provisions of this part in the same manner as attorneys, certified public accountants, enrolled agents, enrolled actuaries, and registered tax return preparers.

(f) *Registered tax return preparers.* (1) Any individual who is designated as a registered tax return preparer pursuant to § 10.4(c) of this part who is not currently under suspension or disbarment from practice before the Internal Revenue Service may practice before the Internal Revenue Service.

(2) Practice as a registered tax return preparer is limited to preparing and signing tax returns and claims for refund, and other documents for submission to the Internal Revenue Service. A registered tax return preparer may prepare all or substantially all of a tax return or claim for refund of tax. The Internal Revenue Service will prescribe by forms, instructions, or other appropriate guidance the tax returns and claims for refund that a registered tax return preparer may prepare and sign.

(3) A registered tax return preparer may represent taxpayers before revenue agents, customer service representatives, or similar officers and employees of the Internal Revenue Service (including the Taxpayer Advocate Service) during an examination if the registered tax return preparer signed the tax return or claim for refund for the taxable year or period under examination. Unless otherwise prescribed by regulation or notice, this right does not permit such individual to represent the taxpayer, regardless of the circumstances requiring representation, before appeals

officers, revenue officers, Counsel or similar officers or employees of the Internal Revenue Service or the Treasury Department. A registered tax return preparer's authorization to practice under this part also does not include the authority to provide tax advice to a client or another person except as necessary to prepare a tax return, claim for refund, or other document intended to be submitted to the Internal Revenue Service.

(4) An individual who practices before the Internal Revenue Service pursuant to paragraph (f)(1) of this section is subject to the provisions of this part in the same manner as attorneys, certified public accountants, enrolled agents, enrolled retirement plan agents, and enrolled actuaries.

(g) *Others.* Any individual qualifying under paragraph (d) of § 10.5 or § 10.7 is eligible to practice before the Internal Revenue Service to the extent provided in those sections.

(h) *Government officers and employees, and others.* An individual, who is an officer or employee of the executive, legislative, or judicial branch of the United States Government; an officer or employee of the District of Columbia; a Member of Congress; or a Resident Commissioner may not practice before the Internal Revenue Service if such practice violates 18 U.S.C. 203 or 205.

(i) *State officers and employees.* No officer or employee of any State, or subdivision of any State, whose duties require him or her to pass upon, investigate, or deal with tax matters for such State or subdivision, may practice before the Internal Revenue Service, if such employment may disclose facts or information applicable to Federal tax matters.

§ 10.4. Eligibility to become an enrolled agent, enrolled retirement plan agent, or registered tax return preparer. (a) *Enrollment as an enrolled agent upon examination.* The Commissioner, or delegate, will grant enrollment as an enrolled agent to an applicant eighteen years of age or older who demonstrates special competence in tax matters by written examination administered by, or administered under the oversight of, the Internal Revenue Service, who possesses a current or otherwise valid preparer tax identification number or other prescribed identifying number, and who has not engaged in any conduct that would justify the suspension or disbarment of any practitioner under the provisions of this part.

(b) *Enrollment as a retirement plan agent upon examination.* The Commissioner, or delegate, will grant enrollment as an enrolled retirement plan agent to an applicant eighteen years of age or older who demonstrates special competence in qualified retirement plan matters by written examination administered by, or administered under the oversight of, the Internal Revenue Service, who possesses a current or otherwise valid preparer tax identification number or other prescribed identifying number, and who has not engaged in any conduct that would justify the suspension or disbarment of any practitioner under the provisions of this part.

(c) *Designation as a registered tax return preparer.* The Commissioner, or delegate, may designate an individual eighteen years of age or older as a registered tax return preparer provided an applicant demonstrates competence in Federal tax return preparation matters by written examination administered by, or administered under the oversight of, the Internal Revenue Service, or otherwise meets the requisite standards prescribed by the Internal Revenue Service, possesses a current or otherwise valid preparer tax identification number or other prescribed identifying number, and has not engaged in any conduct that would justify the suspension or disbarment of any practitioner under the provisions of this part.

(d) *Enrollment of former Internal Revenue Service employees.* The Commissioner, or delegate, may grant enrollment as an enrolled agent or enrolled retirement plan agent to an applicant who, by virtue of past service and technical experience in the Internal Revenue Service, has qualified for such enrollment and who has not engaged in any conduct that would justify the suspension or disbarment of any practitioner under the provisions of this part, under the following circumstances:

(1) The former employee applies for enrollment on an Internal Revenue Service form and supplies the information requested on the form and such other information regarding the experience and training of the applicant as may be relevant.

(2) The appropriate office of the Internal Revenue Service provides a detailed report of the nature and rating of the applicant's work while employed by the Internal Revenue Service and a recommendation whether such employment qualifies the applicant technically or otherwise for the desired authorization.

(3) Enrollment as an enrolled agent based on an applicant's former employment with the Internal Revenue Service may be of unlimited scope or it may be limited to permit the presentation of matters only of the particular specialty or only before the particular unit or division of the Internal Revenue Service for which the applicant's former employment has qualified the applicant. Enrollment as an enrolled retirement plan agent based on an applicant's former employment with the Internal Revenue Service will be limited to permit the presentation of matters only with respect to qualified retirement plan matters.

(4) Application for enrollment as an enrolled agent or enrolled retirement plan agent based on an applicant's former employment with the Internal Revenue Service must be made within three years from the date of separation from such employment.

(5) An applicant for enrollment as an enrolled agent who is requesting such enrollment based on former employment with the Internal Revenue Service must have had a minimum of five years continuous employment with the Internal Revenue Service during which the applicant must have been regularly engaged in applying and interpreting the provisions of the Internal Revenue Code and the regulations relating to income, estate, gift, employment, or excise taxes.

(6) An applicant for enrollment as an enrolled retirement plan agent who is requesting such enrollment based on former employment with the Internal Revenue Service must have had a minimum of five years continuous employment with the

¶202

Internal Revenue Service during which the applicant must have been regularly engaged in applying and interpreting the provisions of the Internal Revenue Code and the regulations relating to qualified retirement plan matters.

(7) For the purposes of paragraphs (d)(5) and (6) of this section, an aggregate of 10 or more years of employment in positions involving the application and interpretation of the provisions of the Internal Revenue Code, at least three of which occurred within the five years preceding the date of application, is the equivalent of five years continuous employment.

(e) *Natural persons.* Enrollment or authorization to practice may be granted only to natural persons.

§ 10.5. Application to become an enrolled agent, enrolled retirement plan agent, or registered tax return preparer. (a) *Form; address.* An applicant to become an enrolled agent, enrolled retirement plan agent, or registered tax return preparer must apply as required by forms or procedures established and published by the Internal Revenue Service, including proper execution of required forms under oath or affirmation. The address on the application will be the address under which a successful applicant is enrolled or registered and is the address to which all correspondence concerning enrollment or registration will be sent.

(b) *Fee.* A reasonable nonrefundable fee may be charged for each application to become an enrolled agent, enrolled retirement plan agent, or registered tax return preparer. See 26 CFR part 300.

(c) *Additional information; examination.* The Internal Revenue Service may require the applicant, as a condition to consideration of an application, to file additional information and to submit to any written or oral examination under oath or otherwise. Upon the applicant's written request, the Internal Revenue Service will afford the applicant the opportunity to be heard with respect to the application.

(d) *Additional information; examination.* (1) As a condition to consideration of an application, the Internal Revenue Service may conduct a Federal tax compliance check and suitability check. The tax compliance check will be limited to an inquiry regarding whether an applicant has filed all required individual or business tax returns and whether the applicant has failed to pay, or make proper arrangements with the Internal Revenue Service for payment of, any Federal tax debts. The suitability check will be limited to an inquiry regarding whether an applicant has engaged in any conduct that would justify suspension or disbarment of any practitioner under the provisions of this part on the date the application is submitted, including whether the applicant has engaged in disreputable conduct as defined in § 10.51. The application will be denied only if the results of the compliance or suitability check are sufficient to establish that the practitioner engaged in conduct subject to sanctions under § § 10.51 and 10.52.

(2) If the applicant does not pass the tax compliance or suitability check, the applicant will not be issued an enrollment or registration card or certificate pursuant to § 10.6(b) of this part. An applicant who is initially denied enrollment or registration for failure to pass a tax compliance check may reapply after the initial denial if the applicant becomes current with respect to the applicant's tax liabilities.

(e) *Temporary recognition.* On receipt of a properly executed application, the Commissioner, or delegate, may grant the applicant temporary recognition to practice pending a determination as to whether status as an enrolled agent, enrolled retirement plan agent, or registered tax return preparer should be granted. Temporary recognition will be granted only in unusual circumstances and it will not be granted, in any circumstance, if the application is not regular on its face, if the information stated in the application, if true, is not sufficient to warrant granting the application to practice, or the Commissioner, or delegate, has information indicating that the statements in the application are untrue or that the applicant would not otherwise qualify to become an enrolled agent, enrolled retirement plan agent, or registered tax return preparer. Issuance of temporary recognition does not constitute either a designation or a finding of eligibility as an enrolled agent, enrolled retirement plan agent, or registered tax return preparer, and the temporary recognition may be withdrawn at any time.

(f) *Protest of application denial..* The applicant will be informed in writing as to the reason(s) for any denial of an application. The applicant may, within 30 days after receipt of the notice of denial of the application, file a written protest of the denial as prescribed by the Internal Revenue Service in forms, guidance, or other appropriate guidance. A protest under this section is not governed by subpart D of this part.

§10.6. Term and renewal of status as an enrolled agent, enrolled retirement plan agent, or registered tax return preparer. (a) *Term.* Each individual authorized to practice before the Internal Revenue Service as an enrolled agent, enrolled retirement plan agent, or registered tax return preparer will be accorded active enrollment or registration status subject to renewal of enrollment or registration as provided in this part.

(b) *Enrollment or registration card or certificate.* The Internal Revenue Service will issue an enrollment or registration card or certificate to each individual whose application to practice before the Internal Revenue Service is approved. Each card or certificate will be valid for the period stated on the card or certificate. An enrolled agent, enrolled retirement plan agent, or registered tax return preparer may not practice before the Internal Revenue Service if the card or certificate is not current or otherwise valid. The card or certificate is in addition to any notification that may be provided to each individual who obtains a preparer tax identification number.

(c) *Change of address.* An enrolled agent, enrolled retirement plan agent, or registered tax return preparer must send notification of any change of address to the address specified by the Internal Revenue Service within 60 days of the change of address. This notification must include the enrolled agent's, enrolled retirement plan agent's, or registered tax return preparer's name, prior address, new address, tax identification number(s) (including preparer tax identificatio⟨...⟩ ⟨...⟩ date the change of a ⟨...⟩ notification ⟨...⟩ poses of a⟨...⟩ propriate ⟨...⟩ responsibl⟨...⟩ be the ad⟨...⟩ tioner's m⟨...⟩ ment or ⟨...⟩ renewal ⟨...⟩ practitior⟨...⟩ tion und⟨...⟩ change ⟨...⟩ dress for purp⟨...⟩ Internal Revenue Code and reg⟨...⟩ thereunder.

[handwritten note:] I'm so bored, it's unreal.... like what is he talking about? 1) O He is terrible. worst class ever! I want a pp (power point)

(d) *Renewal.* (1) *In general.* Enrolled agents, enrolled retirement plan agents, and registered tax return preparers must renew their status with the Internal Revenue Service to maintain eligibility to practice before the Internal Revenue Service. Failure to receive notification from the Internal Revenue Service of the renewal requirement will not be justification for the individual's failure to satisfy this requirement.

(2) *Renewal period for enrolled agents*

(i) All enrolled agents must renew their preparer tax identification number as prescribed by forms, instructions, or other appropriate guidance.

(ii) Enrolled agents who have a social security number or tax identification number that ends with the numbers 0, 1, 2, or 3, except for those individuals who received their initial enrollment after November 1, 2003, must apply for renewal between November 1, 2003, and January 31, 2004. The renewal will be effective April 1, 2004.

(iii) Enrolled agents who have a social security number or tax identification number that ends with the numbers 4, 5, or 6, except for those individuals who received their initial enrollment after November 1, 2004, must apply for renewal between November 1, 2004, and January 31, 2005. The renewal will be effective April 1, 2005.

¶202

(iv) Enrolled agents who have a social security number or tax identification number that ends with the numbers 7, 8, or 9, except for those individuals who received their initial enrollment after November 1, 2005, must apply for renewal between November 1, 2005, and January 31, 2006. The renewal will be effective April 1, 2006.

(v) Thereafter, applications for renewal as an enrolled agent will be required between November 1 and January 31 of every subsequent third year as specified in paragraph (d)(2)(i), (d)(2)(ii), or (d)(2)(iii) of this section according to the last number of the individual's social security number or tax identification number. Those individuals who receive initial enrollment as an enrolled agent after November 1 and before April 2 of the applicable renewal period will not be required to renew their enrollment before the first full renewal period following the receipt of their initial enrollment.

(3) *Renewal period for enrolled retirement plan agents*

(i) All enrolled retirement plan agents must renew their preparer tax identification number as prescribed by the Internal Revenue Service in forms, instructions, or other appropriate guidance.

(ii) Enrolled retirement plan agents will be required to renew their status as enrolled retirement plan agents between April 1 and June 30 of every third year subsequent to their initial enrollment.

(4) *Renewal period for registered tax return preparers* . Registered tax return preparers must renew their preparer tax identification number and their status as a registered tax return preparer as prescribed by the Internal Revenue Service in forms, instructions, or other appropriate guidance.

(5) *Notification of renewal* . After review and approval, the Internal Revenue Service will notify the individual of the renewal and will issue the individual a card or certificate evidencing current status as an enrolled agent, enrolled retirement plan agent, or registered tax return preparer.

(6) *Fee* . A reasonable nonrefundable fee may be charged for each application for renewal filed. See 26 CFR part 300.

(7) *Forms* . Forms required for renewal may be obtained by sending a written request to the address specified by the Internal Revenue Service or from such other source as the Internal Revenue Service will publish in the Internal Revenue Bulletin (see 26 CFR 601.601(d)(2)(ii)(b)) and on the Internal Revenue Service webpage (www.irs.gov).

(e) *Condition for renewal: continuing education*. In order to qualify for renewal as an enrolled agent, enrolled retirement plan agent, or registered tax return preparer, an individual must certify, in the manner prescribed by the Internal Revenue Service, that the individual has satisfied the requisite number of continuing education hours.

(1) *Definitions*

For purposes of this section—

(i) *Enrollment year* means January 1 to December 31 of each year of an enrollment cycle.

(ii) *Enrollment cycle* means the three successive enrollment years preceding the effective date of renewal.

(iii) *Registration year* means each 12-month period the registered tax return preparer is authorized to practice before the Internal Revenue Service.

(iv) The *effective date of renewal* is the first day of the fourth month following the close of the period for renewal described in paragraph (d) of this section.

(2) *For renewed enrollment as an enrolled agent or enrolled retirement plan agent*

(i) *Requirements for enrollment cycle.* A minimum of 72 hours of continuing education credit, including six hours of ethics or professional conduct, must be completed during each enrollment cycle.

(ii) *Requirements for enrollment year.* A minimum of 16 hours of continuing education credit, including two hours of ethics or professional conduct, must be completed during each enrollment year of an enrollment cycle.

(iii) *Enrollment during enrollment cycle.*

... ubject to ... ction, an ... nrollment ... complete ... g educa- ... d during ... for any ... rollment

... dividual who receives initial enrollment during an enrollment cycle must complete two hours of ethics or professional conduct for each enrollment year during the enrollment cycle. Enrollment for any part of an enrollment year is considered enrollment for the entire year.

(3) Requirements for renewal as a registered tax return preparer. A minimum of 15 hours of continuing education credit, including two hours of ethics or professional conduct, three hours of Federal tax law updates, and 10 hours of Federal tax law topics, must be completed during each registration year.

(f) *Qualifying continuing education.*

(1) *General.* (i) *Enrolled agents.* To qualify for continuing education credit for an enrolled agent, a course of learning must:

(A) Be a qualifying continuing education program designed to enhance professional knowledge in Federal taxation or Federal tax related matters (programs comprised of current subject matter in Federal taxation or Federal tax related matters, including accounting, tax return preparation software, taxation, or ethics); and

(B) Be a qualifying continuing education program consistent with the Internal Revenue Code and effective tax administration.

(ii) **Enrolled retirement plan agents**. To qualify for continuing education credit for an enrolled retirement plan agent, a course of learning must:

(A) Be a qualifying continuing education program designed to enhance professional knowledge in qualified retirement plan matters; and

(B) Be a qualifying continuing education program consistent with the Internal Revenue Code and effective tax administration.

(iii) **Registered tax return preparers**. To qualify for continuing education credit for a registered tax return preparer, a course of learning must:

(A) Be a qualifying continuing education program designed to enhance professional knowledge in Federal taxation or Federal tax related matters (programs comprised of current subject matter in Federal taxation or Federal tax related matters, including accounting, tax return preparation software, taxation, or ethics); and

(B) Be a qualifying continuing education program consistent with the Internal Revenue Code and effective tax administration.

(2) *Qualifying Programs.*

(i) *Formal programs.* A formal program qualifies as continuing education programs if it—:

(A) Requires attendance and provides each attendee with a certificate of attendance;

(B) Is conducted by a qualified instructor, discussion leader, or speaker (in other words, a person whose background, training, education, and experience is appropriate for instructing or leading a discussion on the subject matter of the particular program);

(C) Provides or requires a written outline, textbook, or suitable electronic educational materials; and

(D) Satisfies the requirements established for a qualified continuing education program pursuant to §10.9.

(ii) *Correspondence or individual study programs (including taped programs).* Qualifying continuing education programs include correspondence or individual study programs that are conducted by continuing education providers and completed on an individual basis by the enrolled individual. The allowable credit hours for such programs will be measured on a basis comparable to the measurement of a seminar or course for credit in an accredited educational institution. Such programs qualify as continuing education programs only if they—

(A) Require registration of the participants by the continuing education provider;

(B) Provide a means for measuring successful completion by the participants (for example, a written examination), including the issuance of a certificate of completion by the continuing education provider;

(C) Provide a written outline, textbook, or suitable electronic educational materials; and

(D) Satisfy the requirements established for a qualified continuing education program pursuant to § 10.9.

(iii) *Serving as an instructor, discussion leader or speaker*

(A) One hour of continuing education credit will be awarded for each contact hour completed as an instructor, discussion leader, or speaker at an educational program that meets the continuing education requirements of paragraph (f) of this section.

(B) A maximum of two hours of continuing education credit will be awarded for actual subject preparation time for each contact hour completed as an instructor, discussion leader, or speaker at such programs. It is the responsibility of the individual claiming such credit to maintain records to verify preparation time.

(C) The maximum continuing education credit for instruction and preparation may not exceed four hours annually for registered tax return preparers and six hours annually for enrolled agents and enrolled retirement plan agents.

(D) An instructor, discussion leader, or speaker who makes more than one presentation on the same subject matter during an enrollment cycle or registration year will receive continuing education credit for only one such presentation for the enrollment cycle or registration year.

(3) *Periodic examination.*

Enrolled Agents and Enrolled Retirement Plan Agents may establish eligibility for renewal of enrollment for any enrollment cycle by—

(i) Achieving a passing score on each part of the Special Enrollment Examination administered under this part during the three year period prior to renewal; and

(ii) Completing a minimum of 16 hours of qualifying continuing education during the last year of an enrollment cycle.

(g) *Measurement of continuing education coursework*

(1) All continuing education programs will be measured in terms of contact hours. The shortest recognized program will be one contact hour.

(2) A contact hour is 50 minutes of continuous participation in a program. Credit is granted only for a full contact hour, which is 50 minutes or multiples thereof. For example, a program lasting more than 50 minutes but less than 100 minutes will count as only one contact hour.

(3) Individual segments at continuous conferences, conventions and the like will be considered one total program. For example, two 90-minute segments (180 minutes) at a continuous conference will count as three contact hours.

(4) For university or college courses, each semester hour credit will equal 15 contact hours and a quarter hour credit will equal 10 contact hours.

(h) *Recordkeeping requirements*

(1) Each individual applying for renewal must retain for a period of four years following the date of renewal the information required with regard to qualifying continuing education credit hours. Such information includes—

(i) The name of the sponsoring organization;

(ii) The location of the program;

(iii) The title of the program, qualified program number, and description of its content;

(iv) Written outlines, course syllibi, textbook, and/or electronic materials provided or required for the course;

(v) The dates attended;

(vi) The credit hours claimed;

(vii) The name(s) of the instructor(s), discussion leader(s), or speaker(s), if appropriate; and

(viii) The certificate of completion and/or signed statement of the hours of attendance obtained from the continuing education provider.

(2) To receive continuing education credit for service completed as an instructor, discussion leader, or speaker, the following information must be maintained for a period of four years following the date of renewal—

(i) The name of the sponsoring organization;

(ii) The location of the program;

(iii) The title of the program and copy of its content;

(iv) The dates of the program; and

(v) The credit hours claimed.

(i) *Waivers*

(1) Waiver from the continuing education requirements for a given period may be granted for the following reasons—

(i) Health, which prevented compliance with the continuing education requirements;

(ii) Extended active military duty;

(iii) Absence from the United States for an extended period of time due to employment or other reasons, provided the individual does not practice before the Internal Revenue Service during such absence; and

(iv) Other compelling reasons, which will be considered on a case-by-case basis.

(2) A request for waiver must be accompanied by appropriate documentation. The individual is required to furnish any additional documentation or explanation deemed necessary. Examples of appropriate documentation could be a medical certificate or military orders.

(3) A request for waiver must be filed no later than the last day of the renewal application period.

(4) If a request for waiver is not approved, the individual will be placed in inactive status. The individual will be noti-fied that the waiver was not approved and that the individual has been placed on a roster of inactive enrolled agents, enrolled retirement plan agents, or registered tax return preparers.

(5) If the request for waiver is not approved, the individual may file a protest as prescribed by the Internal Revenue Service in forms, instructions, or other appropriate guidance. A protest filed under this section is not governed by subpart D of this part.

(6) If a request for waiver is approved, the individual will be notified and issued a card or certificate evidencing renewal.

(7) Those who are granted waivers are required to file timely applications for renewal of enrollment or registration.

(j) *Failure to comply.* (1) Compliance by an individual with the requirements of this part is determined by the Internal Revenue Service. The Internal Revenue Service will provide notice to any individual who fails to meet the continuing education and fee requirements of eligibility for renewal. The notice will state the basis for the determination of noncompliance and will provide the individual an opportunity to furnish the requested information in writing relating to the matter within 60 days of the date of the notice. Such information will be considered in making a final determination as to eligibility for renewal. The individual must be informed of the reason(s) for any denial of a renewal. The individual may, within 30 days after receipt of the notice of denial of renewal, file a written protest of the denial as prescribed by the Internal Revenue Service in forms, instructions, or other appropriate guidance. A protest under this section is not governed by subpart D of this part.

(2) The continuing education records of an enrolled agent, enrolled retirement plan agent, or registered tax return preparer may be reviewed to determine compliance with the requirements and standards for renewal as provided in paragraph (f) of this section. As part of this review, the enrolled agent, enrolled retirement plan agent or registered

¶202

tax return preparer may be required to provide the Internal Revenue Service with copies of any continuing education records required to be maintained under this part. If the enrolled agent, enrolled retirement plan agent or registered tax return preparer fails to comply with this requirement, any continuing education hours claimed may be disallowed.

(3) An individual who has not filed a timely application for renewal, who has not made a timely response to the notice of noncompliance with the renewal requirements, or who has not satisfied the requirements of eligibility for renewal will be placed on a roster of inactive enrolled individuals or inactive registered individuals. During this time, the individual will be ineligible to practice before the Internal Revenue Service.

(4) Individuals placed in inactive status and individuals ineligible to practice before the Internal Revenue Service may not state or imply that they are eligible to practice before the Internal Revenue Service, or use the terms enrolled agent, enrolled retirement plan agent, or registered tax return preparer, the designations "EA" or "ERPA" or other form of reference to eligibility to practice before the Internal Revenue Service.

(5) An individual placed in inactive status may be reinstated to an active status by filing an application for renewal and providing evidence of the completion of all required continuing education hours for the enrollment cycle or registration year. Continuing education credit under this paragraph (j)(5) may not be used to satisfy the requirements of the enrollment cycle or registration year in which the individual has been placed back on the active roster.

(6) An individual placed in inactive status must file an application for renewal and satisfy the requirements for renewal as set forth in this section within three years of being placed in inactive status. Otherwise, the name of such individual will be removed from the inactive status roster and the individual's status as an enrolled agent, enrolled retirement plan agent, or registered tax return preparer will terminate. Future eligibility for active status must then be reestablished by the individual as provided in this section.

(7) Inactive status is not available to an individual who is the subject of a pending disciplinary matter before the Internal Revenue Service

(k) *Inactive retirement status.* An individual who no longer practices before the Internal Revenue Service may request to be placed in an inactive retirement status at any time and such individual will be placed in an inactive retirement status. The individual will be ineligible to practice before the Internal Revenue Service. An individual who is placed in an inactive retirement status may be reinstated to an active status by filing an application for renewal and providing evidence of the completion of the required continuing education hours for the enrollment cycle or registration year. Inactive retirement status is not available to an individual who is ineligible to practice before the Internal Revenue Service or an individual who is the subject of a pending disciplinary matter under this part.

(l) *Renewal while under suspension or disbarment.* An individual who is ineligible to practice before the Internal Revenue Service by virtue of disciplinary action under this part is required to conform to the requirements for renewal of enrollment or registration before the individual's eligibility is restored.

(m) *Enrolled actuaries.* The enrollment and renewal of enrollment of actuaries authorized to practice under paragraph (d) of § 10.3 are governed by the regulations of the Joint Board for the Enrollment of Actuaries at 20 CFR 901.1 through 901.72.

✳ §10.7. Representing oneself; participating in rulemaking; limited practice; and special appearances. (a) *Representing oneself.* Individuals may appear on their own behalf before the Internal Revenue Service provided they present satisfactory identification.

(b) *Participating in rulemaking.* Individuals may participate in rulemaking as provided by the Administrative Procedure Act. See 5 U.S.C. 553.

(c) *Limited practice.* (1) *In general.* Subject to the limitations in paragraph (c)(2) of this section, an individual who is not a practitioner may represent a taxpayer before the Internal Revenue Service in the circumstances described in this paragraph (c)(1), even if the taxpayer is not present, provided the individual presents satisfactory identification and proof of his or her authority to represent the taxpayer. The circumstances described in this paragraph (c)(1) are as follows:

(i) An individual may represent a member of his or her immediate family.

(ii) A regular full-time employee of an individual employer may represent the employer.

(iii) A general partner or a regular full-time employee of a partnership may represent the partnership.

(iv) A bona fide officer or a regular full-time employee of a corporation (including a parent, subsidiary, or other affiliated corporation), association, or organized group may represent the corporation, association, or organized group.

(v) A regular full-time employee of a trust, receivership, guardianship, or estate may represent the trust, receivership, guardianship, or estate.

(vi) An officer or a regular employee of a governmental unit, agency, or authority may represent the governmental unit, agency, or authority in the course of his or her official duties.

(vii) An individual may represent any individual or entity, who is outside the United States, before personnel of the Internal Revenue Service when such representation takes place outside the United States.

(2) *Limitations.*

(i) An individual who is under suspension or disbarment from practice before the Internal Revenue Service may not engage in limited practice before the Internal Revenue Service under paragraph (c)(1) of this section.

(ii) The Commissioner, or delegate, may, after notice and opportunity for a conference, deny eligibility to engage in limited practice before the Internal Revenue Service under paragraph (c)(1) of this section to any individual who has engaged in conduct that would justify a sanction under § 10.50.

(iii) An individual who represents a taxpayer under the authority of paragraph (c)(1) of this section is subject, to the extent of his or her authority, to such rules of general applicability regarding standards of conduct and other matters as prescribed by the Internal Revenue Service.

(d) *Special appearances.* The Commissioner, or delegate, may, subject to conditions deemed appropriate, authorize an individual who is not otherwise eligible to practice before the Internal Revenue Service to represent another person in a particular matter.

(e) *Fiduciaries.* For purposes of this part, a fiduciary (for example, a trustee, receiver, guardian, personal representative, administrator, or executor) is considered to be the taxpayer and not a representative of the taxpayer.

§10.8 Return preparation and application of rules to other individuals. (a) *Preparing all or substantially all of a tax return.* Any individual who for compensation prepares or assists with the preparation of all or substantially all of a tax return or claim for refund must have a preparer tax identification number. Except as otherwise prescribed in forms, instructions, or other appropriate guidance, an individual must be an attorney, certified public accountant, enrolled agent, or registered tax return preparer to obtain a preparer tax identification number. Any individual who for compensation prepares or assists with the preparation of all or substantially all of a tax return or claim for refund is subject to the duties and restrictions relating to practice in subpart B, as well as subject to the sanctions for violation of the regulations in subpart C.

(b) *Preparing a tax return and furnishing information.* Any individual may for compensation prepare or assist with the preparation of a tax return or claim for refund (provided the individual prepares less than substantially all of the tax return or claim for refund), appear as a witness for the taxpayer before the Internal Revenue Service, or furnish information at the request of the Internal Revenue Service or any of its officers or employees.

(c) *Application of rules to other individuals.* Any individual who for compensation prepares, or assists in the preparation of, all or a substantial portion of a document pertaining to any taxpayer's tax liability for submission to the Internal Revenue Service is subject to the duties and restrictions relating to practice in subpart B, as well as subject to the sanctions for violation of the regulations in subpart C. Unless otherwise a practitioner, however, an individual may not for compensation prepare, or assist in the preparation of, all or substantially all of a tax return or claim for refund, or sign tax returns and claims for refund. For purposes of this paragraph, an individual described in 26 CFR 301.7701-15(f) is not treated as having prepared all or a substantial portion of the document by reason of such assistance.

§10.9 Continuing education providers and continuing education programs.
(a) *Continuing education providers*

(1) *In general.* Continuing education providers are those responsible for presenting continuing education programs. A continuing education provider must—

(i) Be an accredited educational institution;

(ii) Be recognized for continuing education purposes by the licensing body of any State, territory, or possession of the United States, including a Commonwealth, or the District of Columbia;

(iii) Be recognized and approved by a qualifying organization as a provider of continuing education on subject matters within §10.6(f) of this part. The Internal Revenue Service may, at its discretion, identify a professional organization, society or business entity that maintains minimum education standards comparable to those set forth in this part as a qualifying organization for purposes of this part in appropriate forms, instructions, and other appropriate guidance; or

(iv) Be recognized by the Internal Revenue Service as a professional organization, society, or business whose programs include offering continuing professional education opportunities in subject matters within §10.6(f) of this part. The Internal Revenue Service, at its discretion, may require such professional organizations, societies, or businesses to file an agreement and/or obtain Internal Revenue Service approval of each program as a qualified continuing education program in appropriate forms, instructions or other appropriate guidance.

(2) *Continuing education provider numbers*

(i) *In general.* A continuing education provider is required to obtain a continuing education provider number and pay any applicable user fee.

(ii) *Renewal.* A continuing education provider maintains its status as a continuing education provider during the continuing education provider cycle by renewing its continuing education provider number as prescribed by forms, instructions or other appropriate guidance and paying any applicable user fee.

(3) *Requirements for qualified continuing education programs.*

A continuing education provider must ensure the qualified continuing education program complies with all the following requirements—

(i) Programs must be developed by individual(s) qualified in the subject matter;

(ii) Program subject matter must be current;

(iii) Instructors, discussion leaders, and speakers must be qualified with respect to program content;

(iv) Programs must include some means for evaluation of the technical content and presentation to be evaluated;

(v) Certificates of completion bearing a current qualified continuing education program number issued by the Internal Revenue Service must be provided to the participants who successfully complete the program; and

(vi) Records must be maintained by the continuing education provider to verify the participants who attended and completed the program for a period of four years following completion of the program. In the case of continuous conferences, conventions, and the like, records must be maintained to verify completion of the program and attendance by each participant at each segment of the program.

(4) *Program numbers*

(i) *In general.* Every continuing education provider is required to obtain a continuing education provider program number and pay any applicable user fee for each program offered. Program numbers shall be obtained as prescribed by forms, instructions or other appropriate guidance. Although, at the discretion of the Internal Revenue Service, a continuing education provider may be required to demonstrate that the program is designed to enhance professional knowledge in Federal taxation or Federal tax related matters (programs comprised of current subject matter in Federal taxation or Federal tax related matters, including accounting, tax return preparation software, taxation, or ethics) and complies with the requirements in paragraph (a)(2)of this section before a program number is issued.

(ii) *Update programs.* Update programs may use the same number as the program subject to update. An update program is a program that instructs on a change of existing law occurring within one year of the update program offering. The qualifying education program subject to update must have been offered within the two year time period prior to the change in existing law.

(iii) *Change in existing law.* A change in existing law means the effective date of the statute or regulation, or date of entry of judicial decision, that is the subject of the update.

(b) *Failure to comply.* Compliance by a continuing education provider with the requirements of this part is determined by the Internal Revenue Service. A continuing education provider who fails to meet the requirements of this part will be notified by the Internal Revenue Service. The notice will state the basis for the determination of noncompliance and will provide the continuing education provider an opportunity to furnish the requested information in writing relating to the matter within 60 days of the date of the notice. The continuing education provider may, within 30 days after receipt of the notice of denial, file a written protest as prescribed by the Internal Revenue Service in forms, instructions, or other appropriate guidance. A protest under this section is not governed by subpart D of this part.

¶203 RECOGNITION REQUIREMENTS

Whenever a representative seeks to act for a taxpayer in dealing with the IRS, the representative must establish that he or she has been "duly authorized" by the taxpayer to so act. The Internal Revenue Manual guidelines[6] instruct agents that in dealing with representatives they should keep in mind that IRS personnel are prohibited from disclosing confidential tax information to unauthorized persons. They are also reminded that practice before the IRS is restricted to persons properly qualified under Circular 230. To assure that the representative has been properly authorized, the agent must seek evidence of recognition and authorization from the taxpayer[7] (see Exhibit 2-1 at ¶204, Recognition and Authorization Requirements for Persons Appearing Before the Service).

Generally, an individual may be authorized to inspect and receive tax information of a confidential nature, even though the representative does not seek to "act" on behalf of the taxpayer in any fashion beyond the receipt of such

---

[6] IRM Handbook 4.10.1.6.10.

[7] See Exhibit 2-2 at ¶205, relating to limited authorization for return preparers authorizing the IRS to contact paid preparers relating to questions arising during the processing of a return. This limited authorization ends no later than the due date of the succeeding year's return.

information. For example, if a representative merely wishes to know what adjustments a Revenue Agent is proposing without protesting those adjustments, he or she can file a Form 8821, Tax Information Authorization (see Exhibit 2-2 at ¶205). This form authorizes *any* designated person to inspect or receive tax information of a confidential nature.

On the other hand, if the taxpayer's representative seeks to affirmatively "act" on behalf of the taxpayer, then further authorization of the representative is necessary. Because these acts constitute practice before the IRS, they can only be performed by a qualified person and only when evidence of authorization to perform such acts has been furnished to the IRS. The Power of Attorney, Form 2848 (see Exhibit 2-4 at ¶207), is generally used for such authorization. It must be filed if an individual wishes to represent the taxpayer before the IRS or to execute a waiver, consent or closing agreement on behalf of the taxpayer. In addition to giving the representative the right to receive confidential information, the Power of Attorney authorizes the representative to perform *any and all acts* with respect to the tax matters described in the Power of Attorney. This broad authority, however, does not include the power to receive refund checks or to sign tax returns. If Form 2848 is not properly filled out, the form will be returned to the taxpayer, not to the tax practitioner.

Form 2848, Power of Attorney and Declaration of Representative, will no longer be honored for any purpose other than for representation before the IRS. Form 2848, submitted by parties not eligible to practice under Circular 230, will not be honored, and the third party will be advised to either submit Form 8821, or the taxpayer may grant an oral tax information authorization.

If the taxpayer wishes a representative to receive (but not cash or endorse) refund checks or to sign tax returns, these acts must be specifically authorized in the Power of Attorney.[8] If the signing of a tax return is authorized, the specific requirements of the regulations, Reg. § 1.6012-1(a)(5), must be satisfied. In general, a representative is only permitted to sign a return if the taxpayer is unable to do so by reason of (1) disease or injury, or (2) continuous absence from the country for at least sixty days prior to the due date of the return. Specific permission to sign on behalf of a taxpayer also may be requested from the Director for other good cause.

Authorized representatives must sign and submit with their Power of Attorney a written declaration (Part II of Form 2848) stating that (1) they are not currently under suspension or disbarment from practice before the IRS or from practice of their profession, (2) they are aware of the regulations contained in Circular 230, (3) they are authorized to represent the taxpayer, and (4) they are one of the individuals recognized in Circular 230 as having the right to practice before the IRS. The eight classes of individuals having such right to practice before the IRS include attorneys, certified public accountants, enrolled agents,

---

[8] Statement of Procedural Rules, § 601.504(a)(5) and (6).

¶203

officers and full-time employers of the taxpayer, members of the taxpayer's immediate family, enrolled actuaries and registered tax return preparers.

The IRS will accept a Power of Attorney other than one on Form 2848, provided that such document includes all of the information required by the official form.[9] If such information is not included, the representative can cure the defect by executing a completed Form 2848 on behalf of the taxpayer and attaching it to the original power. Although the attached Form 2848 need not be signed by the taxpayer, the representative must sign the required declaration on the back of the form. A signed statement that the original power is valid under the laws of the governing jurisdiction also must be attached to the Form 2848. To be acceptable under these rules, an original power, not on Form 2848, must contemplate by its terms the authorization to handle federal tax matters. Broad language in an original power authorizing a representative to perform any and all acts would meet this requirement.

Either the original or a copy of the Power of Attorney will be accepted by the IRS. A copy of a power received by facsimile transmission (FAX) also is acceptable.[10]

A Power of Attorney is not required by a fiduciary involved in a tax matter. Instead, a fiduciary should file Form 56, Notice Concerning Fiduciary Relationship (see Exhibit 2-5 at ¶ 208).[11] Fiduciaries include trustees, executors, personal representatives, administrators, guardians and receivers. In addition to the Form 56, the IRS may require further verification of the fiduciary relationship.

An authorization to receive tax information or a Power of Attorney can cover a variety of taxes and a variety of tax years or periods. However, the taxpayer must clearly identify the types of taxes and the tax years or periods, as well as the tax form numbers of these taxes, on the authorization or power. A general reference to "all years," "all periods" or "all taxes" will not be accepted by the IRS.

The regulations specify that authorization of a person to receive confidential information must usually be written. However, under certain circumstances, an oral or implied consent for disclosure may be allowed. For example, where both the taxpayer and the representative are present at a conference, an agent may make disclosures concerning the taxpayer's return or income without receiving authorization from the taxpayer.

In most instances, the Power of Attorney will be executed by the named taxpayer. If a joint return was filed, and the representative is to act for both spouses, then both must sign the Power of Attorney. A Power of Attorney on behalf of a partnership must be executed by all partners, or if in the name of the partnership, by a duly authorized partner. If the partnership has been dissolved, the Power of Attorney must be executed by each former partner, or, for a

---

[9] Statement of Procedural Rules, § 601.503(a) and (b). However, for purposes of processing into the Centralized Authorization File (CAF), a Form 2848 must be attached to the nonstandard form. The attached Form 2848 must be completed, but need not be signed by the taxpayer. § 601.503(b)(2).

[10] Statement of Procedural Rules, § 601.504(c)(4).

[11] Statement of Procedural Rules, § 601.503(d).

deceased partner, by the legal representative of his or her estate. However, if state law gives surviving partners the right to wind up the affairs of the partnership upon the death of one partner, then the surviving partners can execute the Power of Attorney. A corporate Power of Attorney must be executed by an officer who has authority to bind the corporation. Where a corporation has been dissolved, the Power of Attorney must be executed by the liquidating trustee or the trustee under dissolution. If there is no such trustee, then it must be executed by the holders of the majority of the voting stock as of the date of dissolution.

Where the taxpayer is deceased, the Power of Attorney can be executed by the executor or administrator if one has been appointed by the court handling probate. The IRS may require submission of evidence of appointment. Normally, Form 56 (see Exhibit 2-5 at ¶ 208) is filed, along with a certified copy of the order of the court showing that the personal representative has been appointed. After an estate is closed, the Power of Attorney must usually be executed by the residuary legatee or a testamentary trustee.

[The Internal Revenue Manual provides that after a Power of Attorney is received, any notice or other written communication given to a taxpayer in a matter before the IRS is also to be given to the taxpayer's recognized representative.]If the taxpayer has more than one representative, the taxpayer can check a box in line 7 of Form 2848 which will authorize the mailing of copies of all documents to two representatives.[12]

A qualified representative has the right to be present whenever his or her client is interviewed, interrogated or required to furnish information to the IRS. In most instances, this will mean that arrangements for direct examination or investigation of the taxpayer are conducted through the representative. Under certain circumstances, the IRS may bypass the taxpayer's representative, even though a valid Power of Attorney is on file.[13] Generally, the taxpayer will be contacted directly only when a representative has unreasonably delayed or hindered an examination by failing, after repeated requests, to furnish information for which there is no privilege. In such a situation, the examiner can report the situation to the Territory Manager and request permission to contact the taxpayer directly for such information. If such permission is granted, the case file will be documented to show how the examination was being delayed or hindered, and written notice of such permission will be given to the representative and to the taxpayer.[14]

Where permission to bypass the representative has been granted, it does not constitute suspension or disbarment of the representative. That representative may continue to represent the client upon making an appearance before the IRS for that purpose. The representative also will be afforded the courtesy of being advised regarding all future appointments with the taxpayer. Of course, in

---

[12] IRM 4.11..55.1.

[13] Statement of Procedural Rules, § 601.506(b); IRM 5.1.1.7.7.

[14] The IRS has held that evidence received from a taxpayer after the representative was bypassed is still admissible evidence and need not be suppressed. See IRS Ltr. Rul. 8206011 (May 29, 1981).

¶203

aggravated situations, the delay or hindrance of the examination may be referred to the Director of Practice for possible disciplinary proceedings.

When a Power of Attorney is received, the IRS assigns a central authorization file (CAF) number to each taxpayer representative.[15] The nine-digit CAF number identifies each representative and the scope of his or her authority. The automated CAF system expedites the mailing of refunds, notices and other correspondence by automatically directing them to authorized representatives.[16]

---

[15] Statement of Procedural Rules, § 601.506(d).   [16] Announcement 82-147, IRB 1982-47, 54.

¶204 Exhibit 2-1

Recognition and Authorization Requirements for Persons Appearing Before the Service

This chart summarizes how these new forms may be used by different types of practitioners depending upon the capacity in which they appear.

Capacity of Person Appearing			Unenrolled Persons who are not Attorneys or CPAs	
	Attorneys and CPAs	Enrolled Agents	Qualified for Limited Practice Under Sec. 10.7 or Cir. 230	All Others
			Return Preparers / Others	
1. As an advocate who is to perform certain acts for taxpayer as prescribed in 26 CFR 601.504(a) (Constitutes "Practice" as defined in Cir. 230).	P/A and D Exception (2) may apply	P/A and D	P/A and D Exception (3) applies	P/A and D Exception (2) may apply	Ineligible
2. As a witness who may receive or inspect confidential tax information (Does not include "Practice" as defined in Cir. 230).	TIA Exception (1) or (2) may apply	TIA	TIA	TIA Exception (2) may apply	TIA
3. As a witness for taxpayer to present his books, records or returns to the examining officer (Does not include "Practice" as defined in Cir. 230).	No Requirements	No Requirements	No Requirements	No Requirements	No Requirements

Code for Requirements

P/A Must present or have a Power of Attorney on file.

TIA Must present or have a Tax Information Authorization or Power of Attorney on file if the taxpayer is not also present.

D Must present or have declaration on file.

Exceptions

(1) Any attorney who prepared the estate tax return and is attorney of record . . . but must have a declaration on file.

(2) A trustee, receiver or attorney may substitute a proper court certificate in lieu of a P/A or TIA.

(3) Unenrolled return preparers are limited to representation during the examination process.

¶205 Exhibit 2-2

Form **8821**	**Tax Information Authorization**	OMB No. 1545-1165

Form **8821**
(Rev. August 2008)
Department of the Treasury
Internal Revenue Service

Tax Information Authorization

▶ Do not sign this form unless all applicable lines have been completed.

▶ Do not use this form to request a copy or transcript of your tax return. Instead, use Form 4506 or Form 4506-T.

OMB No. 1545-1165

For IRS Use Only
Received by:
Name _____
Telephone ( ) _____
Function _____
Date ___ / ___ / ___

1   Taxpayer information. Taxpayer(s) must sign and date this form on line 7.

Taxpayer name(s) and address (type or print)	Social security number(s)	Employer identification number
	Daytime telephone number ( )	Plan number (if applicable)

2   Appointee. If you wish to name more than one appointee, attach a list to this form.

Name and address	CAF No. .... Telephone No. .... Fax No. .... Check if new: Address ☐ Telephone No. ☐ Fax No. ☐

3 Tax matters. The appointee is authorized to inspect and/or receive confidential tax information in any office of the IRS for the tax matters listed on this line. Do not use Form 8821 to request copies of tax returns.

(a) Type of Tax (Income, Employment, Excise, etc.) or Civil Penalty	(b) Tax Form Number (1040, 941, 720, etc.)	(c) Year(s) or Period(s) (see the instructions for line 3)	(d) Specific Tax Matters (see instr.)

4 Specific use not recorded on Centralized Authorization File (CAF). If the tax information authorization is for a specific use not recorded on CAF, check this box. See the instructions on page 4. If you check this box, skip lines 5 and 6 . ▶ ☐

5 Disclosure of tax information (you **must** check a box on line 5a or 5b unless the box on line 4 is checked):

a If you want copies of tax information, notices, and other written communications sent to the appointee on an ongoing basis, check this box . . . . ▶ ☐

b If you do not want any copies of notices or communications sent to your appointee, check this box . . . . . ▶ ☐

6 Retention/revocation of tax information authorizations. This tax information authorization automatically revokes all prior authorizations for the same tax matters you listed on line 3 above unless you checked the box on line 4. If you do not want to revoke a prior tax information authorization, you **must** attach a copy of any authorizations you want to remain in effect **and** check this box . . . . ▶ ☐

To revoke this tax information authorization, see the instructions on page 4.

7 Signature of taxpayer(s). If a tax matter applies to a joint return, **either** husband or wife must sign. If signed by a corporate officer, partner, guardian, executor, receiver, administrator, trustee, or party other than the taxpayer, I certify that I have the authority to execute this form with respect to the tax matters/periods on line 3 above.

▶ **IF NOT SIGNED AND DATED, THIS TAX INFORMATION AUTHORIZATION WILL BE RETURNED.**

▶ **DO NOT SIGN THIS FORM IF IT IS BLANK OR INCOMPLETE.**

Signature	Date	Signature	Date
Print Name	Title (if applicable)	Print Name	Title (if applicable)
☐ ☐ ☐ ☐ ☐ PIN number for electronic signature		☐ ☐ ☐ ☐ ☐ PIN number for electronic signature	

For Privacy Act and Paperwork Reduction Act Notice, see page 4.   Cat. No. 11596P   Form **8821** (Rev. 8-2008)

General Instructions

Section references are to the Internal Revenue Code unless otherwise noted.

Purpose of Form

Form 8821 authorizes any individual, corporation, firm, organization, or partnership you designate to inspect and/or receive your confidential information in any office of the IRS for the type of tax and the years or periods you list on Form 8821. You may file your own tax information authorization without using Form 8821, but it must include all the information that is requested on Form 8821.

Form 8821 does not authorize your appointee to advocate your position with respect to the federal tax laws; to execute waivers, consents, or closing agreements; or to otherwise represent you before the IRS. If you want to authorize an individual to represent you, use Form 2848, Power of Attorney and Declaration of Representative.

Use Form 4506, Request for Copy of Tax Return, to get a copy of your tax return.

Use Form 4506-T, Request for Transcript of Tax Return, to order: (a) transcript of tax account information and (b) Form W-2 and Form 1099 series information.

Use Form 56, Notice Concerning Fiduciary Relationship, to notify the IRS of the existence of a fiduciary relationship. A fiduciary (trustee, executor, administrator, receiver, or guardian) stands in the position of a taxpayer and acts as the taxpayer. Therefore, a fiduciary does not act as an appointee and should not file Form 8821. If a fiduciary wishes to authorize an appointee to inspect and/or receive confidential tax information on behalf of the fiduciary, Form 8821 must be filed and signed by the fiduciary acting in the position of the taxpayer.

When To File

Form 8821 must be received by the IRS within 60 days of the date it was signed and dated by the taxpayer.

Where To File Chart

IF you live in . . .	THEN use this address . . .	Fax Number*
Alabama, Arkansas, Connecticut, Delaware, District of Columbia, Florida, Georgia, Illinois, Indiana, Kentucky, Louisiana, Maine, Maryland, Massachusetts, Michigan, Mississippi, New Hampshire, New Jersey, New York, North Carolina, Ohio, Pennsylvania, Rhode Island, South Carolina, Tennessee, Vermont, Virginia, or West Virginia	Internal Revenue Service Memphis Accounts Management Center PO Box 268, Stop 8423 Memphis, TN 38101-0268	901-546-4115
Alaska, Arizona, California, Colorado, Hawaii, Idaho, Iowa, Kansas, Minnesota, Missouri, Montana, Nebraska, Nevada, New Mexico, North Dakota, Oklahoma, Oregon, South Dakota, Texas, Utah, Washington, Wisconsin, or Wyoming	Internal Revenue Service 1973 N. Rulon White Blvd. MS 6737 Ogden, UT 84404	801-620-4249
All APO and FPO addresses, American Samoa, nonpermanent residents of Guam or the Virgin Islands**, Puerto Rico (or if excluding income under section 933), a foreign country, U.S. citizens and those filing Form 2555, 2555-EZ, or 4563.	Internal Revenue Service International CAF DP: SW-311 11601 Roosevelt Blvd. Philadelphia, PA 19255	215-516-1017

*These numbers may change without notice.

**Permanent residents of Guam should use Department of Taxation, Government of Guam, P.O. Box 23607, GMF, GU 96921; permanent residents of the Virgin Islands should use: V.I. Bureau of Internal Revenue, 9601 Estate Thomas Charlotte Amalie, St. Thomas, V.I. 00802.

Where To File

Generally, mail or fax Form 8821 directly to the IRS. See the *Where To File Chart* on page 2. Exceptions are listed below.

If Form 8821 is for a specific tax matter, mail or fax it to the office handling that matter. For more information, see the instructions for line 4.

Your representative may be able to file Form 8821 electronically with the IRS from the IRS website. For more information, go to *www.irs.gov*. Under the *Tax Professionals* tab, click on *e-services–Online Tools for Tax Professionals*. If you complete Form 8821 for electronic signature authorization, do not file a Form 8821 with the IRS. Instead, give it to your appointee, who will retain the document.

Revocation of an Existing Tax Information Authorization

If you want to revoke an existing tax information authorization and do not want to name a new appointee, send a copy of the previously executed tax information authorization to the IRS, using the *Where To File Chart* on page 2. The copy of the tax information authorization must have a current signature and date of the taxpayer under the original signature on line 7. Write "REVOKE" across the top of Form 8821. If you do not have a copy of the tax information authorization you want to revoke, send a statement to the IRS. The statement of revocation or withdrawal must indicate that the authority of the appointee is revoked, list the tax matters and periods, and must be signed and dated by the taxpayer or representative. If the taxpayer is revoking, list the name and address of each recognized appointee whose authority is revoked. When the taxpayer is completely revoking authority, the form should state "remove all years/periods" instead of listing the specific tax matters, years, or periods. If the appointee is withdrawing, list the name, TIN, and address (if known) of the taxpayer.

To revoke a specific use tax information authorization, send the tax information authorization or statement of revocation to the IRS office handling your case, using the above instructions.

Taxpayer Identification Numbers (TINs)

TINs are used to identify taxpayer information with corresponding tax returns. It is important that you furnish correct names, social security numbers (SSNs), individual taxpayer identification numbers (ITINs), or employer identification numbers (EINs) so that the IRS can respond to your request.

Partnership Items

Sections 6221-6234 authorize a Tax Matters Partner to perform certain acts on behalf of an affected partnership. Rules governing the use of Form 8821 do not replace any provisions of these sections.

Representative Address Change

If the representative's address has changed, a new Form 8821 is not required. The representative can send a written notification that includes the new information and their signature to the location where the Form 8821 was filed.

Specific Instructions

Line 1. Taxpayer Information

Individuals. Enter your name, TIN, and your street address in the space provided. Do not enter your appointee's address or post office box. If a joint return is used, also enter your spouse's name and TIN. Also enter your EIN if applicable.

Corporations, partnerships, or associations. Enter the name, EIN, and business address.

Employee plan or exempt organization. Enter the name, address, and EIN of the plan sponsor or exempt organization, and the plan name and three-digit plan number.

Trust. Enter the name, title, and address of the trustee, and the name and EIN of the trust.

Estate. Enter the name, title, and address of the decedent's executor/personal representative, and the name and identification number of the estate. The identification number for an estate includes both the EIN, if the estate has one, and the decedent's TIN.

Line 2. Appointee

Enter your appointee's full name. Use the identical full name on all submissions and correspondence. Enter the nine-digit CAF number for each appointee. If an appointee has a CAF number for any previously filed Form 8821 or power of attorney (Form 2848), use that number. If a CAF number has not been assigned, enter "NONE," and the IRS will issue one directly to your appointee. The IRS does not assign CAF numbers to requests for employee plans and exempt organizations.

If you want to name more than one appointee, indicate so on this line and attach a list of appointees to Form 8821.

Check the appropriate box to indicate if either the address, telephone number, or fax number is new since a CAF number was assigned.

Line 3. Tax Matters

Enter the type of tax, the tax form number, the years or periods, and the specific tax matter. Enter "Not applicable," in any of the columns that do not apply.

For example, you may list "Income, 1040" for calendar year "2006" and "Excise, 720" for "2006" (this covers all quarters in 2006). For multiple years or a series of inclusive periods, including quarterly periods, you may list 2004 through (thru or a hyphen) 2006. For example, "2004 thru 2006" or "2nd 2005-3rd 2006." For fiscal years, enter the ending year and month, using the YYYYMM format. Do not use a general reference such as "All years," "All periods," or "All taxes." Any tax information authorization with a general reference will be returned.

You may list the current year or period and any tax years or periods that have already ended as of the date you sign the tax information authorization. However, you may include on a tax information authorization only future tax periods that end no later than 3 years after the date the tax information authorization is received by the IRS. The 3 future periods are determined starting after December 31 of the year the tax information authorization is received by the IRS. You must enter the type of tax, the tax form number, and the future year(s) or period(s). If the matter relates to estate tax, enter the date of the decedent's death instead of the year or period.

In **column (d),** enter any specific information you want the IRS to provide. Examples of column (d) information are: lien information, a balance due amount, a specific tax schedule, or a tax liability.

For requests regarding Form 8802, Application for United States Residency Certification, enter "Form 8802" in column (d) and check the specific use box on line 4. Also, enter the appointee's information as instructed on Form 8802.

Note. If the taxpayer is subject to penalties related to an individual retirement account (IRA) account (for example, a penalty for excess contributions) enter, "IRA civil penalty" on line 3, column a.

Line 4. Specific Use Not Recorded on CAF

Generally, the IRS records all tax information authorizations on the CAF system. However, authorizations relating to a specific issue are not recorded.

Check the box on line 4 if Form 8821 is filed for any of the following reasons: (a) requests to disclose information to loan companies or educational institutions, (b) requests to disclose information to federal or state agency investigators for background checks, (c) application for EIN, or (d) claims filed on Form 843, Claim for Refund and Request for Abatement. If you check the box on line 4, your appointee should mail or fax Form 8821 to the IRS office handling the matter. Otherwise, your appointee should bring a copy of Form 8821 to each appointment to inspect or receive information. A specific-use tax information authorization will not revoke any prior tax information authorizations.

Line 6. Retention/Revocation of Tax Information Authorizations

Check the box on this line and attach a copy of the tax information authorization you do not want to revoke. The filing of Form 8821 will not revoke any Form 2848 that is in effect.

Line 7. Signature of Taxpayer(s)

Individuals. You must sign and date the authorization. Either husband or wife must sign if Form 8821 applies to a joint return.

Corporations. Generally, Form 8821 can be signed by: (a) an officer having legal authority to bind the corporation, (b) any person designated by the board of directors or other governing body, (c) any officer or employee on written request by any principal officer and attested to by the secretary or other officer, and (d) any other person authorized to access information under section 6103(e).

Partnerships. Generally, Form 8821 can be signed by any person who was a member of the partnership during any part of the tax period covered by Form 8821. See *Partnership Items* on page 3.

All others. See section 6103(e) if the taxpayer has died, is insolvent, is a dissolved corporation, or if a trustee, guardian, executor, receiver, or administrator is acting for the taxpayer.

Privacy Act and Paperwork Reduction Act Notice

We ask for the information on this form to carry out the Internal Revenue laws of the United States. Form 8821 is provided by the IRS for your convenience and its use is voluntary. If you designate an appointee to inspect and/or receive confidential tax information, you are required by section 6103(c) to provide the information requested on Form 8821. Under section 6109, you must disclose your social security number (SSN), employer identification number (EIN), or individual taxpayer identification number (ITIN). If you do not provide all the information requested on this form, we may not be able to honor the authorization.

The IRS may provide this information to the Department of Justice for civil and criminal litigation, and to cities, states, the District of Columbia, and U.S. possessions to carry out their tax laws. We may also disclose this information to other countries under a tax treaty, to federal and state agencies to enforce federal nontax criminal laws, or to federal law enforcement and intelligence agencies to combat terrorism.

You are not required to provide the information requested on a form that is subject to the Paperwork Reduction Act unless the form displays a valid OMB control number. Books or records relating to a form or its instructions must be retained as long as their contents may become material in the administration of any Internal Revenue law.

The time needed to complete and file this form will vary depending on individual circumstances. The estimated average time is: **Recordkeeping,** 6 min.; **Learning about the law or the form,** 12 min.; **Preparing the form,** 24 min.; **Copying and sending the form to the IRS,** 20 min.

If you have comments concerning the accuracy of these time estimates or suggestions for making Form 8821 simpler, we would be happy to hear from you. You can write to Internal Revenue Service, Tax Products Coordinating Committee, SE:W:CAR:MP:T:T:SP, 1111 Constitution Ave. NW, IR-6526, Washington, DC 20224. **Do not** send Form 8821 to this address. Instead, see the *Where To File Chart* on page 2.

¶206 Exhibit 2-3

Excerpts from Form 1040—Check the Box

Third Party Designee	Do you want to allow another person to discuss this return with the IRS (see instructions)? ☐ **Yes.** Complete below. ☐ **No**		
	Designee's name ▶	Phone no. ▶	Personal identification number (PIN) ▶ ☐☐☐☐☐

Sign Here Joint return? See page 12. Keep a copy for your records.	Under penalties of perjury, I declare that I have examined this return and accompanying schedules and statements, and to the best of my knowledge and belief, they are true, correct, and complete. Declaration of preparer (other than taxpayer) is based on all information of which preparer has any knowledge.		
	Your signature	Date	Your occupation	Daytime phone number
	Spouse's signature. If a joint return, **both** must sign.	Date	Spouse's occupation	

Paid Preparer Use Only	Print/Type preparer's name	Preparer's signature	Date	Check ☐ if self-employed	PTIN
	Firm's name ▶			Firm's EIN ▶	
	Firm's address ▶			Phone no.	

Form **1040** (2010)

Third Party Designee

If you want to allow your preparer, a friend, a family member, or any other person you choose to discuss your 2010 tax return with the IRS, check the "Yes" box in the "Third Party Designee" area of your return. Also, enter the designee's name, phone number, and any five digits the designee chooses as his or her personal identification number (PIN).

If you check the "Yes" box, you, and your spouse if filing a joint return, are authorizing the IRS to call the designee to answer any questions that may arise during the processing of your return. You are also authorizing the designee to:

• Give the IRS any information that is missing from your return,

• Call the IRS for information about the processing of your return or the status of your refund or payment(s),

• Receive copies of notices or transcripts related to your return, upon request, and

• Respond to certain IRS notices about math errors, offsets, and return preparation.

You are not authorizing the designee to receive any refund check, bind you to anything (including any additional tax liability), or otherwise represent you before the IRS. If you want to expand the designee's authorization, see Pub. 947.

The authorization will automatically end no later than the due date (without regard to extensions) for filing your 2011 tax return. This is April 17, 2012, for most people. If you wish to revoke the authorization before it ends, see Pub. 947.

¶207 Exhibit 2-4

Form **2848** (Rev. June 2008) Department of the Treasury Internal Revenue Service	**Power of Attorney** **and Declaration of Representative** ▶ Type or print. ▶ See the separate instructions.	OMB No. 1545-0150 **For IRS Use Only** Received by: Name Telephone Function Date / /

Part I   **Power of Attorney**

     Caution: *Form 2848 will not be honored for any purpose other than representation before the IRS.*

1   **Taxpayer information.** Taxpayer(s) must sign and date this form on page 2, line 9.

Taxpayer name(s) and address	Social security number(s)	Employer identification number
	Daytime telephone number ( )	Plan number (if applicable)

hereby appoint(s) the following representative(s) as attorney(s)-in-fact:

2   **Representative(s)** must sign and date this form on page 2, Part II.

Name and address	CAF No. .... Telephone No. .... Fax No. .... Check if new: Address ☐ Telephone No. ☐ Fax No. ☐
Name and address	CAF No. .... Telephone No. .... Fax No. .... Check if new: Address ☐ Telephone No. ☐ Fax No. ☐
Name and address	CAF No. .... Telephone No. .... Fax No. .... Check if new: Address ☐ Telephone No. ☐ Fax No. ☐

to represent the taxpayer(s) before the Internal Revenue Service for the following tax matters:

3   **Tax matters**

Type of Tax (Income, Employment, Excise, etc.) or Civil Penalty (see the instructions for line 3)	Tax Form Number (1040, 941, 720, etc.)	Year(s) or Period(s) (see the instructions for line 3)

4   **Specific use not recorded on Centralized Authorization File (CAF).** If the power of attorney is for a specific use not recorded on CAF, check this box. See the instructions for **Line 4. Specific Uses Not Recorded on CAF** . . . . ▶ ☐

5   **Acts authorized.** The representatives are authorized to receive and inspect confidential tax information and to perform any and all acts that I (we) can perform with respect to the tax matters described on line 3, for example, the authority to sign any agreements, consents, or other documents. The authority does not include the power to receive refund checks (see line 6 below), the power to substitute another representative or add additional representatives, the power to sign certain returns, or the power to execute a request for disclosure of tax returns or return information to a third party. See the line 5 instructions for more information.

     Exceptions. An unenrolled return preparer cannot sign any document for a taxpayer and may only represent taxpayers in limited situations. See **Unenrolled Return Preparer** on page 1 of the instructions. An enrolled actuary may only represent taxpayers to the extent provided in section 10.3(d) of Treasury Department Circular No. 230 (Circular 230). An enrolled retirement plan administrator may only represent taxpayers to the extent provided in section 10.3(e) of Circular 230. See the line 5 instructions for restrictions on tax matters partners. In most cases, the student practitioner's (levels k and l) authority is limited (for example, they may only practice under the supervision of another practitioner).

     List any specific additions or deletions to the acts otherwise authorized in this power of attorney: ....
....
....
....

6   **Receipt of refund checks.** If you want to authorize a representative named on line 2 to receive, **BUT NOT TO ENDORSE OR CASH**, refund checks, initial here ————— and list the name of that representative below.

     Name of representative to receive refund check(s) ▶

For Privacy Act and Paperwork Reduction Act Notice, see page 4 of the instructions.   Cat. No. 11980J   Form **2848** (Rev. 6-2008)

Form 2848 (Rev. 6-2008)   Page **2**

7   **Notices and communications.** Original notices and other written communications will be sent to you and a copy to the first representative listed on line 2.

a   If you also want the second representative listed to receive a copy of notices and communications, check this box . . . . . ▶ ☐

b   If you do not want any notices or communications sent to your representative(s), check this box . . . . ▶ ☐

8   **Retention/revocation of prior power(s) of attorney.** The filing of this power of attorney automatically revokes all earlier power(s) of attorney on file with the Internal Revenue Service for the same tax matters and years or periods covered by this document. If you **do not** want to revoke a prior power of attorney, check here. . . . . ▶ ☐

YOU MUST ATTACH A COPY OF ANY POWER OF ATTORNEY YOU WANT TO REMAIN IN EFFECT.

9   **Signature of taxpayer(s).** If a tax matter concerns a joint return, **both** husband and wife must sign if joint representation is requested, otherwise, see the instructions. If signed by a corporate officer, partner, guardian, tax matters partner, executor, receiver, administrator, or trustee on behalf of the taxpayer, I certify that I have the authority to execute this form on behalf of the taxpayer.

▶ **IF NOT SIGNED AND DATED, THIS POWER OF ATTORNEY WILL BE RETURNED.**

Signature	Date	Title (if applicable)

Print Name	☐☐☐☐☐ PIN Number	Print name of taxpayer from line 1 if other than individual

Signature	Date	Title (if applicable)

Print Name	☐☐☐☐☐ PIN Number	

Part II	**Declaration of Representative**

Caution: *Students with a special order to represent taxpayers in qualified Low Income Taxpayer Clinics or the Student Tax Clinic Program (levels k and l), see the instructions for Part II.*

Under penalties of perjury, I declare that:

• I am not currently under suspension or disbarment from practice before the Internal Revenue Service;

• I am aware of regulations contained in Circular 230 (31 CFR, Part 10), as amended, concerning the practice of attorneys, certified public accountants, enrolled agents, enrolled actuaries, and others;

• I am authorized to represent the taxpayer(s) identified in Part I for the tax matter(s) specified there; and

• I am one of the following:

  a   Attorney—a member in good standing of the bar of the highest court of the jurisdiction shown below.

  b   Certified Public Accountant—duly qualified to practice as a certified public accountant in the jurisdiction shown below.

  c   Enrolled Agent—enrolled as an agent under the requirements of Circular 230.

  d   Officer—a bona fide officer of the taxpayer's organization.

  e   Full-Time Employee—a full-time employee of the taxpayer.

  f   Family Member—a member of the taxpayer's immediate family (for example, spouse, parent, child, brother, or sister).

  g   Enrolled Actuary—enrolled as an actuary by the Joint Board for the Enrollment of Actuaries under 29 U.S.C. 1242 (the authority to practice before the Internal Revenue Service is limited by section 10.3(d) of Circular 230).

  h   Unenrolled Return Preparer—the authority to practice before the Internal Revenue Service is limited by Circular 230, section 10.7(c)(1)(viii). You must have prepared the return in question and the return must be under examination by the IRS. See **Unenrolled Return Preparer** on page 1 of the instructions.

  k   Student Attorney—student who receives permission to practice before the IRS by virtue of their status as a law student under section 10.7(d) of Circular 230.

  l   Student CPA—student who receives permission to practice before the IRS by virtue of their status as a CPA student under section 10.7(d) of Circular 230.

  r   Enrolled Retirement Plan Agent—enrolled as a retirement plan agent under the requirements of Circular 230 (the authority to practice before the Internal Revenue Service is limited by section 10.3(e)).

▶ **IF THIS DECLARATION OF REPRESENTATIVE IS NOT SIGNED AND DATED, THE POWER OF ATTORNEY WILL BE RETURNED.** See the Part II instructions.

Designation—Insert above letter **(a–r)**	Jurisdiction (state) or identification	Signature	Date

Form **2848** (Rev. 6-2008)

¶208 Exhibit 2-5

Form **56** (Rev. December 2007) Department of the Treasury Internal Revenue Service	**Notice Concerning Fiduciary Relationship** (Internal Revenue Code sections 6036 and 6903)	OMB No. 1545-0013

Part I — Identification

Name of person for whom you are acting (as shown on the tax return)	Identifying number	Decedent's social security no.

Address of person for whom you are acting (number, street, and room or suite no.)

City or town, state, and ZIP code (If a foreign address, see instructions.)

Fiduciary's name

Address of fiduciary (number, street, and room or suite no.)

City or town, state, and ZIP code	Telephone number (optional) ( )

Part II — Authority

1   Authority for fiduciary relationship. Check applicable box:

a(1) ☐ Will and codicils or court order appointing fiduciary . . . . **(2)** Date of death ....

b(1) ☐ Court order appointing fiduciary . . . . **(2)** Date (see instructions) ....

c ☐ Valid trust instrument and amendments

d ☐ Other. Describe ▶ ....

Part III — Nature of Liability and Tax Notices

2   Type of tax (estate, gift, generation-skipping transfer, income, excise, etc.) ▶ ....

3   Federal tax form number (706, 1040, 1041, 1120, etc.) ▶ ....

4   Year(s) or period(s) (if estate tax, date of death) ▶ ....

5   If the fiduciary listed in Part I is the person to whom notices and other written communications should be sent for **all** items described on lines 2, 3, and 4, check here . . . . ▶ ☐

6   If the fiduciary listed in Part I is the person to whom notices and other written communications should be sent for **some** (but not all) of the items described on lines 2, 3, and 4, check here ▶ ☐ and list the applicable federal tax form number and the year(s) or period(s) applicable

    ....

Part IV — Revocation or Termination of Notice

Section A—Total Revocation or Termination

7   Check this box if you are revoking or terminating all prior notices concerning fiduciary relationships on file with the Internal Revenue Service for the same tax matters and years or periods covered by this notice concerning fiduciary relationship . ▶ ☐
    Reason for termination of fiduciary relationship. Check applicable box:

a ☐ Court order revoking fiduciary authority

b ☐ Certificate of dissolution or termination of a business entity

c ☐ Other. Describe ▶

Section B—Partial Revocation

8a   Check this box if you are revoking earlier notices concerning fiduciary relationships on file with the Internal Revenue Service for the same tax matters and years or periods covered by this notice concerning fiduciary relationship . . . . ▶ ☐

b   Specify to whom granted, date, and address, including ZIP code.
    ▶ ....

Section C—Substitute Fiduciary

9   Check this box if a new fiduciary or fiduciaries have been or will be substituted for the revoking or terminating fiduciary and specify the name(s) and address(es), including ZIP code(s), of the new fiduciary(ies) . . . . ▶ ☐
    ▶ ....

For Paperwork Reduction Act and Privacy Act Notice, see back page.   Cat. No. 16375I   Form **56** (Rev. 12-2007)

Form 56 (Rev. 12-2007) Page **2**

| Part V | **Court and Administrative Proceedings** |

Name of court (if other than a court proceeding, identify the type of proceeding and name of agency)	Date proceeding initiated
Address of court	Docket number of proceeding

City or town, state, and ZIP code	Date	Time	a.m.	Place of other proceedings
			p.m.	

| Part VI | **Signature** |

Please Sign Here

I certify that I have the authority to execute this notice concerning fiduciary relationship on behalf of the taxpayer.

| Fiduciary's signature | Title, if applicable | Date |

Form **56** (Rev. 12-2007)

Form 56 (Rev. 12-2007)   Page **3**

General Instructions

Section references are to the Internal Revenue Code unless otherwise noted.

 Form 56 cannot be used to update the last known address of the person for whom you are acting. Use Form 8822, Change of Address, to make this change.

Purpose of Form

You must notify the IRS of the creation or termination of a fiduciary relationship under section 6903 and give notice of qualification under section 6036. You may use Form 56 to provide this notice to the IRS.

Who Should File

The fiduciary (see **Definitions** below) uses Form 56 to notify the IRS of the creation or termination of a fiduciary relationship under section 6903. For example, if you are acting as fiduciary for an individual, a decedent's estate, or a trust, you may file Form 56.

Receivers and assignees for the benefit of creditors also file Form 56 to give notice of qualification under section 6036. However, a bankruptcy trustee, debtor-in-possession, or other like fiduciary in a bankruptcy proceeding is not required to give notice of qualification under section 6036. Trustees, etc., in bankruptcy proceedings are subject to the notice requirements under title 11 of the United States Code (Bankruptcy Rules).

Definitions

Fiduciary. A fiduciary is any person acting in a fiduciary capacity for any other person (or terminating entity), such as an administrator, conservator, designee, executor, guardian, receiver, trustee of a trust, trustee in bankruptcy, personal representative, person in possession of property of a decedent's estate, or debtor-in-possession of assets in any bankruptcy proceeding by order of the court.

Person. A person is any individual, trust, estate, partnership, association, company or corporation.

Decedent's estate. A decedent's estate is a taxable entity separate from the decedent that comes into existence at the time of the decedent's death. It generally continues to exist until the final distribution of the estate's assets is made to the heirs and other beneficiaries.

Terminating entities. A terminating entity, such as a corporation, partnership, trust, etc., only has the legal capacity to establish a fiduciary

relationship while it is in existence. Establishing a fiduciary relationship prior to termination of the entity allows the fiduciary to represent the entity on all tax matters after it is terminated.

When and Where To File

Notice of fiduciary relationship. Generally, you should file Form 56 when you create (or terminate) a fiduciary relationship. File Form 56 with the Internal Revenue Service Center where the person for whom you are acting is required to file tax returns.

Proceedings (other than bankruptcy) and assignments for the benefit of creditors. A fiduciary who is appointed or authorized to act as:

● A receiver in a receivership proceeding or similar fiduciary (including a fiduciary in aid of foreclosure), or

● An assignee for the benefit of creditors, must file Form 56 on, or within 10 days of, the date of appointment with the Advisory Group Manager, Advisory, Insolvency and Quality (AIQ) Office, of the area office of the IRS having jurisdiction over the person for whom you are acting. See Publication 4235, Technical Services (Advisory) Group Addresses, for more information.

The receiver or assignee may also file a separate Form 56 with the service center where the person for whom the fiduciary is acting is required to file tax returns to provide the notice required by section 6903.

Specific Instructions

Part I—Identification

Provide all the information called for in this part. If there is more than one fiduciary, each fiduciary must file (or otherwise give notice) a separate Form 56.

Name. File a separate Form 56 for each person for whom you are acting in a fiduciary capacity. For example, if you will be filing the decedent's final Form 1040 and are the executor/administrator of the decedent's estate, file one Form 56 entering the name of the decedent as the person for whom you are acting and file one Form 56 entering the name of the estate as the name of the person for whom you are acting.

Identifying number. If you are acting for an individual, an individual debtor, or other person whose assets are controlled, the identifying number is the social security number (SSN). If you are acting for a person other than an individual, including an estate or trust, the identifying number is the employer identification number (EIN).

Decedent's SSN. If you are acting on behalf of a decedent, enter the decedent's SSN shown on his or her

final Form 1040 in the space provided. If you are acting on behalf of a decedent's estate that must file a Form 706, United States Estate (and Generation-Skipping Transfer) Tax Return, enter the decedent's SSN in addition to entering the EIN (if applicable) as discussed above under *Identifying number.*

Address. Include the suite, room, or other unit number after the street address.

If the postal service does not deliver mail to the street address and the fiduciary (or person) has a P.O. box, show the box number instead of the street address.

For a foreign address, enter the information in the following order: city, province or state, and country. Follow the country's practice for entering the postal code. Please do not abbreviate the country name.

Part II—Authority

Line 1a. Check the box on line 1a if the decedent died *testate* (i.e., having left a valid will) and enter the decedent's date of death.

Line 1b. Check the box on line 1b if the decedent died *intestate* (i.e., without leaving a valid will). Also, enter the decedent's date of death and write "Date of Death" next to the date.

Assignment for the benefit of creditors. Enter the date the assets were assigned to you and write "Assignment Date" after the date.

Proceedings other than bankruptcy. Enter the date you were appointed or took possession of the assets of the debtor or other person whose assets are controlled.

 You must be prepared to furnish evidence that substantiates your authority to act as a fiduciary for the person for whom you are acting.

Part III—Nature of Liability and Tax Notices

Line 2. Specify the type of tax involved. This line should also identify a transferee tax liability under section 6901 or fiduciary tax liability under 31 U.S.C. 3713(b) when either exists.

Line 5. If you check the box on line 5, we will treat your address as the address for IRS notices and correspondence for the form(s) and period(s) listed on lines 3 and 4.

Line 6. If you check the box on line 6, we will treat your address as the address for IRS notices and correspondence for the form(s) and period(s) that you list on line 6.

Part IV—Revocation or Termination of Notice

Complete this part only if you are revoking or terminating a prior notice concerning a fiduciary relationship. Completing this part will relieve you of any further duty or liability as a fiduciary if used as a notice of termination. However, completing Section B or C does not relieve any new or substitute fiduciary of the requirement to file a Form 56 or to otherwise give notice.

Part V—Court and Administrative Proceedings

Complete this part only if you have been appointed a receiver, trustee, or fiduciary by a court or other governmental unit in a proceeding other than a bankruptcy proceeding.

If proceedings are scheduled for more than one date, time, or place, attach a separate schedule of the proceedings.

Assignment for the benefit of creditors. You must attach the following information:

1. A brief description of the assets that were assigned, and

2. An explanation of the action to be taken regarding such assets, including any hearings, meetings of creditors, sale, or other scheduled action.

Part VI—Signature

Sign Form 56 and enter a title describing your role as a fiduciary (e.g., assignee, executor, guardian, trustee, personal representative, receiver, or conservator).

Paperwork Reduction Act and Privacy Act Notice. We ask for the information on this form to carry out the Internal Revenue laws of the United States. Form 56 is provided for your convenience in meeting this requirement and its use is voluntary. Sections 6903 and 6036 require you to inform the IRS of the creation or termination of a fiduciary relationship. Under section 6109 you must disclose the social security number or other identification number of the individual or entity for which you are acting. The principal purpose of this disclosure is to secure proper identification of the taxpayer. We also need this information to gain access to the tax information in our files and properly respond to your request. We may disclose this information to the Department of Justice for civil or criminal litigation, and to cities, states, and the District of Columbia for use in administering their tax laws. We may also disclose this information to other countries under a tax treaty, to federal and state agencies to enforce federal nontax criminal laws, or to federal law enforcement and intelligence agencies to combat terrorism. If you do not disclose this information, we may suspend processing the notice of fiduciary relationship and not consider this as proper notification until you provide the information. Providing false information may subject you to penalties.

You are not required to provide the information requested on a form that is subject to the Paperwork Reduction Act unless the form displays a valid OMB control number. Books or records relating to a form or its instructions must be retained as long as their contents may become material in the administration of any Internal Revenue law. Generally, tax returns and return information are confidential as required by section 6103.

The time needed to complete and file this form will vary depending on individual circumstances. The estimated average time is:

Recordkeeping . . . . . . 8 min.

Learning about the law or the form . . . . . . 32 min.

Preparing the form . . . . . 46 min.

Copying, assembling, and sending the form to the IRS . 15 min.

If you have comments concerning the accuracy of these time estimates or suggestions for making this form simpler, we would be happy to hear from you. You can write to the Internal Revenue Service, Tax Products Coordinating Committee, SE:W:CAR:MP:T:T:SP, IR-6526, 1111 Constitution Avenue, NW, Washington, DC 20224. Do not send Form 56 to this address. Instead, see *When and Where To File* on the prior page.

¶208

¶221 DISCUSSION QUESTIONS

1. You prepared Henry Helpless' tax return for 2008 and Helpless has been called in by a Revenue Agent. He asks you to attend the meeting.

   (A) Assume that you are Friendly Frank, Helpless' neighbor, who has prepared the return *without compensation*. What document(s), if any, must you file with the IRS *to accompany the taxpayer* and act in the capacities described below?

      (1) To receive or inspect confidential tax information.

      (2) To act as an advocate on behalf of Helpless and perform acts as described in Reg. § 601.504(a).

   (B) Assume the same facts in (A), except that Helpless *is not present* at the meeting. What document(s), if any, must you file in the following capacities:

      (1) To receive or inspect confidential tax information.

      (2) To act as an advocate on behalf of Helpless and perform acts as described in Reg. § 601.504(a).

   (C) Assume that Henry Helpless compensates you for preparing his return. Would your answers to the questions in (A) and (B), above, differ? Why?

2. Assume that you *did not* prepare Henry Helpless' return in Question 1 but that Helpless still wants you to represent him at the audit. What do you need to file in the following situations?

   (A) You are Helpless' representative and he is present at the meeting.

   (B) You are Helpless' representative and he is not present at the meeting.

   (C) You are Helpless' representative and he is not present and the Agent has indicated that he wishes to have the statute of limitations on assessment extended.

3. Your employer, Seville, Inc., is being audited by the IRS. You are assigned to coordinate the responses given to the IRS and to handle any negotiations with them. Assuming you have been granted carte blanche corporate authority, what acts can you perform and what decisions can you make if your status is:

   (A) Bookkeeper for Seville, Inc.?

   (B) Internal auditor for Seville, Inc., and a graduate of High Standards University with a Masters in Taxation?

   (C) Comptroller of Seville, Inc., and a Certified Public Accountant?

   (D) Corporate Counsel for Seville, Inc., and an attorney with a Masters of Law in Taxation?

4. Tammy Terrified received a notice from the IRS Center demanding payment in full of $50,000 of additional tax, $10,000 in penalties and $5,000 in statutory interest. The computerized statement sets out in bold,

capital letters "Final Notice—Payment Due Within Ten (10) Days." Tammy Terrified looks in the Yellow Pages and finds that representation in tax matters seems to be touted by a number of different professions. She seeks your help in deciding which ones she could call for her problem. Terrified tells you that she does owe the tax, penalties and interest, but that she and her nine children have been abandoned, left penniless and are on welfare.

The phone book has the following listings:

ACCOUNTANT—noncertified—enrolled to practice before the IRS.

ACCOUNTANT—Certified Public—licensed to practice in this state.

ATTORNEY—licensed to practice in this state—divorce, real estate, tax, personal injury and Workers' Compensation cases accepted.

BOOKKEEPING SERVICE—accounting and bookkeeping service, general ledger, profit and loss and financial statements, and tax return preparation.

CONSULTANT—tax and related matters, mergers, acquisitions and business closings—MBA and MS in Taxation, High Standards University.

TAXMAN—preparation of Forms 1040EZ, 1040A, 1040, 1040X, 1120, 1120S, 940, 941 and other federal tax forms—inexpensive but good—We talk tax!

(A) Explain in detail which one(s) Tammy Terrified could call, and explain the powers and authority of each representative.

(B) Explain in detail the reason for rejecting any individual, including lack of authority.

(C) If Tammy Terrified asks you to make a single choice, which one would you choose and why?

5. Oscar Obnoxious is a CPA and an ardent champion of taxpayers' rights. He specializes in representing taxpayers in audits and boasts that he has been extremely successful either in resolving audits with little or no tax due or in delaying them so long that the IRS finally gives up. Oscar's aggressive television advertising has resulted in his having many clients whose cases need his attention.

In 2008, on four separate occasions, the IRS has not been able to get information from Oscar in a timely fashion and it has resorted to contacting his clients directly, following the bypass procedure described in IRM 5.1.1.7.7. In two instances the IRS found Oscar had never contacted the taxpayer to get the information; in the other two, the taxpayers had given Oscar the information several months before.

Oscar is concerned that the IRS's use of the bypass procedure will hamper his ability to effectively resolve his clients' situations and will eventually destroy his practice. He wishes to sue the IRS for an injunction against their using the bypass procedure and also for damages for impairing his contracts with his clients and for violations of his constitutional rights. He wants to know his chances in this litigation.

¶221

CHAPTER 3
ETHICAL RESPONSIBILITIES: PROHIBITIONS AND DUTIES REGARDING PRACTICE

¶301 CODE OF CONDUCT

Treasury Department Circular No. 230 provides regulations governing the practice of various tax professionals before the Internal Revenue Service (IRS).[1] Subpart A of Circular 230[2] provides rules governing the authority to practice before the IRS and is discussed in Chapter 2. Subpart B of Circular 230[3] sets forth a code of conduct that representatives must follow in representing taxpayers. Subpart C[4] provides the sanctions for violations of Circular 230. Subpart D[5] contains the procedural rules for disciplinary proceedings when the Treasury Department seeks to suspend or disbar a tax professional from practice before the IRS. Subpart E[6] provides general procedures.

Although Circular 230 provides very stringent requirements with respect to the conduct of tax professionals before the IRS, Circular 230 does not provide any standards with respect to dealing with state or foreign tax authorities. Presumably, the state society of CPAs will govern the standards of accountants while the State Bar Association (not the American Bar Association) will provide standards applicable to dealing with state tax authorities. A foreign tax authority may have its own standards, but it is unlikely that the foreign tax authority would be able to enforce any such standards in the United States.

¶302 DUTIES WITH RESPECT TO PRACTICE BEFORE THE IRS

Diligence. A practitioner must exercise due diligence in any matter before the IRS, which includes determining the correctness of any representations to the IRS.[7] The practitioner may rely on the work product of another, but only after taking reasonable care to determine the accuracy of the work product.[8] Circular 230 further provides that if a practitioner is aware of a mistake made with respect to a return or other paper filed, the practitioner must immediately advise the taxpayer of the error and the subsequent consequences under the tax laws.[9]

---

[1] Regulations Governing The Practice Of Attorneys, Certified Public Accountants, Enrolled Agents, Enrolled Actuaries, Enrolled Retirement Plan Agents, And Appraisers Before The Internal Revenue Service, September 26, 2007.

[2] 31 CFR §§ 10.1-10.8.

[3] 31 CFR §§ 10.20-10.38.

[4] 31 CFR §§ 10.50-10.53.

[5] 31 CFR §§ 10.60-10.82.

[6] 31 CFR §§ 10.90-10.93.

[7] 31 CFR § 10.22(a).

[8] 31 CFR § 10.22(b).

[9] 31 CFR § 10.21.

Occasions arise where there are computational errors in favor of the taxpayer in IRS settlements and/or court cases. These mistakes could cause a reduced deficiency and erroneous refund if not corrected. Although Circular 230 addresses the correction of errors and, purportedly, covers this issue, it does not specifically mention an error by the IRS in the taxpayer's favor. The American Bar Association's Tax Section has issued guidance for attorneys in such a matter. Although these very specific factually-oriented hypotheticals show the tension between the attorney's duty to his client versus the attorney's duty not to make misrepresentations, the attorney must disclose clear computational errors.[10]

The diligence provisions also provide that a tax practitioner may not act merely to delay the administration of any tax.[11]

> **Example 3-1:** A tax protestor is represented by a practitioner that knows the tax protestor's position is wrong. The practitioner should not seek a conference in the Appeals Office that the practitioner knows will not be fruitful just to delay the inevitable assessment and collection of tax.

Conflicts of Interest. A practitioner cannot represent a client before the IRS if the representation involves a conflict of interest. A conflict of interest exists if the representation of the client will be adverse to another client or a personal interest of the practitioner or if there is a significant risk that the representation will materially limit the practitioner's responsibilities to another person.[12] However, if the conflict of interest is fully disclosed to all parties, the parties may waive the conflict in writing and the practitioner may take the representation.[13]

> **Example 3-2:** A CPA has represented a life-long friend in varied business interests. The friend provides funding to a C corporation and wants the CPA to take responsibility for all the corporation's tax matters. The funding agreement could be characterized as either debt or as preferred shares. If the funding constitutes preferred shares, any payments to the friend would constitute dividends that qualify for a favorable 15% tax rate, but do not result in a deduction to the corporation. If the funding is characterized as debt, any payments to the friend will be interest, on which the friend will be taxed at 35%, but for which the corporation will receive an interest expense deduction. CPA has a conflict of interest and, unless he discloses that conflict to both the corporation (the other shareholders) and to his friend and receives a waiver in writing, he may not represent the corporation.

> **Example 3-3:** Attorney has a son who plays on a little league baseball team coached by an IRS Agent. Taxpayer comes to Attorney's office, seeking representation in an audit being conducted by IRS Agent. Because Attorney has a personal interest in seeing that his son is treated well by the IRS Agent at the little league field, Attorney has a conflict of interest. However, if the conflict of interest is fully disclosed to Taxpayer and Taxpayer waives the conflict in writing, Attorney may represent Taxpayer.

---

[10] ABA Section of Taxation's Standard of Tax Practice statement 1999-1, updated March 2000.
[11] 31 CFR § 10.20(a).
[12] 31 CFR § 10.29(a).
[13] 31 CFR § 10.29(b).

Returns. A practitioner, which includes registered return preparers, may not willfully nor recklessly sign a tax return that the practitioner reasonably believes contains a position that[14] (a) lacks a reasonable basis; (b) is an unreasonable position;[15] (c) is a willful attempt to understate the liability for tax or (d) is a reckless or intentional disregard of rules or regulations.[16]

> **Example 3-4:** Neville goes to the local volunteer income tax assistance (VITA) location to have his return prepared by Barry. Neville provides information showing eligibility for the earned income tax credit. Barry completes the return for Neville that includes a refund of the earned income tax credit despite the fact that Barry knows Neville earns over $200,000 a year from illicit activities. Barry has failed to follow the appropriate standards because he knows that taking the earned income credit lacks a reasonable basis.

These standards further apply with respect to the duty of a practitioner to advise clients with respect to potential penalties.[17]

Written Advice. At a minimum, a practitioner may not give written advice, which includes electronic communications, if the practitioner bases the written advice on unreasonable factual or legal assumptions, unreasonably relies on statements of the taxpayer, or does not exercise due diligence in considering all the relevant facts (excluding the possibility of audit) that are important to determination of the issue.[18]

> **Example 3-5:** Aunt Harriet, a U.S. citizen, inherits all of the shares of a foreign corporation (ForCo) from her nephew, Bruce. Aunt Harriet's CPA does not know about ForCo and continues to file Aunt Harriet's return without attaching a Form 5471. A few years later, Aunt Harriet learns about the Form 5471 filing obligation from her butler, Alfred. Subsequently, Aunt Harriet requests that CPA provide advice with respect to her obligation to file Forms 5471. CPA writes a letter to Aunt Harriet stating that she does not have to file Forms 5471 because they are information returns that do not result in any tax and there is little chance that the IRS will discover this issue on audit. The letter fails to mention the possibility of any penalty for failure to file the Forms 5471 under Code Sec. 6038. CPA has made inaccurate legal assumptions and has failed to consider all the relevant facts that are important to the determination of the issue.

Covered Opinions. The standard of care increases if the written advice rises to the level of a covered opinion.[19]

In a covered opinion, a practitioner must use reasonable efforts to identify and ascertain the facts, relate the law to the facts, evaluate each significant federal tax issue, and must provide an overall conclusion.[20] Although this would

---

[14] 31 CFR § 10.34(a).

[15] An unreasonable position is described in Code Sec. 6694(a)(2) and its Regulations.

[16] A reckless or intentional disregard is defined in Code Sec. 6694(b)(2) and its Regulations.

[17] 31 CFR § 10.34(c).

[18] 31 CFR §§ 10.22, 10.37.

[19] 31 CFR § 10.35.

[20] 31 CFR § 10.35(c).

ostensibly seem to be standard practice, the key issue is whether an opinion constitutes a covered opinion. Covered opinions by a practitioner evaluate one or more Federal tax issues arising from:

- a listed transaction;[21]
- tax planning in which the principal purpose[22] is the avoidance of tax;[23] or
- tax planning in which a significant purpose[24] is the avoidance of tax[25] and either:
  - concludes that there is a greater than 50% chance of the taxpayer prevailing so that the taxpayer can avoid penalties (a "reliance opinion");[26]
  - the practitioner has reason to know that the opinion will be used to promote an investment plan (a "marketed opinion");[27]
  - the opinion imposes on the recipient the confidentiality of the practitioner's tax strategies ("conditions of confidentiality");[28] or
  - the opinion is subject to a contractual protection that the fees paid to the practitioner are contingent on the taxpayer realizing tax benefits.[29]

Example 3-6: Suppose a promoter organizes a master limited partnership to exploit the recordings of a musical artist. Promoter approaches various potential investors. If the dealings of the partnership constitute a listed transaction, the practitioner's opinion would be a covered opinion. If the principal purpose of the investment is to evade or avoid tax, the practitioner's opinion is a covered opinion.

If a significant purpose of the investment is to evade or avoid tax (but not the principal purpose), the practitioner's opinion is a covered opinion if (a) the investor seeks an opinion to rely on to avaoid penalties, (b) the promoter is seeking the opinion for purposes of selling investments in the partnership, (c) the practitioner giving the opinion does not want anyone else to know about the tax planning implications of the transaction, or (d) the practitioner giving the opinion to the investor receives a fee based on the taxpayer realizing certain tax benefits from the transaction.

If a practitioner provides written advice with respect to a taxpayer's possibility of prevailing that is not with respect to either a listed transaction or a transaction for which the principal purpose is tax avoidance, the writing is not a covered opinion if a legend prominently discloses that the writing may not be used to avoid penalties (i.e., not a reliance opinion).[30]

Example 3-7: Consider a practitioner who receives an unsolicited e-mail from a taxpayer wondering whether his interest expense is deductible. The

---

[21] 31 CFR § 10.35(b)(2)(A); Reg. § 1.6011-4(b)(2).

[22] A principal purpose exists if that purpose exceeds any other purpose. 31 CFR § 10.35(b)(10).

[23] 31 CFR § 10.35(b)(2)(B)

[24] A significant purpose may exist even if there is not a principal purpose. *Id.*

[25] 31 § 10.35(b)(2)(C).

[26] 31 CFR § 10.35(b)(2)(i)(c)(1) and (b)(4).

[27] 31 CFR § 10.35(b)(2)(i)(C)(2) and (b)(5).

[28] 31 CFR § 10.35(b)(2)(i)(C)(3) and (d)(6).

[29] 31 CFR § 10.35(b)(2)(i)(C)(4) and (d)(7).

[30] 31 CFR § 10.35(b)(4) and (8).

¶302

practitioner replies that interest expense is generally deductible but, due to the lack of facts provided, does not go into all the various nuances with respect to the deductibility of interest contained in the Internal Revenue Code and its regulations. Such a response ostensibly constitutes a covered opinion for which the practitioner has not practiced the appropriate standard of care. However, the reply e-mail contains a legend at the bottom stating that "Any advice expressed in this writing as to tax matters was neither written or intended by the sender to be used and cannot be used by any taxpayer for the purpose of avoiding tax penalties that may be imposed on the taxpayer." As a result, the practitioner is not giving a covered opinion that requires a higher standard of care by Circular 230.

The practitioner in charge of overseeing a firm's tax practice must take reasonable steps to ensure that the firm has adequate procedures in effect for that firm's practitioners with respect to representing taxpayers that are consistent with "best practices."[31] Those best practices include communicating clearly with clients, properly establishing the relevant facts, advising taxpayers regarding the import of the conclusions reached, and acting fairly and with integrity before the IRS.[32]

¶303 DISCIPLINARY PROCEEDINGS AND SANCTIONS

The disciplinary proceedings under Subparts C and D of Circular 230 are conducted by the Office of Professional Responsibility of the IRS.[33] The only effective sanction that the Office can impose is the suspension or disbarment of a person who practices before the IRS. For many professionals their ability to represent taxpayers before the IRS, which includes the preparation of returns, constitutes a substantial portion of their practice. Denial of the right to practice would not only have a significant economic effect on them, but would also result in their loss of professional standing and esteem.

Circular 230 lists specific instances of incompetence and disreputable conduct that may be grounds for disbarment from practice before the IRS.[34] The list contained in Circular 230 does not purport to be exhaustive[35] and result in censure, suspension or disbarment from practice for willful violation of any of the regulations contained in Circular 230 or for recklessness or gross incompetence violating the standards for advising with respect to written materials.[36]

Disciplinary proceedings will be heard by an administrative law judge,[37] with an appeal to the Secretary of the Treasury.[38] An expedited procedure further exists for any practitioner who has lost his license pursuant to a state licensing authority or has been convicted of a crime involving dishonesty or breech of trust.[39]

---

[31] 31 CFR § 10.36.
[32] 31 CFR § 10.33.
[33] T.D. 9527, 2011-27 I.R.B. 1.
[34] 31 CFR § 10.51.
[35] 31 CFR § 10.52.

[36] 31 CFR §§ 10.34 through 10.37.
[37] 31 CFR § 10.71.
[38] 31 CFR §§ 10.77 and 10.88.
[39] 31 CFR § 10.82.

¶304 CIRCULAR 230

Set forth is the current text of Subparts B through E of Circular 230.

PART 10—PRACTICE BEFORE THE INTERNAL REVENUE SERVICE

* * * * *

Subpart B—Duties and Restrictions Relating to Practice Before the Internal Revenue Service

§ 10.20. Information to be furnished. (a) *To the Internal Revenue Service.* (1) A practitioner must, on a proper and lawful request by a duly authorized officer or employee of the Internal Revenue Service, promptly submit records or information in any matter before the Internal Revenue Service unless the practitioner believes in good faith and on reasonable grounds that the records or information are privileged.

(2) Where the requested records or information are not in the possession of, or subject to the control of, the practitioner or the practitioner's client, the practitioner must promptly notify the requesting Internal Revenue Service officer or employee and the practitioner must provide any information that the practitioner has regarding the identity of any person who the practitioner believes may have possession or control of the requested records or information. The practitioner must make reasonable inquiry of his or her client regarding the identity of any person who may have possession or control of the requested records or information, but the practitioner is not required to make inquiry of any other person or independently verify any information provided by the practitioner's client regarding the identity of such persons.

(3) When a proper and lawful request is made by a duly authorized officer or employee of the Internal Revenue Service, concerning an inquiry into an alleged violation of the regulations in this part, a practitioner must provide any information the practitioner has concerning the alleged violation and testify regarding this

information in any proceeding instituted under this part, unless the practitioner believes in good faith and on reasonable grounds that the information is privileged.

(b) *Interference with a proper and lawful request for records or information*. A practitioner may not interfere, or attempt to interfere, with any proper and lawful effort by the Internal Revenue Service, its officers or employees, to obtain any record or information unless the practitioner believes in good faith and on reasonable grounds that the record or information is privileged.

(c) *Effective/applicability date*. This section is applicable beginning August 2, 2011.

⤷ § 10.21. Knowledge of client's omission. A practitioner who, having been retained by a client with respect to a matter administered by the Internal Revenue Service, knows that the client has not complied with the revenue laws of the United States or has made an error in or omission from any return, document, affidavit, or other paper which the client submitted or executed under the revenue laws of the United States, must advise the client promptly of the fact of such noncompliance, error, or omission. The practitioner must advise the client of the consequences as provided under the Code and regulations of such noncompliance, error, or omission.

§ 10.22. Diligence as to accuracy. (a) In general. A practitioner must exercise due diligence—

(1) In preparing or assisting in the preparation of, approving, and filing tax returns, documents, affidavits, and other papers relating to Internal Revenue Service matters;

(2) In determining the correctness of oral or written representations made by the practitioner to the Department of the Treasury; and

(3) In determining the correctness of oral or written representations made by the practitioner to clients with reference to any matter administered by the Internal Revenue Service.

(b) **Reliance on others**. Except as provided in §§ 10.34, 10.35, and 10.37, a practitioner will be presumed to have exer-

cised due diligence for purposes of this section if the practitioner relies on the work product of another person and the practitioner used reasonable care in engaging, supervising, training, and evaluating the person, taking proper account of the nature of the relationship between the practitioner and the person.

(c) *Effective/applicability date*. This section is applicable on September 26, 2007.

§ 10.23. Prompt disposition of pending matters. A practitioner may not unreasonably delay the prompt disposition of any matter before the Internal Revenue Service.

§ 10.24. Assistance from disbarred or suspended persons and former Internal Revenue Service employees. A practitioner may not, knowingly and directly or indirectly:

(a) Accept assistance from or assist any person who is under disbarment or suspension from practice before the Internal Revenue Service if the assistance relates to a matter or matters constituting practice before the Internal Revenue Service.

(b) Accept assistance from any former government employee where the provisions of § 10.25 or any Federal law would be violated.

§ 10.25. Practice by former Government employees, their partners and their associates. (a) *Definitions* . For purposes of this section—

(1) *Assist* means to act in such a way as to advise, furnish information to, or otherwise aid another person, directly or indirectly.

(2) *Government employee* is an officer or employee of the United States or any agency of the United States, including a special Government employee as defined in 18 U.S.C. 202(a), or of the District of Columbia, or of any State, or a member of Congress or of any State legislature.

(3) *Member of a firm* is a sole practitioner or an employee or associate thereof, or a partner, stockholder, associate, affiliate or employee of a partnership, joint venture, corporation, professional association or other affiliation of two or more practitioners who represent nongovernmental parties.

¶304

(4) *Particular matter involving specific parties* is defined at 5 CFR 2637.201(c), or superseding post-employment regulations issued by the U.S. Office of Government Ethics.

(5) *Rule* includes Treasury regulations, whether issued or under preparation for issuance as notices of proposed rulemaking or as Treasury decisions, revenue rulings, and revenue procedures published in the Internal Revenue Bulletin (see 26 CFR 601.601(d)(2)(ii)(*b*)).

(b) *General rules* . (1) No former Government employee may, subsequent to Government employment, represent anyone in any matter administered by the Internal Revenue Service if the representation would violate 18 U.S.C. 207 or any other laws of the United States.

(2) No former Government employee who personally and substantially participated in a particular matter involving specific parties may, subsequent to Government employment, represent or knowingly assist, in that particular matter, any person who is or was a specific party to that particular matter.

(3) A former Government employee who within a period of one year prior to the termination of Government employment had official responsibility for a particular matter involving specific parties may not, within two years after Government employment is ended, represent in that particular matter any person who is or was a specific party to that particular matter.

(4) No former Government employee may, within one year after Government employment is ended, communicate with or appear before, with the intent to influence, any employee of the Treasury Department in connection with the publication, withdrawal, amendment, modification, or interpretation of a rule the development of which the former Government employee participated in, or for which, within a period of one year prior to the termination of Government employment, the former government employee had official responsibility. This paragraph (b)(4) does not, however, preclude any former employee from appearing on one's own behalf or from representing a taxpayer

before the Internal Revenue Service in connection with a particular matter involving specific parties involving the application or interpretation of a rule with respect to that particular matter, provided that the representation is otherwise consistent with the other provisions of this section and the former employee does not utilize or disclose any confidential information acquired by the former employee in the development of the rule.

(c) *Firm representation* . (1) No member of a firm of which a former Government employee is a member may represent or knowingly assist a person who was or is a specific party in any particular matter with respect to which the restrictions of paragraph (b)(2) of this section apply to the former Government employee, in that particular matter, unless the firm isolates the former Government employee in such a way to ensure that the former Government employee cannot assist in the representation.

(2) When isolation of a former Government employee is required under paragraph (c)(1) of this section, a statement affirming the fact of such isolation must be executed under oath by the former Government employee and by another member of the firm acting on behalf of the firm. The statement must clearly identify the firm, the former Government employee, and the particular matter(s) requiring isolation. The statement must be retained by the firm and, upon request, provided to the office(s) of the Internal Revenue Service administering or enforcing this part.

(d) *Pending representation.* The provisions of this regulation will govern practice by former Government employees, their partners and associates with respect to representation in particular matters involving specific parties where actual representation commenced before the effective date of this regulation.

(e) *Effective/applicability date.* This section is applicable beginning August 2, 2011.

§ 10.26. Notaries. A practitioner may not take acknowledgments, administer oaths, certify papers, or perform any official act as a notary public with respect

[handwritten margin note: Can not notarize your own interest]

to any matter administered by the Internal Revenue Service and for which he or she is employed as counsel, attorney, or agent, or in which he or she may be in any way interested.

§ 10.27. **Fees.** (a) *In General.* A practitioner may not charge an unconscionable fee in connection with any matter before the Internal Revenue Service.

(b) *Contingent fees.* (1) Except as provided in paragraphs (b)(2), (3), and (4) of this section, a practitioner may not charge a contingent fee for services rendered in connection with any matter before the Internal Revenue Service.

(2) A practitioner may charge a contingent fee for services rendered in connection with the Service's examination of, or challenge to—

(i) An original tax return; or

(ii) An amended return or claim for refund or credit where the amended return or claim for refund or credit was filed within 120 days of the taxpayer receiving a written notice of the examination of, or a written challenge to the original tax return.

(3) A practitioner may charge a contingent fee for services rendered in connection with a claim for credit or refund filed solely in connection with the determination of statutory interest or penalties assessed by the Internal Revenue Service.

(4) A practitioner may charge a contingent fee for services rendered in connection with any judicial proceeding arising under the Internal Revenue Code.

(c) *Definitions.* For purposes of this section—

(1) *Contingent fee* is any fee that is based, in whole or in part, on whether or not a position taken on a tax return or other filing avoids challenge by the Internal Revenue Service or is sustained either by the Internal Revenue Service or in litigation. A contingent fee includes a fee that is based on a percentage of the refund reported on a return, that is based on a percentage of the taxes saved, or that otherwise depends on the specific result attained. A contingent fee also includes any fee arrangement in which the practitioner will reimburse the client for all or a portion of the client's fee in the event that a position taken on a tax return or other filing is challenged by the Internal Revenue Service or is not sustained, whether pursuant to an indemnity agreement, a guarantee, rescission rights, or any other arrangement with a similar effect.

(2) *Matter before the Internal Revenue Service* includes tax planning and advice, preparing or filing or assisting in preparing or filing returns or claims for refund or credit, and all matters connected with a presentation to the Internal Revenue Service or any of its officers or employees relating to a taxpayer's rights, privileges, or liabilities under laws or regulations administered by the Internal Revenue Service. Such presentations include, but are not limited to, preparing and filing documents, corresponding and communicating with the Internal Revenue Service, rendering written advice with respect to any entity, transaction, plan or arrangement, and representing a client at conferences, hearings, and meetings.

(d) *Effective/applicability date.* This section is applicable for fee arrangements entered into after March 26, 2008.

§ 10.28 **Return of client's records.** (a) In general, a practitioner must, at the request of a client, promptly return any and all records of the client that are necessary for the client to comply with his or her Federal tax obligations. The practitioner may retain copies of the records returned to a client. The existence of a dispute over fees generally does not relieve the practitioner of his or her responsibility under this section. Nevertheless, if applicable state law allows or permits the retention of a client's records by a practitioner in the case of a dispute over fees for services rendered, the practitioner need only return those records that must be attached to the taxpayer's return. The practitioner, however, must provide the client with reasonable access to review and copy any additional records of the client retained by the practitioner under state law that are necessary for the client to comply with his or her Federal tax obligations.

(b) For purposes of this section. , *Records of the client* include all documents or written or electronic materials provided

[handwritten margin note: because they don't pay you]

to the practitioner, or obtained by the practitioner in the course of the practitioner's representation of the client, that preexisted the retention of the practitioner by the client. The term also includes materials that were prepared by the client or a third party (not including an employee or agent of the practitioner) at any time and provided to the practitioner with respect to the subject matter of the representation. The term also includes any return, claim for refund, schedule, affidavit, appraisal or any other document prepared by the practitioner, or his or her employee or agent, that was presented to the client with respect to a prior representation if such document is necessary for the taxpayer to comply with his or her current Federal tax obligations. The term does not include any return, claim for refund, schedule, affidavit, appraisal or any other document prepared by the practitioner or the practitioner's firm, employees or agents if the practitioner is withholding such document pending the client's performance of its contractual obligation to pay fees with respect to such document.

§ 10.29. Conflicting interests. (a) Except as provided by paragraph (b) of this section, a practitioner shall not represent a client before the Internal Revenue Service if the representation involves a conflict of interest. A conflict of interest exists if—

(1) The representation of one client will be directly adverse to another client; or

(2) There is a significant risk that the representation of one or more clients will be materially limited by the practitioner's responsibilities to another client, a former client or a third person, or by a personal interest of the practitioner.

(b) Notwithstanding the existence of a conflict of interest under paragraph (a) of this section, the practitioner may represent a client if—

(1) The practitioner reasonably believes that the practitioner will be able to provide competent and diligent representation to each affected client;

(2) The representation is not prohibited by law; and

(3) Each affected client waives the conflict of interest and gives informed consent, confirmed in writing by each affected client, at the time the existence of the conflict of interest is known by the practitioner. The confirmation may be made within a reasonable period after the informed consent, but in no event later than 30 days.

(c) Copies of the written consents must be retained by the practitioner for at least 36 months from the date of the conclusion of the representation of the affected clients, and the written consents must be provided to any officer or employee of the Internal Revenue Service on request.

(d) *Effective/applicabilty date.* This section is applicable on September 26, 2007.

§ 10.30. Solicitation. (a) *Advertising and Solicitation Restrictions* . (1) A practitioner may not, with respect to any Internal Revenue Service matter, in any way use or participate in the use of any form of public communication or private solicitation containing a false, fraudulent, or coercive statement or claim; or a misleading or deceptive statement or claim. Enrolled agents, enrolled retirement plan agents, or registered tax return preparers, in describing their professional designation, may not utilize the term "certified" or imply an employer/employee relationship with the Internal Revenue Service. Examples of acceptable descriptions for enrolled agents are "enrolled to represent taxpayers before the Internal Revenue Service," "enrolled to practice before the Internal Revenue Service," and "admitted to practice before the Internal Revenue Service." Similarly, examples of acceptable descriptions for enrolled retirement plan agents are "enrolled to represent taxpayers before the Internal Revenue Service as a retirement plan agent" and "enrolled to practice before the Internal Revenue Service as a retirement plan agent." An example of an acceptable description for registered tax return preparers is "designated as a registered tax return preparer by the Internal Revenue Service."

(2) A practitioner may not make, directly or indirectly, an uninvited written or oral solicitation of employment in matters related to the Internal Revenue

Service if the solicitation violates Federal or State law or other applicable rule, e.g., attorneys are precluded from making a solicitation that is prohibited by conduct rules applicable to all attorneys in their State(s) of licensure. Any lawful solicitation made by or on behalf of a practitioner eligible to practice before the Internal Revenue Service must, nevertheless, clearly identify the solicitation as such and, if applicable, identify the source of the information used in choosing the recipient.

⚹ (b) *Fee Information.* (1)(i) A practitioner may publish the availability of a written schedule of fees and disseminate the following fee information—

(A) Fixed fees for specific routine services.

(B) Hourly rates.

(C) Range of fees for particular services.

(D) Fee charged for an initial consultation.

(ii) Any statement of fee information concerning matters in which costs may be incurred must include a statement disclosing whether clients will be responsible for such costs.

(2) A practitioner may charge no more than the rate(s) published under paragraph (b)(1) of this section for at least 30 calendar days after the last date on which the schedule of fees was published.

(c) *Communication of fee information.* Fee information may be communicated in professional lists, telephone directories, print media, mailings, and electronic mail, facsimile, hand delivered flyers, radio, television, and any other method. The method chosen, however, must not cause the communication to become untruthful, deceptive, or otherwise in violation of this part. A practitioner may not persist in attempting to contact a prospective client if the prospective client has made it known to the practitioner that he or she does not desire to be solicited. In the case of radio and television broadcasting, the broadcast must be recorded and the practitioner must retain a recording of the actual transmission. In the case of direct mail and e-commerce communications, the practitioner must retain a copy of the actual communication, along with a list or other description of persons to whom the communication was mailed or otherwise distributed. Treasury Department Circular No. 230 The copy must be retained by the practitioner for a period of at least 36 months from the date of the last transmission or use.

(d) *Improper Associations* . A practitioner may not, in matters related to the Internal Revenue Service, assist, or accept assistance from, any person or entity who, to the knowledge of the practitioner, obtains clients or otherwise practices in a manner forbidden under this section.

(e) *Effective/applicability date.* This section is applicable beginning August 2, 2011.

§10.31. Negotiation of taxpayer checks. A practitioner who prepares tax returns may not endorse or otherwise negotiate any check issued to a client by the government in respect of a Federal tax liability.

§10.32. Practice of law. Nothing in the regulations in this part may be construed as authorizing persons not members of the bar to practice law.

CPA can not practice law

* * *

⚹ **§10.33 Best practices for tax advisors.** (a) *Best practices.* Tax advisors should provide clients with the highest quality representation concerning Federal tax issues by adhering to best practices in providing advice and in preparing or assisting in the preparation of a submission to the Internal Revenue Service. In addition to compliance with the standards of practice provided elsewhere in this part, best practices include the following:

(1) Communicating clearly with the client regarding the terms of the engagement. For example, the advisor should determine the client's expected purpose for and use of the advice and should have a clear understanding with the client regarding the form and scope of the advice or assistance to be rendered.

(2) Establishing the facts, determining which facts are relevant, evaluating the reasonableness of any assumptions or representations, relating the applicable law (including potentially applicable judicial

doctrines) to the relevant facts, and arriving at a conclusion supported by the law and the facts.

(3) Advising the client regarding the import of the conclusions reached, including, for example, whether a taxpayer may avoid accuracy-related penalties under the Internal Revenue Code if a taxpayer acts in reliance on the advice.

(4) Acting fairly and with integrity in practice before the Internal Revenue Service.

(b) *Procedures to ensure best practices for tax advisors.* Tax advisors with responsibility for overseeing a firm's practice of providing advice concerning Federal tax issues or of preparing or assisting in the preparation of submissions to the Internal Revenue Service should take reasonable steps to ensure that the firm's procedures for all members, associates, and employees are consistent with the best practices set forth in paragraph (a) of this section.

(c) *Applicability date.* This section is applicable after June 20, 2005.

§10.34. Standards with respect to tax returns and documents, affidavits and other papers. (a) *Tax returns.* (1) A practitioner may not willfully, recklessly, or through gross incompetence —

(i) Sign a tax return or claim for refund that the practitioner knows or reasonably should know contains a position that —

(A) Lacks a reasonable basis;

(B) Is an unreasonable position as described in section 6694(a)(2) of the Internal Revenue Code (Code) (including the related regulations and other published guidance); or

(C) Is a willful attempt by the practitioner to understate the liability for tax or a reckless or intentional disregard of rules or regulations by the practitioner as described in section 6694(b)(2) of the Code (including the related regulations and other published guidance).

(ii) Advise a client to take a position on a tax return or claim for refund, or prepare a portion of a tax return or claim for refund containing a position, that —

(A) Lacks a reasonable basis;

(B) Is an unreasonable position as described in section 6694(a)(2) of the Code (including the related regulations and other published guidance); or

(C) Is a willful attempt by the practitioner to understate the liability for tax or a reckless or intentional disregard of rules or regulations by the practitioner as described in section 6694(b)(2) of the Code (including the related regulations and other published guidance).

(2) A pattern of conduct is a factor that will be taken into account in determining whether a practitioner acted willfully, recklessly, or through gross incompetence.

(b) *Documents, affidavits and other papers.* (1) A practitioner may not advise a client to take a position on a document, affidavit or other paper submitted to the Internal Revenue Service unless the position is not frivolous.

(2) A practitioner may not advise a client to submit a document, affidavit or other paper to the Internal Revenue Service—

(i) The purpose of which is to delay or impede the administration of the Federal tax laws;

(ii) That is frivolous; or

(iii) That contains or omits information in a manner that demonstrates an intentional disregard of a rule or regulation unless the practitioner also advises the client to submit a document that evidences a good faith challenge to the rule or regulation.

(c) *Advising clients on potential penalties.* (1) A practitioner must inform a client of any penalties that are reasonably likely to apply to the client with respect to—

(i) A position taken on a tax return if—

(A) The practitioner advised the client with respect to the position; or

(B) The practitioner prepared or signed the tax return; and

(ii) Any document, affidavit or other paper submitted to the Internal Revenue Service.

(2) The practitioner also must inform the client of any opportunity to avoid any such penalties by disclosure, if relevant, and of the requirements for adequate disclosure.

(3) This paragraph (c) applies even if the practitioner is not subject to a penalty under the Internal Revenue Code with respect to the position or with respect to the document, affidavit or other paper submitted.

(d) *Relying on information furnished by clients.* A practitioner advising a client to take a position on a tax return, document, affidavit or other paper submitted to the Internal Revenue Service, or preparing or signing a tax return as a preparer, generally may rely in good faith without verification upon information furnished by the client. The practitioner may not, however, ignore the implications of information furnished to, or actually known by, the practitioner, and must make reasonable inquiries if the information as furnished appears to be incorrect, inconsistent with an important fact or another factual assumption, or incomplete.

(e) *Effective/applicability date.* Paragraph (a) of this section is applicable for returns or claims for refund filed, or advice provided, beginning August 2, 2011. Paragraphs (b) through (d) of this section are applicable to tax returns, documents, affidavits, and other papers filed on or after September 26, 2007.

(f) *Effective/applicability date.* Section 10.34 is applicable to tax returns, documents, affidavits, and other paper filed on or after September 26, 2007.

§ 10.35. Requirements for covered opinions. (a) A practitioner who provides a covered opinion shall comply with the standards of practice in this section.

(b) *Definitions* . For purposes of this subpart—

(1) A *practitioner* includes any individual described in § 10.2(a)(5).

(2) *Covered opinion.* (i) *In general.* A *covered opinion* is written advice (in-cluding electronic communications) by a practitioner concerning one or more Federal tax issues arising from—

(A) A transaction that is the same as or substantially similar to a transaction that, at the time the advice is rendered, the Internal Revenue Service has determined to be a tax avoidance transaction and identified by published guidance as a listed transaction under 26 C.F.R. § 1.6011-4(b)(2);

(B) Any partnership or other entity, any investment plan or arrangement, or any other plan or arrangement, the principal purpose of which is the avoidance or evasion of any tax imposed by the Internal Revenue Code; or

(C) Any partnership or other entity, any investment plan or arrangement, or any other plan or arrangement, a significant purpose of which is the avoidance or evasion of any tax imposed by the Internal Revenue Code if the written advice—

(1) Is a *reliance opinion;*

(2) Is a *marketed opinion;*

(3) Is subject to *conditions of confidentiality*; or

(4) Is subject to *contractual protection.*

(ii) *Excluded advice.* A *covered opinion* does not include—

(A) Written advice provided to a client during the course of an engagement if a practitioner is reasonably expected to provide subsequent written advice to the client that satisfies the requirements of this section;

(B) Written advice, other than advice described in paragraph (b)(2)(i)(A) of this section (concerning listed transactions) or paragraph (b)(2)(ii)(B) of this section (concerning the principal purpose of avoidance or evasion) that—

(1) Concerns the qualification of a qualified plan;

(2) Is a *State or local bond opinion*; or

(3) Is included in documents required to be filed with the Securities and Exchange Commission;

(C) Written advice prepared for and provided to a taxpayer, solely for use by that taxpayer, after the taxpayer has filed a tax return with the Internal Revenue Service reflecting the tax benefits of the transaction. The preceding sentence does not apply if the practitioner knows or has reason to know that the written advice will be relied upon by the taxpayer to take a position on a tax return (including for these purposes an amended return that claims tax benefits not reported on a previously filed return) filed after the date on which the advice is provided to the taxpayer;

(D) Written advice provided to an employer by a practitioner in that practitioner's capacity as an employee of that employer solely for purposes of determining the tax liability of the employer; or

(E) Written advice that does not resolve a Federal tax issue in the taxpayer's favor, unless the advice reaches a conclusion favorable to the taxpayer at any confidence level (e.g., not frivolous, realistic possibility of success, reasonable basis or substantial authority) with respect to that issue. If written advice concerns more than one Federal tax issue, the advice must comply with the requirements of paragraph (c) of this section with respect to any Federal tax issue not described in the preceding sentence.

(3) A *Federal tax issue* is a question concerning the Federal tax treatment of an item of income, gain, loss, deduction, or credit, the existence or absence of a taxable transfer of property, or the value of property for Federal tax purposes. For purposes of this subpart, a *Federal tax issue* is significant if the Internal Revenue Service has a reasonable basis for a successful challenge and its resolution could have a significant impact, whether beneficial or adverse and under any reasonably foreseeable circumstance, on the overall Federal tax treatment of the transaction(s) or matter(s) addressed in the opinion.

(4) *Reliance opinion.* (i) Written advice is a *reliance opinion* if the advice concludes at a confidence level of at least more likely than not (a greater than 50 percent likelihood) that one or more significant Federal tax issues would be resolved in the taxpayer's favor.

(ii) For purposes of this section, written advice, other than advice described in paragraph (b)(2)(i)(A) of this section (concerning listed transactions) or paragraph (b)(2)(i)(B) of this section (concerning the principal purpose of avoidance or evasion), is not treated as a *reliance opinion* if the practitioner prominently discloses in the written advice that it was not intended or written by the practitioner to be used, and that it cannot be used by the taxpayer, for the purpose of avoiding penalties that may be imposed on the taxpayer.

(5) *Marketed opinion.* (i) Written advice is a *marketed opinion* if the practitioner knows or has reason to know that the written advice will be used or referred to by a person other than the practitioner (or a person who is a member of, associated with, or employed by the practitioner's firm) in promoting, marketing or recommending a partnership or other entity, investment plan or arrangement to one or more taxpayer(s).

(ii) For purposes of this section, written advice, other than advice described in paragraph (b)(2)(i)(A) of this section (concerning listed transactions) or paragraph (b)(2)(i)(B) of this section (concerning the principal purpose of avoidance or evasion), is not treated as a *marketed opinion* if the practitioner prominently discloses in the written advice that—

(A) The advice was not intended or written by the practitioner to be used, and that it cannot be used by any taxpayer, for the purpose of avoiding penalties that may be imposed on the taxpayer;

(B) The advice was written to support the promotion or marketing of the transaction(s) or matter(s) addressed by the written advice; and

(C) The taxpayer should seek advice based on the taxpayer's particular circumstances from an independent tax advisor.

(6) *Conditions of confidentiality.* Written advice is subject to *conditions of confidentiality* if the practitioner imposes on one or more recipients of the written advice a limitation on disclosure of the tax treatment or tax structure of the transaction and the limitation on disclosure protects the confidentiality of that practitioner's tax

strategies, regardless of whether the limitation on disclosure is legally binding. A claim that a transaction is proprietary or exclusive is not a limitation on disclosure if the practitioner confirms to all recipients of the written advice that there is no limitation on disclosure of the tax treatment or tax structure of the transaction that is the subject of the written advice.

(7) *Contractual protection.* Written advice is subject to *contractual protection* if the taxpayer has the right to a full or partial refund of fees paid to the practitioner (or a person who is a member of, associated with, or employed by the practitioner's firm) if all or a part of the intended tax consequences from the matters addressed in the written advice are not sustained, or if the fees paid to the practitioner (or a person who is a member of, associated with, or employed by the practitioner's firm) are contingent on the taxpayer's realization of tax benefits from the transaction. All the facts and circumstances relating to the matters addressed in the written advice will be considered when determining whether a fee is refundable or contingent, including the right to reimbursements of amounts that the parties to a transaction have not designated as fees or any agreement to provide services without reasonable compensation.

(8) *Prominently disclosed.* An item is prominently disclosed if it is readily apparent to a reader of the written advice. Whether an item is readily apparent will depend on the facts and circumstances surrounding the written advice including, but not limited to, the sophistication of the taxpayer and the length of the written advice. At a minimum, to be prominently disclosed an item must be set forth in a separate section (and not in a footnote) in a typeface that is the same size or larger than the typeface of any discussion of the facts or law in the written advice.

(9) *State or local bond opinion.* A *State or local bond opinion* is written advice with respect to a *Federal tax issue* included in any materials delivered to a purchaser of a State or local bond in connection with the issuance of the bond in a public or private offering, including an official statement (if one is prepared), that concerns only the excludability of interest on a State or local bond from gross income under section 103 of the Internal Revenue Code, the application of section 55 of the Internal Revenue Code to a State or local bond, the status of a State or local bond as a qualified tax-exempt obligation under section 265(b)(3) of the Internal Revenue Code, the status of a State or local bond as a qualified zone academy bond under section 1397E of the Internal Revenue Code, or any combination of the above.

(10) *The principal purpose.* For purposes of this section, the principal purpose of a partnership or other entity, investment plan or arrangement, or other plan or arrangement is the avoidance or evasion of any tax imposed by the Internal Revenue Code if that purpose exceeds any other purpose. The principal purpose of a partnership or other entity, investment plan or arrangement, or other plan or arrangement is not to avoid or evade Federal tax if that partnership, entity, plan or arrangement has as its purpose the claiming of tax benefits in a manner consistent with the statute and Congressional purpose. A partnership, entity, plan or arrangement may have a significant purpose of avoidance or evasion even though it does not have the principal purpose of avoidance or evasion under this paragraph (b)(10).

(c) *Requirements for covered opinions.* A practitioner providing a *covered opinion* must comply with each of the following requirements.

(1) *Factual matters.* (i) The practitioner must use reasonable efforts to identify and ascertain the facts, which may relate to future events if a transaction is prospective or proposed, and to determine which facts are relevant. The opinion must identify and consider all facts that the practitioner determines to be relevant.

(ii) The practitioner must not base the opinion on any unreasonable factual assumptions (including assumptions as to future events). An unreasonable factual assumption includes a factual assumption that the practitioner knows or should know is incorrect or incomplete. For example, it is unreasonable to assume that a transaction has a business purpose or that a transaction is potentially profitable apart from tax benefits. A factual assumption includes reliance on a projection, financial forecast or appraisal. It is unreasonable for a practitioner to rely on a projection, financial forecast or appraisal if the practitioner knows or should know that the projection, financial forecast or appraisal is incorrect or incomplete or was prepared by a person lacking the skills or qualifications necessary to prepare such projection, financial forecast or appraisal. The opinion must identify in a separate section all factual assumptions relied upon by the practitioner.

(iii) The practitioner must not base the opinion on any unreasonable factual representations, statements or findings of the taxpayer or any other person. An unreasonable factual representation includes a factual representation that the practitioner knows or should know is incorrect or incomplete. For example, a practitioner may not rely on a factual representation that a transaction has a business purpose if the representation does not include a specific description of the business purpose or the practitioner knows or should know that the representation is incorrect or incomplete. The opinion must identify in a separate section all factual representations, statements or findings of the taxpayer relied upon by the practitioner.

(2) *Relate law to facts.* (i) The opinion must relate the applicable law (including potentially applicable judicial doctrines) to the relevant facts.

(ii) The practitioner must not assume the favorable resolution of any significant Federal tax issue except as provided in paragraphs (c)(3)(v) and (d) of this section, or otherwise base an opinion on any unreasonable legal assumptions, representations, or conclusions.

(iii) The opinion must not contain internally inconsistent legal analyses or conclusions.

(3) *Evaluation of significant Federal tax issues.* (i) *In general.* The opinion must consider all significant Federal tax issues except as provided in paragraphs (c)(3)(v) and (d) of this section.

(ii) *Conclusion as to each significant Federal tax issue.* The opinion must provide the practitioner's conclusion as to

the likelihood that the taxpayer will prevail on the merits with respect to each significant Federal tax issue considered in the opinion. If the practitioner is unable to reach a conclusion with respect to one or more of those issues, the opinion must state that the practitioner is unable to reach a conclusion with respect to those issues. The opinion must describe the reasons for the conclusions, including the facts and analysis supporting the conclusions, or describe the reasons that the practitioner is unable to reach a conclusion as to one or more issues. If the practitioner fails to reach a conclusion at a confidence level of at least more likely than not with respect to one or more significant Federal tax issues considered, the opinion must include the appropriate disclosure(s) required under paragraph (e) of this section.

(iii) *Evaluation based on chances of success on the merits.* In evaluating the significant Federal tax issues addressed in the opinion, the practitioner must not take into account the possibility that a tax return will not be audited, that an issue will not be raised on audit, or that an issue will be resolved through settlement if raised.

(iv) *Marketed opinions.* In the case of a *marketed opinion*, the opinion must provide the practitioner's conclusion that the taxpayer will prevail on the merits at a confidence level of at least more likely than not with respect to each significant Federal tax issue. If the practitioner is unable to reach a more likely than not conclusion with respect to each significant Federal tax issue, the practitioner must not provide the marketed opinion, but may provide written advice that satisfies the requirements in paragraph (b)(5)(ii) of this section.

(v) *Limited scope opinions.* (A) The practitioner may provide an opinion that considers less than all of the significant Federal tax issues if—

(1) The practitioner and the taxpayer agree that the scope of the opinion and the taxpayer's potential reliance on the opinion for purposes of avoiding penalties that may be imposed on the taxpayer are limited to the Federal tax issue(s) addressed in the opinion;

¶304

(2) The opinion is not advice described in paragraph (b)(2)(i)(A) of this section (concerning listed transactions), paragraph (b)(2)(i)(B) of this section (concerning the principal purpose of avoidance or evasion) or paragraph (b)(5) of this section (a *marketed opinion*); and

(3) The opinion includes the appropriate disclosure(s) required under paragraph (e) of this section.

(B) A practitioner may make reasonable assumptions regarding the favorable resolution of a Federal tax issue (an assumed issue) for purposes of providing an opinion on less than all of the significant Federal tax issues as provided in this paragraph (c)(3)(v). The opinion must identify in a separate section all issues for which the practitioner assumed a favorable resolution.

(4) Overall conclusion. (i) The opinion must provide the practitioner's overall conclusion as to the likelihood that the Federal tax treatment of the transaction or matter that is the subject of the opinion is the proper treatment and the reasons for that conclusion. If the practitioner is unable to reach an overall conclusion, the opinion must state that the practitioner is unable to reach an overall conclusion and describe the reasons for the practitioner's inability to reach a conclusion.

(ii) In the case of a *marketed opinion*, the opinion must provide the practitioner's overall conclusion that the Federal tax treatment of the transaction or matter that is the subject of the opinion is the proper treatment at a confidence level of at least more likely than not.

(d) Competence to provide opinion; reliance on opinions of others. (1) The practitioner must be knowledgeable in all of the aspects of Federal tax law relevant to the opinion being rendered, except that the practitioner may rely on the opinion of another practitioner with respect to one or more significant Federal tax issues, unless the practitioner knows or should know that the opinion of the other practitioner should not be relied on. If a practitioner relies on the opinion of another practitioner, the relying practitioner's opinion must identify the other opinion and set forth the conclusions reached in the other opinion.

(2) The practitioner must be satisfied that the combined analysis of the opinions, taken as a whole, and the overall conclusion, if any, satisfy the requirements of this section.

(e) *Required disclosures.* A covered opinion must contain all of the following disclosures that apply—

(1) *Relationship between promoter and practitioner.* An opinion must prominently disclose the existence of—

(i) Any compensation arrangement, such as a referral fee or a fee-sharing arrangement, between the practitioner (or the practitioner's firm or any person who is a member of, associated with, or employed by the practitioner's firm) and any person (other than the client for whom the opinion is prepared) with respect to promoting, marketing or recommending the entity, plan, or arrangement (or a substantially similar arrangement) that is the subject of the opinion; or

(ii) Any referral agreement between the practitioner (or the practitioner's firm or any person who is a member of, associated with, or employed by the practitioner's firm) and a person (other than the client for whom the opinion is prepared) engaged in promoting, marketing or recommending the entity, plan, or arrangement (or a substantially similar arrangement) that is the subject of the opinion.

(2) *Marketed opinions.* A *marketed opinion* must prominently disclose that—

(i) The opinion was written to support the promotion or marketing of the transaction(s) or matter(s) addressed in the opinion; and

(ii) The taxpayer should seek advice based on the taxpayer's particular circumstances from an independent tax advisor.

(3) *Limited scope opinions.* A limited scope opinion must prominently disclose that—

(i) The opinion is limited to the one or more Federal tax issues addressed in the opinion;

(ii) Additional issues may exist that could affect the Federal tax treatment of the transaction or matter that is the subject of the opinion and the opinion does not consider or provide a conclusion with respect to any additional issues; and

(iii) With respect to any significant Federal tax issues outside the limited scope of the opinion, the opinion was not written, and cannot be used by the taxpayer, for the purpose of avoiding penalties that may be imposed on the taxpayer.

(4) *Opinions that fail to reach a more likely than not conclusion.* An opinion that does not reach a conclusion at a confidence level of at least more likely than not with respect to a significant Federal tax issue must prominently disclose that—

(i) The opinion does not reach a conclusion at a confidence level of at least more likely than not with respect to one or more significant Federal tax issues addressed by the opinion; and

(ii) With respect to those significant Federal tax issues, the opinion was not written, and cannot be used by the taxpayer, for the purpose of avoiding penalties that may be imposed on the taxpayer.

(5) *Advice regarding required disclosures.* In the case of any disclosure required under this section, the practitioner may not provide advice to any person that is contrary to or inconsistent with the required disclosure.

✕ (f) *Effect of opinion that meets these standards.* (1) *In general.* An opinion that meets the requirements of this section satisfies the practitioner's responsibilities under this section, but the persuasiveness of the opinion with regard to the tax issues in question and the taxpayer's good faith reliance on the opinion will be determined separately under applicable provisions of the law and regulations.

(2) *Standards for other written advice.* A practitioner who provides written advice that is not a covered opinion for purposes of this section is subject to the requirements of § 10.37.

(g) *Effective date.* This section applies to written advice that is rendered after June 20, 2005.

✕ **§10.36 Procedures to ensure compliance.** (a) *Requirements for covered opinions.* Any practitioner who has (or practitioners who have or share) principal authority and responsibility for overseeing a firm's practice of providing advice concerning Federal tax issues must take reasonable steps to ensure that the firm has adequate procedures in effect for all members, associates, and employees for purposes of complying with § 10.35. Any such practitioner will be subject to discipline for failing to comply with the requirements of this paragraph if—

(1) The practitioner through willfulness, recklessness, or gross incompetence does not take reasonable steps to ensure that the firm has adequate procedures to comply with § 10.35, and one or more individuals who are members of, associated with, or employed by, the firm are, or have, engaged in a pattern or practice, in connection with their practice with the firm, of failing to comply with § 10.35; or

(2) The practitioner knows or should know that one or more individuals who are members of, associated with, or employed by, the firm are, or have, engaged in a pattern or practice, in connection with their practice with the firm, that does not comply with § 10.35 and the practitioner, through willfulness, recklessness, or gross incompetence, fails to take prompt action to correct the noncompliance.

(b) *Requirements for tax returns and other documents.* Any practitioner who has (or practitioners who have or share) principal authority and responsibility for overseeing a firm's practice of preparing tax returns, claims for refunds, or other documents for submission to the Internal Revenue Service must take reasonable steps to ensure that the firm has adequate procedures in effect for all members, associates, and employees for purposes of complying with Circular 230. Any practitioner who has (or practitioners who have or share) this principal authority will be subject to discipline for failing to comply with the requirements of this paragraph if —

(1) The practitioner through willfulness, recklessness, or gross incompetence does not take reasonable steps to ensure that the firm has adequate procedures to comply with Circular 230, and one or more individuals who are members of, associated with, or employed by, the firm are,

¶304

or have, engaged in a pattern or practice, in connection with their practice with the firm, of failing to comply with Circular 230; or

(2) The practitioner knows or should know that one or more individuals who are members of, associated with, or employed by, the firm are, or have, engaged in a pattern or practice, in connection with their practice with the firm, that does not comply with Circular 230, and the practitioner, through willfulness, recklessness, or gross incompetence fails to take prompt action to correct the noncompliance.

(c) *Effective date.* This section is applicable beginning August 2, 2011.

§ 10.37 Requirements for other written advice. (a) *Requirements.* A practitioner must not give written advice (including electronic communications) concerning one or more Federal tax issues if the practitioner bases the written advice on unreasonable factual or legal assumptions (including assumptions as to future events), unreasonably relies upon representations, statements, findings or agreements of the taxpayer or any other person, does not consider all relevant facts that the practitioner knows or should know, or, in evaluating a Federal tax issue, takes into account the possibility that a tax return will not be audited, that an issue will not be raised on audit, or that an issue will be resolved through settlement if raised. All facts and circumstances, including the scope of the engagement and the type and specificity of the advice sought by the client will be considered in determining whether a practitioner has failed to comply with this section. In the case of an opinion the practi-

tioner knows or has reason to know will be used or referred to by a person other than the practitioner (or a person who is a member of, associated with, or employed by the practitioner's firm) in promoting, marketing or recommending to one or more taxpayers a partnership or other entity, investment plan or arrangement a significant purpose of which is the avoidance or evasion of any tax imposed by the Internal Revenue Code, the determination of whether a practitioner has failed to comply with this section will be made on the basis of a heightened standard of care because of the greater risk caused by the practitioner's lack of knowledge of the taxpayer's particular circumstances.

(b) *Effective date* . This section is applicable to written advice that is rendered after June 20, 2005.

§ 10.38 Establishment of advisory committees. (a) *Advisory committees.* To promote and maintain the public's confidence in tax advisors, the Internal Revenue Service is authorized to establish one or more advisory committees composed of at least six individuals authorized to practice before the Internal Revenue Service. Membership of an advisory committee must be balanced among those who practice as attorneys, accountants, enrolled agents, enrolled actuaries, enrolled retirement plan agents, and registered tax return preparers. Under procedures prescribed by the Internal Revenue Service, an advisory committee may review and make general recommendations regarding the practices, procedures, and policies of the offices described in § 10.1.

(b) *Effective date* . This section is applicable beginning August 2, 2011.

Subpart C—Sanctions for Violation of the Regulations

§ 10.50 Sanctions. (a) *Authority to censure, suspend, or disbar.* The Secretary of the Treasury, or delegate, after notice and an opportunity for a proceeding, may cen-

sure, suspend, or disbar any practitioner from practice before the Internal Revenue Service if the practitioner is shown to be incompetent or disreputable (within the meaning of §10.51), fails to comply with any regulation in this part (under the prohibited conduct standards of §10.52), or with intent to defraud, willfully and knowingly misleads or threatens a client or prospective client. Censure is a public reprimand.

(b) *Authority to disqualify.* The Secretary of Treasury, or delegate, after due notice and opportunity for hearing, may disqualify any appraiser for a violation of these rules as applicable to appraisers.

(1) If any appraiser is disqualified pursuant to this subpart C, the appraiser is barred from presenting evidence or testimony in any administrative proceeding before the Department of Treasury or the Internal Revenue Service, unless and until authorized to do so by the Director of the Office of Professional Responsibility pursuant to §10.81, regardless of whether the evidence or testimony would pertain to an appraisal made prior to or after the effective date of disqualification.

(2) Any appraisal made by a disqualified appraiser after the effective date of disqualification will not have any probative effect in any administrative proceeding before the Department of the Treasury or the Internal Revenue Service. An appraisal otherwise barred from admission into evidence pursuant to this section may be admitted into evidence solely for the purpose of determining the taxpayer's reliance in good faith on such appraisal.

(c) *Authority to impose monetary penalty.* (1) *In general.* (i) The Secretary of the Treasury, or delegate, after notice and an opportunity for a proceeding, may impose a monetary penalty on any practitioner who engages in conduct subject to sanction under paragraph (a) of this section.

(ii) If the practitioner described in paragraph (c)(1)(i) of this section was acting on behalf of an employer or any firm or other entity in connection with the conduct giving rise to the penalty, the Secretary of the Treasury, or delegate, may impose a monetary penalty on the employer, firm, or entity if it knew, or reasonably should have known, of such conduct.

(2) *Amount of penalty.* The amount of the penalty shall not exceed the gross income derived (or to be derived) from the conduct giving rise to the penalty.

(3) *Coordination with other sanctions.* Subject to paragraph (c)(2) of this section—

(i) Any monetary penalty imposed on a practitioner under this paragraph (c) may be in addition to or in lieu of any suspension, disbarment or censure and may be in addition to a penalty imposed on an employer, firm or other entity under paragraph (c)(1)(ii) of this section.

(ii) Any monetary penalty imposed on an employer, firm or other entity may be in addition to or in lieu of penalties imposed under paragraph (c)(1)(i) of this section.

(d) *Sanctions to be imposed.* The sanctions imposed by this section shall take into account all relevant facts and circumstances.

(e) *Effective/applicability date.* This section is applicable to conduct occurring on or after September 26, 2007, except paragraph (c) which applies to prohibited conduct that occurs after October 22, 2004.

§10.51. Incompetence and disreputable conduct. Incompetence and disreputable conduct for which a practitioner may be censured, suspended or disbarred from practice before the Internal Revenue Service includes, but is not limited to—

(a) *Incompetence and disreputable conduct.* Incompetence and disreputable conduct for which a practitioner may be sanctioned under §10.50 includes, but is not limited to—

(1) Conviction of any criminal offense under the Federal tax laws.

(2) Conviction of any criminal offense involving dishonesty or breach of trust.

(3) Conviction of any felony under Federal or State law for which the conduct involved renders the practitioner unfit to practice before the Internal Revenue Service.

(4) Giving false or misleading information, or participating in any way in the giving of false or misleading

information to the Department of the Treasury or any officer or employee thereof, or to any tribunal authorized to pass upon Federal tax matters, in connection with any matter pending or likely to be pending before them, knowing the information to be false or misleading. Facts or other matters contained in testimony, Federal tax returns, financial statements, applications for enrollment, affidavits, declarations, and any other document or statement, written or oral, are included in the term "information."

(5) Solicitation of employment as prohibited under § 10.30, the use of false or misleading representations with intent to deceive a client or prospective client in order to procure employment, or intimating that the practitioner is able improperly to obtain special consideration or action from the Internal Revenue Service or any officer or employee thereof.

(6) Willfully failing to make a Federal tax return in violation of the Federal tax laws, or willfully evading, attempting to evade, or participating in any way in evading or attempting to evade any assessment or payment of any Federal tax.

(7) Willfully assisting, counseling, encouraging a client or prospective client in violating, or suggesting to a client or prospective client to violate, any Federal tax law, or knowingly counseling or suggesting to a client or prospective client an illegal plan to evade Federal taxes or payment thereof.

(8) Misappropriation of, or failure properly or promptly to remit, funds received from a client for the purpose of payment of taxes or other obligations due the United States.

(9) Directly or indirectly attempting to influence, or offering or agreeing to attempt to influence, the official action of any officer or employee of the Internal Revenue Service by the use of threats, false accusations, duress or coercion, by the offer of any special inducement or promise of an advantage, or by the bestowing of any gift, favor or thing of value.

(10) Disbarment or suspension from practice as an attorney, certified public accountant, public accountant or actuary by any duly constituted authority of any State, territory, or possession of the United States, including a Commonwealth, or the District of Columbia, any Federal court of record or any Federal agency, body or board.

(11) Knowingly aiding and abetting another person to practice before the Internal Revenue Service during a period of suspension, disbarment or ineligibility of such other person.

(12) Contemptuous conduct in connection with practice before the Internal Revenue Service, including the use of abusive language, making false accusations or statements, knowing them to be false or circulating or publishing malicious or libelous matter.

(13) Giving a false opinion, knowingly, recklessly, or through gross incompetence, including an opinion which is intentionally or recklessly misleading, or engaging in a pattern of providing incompetent opinions on questions arising under the Federal tax laws. False opinions described in this paragraph (a)(13) include those which reflect or result from a knowing misstatement of fact or law, from an assertion of a position known to be unwarranted under existing law, from counseling or assisting in conduct known to be illegal or fraudulent, from concealing matters required by law to be revealed, or from consciously disregarding information indicating that material facts expressed in the opinion or offering material are false or misleading. For purposes of this paragraph (a)(13), reckless conduct is a highly unreasonable omission or misrepresentation involving an extreme departure from the standards of ordinary care that a practitioner should observe under the circumstances. A pattern of conduct is a factor that will be taken into account in determining whether a practitioner acted knowingly, recklessly, or through gross incompetence. Gross incompetence includes conduct that reflects gross indifference, preparation which is grossly inadequate under the circumstances, and a consistent failure to perform obligations to the client.

(14) Willfully failing to sign a tax return prepared by the practitioner when the practitioner's signature is required by the Federal tax laws unless the

failure is due to reasonable cause and not due to willful neglect.

(15) Willfully disclosing or otherwise using a tax return or tax return information in a manner not authorized by the Internal Revenue Code, contrary to the order of a court of competent jurisdiction, or contrary to the order of an administrative law judge in a proceeding instituted under §10.60.

(16) Willfully failing to file on magnetic or other electronic media a tax return prepared by the practitioner when the practitioner is required to do so by the Federal tax laws unless the failure is due to reasonable cause and not due to willful neglect.

(17) Willfully preparing all or substantially all of, or signing, a tax return or claim for refund when the practitioner does not possess a current or otherwise valid preparer tax identification number or other prescribed identifying number.

(18) Willfully representing a taxpayer before an officer or employee of the Internal Revenue Service unless the practitioner is authorized to do so pursuant to this part.

(b) *Effective/applicability date.* This section is applicable beginning August 2, 2011.

§10.52. Violation subject to sanction. (a) A practitioner may be sanctioned under §10.50 if the practitioner—

(1) Willfully violates any of the regulations (other than §10.33) contained in this part; or

(2) Recklessly or through gross incompetence (within the meaning of §10.51(a)(13)) violates §§10.34, 10.35, 10.36 or 10.37.

(b) *Effective/applicability date.* This section is applicable to conduct occurring on or after September 26, 2007.

§10.53. Receipt of information concerning practitioner. (a) *Officer or em-*

ployee of the Internal Revenue Service. If an officer or employee of the Internal Revenue Service has reason to believe a practitioner has violated any provision of this part, the officer or employee will promptly make a written report of the suspected violation. The report will explain the facts and reasons upon which the officer's or employee's belief rests and must be submitted to the office(s) of the Internal Revenue Service responsible for administering or enforcing this part.

(b) *Other persons.* Any person other than an officer or employee of the Internal Revenue Service having information of a violation of any provision of this part may make an oral or written report of the alleged violation to the office(s) of the Internal Revenue Service responsible for administering or enforcing this part or any officer or employee of the Internal Revenue Service. If the report is made to an officer or employee of the Internal Revenue Service, the officer or employee will make a written report of the suspected violation and submit the report to the office(s) of the Internal Revenue Service responsible for administering or enforcing this part.

(c) *Destruction of report.* No report made under paragraph (a) or (b) of this section shall be maintained unless retention of the report is permissible under the applicable records control schedule as approved by the National Archives and Records Administration and designated in the Internal Revenue Manual. Reports must be destroyed as soon as permissible under the applicable records control schedule.

(d) *Effect on proceedings under subpart D*. The destruction of any report will not bar any proceeding under subpart D of this part, but will preclude the use of a copy of the report in a proceeding under subpart D of this part.

(e) *Effective/applicability date.* This section is applicable beginning August 2, 2011.

Subpart D—Rules Applicable to Disciplinary Proceedings

¶304

§10.60 Institution of proceeding. (a) Whenever it is determined that a practitioner (or employer, firm or other entity, if applicable) violated any provision of the laws governing practice before the Internal Revenue Service or the regulations in this part, the practitioner may be reprimanded or, in accordance with §10.62, subject to a proceeding for sanctions described in §10.50.

(b) Whenever a penalty has been assessed against an appraiser under the Internal Revenue Code and an appropriate officer or employee in an office established to enforce this part determines that the appraiser acted willfully, recklessly, or through gross incompetence with respect to the proscribed conduct, the appraiser may be reprimanded or, in accordance with §10.62, subject to a proceeding for disqualification. A proceeding for disqualification of an appraiser is instituted by the filing of a complaint, the contents of which are more fully described in §10.62.

(c) Except as provided in §10.82, a proceeding will not be instituted under this section unless the proposed re-spondent previously has been advised in writing of the law, facts and conduct warranting such action and has been accorded an opportunity to dispute facts, assert additional facts, and make arguments (including an explanation or description of mitigating circumstances).

(d) *Effective/applicability date.* This section is applicable beginning August 2, 2011.

§10.61. Conferences. (a) *In general.* The Director of the Office of Professional Responsibility may confer with a practitioner, employer, firm or other entity, or an appraiser concerning allegations of misconduct irrespective of whether a proceeding has been instituted. If the conference results in a stipulation in connection with an ongoing proceeding in which the practitioner, employer, firm or other entity, or appraiser is the respondent, the stipulation may be entered in the record by either party to the proceeding.

(b) *Voluntary sanction.* (1) *In general.* In lieu of a proceeding being insti-

¶304

tuted or continued under §10.60(a), a practitioner or appraiser (or employer, firm or other entity, if applicable) may offer a consent to be sanctioned under §10.50.

(2) *Discretion; acceptance or declination.* The Commissioner, or delegate, may accept or decline the offer described in paragraph (b)(1) of this section. When the decision is to decline the offer, the written notice of declination may state that the offer described in paragraph (b)(1) of this section would be accepted if it contained different terms. The Commissioner, or delegate, has the discretion to accept or reject a revised offer submitted in response to the declination or may counteroffer and act upon any accepted counteroffer.

(c) *Effective/applicability date.* This section is applicable beginning August 2, 2011.

§10.62. Contents of complaint.

(a) *Charges.* A complaint must name the respondent, provide a clear and concise description of the facts and law that constitute the basis for the proceeding, and be signed by an authorized representative of the Internal Revenue Service under §10.69(a)(1). A complaint is sufficient if it fairly informs the respondent of the charges brought so that the respondent is able to prepare a defense.

(b) *Specification of sanction.* The complaint must specify the sanction sought against the practitioner or appraiser. If the sanction sought is a suspension, the duration of the suspension sought must be specified.

(c) *Demand for answer.* The respondent must be notified in the complaint or in a separate paper attached to the complaint of the time for answering the complaint, which may not be less than 30 days from the date of service of the complaint, the name and address of the Administrative Law Judge with whom the answer must be filed, the name and address of the person representing the Internal Revenue Service to whom a copy of the answer must be served, and that a decision by default may be rendered against the respondent in the event an answer is not filed as required.

(d) *Effective/applicability date.* This section is applicable beginning August 2, 2011.

§10.63. Service of complaint; service of other papers; service of evidence in support of complaint; filing of papers.

(a) *Service of complaint.* (1) *In general.* The complaint or a copy of the complaint must be served on the respondent by any manner described in paragraphs (a)(2) or (3) of this section.

(2) *Service by certified or first class mail.* (i) Service of the complaint may be made on the respondent by mailing the complaint by certified mail to the last known address (as determined under section 6212 of the Internal Revenue Code and the regulations thereunder) of the respondent. Where service is by certified mail, the returned post office receipt duly signed by the respondent will be proof of service.

(ii) If the certified mail is not claimed or accepted by the respondent, or is returned undelivered, service may be made on the respondent, by mailing the complaint to the respondent by first class mail. Service by this method will be considered complete upon mailing, provided the complaint is addressed to the respondent's last known address as determined under section 6212 of the Internal Revenue Code and the regulations thereunder.

(3) *Service by other than certified or first class mail.* (i) Service of the complaint may be made on the respondent by delivery by a private delivery service designated pursuant to section 7502(f) of the Internal Revenue Code to the last known address (as determined under section 6212 of the Internal Revenue Code and the regulations there under) of the respondent. Service by this method will be considered complete, provided the complaint is addressed to the respondent at the respondent's last known address as determined under section 6212 of the Internal Revenue Code and the regulations thereunder.

(ii) Service of the complaint may be made in person on, or by leaving the complaint at the office or place of business of, the respondent. Service by this method will be considered complete

¶304

and proof of service will be a written statement, sworn or affirmed by the person who served the complaint, identifying the manner of service, including the recipient, relationship of recipient to respondent, place, date and time of service.

(iii) Service may be made by any other means agreed to by the respondent. Proof of service will be a written statement, sworn or affirmed by the person who served the complaint, identifying the manner of service, including the recipient, relationship of recipient to respondent, place, date and time of service.

(4) For purposes of this section, *respondent* means the practitioner, employer, firm or other entity, or appraiser named in the complaint or any other person having the authority to accept mail on behalf of the practitioner, employer, firm or other entity, or appraiser.

(b) *Service of papers other than complaint.* Any paper other than the complaint may be served on the respondent, or his or her authorized representative under § 10.69(a)(2) by:

(1) mailing the paper by first class mail to the last known address (as determined under section 6212 of the Internal Revenue Code and the regulations thereunder) of the respondent or the respondent's authorized representative.

(2) delivery by a private delivery service designated pursuant to section 7502(f) of the Internal Revenue Code to the last known address (as determined under section 6212 of the Internal Revenue Code and the regulations thereunder) of the respondent or the respondent's authorized representative, or

(3) as provided in paragraphs (a)(3)(ii) and (a)(3)(iii) of this section.

(c) *Service of papers on the Internal Revenue Service..* Whenever a paper is required or permitted to be served on the Internal Revenue Service in connection with a proceeding under this part, the paper will be served on the Internal Revenue Service's authorized representative under § 10.69(a)(1) at the address designated in the complaint, or at an address provided in a notice of appearance. If no address is designated in the complaint or provided in

a notice of appearance, service will be made on the office(s) established to enforce this part under the authority of § 10.1, Internal Revenue Service, 1111 Constitution Avenue, NW, Washington, DC 20224.

(d) *Service of evidence in support of complaint.* Within 10 days of serving the complaint, copies of the evidence in support of the complaint must be served on the respondent in any manner described in paragraphs (a)(2) and (3) of this section.

(e) *Filing of papers.* Whenever the filing of a paper is required or permitted in connection with a proceeding under this part, the original paper, plus one additional copy, must be filed with the Administrative Law Judge at the address specified in the complaint or at an address otherwise specified by the Administrative Law Judge. All papers filed in connection with a proceeding under this part must be served on the other party, unless the Administrative Law Judge directs otherwise. A certificate evidencing such must be attached to the original paper filed with the Administrative Law Judge.

(f) *Effective/applicability date.* This section is applicable beginning August 2, 2011.

§ 10.64 Answer; default. (a) *Filing.* The respondent's answer must be filed with the Administrative Law Judge, and served on the Internal Revenue Service, within the time specified in the complaint unless, on request or application of the respondent, the time is extended by the Administrative Law Judge.

(b) *Contents.* The answer must be written and contain a statement of facts that constitute the respondent's grounds of defense. General denials are not permitted. The respondent must specifically admit or deny each allegation set forth in the complaint, except that the respondent may state that the respondent is without sufficient information to admit or deny a specific allegation. The respondent, nevertheless, may not deny a material allegation in the complaint that the respondent knows to be true, or state that the respondent is without sufficient information to form a belief, when the respondent possesses the required information. The respondent also must state affirmatively any special matters of defense on which he or she relies.

(c) *Failure to deny or answer allegations in the complaint.* Every allegation in the complaint that is not denied in the answer is deemed admitted and will be considered proved; no further evidence in respect of such allegation need be adduced at a hearing.

(d) *Default.* Failure to file an answer within the time prescribed (or within the time for answer as extended by the Administrative Law Judge), constitutes an admission of the allegations of the complaint and a waiver of hearing, and the Administrative Law Judge may make the decision by default without a hearing or further procedure. A decision by default constitutes a decision under § 10.76.

(e) *Signature.* The answer must be signed by the respondent or the respondent's authorized representative under § 10.69(a)(2) and must include a statement directly above the signature acknowledging that the statements made in the answer are true and correct and that knowing and willful false statements may be punishable under 18 U.S.C. § 1001.

(f) *Effective/applicability date.* This section is applicable beginning August 2, 2011.

§ 10.65 Supplemental charges. (a) *In general.* Supplemental charges may be filed against the respondent by amending the complaint with the permission of the Administrative Law Judge if, for example —

(1) It appears that the respondent, in the answer, falsely and in bad faith, denies a material allegation of fact in the complaint or states that the respondent has insufficient knowledge to form a belief, when the respondent possesses such information; or

(2) It appears that the respondent has knowingly introduced false testimony during the proceedings against the respondent.

(b) *Hearing.* The supplemental charges may be heard with other charges in the case, provided the respondent is given due notice of the charges and is afforded a reasonable opportunity to prepare a defense to the supplemental charges.

(c) *Effective/applicability date.* This section is applicable beginning August 2, 2011.

§ 10.66 Reply to answer. (a) The Internal Revenue Service may file a reply to the respondent's answer, but unless otherwise ordered by the Administrative Law Judge, no reply to the respondent's answer is required. If a reply is not filed, new matter in the answer is deemed denied.

(b) *Effective/applicability date.* This section is applicable beginning August 2, 2011.

§ 10.67 Proof; variance; amendment of pleadings. In the case of a variance between the allegations in pleadings and the evidence adduced in support of the pleadings, the Administrative Law Judge, at any time before decision, may order or authorize amendment of the pleadings to conform to the evidence. The party who would otherwise be prejudiced by the amendment must be given a reasonable opportunity to address the allegations of the pleadings as amended and the Administrative Law Judge must make findings on any issue presented by the pleadings as amended.

§ 10.68 Motions and requests. (a) *Motions.* (1) *In general.* At any time after the filing of the complaint, any party may file a motion with the Administrative Law Judge. Unless otherwise ordered by the Administrative Law Judge, motions must be in writing and must be served on the opposing party as provided in § 10.63(b). A motion must concisely specify its grounds and the relief sought, and, if appropriate, must contain a memorandum of facts and law in support.

(2) *Summary adjudication.* Either party may move for a summary adjudication upon all or any part of the legal issues in controversy. If the non-moving party opposes summary adjudication in the moving party's favor, the non-moving party must file a written response within 30

days unless ordered otherwise by the Administrative Law Judge.

(3) *Good Faith.* A party filing a motion for extension of time, a motion for postponement of a hearing, or any other non-dispositive or procedural motion must first contact the other party to determine whether there is any objection to the motion, and must state in the motion whether the other party has an objection.

(b) *Response.* Unless otherwise ordered by the Administrative Law Judge, the nonmoving party is not required to file a response to a motion. If the Administrative Law Judge does not order the nonmoving party to file a response, and the nonmoving party files no response, the nonmoving party is deemed to oppose the motion. If a nonmoving party does not respond within 30 days of the filing of a motion for decision by default for failure to file a timely answer or for failure to prosecute, the nonmoving party is deemed not to oppose the motion.

(c) *Oral motions; oral argument.* (1) The Administrative Law Judge may, for good cause and with notice to the parties, permit oral motions and oral opposition to motions.

(2) The Administrative Law Judge may, within his or her discretion, permit oral argument on any motion.

(d) *Orders.* The Administrative Law Judge should issue written orders disposing of any motion or request and any response thereto.

(e) *Effective/applicability date.* This section is applicable on September 26, 2007.

§ 10.69 Representation; ex parte communication. (a) *Representation.* (1) The Internal Revenue Service may be represented in proceedings under this part by an attorney or other employee of the Internal Revenue Service. An attorney or an employee of the Internal Revenue Service representing the Internal Revenue Service in a proceeding under this part may sign the complaint or any document required to be filed in the proceeding on behalf of the Internal Revenue Service.

(2) A respondent may appear in person, be represented by a practitioner, or be represented by an attorney who has not filed a declaration with the Internal Revenue Service pursuant to § 10.3. A practitioner or an attorney representing a respondent or proposed respondent may sign the answer or any document required to be filed in the proceeding on behalf of the respondent.

(b) *Ex parte communication.* This section is applicable beginning August 2, 2011.

(c) *Effective/applicability date.* The Internal Revenue Service, the respondent, and any representatives of either party, may not attempt to initiate or participate in ex parte discussions concerning a proceeding or potential proceeding with the Administrative Law Judge (or any person who is likely to advise the Administrative Law Judge on a ruling or decision) in the proceeding before or during the pendency of the proceeding. Any memorandum, letter or other communication concerning the merits of the proceeding, addressed to the Administrative Law Judge, by or on behalf of any party shall be regarded as an argument in the proceeding and shall be served on the othe party.

§ 10.70 Administrative Law Judge. (a) *Appointment.* Proceedings on complaints for the sanction (as described in § 10.50) of a practitioner, employer, firm or other entity, or appraiser will be conducted by an Administrative Law Judge appointed as provided by 5 U.S.C. 3105.

(b) *Powers of the Administrative Law Judge.* The Administrative Law Judge, among other powers, has the authority, in connection with any proceeding under § 10.60 assigned or referred to him or her, to do the following:

(1) Administer oaths and affirmations;

(2) Make rulings on motions and requests, which rulings may not be appealed prior to the close of a hearing except in extraordinary circumstances and at the discretion of the Administrative Law Judge;

(3) Determine the time and place of hearing and regulate its course and conduct;

(4) Adopt rules of procedure and modify the same from time to time as needed for the orderly disposition of proceedings;

(5) Rule on offers of proof, receive relevant evidence, and examine witnesses;

(6) Take or authorize the taking of depositions or answers to requests for admission;

(7) Receive and consider oral or written argument on facts or law;

(8) Hold or provide for the holding of conferences for the settlement or simplication of the issues with the consent of the parties;

(9) Perform such acts and take such measures as are necessary or appropriate to the efficient conduct of any proceeding; and

(10) Make decisions.

(c) *Effective/applicability date.* This section is applicable on September 26, 2007.

§ 10.71 Discovery. (a) *In general.* Discovery may be permitted, at the discretion of the Administrative Law Judge, only upon written motion demonstrating the relevance, materiality and reasonableness of the requested discovery and subject to the requirements of § 10.72(d)(2) and (3). Within 10 days of receipt of the answer, the Administrative Law Judge will notify the parties of the right to request discovery and the timeframes for filing a request. A request for discovery, and objections, must be filed in accordance with § 10.68. In response to a request for discovery, the Administrative Law Judge may order—

(1) Depositions upon oral examination; or

(2) Answers to requests for admission.

(b) *Depositions upon oral examination.* (1) A deposition must be taken before an officer duly authorized to administer an oath for general purposes or before an officer or employee of the Internal Revenue Service who is authorized to administer an oath in Federal tax law matters.

(2) In ordering a deposition, the Administrative Law Judge will require reasonable notice to the opposing party as to the time and place of the deposition. The opposing party, if attending, will be provided the opportunity for full examination and cross-examination of any witness.

(3) Expenses in the reporting of depositions shall be borne by the party at whose instance the deposition is taken. Travel expenses of the deponent shall be borne by the party requesting the deposition, unless otherwise authorized by Federal law or regulation.

(c) *Requests for admission.* Any party may serve on any other party a written request for admission of the truth of any matters which are not privileged and are relevant to the subject matter of this proceeding. Requests for admission shall not exceed a total of 30 (including any subparts within a specific request) without the approval from the Administrative Law Judge.

(d) *Limitations.* Discovery shall not be authorized if—

(1) The request fails to meet any requirement set forth in paragraph (a) of this section;

(2) It will unduly delay the proceeding;

(3) It will place an undue burden on the party required to produce the discovery sought;

(4) It is frivolous or abusive;

(5) It is cumulative or duplicative;

(6) The material sought is privileged or otherwise protected from disclosure by law;

(7) The material sought relates to mental impressions, conclusions, or legal theories of any party, attorney, or other representative, of a party prepared in anticipation of a proceeding; or

(8) The material sought is available generally to the public, equally to the parties, or to the party seeking the discovery through another source.

(e) *Failure to comply.* Where a party fails to comply with an order of the Administrative Law Judge under this section, the Administrative Law Judge may, among other things, infer that the information would be adverse to the party failing to provide it, exclude the information from evidence or issue a decision by default.

(f) *Other discovery.* No discovery other than that specifically provided for in this section is permitted.

(g) *Effective/applicability date.* This section is applicable to proceedings initiated on or after September 26, 2007.

§ 10.72 Hearings. (a) *In general.* (1) *Presiding officer.* An Administrative Law Judge will preside at the hearing on a complaint filed under § 10.60 for the sanction of a practitioner, employer, firm or other entity, or appraiser.

(2) *Time for hearing.* Absent a determination by the Administrative Law Judge that, in the interest of justice, a hearing must be held at a later time, the Administrative Law Judge should, on notice sufficient to allow proper preparation, schedule the hearing to occur no later than 180 days after the time for filing the answer.

(3) *Procedural requirements.* (i) Hearings will be stenographically recorded and transcribed and the testimony of witnesses will be taken under oath or affirmation.

(ii) Hearings will be conducted pursuant to 5 U.S.C. 556.

(iii) A hearing in a proceeding requested under § 10.82(g) will be conducted de novo.

(iv) An evidentiary hearing must be held in all proceedings prior to the issuance of a decision by the Administrative Law Judge unless—

(A) The Director of the Office of Professional Responsibility withdraws the complaint;

(B) A decision is issued by default pursuant to § 10.64(d);

(C) A decision is issued under § 10.82(e);

(D) The respondent requests a decision on the written record without a hearing; or

(E) The Administrative Law Judge issues a decision under § 10.68(d) or rules on another motion that disposes of the case prior to the hearing.

(b) *Cross-examination.* A party is entitled to present his or her case or defense by oral or documentary evidence, to submit rebuttal evidence, and to conduct cross-examination, in the presence of the Administrative Law Judge, as may be required for a full and true disclosure of the facts. This paragraph (b) does not limit a party from presenting evidence contained within a deposition when the Administrative Law Judge determines that the deposition has been obtained in compliance with the rules of this subpart D.

(c) *Prehearing memorandum.* Unless otherwise ordered by the Administrative Law Judge, each party shall file, and serve on the opposing party or the opposing party's representative, prior to any hearing, a prehearing memorandum containing—

(1) A list (together with a copy) of all proposed exhibits to be used in the party's case in chief;

(2) A list of proposed witnesses, including a synopsis of their expected testimony, or a statement that no witnesses will be called;

(3) Identification of any proposed expert witnesses, including a synopsis of their expected testimony and a copy of any report prepared by the expert or at his or her direction; and

(4) A list of undisputed facts.

(d) *Publicity.* (1) *In general.* All reports and decisions of the Secretary of the Treasury, or delegate, including any reports and decisions of the Administrative Law Judge, under this Subpart D are, subject to the protective measures in paragraph (d)(4) of this section, public and open to inspection within 30 days after the agency's decision becomes final.

(2) *Request for additional publicity.* The Administrative Law Judge may grant a request by a practitioner or

appraiser that all the pleadings and evidence of the disciplinary proceeding be made available for inspection where the parties stipulate in advance to adopt the protective measures in paragraph (d)(4) of this section.

(3) *Returns and return information*. (i) *Disclosure to practitioner or appraiser*. Pursuant to section 6103(l)(4) of the Internal Revenue Code, the Secretary of the Treasury, or delegate, may disclose returns and return information to any practitioner or appraiser, or to the authorized representative of the practitioner or appraiser, whose rights are or may be affected by an administrative action or proceeding under this subpart D, but solely for use in the action or proceeding and only to the extent that the Secretary of the Treasury, or delegate, determines that the returns or return information are or may be relevant and material to the action or proceeding.

(ii) *Disclosure to officers and employees of the Department of the Treasury*. Pursuant to section 6103(l)(4)(B) of the Internal Revenue Code, the Secretary of the Treasury, or delegate, may disclose returns and return information to officers and employees of the Department of the Treasury for use in any action or proceeding under this subpart D, to the extent necessary to advance or protect the interests of the United States.

(iii) *Use of returns and return information*. Recipients of returns and return information under this paragraph (d)(3) may use the returns or return information solely in the action or proceeding, or in preparation for the action or proceeding, with respect to which the disclosure was made.

(iv) *Procedures for disclosure of returns and return information*. When providing returns or return information to the practitioner or appraiser, or authorized representative, the Secretary of the Treasury, or delegate, will—

(A) Redact identifying information of any third party taxpayers and replace it with a code;

(B) Provide a key to the coded information; and

(C) Notify the practitioner or appraiser, or authorized representative, of the restrictions on the use and disclosure of the returns and return information, the applicable damages remedy under section 7431 of the Internal Revenue Code, and that unauthorized disclosure of information provided by the Internal Revenue Service under this paragraph (d)(3) is also a violation of this part.

(4) *Protective measures*. (i) *Mandatory protective order*. If redaction of names, addresses, and other identifying information of third party taxpayers may still permit indirect identification of any third party taxpayer, the Administrative Law Judge will issue a protective order to ensure that the identifying information is available to the parties and the Administrative Law Judge for purposes of the proceeding, but is not disclosed to, or open to inspection by, the public.

(ii) *Authorized orders*. (A) Upon motion by a party or any other affected person, and for good cause shown, the Administrative Law Judge may make any order which justice requires to protect any person in the event disclosure of information is prohibited by law, privileged, confidential, or sensitive in some other way, including, but not limited to, one or more of the following—

(1) That disclosure of information be made only on specified terms and conditions, including a designation of the time or place;

(2) That a trade secret or other information not be disclosed, or be disclosed only in a designated way.

(iii) *Denials*. If a motion for a protective order is denied in whole or in part, the Administrative Law Judge may, on such terms or conditions as the Administrative Law Judge deems just, order any party or person to comply with, or respond in accordance with, the procedure involved.

(iv) *Public inspection of documents*. The Secretary of the Treasury, or delegate, shall ensure that all names, addresses or other identifying details of third party taxpayers are redacted and replaced with the code assigned to the corresponding taxpayer in all documents prior to public inspection of such documents.

(e) *Location.* The location of the hearing will be determined by the agreement of the parties with the approval of the Administrative Law Judge, but, in the absence of such agreement and approval, the hearing will be held in Washington, D.C.

(f) *Failure to appear.* If either party to the proceeding fails to appear at the hearing, after notice of the proceeding has been sent to him or her, the party will be deemed to have waived the right to a hearing and the Administrative Law Judge may make his or her decision against the absent party by default.

(g) *Effective/applicability date.* This section is applicable beginning August 2, 2011

§ 10.73 Evidence. (a) *In general.* The rules of evidence prevailing in courts of law and equity are not controlling in hearings or proceedings conducted under this part. The Administrative Law Judge may, however, exclude evidence that is irrelevant, immaterial, or unduly repetitious,

(b) *Depositions.* The deposition of any witness taken pursuant to § 10.71 may be admitted into evidence in any proceeding instituted under § 10.60.

(c) *Requests for admission.* Any matter admitted in response to a request for admission under § 10.71 is conclusively established unless the Administrative Law Judge on motion permits withdrawal or modification of the admission. Any admission made by a party is for the purposes of the pending action only and is not an admission by a party for any other purpose, nor may it be used against a party in any other proceeding.

(d) *Proof of documents.* Official documents, records, and papers of the Internal Revenue Service and the Office of Professional Responsibility are admissible in evidence without the production of an officer or employee to authenticate them. Any documents, records, and papers may be evidenced by a copy attested to or identified by an officer or employee of the Inter-

nal Revenue Service or the Treasury Department, as the case may be.

(e) *Withdrawal of exhibits.* If any document, record, or other paper is introduced in evidence as an exhibit, the Administrative Law Judge may authorize the withdrawal of the exhibit subject to any conditions that he or she deems proper.

(f) *Objections.* Objections to evidence are to be made in short form, stating the grounds for the objection. Except as ordered by the Administrative Law Judge, argument on objections will not be recorded or transcribed. Rulings on objections are to be a part of the record, but no exception to a ruling is necessary to preserve the rights of the parties.

(g) *Effective/applicability date.* This section is applicable on September 26, 2007.

§ 10.74 Transcript. In cases where the hearing is stenographically reported by a Government contract reporter, copies of the transcript may be obtained from the reporter at rates not to exceed the maximum rates fixed by contract between the Government and the reporter. Where the hearing is stenographically reported by a regular employee of the Internal Revenue Service, a copy will be supplied to the respondent either without charge or upon the payment of a reasonable fee. Copies of exhibits introduced at the hearing or at the taking of depositions will be supplied to the parties upon the payment of a reasonable fee (Sec. 501, Public Law 82-137)(65 Stat. 290)(31 U.S.C. 483a).

§ 10.75 Proposed findings and conclusions. Except in cases where the respondent has failed to answer the complaint or where a party has failed to appear at the hearing, the parties must be afforded a reasonable opportunity to submit proposed findings and conclusions and their supporting reasons to the Administrative Law Judge.

§ 10.76 Decision of Administrative Law Judge. (a) *In general.* (1) *Hearings.* Within 180 days after the conclusion of a hearing and the receipt of any proposed findings and conclusions timely submitted by the parties, the Administrative

¶304

Law Judge should enter a decision in the case. The decision must include a statement of findings and conclusions, as well as the reasons or basis for making such findings and conclusions, and an order of censure, suspension, disbarment, monetary penalty, disqualification, or dismissal of the complaint.

(2) *Summary adjudication.* In the event that a motion for summary adjudication is filed, the Administrative Law Judge should rule on the motion for summary adjudication within 60 days after the party in opposition files a written response, or if no written response is filed, within 90 days after the motion for summary adjudication is filed. A decision shall thereafter be rendered if the pleadings, depositions, admissions, and any other admissible evidence show that there is no genuine issue of material fact and that a decision may be rendered as a matter of law. The decision must include a statement of conclusions, as well as the reasons or basis for making such conclusions, and an order of censure, suspension, disbarment, monetary penalty, disqualification, or dismissal of the complaint.

(3) *Returns and return information.* In the decision, the Administrative Law Judge should use the code assigned to third party taxpayers (described in § 10.72(d)).

(b) *Standard of proof.* If the sanction is censure or a suspension of less than six months' duration, the Administrative Law Judge, in rendering findings and conclusions, will consider an allegation of fact to be proven if it is established by the party who is alleging the fact by a preponderance of the evidence in the record. If the sanction is a monetary penalty, disbarment or a suspension of six months or longer duration, an allegation of fact that is necessary for a finding against the practitioner must be proven by clear and convincing evidence in the record. An allegation of fact that is necessary for a finding of disqualification against an appraiser must be proved by clear and convincing evidence in the record.

(c) *Copy of decision.* The Administrative Law Judge will provide the decision to the Internal Revenue Service's authorized representative, and a copy of the decision to the respondent or the respondent's authorized representative.

(d) *When final.* In the absence of an appeal to the Secretary of the Treasury or delegate, the decision of the Administrative Law Judge will, without further proceedings, become the decision of the agency 30 days after the date of the Administrative Law Judge's decision.

(e) *Effective/applicability date.* This section is applicable beginning August 2, 2011.

§10.77 Appeal of Decision of administrative Law Judge. (a) *Appeal.* Any party to the proceeding under this subpart D may appeal the decision of the Administrative Law Judge by filing a notice of appeal with the Secretary of the Treasury, or delegate deciding appeals. The notice of appeal must include a brief that states exceptions to the decision of Administrative Law Judge and supporting reasons for such exceptions.

(b) *Time and place for filing of appeal.* The notice of appeal and brief must be filed, in duplicate, with the Secretary of the Treasury, or delegate deciding appeals, at an address for appeals that is identified to the parties with the decision of the Administrative Law Judge. The notice of appeal and brief must be filed within 30 days of the date that the decision of the Administrative Law Judge is served on the parties. The appealing party must serve a copy of the notice of appeal and the brief to any non appealing party or, if the party is represented, the non-appealing party's representative.

(c) *Response.* Within 30 days of receiving the copy of the appellant's brief, the other party may file a response brief with the Secretary of the Treasury, or delegate deciding appeals, using the address identified for appeals. A copy of the response brief must be served at the same time on the opposing party or, if the party is represented, the opposing party's representative.

(d) *No other briefs, responses or motions as of right.* Other than the appeal brief and response brief, the parties are not permitted to file any other briefs, responses or motions, except on a grant of leave to do so after a motion demonstrating sufficient cause, or unless otherwise ordered by the Secretary of the Treasury, or delegate deciding appeals.

(e) *Additional time for briefs and responses.* Notwithstanding the time for filing briefs and responses provided in paragraphs (b) and (c) of this section, the Secretary of the Treasury, or delegate deciding appeals, may, for good cause, authorize additional time for filing briefs and responses upon a motion of a party or upon the initiative of the Secretary of the Treasury, or delegate deciding appeals.

(f) *Effective/applicability date.* This section is applicable beginning August 2, 2011.

§10.78 Decision on review. (a) *Decision on review.* On appeal from or review of the decision of the Administrative Law Judge, the Secretary of the Treasury, or delegate, will make the agency decision. The Secretary of the Treasury, or delegate, should make the agency decision within 180 days after receipt of the appeal.

(b) *Standard of review.* The decision of the Administrative Law Judge will not be reversed unless the appellant establishes that the decision is clearly erroneous in light of the evidence in the record and applicable law. Issues that are exclusively matters of law will be reviewed de novo. In the event that the Secretary of the Treasury, or delegate, determines that there are unresolved issues raised by the record, the case may be remanded to the Administrative Law Judge to elicit additional testimony or evidence.

(c) *Copy of decision on review.* The Secretary of the Treasury, or delegate, will provide copies of the agency decision to the authorized representative of the Internal Revenue Service and the respondent or the respondent's authorized representative.

(d) *Effective/applicability date.* This section is applicable beginning August 2, 2011.

§10.79 Effect of disbarment, suspension, or censure. (a) *Disbarment.* When the final decision in a case is against the respondent (or the respondent has offered his or her consent and such consent has been accepted by the Internal Revenue Service) and such decision is for disbarment, the respondent will not be permitted to practice before the Internal Revenue Service unless and until authorized to do so by the Internal Revenue Service pursuant to §10.81.

(b) *Suspension.* When the final decision in a case is against the respondent (or the respondent has offered his or her consent and such consent has been accepted by the Internal Revenue Service) and such decision is for suspension, the respondent will not be permitted to practice before the Internal Revenue Service during the period of suspension. For periods after the suspension, the practitioner's future representations may be subject to conditions as authorized by paragraph (d) of this section.

(c) *Censure.* When the final decision in the case is against the respondent (or the Internal Revenue Service has accepted the respondent's offer to consent, if such offer was made) and such decision is for censure, the respondent will be permitted to practice before the Internal Revenue Service, but the respondent's future representations may be subject to conditions as authorized by paragraph (d) of this section.

(d) *Conditions.* After being subject to the sanction of either suspension or censure, the future representations of a practitioner so sanctioned shall be subject to specified conditions designed to promote high standards of conduct. These conditions can be imposed for a reasonable period in light of the gravity of the practitioner's violations. For example, where a practitioner is censured because the practitioner failed to advise the practitioner's clients about a potential conflict of interest or failed to obtain the clients' written consents, the practitioner may be required to provide the Internal Revenue Service with a copy of all consents obtained by the practitioner for an appropriate period following censure, whether or not such consents are specifically requested.

(e) *Effective/applicability date.* This section is applicable beginning August 2, 2011.

§10.80 Notice of disbarment, suspension, censure, or disqualification. (a) *In general.* On the issuance of a final order censuring, suspending, or disbarring a practitioner or a final order disqualifying an appraiser, notification of the censure, suspension, disbarment or disqualification will be given to appropriate officers and employees of the Internal Revenue Service and interested departments and agencies of the Federal government. The Internal Revenue Service may determine the manner of giving notice to the proper authorities of the State by which the censured, suspended, or disbarred person was licensed to practice.

(b) *Effective/applicability date.* This section is applicable beginning August 2, 2011.

§10.81 Petition for reinstatement. (a) *In general.* A disbarred practitioner or a disqualified appraiser may petition for reinstatement before the Internal Revenue Service after the expiration of 5 years following such disbarment or disqualification. Reinstatement will not be granted unless the Internal Revenue Service is satisfied that the petitioner is not likely to conduct himself, thereafter, contrary to the regulations in this part, and that granting such reinstatement would not be contrary to the public interest.

(b) *Effective/applicability date.* This section is applicable beginning August 2, 2011.

§10.82 Expedited suspension. (a) *When applicable.* Whenever the Commissioner, or delegate, determines that a practitioner is described in paragraph (b) of this section, proceedings may be instituted under this section to suspend the practitioner from practice before the Internal Revenue Service.

(b) *To whom applicable.* This section applies to any practitioner who, within 5 years of the date a complaint insti-

tuting a proceeding under this section is served:

(1) Has had a license to practice as an attorney, certified public accountant, or actuary suspended or revoked for cause (not including a failure to pay a professional licensing fee) by any authority or court, agency, body, or board described in §10.51(a)(10).

(2) Has, irrespective of whether an appeal has been taken, been convicted of any crime under title 26 of the United States Code, any crime involving dishonesty or breach of trust, or any felony for which the conduct involved renders the practitioner unfit to practice before the Internal Revenue Service.

(3) Has violated conditions imposed on the practitioner pursuant to §10.79(d).

(4) Has been sanctioned by a court of competent jurisdiction, whether in a civil or criminal proceeding (including suits for injunctive relief), relating to any taxpayer's tax liability or relating to the practitioner's own tax liability, for—

(i) Instituting or maintaining proceedings primarily for delay;

(ii) Advancing frivolous or groundless arguments; or

(iii) Failing to pursue available administrative remedies.

(c) *Instituting a proceeding.* A proceeding under this section will be instituted by a complaint that names the respondent, is signed by the Director of the Office of Professional Responsibility or a person representing the Director of the Office of Professional Responsibility under §10.69(a)(1), is filed in the Director of the Office of Professional Responsibility's office, and is served according to the rules set forth in paragraph (a) of §10.63. The complaint must give a plain and concise description of the allegations that constitute the basis for the proceeding. The complaint must notify the respondent—

(1) Of the place and due date for filing an answer;

(2) That a decision by default may be rendered if the respondent fails to file an answer as required;

(3) That the respondent may request a conference with the Director

of the Office of Professional Responsibility to address the merits of the complaint and that any such request must be made in the answer; and

(4) That the respondent may be suspended either immediately following the expiration of the period within which an answer must be filed or, if a conference is requested, immediately following the conference.

(d) *Answer.* The answer to a complaint described in this section must be filed no later than 30 calendar days following the date the complaint is served, unless the Director of the Office of Professional Responsibility extends the time for filing. The answer must be filed in accordance with the rules set forth in § 10.64, except as otherwise provided in this section. A respondent is entitled to a conference with the Director of the Office of Professional Responsibility only if the conference is requested in a timely filed answer. If a request for a conference is not made in the answer or the answer is not timely filed, the respondent will be deemed to have waived his or her right to a conference and the Director of the Office of Professional Responsibility may suspend such respondent at any time following the date on which the answer was due.

(e) *Conference.* An authorized representative of the Internal Revenue Service will preside at a conference described in this section. The conference will be held at a place and time selected by the Internal Revenue Service, but no sooner than 14 calendar days after the date by which the answer must be filed with the Internal Revenue Service, unless the respondent agrees to an earlier date. An authorized representative may represent the respondent at the

conference. Following the conference, upon a finding that the respondent is described in paragraph (b) of this section, or upon the respondent's failure to appear at the conference either personally or through an authorized representative, the respondent may be immediately suspended from practice before the Internal Revenue Service.

(f) *Duration of suspension.* A suspension under this section will commence on the date that written notice of the suspension is issued. The suspension will remain effective until the earlier of the following:

(1) The Internal Revenue Service lifts the suspension after determining that the practitioner is no longer described in paragraph (b) of this section or for any other reason; or

(2) The suspension is lifted by an Administrative Law Judge or the Secretary of the Treasury in a proceeding referred to in paragraph (g) of this section and instituted under § 10.60.

(g) *Proceeding instituted under § 10.60.* If the Director of the Office of Professional Responsibility suspends a practitioner under this section, the practitioner may ask the Director of the Office of Professional Responsibility to issue a complaint under § 10.60. The request must be made in writing within 2 years from the date on which the practitioner's suspension commences. The Director of the Office of Professional Responsibility must issue a complaint requested under this paragraph within 30 calendar days of receiving the request.

(h) *Effective/applicability date.* This section is applicable beginning August 2, 2011.

Subpart E—General Provisions

§ 10.90 Sanctions. (a) *Roster.* The Internal Revenue Service will maintain and make available for public inspection in the time and manner prescribed by the Secretary, or delegate, the following rosters —

(1) Individuals (and employers, firms, or other entities, if applicable) censured, suspended, or disbarred from practice before the Internal Revenue Service or upon whom a monetary penalty was imposed.

(2) Enrolled agents, including individuals —

(i) Granted active enrollment to practice;

(ii) Whose enrollment has been placed in inactive status for failure to meet the requirements for renewal of enrollment;

(iii) Whose enrollment has been placed in inactive retirement status; and

(iv) Whose offer of consent to resign from enrollment has been accepted by the Internal Revenue Service under § 10.61.

(3) Enrolled retirement plan agents, including individuals —

(i) Granted active enrollment to practice;

(ii) Whose enrollment has been placed in inactive status for failure to meet the requirements for renewal of enrollment;

(iii) Whose enrollment has been placed in inactive retirement status; and

(iv) Whose offer of consent to resign from enrollment has been accepted under § 10.61.

(4) Registered tax return preparers, including individuals —

(i) Authorized to prepare all or substantially all of a tax return or claim for refund;

(ii) Who have been placed in inactive status for failure to meet the requirements for renewal;

(iii) Who have been placed in inactive retirement status; and

(iv) Whose offer of consent to resign from their status as a registered tax return preparer has been accepted by the Internal Revenue Service under § 10.61.

(5) Disqualified appraisers.

(6) Qualified continuing education providers, including providers —

(i) Who have obtained a qualifying continuing education provider number; and

(ii) Whose qualifying continuing education number has been revoked for failure to comply with the requirements of this part.

(b) *Other records.* Other records of the Director of the Office of Professional Responsibility may be disclosed upon specific request, in accordance with the applicable law.

(c) *Effective/applicability date.* This section is applicable beginning August 2, 2011.

§ 10.91. Saving provision. Any proceeding instituted under this part prior to July 26, 2002, for which a final decision has not been reached or for which judicial review is still available will not be affected by these revisions. Any proceeding under this part based on conduct engaged in prior to September 26, 2007, which is instituted after that date, will apply subpart D and E or this part as revised, but the conduct engaged in prior to the effective date of these revisions will be judged by the regulations in effect at the time the conduct occurred.

§ 10.92. Special orders. The Secretary of the Treasury reserves the power to issue such special orders as he or she deems proper in any cases within the purview of this part.

§ 10.93. Effective date. Except as otherwise provided in each section and Subject to § 10.91, Part 10 is applicable on July 26, 2002.

¶304

¶311 DISCUSSION QUESTIONS

1. PUB Corp. is a publicly held company and for several years its certified audit has been done by Final 4, a nationally known accounting firm. Annabel Aggressive, certified public accountant, a recent graduate of a Master of Taxation program and the self-styled "fireball" of Final 4, has just received a summons from the IRS. Annabel worked on the certified audit of PUB Corp. and prepared the tax accrual workpapers regarding PUB Corp. The summons seeks production of the tax accrual workpapers, a step the agent has resorted to because Annabel refuses to produce them (or anything else if she can get away with it) voluntarily.

   Annabel knows that you are still a student in the Master of Taxation program and also knows that in your course you are discussing the FATP privilege and the *Arthur Young* case, 465 U.S. 805, 104 S.Ct. 1475 (1984), 84-1 USTC ¶9305, concerning a privilege for accountant's tax accrual workpapers. (Chapter 7, IRS position on seeking accrual workpapers). Annabel wants to claim privilege solely to delay the agent in his audit. She wants to know whether her actions are prohibited by Circular 230.

2. You normally prepare the tax return for ABC Manufacturing, an S corporation. The sole shareholder of the corporation submits all of the year-end figures except the closing inventory. The owner tells you that they are still in the process of extending the inventory, but that you should start working on those portions of the return that you can do without the closing inventory. He suggests you use $250,000 as an estimate for the closing inventory.

   After you have the return sketched out, you call the owner to get the closing inventory figures. The conversation goes as follows:

   You: I have sketched out your return using the $250,000 estimate for the closing inventory. Do you have any accurate figures for the closing inventory yet?

   Owner: No, we're just finishing that up right now. Tell me, how does the year look using the estimated figure?

   You: Well, it looks like you had a pretty good profit. It's hard to say without all the figures, but I would guess your profit could be as high as $145,000 this year.

   Owner: You say that I could have a $145,000 profit this year?

   You: That assumes that your inventory will close at $250,000.

   Owner: What will my profit be if the closing inventory is only $175,000?

   You: It looks like your profit will only be $70,000.

   Owner: What if the ending inventory is only $125,000?

   You: Then your profit will probably be about $20,000. Why do you ask?

   About an hour later the owner comes in. He says, "I just got the figures for the closing inventory. We had to do a lot of computing to come up with an accurate figure, but I'm pretty sure this is it." He hands you a sheet of paper showing the closing inventory to be $95,000.

(A) What does Circular 230 tell you to do in such a situation?

(B) As a practical matter, what should you do in this situation?

3. Alex Alert is the in-house Certified Public Accountant for a large manufacturing firm. He is asked to prepare a pro forma schedule to be used by the president's personal tax preparer in the preparation of the president's individual income tax return.

When Alert receives the figures from the president, he notes that the only income items are the president's already sizable salary and two cash dividends paid to all stockholders during that year. Alert knows that the maintenance staff of the company has rebuilt the president's summer cottage during that year with "surplus goods" rerouted from the plant expansion site. Alert has been reviewing some of the cost overruns on the plant expansion, and he estimates that the cost of labor and materials that went into the president's four-bedroom, three-bath "cottage" is approximately $500,000.

(A) What, if anything, does Circular 230 require Alert to do in this situation?

(B) What should be done as a practical matter?

4. You work for Modmfg as an internal accountant. Modmfg is a very successful sole proprietorship. During the year, Peter Proprietor sells his business, Modmfg, to Newton Owner. Owner asks you to stay on as internal accountant and you agree. At the same time, Proprietor wishes you to continue to prepare his personal tax returns, something you have done for fifteen years.

When it comes time to prepare Peter Proprietor's personal return, you review the contract for the sale of the business. You notice for the first time that the contract drafted by Owner's attorney has allocated 100% of the purchase price to the tangible assets of the business, with no amount allocated to goodwill at all. You believe that this is an unreasonable allocation, so in reporting the gain on Proprietor's return, you allocate 50% of the purchase price to goodwill. You are not involved in the preparation of the personal return for Newton Owner, since that task is handled by the outside accountant who worked with Owner's attorney in drafting the contract for the purchase of the business.

Approximately a year later, Proprietor receives a notice that he has been called in for an office examination for a review of the sale of the business. Proprietor asks you to represent him before the IRS in connection with this audit. At the same time, your responsibilities at Modmfg have been growing and Newton Owner has just asked you to be its senior representative in dealing with the IRS in connection with a field audit that is about to be conducted of the operations of Modmfg. You realize that Proprietor's and Owner's interests are adverse as to the allocation of the purchase price and that you may have a potential conflict of interest in seeking to represent both of them.

(A) Under Circular 230, can you represent both of them?

(B) What could you do if you wish to represent them both?

(C) Can they agree on an allocation of the purchase price between themselves prior to the time that the audits are scheduled?

5. Joseph Argue, an attorney, is approached by Warren Investor. Investor is considering an investment in a life insurance arrangement, which seems very complex and which Investor will not invest in unless he is more likely than not to prevail on the desired tax benefits if examined by the IRS. Is the opinion Joe Argue gives with respect to this investment a covered opinion? Why or why not?

6. Betsy Ross, a U.S. citizen and a loyal patriot of the United States, operates a branch that makes flags in the United Kingdom (the "U.K."). Betsy describes to attorney what the attorney believes to be a very fraudulent scheme to defraud the U.K. tax authority. After your explanation, Betsy says "I don't care about those darn Redcoats. I don't get to vote in the U.K. so this is taxation without representation." What obligations does Betsy's attorney have under Circular 230?

CHAPTER 4
EXAMINATION OF RETURNS

¶401 INTRODUCTION

Under the federal taxation system, the taxpayer files a return disclosing income and expenses and pays the tax based on the taxable income shown on the return. While the Internal Revenue Service (IRS) depends primarily on voluntary compliance with the self-assessment system, it also examines and audits returns. An IRS audit consists of an examination of a taxpayer's tax return. The tax return is audited by the IRS examining the books and records upon which the entries on the return are based. Generally, when the books and records support the entries on the return, then the audit work is complete and the audit will be closed as an agreed case. For many taxpayers the possibility that the IRS will examine their returns encourages voluntary compliance. The actual chances of examination vary depending on geographical location, type of return and the amount of taxable income.

Audit Procedures

¶402 IRS CAMPUS

The audit process begins at the Internal Revenue Service Campus where computers and personnel routinely check for such obvious errors as missing signatures and social security numbers and mathematical mistakes. A magnetic tape with pertinent information from each return is sent to the national computer center in Martinsburg, West Virginia, where each return is rated by computer for potential errors by means of a mathematically-based technique known as Discriminate Inventory Function (DIF). Numerical weights are assigned to items on the return and the computers produce a composite score for each return. Some corporate and all individual returns are rated under the DIF system. The higher the DIF score, the greater the probability of error on the return.[1]

A number of different formulas for computing a return's error potential exist, but the exact makeup of the formula is not publicly disclosed.[2] Variables probably include amount of income and its source, number and type of dependents, size and nature of certain itemized deductions, and the taxpayer's marital status.

---

[1] IRS Pub. 556 (Rev. May 2008).

[2] Code Sec. 6103(b)(2) provides that nothing "shall be construed to require the disclosure of standards used or to be used for the selection of returns for examination, or data used or to be used for determining such standards, if the Secretary determines that such disclosure will seriously impair assessment, collection, or enforcement under the Internal Revenue Laws." This provision was added by Act §701(a) of the Economic Recovery Tax Act of 1981, P.L. 97-34, and was intended to reverse the result in cases such as *Long v. Bureau of Economic Analysts,* 646 F2d 1310 (9th Cir. 1981), 81-1 USTC ¶9439.

When the computer selects a return with a high DIF score, a classifying officer inspects the return for some obvious or innocent explanation. If the classifying officer sees no ready explanation, the questionable return is forwarded for examination.

In addition to computer selected returns, other returns are manually selected under various IRS programs designed to probe for specific tax problems. Manual identification includes tax returns made available for classification other than by computer identification—e.g., amended returns, information reports (Form 1099 matching program), claims for refund, etc. When a return reviewed by a classifying officer does not warrant examination, it is stamped "Accepted as Filed by Classification" on the face of the return to indicate its status.[3]

¶403 AUTOMATED UNDERREPORTER PROGRAM

The IRS presently conducts five major types of audit programs. The first, the Automated Underreporter Program, is the simplest audit and is conducted at the Campus. The IRS computers simply match items reported on individual tax returns with information reported by payers on forms such as Form W-2 and Form 1099.[4] The taxpayers audited under this program receive a computer-printed notice proposing a correction to the tax. (The IRS, through the screening of information returns, also detects those taxpayers who fail to filed income tax return for the year.) These are not considered an "examination" and so the IRS can later do a formal examination without violating the one examination rule. Rev. Proc. 2005-32, 2005-23 IRB 1206.

> **Example 4-1:** Happy At Home received a computer-printed notice from the IRS that stated Happy had claimed too may exemptions for the tax years. The notice stated that $200 was due to the IRS. Happy double-checked her records and concluded that the IRS was correct. So Happy paid the $200.

¶404 CORRESPONDENCE EXAMINATION

The second of the five major types of audit programs is a correspondence examination. This type of audit is usually conducted by IRS Campuses. As its name implies, the IRS sends a letter questioning a single tax issue. The types of issues handled by correspondence include: payments to a Keogh plan, payments to an IRA, interest penalty on early withdrawal of savings, disability income exclusion, small casualty or theft loss, itemized deductions for interest, taxes, contributions, medical expenses and miscellaneous deductions other than office in home, travel and entertainment or education and credits for child care, elderly, residential energy and political contributions.[5] The letter indicates what item on the return is in doubt and asks the taxpayer to mail supporting documents to the IRS.

Substantiation by the taxpayer might be a receipt or cancelled check or a written explanation of how the person arrived at a particular figure entered on the return. In a correspondence examination, the IRS will wait for the taxpayer to

---

[3] IRM 4.1.5.1.5.1.1.   [5] See IRM 4.19.11.
[4] IRM 1.4.19.1.

submit substantiation before proposing any changes on the return. Unless specifically required to produce originals, a taxpayer should only produce copies of documents to the IRS.

> **Example 4-2:** Coach Potato received a letter from the IRS questioning his itemized deduction for his home mortgage interest. The letter asks Coach Potato to mail in any document that support the deduction. Coach Potato looked and found the year-end bank statement that supports the deduction. The IRS was satisfied and closed the audit.

¶405 OFFICE EXAMINATION

The third of the five major types of audit programs is the office examination. In this audit the taxpayer is asked to visit the IRS. The taxpayer receives a letter (see Exhibit 4-1 at ¶421) which specifies the date and time for the appointment. The letter also indicates the areas under audit and the records and information that the taxpayer should bring to the appointment. Some IRS offices issue audit letters to taxpayers requesting that they call the office and arrange a time and date that is convenient to them. The audit letter also provides the taxpayer with the office location for the interview.

The place of the examination will be based upon the address shown on the tax return.[6] This will be the IRS office closest to the taxpayer's residence. In those situations where the nearest IRS office does not have the appropriate personnel, it will be considered reasonable to conduct the audit at the closest office that has such personnel.

Although office examinations are generally conducted at the nearest IRS office, it is possible to have them held at another location. As an example, if the taxpayer can show a clear need for the audit to take place somewhere else, the IRS will accommodate that situation. Such would be the case if a taxpayer was of advanced age, was infirm or where the taxpayer's books, records and source documents were too cumbersome to bring to an IRS office.[7] A request to change the place of examination should be in writing. The IRS normally will not consider a request that is based on the location of the taxpayer's representative or requires the reassignment of the case to an office that would have difficulty accommodating the audit. The taxpayer must agree to extend the statute of limitations for up to one year if it would expire within thirteen months of the requested transfer.[8]

The office examination is conducted by an interview with the taxpayer, his representative or both.[9] If the taxpayer attends alone, the interview will be suspended at any time the taxpayer asks to consult with an attorney, a CPA or any other person permitted to represent that taxpayer before the IRS.[10] The taxpayer also is permitted to make an audio recording of the interview, provided he or she makes the request at least ten days in advance of the interview, bears

---

[6] Reg. § 301.7605-1(d).

[7] Reg. § 301.7605-1(c)(2)

[8] Reg. § 301.7605-1(e)(4).

[9] Code Sec. 7521(c) provides that the taxpayer need not attend with his representative unless required to do so by an IRS summons.

[10] Code Sec. 7521(b)(2).

the cost of such recording and allows the IRS to make its own recording.[11] If the taxpayer does not record the interview, the IRS nevertheless may make its own recording, but only upon giving at least ten days advance notice to the taxpayer.[12]

Typical issues covered at an office examination include income from tips, capital gains, charitable contributions, dependency exemptions, travel and entertainment expenses, education expenses, medical expenses and bad debts. Although the entire return is technically subject to audit, the IRS generally stays close to the items in question unless a very obvious issue comes up at the examination.

Previously, an office examination was generally limited to individuals who did not have significant business income. The complexity of business returns being audited in this program has been expanded in recent years.

As part of any examination of a business return, the examiner[13] will probe gross receipts.[14] The taxpayer will be questioned regarding sources of income, standard of living, purchases of assets, balances of cash on hand, loan payments and the receipt of borrowed funds. If, based on the answers to these questions, the examiner has a reasonable indication of unreported income, the examiner will probe further by use of one of the indirect methods for reconstructing income.[15] In office audits, this is most commonly the cash transaction or T-account method. The bank-deposits method or source-and-application-of-funds method also may be used by the examiner.

If the T-account or other analysis discloses no discrepancy in reported income, the examination will proceed to a verification of the specific items requested in the appointment letter (see Exhibit 4-1 at ¶ 421). After all the evidence has been presented, the examiner will afford the taxpayer or his representative an opportunity for a conference. During the conference the examiner will explain the findings and the amount of any additional tax to be proposed. When the examiner and the taxpayer are unable to agree on all the adjustments, the examiner will submit a Form 4549, Income Tax Examination Changes (see Exhibit 4-2 at ¶ 422), to the taxpayer using either Transmittal Letter 915 (see Exhibit 4-3 at ¶ 423) or Letter 950 (see Exhibit 4-4 at ¶ 424). The first letter gives the taxpayer an opportunity to submit additional evidence or information within thirty days, or to request a review by the Appeals Officer. This letter is generally used in connection with a correspondence examination or an office audit when very little interviewer contact has been had with the taxpayer. When the examiner and the taxpayer have had a full discussion of the issues, Letter 950 is submitted to the taxpayer, together with a Form 870, Waiver of Restrictions on

---

[11] Code Sec. 7521(a)(1); Notice 89-51, 1989-1 CB 691.

[12] Code Sec. 7521(a)(2); Notice 89-51, 1989-1 CB 691.

[13] The title of the examiner in the Office Examination program has been changed from "Office Auditor" or "Office Examiner" to "Tax Compliance Officer" (TCO) as part of the IRS reorganization.

[14] IRM 4.10.4.3.

[15] Code Sec. 7602(e) limits the use of these indirect methods without a "reasonable indication that there is a likelihood of unreported income." See Chapter 19, *infra*, for discussion of these indirect methods.

¶405

Assessment (see Exhibit 4-5 at ¶ 425). Publication 5, Appeal Rights and Preparation of Protests for Unagreed Cases, which explains a taxpayer's appeal rights, is enclosed with both letters (see Exhibit 4-6 at ¶ 426).

> **Example 4-3:** Mary Mobile received an IRS letter requesting that Mary come to a specific IRS office on a given date and time and bring all of her books and records on her candy-making company that she runs as a sole proprietorship. The IRS office was not far away and it was easy to bring her books and records. Mary was interviewed by a Revenue Agent. The focus was on items of gross income, just as the IRS letter said it would be. Mary was able to use her books and records to answer the questions. The IRS was satisfied and there was no charge made to Mary's return.

¶406 FIELD EXAMINATION

The field examination, the fourth type of the five types of audit programs, is used for most business returns and the larger, more complex individual returns. The revenue agent normally advises the taxpayer that the return has been assigned for examination and schedules an appointment at a mutually convenient time, date and place (see Exhibit 4-7 at ¶ 427). Generally, the examination must be scheduled during the IRS's normal workday and business hours. The IRS may schedule examinations without regard to seasonal fluctuations of the taxpayer's business, but will attempt to accommodate the taxpayer to minimize any adverse effects an examination might have on the taxpayer's business.[16]

A field examination normally is required to be conducted at the location where the taxpayer maintains books, records and other relevant documents. Typically, this will be the taxpayer's principal place of business or personal residence. However, if a business is so small that an on-site examination would essentially require the business to close or unduly disrupt its operations, the IRS will change the place of examination to an IRS office.[17] The IRS may also move the examination to an IRS office if a taxpayer conditions access to the audit site on IRS employees' compliance with requests for personal identification, surrender of credentials or permission to copy such credentials.[18] Regardless of where the audit occurs, the IRS reserves the right to visit the business premises or the taxpayer's residence to verify facts that can only be established by such a visit.

A taxpayer's written request to change the place of examination will be considered by the IRS on a case-by-case basis.[19] Such a request normally will be granted if the taxpayer has moved or the books and records are being maintained at some other location. No consideration will be given, however, to the location or convenience of the taxpayer's representative. The IRS will take into account the place at which the examination can be performed most efficiently and the resources that are available at the IRS office to which the transfer is requested. A change also will be considered if other factors indicate that examination at the

---

[16] Reg. § 301.7605-1(b)(1).
[17] Reg. § 301.7605-1(d)(3)(ii).

[18] CCA 200206054. The only information required to be provided by an IRS employee is the employee's name and unique identifying number.
[19] Reg. § 301.7605-1(e)(1).

location set by the IRS could pose undue inconvenience to the taxpayer. As a condition for granting a request for transfer, the taxpayer must agree to extend the statute of limitations for up to one year if it will expire within thirteen months of the transfer.[20]

When an IRS agent contacts a taxpayer to examine a return, the agent is required to furnish an explanation of the audit process and the taxpayer's rights relating to that process.[21] If the taxpayer wishes to consult with a representative, the agent must hold the interview in abeyance to allow time for the taxpayer to meet with his or her representative. In many instances, the agent will ask the representative to have the taxpayer present at the meeting. The taxpayer is not required to attend the meeting, however, unless he or she has been given a summons to appear.[22] A taxpayer may make an audio recording of the meeting, provided that ten days advance notice be given to the IRS that the taxpayer intends to record the interview. The recording must be done with the taxpayer's equipment and at the taxpayer's own expense. In these situations, the IRS may also record the interview.[23] To fully appreciate the scope of the field examination, it is helpful to reflect on the power given to the IRS to examine returns. Section 7602 of the Internal Revenue Code (the Code) authorizes the Treasury Department to examine any books, papers, records or other data which may be relevant or material to ascertaining the correctness of any return. A field examination conducted by a revenue agent is in essence a complete review of the entire financial workings of the taxpayer. The agent will examine the history of the taxpayer, including a study of any pertinent business agreements or documents. In the case of a corporation, the corporate minutes and any other written documentation of the actions of the corporation for the years under audit will be examined.

Determining the scope of an examination is the process by which an examiner selects issues warranting examination. Examiners should select issues so that, with reasonable certainty, all items necessary for a substantially proper determination of the tax liability have been considered. Examiners must assess the facts and apply judgment in determining the scope of the examination. The scope of the examination will be determined by the revenue agent.[24] Examiners are expected to continually exercise judgment throughout the examination process to expand or contract the scope as needed. If, during the course of the examination, the scope of the examination is expanded to include another tax period and the taxpayer has representation, the taxpayer should be notified of the expansion and given time to secure a power-of-attorney for the additional tax period, before any examination action is taken.[25]

The revenue agent will look into the method of accounting employed by the taxpayer (cash or accrual) and determine whether income and expenses have been reported consistently with that method. A comparison of the original books of entry with the tax return will also be made. The agent will seek to reconcile

---

[20] Reg. § 301.7605-1(e)(4).

[21] Code Sec. 7521(b)(1).

[22] Code Sec. 7521(c).

[23] Code Sec. 7521(a).

[24] IRM 4.10.2.6.1.

[25] IRM 4.10.2.6.1.

book income with tax return income. Usually this reconciliation will require an analysis of the year-end adjusting entries as well as the journals and ledgers. Special analysis of reserve accounts for bad debts and depreciation can be expected. A test of gross receipts either through the use of a simple T-account, a bank deposit analysis or a spot check is usually required. The agent may also seek inventory verification in the case of a business in which inventory is a material income producing factor. Compensation of officers, accumulation of earnings and related-party transactions are three other prime objects of field examination verification. In these instances, the taxpayer will be asked to furnish the foundation for deductions taken on the return.

An item that is common to both field and office audits is the verification of travel and entertainment expenses. Under Code Sec. 274, specific criteria must be met before a deduction can be taken for these expenses. The revenue agent will be interested in verifying not only the amount of the expenditure but also whether the expenditure meets the requirements of Code Sec. 274.

As part of an audit, the revenue agent may request file copies of a variety of other tax returns. It ensures that all required returns have been filed and the information correctly reported. As an example, a revenue agent auditing a corporation may ask the principal officers for copies of their individual returns. The "inspection" of these file copies does not constitute an audit but is merely a verification to ensure that a return was filed and that income on that return corresponds to those items from the corporate audit that should be reported by the individual. In the event of a discrepancy on the individual return, the agent generally will open that return for examination and conduct an audit of the individual taxpayer. In a "package audit" of a business, the agent also will ask for copies of employment tax returns to determine that such returns have been filed and that the reported information reconciles with the tax return deductions of the business.

During an audit, questions frequently arise concerning the valuation, depreciation, obsolescence or depletion of particular assets. Such issues are often referred to an engineering group which services the local examination area.

> **Example 4-4:** IRS Agents set an appointment at Field Company to conduct a field examination. The IRS and Field personnel held an opening conference during which the IRS informed Field what issues it was going to examine. Thereafter, the IRS began issuing a series of Information Document Requests asking for certain documents. Field Company complies with these requests. By the end of the field examination, there was only one issue upon which the IRS and the Field Company did not agree. The Field Company took the issue to IRS Appeals.

¶407 RESEARCH AUDIT

The final type of the five audit programs is a research audit. Returns are chosen at random from a scientific sample based on the ending digits of the taxpayer's social security number. The return is subjected to a thorough audit in which every item on the return is covered regardless of dollar amount. Although some taxpayers have objected to such an in-depth scrutiny for research purposes, both *United States v. Flagg*[26] and *United States v. First National Bank of Dallas*[27] have held that a taxpayer cannot refuse to comply with the requirements of a research audit.

In order to protect the validity of the statistical sample, revenue agents are required to complete an assigned research audit, even though there is no apparent error on the tax return. The failure to complete the audit would impair the sampling technique.

> **Example 4-5:** The current version of the research audit is the National Research Program (NRP), which was updated in June of 2007. According to IR-2007-113, the new NRP is designed to provide the IRS with more accurate audit selection tools, with the desired result to reduce the nation's "tax gap." The tax gap is the difference between the amount of tax owed and the amount of tax collected. The new NRP will be conducted annually by selecting at random approximately 13,000 returns. The unique feature of this new NRP is that it will be conducted each year. The NRP will result in a multi-year rolling methodology that is expected to burden fewer taxpayers and yield more timely feedback to the IRS.

¶408 TAXPAYER RIGHTS

The Secretary of the Treasury is required to prepare and distribute a statement explaining in simple language the rights of taxpayers when dealing with the IRS. That statement must be furnished to all taxpayers contacted by the IRS for the purpose of determining or collecting taxes. Publication No. 1, Your Rights as a Taxpayer (see Exhibit 4-8 at ¶428) issued by the IRS, sets forth in nontechnical terms the following rights:

1. The rights of the taxpayer and obligations of the IRS during the audit;

2. The right to a representative;

3. How adverse decisions are appealed;

4. How refunds can be claimed;

5. How the taxpayers may file complaints; and

6. How and by what procedures the IRS assesses and collects tax.

At the initial interview, revenue agents and auditors also are required to orally explain to the taxpayer the audit process and the rights of the taxpayer with respect to such process. They must clearly advise the taxpayer of his or her right to appeal.

In addition, the IRS is now prohibited from contacting any person, other than the taxpayer, regarding the determination or collection of the taxpayer's tax liability without providing reasonable advance notice to the taxpayer.[28] However, disclosure need not be made for any contact (1) authorized by the taxpayer;

---

[26] 634 F2d 1087 (8th Cir. 1980), 80-2 USTC ¶9795 cert. denied, 451 U.S. 909 (1981).

[27] 635 F2d 391 (5th Cir. 1981), 81-1 USTC ¶9159.
[28] Code Sec. 7602(c).

(2) situations where notice would jeopardize collection; and (3) contacts during a pending criminal investigation.

¶409 INTERNAL REVENUE MANUAL

The Internal Revenue Manual (IRM) is the single official source of IRS instructions to its staff including procedures, guidelines, policies and delegations of authority. It is the intent of the IRS that various types of instructions to staff such as job aids, desk guides and the like be incorporated in the IRM. The IRM is organized into parts based upon the type of work process. For example, Part Four deals with Examining Process, Part Five deals with the Collecting Process, Part Eight deals with Appeals and Part Nine deals with Criminal Investigation. Within each part are chapters dealing with a specific topic. Chapter 4.10 deals with Examination of Returns, Chapter 4.11 is the Examining Officers Guide, Chapter 4.23 deals with Employment Tax, Chapter 4.41 deals with the Oil and Gas Industry and Chapter 4.42 deals with the Insurance Industry. Part 25 contains policies and procedures that apply to more than one work process. Among the items contained in Part 25 are policies and procedures dealing with Fraud (25.1), Summons (25.5), Statute Of Limitations (25.6) and Relief from Joint and Several Liability (25.15).

The IRM contains Official Use Only (OUO) materials that are not available to the public. OUO materials includes guidance or information that if released would hinder the law enforcement process and instructions relating to enforcement strategies, methods, procedures, tolerances and criteria. Law Enforcement Manuals (LEM) are units of issue that consist entirely of OUO material. LEMs are issued and published separately.

¶410 BURDEN OF PROOF

An audit is basically an adversary proceeding, but unlike a criminal trial in which the defendant is presumed innocent until proven guilty, historically, an audit placed the burden of proof on the taxpayer. In one of its most publicized provisions, the IRS Restructuring and Reform Act of 1998[29] altered the historical rule.[30] Code Sec. 7491 provides that the IRS will have the burden of proof in any court proceedings arising out of examinations beginning after July 22, 1998, if the taxpayer introduces "credible evidence" on any factual issue relevant to ascertaining the taxpayer's liability for any income, estate, or gift tax, provided that (1) the taxpayer has complied with any requirement to substantiate any item,[31] (2) the taxpayer has maintained records required under the Code and has cooperated with reasonable requests by the IRS for witnesses, information, documents, meetings and interviews, and (3) in the case of a partnership, corporation, or trust, the taxpayer has a net worth of no more than seven million dollars. The term "credible evidence" is the "quality of evidence which, after the critical analysis, the court would find sufficient upon which to base a decision if no contrary evidence were submitted (without regard to the judicial presumption of

---

[29] P.L. 105-206.

[30] Code Sec. 7491.

[31] *Sowards v. Comm'r*, T.C. Memo 2003-180

Internal Revenue Service correctness)."[32] Code Sec. 7491's cooperation requirement demands that, among other things, the taxpayer exhaust all administrative remedies, including any appeal rights. The taxpayer is not, however, required to agree to extend the statute of limitations. The taxpayer must establish the applicability of any claimed privilege. The taxpayer has the burden of proving that he or she meets the requirements for shifting the burden of proof under Code Sec. 7491.

The IRS will also have the burden of proof on any item of income that is reconstructed through the use of statistical information of unrelated taxpayers.[33] In addition, under Code Sec. 7491(c), the IRS will have the burden of proof in any court proceeding involving imposition of a civil penalty on any individual.

The perceived importance of the burden shift from the taxpayer makes it critical for accountants, attorneys, and others who represent taxpayers during audits to ensure that the prerequisites for the burden shift are met, if possible. In situations where the taxpayer failed to shift the burden, it will be necessary to present a persuasive defense. A practitioner should prepare for an audit in the same way an attorney prepares for a courtroom appearance. The practitioner should marshal all the evidence and should have all receipts and cancelled checks classified and verified with adding machine tapes. The practitioner also should verify that all books of account correspond with the items in the tax return.

Generally, it is better for the practitioner not to volunteer any extraneous information and only to present evidence or documents pertaining to those areas about which the agent has inquired. After the agent completes the examination, he or she will tell the taxpayer or practitioner what the results are. At this stage, depending on the nature of the issue, arguments can be presented in an attempt to resolve the case.

¶411 RESOLUTION EFFORTS

While there is no general rule for the best time or manner to resolve a tax case, it is usually best to attempt to dispose of a case at the lowest possible level, that is, with the revenue agent. The agent who has conducted the examination will be familiar with all the facts and circumstances surrounding the items in issue. In most cases, the taxpayer has nothing to lose by an intensive effort to resolve a tax controversy immediately. If negotiations are unsuccessful, at least the taxpayer will know what issues are in doubt and where he or she stands. This will allow the taxpayer time to prepare the case and to consider the various alternative actions available.

The distinction between resolution authority and settlement authority possessed by revenue agents at the examination level is critical in understanding how to conclude a dispute on favorable terms at the examination level. Settlement authority includes the discretion to settle the dispute on a percentage of tax

---

[32] Sen. Comm. Rep. to P.L. 105-206; *Higbee v. Comm'r*, 116 T.C. 438, 442-3 (2001); *Forste v. Comm'r*, T.C. Memo 2003-103.

[33] Code Sec. 7491(b).

owed basis due to the hazards of litigation each party is likely to encounter in court. Hazards of litigation are influenced most heavily by legal considerations. Resolution authority, on the other hand, is influenced most heavily by the facts and circumstances peculiar to the dispute at hand. Although a revenue agent technically has no settlement authority, in practice, the agent has discretion in a number of areas to resolve a dispute. A revenue agent does not have authority or discretion in areas where the Commissioner has indicated that the IRS will not follow a court decision or has issued adverse regulations or revenue rulings. Therefore, it is important to determine whether the issues raised by the agent are of a factual or a legal nature.

> **Example 4-6:** For example, reasonableness of compensation and deductibility of travel and entertainment expenses are factual issues. On such issues, the agent may have substantial authority to resolve a case.

When a legal issue is involved and the IRS has clearly articulated its position, an impasse will quickly be reached with the revenue agent in any resolution attempt. In such a situation, the practitioner should indicate that the agent's opinion is respected and that the representative realizes the agent has no choice on the issue. At the same time, the practitioner should explain that he or she must disagree in order to represent the client's best interests. The practitioner should attempt to isolate the agreed from the unagreed issues and, if possible, to have the agent's report reflect only the unagreed issues. Finally, the practitioner should make sure that the agent has a complete and accurate picture of each transaction, because the statement of facts in the agent's report will be relied upon by the IRS in all future settlement discussions.

Another means of settling legal issues is to obtain a National Office Technical Advice Memorandum. Technical advice is furnished by the National Office of the Internal Revenue Service to help IRS personnel close cases and to establish and maintain consistent holdings on issues. Such advice can be obtained during the course of the examination or when the case has been forwarded to the Appeals Office for review. A technical advice conclusion that is adverse to the taxpayer does not preclude the taxpayer from litigating the issue. The rules for obtaining a Technical Advice Memorandum are discussed in Chapter 16.

If a full resolution has been reached, the revenue agent will prepare a Form 4549, Income Tax Examination Changes (see Exhibit 4-2 at ¶422). This form will set forth in summary the adjustments to income or expenses that have been made as a result of the audit, the years being adjusted, the amount of additional tax and penalties, if any, and with whom the examination changes were discussed. The Form 4549 is to be signed by the examiner and consented to by the taxpayer. Execution of a Form 4549 constitutes a consent to the assessment of the deficiencies shown on the form and eliminates the need for the IRS to follow the formal assessment procedures required by Code Sec. 6212. The execution of Form 4549 at this stage of the proceedings will stop the running of interest thirty days after the consent to assessment is filed with the IRS.[34]

---

[34] Code Sec. 6601(c).

In cases in which there has been a partial agreement, the revenue agent may request that the taxpayer sign a Form 870, Waiver of Restrictions on Assessment and Collection of Deficiency in Tax and Acceptance of Overassessment (see Exhibit 4-5 at ¶425). Execution of this waiver by the taxpayer will allow the immediate assessment of the tax on agreed issues without the need to issue a formal statutory notice of deficiency. Since Form 870 generally does not detail the audit changes, it will be accompanied by a Form 4549-A, Discrepancy Adjustments (see Exhibit 4-9 at ¶429 and Exhibit 4-10 at ¶430, Form 886-A, Explanation of Items).

Any agreement reached with the revenue agent or auditor is not binding on the IRS. It is subject to review by the Technical Services (TS) servicing the local office. TS checks the report and the workpapers prepared by the agent to see if all relevant issues have been examined. TS will also review the recommended treatment of items by the agent to see if such treatment conforms to the IRS rules. This is an extension of the IRS's attempt to apply the law uniformly throughout the country to all taxpayers. At times, TS will question whether the agent's proposed allowance or disallowance of a deduction or exclusion of income is appropriate. In such a situation, the case may be sent back to the examiner to develop further facts supporting the conclusion reached. At other times, the review staff will instruct the agent that the proposed treatment is wrong because of an error in the agent's interpretation of the law. Cases subject to mandatory review by TS include Joint Committee cases and Employee audits. Although there are a limited number of identified mandatory review categories, territory managers have the discretion to designate any type or group of cases as a 100-percent review category if reviews are considered essential.[35] In addition, cases are reviewed on a random sample basis.

It is only when the local office issues a report accepting the return as filed or notifying the taxpayer of any agreed adjustment to his or her tax liability that any resolution reached with the agent can be considered final. The letter notifying the taxpayer of final action is set forth as Exhibit 4-11 at ¶431.

¶412 UNAGREED CASES

If a resolution cannot be reached with the examiner, a report is prepared detailing the reasons for the inclusion of additional income or disallowance of expenses, credits, etc. A summary of the changes is reflected on Form 4549-A (see Exhibit 4-9 at ¶429). This form along with the full explanation of adjustments is sent to the taxpayer along with a Form 870. A transmittal letter commonly known as a "30-day letter" (see Exhibit 4-4 at ¶424) also accompanies this report. The transmittal letter sets out the following options:

1. The taxpayer can accept the findings of the examiner and execute a Waiver of Restrictions on Assessment (Form 870). If this course is followed, the taxpayer is billed for any additional tax resulting from the examination. This does not preclude the taxpayer from contesting the

---

[35] IRM 4.8.4.2.

deficiency in court, but it does mean that the tax will have to be paid and then a claim for refund filed.[36]

2. The taxpayer can request a conference with the local Appeals office. This request normally must be received within thirty days of the issuance of the transmittal letter. When the deficiency in tax is more than $25,000, the request must include a written protest setting forth the taxpayer's position.[37] The examiner will then forward the file along with the protest to the Appeals Office.

3. The taxpayer can do nothing, in which case the taxpayer will receive a "Statutory Notice of Deficiency," commonly referred to as a "90-day letter" (see Exhibit 4-12 at ¶432). This form indicates that the tax will be assessed unless a petition is filed with the Tax Court of the United States. A waiver, Form 4089, is enclosed with the 90-day letter (see Exhibit 4-13 at ¶433).

Example 4-7: George received an IRS report with details as to why the IRS disagreed with certain aspects of his tax return, along with a summary report on Form 4549-A, a Form 870, and a 30-day letter. George has the following options:

1. Accept the IRS changes and sign the Form 870 which will allow the IRS to bill George for any amounts due.

2. Seek a meeting with the IRS Appeals. If the amount in dispute exceeds $25,000 this request must include a formal written protest.

3. Do nothing. George will receive a Statutory Notice of Deficiency that will make clear the IRS will assess the tax unless George files a petition in the U.S. Tax Court within 90 days of the date on the Notice of Deficiency.

---

[36] See Chapter 15, *infra.*   [37] See Chapter 12, *infra.*

Letter 2201 (handwritten)

¶421 Exhibit 4-1

Internal Revenue Service   **Department of the Treasury**

Date:

Taxpayer Identification Number:

Tax Year:

Form Number:

Person to Contact:

Employee Identification Number:

Contact Telephone Number:

Fax Number:

Dear

   Your federal income tax return for the year shown above has been selected for examination. We examine tax returns to verify the correctness of income, deductions, exemptions, and credits.

WHAT YOU NEED TO DO
Please call our appointment clerk **WITHIN 10 DAYS** to schedule an appointment. For your convenience we have provided space below to record your appointment.

   Place: Date:

                                                   Time:

   Attached to this letter is a list of the items on your return which will be examined. In an effort to save time, you should organize your records according to the category as deducted on your return. For further information see the enclosed Publication 1, *Your Rights as a Taxpayer,* and Notice 609, *Privacy Act Notice.*

WHAT TO EXPECT AT THE EXAMINATION
Generally an examination is scheduled to last two to four hours. After the completion of the initial interview, additional information still may be needed. You may submit this information by mail or by scheduling a follow-up appointment. When the examination is completed, you may owe additional tax, be due a refund, or there may be no change to your return.

WHO MAY COME TO THE EXAMINATION
If you filed a joint return, you and/or your spouse may attend. You also may elect to have someone else represent you. If you will not attend with your representative, you must provide a completed Form 2848, *Power of Attorney,* or Form 8821, *Tax Information Authorization,* by the start of the examination. You can get these forms from our office.

                         (over)   **Letter 2201 (DO) (Rev. 12-1999)**
                                                     Catalog Number 63748H

WHAT WILL HAPPEN IF YOU DO NOT RESPOND
If you do not keep your appointment or provide the requested records, we will issue an examination report showing additional tax due. Therefore, it is to your advantage to keep your appointment and to provide the records. If you are uncertain about the records needed or the examination process, we will answer your questions when you call to schedule your appointment.

Sincerely yours,

Enclosures:
Publication 1
Notice 609

Letter 2201 (DO) (Rev. 12-1999)
Catalog Number 63748H

¶421

Please bring records to support the following items reported on your tax return for _____ .

☐ Automobile Expenses	☐ Energy Credit	☐ Sale or Exchange of Residence
☐ Bad Debts	☐ Exemptions (Child/Children, Other)	☐ Taxes
☐ Capital Gains and Losses	☐ Filing Status	☐ Uniform, Equipment, and Tools
☐ Casualty Losses	☐ Income	☐
☐ Contributions	☐ Interest Expenses	☐
☐ Credit for Child and	☐ Medical and Dental Expenses	☐
Dependent Care Expenses	☐ Miscellaneous Expenses	
☐ Education Expenses	☐ Moving Expenses	
☐ Employee Business Expenses	☐ Rental Income and Expenses	

Schedule C

☐ Books and records about your income, expenses, and deductions
☐ Workpapers used in preparing your return
☐ Savings account passbooks, brokerage statements, and other information related to foreign and domestic investments
☐ Bank statements, canceled checks, and duplicate deposit slips covering the period from _____ to _____ .
☐ Information on loans, repayments, and other nontaxable sources of income

☐ All Business Expenses	☐ Gross Receipts	☐ Salaries and Wages
☐ Bad Debts	☐ Insurance	☐ Supplies
☐ Car and Truck Expenses	☐ Interest	☐ Taxes
☐ Commissions	☐ Legal and Professional Services	☐ Travel and Entertainment
☐ Cost of Goods Sold	☐ Rent	
☐ Depreciation	☐ Repairs	
☐	☐	

Schedule F

☐ Books and records about your income, expenses, and deductions
☐ Workpapers used in preparing your return
☐ Savings account passbooks, brokerage statements, and other information related to foreign and domestic investments
☐ Bank statements, canceled checks, and duplicate deposit slips covering the period from _____ to _____ .
☐ Information on loans, repayments, and other nontaxable sources of income

☐ All Farm Expenses	☐ Insurance	☐ Repairs and Maintenance
☐ Depreciation	☐ Inventories	☐ Supplies Purchases
☐ Feed Purchases	☐ Labor Hired	☐ Taxes
☐ Fertilizers and Lime	☐ Machine Hire	☐
☐ Gross Receipts	☐ Other Farm income	☐
☐		

Letter 2201 (DO) (Rev. 12-1999)
Catalog Number 63748H

¶421

¶422 Exhibit 4-2

← EXaM

Form **4549** (Rev. March 2005)	Department of the Treasury-Internal Revenue Service **Income Tax Examination Changes**		Page _____ of _____
Name and Address of Taxpayer		Taxpayer Identification Number	Return Form No.:
		Person with whom examination changes were discussed.	Name and Title:

1. **Adjustments to Income**	Period End	Period End	Period End
a.			
b.			
c.			
d.			
e.			
f.			
g.			
h.			
i.			
j.			
k.			
l.			
m.			
n.			
o.			
p.			
2. **Total Adjustments**			
3. Taxable Income Per Return or as Previously Adjusted			
4. **Corrected Taxable Income** Tax Method Filing Status			
5. **Tax**			
6. Additional Taxes / Alternative Minimum Tax			
7. Corrected Tax Liability			
8. **Less** **Credits** a. b. c. d.			
9. **Balance** *(Line 7 less Lines 8a through 8d)*			
10. Plus Other Taxes a. b. c. d.			
11. Total Corrected Tax Liability *(Line 9 plus Lines 10a through 10d)*			
12. Total Tax Shown on Return or as Previously Adjusted			
13. Adjustments to: a. b.			
14. Deficiency-Increase in Tax or *(Overassessment-Decrease in Tax)* *(Line 11 less Line 12 adjusted by Lines 13a plus 13b)*			
15. Adjustments to Prepayment Credits - Increase *(Decrease)*			
16. **Balance Due or** *(Overpayment)* - *(Line 14 adjusted by Line 15)* *(Excluding interest and penalties)*			

The Internal Revenue Service has agreements with state tax agencies under which information about federal tax, including increases or decreases, is exchanged with the states. If this change affects the amount of your state income tax, you should amend your state return by filing the necessary forms.

You may be subject to backup withholding if you underreport your interest, dividend, or patronage dividend income you earned and do not pay the required tax. The IRS may order backup withholding *(withholding of a percentage of your dividend and/or interest income)* if the tax remains unpaid after it has been assessed and four notices have been issued to you over a 120-day period.

Catalog Number 23105A	www.irs.gov	Form **4549** (Rev. 3-2005)

¶422

Form **4549** (Rev. March 2005)	Department of the Treasury-Internal Revenue Service **Income Tax Examination Changes**	Page_____ of _____
Name of Taxpayer	Taxpayer Identification Number	Return Form No.:

17. Penalties/ Code Sections	Period End	Period End	Period End
a.			
b.			
c.			
d.			
e.			
f.			
g.			
h.			
i.			
j.			
k.			
l.			
m.			
18. **Total Penalties**			
Underreporter attributable to negligence: *(1981-1987)* *A tax addition of 50 percent of the interest due on the underpayment will accrue until it is paid or assessed.*			
Underreporter attributable to fraud: *(1981-1987)* *A tax addition of 50 percent of the interest due on the underpayment will accrue until it is paid or assessed.*			
Underreporter attributable to Tax Motivated Transactions *(TMT).* The interest will accrue and be assessed at 120% of the under-payment rate in accordance with IRC §6621(c)			
19. **Summary of Taxes, Penalties and Interest:**			
a. Balance due or *(Overpayment)* Taxes - *(Line 16, Page 1)*			
b. Penalties *(Line 18)* - computed to			
c. Interest *(IRC § 6601)* - computed to			
d. TMT Interest - computed to *(on TMT underpayment)*			
e. Amount due or *(refund)* - *(sum of Lines a, b, c and d)*			

Other Information:

Examiner's Signature:	Employee ID:	Office:	Date:

Consent to Assessment and Collection- I do not wish to exercise my appeal rights with the Internal Revenue Service or to contest in the United States Tax Court the findings in this report. Therefore, I give my consent to the immediate assessment and collection of any increase in tax and penalties, and accept any decrease in tax and penalties shown above, plus additional interest as provided by law. It is understood that this report is subject to acceptance by the Area Director, Area Manager, Specialty Tax Program Chief, or Director of Field Operations.

PLEASE NOTE: If a joint return was filed. **BOTH** *taxpayers must sign*			
Signature of Taxpayer	Date:	Signature of Taxpayer	Date:
By:		Title:	Date:

Catalog Number 23105A   www.irs.gov   Form **4549** (Rev. 3-2005)

¶423 Exhibit 4-3

Internal Revenue Service   **Department of the Treasury**

Date:

Taxpayer Identification Number:

Form:

Tax Period(s) Ended:

Person to Contact:

Contact Telephone Number:

Employee Identification Number:

Refer Reply to:

Last Date to Respond to this Letter:

Dear

   We have enclosed two copies of our examination report showing the changes we made to your tax for the period(s) shown above. Please read the report and tell us whether you agree or disagree with the changes. (This report may not reflect the results of later examinations of partnerships, "S" Corporations, trusts, etc., in which you have an interest. Changes made to those tax returns could affect your tax.)

   IF YOU AGREE with the changes in the report please sign, date, and return one copy to us by the response date shown above. If you filed a joint return, both taxpayers must sign the report. If you owe additional tax, please include payment for the full amount to limit penalty and interest charges to your account.

   IF YOU CAN'T PAY the full amount you owe now, pay as much as you can. If you want us to consider an installment agreement, please complete and return the enclosed Form 9465, *Installment Agreement Request*. If we approve your request, we will charge a $43.00 fee to help offset the cost of providing this service. We will continue to charge penalties and interest until you pay the full amount you owe.

   IF YOU DON'T AGREE with the changes shown in the examination report, you should do one of the following by the response date.

- Mail us any additional information that you would like us to consider

- Discuss the report with the examiner

- Discuss your position with the examiner's supervisor

- Request a conference with an Appeals Officer, as explained in the enclosed Publication 3498, *The Examination Process*. Publication 3498 also explains *Your Rights as a Taxpayer* and *The Collection Process*.

Letter 915 (DO) (Rev. 9-2000)
Catalog Number 62712V

IF YOU DON'T TAKE ANY ACTION by the response date indicated in the heading of this letter, we will process your case based on the information shown in the report. We will send you a statutory notice of deficiency that gives you 90 days to petition the United States Tax Court. If you allow the 90-day period to expire without petitioning the tax court, we will bill you for any additional tax, interest, and penalties.

If you have any questions, please contact the person whose name and telephone number are shown in the heading of this letter. When you write to us, please include your telephone number and the best time for us to call you if we need more information. We have enclosed an envelope for your convenience.

Thank you for your cooperation.

                                   Sincerely yours,

Enclosures:
Examination Report (2)
Form 9465
Publication 3498
Envelope

                                                                  Letter 915 (DO) (Rev. 9-2000)
                                                                  Catalog Number 62712V

¶424 Exhibit 4-4

EXAM Letter 950

Internal Revenue Service

Department of the Treasury

Taxpayer Identification Number:

Date:

Form:

Tax Period(s) Ended and Deficiency Amount(s):

Person to Contact:

Contact Telephone Number:

Employee Identification Number:

Last Date to Respond to this Letter:

Dear

We have enclosed an examination report showing proposed changes to your tax for the period(s) shown above. Please read the report, and tell us whether you agree or disagree with the changes by the date shown above. (This report may not reflect the results of later examinations of partnerships, "S" Corporations, trusts, etc., in which you may have an interest. Changes to those accounts could also affect your tax.)

If you agree with the proposed changes...

1. Sign and date the enclosed agreement form. If you filed a joint return, both taxpayers must sign the form.

2. Return the signed agreement form to us.

3. Enclose payment for tax, interest and any penalties due. Make your check or money order payable to the **United States Treasury.** You can call the person identified above to determine the total amount due as of the date you intend to make payment.

4. After we receive your signed agreement form, we will close your case.

If you pay the full amount due now, you will limit the amount of interest and penalties charged to your account. If you agree with our findings, but can only pay part of the bill, please call the person identified above to discuss different payment options. We may ask you to complete a collection information statement to determine your payment options, such as paying in installments. You can also write to us or visit your nearest IRS office to explain your circumstances. If you don't enclose payment for the additional tax, interest, and any penalties, we will bill you for the unpaid amounts.

If you are a "C" Corporation, Section 6621(c) of the Internal Revenue Code provides that an interest rate 2% higher than the standard rate of interest will be charged on deficiencies of $100,000 or more.

If you don't agree with the proposed changes...

1. You may request a meeting or telephone conference with the supervisor of the person identified in the heading of this letter. If you still don't agree after the meeting or telephone conference, you can:

Letter 950(DO) (Rev. 8-2005)
Catalog Number 40390D

¶424

2. Request a conference with our Appeals Office. If the total proposed change to your tax and penalties is:

- $25,000 or less for *each* referenced tax period, send us a letter requesting consideration by Appeals. Indicate the issues you don't agree with and the reasons why you don't agree. If you don't want to write a separate letter, you can complete the enclosed Form 13683, *Statement of Disputed Issues,* and return it to us.

- More than $25,000 for *any* referenced tax period; you must submit a formal protest.

The requirements for filing a formal protest are explained in the enclosed Publication 3498, *The Examination Process.* Publication 3498 also includes information on your *Rights as a Taxpayer* and the *IRS Collection Process.*

If you request a conference with our Appeals Office, an Appeals Officer will call you (if necessary) for an appointment to take a fresh look at your case. The Appeals Office is an independent office and most disputes considered by the Appeals Office are resolved informally and promptly. By requesting a conference with our Appeals Office you may avoid court costs (such as the Tax Court filing fees), resolve the matter sooner, and/or prevent interest and any penalties from increasing on your account.

If you decide to bypass the Appeals Office and petition the Tax Court directly, your case will usually be sent to an Appeals Office first to try to resolve the issue(s). Certain procedures and rights in court (for example, the burden of proof and potential recovery of litigation costs) depend on you fully participating in the administrative consideration of your case, including consideration by the IRS Appeals Office.

If you don't reach an agreement with our Appeals Office or if you don't respond to this letter, we will send you another letter that will tell you how to obtain Tax Court Review of your case.

You must mail your signed agreement form, completed Statement of Disputed Issues, or a formal protest to us by the response date shown in the heading of this letter. If you decide to request a conference with the examiner's supervisor, your request should also be made by the response date indicated.

MAIL RESPONSES TO: **Internal Revenue Service**
                                  Attn:

If you have any questions, please contact the person whose name and telephone number are shown above.

Thank you for your cooperation.

                               Sincerely yours,

Enclosures:
Copy of this letter
Examination Report
Agreement Form
Form 13683
Publication 3498
Envelope

                                             Letter 950(DO) (Rev. 8-2005)
                                             Catalog Number 40390D

✗EXAM

¶425 Exhibit 4-5

Form **870** (Rev. March 1992)	Department of the Treasury — Internal Revenue Service **Waiver of Restrictions on Assessment and Collection of Deficiency in Tax and Acceptance of Overassessment**	Date received by Internal Revenue Service
Names and address of taxpayers *(Number, street, city or town, State, ZIP code)*		Social security or employer identification number

		Increase (Decrease) in Tax and Penalties			
Tax year ended	Tax			Penalties	
	$	$	$	$	$
	$	$	$	$	$
	$	$	$	$	$
	$	$	$	$	$
	$	$	$	$	$
	$	$	$	$	$
	$	$	$	$	$

(For instructions, see back of form)

Consent to Assessment and Collection

I consent to the immediate assessment and collection of any deficiencies *(increase in tax and penalties)* and accept any overassessment *(decrease in tax and penalties)* shown above, plus any interest provided by law. I understand that by signing this waiver, I will not be able to contest these years in the United States Tax Court, unless additional deficiencies are determined for these years.

YOUR SIGNATURE⟶ HERE		Date
SPOUSE'S SIGNATURE⟶		Date
TAXPAYER'S REPRESENTATIVE HERE ⟶		Date
CORPORATE NAME ⟶		

		Title	Date
CORPORATE OFFICER(S) SIGN HERE		Title	Date

Catalog Number 16894U   Form **870** (Rev. 3-92)

Instructions

General Information

If you consent to the assessment of the deficiencies shown in this waiver, please sign and return the form in order to limit any interest charge and expedite the adjustment to your account. Your consent will not prevent you from filing a claim for refund *(after you have paid the tax)* if you later believe you are so entitled. It will not prevent us from later determining, if necessary, that you owe additional tax; nor extend the time provided by law for either action.

We have agreements with State tax agencies under which information about Federal tax, including increases or decreases, is exchanged with the States. If this change affects the amount of your State income tax, you should file the required State form.

If you later file a claim and the Service disallows it, you may file suit for refund in a district court or in the United States Claims Court, but you may not file a petition with the United States Tax Court.

We will consider this waiver a valid claim for refund or credit of any overpayment due you resulting from any decrease in tax and penalties shown above, provided you sign and file it within the period established by law for making such a claim.

Who Must Sign

If you filed jointly, both you and your spouse must sign. If this waiver is for a corporation, it should be signed with the corporation name, followed by the signatures and titles of the corporate officers authorized to sign. An attorney or agent may sign this waiver provided such action is specifically authorized by a power of attorney which, if not previously filed, must accompany this form.

If this waiver is signed by a person acting in a fiduciary capacity *(for example, an executor, administrator, or a trustee)* Form 56, Notice Concerning Fiduciary Relationship, should, unless previously filed, accompany this form.

∗U.S. GPO:1992-312-711/50896

¶426 Exhibit 4-6

Your Appeal Rights and How To Prepare a Protest If You Don't Agree

Department of the Treasury
Internal Revenue Service

www.irs.ustreas.gov

Publication 5 (Rev. 01-1999)
Catalog Number 46074I

Introduction

This Publication tells you how to appeal your tax case if you don't agree with the Internal Revenue Service (IRS) findings.

If You Don't Agree

If you don't agree with any or all of the IRS findings given you, you may request a meeting or a telephone conference with the supervisor of the person who issued the findings. If you still don't agree, you may appeal your case to the Appeals Office of IRS.

If you decide to do nothing and your case involves an examination of your income, estate, gift, and certain excise taxes or penalties, you will receive a formal Notice of Deficiency. The Notice of Deficiency allows you to go to the Tax Court and tells you the procedure to follow. If you do not go to the Tax Court, we will send you a bill for the amount due.

If you decide to do nothing and your case involves a trust fund recovery penalty, or certain employment tax liabilities, the IRS will send you a bill for the penalty. If you do not appeal a denial of an offer in compromise or a denial of a penalty abatement, the IRS will continue collection action.

If you don't agree, we urge you to appeal your case to the Appeals Office of IRS. The Office of Appeals can settle most differences without expensive and time-consuming court trials. [Note: Appeals can not consider your reasons for not agreeing if they don't come within the scope of the tax laws (for example, if you disagree solely on moral, religious, political, constitutional, conscientious, or similar grounds.)]

The following general rules tell you how to appeal your case.

Appeals Within the IRS

Appeals is the administrative appeals office for the IRS. You may appeal most IRS decisions with your local Appeals Office. The Appeals Office is separate from - and independent of - the IRS Office taking the action you disagree with. The Appeals Office is the only level of administrative appeal within the IRS.

Conferences with Appeals Office personnel are held in an informal manner by correspondence, by telephone or at a personal conference. There is no need for you to have representation for an Appeals conference, but if you choose to have a representative, see the requirements under *Representation.*

If you want an Appeals conference, follow the instructions in our letter to you. Your request will be sent to the Appeals Office to arrange a conference at a convenient time and place. You or your representative should prepare to discuss all issues you don't agree with at the conference. Most differences are settled at this level.

In most instances, you may be eligible to take your case to court if you don't reach an agreement at your Appeals conference, or if you don't want to appeal your case to the IRS Office of Appeals. See the later section *Appeals To The Courts.*

Protests

When you request an appeals conference, you may also need to file a formal written protest or a small case request with the office named in our letter to you. Also, see the special appeal request procedures in Publication 1660, Collection Appeal Rights, if you disagree with lien, levy, seizure, or denial or termination of an installment agreement.

You need to file a written protest:

- In all employee plan and exempt organization cases without regard to the dollar amount at issue.

- In all partnership and S corporation cases without regard to the dollar amount at issue.

- In all other cases, unless you qualify for the small case request procedure, or other special appeal procedures such as requesting Appeals consideration of liens, levies, seizures, or installment agreements. See Publication 1660.

How to prepare a protest:

When a protest is required, **send it within the time limit specified in the letter you received.** Include in your protest:

1) Your name and address, and a daytime telephone number,

2) A statement that you want to appeal the IRS findings to the Appeals Office,

3) A copy of the letter showing the proposed changes and findings you don't agree with (or the date and symbols from the letter),

4) The tax periods or years involved,

5) A list of the changes that you don't agree with, and why you don't agree.

6) The facts supporting your position on any issue that you don't agree with,

7) The law or authority, if any, on which you are relying.

8) You must sign the written protest, stating that it is true, under the penalties of perjury as follows:

"Under the penalties of perjury, I declare that I examined the facts stated in this protest, including any accompanying documents, and, to the best of my knowledge and belief, they are true, correct, and complete."

If your representative prepares and signs the protest for you, he or she must substitute a declaration stating:

1) That he or she submitted the protest and accompanying documents and

2) Whether he or she knows personally that the facts stated in the protest and accompanying documents are true and correct.

We urge you to provide as much information as you can, as this will help us speed up your appeal. This will save you both time and money.

Small Case Request:

If the total amount for any tax period is not more than $25,000, you may make a small case request instead of filing a formal written protest. In computing the total amount, include a proposed increase or decrease in tax (including penalties), or claimed refund. For an offer in compromise, in calculating the total amount, include total unpaid tax, penalty and interest due. For a small case request, follow the instructions in our letter to you by: sending a letter requesting Appeals consideration, indicating the changes you don't agree with, and the reasons why you don't agree.

Representation

You may represent yourself at your appeals conference, or you may have an attorney, certified public accountant, or an individual enrolled to practice before the IRS represent you. Your representative must be qualified to practice before the IRS. If you want your representative to appear without you, you must provide a properly completed power of attorney to the IRS before the representative can receive or inspect confidential information. Form 2848, Power of Attorney and Declaration of Representative, or any other properly written power of attorney or authorization may be used for this

¶426

purpose. You can get copies of Form 2848 from an IRS office, or by calling 1-800-TAX-FORM (1-800-829-3676).

You may also bring another person(s) with you to support your position.

Appeals To The Courts

If you and Appeals don't agree on some or all of the issues after your Appeals conference, or if you skipped our appeals system, you may take your case to the United States Tax Court, the United States Court of Federal Claims, or your United States District Court, after satisfying certain procedural and jurisdictional requirements as described below under each court. (However, if you are a nonresident alien, you cannot take your case to a United States District Court.) These courts are independent judicial bodies and have no connection with the IRS.

Tax Court

If your disagreement with the IRS is over whether you owe additional income tax, estate tax, gift tax, certain excise taxes or penalties related to these proposed liabilities, you can go to the United States Tax Court. (Other types of tax controversies, such as those involving some employment tax issues or manufacturers' excise taxes, cannot be heard by the Tax Court.) You can do this after the IRS issues a formal letter, stating the amounts that the IRS believes you owe. This letter is called a notice of deficiency. You have 90 days from the date this notice is mailed to you to file a petition with the Tax Court (or 150 days if the notice is addressed to you outside the United States). The last date to file your petition will be entered on the notice of deficiency issued to you by the IRS. If you don't file the petition within the 90-day period (or 150 days, as the case may be), we will assess the proposed liability and send you a bill. You may also have the right to take your case to the Tax Court in some other situations, for example, following collection action by the IRS in certain cases. See Publication 1660.

If you discuss your case with the IRS during the 90-day period (150-day period), the discussion will not extend the period in which you may file a petition with the Tax Court.

The court will schedule your case for trial at a location convenient to you. You may represent yourself before the Tax Court, or you may be represented by anyone permitted to practice before that court.

Note: If you don't choose to go to the IRS Appeals Office before going to court, normally you will have an opportunity to attempt settlement with Appeals before your trial date.

If you dispute not more than $50,000 for any one tax year, there are simplified procedures. You can get information about these procedures and

other matters from the Clerk of the Tax Court, 400 Second St. NW, Washington, DC 20217.

Frivolous Filing Penalty

Caution: If the Tax Court determines that your case is intended primarily to cause a delay, or that your position is frivolous or groundless, the Tax Court may award a penalty of up to $25,000 to the United States in its decision.

District Court and Court of Federal Claims

If your claim is for a refund of any type of tax, you may take your case to your United States District Court or to the United States Court of Federal Claims. Certain types of cases, such as those involving some employment tax issues or manufacturers' excise taxes, can be heard only by these courts.

Generally, your District Court and the Court of Federal Claims hear tax cases only after you have paid the tax and filed a claim for refund with the IRS. You can get information about procedures for filing suit in either court by contacting the Clerk of your District Court or the Clerk of the Court of Federal Claims.

If you file a formal refund claim with the IRS, and we haven't responded to you on your claim within 6 months from the date you filed it, you may file suit for a refund immediately in your District Court or the Court of Federal Claims. If we send you a letter that proposes disallowing or disallows your claim, you may request Appeals review of the disallowance. If you wish to file a refund suit, you must file your suit no later than 2 years from the date of our notice of claim disallowance letter.

Note: Appeals review of a disallowed claim doesn't extend the 2 year period for filing suit. However, it may be extended by mutual agreement.

Recovering Administrative and Litigation Costs

You may be able to recover your reasonable litigation and administrative costs if you are the prevailing party, and if you meet the other requirements. You must exhaust your administrative remedies within the IRS to receive reasonable litigation costs. You must not unreasonably delay the administrative or court proceedings.

Administrative costs include costs incurred on or after the date you receive the Appeals decision letter, the date of the first letter of proposed deficiency, or the date of the notice of deficiency, whichever is earliest.

Recoverable litigation or administrative costs may include:

- Attorney fees that generally do not exceed $125 per hour. This amount will be indexed for a cost of living adjustment.

- Reasonable amounts for court costs or any administrative fees or similar charges by the IRS.

- Reasonable expenses of expert witnesses.

- Reasonable costs of studies, analyses, tests, or engineering reports that are necessary to prepare your case.

You are the prevailing party if you meet all the following requirements:

- You substantially prevailed on the amount in controversy, or on the most significant tax issue or issues in question.

- You meet the net worth requirement. For individuals or estates, the net worth cannot exceed $2,000,000 on the date from which costs are recoverable. Charities and certain cooperatives must not have more than 500 employees on the date from which costs are recoverable. And taxpayers other than the two categories listed above must not have net worth exceeding $7,000,000 and cannot have more than 500 employees on the date from which costs are recoverable.

You are not the prevailing party if:

- The United States establishes that its position was substantially justified. If the IRS does not follow applicable published guidance, the United States is presumed to not be substantially justified. This presumption is rebuttable. Applicable published guidance means regulations, revenue rulings, revenue procedures, information releases, notices, announcements, and, if they are issued to you, private letter rulings, technical advice memoranda and determination letters. The court will also take into account whether the Government has won or lost in the courts of appeals for other circuits on substantially similar issues, in determining if the United States is substantially justified.

You are also the prevailing party if:

- The final judgment on your case is less than or equal to a "qualified offer" which the IRS rejected, and if you meet the net worth requirements referred to above.

A court will generally decide who is the prevailing party, but the IRS makes a final determination of liability at the administrative level. This means you may receive administrative costs from the IRS without going to court. You must file your claim for administrative costs no later than the 90th day after the final determination of tax, penalty or interest is mailed to you. The Appeals Office makes determinations for the IRS on administrative costs. A denial of administrative costs may be appealed to the Tax Court no later than the 90th day after the denial.

¶427 Exhibit 4-7

Internal Revenue Service	**Department of the Treasury**

Date:

Taxpayer Identification Number:

Form:

Tax Period(s):

Person to Contact:

Contact Telephone Number:

Contact Fax Number:

Employee Identification Number:

Dear

Your federal return for the period(s) shown above has been selected for examination.

What You Need To Do

Please call me on or before   . I can be contacted from   to   at the contact telephone number provided above.

During our telephone conversation, we will talk about the items I'll be examining on your return, the types of documentation I will ask you to provide, the examination process, and any concerns or questions you may have. We will also set the date, time, and agenda for our first meeting.

Someone May Represent You

You may have someone represent you during any part of this examination. If you want someone to represent you, please provide me with a completed Form 2848, *Power of Attorney and Declaration of Representative*, at our first appointment.

If you prefer, you may mail or fax the form to me prior to our first appointment. You can get this form from our office, or from our web site www.irs.gov, or by calling 1-800-829-3676. If you decide that you wish to get representation after the examination has started, we will delay further examination activity until you can secure representation.

Letter 2205 (Rev. 10-2005)
Catalog Number 63744P

Your Rights As A Taxpayer

We have enclosed Publication 1, *Your Rights as a Taxpayer,* and Notice 609, *Privacy Act Notice.* We encourage you to read the Declaration of Taxpayer Rights found in Publication 1. This publication discusses general rules and procedures we follow in examinations. It explains what happens before, during, and after an examination, and provides additional sources of information.

Thank you for your cooperation and I look forward to hearing from you by

Sincerely,

Internal Revenue Agent

Enclosure:
Publication 1
Notice 609

Letter 2205 (Rev. 10-2005)
Catalog Number 63744P

¶428 Exhibit 4-8

Department of the Treasury
Internal Revenue Service

Publication 1
(Rev. May 2005)

Catalog Number 64731W

www.irs.gov

Your Rights as a Taxpayer

The first part of this publication explains some of your most important rights as a taxpayer. The second part explains the examination, appeal, collection, and refund processes. This publication is also available in Spanish.

Declaration of Taxpayer Rights

I. Protection of Your Rights

IRS employees will explain and protect your rights as a taxpayer throughout your contact with us.

II. Privacy and Confidentiality

The IRS will not disclose to anyone the information you give us, except as authorized by law. You have the right to know why we are asking you for information, how we will use it, and what happens if you do not provide requested information.

III. Professional and Courteous Service

If you believe that an IRS employee has not treated you in a professional, fair, and courteous manner, you should tell that employee's supervisor. If the supervisor's response is not satisfactory, you should write to the IRS director for your area or the center where you file your return.

IV. Representation

You may either represent yourself or, with proper written authorization, have someone else represent you in your place. Your representative must be a person allowed to practice before the IRS, such as an attorney, certified public accountant, or enrolled agent. If you are in an interview and ask to consult such a person, then we must stop and reschedule the interview in most cases.

You can have someone accompany you at an interview. You may make sound recordings of any meetings with our examination, appeal, or collection personnel, provided you tell us in writing 10 days before the meeting.

V. Payment of Only the Correct Amount of Tax

You are responsible for paying only the correct amount of tax due under the law—no more, no less. If you cannot pay all of your tax when it is due, you may be able to make monthly installment payments.

VI. Help With Unresolved Tax Problems

The Taxpayer Advocate Service can help you if you have tried unsuccessfully to resolve a problem with the IRS. Your local Taxpayer Advocate can offer you special help if you have a significant hardship as a result of a tax problem. For more information, call toll free 1–877–777–4778 (1–800–829–4059 for TTY/TDD) or write to the Taxpayer Advocate at the IRS office that last contacted you.

VII. Appeals and Judicial Review

If you disagree with us about the amount of your tax liability or certain collection actions, you have the right to ask the Appeals Office to review your case. You may also ask a court to review your case.

VIII. Relief From Certain Penalties and Interest

The IRS will waive penalties when allowed by law if you can show you acted reasonably and in good faith or relied on the incorrect advice of an IRS employee. We will waive interest that is the result of certain errors or delays caused by an IRS employee.

THE IRS MISSION

PROVIDE AMERICA'S TAXPAYERS TOP QUALITY SERVICE BY HELPING THEM UNDERSTAND AND MEET THEIR TAX RESPONSIBILITIES AND BY APPLYING THE TAX LAW WITH INTEGRITY AND FAIRNESS TO ALL.

Examinations, Appeals, Collections, and Refunds

Examinations (Audits)

We accept most taxpayers' returns as filed. If we inquire about your return or select it for examination, it does not suggest that you are dishonest. The inquiry or examination may or may not result in more tax. We may close your case without change; or, you may receive a refund.

The process of selecting a return for examination usually begins in one of two ways. First, we use computer programs to identify returns that may have incorrect amounts. These programs may be based on information returns, such as Forms 1099 and W-2, on studies of past examinations, or on certain issues identified by compliance projects. Second, we use information from outside sources that indicates that a return may have incorrect amounts. These sources may include newspapers, public records, and individuals. If we determine that the information is accurate and reliable, we may use it to select a return for examination.

Publication 556, Examination of Returns, Appeal Rights, and Claims for Refund, explains the rules and procedures that we follow in examinations. The following sections give an overview of how we conduct examinations.

By Mail

We handle many examinations and inquiries by mail. We will send you a letter with either a request for more information or a reason why we believe a change to your return may be needed. You can respond by mail or you can request a personal interview with an examiner. If you mail us the requested information or provide an explanation, we may or may not agree with you, and we will explain the reasons for any changes. Please do not hesitate to write to us about anything you do not understand.

By Interview

If we notify you that we will conduct your examination through a personal interview, or you request such an interview, you have the right to ask that the examination take place at a reasonable time and place that is convenient for both you and the IRS. If our examiner proposes any changes to your return, he or she will explain the reasons for the changes. If you do not agree with these changes, you can meet with the examiner's supervisor.

Repeat Examinations

If we examined your return for the same items in either of the 2 previous years and proposed no change to your tax liability, please contact us as soon as possible so we can see if we should discontinue the examination.

Appeals

If you do not agree with the examiner's proposed changes, you can appeal them to the Appeals Office of IRS. Most differences can be settled without expensive and time-consuming court trials. Your appeal rights are explained in detail in both Publication 5, Your Appeal Rights and How To Prepare a Protest If You Don't Agree, and Publication 556, Examination of Returns, Appeal Rights, and Claims for Refund.

If you do not wish to use the Appeals Office or disagree with its findings, you may be able to take your case to the U.S. Tax Court, U.S. Court of Federal Claims, or the U.S. District Court where you live. If you take your case to court, the IRS will have the burden of proving certain facts if you kept adequate records to show your tax liability, cooperated with the IRS, and meet certain other conditions. If the court agrees with you on most issues in your case and finds that our position was largely unjustified, you may be able to recover some of your administrative and litigation costs. You will not be eligible to recover these costs unless you tried to resolve your case administratively, including going through the appeals system, and you gave us the information necessary to resolve the case.

Collections

Publication 594, The IRS Collection Process, explains your rights and responsibilities regarding payment of federal taxes. It describes:

- What to do when you owe taxes. It describes what to do if you get a tax bill and what to do if you think your bill is wrong. It also covers making installment payments, delaying collection action, and submitting an offer in compromise.

- IRS collection actions. It covers liens, releasing a lien, levies, releasing a levy, seizures and sales, and release of property.

Your collection appeal rights are explained in detail in Publication 1660, Collection Appeal Rights.

Innocent Spouse Relief

Generally, both you and your spouse are each responsible for paying the full amount of tax, interest, and penalties due on your joint return. However, if you qualify for innocent spouse relief, you may be relieved of part or all of the joint liability. To request relief, you must file Form 8857, Request for Innocent Spouse Relief no later than 2 years after the date on which the IRS first attempted to collect the tax from you. For example, the two-year period for filing your claim may start if the IRS applies your tax refund from one year to the taxes that you and your spouse owe for another year. For more information on innocent spouse relief, see Publication 971, Innocent Spouse Relief, and Form 8857.

Potential Third Party Contacts

Generally, the IRS will deal directly with you or your duly authorized representative. However, we sometimes talk with other persons if we need information that you have been unable to provide, or to verify information we have received. If we do contact other persons, such as a neighbor, bank, employer, or employees, we will generally need to tell them limited information, such as your name. The law prohibits us from disclosing any more information than is necessary to obtain or verify the information we are seeking. Our need to contact other persons may continue as long as there is activity in your case. If we do contact other persons, you have a right to request a list of those contacted.

Refunds

You may file a claim for refund if you think you paid too much tax. You must generally file the claim within 3 years from the date you filed your original return or 2 years from the date you paid the tax, whichever is later. The law generally provides for interest on your refund if it is not paid within 45 days of the date you filed your return or claim for refund. Publication 556, Examination of Returns, Appeal Rights, and Claims for Refund, has more information on refunds.

If you were due a refund but you did not file a return, you generally must file your return within 3 years from the date the return was due (including extensions) to get that refund.

Tax Information

The IRS provides the following sources for forms, publications, and additional information.

- *Tax Questions:* 1–800–829–1040 (1–800–829–4059 for TTY/TDD)
- *Forms and Publications:* 1–800–829–3676 (1–800–829–4059 for TTY/TDD)
- *Internet:* www.irs.gov
- *Small Business Ombudsman:* A small business entity can participate in the regulatory process and comment on enforcement actions of IRS by calling 1-888-REG-FAIR.
- *Treasury Inspector General for Tax Administration:* You can confidentially report misconduct, waste, fraud, or abuse by an IRS employee by calling 1–800–366–4484 (1–800–877–8339 for TTY/TDD). You can remain anonymous.

¶429 Exhibit 4-9

Form **4549-A** (Rev. March 2005)	Department of the Treasury-Internal Revenue Service **Income Tax Discrepancy Adjustments**		Page _____ of _____	
Name and Address of Taxpayer		Taxpayer Identification Number		Return Form No.:
		Person with whom examination changes were discussed.	Name and Title:	
1. Adjustments to Income		**Period End**	**Period End**	**Period End**
a.				
b.				
c.				
d.				
e.				
f.				
g.				
h.				
i.				
j.				
k.				
l.				
m.				
n.				
o.				
p.				
2. **Total Adjustments**				
3. Taxable Income Per Return or as Previously Adjusted				
4. **Corrected Taxable Income** Tax Method Filing Status				
5. **Tax**				
6. **Additional Taxes / Alternative Minimum**				
7. Corrected Tax Liability				
8. **Less** a. **Credits** b. c. d.				
9. **Balance** *(Line 7 less total of Lines 8a thru 8d)*				
10. Plus a. Other b. Taxes c. d.				
11. Total Corrected Tax Liability *(Line 9 plus Lines 10a thru 10d)*				
12. Total Tax Shown on Return or as Previously Adjusted				
13. Adjustments to: a. b. c. d.				
14. Deficiency-Increase in Tax or *(Overassessment - Decrease in Tax)* *(Line 11 less Line 12 adjusted by Lines 13a thru 13d)*				
15. Adjustments to Prepayment Credits-Increase *(Decrease)*				
16. **Balance Due or (Overpayment)** - *(Line 14 adjusted by Line 15)* *(Excluding interest and penalties)*				

Catalog Number 23110T   www.irs.gov   Form **4549-A** (Rev. 3-2005)

Form **4549-A** (Rev. March 2005)	Department of the Treasury-Internal Revenue Service **Income Tax Discrepancy Adjustments**		Page_____ of _____
Name of Taxpayer		Taxpayer Identification Number	Return Form No.:

17. Penalties/ Code Sections	Period End	Period End	Period End
a.			
b.			
c.			
d.			
e.			
f.			
g.			
h.			
i.			
j.			
k.			
l.			
m.			
n.			
18. Total Penalties			
Underreporter attributable to negligence: *(1981-1987)* *A tax addition of 50 percent of the interest due on the underpayment will accrue until it is paid or assessed.*			
Underreporter attributable to fraud: *(1981-1987)* *A tax addition of 50 percent of the interest due on the underpayment will accrue until it is paid or assessed.*			
Underreporter attributable to Tax Motivated Transactions *(TMT).* Interest will accrue and be assessed at 120% of underpayment rate in accordance with IRC 6621(c).			
19. Summary of Taxes, Penalties and Interest:			
a. Balance due or *(Overpayment)* Taxes - *(Line 16, Page 1)*			
b. Penalties *(Line 18)* - computed to			
c. Interest *(IRC § 6601)* - computed to			
d. TMT Interest - computed to *(on TMT underpayment)*			
e. Amount due or refund - *(sum of Lines a, b, c and d)*			

Other Information:

Examiner's Signature: Name	Employee ID:	Office:	Date:

The Internal Revenue Service has agreements with state tax agencies under which information about federal tax, including increases or decreases, is exchanged with the states. If this change affects the amount of your state income tax, you should amend your state return by filing the necessary forms.

You may be subject to backup withholding if you underreport your interest, dividend, or patronage dividend income you earned and do not pay the required tax. The IRS may order backup withholding *(withholding of a percentage of your dividend and/or interest payments)* if the tax remains unpaid after it has been assessed and four notices have been issued to you over a 120-day period.

Catalog Number 23110T	www.irs.gov	Form **4549-A** (Rev. 3-2005)

¶429

¶430 Exhibit 4-10

Form **886-A** (REV JANUARY 1994	**EXPLANATIONS OF ITEMS**	SCHEDULE NO. OR EXHIBIT
NAME OF TAXPAYER	TAX IDENTIFICATION NUMBER	YEAR/PERIOD ENDED

FORM **886-A** (REV. 01-94)   Page ____   Cat. No. 20810W   DEPARTMENT OF THE TREASURY — INTERNAL REVENUE SERVICE

*U.S. GPO: 1997-417-690/51721

¶431 Exhibit 4-11

Internal Revenue Service   **Department of the Treasury**

Taxpayer Identification Number:

Tax Year:

Form Number:

Date:

Person to Contact:

Employee Identification Number:

Contact Telephone Number:

Dear

You were previously provided with an examination report with changes to your tax return(s) for the periods noted above.

We have reviewed the examination report and taken the following action:

☐   We made no changes to the original report.

☐   We made changes shown on the enclosed corrected examination report.

(We do not plan to make any additional changes to your return(s) unless we change a partnership, S-Corporation, trust, or estate tax return in which you have an interest. Changes to these types of returns could affect your return.)

Please call us at the telephone number shown above with any questions you may have. Thank you for your cooperation.

Sincerely,

Enclosure:
☐ Corrected examination report

Letter 987 (Rev. 12-2005)
Catalog Number 40421R

¶432 **Exhibit 4-12**   *Letter 531*

Internal Revenue Service	**Department of the Treasury**

Taxpayer Identification Number:

Tax Form(s):

Tax Year(s) Ending:

Person to Contact:

Date:

Employee Number:

Contact Hours:

Fax Number:

Deficiency (increase in tax):

Last Day to File a Petition With the
United States Tax Court:

Dear

NOTICE OF DEFICIENCY

We have determined that you owe additional tax or other amounts, or both, for the tax year(s) identified above. This letter is your NOTICE OF DEFICIENCY, as required by law. The enclosed statement shows how we figured the deficiency.

If you want to contest this determination in court before making any payment, you have 90 days from the date of this letter (150 days if this letter is addressed to you outside of the United States) to file a petition with the United States Tax Court for a redetermination of the deficiency. You can get a copy of the rules for filing a petition and a petition form you can use by writing to the address below.

United States Tax Court, 400 Second Street, NW, Washington, DC 20217

The Tax Court has a simplified procedure for small tax cases when the amount in dispute for each tax year is $50,000 or less. If you intend to file a petition for multiple tax years and the amount in dispute for any one or more of the tax years exceeds $50,000, this simplified procedure is not available to you. If you use this simplified procedure, you cannot appeal the Tax Court's decision. You can get information pertaining to the simplified procedure for small cases from the Tax Court by writing to the court at the above address or from the court's internet site at www.ustaxcourt.gov.

Send the completed petition form, a copy of this letter, and copies of all statements and/or schedules you received with this letter to the Tax Court at the above address. The Court cannot consider your case if the petition is filed late. The petition is considered timely filed if the postmark date falls within the prescribed 90 or 150 day period and the envelope containing the petition is properly addressed with the correct postage.

The time you have to file a petition with the court is set by law and cannot be extended or suspended. Thus, contacting the Internal Revenue Service (IRS) for more information, or receiving other correspondence from the IRS won't change the allowable period for filing a petition with the Tax Court.

Letter 531 (Rev. 4-2006)
Catalog Number 40223L

As required by law, separate notices are sent to husbands and wives. If this letter is addressed to both husband and wife, and both want to petition the Tax Court, both must sign and file the petition or each must file a separate, signed petition. If more than one tax year is shown above, you may file one petition form showing all of the tax years you are contesting.

You may represent yourself before the Tax Court, or you may be represented by anyone admitted to practice before the Tax Court.

If you decide not to file a petition with the Tax Court, please sign the enclosed waiver form and return it to us at the IRS address on the top of the first page of this letter. This will permit us to assess the deficiency quickly and can help limit the accumulation of interest.

If you decide not to sign and return the waiver, and you do not file a petition with the Tax Court within the time limit, the law requires us to assess and bill you for the deficiency after 90 days from the date of this letter (150 days if this letter is addressed to you outside the United States).

NOTE: If you are a C-corporation, section 6621(c) of the Internal Revenue Code requires that we charge an interest rate two percent higher than the normal rate on corporate under payments in excess of $100,000.

If you have questions about this letter, you may write to or call the contact person whose name, telephone number, and IRS address are shown on the front of this letter. If you write, please include your telephone number, the best time for us to call you if we need more information, and a copy of this letter to help us identify your account. Keep the original letter for your records. If you prefer to call and the telephone number is outside your local calling area, there will be a long distance charge to you.

The contact person can access your tax information and help you get answers. You also have the right to contact the office of the Taxpayer Advocate. Taxpayer Advocate assistance is not a substitute for established IRS procedures such as the formal appeals process. The Taxpayer Advocate is not able to reverse legally correct tax determinations, nor extend the time fixed by law that you have to file a petition in the U.S. Tax Court. The Taxpayer Advocate can, however, see that a tax matter that may not have been resolved through normal channels gets prompt and proper handling. If you want Taxpayer Advocate assistance, please contact the Taxpayer Advocate for the IRS office that issued this notice of deficiency. Please visit our website at www.irs.gov/advocate/content/0,,id=150972,00.html for the Taxpayer Advocate telephone numbers and addresses for this location.

Thank you for your cooperation.

Sincerely,

Commissioner
By

Enclosures:
Explanation of the tax changes
Waiver

Letter 531 (Rev. 4-2006)
Catalog Number 40223L

¶433 Exhibit 4-13

Form **4089** (Rev. January 1983)	Department of the Treasury — Internal Revenue Service **Notice of Deficiency-Waiver**	Symbols

Name, SSN or EIN, and Address of Taxpayer(s)

Kind of Tax   ☐ Copy to Authorized Representative

	Deficiency	
Tax Year Ended	Increase in Tax	Penalties

See the attached explanation for the above deficiencies

I consent to the immediate assessment and collection of the deficiencies (increase in tax and penalties) shown above, plus any interest provided by law.

Your Signature ▶ _____ _____
(Date signed)

Spouse's Signature, If A Joint Return Was Filed ▶ _____ _____
(Date signed)

Taxpayer's Representative Sign Here ▶ _____ _____
(Date signed)

Corporate Name: _____

Corporate Officers Sign Here
▶ _____ _____ _____
(Signature)   (Title)   (Date signed)
▶ _____ _____ _____
(Signature)   (Title)   (Date signed)

Note:

If you consent to the assessment of the amounts shown in this waiver, please sign and return it in order to limit the accumulation of interest and expedite our bill to you. Your consent will not prevent you from filing a claim for refund (after you have paid the tax) if you later believe you are entitled to a refund. It will not prevent us from later determining, if necessary, that you owe additional tax; nor will it extend the time provided by law for either action.

If you later file a claim and the Internal Revenue Service disallows it, you may file suit for refund in a district court or in the United States Claims Court, but you may not file petition with the United States Tax Court.

Who Must Sign

If this waiver is for any year(s) for which you filed a joint return, both you and your spouse must sign the original and duplicate of this form. Sign your name exactly as it appears on the return. If you are acting under power of attorney for your spouse, you may sign as agent for him or her.

For an agent or attorney acting under a power of attorney, a power of attorney must be sent with this form if not previously filed.

For a person acting in a fiduciary capacity (executor, administrator, trustee), file Form 56, Notice Concerning Fiduciary Relationship, with this form if not previously filed.

For a corporation, enter the name of the corporation followed by the signature and title of the officer(s) authorized to sign.

If you agree, please sign one copy and return it; keep the other copy for your records.

Form **4089** (Rev. 1-83)

¶441 DISCUSSION QUESTIONS

1. Andy Antagonistic comes to your office with a letter he has received from the IRS scheduling an examination by the tax compliance officer. The letter explains that among the items to be reviewed at the examination is the verification of gross receipts from Andy's business (retailer of used automobiles). Andy explains that his operation is not very large but that he does not want to have to transport the records to the suburban office of the IRS where the examination is scheduled. Andy assumes that revenue agents of the IRS are more experienced and more reasonable to deal with and asks you to request that the audit be transferred to a revenue agent in SB/SE. What is your advice?

2. You have just been retained by Nick L. Nockdown in connection with the examination of his return. Nick runs a tavern with reported gross sales of $250,000. Nick has met with the IRS on numerous occasions. You attend the first conference with the examiner and he runs a preliminary "T-account" to attempt to verify gross receipts. Because Nick is not with you at the conference, there is no information available as to his "cash on hand." The examiner also does not have much information regarding personal expenses (other than the listed itemized deductions), but a reasonable estimate is $10,000. The preliminary T-account reflects a potential understatement of gross receipts of $50,000.

   You return to your office and discuss the potential understatement with the taxpayer. Nick explains that his wife has worked as a restroom custodian at the Big Bucks Hotel for the past 25 years. She receives nominal wages and "cash tips". She has always been able to save a substantial portion of her cash tips. When they were putting an addition on the tavern, Nick's wife took her money out of the mason jars in the basement and paid the contractor for the addition. The amount paid was approximately $50,000, and Nick explains that this is where the understatement must be coming from.

   (A) If you are representing Nick, how do you deal with the information that he has given you regarding the explanation of the understatement?

   (B) If this story is presented to the examiner, will the statement of the taxpayer given under oath be sufficient or must other evidence be submitted to back it up?

   (C) Who will bear the burden of proof on the reliability of the explanation?

   (D) Can an explanation like this be used in court as a defense to an assessment by the IRS?

3. Assume in Question 2 that the examiner has also requested the individual checks and bank statements to confirm the estimated personal expenses. Must you provide the information? What can happen if you do not?

4. If you are consulted regarding a field audit and you discover that the agent and the taxpayer have already met at the place of business, how do you proceed in each of the following circumstances:

   (A) The president of the corporation tells you that he had a personality conflict with the examiner and threw the examiner out of the office?

   (B) You have had previous dealings with the IRS Agent, Oscar Obnoxious, and you have found him to be arrogant, insufferable and completely impossible to work with?

   (C) The audit is disrupting the business operations of the taxpayer?

5. You are contacted to represent a taxpayer in a field audit. Bob Butcher, the bookkeeper, prepared the return. In reviewing the records, you find substantial errors which will be very obvious to the agent, i.e., income improperly posted and not included in gross receipts, duplicated expenditures and depreciation claimed on retired assets. The Agent is scheduled to come in the following day. When, if at all, do you disclose these errors to the Agent?

6. At the conclusion of his corporate audit, the Revenue Agent questions the reasonableness of the corporation's accumulated earnings. For the current year, the corporation has total additions to accumulated earnings of $300,000. The balance at the beginning of the year was $750,000, and there is a plethora of liquid assets reflected on the corporate balance sheet. The corporation manufactures computer parts and has two shareholders, Mr. Greed and Mr. Glutt. Dividends have not been declared in the last 10 years. However, the corporate minutes reflect various anticipated needs of the business as reasons for the accumulation of earnings, including an acquisition of or an expansion into other businesses.

   (A) Should you discuss with the agent the grounds on which the corporation relies to establish the reasonableness of its accumulated earnings?

   (B) Should you wait to discuss the issue with the Appeals Office? See Code Sec. 534.

CHAPTER 5
LARGE CASE AUDITS

¶500 LARGE BUSINESS AND INTERNATIONAL OPERATING DIVISION

The focus of this chapter is on large case audits. These complex audits are conducted by the Large Business & International ("LB&I") operating division of the IRS, which is one of the four operating divisions of the IRS created as a result of the 1998 IRS Restructuring and Reform Act ("the Act").

In his remarks to a conference held in 2008 to mark the ten year anniversary of the Act, IRS Commissioner Douglas Shulman emphasized the impact the Act is having on tax administration:

> Perhaps the most dramatic change brought about by the Act was the structural reorganization of the agency. [Before the Act] the IRS was geographically based with a National Office in Washington, DC, and field offices across the country. The field consisted of four regions. Within those four regions were 33 districts, 10 service centers and two computing centers. . . .

> We are now all very familiar with the notion of the four operating divisions–Wage and Investment, Small Business/Self-Employed, Large and Mid-Sized Business and Tax Exempt and Government Entities. . . . By focusing on a taxpayer segment, the operating division can tailor programs that are best suited to meet the needs of their taxpayer base. . . . For example, I believe the recent success the IRS has had in combating abusive shelters, was, in no small part, attributable to the existence of LB&I.

LB&I serves taxpayers with assets over $10 million. LB&I itself is further organized around six distinct industry segments: Financial Services; Retailers, Food, Pharmaceuticals & Healthcare; Natural Resources & Construction; Communications, Technology & Media; Heavy Manufacturing & Transportation; and Global High Wealth. Each of LB&I's industry segments is headed by an Industry Director who leads the implementation of LB&I's enforcement initiatives for industries in each segment. See Exhibit 5-1 at ¶511, LB&I Organizational Structure as of May 18, 2011.

> **Example 5-1:** The IRS selects a healthcare company with $20 million in assets and $100 million in gross revenues. LB&I will be the operating division that examines this company.

¶501 LB&I EXAMINATIONS

LB&I has the responsibility for the examination of both Coordinated Industry Cases[1] and Industry Cases. A Coordinated Industry Case (CIC) is a case assigned

---

[1] The program was previously known as the Co-ordinated Examination Program (CEP).

to LB&I where the taxpayer and its effectively controlled entities warrant the application of the team examination procedures employed by LB&I. The team examination procedures result in a team of specialists being assigned to examine the case, which is coordinated by a revenue agent called a Team Coordinator and led by the Team Manager. Generally, large cases that score 12 or more points under the CIC scoring methodology set forth in IRM 4.46.2 may be designated CIC. The point criteria can be complex but focuses generally on the following factors: gross assets; gross receipts; operating entities; multiple industry status; total foreign assets; and total related transactions as those terms are defined in the IRM 4.46.2.

Cases within LB&I that are not classified as Coordinated Industry Cases are designated as Industry Cases (IC). IC examinations do not necessarily result in the application of the team examination procedures. Instead, the team coordinator may request that a specialist be assigned to the team after the IC examination is underway and after a significant specialized issue is identified to be developed further.

> **Example 5-2:** XYZ, a retailer with $1 billion in assets, $1 billion in gross receipts, and half of its operations outside the United States will "score out" as a CIC taxpayer.

¶502 LB&I EXAMINATION PROCESS

The LB&I case team manager is responsible for organizing, controlling and directing the team examination, whether that is a CIC or IC case. The supporting team usually includes not only groups of revenue agents throughout LB&I, but also industry and other specialists, such as engineers, excise tax agents, economists, international examiners, computer audit specialists, employment tax agents and employee and exempt organization specialists.[2]

The team manager organizes and sets the scope of the audit in a five-step process. The first step is a series of preliminary meetings with the taxpayer to plan the examination in cooperative manner and to ensure the best use of the resources of both the IRS and the taxpayer. The IRS believes that taxpayer involvement in the planning process is essential to efficient and effective examination. The joint planning meeting should allow the parties to discuss commitments and mutual goals such as completing the examination in a timely manner.[3]

The second step is one or more formal planning meetings with the examination team (sometimes referred to as "strategy meetings") where the IRS personnel review all the available information needed to form the basis for an examination plan. The team manager arranges the meeting with the complete examination team, which normally includes specialists, specialist managers, team coordinators and team members. Other individuals may be invited including LB&I Counsel. The participants review all related returns, the planning file, commercial services and public records, including information from the internet. If an Appeals Officer is invited to any pre-conference meeting then, in accordance

---

[2] IRM 4.46.3.3.2.1.   [3] IRM 4.46.3.3.1.

with the provisions of the Act which forbid *ex parte* communications between the examination function of the IRS and the Office of Appeals, the team manager will inform the taxpayer and invite the taxpayer to any meeting where Appeals will be in attendance.[4]

The third step is a formal opening conference with the taxpayer where the parties discuss agreements on coordination and accommodations and discuss the scope and depth of the examination. At this meeting the IRS attempts to firm-up commitments made during the preliminary meetings. The team manager conducts the meeting and the team coordinator also attends the meeting. Other team members, specialist managers and Area Counsel may be invited to attend. At this meeting, the parties can discuss any accommodations that may be possible to facilitate the audit or minimize the disruption to business operations.[5]

The fourth step is preliminary examination work. This step entails the selection of issues to be included in the examination plan. See ¶503 for further discussion. The team will review the tax return, Schedule M (M-2 and M-3), corporate minutes, Annual Reports, internal controls, internal management reports and accounting manuals and systems. The team members will review the records and identify the procedures necessary to examine areas of noncompliance, identify other unusual and questionable items not detected during the initial review, and modify decisions made during the initial review.[6]

The fifth step is the finalization of the examination plan, which is a written document that contains topics such as work assignments for each specialist, scope of the examination issues, examination procedures, and time estimates for each phase of the examination. See ¶504 for further discussion.[7]

In summary, it should be noted that the bright line distinctions the IRS used to make between the old Coordinated Examination Program taxpayers and all other taxpayers no longer formally exist. Now all taxpayers with assets in excess of $10 million are examined by the LB&I operating division. LB&I taxpayers are divided into CIC and IC taxpayers and, depending upon the size and complexity of the IC taxpayer, LB&I may undertake all five of the above steps in planning for an IC examination.

¶503 SELECTION OF ISSUES IN LB&I EXAMINATIONS

As Commissioner Schulman's remarks set forth above indicate, LB&I played a significant role in combating abusive tax shelters in the late 1990s and early 2000s. The Office of Tax Shelter Analysis, which serves as a clearinghouse of information relating to potentially improper tax shelter activities, is located within LB&I.[8] In place of the old distinctions between the old Coordinated Examination Program taxpayers and all other taxpayers, LB&I is taking the experience it developed in creating focus around abusive tax shelters and is employing that experience in identifying, developing and resolving industry

---

[4] IRM 4.46.3.3.2.4.
[5] IRM 4.46.3.3.3.
[6] IRM 4.46.3.4.

[7] IRM 4.46.3.5.
[8] IRM 4.40.1.1.1.1.

based examination issues LB&I refers to as Tier I, Tier II and Tier III examination issues. See Exhibits 5-4, 5-5, and 5-6 for a listing and discussion of these issues.

The LB&I tiering procedures apply to CIC and IC cases alike. LB&I has established procedures regarding the involvement of Issue Management Teams (IMT) comprised of LB&I Executives, Senior Leaders, Technical Advisors, Specialists, and Counsel in ongoing examinations where industry-aligned cases are not under the direct line authority of the related Industry Director. Each IMT is led by an Issue Owner Executive with designated authority to oversee and resolve specific tax issues. Each IMT also has a representative from the Office of Appeals. A new IRM section has been published to formalize the industry focused approach that LB&I takes in its examinations. See Exhibit 5-2 at ¶512 for a copy of IRM section 4.51.1 and 4.51.5.

Issue tiering focuses LB&I resources on significant compliance risks. The new Tiering procedures classify issues as Tier I, Tier II, or Tier III in accordance with their compliance risk. One purpose of issue tiering is to provide clear and consistent guidance to exam personnel so that similar tax issues are administered and resolved in a similar manner regardless of where the issue arises geographically. Another purpose for employing issue tiering is to infuse greater flexibility into tax administration: LB&I can change direction quickly by adding (or removing) an issue, thereby keeping pace with ever changing tax positions developed by taxpayers.

Tier I issues are defined by the Service as issues that present the highest compliance risk across multiple LB&I industries. Tier I issues generally include large numbers of taxpayers, significant dollar risk, significant compliance risk or are highly visible issues. For this reason, Tier I issues include listed transactions and transactions that are substantially similar to listed transactions. See Exhibit 5-3 at ¶513 for a complete roster of Listed Transactions. Tier I issues also include several accounting methods issues (e.g., mixed service costs), several international tax issues (e.g., section 482 cost sharing agreements), and issues involving tax credits and exclusions from income (e.g., section 118 contributions to capital). See Exhibit 5-4 at ¶514 for a listing of Tier I issues.

The Service defines Tier II issues as those involving areas of potential or actual high non-compliance risk affecting one or more LB&I industry segments. Tier II issues include emerging issues with fairly well-established law that need further development, clarification, direction, and guidance concerning LB&I's position. For example, in the retail industry, how the deferral of gift card income should be identified, developed and resolved is a Tier II issue. See Exhibit 5-5 at ¶515 for a list of Tier II issues.

Tier III issues are defined by the Service as high compliance risk issues but for only one LB&I industry. Tier III issues typically require unique treatment within the affected LB&I industry in order to be properly developed and resolved. See Exhibit 5-6 at ¶516 for a list of Tier III issues.

Decision making concerning tiered issues resides at different levels of LB&I, depending upon the tier to which the issue has been assigned.

¶503

Tier I issues are mandatory examination issues that require oversight and control by an Issue Owner Executive (IOE). That IOE is responsible for ensuring that the issue is identified, developed and resolved in a consistent manner across all LB&I cases involving similarly situated taxpayers. The disposition or resolution of a Tier I issue must be in accordance with that IOE's active guidance.

More recently, Tier I issues have been further categorizes as "active status" or "monitoring status" issues. Active status Tier I issues require continual coordination by the IMT. Monitoring status Tier I issues can be evaluated and resolved pursuant to existing guidance provided by the IMT. See Exhibit 5-7 at ¶517 for a listing of currently active Tier I issues.

Tier II issues require coordination with the IOE, as opposed to oversight and control by the IOE. The IOE is responsible for ensuring the disposition or resolution of Tier II issues does not hinder LB&I's broader direction or guidance.

Finally, Tier III issues are those that have been indentified by a particular industry and should be considered by examination teams within that industry when conducting their risk analyses. Exam teams selecting Tier III issues to exam should develop and resolve them in a manner consistent with published guidance, such as Audit Technique Guides.

In summary, LB&I now employs an industry and issue-driven approach to examining significant tax issues. LB&I has jurisdiction to examine all taxpayers with assets over $10 million and does not limit its examinations to the very largest taxpayers only. Nor does LB&I limit its examination to only Tier I, II and III issues. LB&I does employ its institutional experience from the abusive tax shelter era to identify, develop and resolve significant tax issues in a coordinated manner. See Exhibit 5-7 at ¶517 for a diagram of the Issue Tiering Strategy Decision Tree.

¶504 WRITTEN PLAN — Not needed on exam

Once an LB&I exam team makes an initial determination of the issues for examination, the team prepares an audit plan. The LB&I Audit Plan is a written document that contains all agreements reached with the taxpayer, necessary information for IRS personnel, work assignments, examination scope, examination procedures, time estimates, and special instructions. The purpose of the LB&I Audit Plan is two-fold. First, it formalizes the general examination procedures to be followed. Second, it reduces misunderstandings as to agreements reached during the pre-examination conferences by reducing them to writing. The taxpayer is clearly apprised that the Audit Plan may be modified to meet the needs of the examination. Expansion will occur if high risk transactions such as Listed Transactions and other Tier I issues are identified and expansion likely will occur if Tier II and Tier III issues are identified.

¶505 EXAMINATION

Because the roles and responsibilities of the various LB&I examination team members differ, it is important for taxpayers to understand the distinction in roles between and among the team members. Similarly, it is important for taxpayers to understand the responsibility and authority that each team member possesses. The roles and responsibilities of LB&I team members can be understood by a review of the rules of engagement in an LB&I examination.

Normal rules of engagement are to be followed when a taxpayer wants to elevate a case-specific issue to the upper management of LB&I.

> Consider for example a situation in which Narrow Co. considers the scope of an Information Document Request (IDR) to be too broad. Narrow Co. should first discuss that language with the team coordinator or specialist who drafted the IDR. Barring a resolution of the issue at that level, Narrow Co. may request a meeting with the team manager. Narrow Co. will learn that an LB&I team manager has "51 percent of the vote" when it comes to resolving issues such as the scope of a routine IDR.

Most disputes are resolved on case-specific issues with the assistance of the team manager. In the infrequent instances where resolution at this level of engagement is not achieved, a taxpayer may request a meeting with the territory manager or even the director of field operations. Rarely would a taxpayer meet with an industry director unless the meeting involved a Tier I issue.

Special "rules of engagement" apply where LB&I examination issues are controlled by Issue Owner Executives resident in a different industry sector than the Line Owner Executives controlling the overall examination. These across-industry situations arise because, in 2003, LB&I reorganized along geographic lines. When that happened Issue Owner Executives became separated from Line Owner Executives. LB&I's geographic reorganization was another reason that LB&I created the Tier I, II and III issue categories: Tier I industry issues that are, for geographic reasons, examined by employees of a different industry segment remain under the control of the original Industry Director in his or her capacity as the Issue Owner Executive.

> Consider, for example, Mining Co., a mining company with its headquarters in the Midwest. Historically, all mining companies were subject to the line authority and the issue resolution authority of the Natural Resources & Construction (NRC) industry segment of LB&I. After 2003, Mining Co. is examined by the Retailers, Food, Pharmaceutical & Healthcare (RFPH) industry segment because those personnel reside in the Midwest. Mining Co. raises an objection to how a Tier I mining issue is being handled by the local exam team. Mining Co. should employ the "guidelines for taxpayers when across-industry contact is necessary" found in IRM 4.51.1. Essentially, those guidelines provide that Mining Co. should elevate the issue through the Line Authority Executive of RFPH and then over to the Issue Owner Executive of NRC.

During LB&I examinations, IRS attorneys in the Chief Counsel's local office are more directly involved than in non-LB&I examinations. Officially, they are available to offer legal advice on complex issue and to provide assistance in the development of facts relating to those issues. Although taxpayers have voiced concern regarding such intimate involvement by Counsel attorneys during the

¶505

examination phase, the IRS maintains that such involvement promotes early development and resolution of the significant legal issues.[9]

The Tax Court has been critical of the active participation by an IRS attorney in an ongoing examination at the same time the attorney was acting as trial counsel in a docketed case against the same taxpayer for earlier years involving identical issues. In *Westreco, Inc. v. Commissioner,*[10] the IRS trial attorney was ordered to discontinue participation in the audit. The IRS was further ordered not to use in the Tax Court proceedings any evidence obtained by summons or any other means during the examination of the more recent years. The Tax Court was concerned that the IRS was attempting to circumvent the Court's limited discovery rules by allowing trail attorneys to obtain testimony and other evidence during an examination by use of broad investigative powers not available to the IRS in pretrial discovery under the Rules of the Tax Court. However in a 1996 case, *Mary Kay Ash v. Commissioner,*[11] the Tax Court modified its position in Westreco and denied petitioner's motion for a protective order. The court noted that while the compelling facts in Westreco justified a protective order, not all cases could be seen as an attempt to circumvent the Tax Court's discovery rules. The summonses in Mary Kay Ash were issued before any litigation commenced and thus the dangers of information being used improperly by an IRS attorney in a proceeding were not present. The court did not rule that a protective order could never be granted, but that a protective order would only be justified when the facts of a particular case warranted.

Upon completion of the LB&I examination, the taxpayer may object to any proposed tax adjustments by filing a protest with the IRS Office of Appeals.[12]

¶506 RESOLVING EXAMINATION ISSUES

Once the audit has begun, the IRS will use Form 4564, Information Document Request (see Exhibit 5-9 at ¶519), to make any information requests.[13] As the IRS makes each adjustment during the audit, it will give the taxpayer notice on Form 5701, Notice of Proposed Adjustment (see Exhibit 5-8 at ¶518). Presented with Form 5701, the taxpayer may either sign the form indicating that it agrees with the adjustment, disagrees or will supply further information.[14]

Certain issues on which there is disagreement may be settled by the team manager under the authority of Code Sec. 7121. This authority exists where the Appeals Office has previously approved a settlement agreement involving the same issue in an LB&I case examination in a prior year involving the same taxpayer or a taxpayer directly involved in the taxable transaction.[15] The following conditions must be present for the team manager to have jurisdiction to settle an issue: (1) substantially the same facts must be involved in both examination years, (2) the legal authority must not have changed, (3) the issue must have been settled on its merits and not have been settled in exchange for the taxpayer's

---

[9] Daily Tax Report, BNA, at E-1 (Mar. 4, 1991).

[10] 60 TCM 824, TC Memo. 1990-501, CCH Dec. 46,882(M).

[11] 96 TC 459 (1991), CCH Dec. 47,221.

[12] See Chapter 12 infra.

[13] IRM 4.45.4.4.

[14] IRM 4.46.3.3.3.4(2).

[15] IRM 4.45.5.4.

concession on another issue, and (4) the issue must concern the same taxpayer or a taxpayer who was directly involved in the settled transaction.

¶507 TAXPAYER OPTIONS

Issue resolution techniques exist throughout the life-cycle of a tax return. Certain issue resolution techniques exist that are available for use by taxpayers prior to examination of a tax return (even prior to filing the tax return in some instances). Other issue resolution techniques are available while the tax return is under examination. Finally, still other issue resolution techniques exist after the examination has concluded. While this chapter does not exhaust the subject, several pre-exam, during exam, and post-exam issue resolution techniques are discussed.

Pre-Examination

Issue resolution techniques that are available prior to examination are intended to reduce taxpayer burden by eliminating or significantly reducing the need for a post filing examination. They include:

- **Industry Issue Resolution** (IIR) under Rev. Proc. 2003-6.[16] Generally the types of issues that are most appropriate for this industry-wide type of issue resolution opportunity have two or more of the following characteristics:

  — common factual situations with significant tax issues affecting a large population of taxpayers generally specific to one or more industries;

  — where the proper tax treatment is uncertain;

  — resulting in numerous repetitive examinations;

  — and therefore in taxpayer burden that may be alleviated if the Service was to understand industry practices and viewpoints on the issue.

- **Pre-Filing Agreements** under Rev. Proc. 2009-14.[17] Pre-Filing examinations can often resolve issues more effectively and efficiently than a post-filing examination because the taxpayer and the Service have more timely access to the records and personnel relevant to the issue.

  — Pre-Filing Agreements allow a taxpayer to request examination of specific issues involving factual questions and well-settled principles of law before the return is filed.

  — If the taxpayer and LB&I are able to resolve the selected issues prior to filing the return, then the parties may execute an LB&I Pre-Filing Agreement (PFA).

- **Advance Pricing Agreements** under Rev. Procs. 2006-9 and 2008-31. The Advance Pricing Agreement (APA) Program is designed to resolve actual or potential transfer pricing disputes in a non adversarial manner.

(handwritten margin note: "not tested on")

---

[16] 2003-1 C.B. 85; See also IRM 4.45.5.7.   [17] 2009- C.B.; See also IRM 4.46.5.6.12.

— An APA is a binding contract between the IRS and a taxpayer

— The IRS agrees not to seek a transfer pricing adjustment under IRC § 482 for a covered transaction if the taxpayer files its tax return for a covered year consistent with the agreed transfer pricing method.

— Covered years may include as many as 5 years into the future. And the method employed in the APA might be rolled back into open appeals and examination years, resulting in increased certainty.

- **Compliance Assurance Process**–Ann. 2005-87. The IRS continues to conduct this issue resolution technique as a permanent program. The Compliance Assurance Process (CAP) is designed for large business taxpayers and is available only upon invitation by LB&I.

  — LB&I works with large business taxpayers to identify and resolve issues prior to the filing of a tax return through contemporaneous exchange of information.

  — The goal is to reduce taxpayer burden and uncertainty while assuring the IRS of the accuracy of entire tax returns prior to filing.

  — With CAP the Service hopes to shorten examination cycles and increase currency for taxpayers while enhancing the accurate, efficient, and timely final resolution of increasingly complex corporate tax issues.

  — Finally, the program results in increased financial statement certainty.

- **Determination Letters and Letter Rulings**–Rev. Procs. 2009-1, 2009-3, 2009-Characteristics of these pre-filing issue resolution tools include:

  — Both are subject to a user fee;

  — IRS and taxpayer agree on treatment of completed transaction prior to return filing;

  — Both apply principles and precedents previously announced to a specific set of facts;

  — Inspection or review of books and records prior to filing is not considered an audit;

  — Not concluded with a Closing Agreement so there is less finality;

  — Decisions made public without identifying information;

  — Both are attached to the return when filed;

  — Determination letters are reviewed by the examination division but not by the Office of Chief Counsel;

  — Taxpayer requests a PLR from the Office of Chief Counsel that applies the tax laws to the taxpayer's specific facts;

¶507

— PLRs may cover a proposed or completed transaction prior to the filing of the return and any identical issue was not previously examined, in Appeals, or in litigation.

Under Examination

Issue resolution techniques available to taxpayers and the IRS while a case is under the jurisdiction of examination include:

- **Technical Advice**–Rev. Proc. 2009-2. A technical advice memorandum, or TAM, is written legal guidance issued by the Office of Chief Counsel upon the request of an exam team in response to technical or procedural questions that arise.

  — Issues generally arise from an examination, or a claim for a refund or credit, but may arise from any other matter pending in examination or in Appeals.

  — TAMs are issued on closed transactions and provide the IRS interpretation of proper application of tax laws, tax treaties, regulations, revenue rulings or other precedents.

  — TAMs represent the IRS's final determination of the position for the specific issue(s) under consideration as applied to the particular taxpayer at issue.

  — TAMs are generally made public after all information has been removed that might identify the taxpayer at issue.

- **Fast Track Settlement Program**–Rev. Proc. 2003-40. Fast Track Settlement program (FTS) offers taxpayers issue resolution at the earliest possible stage in the examination process.

  — FTS adds an Appeals officer into resolution of issues still under the jurisdiction of examination, thereby granting all parties a "voice" in the resolution,

  — The Appeals officer brings mediation skills and settlement authority to the examination, and

  — FTS applications are simple and a formal written protest is not required.

  — FTS is designed to conclude within 120. Either party may withdraw at any time from FTS or unresolved issues may still be taken to regular Appeals.

- **Settlement Authority–Delegation Order 4-24 and 4-25** grant settlement authority to team managers they would not otherwise possess when the precise terms of those orders are applicable.

- **Accelerated Issue Resolution**–Rev. Proc. 94-67. This alternative dispute resolution option is available in examination where the agreed issue (or issues) is present in subsequent tax returns already filed but not yet under examination.

— Rev. Proc. 94-67 and Rev. Proc. 68-16 provide guidance when considering the utilization of AIR procedures.

— Counsel assistance is mandatory.

— While the AIR process applies to CIC and IC taxpayers alike, the AIR process may be limited in IC examinations where it is not practical to include subsequently filed returns as part of the current examination cycle.

— The AIR process does not constitute a formal examination of the taxpayer's books and records.

— The AIR process does not grant team managers additional settlement authority like Delegation Orders 4-24 and 4-25 do.

— The AIR process does not alter the application of Policy Statement P-4-5 (that examination team members generally may not examine a taxpayer for more than 60 consecutive months) to subsequent years included but not examined.

- **Early Referral to Appeals**–Rev. Proc. 99-28. This alternative dispute resolution option is available for taxpayers under examination whose unagreed issue is developed and ready for Appeals consideration (prior to issuance of the 30-day letter).

— The team manager must agree issue should be referred early;

— Appeals is expected to resolve the issue before examination of remaining issues will be complete;

— Certain issues are not eligible (e.g., Appeals Coordinated Issues);

— Upon agreement the early referred issue results in a Closing Agreement;

— If the early referred issue is not resolved then post-appeals mediation or litigation remain available.

Post Examination

Finally, where issues are not resolved before filing or by the conclusion of the examination and appeals processes, two post-appeals procedures may be available.

- **Post Appeals Mediation**–Rev. Proc. 2002-44. This alternative dispute resolution option is available for certain issues:

— Contain qualifying issues–as those are defined in section 4.02 of Revenue Procedure 2002-44;

— Are non-docketed cases in the Appeals administrative process; and

— Will be mediated by an objective and neutral third party whose task is to assist the parties in reaching agreement; however, the authority to agree with the mediator's position remains with the taxpayer and Appeals.

- **Appeals Arbitration**–Rev. Proc. 2006-44. Issues that are eligible for post-appeals arbitration are those that:

    — contain facts already in the Appeals administrative process;

    — the taxpayer and Appeals have first attempted a resolution before requesting arbitration; and

    — the parties have jointly request binding arbitration on the unresolved issues.

¶511 Exhibit 5-1

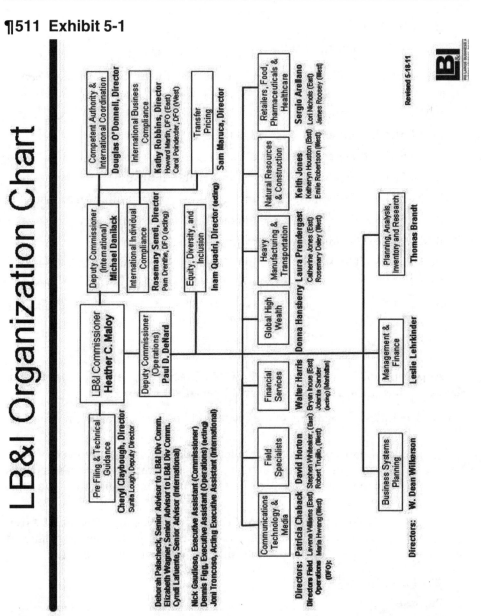

LB&I Organization Chart

¶512 Exhibit 5-2

4.51.1 Rules of Engagement

IRM 4.51.1.1, Applicability: Case Interactions by LB&I Executives, Senior Leaders, Team Managers, Technical Advisors, and Field Specialist Leaders

IRM 4.51.1.2, Purpose

IRM 4.51.1.3, Definitions

IRM 4.51.1.4, Roles and Responsibilities

IRM 4.51.1.5, Elevating Case Interactions Within Industries

IRM 4.51.1.5.1, Criteria for Elevating Case Interactions Within an Industry

IRM 4.51.1.5.2, Protocol for Case Interactions Within an Industry

IRM 4.51.1.6, Elevating Case Interactions Across Industries

IRM 4.51.1.6.1, Criteria for Elevating Case Interactions Across Industries

IRM 4.51.1.6.2, Protocol for Managing Case Interactions Across Industries

IRM 4.51.1.6.3, Guidelines for Taxpayers When Across-Industry Contact Is Necessary

4.51.1.1 (04-01-2007)

Applicability: Case Interactions by LB&I Executives, Senior Leaders, Team Managers, Technical Advisors, and Field Specialist Leaders

1. The Rules of Engagement are intended to provide guidance in situations where:
   A. An LB&I Executive or Senior Leader could be involved with a taxpayer or a group of taxpayers (corporations and partnerships with partnerships with over $10,000,000 in assets) in a pre/post filing activity.
   B. An LB&I Executive, Senior Leader, Team Manager, Technical Advisor, Field Specialist Leader could be involved when industry aligned cases are not under the line authority of the Industry Director.

4.51.1.2 (04-01-2007)

Purpose

1. For case interactions described in 4.51.1.1, the Rules of Engagement are intended to:
   A. Clarify individual roles, responsibilities and lines of authority to
      1. Help ensure end-to-end accountability, and
      2. Provide clear procedural guidance on how to manage tax case interactions;

    B. Facilitate getting to the right answer for a particular case or issue;

    C. Promote consistent tax treatment between similarly situated taxpayers or cases; and

    D. Reinforce the importance of integrity and ethical behavior in all case-related decision making.

4.51.1.3 (04-01-2007)

Definitions

Case	A taxpayer or a group of taxpayers
Case *Interaction*	A case-related positive contact to achieve a shared outcome. Such interactions may occur at any phase of post-filing, the filing of tax return, through the examination/processing phase, to the collection phase. In addition, case interactions may occur in pre-filing (e.g., Industry Issue Resolution, Pre-Filing Agreement, and Advanced Pricing Agreement).
Director of Field Operations	For purposes of this IRM, the title, *director field operations* is assumed to include *deputy director , field specialists*.
Industry Director	For purposes of this IRM, the title, industry director is assumed to include director, field specialists
Issue Owner Executive	Any LB&I director (or delegate) with designated authority to oversee and resolve specific tax issues.
Line Authority Executive	An industry director (or delegate) with direct chain-of-command responsibility for personnel working on a given tax case.
Team	A tax examination team. The team includes all LB&I personnel required to review, evaluate, adjust and approve a tax case. The team's makeup is flexible and may consist of a few members or many members, depending on the nature and complexity of the issues and/or case to be examined. A team may include examiners, managers, senior managers, specialists, counsel, and others.
Tier I - Issues of High Strategic Importance	Tier I issues are tax issues of high strategic importance to LB&I which have significant impact on one or more Industries. Tier I issues could areas involving a large number of taxpayers, significant dollar risk, substantial compliance risk or high visibility, where are established legal positions and/or LB&I direction. Tier I issues require oversight and control by an issue Owner Executive. The Issue Owner Executive is responsible for ensuring that the issue is identified, developed and resolved in a consistent manner across all LB&I cases involving similarly situated taxpayers. The disposition or resolution of the issue must be in accordance with that Executive's guidance. The LB&I Compliance Strategy Council will designate Tier I issues.

Tier II - Issues of Significant Compliance Risk	Tier II issues are those involving areas of potential high non-compliance and/or significant compliance risk to LB&I or and Industry. Tier II includes emerging issues, where the law is fairly well established, but there is a need for further development, clarification, direction and guidance on LB&I's position. Tier II issues require coordination with the Issue Owner Executive. The Executive is responsible for ensuring the disposition or resolution of issues, so as not to hinder LB&I's broader direction and/or guidance. The LB&I Compliance Strategy Council will designate Tier II issues.
Tier III - Issues of Industry Importance	Tier III issues typically are industry-related, and have been identified as issues that should be considered by LB&I teams when conducting their risk analyses. Teams selecting Tier III issues for examination should use available direction, guidance and/or Audit Technique Guidelines in the development and resolution of the issue to ensure consistency throughout LB&I. LB&I Industries, working in conjunction with other examiners, technical advisors and specialists, will identify Tier III issues.

4.51.1.4 (04-01-2007)

Roles and Responsibilities

1. Roles vary across the different levels of LB&I leadership, reflecting the distribution of strategic and tactical responsibilities. Understanding roles is important when considering how to achieve consistent treatment of cases not under line authority. (See Figures 4.51.1-1 and 4.51.1-2)

Figure 4.51.1-1

Team Manager	Technical Advisor	Specialist Leadership
• Identify emerging issues and provide support to develop them	• Determine cases under audit	• Mentor and coach specialist at all levels
• Communicate industry and emerging issues to team	• Notify Industry Director of significant cases	• Promote issue resolution at case level
• Provide updated industry and emerging issues to team	• Communicate with CIC and IC agents regardless of industry alignment	• Identify and communicate with Industry Leadership on possible emerging issues and provide support to develop them
• Identify industry and emerging issues in the audit plan	• Provide teams with timely updated information	• Ensure that field team and specialists operate as a team
• Ensure review of Technical Advisor Web site	• Maintain mailing list for employees working industry and emerging issues	• Help identify and develop best practices
• Contact Technical Advisor in early stages of audit process	• Contact teams with industry and emerging issues	• Support resource allocation decisions with respect to compliance strategy
• Discuss with Territory Manager industry and emerging issues	• Provide value added input to team	• Ensure specialists receive industry training as it relates to case assignments

Team Manager	Technical Advisor	Specialist Leadership
• Ensure examiners receive industry-related training	• Develop and maintain auditing guidelines and techniques	• Promote and ensure Issue Management Strategy implementation
• Communicate with taxpayer on industry and emerging issues and provide support	• Communicate with the team in the early stages of audit	• Contact point for external specialist associations
	• Be part of the team and ensure timely resolution of issue	• Assist team leadership as appropriate in resolution of significant issues
	• Ensure that Tier I and Tier II issue are identified, coordinated and property developed in accordance with guidance from Issue Owner Executive(s).	• Secure expertise outside field team and beyond territory
	• Work with Issue Owner Executive(s) and Line Authority Executive(s) as necessary to reinforce consistent treatment of similarly situated taxpayers with respect to specific issues.	• Facilitate positive relationship with taxpayer

Figure 4.51.1-2

Territory Manager	Director Field Operations	Industry Director	Industry Director
• Mentor and coach at all levels, with immediate focus on Team Manager and field team	• Mentor and coach at all levels, with immediate focus on Territory Manager, Team Manager and field team	• LB&I industry directors are responsible and accountable for ensuring appropriate application and administration of the Rules of Engagement in case interactions within their Industries.	• Mentor and coach LB&I employees at all levels
• Promote issue resolution at case level	• Push decisions down to level closest to the facts	• Mentor and coach at all levels, with immediate focus on DFOs and Territory Managers	• Refer issues to Industry Directors and below as appropriate
• Monitor progress	• Identify/champion emerging issues on first case where issue appears	• Push issues down to level closest to the facts	• Work with Chief Counsel to carry issues to Treasury
• Identify possible emerging issues and provide support to develop them	• Mediate within team on impasses on issues or processes	• Execute pre-filing agreement process responsibilities	• Resolve impasses within LB&I

Territory Manager	Director Field Operations	Industry Director	Industry Director
• Ensure that field team operates as a unit	• Identify/promote best practices	• Assist in resolving cross-industry issues	• Showcase best practices
• Facilitate team and taxpayer planning issue development and resolution	• Secure expertise outside field team and beyond territory	• Mediate unresolved issues within own industry	• Champion Issue Management Strategy
• Secure expertise outside field team	• Promote and ensure implementation of Issue Management Strategy	• Work with Industry Analysts to develop industry practices based on cases	• Support compliance resource strategy allocation across and outside LB&I
• Facilitate positive relationship with taxpayer	• Facilitate resource reallocation consistent with compliance strategy	• Promote best practices specific to own industry	
• Help identify and develop best practices and ensure that Team Manager implements them	• Communicate industry and emerging issues with other Directors, Field Operations	• Help determine impact on emerging issue with other Industry Directors and Counsel	
• Ensure implementation of Issue Management Strategy	• Communicate industry and emerging issues with Industry Director	• Champion Issue Management Strategy	
• Ensure that resources are deployed consistent with LB&I compliance strategy		• Support resource allocation decisions with respect to compliance strategy	
• Communicate industry and emerging issues with the team manager and team			
• Communicate with team manager and team to ensure consistent treatment			
• Provide updated industry and emerging issues to team manager and team			
• Review audit plan to ensure industry issues are addressed by team			

Territory Manager	Director Field Operations	Industry Director	Industry Director
• Communicate with Manager, Technical Advisor or Industry on emerging issues			
• Communicate with Specialist Leadership on emerging issues			
• Serve as contact person for external stakeholders			

4.51.1.5 (04-01-2007)

Elevating Case Interactions Within Industries

1. Case interactions can be triggered by teams or by leaders for a variety of reasons. In most instances, a team invites interaction from senior leaders in response to particular needs. In other instances, a leader may proactively become involved after identifying the need for interaction or uncovering a situational opportunity that warrants involvement.

4.51.1.5.1 (04-01-2007)

Criteria for Elevating Case Interactions Within an Industry

1. Teams may identify a need to invite senior leader or executive interaction. Typical reasons include:

   A. Questions regarding availability of team resources; ability of the team to handle or resolve a particular issue or situation; team/manager experience levels; competing resource demands; and scheduling concerns resulting from taxpayer's untimely furnishing of documents

   B. Disputes within teams; disputes between teams and taxpayers, difficulties dealing with contentious taxpayers; taxpayer requests for senior leader or executive interactions; or taxpayer's need to elevate issues or discussions within its own organization

   C. Potential impact or visibility of an issue; potential for precedent-setting and/or concerns about undermining the tax system; need to coordinate issues across LB&I; lack of published guidance on a particular issue; the need for strategic industry input or assistance; need to ensure consistent industry treatment of issues; resolution that requires additional technical and/or procedural guidance or support; and emerging industry/specialist needs.

2. Senior leaders or executives may determine a need for interaction. Typical reasons include:

   A. Requests from team leaders or taxpayers; involvement of new taxpayers; need to improve service to taxpayers; Trade Association or

Industry group contact; or for other "relationship management" purposes.

B. Increase understanding of particular cases / issues; ensure consistent industry treatment; propagate best practices; introduce new initiatives; instill the values of and apply Issues Management Strategy.

4.51.1.5.2 (04-01-2007)

Protocol for Case Interactions Within an Industry

1. The within-industry process for elevating case interactions to include senior leaders or executives is intended to ensure continued team involvement and decision-making at the level closest to the facts. In general, before interacting in a particular case-related issue, a senior leader or executive will attempt to verify that other leaders closer to the facts have been fully engaged in trying to resolve the particular situation or issue; and that such elevated case interactions are warranted.

4.51.1.6 (04-01-2007)

Elevating Case Interactions Across Industries

1. The need for across-industry case interactions typically arises when a team aligned within one particular LB&I Industry is examining a taxpayer affiliated with a different Industry. The exam team may request support or guidance from an Issue Owner Executive relative to the interpretation or treatment of a particular issue within the taxpayer's industry. Similarly, an Issue Owner Executive may proactively become involved in order to ensure that LB&I treats all similarly situated taxpayers in a fair and consistent manner. The Line Authority Executive will work with the Issue Owner Executive to ensure that access is granted to Tier I and II cases for the above purpose.

4.51.1.6.1 (04-01-2007)

Criteria for Elevating Case Interactions Across Industries

1. Teams, senior leaders or executives may determine that the need exists to elevate case interactions across industries. Such cross industry interactions might be appropriate when it is determined that a case is not aligned with the proper industry; the case consists of clear industry-specific issues that require guidance or leadership from Issue Owner Executive; potential exists for the case to be designated as a litigating vehicle; the impact of an issue on a particular industry is significant; the potential for setting precedent within the industry exists; and the issue has high visibility with an industry group.

4.51.1.6.2 (04-01-2007)

Protocol for Managing Case Interactions Across Industries

1. Interactions across industries should be managed carefully; following this protocol is critical to ensure the benefits of industry alignment and consistent issue treatment.

2. To ensure consistent treatment of identified industry issues, the Line Authority Industry Executive controls the case while the Issue Owner Executive controls and/or influences the identification, development and resolution of the specific industry issue.

   A. It is essential that all parties involved interact in a collaborative manner ensuring:

   • Involvement of executives adds value and builds trust

   • There is fairness and consistency in tax administration

3. Issue Owner Executives will have access to significant industry aligned cases regardless of geographic location or assigned industry.

   A. Issue Owner Executive (ID/DFO or delegate) will contact and coordinate with the Line Authority Executive to secure briefing from the team, contact and/or visit team, exchange information, and provide assistance and guidance on specific industry issues.

   B. The Issue Owner Executive will be sensitive to established line authority relationships as they provide guidance and direction on specific Industry issues(s).

4. On Strategic/Significant Industry (Tier I) issues, Issue Owner Executives will retain nationwide jurisdiction including issue resolution.

   A. The Compliance Strategy Council will approve Tier I issues per IRM 4.51.5.

5. On significant Compliance Risk (Tier II) issues, the Line Authority Executive will coordinate on issue resolution with the Issue Owner Executive. If agreement cannot be reached as to the ultimate disposition of an issue, it will be elevated to the next higher level of management.

   A. The Compliance Strategy Council will approve Tier II issues per IRM 4.51.5.

6. On Industry (Tier III) issues, LB&I teams will familiarize themselves with industry issues through contacting Technical Advisors and/or obtaining information from Industry and PFTG websites. The Line Authority Industry Executive retains unilateral decision making authority including ultimate disposition and resolution.

4.51.1.6.3 (04-01-2007)

Guidelines for Taxpayers When Across-Industry Contact Is Necessary

1. Taxpayers and teams should observe the following guidelines when taxpayers are seeking interaction with an Issue Owner Executive.

A. Case related contacts should be made at the team level.

B. Industry issue contacts should be made for strategic issues or assistance directly to the specific industry director.

C. If the level of contact is unclear, taxpayer should rely on any IRS contact to determine the appropriate industry and level of contact, following the rules of interaction.

D. While cross-industry involvement of all appropriate team members should result in resolutions, taxpayers can elevate unresolved issues to the next level of interaction.

E. Taxpayers may elevate unresolved industry-related issues through the Line Authority Executive to the Issue Owner Executive.

F. Taxpayers may directly request industry aligned involvement and any disputes will be resolved through industry protocol.

G. Field agents and teams are expected to recognize elevation is part of the audit process.

4.51.5 Industry Focus and Control of LB&I Compliance Issues

IRM 4.51.5.1, Overview and Definitions

IRM 4.51.5.2, Process of Identifying and Ranking Industry Issues

IRM 4.51.5.3, Compliance Strategy Council (CSC) Designation of Tier I and II Issues

IRM 4.51.5.4, Direction and Control of Tier I Issues

IRM 4.51.5.5, Direction and Control of Tier II Issues

IRM 4.51.5.6, Monthly Report to CSC

IRM 4.51.5.7, Tier III – Direction and Control of Issues of Industry Importance

IRM Exhibit 4.51.5-1, Industry Issue Coordinator – Roles and Responsibilities

IRM Exhibit 4.51.5-2, LB&I Tier I–II Directive

IRM Exhibit 4.51.5-3, LB&I Significant Tax Compliance Issue

4.51.5.1 (04-01-2007)

Overview and Definitions

1. To strengthen the Industry focus within LB&I, new rules for designating and controlling industry issues are being implemented. The extent to which these issues are controlled and the operation of the rules of engagement functions will depend largely on the importance or impact of the issue. Industry issues will be designated as follows:

   • **Tier I – High Strategic Importance.** Tier I issues are of high strategic importance to LB&I and have significant impact on one or more Industries. Tier I issues could include areas involving a large number of taxpayers, significant dollar risk, substantial compliance risk or high visibility, where there are established legal positions and/or LB&I direction.

- **Tier II – Significant Compliance Risk.** Tier II issues reflect areas of potential high non-compliance and/or significant compliance risk to LB&I or an Industry. Tier II includes emerging issues, where the law is fairly well established, but there is a need for further development, clarification, direction and guidance on LB&I's position.

- **Tier III – Industry Importance.** Tier III issues typically are industry-related, and have been identified as issues that should be considered by LB&I teams when conducting their risk analyses.

4.51.5.2 (04-01-2007)

Process of Identifying and Ranking Industry Issues

1. Each LB&I director will identify an industry issue coordinator to manage the process of identifying and ranking industry issues. See Exhibit 4.51.5-1 for Roles and Responsibilities of Industry Issue Coordinators.

2. Industry issues will be identified for each sub-industry from various sources and sent to the industry issue coordinator. These sources would include both internal (examinations) and external sources (outside stake-holders, new legislation). Issues will be received from the Pre-Filing and Technical Guidance (PFTG) technical advisors, Industry Counsel, Schedule M-3 reviews, and other specialist programs (International and Field Specialists). Known cross-industry issues will be submitted by technical advisors or other submitters to all industries impacted for consideration. Additionally, Industry Directors, Director Field Specialists and Directors of Field Operations will gather information to identify issues for each sub-industry through attendance at sub-industry meetings and field visits.

3. Each Industry Director in coordination with the Directors International Compliance Strategy and Policy, Field Specialists, and PFTG will evaluate issues received at least annually to determine which issues are of industry importance. In doing so, the industry will consider both issues unique to the industry and cross industry issues.

4. In determining industry importance the following factors should be considered:

- Visibility and public uncertainty of the tax treatment due to new legislation or litigation.

- Materiality (affects a significant number of taxpayers, large permanent or long-term timing adjustments, undue amount of time spent auditing issue).

- Potentially an abusive tax avoidance transaction or promotion.

5. The evaluation process reviewers will include the industry issue coordinator, technical advisors, Field/Issue Counsel and other specialist (Field

Specialist/International) as needed. Some issues will need further development of their compliance impact or technical merits and need to be assigned to a technical advisor or other specialist for development.

6. Issues that are sufficiently developed and determined to be of importance, will be sent by the Industry Directors to peers for review in order to further identify cross-industry issues. Copies will also be sent to the Directors, PFTG, International Compliance Strategy and Policy, and Field Specialists. Section I of Exhibit 4.51.5-3 will be completed and circulated for this purpose. Feedback will be sent to the industry issue coordinator who will then reconcile similarities and differences for each cross-industry issue for the Industry Director to identify the issue owner. Industry Directors will work with the Directors of International Compliance Strategy and Policy, Field Specialist, and PFTG to assign ownership of cross-industry issues.

7. After cross-industry issues have been identified and assigned, issues of industry importance owned by the industry will be reviewed by the Industry Director or delegate to determine if they should be designated as Tier I or II as defined in section 4.51.5.1. If not, they will be designated as Tier III to be considered by examiners in their examinations per IRM 4.51.5.7.

4.51.5.3 (04-01-2007)

Compliance Strategy Council (CSC) Designation of Tier I and II Issues

1. **Presentation to the CSC.** Proposed Tier I and II issues will be presented to the CSC for approval. In advance of the meeting the industry/or specialty issue coordinator will complete Sections I and II of Exhibit 4.51.5-3, Compliance Strategy Council Reporting Template. This report includes the proposed tier designation, issue summary, findings to date on compliance impact, and proposed industry direction. Cross-industry issues without clear ownership affiliations can be presented to the CSC by the Directors of PFTG, Field Specialists, or International Compliance Strategy and Policy for Tier I or II designation. Approval will also be requested in this manner from the CSC to change an issue's level of importance (Tier II to Tier I, Tier I to Tier III, etc.) because of new findings or further issue development.

2. **CSC Designation of Tier I or II Issue.**

   A. Upon approval, the CSC will assign ownership to an industry or specialty area.

   B. Upon CSC designation of an issue as a Tier I or II issue, notice should be provided to the Appeals Division. Appeals will establish a contact who will coordinate each Tier I and II issue and will represent Appeals on the issue management team.

   C. Tier I projects approved by the CSC are national strategic initiatives. Per IRM 4.17.1.3 these projects are not subject to compliance initiative project procedures. The Director, SRPP will approve information gathering/selecting returns for examination on these projects using the Exhibit 4.51.5-3 template. If other functions will be significantly impacted, their approval will also be obtained on the template. Details of the project and request for project codes, etc. will be coordinated with the LB&I SRPP Operation Support analyst. Details should be entered in item 8 per instructions.

3. **Announcement of CSC Designation.** PFTG will post to a centralized web site all Tier I and II issues designated by the CSC. The listing will include the Issue Owner Executive (IOE) and brief description of the issue. IOE will establish a web page linking to the central site for each Tier I and II issue.

4.51.5.4 (04-01-2007)
Direction and Control of Tier I Issues

1. **Issuance of Industry Directive.** An industry directive will be issued upon CSC designation to all examiners for each Tier I issue naming the IOE and provide guidance on identifying, and developing each Tier I issue. The directive may or may not initially provide guidance on resolving the issue. If not, as the issue resolution strategy is developed additional directive(s) will be issued to the field. The directive will also specify how cases with the issue will be tracked. A Uniform Issue List (UIL) number should be assigned to each Tier I issue to enable issue tracking on open and closed cases. A three digit second tier Standard Audit Index Number (SAIN) may also be assigned to allow tracking of issues within LB&I where there is more than one applicable UIL number or to allow for more precise tracking. Request for new UIL and second tier SAIN numbers to track issues should be emailed to PFTS@irs.gov identifying the applicable code section and issue. See Exhibit 4.51.5-2, LB&I Tier I-II Directive, for instructions in preparing the directive. An issue management team should also be assigned to further develop the issue and coordinate resolutions.

2. **Rules of Engagement.** Tier I issues require oversight and control by an IOE. The Executive has national jurisdiction and is responsible for ensuring that the issue is identified, developed and resolved in a consistent manner across all LB&I cases involving similarly situated taxpayers. The disposition or resolution of the issue must be in accordance with the above Executive's guidance. The line Authority Executive will work with the IOE to ensure that access is granted to Tier I cases for the above purpose.

4.51.5.5 (04-01-2007)

Direction and Control of Tier II Issues

1. **Issuance of Industry Directive.** An industry directive in the form of an alert announcing the issue or a directive with specific audit techniques will be issued upon CSC designation to all examiners for each Tier II issue naming the IOE using the format in Exhibit 4.51.5-2. The IOE will establish coordination contacts for line executives and allocate resources to further develop the issue through the emerging issue process (see IRM 4.51.2 - LB&I Administrative Guidance). Additional directives may be issued as guidance is developed. Emerging issue teams may later evolve into an issue management team to develop and coordinate resolutions. A UIL number should be assigned to each Tier II issue to enable issue tracking. Second tier SAINs may also be assigned to track the issue.

2. **Rules of Engagement.** Tier I issues require oversight and control by an IOE. The Executive has national jurisdiction and is responsible for ensuring that the issue is identified, developed and resolved in a consistent manner across all LB&I cases involving similarly situated taxpayers. The disposition or resolution of the issue must be in accordance with the above Executive's guidance. The Line Authority Executive will work with the IOE to ensure that access is granted to Tier II cases for the above purpose.

4.51.5.6 (04-01-2007)

Monthly Report to CSC

1. The IOE will report to the CSC the status of each Tier I issue monthly. The status of Tier II will be reported to the CSC on an exception basis when significant events occur impacting the issue's resolution. See Exhibit 4.51.5-3, Compliance Strategy Council Reporting Template, for information to be contained in the report.

4.51.5.7 (04-01-2007)

Tier III – Direction and Control of Issues of Industry Importance

1. **Listing of Tier III Issues.** Tier III issues will be listed on the centralized web site by industry along with Tier I and Tier II issues. Links will be embedded to available guidance (e.g. Audit Technique Guidelines) on the industry or technical advisor web sites to promote consistent development and resolution of the issue throughout LB&I.

2. **Rules of Engagement.** The Line Authority Industry Executive retains unilateral decision making authority, including ultimate disposition and resolution, over Tier III issues.

Exhibit 4.51.5-1 (04-01-2007)

Industry Issue Coordinator – Roles and Responsibilities

1. Focal point for communications relating to industry issues. Acts as a liaison between LB&I technical advisors/specialist and other industry coordinators. Maintains open lines of communication with Appeals, Counsel, other business operating divisions and government agencies regarding industry issues to be aware of all activities that will affect the issue.

2. Solicitation and Control of Industry Issues [IRM 4.51.5.2(1)]. Encourages the submission of issues by technical advisors, specialists and examiners closest to the facts. Gathers information from sub-industry meetings to gain insight on new issues. Maintains industry records on issues submitted and their disposition.

3. Evaluation of Industry Issues [IRM 4.51.5.2(4)]. Coordinates the preliminary review of new issues within the industry using technical advisor teams, counsel and other specialists. Continuously briefs the Industry Director on potential industry issues.

4. Peer Issue Circulation [IRM 4.51.5.2(5)]. Circulates issues to other coordinators to identify cross industry issues. Directs the review of the issues being circulated by coordinators from outside the industry.

5. Industry Tier Designations [IRM 4.51.5.2(6)]. Arranges briefings with the Industry Director on issue findings. Works with the Industry Director or Delegate to recommend issues warranting continuing coordination as Tier I-II Issues.

6. Presentations to Compliance Strategy Council (CSC) [IRM 4.51.5.3]. Coordinates the preparation of reports (tier, summary, findings and proposed direction to examiners) with the technical advisors, emerging issue teams and others for CSC approval of proposed Tier I-II issue/ changes.

7. Industry Directives [IRM 4.51.5.4]. Coordinates the circulation and processing of directives on Tier I and II issues working with emerging issue/issue management teams. Requests assignment of UIL/SAIN number to issues.

8. CSC Status Reports [IRM 4.51.5.6]. Gathers Tier I and II status reports prepared by IOEs for review by Industry Directors before forwarding to SRPP.

9. Tier II – [IRM 4.51.5.5]. Works with the Industry Director to coordinate the establishment (or continuation) of emerging issues teams for fact finding/legal analysis, if needed.

10. Tier I – [IRM 4.51.5.4]. Works with the Industry Director to coordinate the establishment of issue management team to control issue development and closure, if needed.

11. Tier I – III Industry/TA WEB page and IRS.gov. Coordinates with PFTS and C&L the distribution of Tier I-III issue announcements and procedural directives to internal and external stakeholders, as required.

12. Provide communications to ensure that an issue expert is available to assist management and examiners in properly planning, developing and resolving Tier I issues. Assists in the coordination of issue seminars/ training, as requested.

13. Acts as a point of contact for the Industry Director to facilitate in obtaining the director's concurrence of the disposition of the Tier I issue that adopts a position contrary to that reflected in ID guidance.

14. Coordinates with Appeals and Counsel the tracking of Tier I and II issues in those functions to determine the progress and effectiveness of guidance.

Exhibit 4.51.5-2 (04-01-2007)

LB&I Tier I–II Directive

To: INDUSTRY DIRECTORS
DIRECTOR, FIELD SPECIALISTS
DIRECTOR, PREFILING AND TECHNICAL GUIDANCE
DIRECTOR, INTERNATIONAL COMPLIANCE STRATEGY AND POLICY

Form: LB&I Director

Subject: Tier I (or Tier II) issue (Title as listed on web) Directive [Insert #] (or Alert)

This memorandum provides field direction on Tier I Issue (Title) or Tier II Issue (Title). [Or This memorandum provides notice of Tier II (Title)]. The issue owner executive is (name and title).

Background/Strategic Importance: [Include Issue Description, Legal Opinions & Areas of Controversy]

Issue Tracking: Include UIL Code(s), SAIN Numbers and any other reporting requirements.]

Planning and Examination Guidance:

Note:

For an alert only include Issue Identification in this section.

Issue identification
[Discussion on how the issue is identified (tax return, Schedule M-3, claims). Address whether it is being assigned as part of a compliance initiative project.]

Planning and Examination Risk Analysis
[Discussion on whether the issue is a mandatory examination item. And if examined, what are the mandatory coordination and examination actions.]

Audit Techniques
[Include audit steps and records to requests (Performa IDRs)]

Audit Evaluation
[Provide direction on evaluating information gathered. What factual patterns should be pursued/ sustainable in the post-audit process.]

¶512

LB&I Position:
[State either "pending" or LB&I resolution instructions. Instructions should include: What LB&I position is to be followed (coordinated issue paper, generic legal advice, or published guidance) and. case closing instructions. If settlement offered or safe harbor option exists, address action required on those that do not take it. Include discussion on penalties.]

Effect on Other Guidance:
[Indicate whether any previous LB&I directive needs to be made obsolete or amended.]

Contact:
[Include in technical contact name and phone number in directive or cover memorandum)

This Directive is not an official pronouncement of law, and cannot be used, cited, or relied upon as such.

Note: Any line containing OUO data should marked with #. A footer should be added "Any line marked with a # is for Official Use Only".

CC: Commissioner, LB&I
Deputy Commissioner, Operations
Deputy Commissioner, International
Division Counsel, LB&I
Chief, Appeals
Directors, Field Operations
Director, Performance, Quality and Audit Assistance

Exhibit 4.51.5-3 (04-01-2007)

LB&I Significant Tax Compliance Issue

| LB&I Significant Tax Compliance Issue: | Issue Owner: |
| | Date: |

I.	1. Issue Description
	2. Legal Opinions and Areas of Controversy
	3. Number of Returns/Taxpayers
	4. Revenue Impact and Impacted Functions
	5. How Identified
II	6. Proposed LB&I Direction and Strategy — (Narrative discussion on plans to address the issue)
	7. Issue Tracking — (List UIL codes, SAIN #s, and other reporting requirements)
III	8. Approval to Conduct Information Gathering /Select Returns for Examination
	Signature of the Director, SRPP
	Signature of Other Operating Divisions Impacted
	At the time of implementation, enter specific details regarding taxpayer/return selection criteria and any alternative treatments.

IV	**9. List Key Milestones with Target Completion Dates** (Examples of Key Milestones: IMT Establishment; Fact-finding and Analysis; Legal Guidance; Inventory Identification; LB&I Direction; and Inventory Resolution)	(Provide assessment of each key milestone)
	10. Comments/Next Steps	

Sections I and II will be completed for Tier I and II CSC approval per IRM 4.51.5.3(1). Subsequent changes to these items will be highlighted in monthly reports.

Section III will be completed for approval of projects requiring returns to be selected for examination per IRM 4.51.5.3(2)(c).

Section IV will be updated monthly for reporting to the CSC on Tier I (when applicable Tier II) issues per IRM 4.51.5.6.

¶513 Exhibit 5-3

Recognized Abusive and Listed Transactions–LB&I Tier I Issues in Alphabetical Order

- §§302/318 Basis Shifting - Notice 2001-45
- §461(f) Contested Liabilities - Notice 2003-77
- Abusive Charitable Remainder Trusts - Treasury Reg. 1.643(a)-8
- Abusive Trust Arrangements Utilizing Cash Value Life Insurance Policies Purportedly to Provide Welfare Benefits - Notice 2007-83
- ASA Investering Partnership v. Commissioner
- Certain Accelerated Deductions for Contributions to a Qualified Cash or Deferred Arrangement or Matching Contributions to a Defined Contribution Plan - Revenue Ruling 90-105
- Collectively Bargained Welfare Benefit Funds - Notice 2003-24
- Common Trust Fund Straddles - Notice 2002-50
- Contingent Liabilities - Notice 2001-17
- Contributions to Roth IRA - Notice 2004-8
- Corporate Distributions of Encumbered Property (BOSS) - Notice 99-59
- Custom Adjustable Rate Debt (CARD) - Notice 2002-21
- Debt Straddles - Revenue Ruling 2000-12
- Distressed Asset Debt - Trust Variation (DAD Trust) -Notice 2008-34
- Distressed Asset/Debt
- Foreign Tax Credit Intermediary - Notice 2004-20
- Guam Trust - Notice 2000-61
- Intercompany Financing Using Guaranteed Payments - Notice 2004-31
- Intermediary Transactions - Notice 2001-16
- Lease-In/Lease-Out or LILO - Revenue Ruling 2002-69
- Lease Strips/Inflated Basis - Notice 2003-55
- Loss Importation Transactions - Notice 2007-57
- Major/Minor Tax Avoidance Using Offsetting Foreign currency Option Contracts - Notice 2003-81
- Notional Principal Contracts (NPC) - Notice 2002-35
- Offshore Deferred Compensation Arrangements - Notice 2003-22
- Partnership Straddle - Notice 2002-50
- Pass-Through Entity Straddle - Notice 2002-65
- Pension Plans Involving Insurance Policies with Excess Benefits - Revenue Ruling 2004-20
- Prohibited Allocations of Employer Securities in an S corporation ESOP - Revenue Ruling 2004-04

- Redemption Bogus Optional Basis
- S Corporation ESOPS - Revenue Ruling 2003-6
- S Corporation Tax Shelter - Notice 2004-30
- Sale-In/Sale-Out or SILO Transactions - Notice 2005-13
- Son of BOSS - Notice 2000-44
- Step Down Preferred/Fast Pay Stock - Treasury Reg. § 1.7701(1)-3
- Stock Compensation Transactions - Notice 2000-60
- Transfers of Compensatory Stock Options to Related Persons - Notice 2003-47
- Voluntary Employee Beneficiary Association - Notice 95-34

Recognized Abusive and Listed Transactions–LB&I Tier I Issues

1. Revenue Ruling 90-105–Certain Accelerated Deductions for Contributions to a Qualified Cash or Deferred Arrangement or Matching Contributions to a Defined Contribution Plan

2. Notice 95-34 - Voluntary Employee Beneficiary Association

3. ASA Investering Partnership v. Commissioner -Transactions similar to that described in the ASA Investering litigation and in ACM Partnership v. Commissioner

4. Treasury Regulation § 1.643(a)-8 – Certain Distributions from Charitable Remainder Trusts

5. Notice 99-59 - Corporate Distributions of Encumbered Property (BOSS)

6. Step-Down Step Down Preferred/Fast Pay Stock § 1.7701(1)-3

7. Revenue Ruling 2000-12 – Debt Straddles

8. Notice 2000-44 – Inflated Partnership Basis Transactions (Son of Boss)

9. Notice 2000-60 Stock Compensation Stock Compensation Transactions

10. Notice 2000-61 – Guam Trust

11. Notice 2001-16 – Intermediary Transactions

12. Notice 2001-17 - § 351 Contingent Liability

13. Notice 2001- 45 - § 302 Basis-Shifting Transactions

14. Notice 2002-21 - Inflated Basis "CARDS" Transactions

15. Notice 2002-35 - Notional Principal Contracts

16. Common Trust Fund Straddles (Notice 2003-54), Pass-Through Entity Straddle (Notice 2002-50), and S Corporation Tax Shelter Transaction (Notice 2002-65)

17. Revenue Ruling 2002-69 - Lease In / Lease Out or LILO Transactions

18. Revenue Ruling 2003-6 - Abuses Associated with S Corp ESOPs

19. Notice 2003-22 - Offshore Deferred Compensation Arrangements

20. Notice 2003-24 - Certain Trust Arrangements Seeking to Qualify for Exception for Collectively Bargained Welfare Benefit Funds under § 419A(f)(5)

21. Notice 2003-47 - Transfers of Compensatory Stock Options to Related Persons

22. Notice 2003-55 - Accounting for Lease Strips and Other Stripping Transactions

23. Notice 2003-77 - Improper use of contested liability trusts to attempt to accelerate deductions for contested liabilities under IRC 461(f)

24. Notice 2003-81 - Major/Minor Tax Avoidance Using Offsetting Foreign currency Option Contracts

25. Notice 2004-8 - Abusive Roth IRA Transactions

26. Revenue Ruling 2004-4 - S Corporations ESOP

27. Revenue Ruling 2004-20 - Abusive Transactions Involving Insurance Policies in IRC 412(i) Retirement Plans

28. Notice 2004-20 - Abusive Foreign Tax Credit Transactions

29. Notice 2004-30 - S Corporation Tax Shelter Involving Shifting Income to Tax Exempt Organization

30. Notice 2004-31 - Intercompany Financing Through Partnerships

31. Notice 2005-13 - Sale-In Lease-Out transactions

32. Notice 2007-57 - Loss Importation Transaction

33. Notice 2007-83 - Abusive Trust Arrangements Utilizing Cash Value Life Insurance Policies Purportedly to Provide Welfare Benefits

34. Notice 2008-34 - Distressed Asset Trust (DAT) Transaction

"De-Listed" Transactions

Recognized Abusive Transactions - Not Listed Transactions

- Distressed Asset/Debt - Larry Barnes, Director, Field Operations East, Heavy Manufacturing and Transportation

    — Coordinated Issue Paper - 04-18-2007

- Redemption Bogus Optional Basis - Patricia Chaback, Industry Director, Communications, Technology, and Media

    — Coordinated Issue Paper - 01-31-2006

Tax Shelter Issues and Issue Owners

Revenue Ruling 90-105 – Certain Accelerated Deductions for Contributions to a Qualified Cash or Deferred Arrangement or Matching Contributions to a Defined Contribution Plan (transactions in which taxpayers claim deductions for contributions to a qualified cash or deferred arrangement or matching contributions to a defined contribution plan where the contributions are attributable to compensation earned by plan participants after the end of the taxable year (identified as "listed transactions" on February 28, 2000)). See also Rev. Rul.

¶513

2002-46, 2002-2 C.B. 117 (result is the same, and transactions are substantially similar, even though the contributions are designated as satisfying a liability established before the end of the taxable year), modified by Rev. Rul. 2002-73, 2002-2 C.B. 805

- Coordinated Issue Paper - Deduction of Contributions to IRC section 401(k) Plans Attributable to Compensation Paid After Year End Under IRC section 404(a)(6) - Revised 9-24-2004.

- Revenue Ruling 2002-46–§ 401k Accelerators

- Revenue Ruling 2002-73 - modifies RR 2002-46 for taxpayers electing to change method of accounting.

Voluntary Employee Beneficiary Association

Notice 95-34 – Certain Trusts Purported to be Multiple Employer Welfare Funds Exempted from the Lists of §§ 419 and 419A(certain trust arrangements purported to qualify as multiple employer welfare benefit funds exempt from the limits of §§ 419 and 419A of the Internal Revenue Code (identified as "listed transactions" on February 28, 2000)). See also § 1.419A(f)(6)-1 of the Income Tax Regulations (10 or more employer plans)).

ASA Investering Partnership v. Commissioner -Transactions similar to that described in the ASA Investering litigation and in ACM Partnership v. Commissioner, 157 F.3d 231 (3rd Cir. 1998) (transactions involving contingent installment sales of securities by partnerships in order to accelerate and allocate income to a tax-indifferent partner, such as a tax-exempt entity or foreign person, and to allocate later losses to another partner (identified as "listed transactions" on February 28, 2000)).

Treasury Regulation § 1.643(a)-8 – Certain Distributions from Charitable Remainder Trusts (transactions involving distributions described in § 1.643(a)-8 from charitable remainder trusts (identified as "listed transactions" on February 28, 2000)).

Corporate Distributions of Encumbered Property (BOSS)

Notice 99-59 – Transactions involving the distributions of encumbered property in which losses claimed for capital outlays have been recovered (aka BOSS transactions) (transactions involving the distribution of encumbered property in which taxpayers claim tax losses for capital outlays that they have in fact recovered (identified as "listed transactions" on February 28, 2000)). See also § 1.301-1(g) of the Income Tax Regulations;

Step Down Preferred/Fast Pay Stock § 1.7701(1)-3

Treasury Regulation § 1.7701(I)-3 – Fast Pay or Step-Down Preferred Transactions (transactions involving fast-pay arrangements as defined in § 1.7701(l)-3(b) (identified as "listed transactions" on February 28, 2000));

Revenue Ruling 2000-12 – Debt Straddles (certain transactions involving the acquisition of two debt instruments the values of which are expected to change significantly at about the same time in opposite directions (identified as "listed transactions" on February 28, 2000));

Notice 2000-44 – Inflated Partnership Basis Transactions (Son of Boss) (transactions generating losses resulting from artificially inflating the basis of partnership interests (identified as "listed transactions" on August 11, 2000)). See also § 1.752-6T of the temporary Income Tax Regulations and §§ 1.752-1(a) and 1.752-7 of the proposed Income Tax Regulations;

Son of Boss Settlement Initiative

- IRS Collects $3.2 Billion from Son of Boss
- Strong response to "Son of Boss" Settlement Initiative -- Over 1,500 taxpayers responded by the June 21 deadline to settle under Announcement 2004-46.
- IRS News Release Announcing Settlement Initiative
- IRS Fact Sheet, Son of Boss Settlement Initiative
- Announcement 2004-46, Son of Boss Settlement Initiative
- FAQs (updated 5-28-04 with eligibility information)
- Supplemental FAQs (11-1-04)
- Form 13582, Notice of Election to Participate in Settlement Initiative
- Form 13586, Additional Information and Documentation
- Form 13586-A, Settlement Initiative Declaration
- Initial RA Letter to Taxpayer
- Rejection Letter
- Closing Agreement Letter
- CCN 2003-20 - Chief Counsel Guidance

Stock Compensation Transactions

Notice 2000-60 – Stock Compensation Transactions (transactions involving the purchase of a parent corporation's stock by a subsidiary, a subsequent transfer of the purchased parent stock from the subsidiary to the parent's employees, and the eventual liquidation or sale of the subsidiary (identified as "listed transactions" on November 16, 2000));

Notice 2000-61 – Guam Trust (transactions purporting to apply § 935 to Guamanian trusts (identified as "listed transactions" on November 21, 2000));

Notice 2001-16 – Intermediary Transactions (transactions involving the use of an intermediary to sell the assets of a corporation (identified as "listed transactions" on January 18, 2001));

- **Notice 2008-111** - (12/01/2008) – Clarifies Notice 2001-16 (2001-1 C.B. 730) that identified and described the intermediary transaction tax shelter as a listed transaction and supersedes Notice 2008-20 (2008-6 I.R.B. 406). The Notice defines an intermediary transaction in terms of its plan and of more objective components. Also, the Notice specifies when a person is engaged in a transaction as part of a plan and clarifies that a transaction may be an intermediary transaction for one person and not another.

- Coordinated Issue Paper - Intermediary Transactions

- LB&I Industry Director Guidance - Examination of Multiple Parties in Intermediary Transactions

Notice 2001-17 - § 351 Contingent Liability (transactions involving a loss on the sale of stock acquired in a purported § 351 transfer of a high basis asset to a corporation and the corporation's assumption of a liability that the transferor has not yet taken into account for federal income tax purposes (identified as "listed transactions" on January 18, 2001));

Notice 2001-45 – § 302 Basis-Shifting Transactions (certain redemptions of stock in transactions not subject to U.S. tax in which the basis of the redeemed stock is purported to shift to a U.S. taxpayer (identified as "listed transactions" on July 26, 2001));

Notice 2002-21 – Inflated Basis "CARDS" Transactions (transactions involving the use of a loan assumption agreement to inflate basis in assets acquired from another party to claim losses (identified as "listed transactions" on March 18, 2002));

- Notice 2002-21 Coordinated Issue Paper

- Appeals Settlement Guidelines (redacted)

Notice 2002-35 – Notional Principal Contracts (transactions involving the use of a notional principal contract to claim current deductions for periodic payments made by a taxpayer while disregarding the accrual of a right to receive offsetting payments in the future (identified as "listed transactions" on May 6, 2002));

- Notice 2006-16, Tax Avoidance Using Notional Principal Contracts.

- Explanation of Notice 2006-16, Impact on Required Disclosures.

Common Trust Fund Straddles, Pass-Through Entity Straddle, and S Corporation Tax Shelter transaction

Notice 2002-50–Partnership Straddle Tax Shelter (transactions involving the use of a straddle, a tiered partnership structure, a transitory partner, and the absence of a § 754 election to claim a permanent noneconomic loss (identified as "listed transactions" on June 25, 2002)); Notice 2002-65, 2002-2 C.B. 690 (transactions involving the use of a straddle, an S corporation or a partnership, and one or more transitory shareholders or partners to claim a loss while deferring an offsetting gain are substantially similar to transactions described in Notice 2002-50); and Notice 2003-54, 2003-33 I.R.B. 363 (transactions involving the use of economically offsetting positions, one or more tax indifferent parties, and the common trust fund accounting rules of § 584 to allow a taxpayer to claim a noneconomic loss are substantially similar to transactions described in Notice 2002-50 and Notice 2002-65);

¶513

- Coordinated Issue Paper on Notice 2002-50 Transactions
- Notice 2003-54 - Common Trust Fund Straddle Tax Shelter
- Notice 2002-65–Passthrough Entity Straddle Tax Shelter
- Coordinated Issue Paper on Notice 2002-65 Transactions

Revenue Ruling 2002-69, Lease In / Lease Out or LILO Transactions (transactions in which a taxpayer purports to lease property and then purports to immediately sublease it back to the lessor (often referred to as lease-in/lease-out; or LILO transactions) (identified as listed transactions on February 28, 2000)

- **LILO/SILO SETTLEMENT INITIATIVE** - On August 6, 2008, IRS Commissioner Douglas Shulman announced that settlements would be offered to taxpayers who participated in Lease-In/Lease-Out (LILO) and Sale-In/Sale-Out (SILO) transactions. IRS sent out letters giving taxpayers 30 days to make a decision on whether to accept the offer terms.
  — IRS Commissioner's Remarks 08-06-2008
  — LILO/SILO Initiative Frequently Asked Questions

Revenue Ruling 2003-6, Abuses Associated with S Corp ESOPs (certain arrangements involving the transfer of employee stock ownership plans (ESOPs) that hold stock in an S corporation for the purpose of claiming eligibility for the delayed effective date of § 409(p) (identified as "listed transactions" on December 17, 2002));

Notice 2003-22 - Offshore Deferred Compensation Arrangements (certain arrangements involving leasing companies that have been used to avoid or evade federal income and employment taxes (identified as "listed transactions" on April 4, 2003));

Notice 2003-24 - Certain Trust Arrangements Seeking to Qualify for Exception for Collectively Bargained Welfare Benefit Funds under § 419A(f)(5) (certain arrangements that purportedly qualify as collectively-bargained welfare benefit funds excepted from the account limits of §§ 419 and 419A (identified as "listed transactions" on April 11, 2003));

Transfers of Compensatory Stock Options to Related Persons

Notice 2003-47 - Transfers of Compensatory Stock Options to Related Persons (transactions involving compensatory stock options and related persons to avoid or evade federal income and employment taxes (identified as "listed transactions" on July 1, 2003));

- Announcement 2005-39 - Additional Guidance relating to Announcement 2005-19
- Announcement 2005-19 - Stock Option Settlement Initiative
- Frequently Asked Questions - Stock Option Settlement
- Stock Option Settlement Press Release
- Stock Option Settlement Fact Sheet
- Form 13656 - Settlement Election For Executives and Related Parties
- Form 13567 - Settlement Election for Corporations

Notice 2003-55 - Accounting for Lease Strips and Other Stripping Transactions (transactions in which one participant claims to realize rental or other income from property or service contracts and another participant claims the deductions related to that income (often referred to as "lease strips")), modifying and superseding Notice 95-53, 1995-2 C.B. 334 (identified as "listed transactions" on February 28, 2000);

- Notice 95-53 – Lease Strips - Modified and superseded by Notice 2003-55 above

Notice 2003-77 - Improper use of contested liability trusts to attempt to accelerate deductions for contested liabilities under IRC 461(f) (certain transactions that use contested liability trusts improperly to accelerate deductions for contested liabilities under § 461(f) (identified as "listed transactions" on November 19, 2003)). See also § 1.461-2 of the Income Tax Regulations. See Rev. Proc. 2004-31, 2004-22 I.R.B. 986, for procedures which taxpayers must use to change their methods of accounting for deducting under § 461(f) amounts transferred to trusts in transactions described in Notice 2003-77.

- Lead Executive Memorandum -- Advises that settlements will not be offered on these issues
- Treasury News Release - Announcing Notice 2003-77
- TD 9095
- Regulation 136890-02
- Revenue Procedure 2004-31 - Change of accounting methods for improper contested liability trust transactions described in Notice 2003-77.
- Treasury News Release - Announcing Revenue Procedure 2004-31

Major/Minor Tax Avoidance Using Offsetting Foreign currency Option Contracts

Notice 2003-81 - Offsetting Foreign Currency Option Contracts (certain transactions in which a taxpayer claims a loss upon the assignment of a § 1256 contract to a charity but fails to report the recognition of gain when the taxpayer's obligation under an offsetting non-section 1256 contract terminates (identified as "listed transactions" on December 4, 2003));

- Coordinated Issue Paper

Notice 2004-8 - Abusive Roth IRA Transactions (certain transactions designed to avoid the limitations on contributions to Roth IRAs described in § 408A (identified as "listed transactions" on December 31, 2003));

- Treasury Department News Release

S Corporations ESOP

Revenue Ruling 2004-04 - Prohibited Allocations of Securities in an S Corporation (transactions that involve segregating the business profits of an ESOP-owned S corporation in a qualified subchapter S subsidiary, so that rank-and-file employees do not benefit from participation in the ESOP (identified as "listed transactions" on January 23, 2004));

- Treasury Department Press Release

¶513

Revenue Ruling 2004-20 - Abusive Transactions Involving Insurance Policies in IRC 412(i) Retirement Plans (certain arrangements in which an employer deducts contributions to a qualified pension plan for premiums on life insurance contracts that provide for death benefits in excess of the participant's death benefit, where under the terms of the plan, the balance of the death benefit proceeds revert to the plan as a return on investment) (identified as "listed transactions" on February 13, 2004)). See also Rev. Rul. 2004-21, 2004-10 I.R.B. 544, §§ 1.79-1(d)(3), 1.83-3(e) and 1.402(a)-1(a)(1) and (2) of the proposed Income Tax Regulations, and Rev. Proc. 2004-16, 2004-10 I.R.B. 559;

- Revenue Ruling 2004-21

- Proposed Regulation 126967-03

- Revenue Procedure 2004-16

- News Release IR-2004-21

Notice 2004-20 - Abusive Foreign Tax Credit Transactions (transactions in which, pursuant to a prearranged plan, a domestic corporation purports to acquire stock in a foreign target corporation and to make an election under § 338 before selling all or substantially all of the target corporation's assets in a preplanned transaction that generates a taxable gain for foreign tax purposes (but not for U.S. tax purposes) (identified as "listed transactions" on February 17, 2004));

- Treasury Department Press Release

- Notice 2004-19 -- Withdraws

- Notice 98-5 and describes strategy to address abusive FTC transactions

Notice 2004-30 - S Corporation Tax Shelter Involving Shifting Income to Tax Exempt Organization (transactions in which S corporation shareholders attempt to transfer the incidence of taxation on S corporation income by purportedly donating S corporation nonvoting stock to an exempt organization while retaining the economic benefits associated with that stock (identified as "listed transactions" on April 1, 2004));

- Lead Executive Memo regarding settlements (4/6/05)

- IRS Press Release 2004-44

Notice 2004-31 - Intercompany Financing Through Partnerships (transactions in which corporations claim inappropriate deductions for payments made through a partnership (identified as "listed transactions" on April 1, 2004)).

- Treasury Press Release dated 4/1/04

Notice 2005-13, Sale-In Lease-Out transactions

- Treasury Press Release

- Coordinated Issue Paper - Losses Claimed and Income to be Reported from Sale In/Lease Out (SILO)

- LILO/SILO SETTLEMENT INITIATIVE- On August 6, 2008, IRS Commissioner Douglas Shulman announced that settlements would be offered to taxpayers who participated in Lease-In/Lease-Out (LILO) and Sale-In/Sale-Out (SILO) transactions. IRS sent out letters giving taxpayers 30 days to make a decision on whether to accept the offer terms.
  — IRS Commissioner's Remarks 08-06-2008
  — LILO/SILO Initiative Frequently Asked Questions

Notice 2007-57 - Loss Importation Transaction (IRB 2007-29) (transactions in which a U.S. taxpayer uses offsetting positions with respect to foreign currency or other property for the purpose of importing a loss, but not the corresponding gain, in determining U.S. taxable income (identified as "listed transactions" on July 16, 2007)).

- Coordinated Issue Announcement

Notice 2007-83 - Abusive Trust Arrangements Utilizing Cash Value Life Insurance Policies Purportedly to Provide Welfare Benefits - 2007-45 I.R.B. 1 (transactions in which certain trust arrangements claiming to be welfare benefit funds and involving cash value life insurance policies that are being promoted to and used by taxpayers to improperly claim federal income and employment tax benefits (identified as "listed transactions" on October 17, 2007)).

Notice 2008-34 - Distressed Asset Trust (DAT) Transaction -2008-12 I.R.B. 1 (transactions in which a tax indifferent party, directly or indirectly, contributes one or more distressed assets (for example, a creditor's interests in debt) with a high basis and low fair market value to a trust or series of trusts and sub-trusts, and a U.S. taxpayer acquires an interest in the trust (and/or series of trusts and/or sub-trusts) for the purpose of shifting a built-in loss from the tax indifferent party to the U.S. taxpayer that has not incurred the economic loss (identified as listed transactions on February 27, 2008)).

"De-Listed" Transactions

- Notice 2004-65 - De-lists Producer Owned Reinsurance Companies (PORC) as a listed transaction
  — News Release dated 09-24-2004
- Notice 2004-64 Modification of exemption from tax for small property and casualty insurance companies.
- Notice 2002-70 modified by Notice 2004-65.

¶514 Exhibit 5-4

TIER I ISSUES

Research Credit Claims—Research Claims (informal claims brought against an on-going IRS examination or formal claims on amended returns) based on studies without contemporaneous documentation to support the claims, using high-level estimates, invalid assumptions, lack of nexus between qualified research expenses (QREs) and the business component, prepared by outside consultants on a contingency fee basis.

Mixed Service Costs—Filing of Forms 3115, Applications for Change in Account Method, requesting a change in method of accounting for mixed service costs from the "facts and circumstances" method provided by Treas. Reg. section 1.263A-1(f) to the Simplified Service Cost Method (SSCM) provided by Treas. Reg. section 1.263A-1(h), resulting in current expensing of billions in costs that the Service believes should be capitalized and depreciated.

Section 118 Abuse—(1) Universal Service Fund disbursements from the federal or state government affects telecommunications providers; (2) Bio-energy program subsidies affecting primarily the agriculture industry concerning the increased ethanol production subsidy payments; and (3) Environmental remediation issue affects primarily the petroleum industry and others removing underground storage tanks followed by a reimbursement for their related section 162 expenses.

Government Settlements—Whether settlements between a governmental entity and a defendant under any law in which a penalty may be assessed is deductible in its entirety under section 162(a) or is partially non-deductible under section 162(f).

Section 936 exit strategies—these issues focus on the outbound transfer and transfer pricing issues related to the offshore migration of intangibles from formerly tax-favored Puerto Rican corporations.

Domestic production deduction Code Sec. 199—these issues focus on the allocation of expenses, such as compensation, to and away from qualified production activities income.

International hybrid instrument transactions—these issues focus on the inconsistent treatment of financial instruments as either debt in the United States and equity in a foreign country or equity in the United States and debt in a foreign country.

Backdated stock options—The issue is whether a company backdated stock options excise prices to give the taxpayer lower costs in acquiring the underlying stock, and therefore a larger gain on excise.

Mixed service costs—the issue is whether the taxpayer used the simplified service cost method for self-constructed assets and failed to capitalize enough of the mixed service costs.

Cost-sharing arrangements with buy-in payments—these issues focus on cost-sharing arrangements under the transfer pricing rules, including the amount of any buy-in payment by a new participant to an existing participant for previously-existing intangibles and the measurement of reasonably anticipated benefits; and

Reporting and withholding on U.S.-source fixed, determinable, annual, or periodic income—these issues focus on the compliance of U.S. withholding agents who make these payments.

Repairs v. Capitalization Change for Account Method (CAM)—this issue focuses on the Forms 3115 taxpayers are filing in which they request a change in accounting method that would determine the Unit of Property (UOP) in such a way that the project may be expensed or it may be capitalized, but more often that is expensed.

¶515 Exhibit 5-5

TIER II ISSUES AT A GLANCE

Casualty Loss: Single Identifiable property/Capital v. Repairs—the issue is whether taxpayers may deduct casualty losses under section 165 and then deduct the costs of restoration under 162 (v. capitalixe those costs)

Cost-Sharing Stock-Based Compensation—the issue is a transfer pricing issue and is whether stockpiled compensation should be included as part of intangible development costs that must be shared by participants in a cost sharing arrangement

Gift Cards: Deferral of Income—the issue is whether the sale of gift cards must be taken into income or may be deferred from taking into income depending upon the facts and circumstances.

Interchange Merchant Discount Fees—the issue is whether any of these fees are interest deferred under 1272(a)(6) or services and currently includible in income.

Non-Performing Loans—the issue is when may a regulated bank stop accruing interest on non-performing loans for at purposes.

Super Completed Method of Accounting—the issue is whether some taxpayers are using the completed contract method where it is not allowable or are improperly deferring completion under the method.

Section 43 Enhanced Oil Recovery Credit—the issues are claims by taxpayers that they "significantly expanded" a pre-1991 enhanced oil recovery project (which makes the project qualify for the credit) and second claims that certain costs incurred were "tertiary injectant cost" which costs are eligible for the credit.

Extraterritorial Income Exclusion (Effective Date and Transition Rules)—the issues are taxpayers use of the effective dates and the transaction rules of the exclusion.

Section 172(f)-Specified Liability Losses-Specified Liability Losses—the issue is whether taxpayer claims really are for "qualified specified liability losses" under section 172.

Healthcare accounting issue contractual allowance—the issue is whether taxpayers are following GAAP in their tax returns regarding contractual allowances, or otherwise improperly reporting taxable income.

Upfront Fees, Milestone Payments, Royalities in the Bio-Tech and Pharmaceutical Industries—the issues are whether the upfront fees and milestone payments constitute section 174 and therefore section 41 amounts or should be capitalized.

¶516 Exhibit 5-6

TIER III ISSUES AT A GLANCE

Amortization of Intangibles: Licensed Program Contract Right—the issue is whether to accrue their license fee liabilities upon execution of the contract and amortize the fees over the 3 to 5 years of the contract, or whether to accrue the fees as the games are played.

Carriage/Launch Fees Paid to Cable/Satellite/T.V. Operators by Programmers/Content Providers—whether proper to receive launch fee income from affiliates and then defer them using Rev. Proc. 71-21.

Cost Segregation Studies—the issue is whether an asset has been placed in service and in the appropriate category (e.g. 5 vs. 39 years).

Delay Rentals—the issue is whether these payments are subject to capitalization (IRS position).

Loyalty Programs in Service Industries—the issue is whether revenues generated by programs such as the frequent flyers program are subject to deferral under Rev. Proc. 71-21 or Rev. Proc. 2004-34.

Motor Vehicle Dealers and 263A (Uniform Capitalization/UNICAP)—the issue is how to deal with an industry that in not uniformly following a 2007 TAM on the capitalization of certain amounts.

Premium Deficiency Reserves—an insurance industry issue and its treatment of premium deficiency reserves.

REMIC—the issue is the IRS concern and therefore study of whether REMIC sponsors are understating reportable gain on the retention of the sale of regular REMIC interests.

Vendor Allowances—the issue is whether vendor allowances are (1) gross income or (2) discounts that reduce the invoice price under Regulation section 1.471.3(b) or (3) reimbursements of expenses.

Section 198 Expensing of Environmental Remediation Costs—the issue is whether to capitalize these costs or to deduct them currently.

¶517 Exhibit 5-7

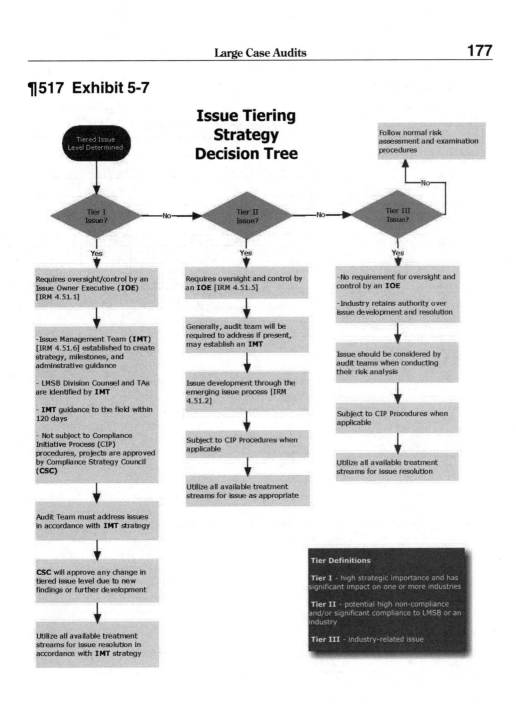

Issue Tiering Strategy Decision Tree

Tiered Issue Level Determined

Follow normal risk assessment and examination procedures

Tier I Issue? —No→ Tier II Issue? —No→ Tier III Issue? —No→

Tier I — Yes:

Requires oversight/control by an Issue Owner Executive (**IOE**) [IRM 4.51.1]

-Issue Management Team (**IMT**) [IRM 4.51.6] established to create strategy, milestones, and adminstrative guidance

- LMSB Division Counsel and TAs are identified by **IMT**

- **IMT** guidance to the field within 120 days

- Not subject to Compliance Initiative Process (CIP) procedures, projects are approved by Compliance Strategy Council (**CSC**)

Audit Team must address issues in accordance with **IMT** strategy

CSC will approve any change in tiered issue level due to new findings or further development

Utilize all available treatment streams for issue resolution in accordance with **IMT** strategy

Tier II — Yes:

Requires oversight and control by an **IOE** [IRM 4.51.5]

Generally, audit team will be required to address if present, may establish an **IMT**

Issue development through the emerging issue process [IRM 4.51.2]

Subject to CIP Procedures when applicable

Utilize all available treatment streams for issue as appropriate

Tier III — Yes:

-No requirement for oversight and control by an **IOE**

-Industry retains authority over issue development and resolution

Issue should be considered by audit teams when conducting their risk analysis

Subject to CIP Procedures when applicable

Utilize all available treatment streams for issue resolution

Tier Definitions

Tier I - high strategic importance and has significant impact on one or more industries

Tier II - potential high non-compliance and/or significant compliance to LMSB or an industry

Tier III - industry-related issue

¶518 Exhibit 5-8

Form **5701** (Rev. September 2006)	Department of the Treasury - Internal Revenue Service **Notice of Proposed Adjustment**	
Name of taxpayer		Issue No.
Name and title of person to whom delivered		Date
Entity for this proposed adjustment		

Based on the information we now have available and our discussions with you, we believe the proposed adjustment listed below should be included in the revenue agent's report. However, if you have additional information that would alter or reverse this proposal, please furnish this information as soon as possible.

Years	Amount	Account or return line	SAIN NO.	Issue Code

Reasons for Proposed Adjustment *(If the explanation of the adjustment will be longer than the space provided below, the entire explanation should begin on Form 886-A (Explanation of Items.)*

Taxpayer Representative's action

☐ Agreed   ☐ Agreed in Part   ☐ Disagreed   ☐ Have additional information; will submit by:

If Disagreed in Part or in Full - Check here for consideration of Fast Track Settlement

☐ Taxpayer   ☐ IRS

Team Manager		Date

Part 1 - Taxpayer's File Copy   Cat. No. 42770J   www.irs.gov   Form **5701** (Rev. 09-2006)

¶519 Exhibit 5-9

Form **4564** (Rev. June 1988)	Department of the Treasury — Internal Revenue Service **Information Document Request**	Request Number 15

To: *(Name of Taxpayer and Company Division or Branch)*	Subject Corporate Return 9609	
	SAIN Number	Submitted to: POA
OFFSHORE EXPORTERS LTD.	Dates of Previous Requests	
Please return Part 2 with listed documents to requester identified below.	None	

Description of Documents Requested

1. Please provide a listing of projects worked during the fiscal year under audit.

2. At what point is revenue reported? What makes up the unbilled work-in-process on the balance sheet?

3. What is the average length of a project?

4. Does the corporation have any foreign bank accounts?

5. Please provide the loan documents for the 2.9 million dollar loan dated August 26, 1996.

Information Due By _____2-12-98_____   At Next Appointment ☐   Mail In ☐

From:	Name and Title of Requester Larry Lukenfer	Date 1-15-98
	Office Location Downtown District	Telephone Number 555-1212

Catalog No. 23145K   Part 1 — Taxpayer's File Copy   Form **4564** (Rev. 6-88)

¶520 DISCUSSION QUESTIONS

1. ABC Corporation, a calendar year taxpayer, purchased a business in January 2009. The tax department wants to authoritatively determine the basis for the acquired assets prior to filing its 2009 return. What course of action would you advise? What are the appeal rights for your suggested course of action?

2. During an examination, the IRS proposes an adjustment based upon a revenue ruling which appears to be squarely in point. However, taxpayer contends that the revenue ruling is contrary to established tax law. How can taxpayer expedite resolution of this matter?

3. XYZ Corporation, a large multi-national entity, "managed" the prior IRS examination as follows. The IRS audit team, including a member of IRS Counsel, was housed in a large comfortable room adjoining the accounting department. The Controller, an especially busy person, dealt directly with the various IRS auditors. These interactions were friendly and informal. The modus operandi for handling IRS written requests for records was for the Controller to assign the Revenue Agents to deal directly with the accounting personnel responsible for the applicable records. This worked well for the IRS because it resulted in a prompt receipt of requested information. Furthermore, the Revenue Agents informally obtained additional information and records from the recordkeepers and, thereby, developed many issues well beyond the scope of the original written requests. The company kept no records with respect to information or records turned over to the IRS.

   On the other hand, this "system" did not work well for the taxpayer. At the end of the audit, the IRS raised numerous, often meritorious, issues which generally came as a complete surprise to the Controller. Some of the issues were later resolved at Appeals, but other issues currently await trial in Tax Court.

   XYZ Corporation has been informed that the IRS is commencing a new audit cycle. What advice would you give XYZ Corporation on how to establish procedures for this new IRS audit?

CHAPTER 6
PARTNERSHIP AUDIT PROCEDURES

Partnerships in General

¶601 INTRODUCTION

Under general concepts of tax law, a partnership is not a taxable entity. For this reason, the law prior to 1982 provided that tax adjustments to partnership items were made at the partner level. The Internal Revenue Service (IRS) would audit each partner's return to adjust partnership items, and the adjustment of one partner's return could not be based on the audit of another partner.

The Tax Equity and Fiscal Responsibility Act of 1982[1] (TEFRA) significantly changed this process. Under TEFRA, proceedings for the assessment or refund of a tax arising out of a partner's distributive share of income or loss are now conducted at the partnership level. The Taxpayer Relief Act of 1997 (the 1997 Act) further refined the partnership audit procedure and created a set of procedural rules for an "electing large partnership" (see ¶614) by enacting Code Secs. 6240 through 6255 and amending various other relevant sections.[2]

Any partnership[3] required[4] to file a return is treated as a "partnership" subject to the TEFRA procedural rules. However, an exception exists for "small partnerships" having ten or fewer partners each of whom is an individual, a C corporation, or the estate of a deceased partner.[5] A partner that is a Section 501(a) tax-exempt organization that meets the definition of a C corporation is considered a C corporation.[6] For purposes of the small partnership exception, the statute treats a husband and wife (and their estates) as one partner. Regardless of the size of a partnership, if another partnership, a trust, or a non-C corporation is a partner, the entity will not be classified as a "small partnership."

Although normally exempt, a qualifying "small partnership" may elect to be governed by the TEFRA audit provisions. The election can be made for any taxable year and will become binding as to all subsequent taxable years unless revoked with the consent of the IRS. The election normally would be made if it is more economical to have only one proceeding instead of separate audits of each partner.

---

[1] P.L. 97-248, Title IV, §§ 401-06, 96 Stat. 324.

[2] The Taxpayer Relief Act of 1997, P.L. 105-34, Title XII, §§ 111 Stat. 788 (1997).

[3] Code Sec. 761(a).

[4] Code Sec. 6031(a).

[5] Code Sec. 6231(a)(1)(B).

[6] Rev. Rul. 2003-69, 2003-26 IRB 1118.

Congress originally extended TEFRA partnership treatment to S corporation items as well.[7] However, in 1996, Congress repealed Code Secs. 6241–6245 for tax years beginning after December 31, 1996.[8]

¶602 CONSISTENCY REQUIREMENT

A cornerstone of the TEFRA provisions is the requirement that a partner treat all "partnership item[s]" consistently with the treatment on the partnership return.[9] If the partner chooses to report an item inconsistently with the partnership return, the partner is required to disclose the inconsistency in the filing of his or her return.[10] To facilitate consistent reporting, the Code requires each partnership to furnish a copy of the information contained in the partnership return to each partner.

If a partner fails to report an item consistently with the partnership return, and if the inconsistency results in a deficiency in tax, the IRS can make an immediate assessment of the deficiency (a computational adjustment) without issuing a notice of deficiency to the partner. In addition, this assessment can be made prior to the commencement of a partnership audit proceeding and prior to the issuance of any notice to any other partner. Finally, the underpayment resulting from the inconsistent reporting will be subject to the penalties under Code Secs. 6662–6664 relating to inaccuracy and fraud.

Partnership Audit Procedures

¶603 NOTICE REQUIREMENTS

Partnership items are audited at the partnership level by an examination of the partnership return. This audit is commenced by issuance of a notice of commencement of an administrative proceeding.[11] If the proper notice requirements are met, the audit at the partnership level will apply to all partners. The notice of the commencement of the audit must be mailed to the tax matters partner (TMP) and to each notice partner in the partnership.

¶604 TAX MATTERS PARTNER

The TMP is the general partner who has been designated by the partnership to act as the TMP.[12] This individual will be treated by the IRS as the primary representative of the partnership. If no general partner has been designated by the partnership itself, the Code provides that the general partner having the largest profit interest at the close of the tax year involved will be the TMP.[13] If more than one general partner has the same largest profit percentage at the end of the year involved, then the partner first in alphabetical order will be the TMP. Finally, if no partner can be chosen under these methods, the IRS has the power to choose a TMP. Where the IRS selects the TMP or requires the resignation of a

---

[7] Subchapter S Revision Act of 1982, P.L. 97-354, § 4(a), 96 Stat. 1691.

[8] Small Business Job Protection Act of 1996, P.L. 104-188, Title I, § 1307(c)(1), 110 Stat. 1781.

[9] Code Sec. 6222.

[10] Form 8082, "Notice of Inconsistent Treatment or Administrative Adjustment Request (AAR)."

[11] Code Sec. 6223(a).

[12] Code Sec. 6231(a)(7)(A).

[13] Code Sec. 6231(a)(7)(B).

TMP, it must, within 30 days, notify all partners required to receive notice under Code Sec. 6223(a) of the name and address of the individual selected.[14]

> **Example 6-1:** Tim Palmer is a 5% partner in PMT partnership. He is not designated to be the TMP by the partnership and he does not have the largest profit interest in PMT. The IRS just chose Tim Palmer to be the TMP, and so he is.

There are also circumstances where a partner, having been designated as the TMP for the tax year under audit, will continue to have authority to act as the TMP even after having resigned as a partner in the partnership or where under criminal investigation.

> **Example 6-2:** For example, in *Monetary II Limited Partnership v. Commissioner*[15] the Court of Appeals upheld a Tax Court determination that a former partner's consent to extend the statute of limitations for assessment of tax was valid.

> **Example 6-3:** In another situation involving authority to extend the limitations period, a TMP who was cooperating with the IRS in a criminal tax fraud investigation of the partnership where his cooperation could influence his own sentence and who had signed the partnership returns for the years under audit was held not to have lost his TMP status thereby.[16]

The responsibilities of the TMP include receiving notice of the commencement of a partnership audit and of final partnership administrative adjustments, forwarding that notice to partners who do not receive notice, keeping all partners informed of all administrative and judicial proceedings regarding the partnership, extending the statute of limitations with respect to all partners, and entering into settlements which will bind all partners who are not notice partners. Further, after the IRS proposes final partnership adjustments, the TMP has sole authority to seek judicial review of the audit adjustment during the first 90 days after the notice of final partnership audit adjustment.

Generally, the IRS will deal with the TMP in obtaining the books and records of the partnership and in verifying any items that come up during the audit. The TMP is required to keep all partners informed of administrative and judicial proceedings relating to the adjustment of partnership items. However, the TMP's failure to inform the other partners will not affect the validity of the partnership proceedings as to such partners.

¶605 NOTIFICATION OF PARTNERS

The IRS is required to send notice of the commencement and completion of the partnership audit to each "notice partner."[17] A notice partner is one whose name, address, and profit interest appear on the partnership return or whose identity has been furnished to the IRS at least 30 days prior to the giving of notice to the

---

[14] *Id.*

[15] 47 F.3d 342 (9th Cir. 1995), 95-1 USTC ¶50,073.

[16] *Transpac Drilling Venture v. United States*, 32 Fed. Cl. 810 (1995), 95-1 USTC ¶50,192, *aff'd on other grounds*, 83 F.3d 1410 (1995), 96-1 USTC ¶50,271.

[17] Code Sec. 6223(a).

TMP. If a partnership has more than one hundred partners, the IRS is not required to give notice to any single partner who has less than a one percent interest in the profits of the partnership determined as of the end of the relevant taxable year. However, a group of partners in a partnership of more than one hundred persons may band together and designate one of their members to receive notice provided that the group as an aggregate has a five percent or more interest in the profits.

If the IRS receives notice that an indirect partner has an interest in the profits by ownership of a beneficial interest of a passthrough partner (a partnership, S corporation, or trust), then the IRS will give notice to the indirect partner rather than to the passthrough partner. A passthrough partner is required to forward notices from the IRS to its indirect partners within 30 days of receiving the notice.

> **Example 6-4:** Consider that Partners A, B, C, D and E of a large partnership together hold more than 5 percent of the profits interests in the partnership. They will choose one of them to contact the IRS and be designated a notice partner to receive notice of relevant partnership matters.

¶606 PARTNERS' DEALINGS WITH THE INTERNAL REVENUE SERVICE

All partners, whether or not notice partners, have the right to participate in the partnership proceedings regarding the tax treatment of any partnership item.[18] A partner will be able to attend any meeting with the IRS to discuss the matter; however, the time and place of that meeting is determined by the IRS and the TMP. A partner may waive any right he or she has under the unified audit procedures, including the restrictions on assessment or collection. This waiver is made by filing a signed statement with the IRS.

If during the conduct of the audit any partner enters into a settlement agreement with the IRS, that agreement will be binding on the IRS and on the partners participating in the settlement unless the settlement document otherwise provides or unless there is fraud, malfeasance, or misrepresentation of fact.[19] (See Form 870-P, Agreement to Assessment and Collection of Deficiency in Tax for Partnership Adjustments, Exhibit 6-1 at ¶620.) Nonparticipating partners who make a request will be offered settlement terms that are consistent with such agreement. The offer of consistent settlement terms will not be available, however, unless the initial agreement was entered into before a final partnership audit notice was mailed to the TMP and the request for consistent terms was made within 150 days of such mailing.

An indirect partner will be bound by any settlement entered into by the passthrough partner from which he or she derives his or her interest, unless the indirect ownership has been disclosed to the IRS. If the TMP enters into a settlement, that settlement will be binding on any partner who is not a notice

---

[18] Code Sec. 6224(a).

[19] The IRS Restructuring and Reform Act of 1998 (P.L. 105-206) has incorporated into the partnership audit procedures provisions for raising the innocent spouse defense of Code Sec. 6015(e). These provisions allow an innocent spouse of a partner to be relieved of liability for tax, penalties and interest if certain conditions are met. See Code Sec. 6230(c)(5).

partner (or a member of a five-percent notice group) if the settlement expressly states that it is to be binding on other partners. However, if a partner who is not a notice partner has filed a statement with the IRS that the TMP has no authority to enter into a settlement on his or her behalf, then the settlement is not binding as to that partner.

Upon completion of a TEFRA partnership audit, the revenue agent will provide the TMP with a summary report detailing the proposed adjustments. The TMP will be offered a closing conference to discuss the report. After the closing conference, the agent will prepare a report utilizing the same procedure as in an individual examination.

The report will be reviewed by the local QMS staff and, when approved, will be sent to the TMP along with a 60-day letter explaining the partners' appeal rights. A Form 870-P will also accompany the report. Copies of the 60-day letter and the Form 870-P are sent to all partners at the same time to give them an opportunity to agree with the proposed determination. If the TMP agrees with the IRS determination, he or she can execute the Form 870-P. However, if any partner submits an acceptable written protest, the entire partnership case file will be transferred to the appropriate Appeals Office for the partnership, the settlement reached with the TMP will be temporarily suspended, and the consolidated appeals procedure outlined at ¶607 is then followed. The 60-day letter does not constitute a final partnership administrative adjustment (see ¶608 below) and does not confer jurisdiction on the Tax Court to resolve the matter.[20]

> **Example 6-5:** If small partner disagrees with the final examination results and files adequate written protest to appeals, the entire case will be transferred to appeals, the settlement reached between the IRS and the TMP is temporarily superseded and the special consolidated appeals procedures control the case.

¶607 PARTNERSHIP APPEAL PROCEDURES

Appeals Office procedures exist for partnerships in TEFRA proceedings. Under the Appeals Office procedures, if any partner requests an Appeals conference regarding the proposed partnership adjustments, Appeals will hold a consolidated conference in the Appeals Office servicing the area where the partnership has its principal place of business. All partners have the right to attend this conference, but any partner planning to attend must notify the TMP of his or her plan to be present.[21]

Prior to the conference the TMP must furnish the names of the partners or representatives who will be attending and must submit valid power of attorney forms for those partners who send representatives. Appeals then schedules the conference and communicates the time, date, and location to the TMP who must furnish the information to all other persons planning to attend.

---

[20] See *Clovis I v. Comm'r*, 88 TC 980 (1987), CCH Dec. 43,856.

[21] IRM 8.19.3.5.

If the Appeals proceedings result in a change in the original settlement proposal, a revised Form 870-P is given to the TMP, who must send a copy to all partners who did not assent to the original report. The TMP is responsible for advising all nonassenting partners of any settlement terms. If a partner executes the revised Form 870-P, he or she is bound by that settlement. The form will be forwarded to the appropriate Campus, which will release that partner's return from the suspense unit for assessment of any resulting deficiency.

If the TMP executes the revised Form 870-P, that settlement will be binding on all non-notice partners, unless the non-notice partner has filed a statement with the IRS denying the TMP authority to bind him or her.

If any partner does not agree to the settlement, Appeals is responsible for preparation of the final partnership administrative adjustment (FPAA). This commences the 90-day period in which the TMP can file a suit regarding the FPAA.

¶608 FINAL PARTNERSHIP ADMINISTRATIVE ADJUSTMENT

No deficiency in tax attributable to partnership items may be assessed until 150 days after the mailing of the final partnership administrative adjustment (FPAA) to the TMP.[22] The FPAA may not be mailed to the TMP until 120 days after the notice of commencement of the partnership audit. The FPAA is similar to a statutory notice of deficiency, and the mailing of the FPAA tolls the statute of limitations on assessment of partnership items. The IRS must also send notice of the FPAA to each notice partner within 60 days of sending it to the TMP. Finally, the IRS may issue only one FPAA per partnership per taxable year.

¶609 JUDICIAL REVIEW OF FPAA

Within 90 days of the mailing of the FPAA, the TMP may file a petition for readjustment of the partnership items with the United States Tax Court, the United States District Court for the district in which the partnership's principal place of business is located, or the United States Court of Federal Claims. During this period, no other partner may file a petition for judicial review.[23]

If the TMP does not file a readjustment petition within ninety days, any notice partner or any five-percent group may file a petition in the Tax Court, the District Court, or the Court of Federal Claims within the next sixty days. However, if a notice partner or five-percent group files prematurely within the ninety-day period allowed for the TMP, and no action is otherwise brought within the sixty-day period which is not dismissed, the prematurely-filed petition will be treated as filed on the last day of the sixty-day period.[24] If more than one partner files a petition for readjustment, then the first petition filed in the Tax Court obtains priority. If no Tax Court action is brought, the first action in either

---

[22] Mailing to the TMP at the address of the partnership is sufficient. Treas. Reg. § 301.6223(a)-1. To be valid, an FPAA need not be mailed to a specifically named TMP. See *Seneca, Ltd. v. Comm'r*, 92 TC 363, 366-68 (1989), CCH Dec. 45,492; *Chomp Assocs.*

v. Comm'r, 91 TC 1069, 1072-74 (1988), CCH Dec. 45,217.

[23] Code Secs. 6226(a).

[24] *Id.* Code Sec. 6226(b)(1).

the Court of Federal Claims or the District Court is given priority and all other actions are dismissed. The TMP may intervene in any such proceedings.[25]

To file a petition in either the District Court or the Court of Federal Claims, the TMP must deposit with the IRS an amount equal to the deficiency in tax that would result if the FPAA were upheld.[26] The court that acquires jurisdiction of the FPAA has authority to determine all partnership items of the partnership taxable year to which the FPAA relates. If a partner has already been involved in a judicial determination of tax liability resulting from nonpartnership items, an adjustment of the partner's liability for partnership items still may be made following resolution of the FPAA.

> **Example 6-6:** Terry TMP received the Final Partnership Administrative Adjustment (FPAA) on June 18, 2010, for the 2008 taxable year. Unfortunately all of the other partners assumed that Terry would file the petition for judicial reviews, but Terry got caught up with the canoe he was building and missed the September 17, 2010 deadline. He did file a petition on November 7, 2010. The IRS was successful in its motion to dismiss for lack of jurisdiction because the petition was late.

¶610 PARTNERSHIP ITEMS

The partnership audit provisions apply only to partnership items. The term "partnership item" includes any item to the extent that regulations provide that such item is more appropriately determined at the partnership level than at the partner level.[27] The regulations include as partnership items virtually all income, expenditures, credits, assets, liabilities, investments, transactions, accounting practices and other items which relate to the operation of the partnership and which may affect the individual partners' tax liabilities.[28]

A partnership item may become a nonpartnership item under the following circumstances:

1. The IRS fails to give notice of the commencement of a partnership audit;

2. The IRS mails to a partner a notice that an item is to be treated as a nonpartnership item;

3. The IRS enters into a settlement agreement with a partner regarding such item;

4. A partner files suit regarding the failure of the IRS to allow an administrative adjustment request with respect to any such item;

5. When a partner treats an item inconsistently with the partnership return and notifies the IRS of the inconsistency, then the IRS has the discretion to treat that item as a nonpartnership item;

6. If a partner has filed a request for administrative adjustment which would result in the item's being treated inconsistently with the treatment

---

[25] Code Sec. 6226(b)(6).
[26] *Id.* Code Sec. 6226(e)(1).

[27] *Id.* Code Sec. 6231(a)(3).
[28] Reg. § 301.6231(a)(3)-1.

on the partnership return, the IRS has discretion to treat that item as a nonpartnership item; and

7. If a husband and wife hold partnership interests as community property, partnership items of the husband will be treated as nonpartnership items where the husband is named as a debtor in a bankruptcy proceeding.[29]

If a partnership item becomes a nonpartnership item, the normal deficiency procedures may be used with respect to that item.

¶611 REQUEST FOR ADMINISTRATIVE ADJUSTMENT

Within three years of the time the partnership return was filed, any partner may file a request for administrative adjustment (RAA) for any partnership item for that year.[30] This request must be filed before the mailing of a notice of FPAA to the TMP for that taxable year. However, where the limitations period has been extended under a settlement agreement made pursuant to Code Sec. 6229(b), the time for filing the RAA will equal the extension of time under the agreement, plus six months. The time for filing an RAA relating to deductions for bad debts and worthless securities is seven years and before the mailing of the FPAA for the taxable year.[31] The RAA is analogous to an amended return or a claim for refund.

If the RAA is filed by the TMP and the TMP requests that the IRS treat it as a substitute return, then the IRS may assess any additional tax on the basis of the changes in the RAA without issuance of a notice of deficiency to any partner. The changes are treated as a correction of a clerical or mathematical error for which no notice of deficiency is required. If the TMP does not designate the RAA as a substitute return, the IRS may either allow the changes requested, commence a partnership audit proceeding or take no action on the request. If the IRS does not allow the RAA in full, the TMP may file a petition for readjustment of the disallowed items with the Tax Court, the District Court or the Court of Federal Claims. The petition may not be filed until six months after the date the RAA was filed and must be filed before two years after the date the RAA was filed. No petition may be filed if the IRS has notified the TMP that it is conducting a partnership proceeding.

If the petition for review of the RAA has been filed and a timely notice of FPAA is mailed, the proceeding will be treated as a proceeding with respect to the FPAA. However, a deposit will not be required to establish jurisdiction in the appropriate District Court or Court of Federal Claims. Judicial review of an RAA filed by the TMP is limited to those items which the IRS disallows or asserts as an offset to the requested adjustments.

Parties to an action for review of the RAA are the same parties eligible as parties for review of an FPAA. Thus, all partners who were partners at any time during the tax year in question may be parties to the action.

---

[29] See *Dubin v. Comm'r*, 99 TC 325 (1992), CCH Dec. 48,500; Acq. In Result, IRB 1999-40.

[30] Code Sec. 6227(a).
[31] Code Sec. 6227(e).

If the RAA is filed by a partner other than the TMP, the IRS has four options: (1) it may treat the request as though it were a claim for refund based on nonpartnership items, (2) it may assess any additional tax resulting from the adjustments, (3) it may notify the partner that all partnership items of that partner for that year are being converted to nonpartnership items, or (4) it may commence a partnership audit proceeding. A partner who is notified that the partnership items are being treated as nonpartnership items may file a claim for refund attributable to those items within two years of receiving the notice from the IRS. If any portion of the request for administrative adjustment is not allowed, suit may be commenced after the expiration of six months from the date of filing the RAA and must be brought within two years of such filing date. Unlike a suit on an RAA filed by a TMP, a suit filed by an individual partner will not bind other partners.

> **Example 6-7:** The RAA is similar to an amended return or a claim for refund. Susie small partner files an RAA seeking a refund in fuel. The IRS responds that it is treating the RAA as a claim for refund based on nonpartnership items. The IRS disallowed the claim. In response, Susie files a suit for refund well within the two year time limit.

¶612 STATUTE OF LIMITATIONS ON ASSESSMENTS

The general period for assessment against any person with respect to partnership items for any partnership taxable year is three years from the date of the filing of the partnership return or, if later, the last date prescribed for filing such return determined without extension.[32] An individual partner may enter into an agreement with the Secretary to extend the assessment period for that partner. Additionally, the filing of a Title 11 bankruptcy petition naming the partner as a debtor will toll the running of the limitations period for the time during which the Secretary is prohibited from making an assessment because of the bankruptcy proceeding, plus sixty days.[33]

For partnership items that become nonpartnership items for an individual partner as the result of a settlement agreement covering those items, the period for assessing tax is one year after the date the partnership items convert to nonpartnership items. However, where a settlement agreement relates only to some, but not all, of the disputed partnership items, the period for assessing tax attributable to the settled items is determined as though the settlement agreement had not been entered into.[34] The practical effect is that the limitations period applicable to the last item resolved by settlement will control with respect to the remaining disputed partnership items.[35]

The assessment period will be suspended where the TMP files a petition for readjustment of partnership items following receipt of the FPAA.[36] Under TEFRA, only the filing of a *timely* petition tolls the running of the statute of limitations.

---

[32] Code Sec. 6229(a).
[33] Code Sec. 6229(h).
[34] Code Sec. 6229(f).

[35] See H.R. Rep. No. 105-34. (Found at 143 Cong. Rec. H6470, H6586 [daily ed. July 30, 1997].)
[36] Code Sec. 6229(d).

The TMP, or any other person authorized in writing by the partnership, has authority to extend the assessment period for all partners.[37] If the TMP is a debtor in bankruptcy at the time the agreement is signed, the agreement will bind all partners unless the Secretary has been notified pursuant to Treasury Regulations of the bankruptcy proceeding.[38]

An extension agreement must be entered into before the expiration of the statute. Form 872-P (see Exhibit 10-5 at ¶ 1035) is used to extend the statute to a specific date. As an alternative, the partnership can use Form 872-O (see Exhibit 10-6 at ¶ 1036) which extends the statute until ninety days after the extension is terminated by submitting Form 872-N (see Exhibit 10-7 at ¶ 1037).

Assessments may be made at any time against partners who sign or actively participate in the preparation of a fraudulent return with the intent to evade tax. The period is also extended from three years to six years with respect to all other partners in the case of a false partnership return.[39] Similarly, if the partnership omits an amount from gross income which exceeds twenty-five percent of reported gross income, the assessment period is extended to six years.[40] When no partnership return has been filed, assessment may be made at any time.

If a partner is not properly identified on the partnership return and the IRS timely mails a notice of the FPAA to the TMP, the period for assessment does not expire until one year after the name, address and taxpayer identification number of the partner are mailed to the IRS.[41] The IRS has ruled that partners may be assessed based upon a TEFRA proceeding in year 2 even though the period for assessing tax has expired for year 1, where the losses that are subject of the assessment in year 2 arose in year 1.[42]

> **Example 6-8:** Tom TMP filed the partnership return, early, on February 15, 2010, even though it was not due until June 15, 2010 (not counting extensions to file). The IRS issued the FPAA on June 14, 2013. The IRS action was timely.

¶613 ERRONEOUS INTERNAL REVENUE SERVICE COMPUTATIONAL ADJUSTMENTS

Once the proper treatment of partnership items has been determined at the partnership level, the IRS must then convert these items into tax adjustments for each of the individual partners.[43] When the IRS errs in making these "computational adjustments" to reflect the proper treatment of the partnership items on the individual returns of the partners, special rules permit a partner to file a claim for refund of the tax attributable to such error.[44] If the IRS mails a notice of

---

[37] Code Sec. 6229(b); *see generally* Ronald A. Stein, *Statutes of Limitation: Who May Extend Them for TEFRA Partners?*, TAXES, Sept. 1994, 560.

[38] Code Sec. 6229(b).

[39] Code Sec. 6229(c)(1).

[40] Code Sec. 6229(c)(2); See Chapter 9, Statute of Limitations on Assessment, *infra*.

[41] Code Sec. 6229(e).

[42] CCA 200414045.

[43] Where there is a delay in making a computational adjustment following a settlement under Code Sec. 6224(c) in which partnership items are converted to nonpartnership items pursuant to Code Sec. 6231(b)(1)(C), interest on any deficiency will be suspended in those circumstances provided in Code Sec. 6601(c).

[44] Code Sec. 6230(c).

the computational adjustment to a partner, a claim for refund due to an error in the computation must be filed within six months after the notice was mailed. On the other hand, if the IRS does not make a computational adjustment and thereby fails to allow a proper refund or credit, a partner must file a claim for refund within two years after: (1) the date the settlement was entered into, (2) the date on which the period expired to file a petition in response to the FPAA, or (3) the date on which the decision of the court became final. If the claim is disallowed by the IRS, the partner may file a suit for refund within two years after the notice of disallowance is mailed out.

¶614 ELECTING LARGE PARTNERSHIPS

A partnership with more than 100 partners during the preceding tax year, not counting "service partners,"[45] may elect to be governed by simplified procedural rules, unless the partnership's principal business is either dealing in commodities or the performance of services, with all partners performing such services on behalf of the partnership.[46]

Adjustments to the income or deductions of an electing large partnership will ordinarily affect only the persons who are partners in the year that the adjustment becomes final, rather than the persons who were partners when the adjusted item actually arose.[47] An electing large partnership may either pass through the adjustment to the partners in the year the adjustment becomes final, in which case the partners report the adjustment on their personal income tax returns like any other operating or capital item of the partnership,[48] or it may pay directly the deficiency, interest and penalties associated with the adjustment,[49] so that the partners do not report any of the adjustment on their personal returns. If the partnership chooses to pay the deficiency, the deficiency will be based on the highest personal or corporate income tax rate in effect in the year the adjustment becomes final. Only one type of adjustment must flow through to the persons who were partners in the year to which the adjustment relates; that is, an adjustment to the partners' respective distributive shares, must be picked up by the partners whose distributive shares are adjusted and must be reflected in the partners' personal income tax returns for the year to which the adjustment relates.[50]

Although most of the procedural rules and deadlines discussed above also apply to an electing large partnership, the differences are nonetheless significant and generally enhance the ability of the partnership and the IRS to dispose of partnership item disputes more simply, at the cost of eliminating the individual partners' ability to influence the outcome of the dispute either at the partnership level or with regard to the partner's personal income tax return. Thus, a partner in an electing large partnership *must* report all partnership items consistently with the partnership's reporting.[51] Disclosure will not relieve the partner of

---

[45] Code Sec. 775(b)(1).
[46] Code Secs. 775 and 6240.
[47] Code Sec. 6241(c)(1).
[48] Code Sec. 6242(a).
[49] Code Sec. 6242(b).
[50] Code Secs. 704 and 6241(c)(2).
[51] Code Sec. 6241(a) and (b).

penalties and the IRS can unilaterally and unappealably assess additional taxes and negligence and fraud penalties against a partner who takes inconsistent positions. Furthermore, the IRS is not required to notify partners of the beginning of a partnership audit or inform them of the terms of proposed adjustments to partnership items.[52] The IRS can select a representative for the partnership, without regard to the representative's relative partnership interest and, unless the partnership designates a different person to represent it, the IRS's representative can bind the partnership and all of its current and past partners.[53] In addition, only the partnership can file for judicial review of a proposed IRS adjustment or for a request for administrative adjustment.[54] If the partnership fails to do so, none of the individual partners have the right to seek judicial review or request an administrative adjustment.

Lastly, an electing large partnership *must* provide its partners with the Form 1065, Schedule K-1, Beneficiary's Share of Income, Deductions, Credits, etc., information returns on or before March 15th following the close of the partnership's taxable year, regardless of whether the partnership itself will file its own information return on that date.[55]

¶615 DECLARATORY JUDGMENT PROCEEDINGS

A taxpayer whose "oversheltered return" has been audited can obtain judicial review of the proposed adjustment even if the proposed adjustment does not produce a tax deficiency. An "oversheltered return" is a return that (1) contains both partnership and nonpartnership items, (2) shows no taxable income for the year, and (3) shows a net loss from partnership items that are subject to the partnership audit rules described above.[56] If the IRS audits such a return and adjusts the nonpartnership items, and the adjustments, if correct, would lead to a deficiency in taxes in the absence of the partnership net losses, the taxpayer can seek a declaratory judgment in Tax Court to determine the correctness of the proposed nonpartnership item adjustments.[57]

If the IRS follows this audit procedure, it must issue a notice of adjustment, rather than the notice of deficiency of the conventional audit. If the taxpayer timely petitions the Tax Court with respect to the notice of adjustment, the IRS cannot issue either a second notice of adjustment or a notice of deficiency (except to the extent of a later adjustment of the taxpayer's partnership items) with respect to that tax year absent fraud, malfeasance or misrepresentation of a material fact.[58]

The procedural rules for Tax Court review are the same as those governing review of a notice of deficiency. Once the taxpayer is in Tax Court for review of a notice of adjustment, the Tax Court may exercise its authority to address all items on the taxpayer's return, except for partnership items. Ordinarily, no tax will become due merely because the notice of adjustment is upheld, because the

---

[52] Code Sec. 6245(b).
[53] Code Sec. 6255(b).
[54] Code Sec. 6247(a).
[55] Code Sec. 6031(b).

[56] Code Sec. 6234(b).
[57] Code Sec. 6234(a) and (c).
[58] Code Sec. 6234(f).

taxpayer still will be in a net loss position owing to the net loss on his or her partnership items. If the partnership items are later finally adjusted to change the taxpayer's position from a net loss to net taxable income, however, the taxpayer will be assessed for additional tax reflecting both the nonpartnership items in the notice of adjustment and the subsequent partnership item adjustments.[59]

An oversheltered taxpayer has a second chance to contest items in the notice of adjustment if the taxpayer failed to seek a declaratory judgment review in the Tax Court. If and when the taxpayer's partnership items are finally determined, leading to an underpayment of tax reflecting both the partnership items and the nonpartnership items in the notice of adjustment, the taxpayer may file for a refund claim with the IRS, based on the nonpartnership items in the notice of adjustment, and is entitled to the full panoply of judicial review if the IRS denies the claim.[60]

Reportable Transaction Audit Techniques

¶616 TAX SHELTER AND REPORTABLE TRANSACTION REQUIREMENTS

The American Job Creations Act of 2004 mandated that all "material advisors" with respect to reportable transactions, including listed transactions, file an information return. That form is form 8918, Material Advisor Disclosure Statement. A "material advisor" is any person who (1) provides any material aid, assistance, or advice with respect to organizing, managing, promoting, selling, implementing, insuring, or carrying out any reportable transaction, and (2) who directly or indirectly derives gross income in excess of the threshold amount.[61] The threshold amount is $50,000 in the case of a reportable transaction where substantially all of the tax benefits are provided to natural persons and $250,000 in all other cases.

The penalty for failure to file Form 8918 is $50,000 unless the transaction is a listed transaction, in which case the amount of the penalty would be the greater of $200,000 or 50% of the gross income derived by such person. If the failure to act was intentional, the penalty would by 75%, not 50%.[62]

¶617 REPORTABLE TRANSACTION DISCLOSURE REQUIREMENTS

A second element in the IRS's attack on abusive tax shelters is the requirement of taxpayer disclosure. In the past, the IRS had used an "after the fact" approach to identify tax shelters. With publication of final regulations in 2003,[63] a person who participated in any reportable transaction must disclose such participation by attaching a disclosure statement (Form 8886) (See Exhibit 6-3 at ¶622) to the tax return filed for the year in which such participation occurred. The regulations apply generally to tax returns filed after February 28, 2003, and other reporting requirements are imposed on earlier-filed returns.

---

[59] Code Sec. 6234(g).
[60] Code Sec. 6234(d)(2).
[61] Code Sec. 6111(b)(1)(A).

[62] Code Sec. 6707.
[63] See Reg. § 1.6011-4(a).

The term "transaction" is very broad, and includes all of the factual elements "relevant to the expected tax treatment of any investment, entity, plan or arrangement," and also "includes any series of steps carried out as part of a plan."[64]

Reportable Transaction. There are seven categories of reportable transactions:

1. Listed Transaction;
2. Confidential Transactions;
3. Transactions with contractual protection;
4. Loss Transactions;
5. Transactions with a significant book-tax difference;[65]
6. Transactions involving a brief asset holding period;[66] and
7. Transactions of interest.[67]

Treasury and the IRS issued final reportable transaction regulations under section 6011 on July 31, 2007, which are generally effective for transactions entered into on or after August 3, 2007.[68] Otherwise, the rules that apply with respect to transactions entered into before August 3, 2007, are contained in the section 6011 regulations in effect prior to August 3, 2007.[69]

The IRS and Treasury recently issued proposed regulations identifying "patented transactions" as an additional reportable transaction category.[70] The proposed regulations advise that the final patented transaction disclosure requirement will apply to transactions entered into on or after September 26, 2007.[71]

Listed Transactions. A "listed transaction" is the same as, or is substantially similar to, one of the types of transactions the IRS has determined to be a tax avoidance transaction and is identified by the IRS in published guidance as a listed transaction.[72] The regulations define the term "substantially similar" to

---

[64] Treas. Reg. section 1.6011-4.

[65] Notice 2006-6, 2006-5 I.R.B. 385 removed the significant book-tax difference category and was effective on January 6, 2006.

[66] This reportable transaction category has been eliminated for transactions entered into on or after August 3, 2007. See T.D. 9350 (July 31, 2007).

[67] See Reg. § 1.6011-4(b)(6).

[68] However, the rules with respect to transactions of interest are effective for transactions entered into on or after November 2, 2006. See Reg. § 1.6011-4(h)(1).

[69] See Reg. § 1.6011-4(h)(1).

[70] See 72 Fed. Reg. 54615 (September 26, 2007). A patented transaction is a transaction for which a taxpayer pays a fee to a patent holder or the patent holder's agent for the legal right to use a tax planning method that the taxpayer knows or has reason to know is the subject of a patent. A patented transaction also includes any transaction in which a tax-

payer (i.e. the patent holder or patent holder's agent) has the right to payment for another person's use of a tax planning method that is subject to a patent. Prop. Reg. § 1.6011-4(b)(7)(i). A "taxpayer" participates in a patented transaction if (1) the taxpayer's return reflects a tax benefit from the transaction, or (2) the taxpayer is the patent holder (or agent) and the taxpayer's return reflects a tax benefit in relation to obtaining a patent for a tax planning method or reflects income from a payment received from another person for use of the tax planning method that is subject to the patent. Prop. Reg. § 1.6011-4(c)(3)(i)(F). In addition to the issuance of proposed regulations regarding patented transactions by the Treasury and IRS, the United States House of Representatives recently passed legislation banning tax strategy patents. H.R. 1908 (September 7, 2007). The ban would apply to patent applications filed on or after the bill is enacted.

[71] See Prop. Reg. § 1.6011-4(h)(2).

[72] See Reg. § 1.6011-4(b)(2).

include "any transaction that is expected to obtain the same or similar types of tax consequences and that is either factually similar or based on the same or similar tax strategy."[73] The term must be broadly construed in favor of disclosure.[74] According to the regulations, a taxpayer has "participated" in a listed transaction if (1) the taxpayer's return reflects tax consequences of a tax strategy described in published guidance identifying the transaction as a listed transaction, or (2) the taxpayer knows or has reason to know that the tax benefits are derived directly or indirectly from the tax consequences or a tax strategy included in such guidance.[75]

The IRS has published a comprehensive list of each listed transaction in Notice 2009-59.[76]

> **Example 6-9:** Lo Tax, someone who is always looking for a good deduction, invests in a transaction designed to boast the basis in an asset so that the gain in the other asset to be sold can be shuttered. If the scheme were to work then no tax would be paid on the gain. The IRS announced that the basis booster is a "Limited Transaction." Therefore, Lo Tax must disclose his participation on Form 8886, Reportable Transaction Disclosure Statement.

Confidential Transactions. A confidential transaction is a transaction offered by a tax advisor for a minimum fee that limit's a taxpayer's ability to disclose the tax treatment or tax structure of the transaction protecting the confidentiality of the tax strategy.[77] The minimum fee is $250,000 for a transaction in which the taxpayer is a corporation (or partnership or trust and all of the owners or beneficiaries of which are corporations (looking through any partners or beneficiaries that are themselves partnerships or trusts)) and $50,000 for all other transactions.[78] The minimum fee determination captures consideration paid in any form (e.g., cash, in-kind services) related to any component of the confidential transaction (e.g., implementation, documentation).[79] According to the regulations, a taxpayer has "participated" in a confidential transaction when the tax return reflects a tax benefit from the transaction, and the taxpayer's ability to disclose the tax treatment or tax structure is limited (as described above).[80]

Transactions with Contractual Protection. A transaction with contractual protection is a transaction in which the taxpayer (or a related party) has the right to a full or partial refund of fees if all (or a portion of) the intended tax consequences from the transaction are not sustained.[81] A transaction with contractual protection also includes a transaction in which the fees are contingent on a taxpayer's realization of tax benefit from the transaction.[82] In determining whether a fee is refundable or contingent, all the facts and circumstances relating to the transaction are considered.[83] Fees include those fees paid by or on behalf of

---

[73] See Reg. § 1.6011-4(c)(4).

[74] See Reg. § 1.6011-4(c)(4).

[75] See Reg. § 1.6011-4(c)(3)(i)(A).

[76] See 2009-59 I.R.B. 1.

[77] See Reg. § 1.6011-4(b)(3)(i) and (ii).

[78] See Reg. § 1.6011-4(b)(3)(iii)(A) and (B).

[79] See Reg. § 1.6011-4(b)(3)(iv).

[80] See Reg. § 1.6011-4(c)(3)(i)(B).

[81] See Reg. § 1.6011-4(b)(4)(i).

[82] See Reg. § 1.6011-4(b)(4)(i).

[83] See Reg. § 1.6011-4(b)(4)(i).

the taxpayer to any person who makes or provides an oral or written statement to the taxpayer with respect to the potential tax consequences that may result from the transaction.[84] According to the regulations, a taxpayer has "participated" in a transaction with contractual protection if the taxpayer's tax return reflects a tax benefit from the transaction, and the taxpayer has the right to a partial or full refund of the fees (or the fees are contingent).[85]

A transaction is not considered to have contractual protection solely because a party to the transaction has the right to terminate the transaction upon the happening of an event affecting the taxation of one or more parties to the transaction.[86] In addition, if (1) a person makes or provides a statement to a taxpayer as to the potential tax consequences that may result from a transaction only after the taxpayer has entered into the transaction and reported the consequences of the transaction on a filed tax return, and (2) the person has not previously received fees from the taxpayer relating to the transaction, then any refundable or contingent fees are not taken into account in determining whether the transaction has contractual protection.[87] In Rev. Proc. 2007-20,[88] the IRS identified certain transactions with contractual protection that are not reportable for purposes of Treas. Reg. § 1.6011-4(b)(4).

Loss Transactions. A loss transaction results in the taxpayer claiming a section 165 loss of at least (1) $10 million in any single taxable year or $20 million in any combination of taxable years for corporations (or partnerships that have only corporations as partners, looking through any partners that are themselves partnerships, whether or not any losses flow through one or more partners), (2) $2 million in any single taxable year or $4 million in any combination of taxable years for all other partnerships, individuals, S Corporations or trusts (whether or not any losses flow through to one or more partners, one or more shareholders, or one or more beneficiaries), or (3) $50,000 for any single taxable year for individuals or trusts (whether or not the loss flows through from an S corporation or partnership) if the loss arises with respect to a section 988 transaction.[89] When evaluating the monetary threshold for a combination of taxable years, the losses claimed in the taxable year of the transaction and five succeeding taxable years are considered.[90] According to the regulations, a taxpayer has "participated" in a loss transaction if the taxpayer's tax return reflects a section 165 loss, and the amount of the loss equals or exceeds the (applicable) threshold amount (discussed above).[91] In addition, in Rev. Proc. 2004-66,[92] the IRS identified certain losses that are not to be taken into account in determining whether a transaction is a loss transaction under the reportable transaction rules.

> **Example 6-10:** Buffie is a member of an investment club that invests in foreign currencies. The club experienced a bad year this past year. Buffie lost

---

[84] See Reg. § 1.6011-4(b)(4)(ii).
[85] See Reg. § 1.6011-4(c)(3)(i)(C).
[86] See Reg. § 1.6011-4(b)(4)(iii)(A).
[87] See Reg. § 1.6011-4(b)(4)(iii)(B).
[88] 2007-7 I.R.B. 517, *modifying and superseding* Rev. Proc. 2004-65, 2004-59 I.R.B. 965.

[89] See Reg. § 1.6011-4(b)(5)(i).
[90] See Reg. § 1.6011-4(b)(5)(ii).
[91] See Reg. § 1.6011-4(c)(3)(i)(D).
[92] See 2004-50 I.R.B. 966.

$51,000 in one year on foreign currency transactions. Buffie has entered a reportable transaction and must disclose her loss on Form 8886, Reportable Transaction Disclosure Statement.

Transactions Involving a Brief Asset Holding Period. A transaction involving a brief asset holding period is any transaction that results in the taxpayer claiming a tax credit, including a foreign tax credit, exceeding $250,000 if the underlying asset giving rise to the credit is held for 45 days or less.[93]

Transaction of Interest. A transaction of interest is a transaction that is that same as or substantially similar to one of the types of transactions that the IRS has identified by notice, regulation, or other form of published guidance as a "transaction of interest."[94] According to the regulations, a taxpayer has "participated" in a transaction of interest if the taxpayer is one of the types or classes of persons identified as participants in the published guidance describing the transaction of interest.[95] The final reportable transaction regulations (issued in July 2007) apply to any transaction of interest entered into on or after November 2, 2006.[96]

Reportable Transaction Disclosure Obligations. If a taxpayer participates in a reportable transaction, the taxpayer generally must file Form 8886 ("Reportable Transaction Disclosure Statement") by attaching it to the tax returns of the taxpayer for each taxable year for which a taxpayer participates in the reportable transaction.[97] In certain circumstances, however, a disclosure statement also must be filed with the Office of Tax Shelter Analysis ("OTSA") within 90 calendar days after the date on which the transaction becomes a listed transaction or transaction of interest (regardless of whether the taxpayer participated in the transaction in the year the transaction became a listed transaction or a transaction of interest).[98] The special 90-day filing rule applies where a transaction becomes a listed transaction or a transaction of interest after the filing of the taxpayer's return (including an amended return) that reflects a taxpayer's participation in the listed transaction or transaction of interest and before the end of the period of limitations for assessment of tax for any taxable year (in which the taxpayer participated in the listed transaction or transaction of interest). The taxpayer must also separately file a copy of the disclosure statement with OTSA at the same time that any disclosure statement is first filed by the taxpayer.[99]

---

[93] See Reg. § 1.6011-4(b)(7). See Rev. Proc. 2004-68, 2004-50 I.R.B. 968, which exempts certain brief asset holding period transactions from the disclosure requirement.

[94] See Reg. § 1.6011-4(b)(6). To date, the Service has identified four transactions of interest. See Notice 2009-55, 2009-31 I.R.B. 1. See also Notice 2007-72, 2007-36 I.R.B. 544 (contribution of a successor membership interest to charity); Notice 2007-73, 2007-36 I.R.B. 545 (toggling grantor trust); Notice 2008-99, 2008-47 I.R.B. 1194 (dealing with certain sales through charitable remainder trust interests); and Notice 2009-7, 2009-3 I.R.B. 312 (subpart F income partnership blocker).

[95] See Reg. § 1.6011-4(c)(3)(i)(E).

[96] See Reg. § 1.6011-4(h)(1).

[97] See Reg. § 1.6011-4(d) and (e)(1).

[98] See Reg. § 1.6011-4(e)(2)(i); for taxpayer disclosure obligations regarding transactions entered into after December 28, 2003, and before August 3, 2007, see T.D. 9046, 2-28-03, and amended by T.D. 9108, 12-29-03, and T.D. 9295, 11-01-06.

[99] See Reg. § 1.6011-4(d) and (e). The disclosure statement must also be attached to each amended return that reflects a taxpayer's participation in a reportable transaction, and if a reportable transaction results in a loss that is carried back to a prior year, the disclosure statement must be attached to the taxpayer's application for tentative refund or amended tax return for that prior year. Id. The final

Section 6707A–Penalty for Failure to Disclose a Reportable Transaction. There is a penalty[100] on any person who fails to disclose a reportable transaction as required.[101] The penalty amount for the failure to disclose a reportable transaction (other than a listed transaction) is $10,000 for a natural person and $50,000 in all other cases.[102] The penalty amount for failing to disclose a listed transaction is $100,000 for a natural person and $200,000 in any other case.[103] Section 6707A does not incorporate a reasonable cause exception. The IRS Commissioner, however, may rescind all or a portion of a penalty imposed under section 6707A if (1) the violation does not involve a listed transaction, and (2) the restriction of the penalty promotes compliance with the tax law and effective tax administration.[104]

A taxpayer that is an SEC registrant must disclose the payment of certain tax shelter penalties (under section 6662(h), section 6662A or section 6707A) on reports filed with the SEC.[105] Rev. Proc. 2005-51,[106] which is amplified by Rev. Proc. 2007-25,[107] provides guidance on the method of disclosure and related disclosure issues.

¶618 TAX SHELTER LIST MAINTENANCE REQUIREMENTS

In addition to the disclosure requirements placed on taxpayers, the IRS also finalized regulations in February 2003 that subject all tax professionals to "list maintenance" requirements. These regulations require that each material advisor with respect to any reportable transaction maintain a list of the persons involved with such transaction. A separate list must be maintained that identifies all substantially similar transactions.

The regulations define "reportable transactions" as any transaction that is (a) listed among one of the seven categories of reportable transactions listed under § 1.6011-4 of the regulations.

Any person who makes any statement, oral or written, as to the potential tax consequences of that transaction before the tax return reflecting the tax benefit is filed and receives or expects to receive a minimum fee[108] with respect to that transaction is a "material advisor." However, a person who makes a tax state-

---

(Footnote Continued)

Reg. § 1.6011-4 regulations, effective August 3, 2007, state in the preamble: "The IRS and Treasury Department have decided that investors are no longer required to file Forms 8271 otherwise due on or after August 3, 2007. The Form 8271 will be obsoleted. Taxpayers required to file Form 8886 . . . pursuant to § 1.6011-4(d) and Form 8271 with respect to the same transaction only need to report the registration number on Form 8886".

[100] See § 6707A.

[101] See § 6707A(a).

[102] See § 6707A(b)(1).

[103] See § 6707A(b)(2).

[104] See § 6707A(d). In September 2008, the Service issued proposed and temporary regulations under section 6707A (73 F.R. 52784-52788, T.D. 9425), which provide guidance on the IRS Commissioner's authority to rescind a penalty under section 6707A. See also Rev. Proc. 2007-21, 2007-9 I.R.B. 613 (provides guidance for persons seeking rescission of penalty under § 6707A (or § 6707)).

[105] See § 6707A(e).

[106] See 2005-33 I.R.B. 296.

[107] See 2007-12 I.R.B. 761.

[108] Generally the minimum fee is $250,000 for a transaction in which all participants are C corporations, and $50,000 for any other type of person or entity, See. Reg. 301.6111-3(b).

ment solely in the person's capacity as an employee, shareholder, partner or agent is not considered a material advisor.

For each transaction, the "list" must contain certain information, including the name and address of each person required to be on the list,[109] and must be retained for a period of seven years. Upon request by the IRS, the list must be furnished to the IRS. Formerly, the penalty for failure to comply with the list maintenance rules was $50 for each person not properly included on a list, with a maximum penalty of $100,000 per advisor per calendar year.[110] Failure to provide the list to the IRS within 20 business days after requested by the IRS is now subject to a $10,000 per day penalty after the 20th day.[111]

¶619 INJUNCTIONS AGAINST TAX PROMOTERS

The IRS employs injunctions against promoters as a means of curbing abusive tax shelters.[112] An "injunction" is generally a legal action in which a court forbids a person from performing some act. In the case of tax shelters, the injunction is intended to prevent widespread marketing of the tax shelter by the promoter. Thus, in most cases, the injunction prohibits the promoter from organizing and selling the abusive tax shelter. The promoter also may be enjoined from organizing, promoting or selling interests in other abusive tax shelters. As part of the injunctive relief, the promoter may be required to notify the IRS of its involvement in any type of tax shelter and to submit all promotional materials related to tax shelters to the IRS for a specified period of time.

The injunction may be applied against all persons engaged in the promotion of the abusive tax shelter. Such persons include the entity or organization that set up the shelter (for example, a partnership or corporation), the officers of such entity or organization and the salespersons who market the shelter for the promoter. The injunction may also be applied to material advisors[113] or persons who failed to maintain or provide to the IRS investor lists as required.[114] Furthermore, the IRS will enforce the injunction on a nationwide basis and not just in the locality where the injunction was obtained. Thus, the use of the injunction is a most potent technique for curbing abusive tax shelters, and it has been used with increasing frequency by the IRS.

---

[109] Each piece of information the list must contain is set forth in Reg. 301.6112-1(b)(3).

[110] Code Sec. 6708.

[111] Code Sec. 6708(a).

[112] Code Sec. 7408.

[113] Code Sec. 6111.

[114] Code Sec. 6112.

¶620 Exhibit 6-1

Form **870-P** (Rev. 6-2006)	Department of the Treasury — **Internal Revenue Service** **AGREEMENT TO ASSESSMENT AND COLLECTION OF** **DEFICIENCY IN TAX FOR PARTNERSHIP ADJUSTMENTS**	IN REPLY REFER TO:
Taxpayer(s) name(s), address and ZIP code:	Name of Partnership: Taxpayer Identifying Number:	Tax Year(s) Ended:
	Name of Tax Matters Partner:	
Taxpayer Identifying Number:		

OFFER OF AGREEMENT FOR PARTNERSHIP ITEMS

Under the provisions of section 6224(c) and 7121 of the Internal Revenue Code (IRC), the Commissioner of the Internal Revenue Service and the undersigned taxpayer(s) agree to the determination of partnership items of the partnership for the years shown on the attached schedule of adjustments. The undersigned taxpayer(s), in accordance with IRC sections 6224(b) and 6213(d), also waive(s) the restrictions provided in IRC sections 6225(a) and 6213(a) and consent(s) to the assessment and collection of any deficiency attributable to partnership items as determined in this agreement (with interest as required by law).

This agreement is conditional, and will not become effective or final until this agreement form is returned to Internal Revenue and is signed for the Commissioner. The one year extension of the period of limitations on assessment under IRC section 6229(f) will not begin to run until the date the Commissioner's representative signs this form for the Commissioner. If this is a partial agreement, the period of limitations for assessing any tax attributable to the settled items shall be determined as if this agreement had not been entered into.

If this agreement form is signed for the Commissioner, the treatment of partnership items under this agreement will not be reopened in the absence of fraud, malfeasance, or misrepresentation of fact; and no claim for an adjustment of partnership items, or for a refund or credit based on any change in the treatment of partnership items may be filed or prosecuted.

Signature of Taxpayer	Date Signed	Phone Number
Signature of Taxpayer	Date Signed	Phone Number
By (Signature and Title)	Date Signed	Phone Number

FOR INTERNAL REVENUE USE ONLY	Date accepted for Commissioner	Signature
	Office	Title

Catalog Number 61175O	www.irs.gov	(See instructions for Signing Agreement)	Form **870-P** (Rev. 6-2006)

INSTRUCTIONS FOR SIGNING FORM 870-P

1. Sign the agreement if you wish to agree to the partnership items as shown on the attached Schedule of Adjustments. The execution and filing of this offer will expedite the adjustment of tax liability.

2. If a JOINT RETURN OF A HUSBAND AND WIFE was filed and both spouses intend to agree, both spouses should sign Form 870-P. One spouse may sign as agent for the other if acting under a power of attorney, which, if not previously filed, must accompany this form. The IRS may accept the signature of only one spouse at its discretion. However, the agreement will only be binding on the signing spouse.

3. If the taxpayer is a corporation, the agreement must be signed with the corporate name followed by the signature and title of the officer authorized to sign Form 870-P.

4. Your attorney or agent may sign for you if this action is specifically authorized by a power of attorney, which if not previously filed, must accompany this form.

5. If this offer is signed by a trust, the agreement must be signed with the trust name, followed by the signature and title of the person authorized to sign on behalf of the trust.

6. For a partner who is a member of a consolidated group, the agreement should be signed by a currently authorized officer of the corporation who was the common parent corporation of the consolidated group for the relevant consolidated return year(s). The common parent corporation signs the agreement in its own name. The signature and title of a current officer of the common parent corporation, who is authorized to bind the common parent corporation, should be displayed in the signature block. See Treas. Reg. § 1.1502-77A(a).

7. If the Tax Matters Partner signs this offer, please include the title with the signature.

8. For a Tax Matters Partner who is a subsidiary corporation in a consolidated group, a currently authorized officer of the corporation who was the common parent corporation of the consolidated group for such consolidated return year should sign the agreement on behalf of the Tax Matters Partner. The signature and title of a current officer of the common parent corporation, who is authorized to bind the common parent corporation, should be displayed in the signature block. See Treas. Reg. § 1.1502-77A(a). An authorized officer for the subsidiary corporation should also sign if it, as the Tax Matters Partner, is binding non-notice partners under the agreement.

NOTE: The submission of this offer by you and the acceptance of the offer for the Commissioner may result in an additional tax liability to you plus interest as provided by law. If the result is a decrease in tax, the amount of the decrease will be sent to you with interest as provided by law.

Department of the Treasury — **Internal Revenue Service**

AGREEMENT TO ASSESSMENT AND COLLECTION OF DEFICIENCY IN TAX FOR PARTNERSHIP ADJUSTMENTS

SCHEDULE OF ADJUSTMENTS

NAME OF PARTNERSHIP	TAX YEAR(S) ENDED		
TAXPAYER IDENTIFYING NUMBER			
DETAIL OF ADJUSTMENTS TO ORDINARY INCOME			
TOTAL ADJUSTMENTS TO ORDINARY INCOME			
OTHER ADJUSTMENTS			
A.			
(1) ADJUSTMENT			
(2) AS REPORTED			
(3) CORRECTED			
B.			
(1) ADJUSTMENT			
(2) AS REPORTED			
(3) CORRECTED			

REMARKS

Catalog Number 611750   www.irs.gov   Form **870-P** (Rev. 6-2006)

Form 870-P, Other Adjustments (Continued) Page ____ of ____

NAME OF PARTNERSHIP	TAX YEAR(S) ENDED		
TAXPAYER IDENTIFYING NUMBER			
C.			
(1) ADJUSTMENT			
(2) AS REPORTED			
(3) CORRECTED			
D.			
(1) ADJUSTMENT			
(2) AS REPORTED			
(3) CORRECTED			
E.			
(1) ADJUSTMENT			
(2) AS REPORTED			
(3) CORRECTED			
F.			
(1) ADJUSTMENT			
(2) AS REPORTED			
(3) CORRECTED			
G.			
(1) ADJUSTMENT			
(2) AS REPORTED			
(3) CORRECTED			
H.			
(1) ADJUSTMENT			
(2) AS REPORTED			
(3) CORRECTED			
I.			
(1) ADJUSTMENT			
(2) AS REPORTED			
(3) CORRECTED			

Catalog Number 611750   www.irs.gov   Form **870-P** (Rev. 6-2006)

¶621 Exhibit 6-2

Form **8918**	**Material Advisor Disclosure Statement**	OMB No. 1545-0865
(Rev. October 2007) Department of the Treasury Internal Revenue Service	▶ See separate instructions.	**FOR IRS USE ONLY**

Note: The reportable transaction number will be sent to the material advisor's address below.

Material Advisor's Name (see instructions)	Identifying number	Telephone number ( ) –

Number, street, and room or suite no.

City or town, state, and ZIP code

A Contact person name (last name, first name, middle initial)	Title	Telephone number ( ) –

B   Is this a protective disclosure? (see instructions)   ☐ Yes   ☐ No   If "Yes," see line 6a instructions.

C   Is this the original Form 8918 for this reportable transaction?   ☐ Yes   ☐ No
If "Yes," go to line 1. If "No," enter the reportable transaction number previously issued for this reportable transaction or tax shelter.
Reportable Transaction Number ▶

1   Name of reportable transaction (see instructions)

2   Identify the type of reportable transaction. Check all the box(es) that apply (see instructions).

  a ☐ Listed   **c** ☐ Contractual protection   **e** ☐ Transaction of interest
  b ☐ Confidential **d** ☐ Loss   **f** ☐ Brief asset holding period

3   If you checked box 2a or 2e, enter the published guidance number for the listed transaction or transaction of interest ▶ _____

4   Enter the date the Material Advisor became a material advisor with respect to the reportable transaction (see instructions) ▶ _____

5   If you are a party to a designation agreement, identify the other parties (see instructions).

Name	Identifying number (if known)

Address (Number, street, and room or suite no.)

City or town, state, and ZIP code

Contact name	Telephone number ( ) –

6a Provide a brief description of the type of material aid, assistance, or advice you provided (see instructions).

_____

_____

_____

  b Describe the role of any other entity(ies) or individual(s) who you know or have reason to know provided material aid, assistance, or advice to this transaction and include each entity's and individual's complete name, identifying number (if known), and address.

_____

_____

7a To obtain the intended tax benefits generated by the transaction:
  Is a related entity(ies) or individual(s) needed?   ☐ Yes   ☐ No
  Is a foreign entity(ies) or individual(s) needed?   ☐ Yes   ☐ No
  Is a tax-exempt entity(ies) needed?   ☐ Yes   ☐ No

  b If you answered "Yes" to any of the above questions, describe the role of each individual or entity. Also identify the individual's or entity's country of existence if a particular country is required to obtain the intended tax benefits.

_____

_____

_____

8a To obtain the intended tax benefits generated by the transaction, is income or gain from the transaction allocated directly or indirectly to an individual(s) or entity(ies) that has a net operating loss and/or unused loss or credits?   ☐ Yes   ☐ No

  b If "Yes," describe the role of each individual or entity in the transaction.

_____

_____

_____

For Privacy Act and Paperwork Reduction Act Notice, see separate instructions.	Cat. No. 39533A	Form **8918** (Rev. 10-2007)

9 Identify the types of financial instruments used in this transaction (see instructions).

_____

_____

10 Estimated Tax Benefits—Identify the type of tax benefit generated by the transaction that you expect the taxpayer to claim in each year. Check all boxes that apply (see instructions).

☐ Deductions ☐ Exclusions from gross income ☐ Tax credits ☐ Other _____

☐ Capital loss ☐ Nonrecognition of gain ☐ Deferral

☐ Ordinary loss ☐ Adjustments to basis ☐ Absence of adjustments to basis

11 Timing of Tax Benefits—If you checked one or more boxes on line 10, check the applicable box(es) below to identify the period in which such tax benefits are claimed. Check each box that applies.

☐ Tax benefits generated by the transaction are required to be claimed in the first year of participation by the taxpayer.

☐ Tax benefits may be claimed in another year by the taxpayer.

12 Enter the Internal Revenue Code section(s) used to claim tax benefit(s) generated by the transaction. (Attach additional sheets if necessary.)

13 Describe the reportable transaction for which you provided material aid, assistance or advice, including but not limited to the following: the nature of the expected tax treatment and expected tax benefits generated by the transaction for all affected years, the years the tax benefits are expected to be claimed, the role of the entities or individuals mentioned in lines 7a or 8a (if any) and the role of the financial instruments mentioned in line 9 (if any). Explain how the Internal Revenue Code sections listed in line 12 are applied and how they allow the taxpayer to obtain the desired tax treatment. Also, include a description of any tax result protection with respect to the transaction.

_____

_____

_____

_____

_____

_____

_____

_____

_____

_____

_____

_____

_____

_____

_____

_____

_____

_____

Under penalties of perjury, I declare that I have examined this return, and to the best of my knowledge and belief, it is true, correct, and complete.

Please Sign Here

▶ _____ | _____ | _____
Signature of Material Advisor Date Title

▶ _____
Print name

Form **8918** (Rev. 10-2007)

¶622 Exhibit 6-3

Form **8886**	**Reportable Transaction Disclosure Statement**	OMB No. 1545-1800
(Rev. December 2007) Department of the Treasury Internal Revenue Service	▶ **Attach to your tax return.** ▶ **See separate instructions.**	Attachment Sequence No. **137**

Name(s) shown on return (individuals enter last name, first name, middle initial)	Identifying number

Number, street, and room or suite no.

City or town, state, and ZIP code

A   If you are filing more than one Form 8886 with your tax return, sequentially number each Form 8886 and enter the statement number for this Form 8886 . . . . ▶ Statement number _____ of _____

B   Enter the form number of the tax return to which this form is attached or related . . . . ▶ _____

   Enter the year of the tax return identified above . . . . ▶ _____

   Is this Form 8886 being filed with an amended tax return?   ☐ Yes   ☐ No

C   Check the box(es) that apply (see instructions).   ☐ Initial year filer   ☐ Protective disclosure

1a Name of reportable transaction

1b Initial year participated in transaction	**1c** Reportable transaction or tax shelter registration number (9 digits or 11 digits)

2   Identify the type of reportable transaction. Check all boxes that apply (see instructions).

  a ☐ Listed   **c** ☐ Contractual protection   **e** ☐ Brief asset holding period
  b ☐ Confidential   **d** ☐ Loss   **f** ☐ Transaction of interest

3   If you checked box 2a or 2f, enter the published guidance number for the listed transaction or transaction of interest . . . . ▶ _____

4   Enter the number of "same as or substantially similar" transactions reported on this form . . . . . ▶ _____

5   If you participated in the transaction through another entity, check all applicable boxes and provide the information below for the entity (see instructions). (Attach additional sheets, if necessary.)

  a Type of entity:

☐ Partnership	☐ Partnership
☐ S corporation	☐ S corporation
☐ Trust	☐ Trust
☐ Foreign	☐ Foreign

  b Name . . . . ▶

  c Employer identification number (EIN), if known . . . . ▶

  d Date Schedule K-1 received from entity (enter "none" if Schedule K-1 not received) . . . . ▶

6   Enter below the name and address of each individual or entity to whom you paid a fee with regard to the transaction if that individual or entity promoted, solicited, or recommended your participation in the transaction, or provided tax advice related to the transaction. (Attach additional sheets, if necessary.)

a Name	Identifying number (if known)	Fees paid $
Number, street, and room or suite no.		
City or town, state, and ZIP code		

b Name	Identifying number (if known)	Fees paid $
Number, street, and room or suite no.		
City or town, state, and ZIP code		

For Paperwork Reduction Act Notice, see separate instructions.   Cat. No. 34654G   Form **8886** (Rev. 12-2007)

¶622

Form 8886 (Rev. 12-2007)   Page **2**

7   **Facts**

a   Identify the type of tax benefit generated by the transaction. Check all the boxes that apply (see instructions).

☐ Deductions   ☐ Exclusions from gross income   ☐ Tax credits   ☐ Other _____

☐ Capital loss   ☐ Nonrecognition of gain   ☐ Deferral

☐ Ordinary loss   ☐ Adjustments to basis   ☐ Absence of adjustments to basis

b   Further describe the amount and nature of the expected tax treatment and expected tax benefits generated by the transaction for all affected years. Include facts of each step of the transaction that relate to the expected tax benefits including the amount and nature of your investment. Include in your description your participation in the transaction and all related transactions regardless of the year in which they were entered into. Also, include a description of any tax result protection with respect to the transaction.

8   Identify all tax-exempt, foreign, and related entities and individuals involved in the transaction. Check the appropriate box(es) (see instructions). Include their name(s), identifying number(s), address(es), and a brief description of their involvement. For each foreign entity, identify its country of incorporation or existence. For each related entity, explain how it is related. (Attach additional sheets, if necessary.)

a   Type of entity: ☐ Tax-exempt   ☐ Foreign   ☐ Related   Identifying number

Name

Address

Description

b   Type of entity: ☐ Tax-exempt   ☐ Foreign   ☐ Related   Identifying number

Name

Address

Description

Form **8886** (Rev. 12-2007)

¶623 DISCUSSION QUESTIONS

1. The IRS is conducting an examination of the returns of Aggressivity, Ltd., a partnership in which Nellie Neglect is a 10-percent partner and also the designated Tax Matters Partner (TMP). The Tax Equity and Fiscal Responsibility Act of 1982 (TEFRA; P.L. 97-248) procedures have been scrupulously followed by the IRS, and a Final Partnership Administrative Adjustment (FPAA) was issued to Nellie on June 18, 2009, for the 2007 taxable year. The FPAA provided that the TMP had 90 days in which to file a petition for judicial review of the FPAA.

   On the same day, the IRS sent copies of the FPAA to all notice partners as required by the TEFRA provisions. All of these partners assume that Nellie would be filing a petition for judicial review on behalf of the partnership, because she had previously advised them of that strategy. For that reason, none of the other partners ever filed a petition for judicial review.

   Unfortunately, Nellie got occupied with other things and failed to file the petition by September 17, 2009. However, on November 12, 2009, Nellie realized her error and quickly filed a petition for judicial review of the FPAA with the Court of Federal Claims.

   The IRS, in responding to the petition, files a motion to dismiss for lack of jurisdiction with the Court on two separate grounds:

   (A) Nellie did not file a petition for readjustment within the 90 days of the FPAA as required by Code Sec. 6226(a).

   (B) Nellie in petitioning the Court only made a deposit of the tax liability, not the interest. Thus, she failed the TMP to meet the jurisdictional requirements of Code Sec. 6226(e)(1).

   Which party should prevail?

2. Constance C. Enshus, the limited partner in Bilda Brickhouse, a real estate partnership, received a copy of financial information prepared by the general partners of the partnership. In reviewing the information, Connie finds what she believes should be an additional deduction for the partnership for the preceding year. Connie writes to the general partner (who is also the TMP) asking that he prepare an amended return. The general partner disagrees with Connie and informs her of his decision. Connie still believes she is right and proceeds to file a Request for Administrative Adjustment (RAA) seeking a refund of $4,050, her proportionate share of the refund due as a result of the adjustment at the partnership level. Connie is notified by the IRS on September 15, 2009, that her RAA has been treated as requesting a refund for a nonpartnership item.

   (A) Assuming the IRS decides the TMP was correct and no refund is allowable, what is the last day that Connie can commence an action in federal court to litigate the matter?

(B) What action, if any, is required as a condition precedent to Connie's commencing legal action?

(C) Does it matter that the partnership has elected to be governed by the large partnership rules?

3. Larry Landowner is a partner in Water Street Ventures. The partnership has been undergoing an audit of its 2008 tax return. In an agreement with the tax matters partner and all other partners, Larry signs the Form 870-P—Agreement to Assessment and Collection of Deficiency in Tax for Partnership Adjustments, and pays his portion of the proposed deficiency.

Later that day Larry attends the O.P.E. (Overpaid Executives) luncheon. The speaker is discussing ways to deal with the IRS. He described a situation where a taxpayer entered an agreement with an Appeals Officer by executing a Form 870-AD—Offer to Waive Restrictions on Assessment and Collection of Tax Deficiency and to Accept Overassessment (see Chapter 12), which states that "no claim for refund or credit shall be filed or prosecuted" for the years involved. In the form, the IRS also promises that the case will not be reopened by the Commissioner "in the absence of fraud, malfeasance, concealment or misrepresentation of fact." Despite this language, the speaker explains that some courts have allowed claims for refund even though a Form 870-AD was signed by the taxpayer.

Recognizing that the same language is incorporated in Form 870-P, Larry would like to know whether he would be able to reopen his case on the same basis as Form 870-AD.

4. The IRS has recently concluded an examination of the returns of WWW.Com.Ltd, a partnership in which HTTP, Inc., is the Tax Matters Partner (TMP). HTTP, Inc. is an S corporation. It owns a 10% interest in the partnership. HTTP, Inc.'s shareholders are John E. Mail and his brother Jack E. Mail. As a result of the audit of the partnership, the ultimate tax liability of John E. Mail will be $50,000. Jack E. Mail, on the other hand, due to other investment losses, will have no tax liability as a result of this audit.

The partnership has directed the TMP not to file a petition for judicial review of the FPAA with the Tax Court of the United States. It desires to either go to the United States District Court or the United States Court of Federal Claims. The TMP has asked what amount, if any, it must deposit in order to acquire jurisdiction in the United States District Court or the United States Court of Federal Claims.

=C

CHAPTER 7
INVESTIGATIVE AUTHORITY OF THE INTERNAL REVENUE SERVICE

¶701 GENERAL AUTHORITY TO EXAMINE

The IRS has broad powers to examine records and question individuals for the purpose of determining whether there has been compliance with the tax laws. Internal Revenue Code Section 7602(a)(1) specifically authorizes the IRS to examine any books, papers, records or other data, which includes output of computers,[1] that may be relevant or material to ascertaining the correctness of any return, determining the tax liability of any person, or collecting any tax. Since most taxpayers and other individuals voluntarily produce records and answer questions when requested to do so by the IRS, this general authority in itself is normally sufficient to obtain the necessary information.

During an audit, a taxpayer may be asked informally for certain records or documents. Although such requests may be verbal, written requests specifically describing the documents or information to be produced frequently are made on Form 4564, Information Document Request (See Exhibit 5-9 at ¶519). This form provides a permanent record of what was requested, received and returned to the taxpayer.

¶702 NOTICE OF THIRD-PARTY CONTACT

Most likely your employer

As part of its enforcement efforts, the IRS may also seek to gather information from third parties in connection with the examination of a taxpayer. For many years the IRS did not have to give notice in advance of a third-party contact. The lack of prior notice often led to a chilling affect on a taxpayer's business or damaged the taxpayer's reputation because the taxpayer was denied the opportunity to resolve issues and volunteer information before the IRS actually contacted third parties.

The IRS must now provide reasonable notice of the fact that it will contact "a third party" with respect to the examination or collection activities regarding the taxpayer.[2] However, the IRS is not under an obligation to provide the names or identity of the third parties prior to actual contact. Upon the taxpayer's request, or at least annually, the IRS must provide a taxpayer with a record of persons contacted during that period.[3]

---

[1] *United States v. Davey*, 76-2 USTC ¶9724 (2d Cir), but see limitation on obtaining source codes in ¶705.

[2] Code Sec. 7602(c)(1).
[3] Code Sec. 7602(c)(2).

Example 7-1: FoodCo, a food processor, sells its products to major food retailers. Pursuant to an audit of FoodCo, the focus of which is the underreporting of gross receipts, the IRS contacts major retailers regarding their payments to FoodCo. As a result, the major food retailers, wanting to avoid dealing with the IRS, stop purchasing from FoodCo. However, if FoodCo had notice that the IRS would contact third-parties, FoodCo would have an opportunity to talk to its major customers in order to alleviate the impact of the potential IRS contact.

A third-party contact is considered as having been made when an employee of the IRS contacts a person other than the taxpayer and asks questions about a taxpayer with respect to the determination or collection of that taxpayer's liability.[4] The receipt of unsolicited information from a third party,[5] a foreign country pursuant to an exchange of information clause, or contacts made by the IRS to respond to a request from a treaty partner,[6] are not considered third-party contacts. Furthermore, searches made on computer databases that do not require any personal involvement on the other end (e.g., Lexis or Information America)[7] or contacts made for the purpose of obtaining information about an industry or market segment where specific taxpayers have not been identified are also not considered third-party contacts.[8]

Example 7-2: The IRS audits RealtyCo, a real estate company. During the audit, the IRS accesses a computer database listing the owners of all the real estate in a particular state. Because there is no personal involvement on behalf of the database, accessing the database does not constitute a third-party contact.

If a third-party contact is necessary, the IRS must provide a Letter 3104 to the taxpayer. If the tax liability is due to a jointly filed return, the IRS must provide a separate Letter 3164 to each spouse. In order to allow the U.S. Post Office sufficient time to deliver the notice, IRS employees are instructed not to make any third-party contacts until ten days after the mailing date of the Letter 3164.[9] If the IRS hands the letter to the taxpayer, contacts may be made immediately, although the regulations merely require reasonable notice and do not specify any number of days.[10] The IRS must also provide a copy of Letter 3164 to the Power of Attorney.[11] When a third-party contact is made, the IRS employee must also complete a Form 12175, Third Party Contact Report.[12]

Four situations do not require notification.[13] The situations are: (i) when the taxpayer (verbally or in writing) authorizes a third-party contact; (ii) when notice of such contact would jeopardize collection of any tax; (iii) when notice may involve reprisals against any person (i.e., an abusive spouse situation); and (iv) when there is a pending criminal investigation.[14] If a taxpayer authorizes a third-

---

[4] Reg. §301.7602-2(b).
[5] Reg. §301.7602-2(c)(1)(i)(A).
[6] Reg. §301.7602-2(c)(3)(i)(C).
[7] Reg. §301-7602-2(c)(2)(i)(B).
[8] Code Sec. 7602(c); IRM 4.10.1.6.12.1.
[9] IRM 4.11.57.4.1.

[10] Reg. §301.7602-2(d)(1).
[11] IRM 4.10.1.6.12.2.1.
[12] IRM 4.10.1.6.12.3.1.
[13] Code Sec. 7602(c).
[14] Code Sec. 7602(c)(2).

party contact, the IRS employee prepares Form 12180, Third Party Contact Authorization (see Exhibit 7-1 at ¶721) or obtains other written evidence listing the names of all third parties the taxpayer has authorized the employee to contact. Although not statutorily excluded, judicial proceedings are also exempt from the notification requirements.[15]

> **Example 7-3:** FoodCo, a food processor, sells its products to major food retailers. Pursuant to an audit of FoodCo, the focus of which is the underreporting of gross receipts, the IRS contacts major retailers regarding their payments to FoodCo. FoodCo's Tax Director tells the IRS Agent that "If you don't believe our gross receipts, you can contact the major food retailers that are our customers." Accordingly, the IRS Agent prepares a Form 12180.

Taxpayer representatives who are attorneys, CPAs and enrolled agents can authorize third-party contacts on behalf of their clients. This authority does not extend to other types of representatives such as family members, unenrolled agents or tax return preparers.[16]

¶703 THE SUMMONS POWER

To give force and meaning to this general authority to examine, the IRS has the power to compel a taxpayer or any other person to produce records and to testify under oath. This compulsory process is the administrative summons authorized by Code Sec. 7602(a)(2). The IRS may summon any person to appear at a reasonable time and place named in the summons for the purpose of giving testimony under oath and producing books, papers, records, or other data. The authority to issue summonses has been delegated generally to those agents and other personnel within the IRS who are responsible for the examination of returns, the collection of taxes, and the investigation of tax offenses.[17] Therefore, revenue agents, tax auditors, revenue officers, and special agents are all permitted to issue a summons.

The IRS serves a summons either by handing an attested copy to the person to whom it is directed or by leaving it at that person's "last and usual place of abode."[18] If the IRS cannot make personal service, the IRS must leave the summons at the place of residence either with some other person who is present or in a place where the person summoned will be likely to find it.[19] The IRS must leave the summons with someone of suitable age and discretion when personal service is not possible.[20] Simply leaving the summons at the last and usual place of residence is sufficient.

---

[15] *Seawright v. Commissioner*, 117 T.C. 294 (2004).

[16] Reg. §301.7602-2(f)(7). IRM 13.1.7.3.3.3. The taxpayer and the representative must have executed a valid Form 2848, Power of Attorney and Declaration of Representative. Form 2848 provides that "the representatives are authorized to . . . perform any and all acts that I (we) can perform with respect to tax matters described on line 3 [Form 2848], for example, the authority to sign any agreement, consent or other documents." This language is consid-

ered sufficient to allow a taxpayer's representative to authorize a Code Sec. 7602(c) third-party contact.

[17] Reg. §301.7602-1(b)(1).

[18] Code Sec. 7603(a).

[19] IRM 5.17.6.7.

[20] *See* IRM 25.5.3.2, where the IRS has softened the standard received in favorable court decisions. *See also United States v. Bichara*, 826 F.2d 1037 (11th Cir. 1987); *United States v. Gilleran*, 992 F.2d 232 (9th Cir. 1993), 93-1 USTC ¶50,356.

Example 7-4: In the 10 previous times that the IRS has been to Taxpayer's apartment, Taxpayer has not been there to receive personal service of a summons. On the 11th time, the door is answered by a six-year-old boy, the only person home, who was in the process of spilling milk from his cereal bowl on his race car pajamas. The six-year-old would not be considered a person of suitable age and discretion and, accordingly, the IRS Agent may not leave the summons with him. On the 12th time to Taxpayer's apartment, a bespeckled fifteen-year-old boy holding an advanced placement government textbook answers the door. The IRS can leave the summons with the fifteen-year-old boy because he is of suitable age and discretion.

When a corporation is under examination, the IRS may direct the summons to either a specific corporate officer or the corporation itself. The summons should indicate the officer's corporate position or title. When a summons is directed to the corporation, the IRS must serve an officer, director, managing agent, or other person authorized to accept service of process on behalf of the corporation.[21]

After service of the summons, the server prepares and signs a certificate of service on the reverse side of the Form 2039, Summons, retained by the IRS (see Exhibit 7-2 at ¶722). The server enters the date, time and manner of service on the certificate. In any judicial proceeding to enforce the summons, the signed certificate of service is evidence of the facts it states.[22]

¶704 SCOPE OF THE POWER

The scope of the summons power in Code Sec. 7602 extends to the production of records stored on magnetic tape.[23] It also requires the production of videotapes[24] and microfiche copies of records.[25] The U.S. Supreme Court has even approved the use of a summons to compel an individual to prepare handwriting exemplars before the examining agent.[26] However, the summons cannot require a person to create any documents, such as lists or schedules of factual information, that did not exist at the time the summons was issued.[27]

Although the authority to summon and to examine books and records is very extensive, it has limits. Code Sec. 7605(b) provides that a taxpayer shall not incur an unnecessary examination. It also prohibits more than one inspection of the taxpayer's books for each taxable year unless the taxpayer requests otherwise or unless the IRS notifies the taxpayer in writing that an additional inspection is necessary. The courts, as well as the IRS, generally have taken the position that there is no second inspection, even though the requested records were inspected

---

[21] IRM 25.5.3.2.

[22] Code Sec. 7603(a).

[23] *United States v. Davey,* 543 F.2d 996 (2d Cir. 1976), 76-1 USTC ¶9724.

[24] *United States v. Schenk,* 581 F. Supp. 218 (S.D. Ind. 1984), 84-1 USTC ¶9197; *United States v. Norton,* 81-1 USTC ¶9398 (N.D. Cal. 1981).

[25] *United States v. Mobil Corp.,* 543 F. Supp. 507 (N.D. Tex. 1982), 82-1 USTC ¶9242.

[26] *United States v. Euge,* 444 U.S. 707 (1980), 80-1 USTC ¶9222.

[27] *United States v. Davey, supra.*

previously, if the IRS has not completed or closed the examination or investigation for the taxable year.[28]

Example 7-5: Suppose that a taxpayer fails to report an item of income for which the payor issues a Form 1099-MISC. The IRS may send a notice requiring the payment of tax with respect to that item of income. Should the IRS later decide to audit the taxpayer, the taxpayer could not object that it is an unnecessary second examination.

The date fixed in the summons for compliance cannot be less than ten days from the date of the summons.[29] This minimum allowable time for compliance is for the benefit of the summoned party, who may waive it by voluntary complying.

The issuance of a summons and even its enforcement does not extend the statute of limitations.

Example 7-6: A distributor of computers, USAco, is a subsidiary of AsiaCo and files its return for taxable year 20X0, pursuant to an extension on September 15, 20X1. The IRS conducts a transfer pricing audit of USAco's purchases of computers from AsiaCo, but USAco fails to respond to any Information Document Requests. With the three-year statute of limitations set to expire on September 15, 20X4, the IRS serves a summons on September 1, 20X4. Considering that USAco has ten days to respond to a summons, which would be September 11, 20X4, the IRS will only have four days after receiving the summoned information to make an assessment because a summons does not toll the statute of limitations.

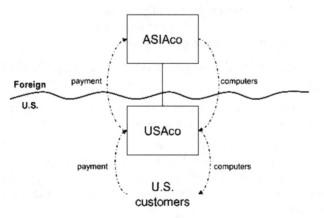

The IRS may issue a designated summons that unilaterally extends the statute of limitations for 120 days, depending on whether the court order compliance.[30] However, the use of a designated summons[31] is limited because the

---

[28] IRM 25.5.4.4.3; *United States v. Gilpin*, 542 F.2d 38 (7th Cir. 1876).

[29] Code Sec. 7605(a). A longer period is required for third-party recordkeeper summonses. See ¶709, *infra.*

[30] Code Sec. 6503(j).

[31] *See* ¶1704, *infra.*

IRS must issue the designated summons 60 days before the expiration of the statute of limitations and numerous IRS personnel must approve issuance of the designated summons.[32]

¶705 PROTECTION OF COMPUTERS AND SOFTWARE

In order to protect the intellectual and property rights of the developers and owners of computer programs, the IRS may not issue a summons or enforcing a summons to produce or analyze any tax related computer software and source code.[33]

There are, however, several exceptions the IRS may issue: a summons for (a) the tax related computer source code in connection with an inquiry into any offense connected with the administration or enforcement of federal tax laws,[34] (b) the tax related computer software source code acquired or developed by the taxpayer or a related person primarily for internal use rather than commercial distribution,[35] or (c) the tax-related computer software source code if the IRS is unable to otherwise reasonably ascertain the correctness of any return.[36]

> **Example 7-7:** Consider the tax department of a large multi-national corporation that develops its own software to calculate the foreign tax credit. The IRS may issue a summons for this tax-related software because the software was internally developed. However, once the IRS has acquired the software source code, the IRS is subject to specific requirements against its disclosure and improper use.[37]

The IRS must follow special procedures with respect to accessing a taxpayer's custom-designed computer software.[38] More specifically, the IRS must formally request the materials from both the taxpayer and the software owner, who have 180 days to respond.[39] A court enforcing the summons may also issue an order to prevent the disclosure of the software.

¶706 PROPER USE OF INTERNAL REVENUE SERVICE SUMMONS

The IRS may only use a summons[40] to verify, determine and collect the tax liability of any person, which includes investigating any criminal tax offense.[41]

A court will not enforce a summons that the IRS has issued for an improper purpose, such as to harass the taxpayer, pressure settlement of a collateral dispute, or for any other purpose reflecting on the good faith of the particular investigation.[42] Enforcement of such a summons constitutes an abuse of the summons power.[43]

---

[32] Code Sec. 6503(j)(2)(A).

[33] Code Sec. 7612(a)(1).

[34] Code Sec. 7612(b)(2)(A).

[35] Code Sec. 7612(b)(2)(B).

[36] Code Sec. 7612(b)(1).

[37] Code Sec. 7612(a)(2).

[38] *See* CCA 200550002.

[39] Code Sec. 7612.

[40] Code Sec. 7602.

[41] Code Sec. 7602(b).

[42] *United States v. Powell,* 379 U.S. 48 (1964), 64-2 USTC ¶9858.

[43] For an excellent discussion of the possible abuse of process and improper use of an IRS summons demanding appearance at a police station for the taking of fingerprints, see *United States v.*

Criminal Tax Investigations. The Code has a bright-line rule for the use of summonses in criminal tax investigations. More specifically, the IRS may issue a summons for "the purpose of inquiring into any offense connected with the administration or enforcement of the internal revenue laws."[44] Furthermore, the authority to issue a summons in a criminal investigation terminates once there is a "Justice Department referral in effect" with respect to the person under investigation.[45] Such a "referral" is in effect when the IRS recommends to the Attorney General either the criminal prosecution or a grand jury investigation of such person. A "referral" is also in effect if any request is made in writing by the Attorney General to the IRS for the disclosure of any tax return or return information relating to such person.

This limitation on the issuance of a summons ceases when the Attorney General notifies the IRS in writing that the person involved will neither be prosecuted nor be the subject of a grand jury investigation. The limitation also ceases when a final disposition of any criminal proceeding instituted against such person occurs.

> **Example 7-8:** Suppose that the IRS's Criminal Investigation Division has investigated a tax evasion case that the IRS Area Counsel ultimately approves and refers to the Department of Justice (the Attorney General's office). The IRS's Criminal Investigation Division could have used the power of the summons until referral of the case to the Department of Justice. However, once referred to the Department of Justice, the IRS may not use a summons to obtain information. Should the Department of Justice decide against prosecuting the taxpayer, the IRS regains the right to use the summons power.

Tax Court Proceedings. The use of administrative summonses by the IRS during Tax Court proceedings has raised objections by taxpayers. The Tax Court discovery rules permitting both parties to obtain relevant information before trial are much more restricted in their scope than the summons power available to the IRS. In certain situations, the Tax Court has held that to allow the IRS in a pending case to use evidence obtained by the issuance of a summons would give the government an unfair advantage over the taxpayer. In substance, such use of the summons would permit the IRS to circumvent the limitations of the Tax Court's discovery rules. The Tax Court can issue protective orders to preclude the IRS from using information obtained by such abusive use of the administrative summons.[46]

In *Ash v. Commissioner*,[47] the Tax Court set forth guidelines that it would follow to determine whether it should issue such a protective order when the IRS obtains information during a pending case by means of a summons.

(Footnote Continued)

Michaud, 907 F.2d 750 (7th Cir. 1990), 90-2 USTC ¶50,425.

[44] Code Sec. 7602(b); see Chapter 18, Criminal Tax Procedure, *infra*, for a discussion of the various criminal tax offenses.

[45] Code Sec. 7602(d).

[46] Tax Court Rule 103.

[47] 96 TC 459 (1991), CCH Dec. 47,221.

In the first situation, where litigation has commenced by the filing of a petition by the taxpayer and the IRS subsequently issues a summons with regard to the same taxpayer and taxable year, then the Tax Court will issue a protective order to prevent the IRS from using any of the summoned evidence in the litigation.[48] However, in such a situation, the Court will not issue a protective order if the IRS can show that it served the summons for a sufficient reason that was independent of the pending litigation.

In the second situation, the IRS serves the summons before the taxpayer files a Tax Court petition. Accordingly, the Tax Court will not issue an order with respect to any information obtained as a result of the summons. The Tax Court reasoned in *Ash* that, before a taxpayer files a petition, the Court does not have jurisdiction and no basis exists for viewing the summons as an attempt to undermine the Court's discovery rules.

In the third situation described in *Ash,* litigation had commenced and the IRS served a summons with regard to a different taxpayer or a different taxable year. The Tax Court concluded that it would not issue a protective order.[49] However, the Court stated that it would do so if the taxpayer could show that the IRS lacked an independent and sufficient reason for the summons.

Other Objections. In addition to the potential challenges to a summons for improper use, a summoned individual may raise additional objections based on constitutional rights or common-law privileges. These include, among others, the Fourth Amendment protection against unreasonable searches and seizures,[50] the Fifth Amendment privilege against self-incrimination,[51] and the common-law privilege that protects confidential communications between attorney and client. These rights and privileges are discussed in Chapter 18, Criminal Tax Procedure, *infra.*

¶707 ENFORCEMENT OF SUMMONS

When a summonsed person refuses to comply, the government can seek enforcement of the summons in the U.S. District Court for the district in which the summoned party resides.[52] Before the Court may order the summoned person to comply, the IRS is initially required to prove the following elements:

---

[48] The Tax Court issued such an order in *Universal Manufacturing Co. v. Comm'r,* 93 TC 589 (1989), CCH Dec. 46,154.

[49] In an earlier case involving this type of situation, the issuance of a protective order was justified by the "compelling facts." *Westreco, Inc. v. Comm'r,* 60 TCM 824 (1990), CCH Dec. 46,882(M).

[50] *Vaughn v. Baldwin,* 950 F.2d 331 (6th Cir. 1991). Taxpayer's Fourth Amendment rights were violated when the IRS refused to return the taxpayer's papers, which he had voluntarily turned over to the IRS pursuant to a summons, after the taxpayer had formally demanded their return and revoked his consent to have them copied.

[51] *U.S. v. Wirenius,* 94-1 USTC ¶50,132. The court upheld the taxpayer's Fifth Amendment claim and

refused to enforce an IRS summons because testimony by the taxpayer could have lead to criminal prosecution and the taxpayer reasonably and legitimately feared his testimony would lead to criminal prosecution.

[52] Code Secs. 7604(a) and 7402(b). Failure to comply with a summons will neither be punished as a criminal offense under Code Sec. 7210, nor subject a person to attachment and arrest under Code Sec. 7604(b), if good faith objections to the summons have been raised and there has not been a complete default or contumacious refusal to comply. *Reisman v. Caplin,* 375 U.S. 440 (1964), 64-1 USTC ¶9202. For a discussion of the suspension of the statute of limitations on assessment when a "designated summons" to a corporation is contested, see ¶704, *supra.*

1. The information sought by the summons is relevant;

2. The purpose of the inquiry is legitimate;

3. The information sought is not already in the government's possession; and

4. The IRS has followed the administrative steps the Code requires.[53]

Example 7-9: Consider an audit of a taxpayer for the taxable year 2011, where the only issue is the price charged for goods between the taxpayer and its foreign-related party. If the IRS had already received a copy of the intercompany sales agreement pursuant to a request from a treaty partner country, the IRS could not seek such a document from the taxpayer via issuing and enforcing a summons.

If the government meets this initial burden of proof and the defenses raised by the summoned party are rejected, the Court will order compliance with the summons. The civil and criminal contempt powers of the Court are available to enforce compliance with the order. A finding of contempt can result in the imposition of monetary penalties[54] or incarceration.[55]

¶708 REPRESENTATION AND RECORDING OF TESTIMONY

The individual to whom a summons is directed may have representation when appearing in response to a summons. When a third-party witness is summoned, others may appear at the interview as observers if the witness requests their presence and obtains a waiver of the taxpayer's right to confidentiality.[56] The taxpayer and his or her representative, however, generally do not have a right to be present during the interview of a third-party witness.[57] When a witness requests representation at an appearance by the same representative that the taxpayer has retained, a conflict-of-interest may arise. If such a question of dual representation occurs, the representative normally will not be excluded from the interview of the witness unless the representative acts to impede or obstruct the investigation.[58]

A taxpayer appearing in response to a summons has the right to make an audio or stenographic recording, provided she gives advance notice to the IRS of such intention.[59] If the IRS makes its own recording, the taxpayer normally is entitled to a copy or transcript upon request. In criminal tax investigations, the IRS will also furnish a witness a copy of a transcript of his testimony (or

---

[53] *United States v. Powell*, 379 U.S. 48 (1964), 64-2 USTC ¶9858.

[54] See, for example, *United States v. Chase Manhattan Bank*, 590 F. Supp. 1160 (S.D.N.Y. 1984), 84-2 USTC ¶9749, and *United States v. Darwin Construction Co.*, 873 F.2d 730 (4th Cir. 1989), 89-2 USTC ¶9425, imposing a fine of $5,000 per day for failure to comply with a summons enforcement order.

[55] See, for example, *Ex Parte Tammen*, 438 F. Supp. 349 (N.D. Tex. 1977), 78-1 USTC ¶9302, and *United States v. Lillibridge*, 80-2 USTC ¶9694 (6th Cir. 1980).

[56] *United States v. Finch*, 434 F. Supp. 1085 (D. Colo. 1977), 78-1 USTC ¶9135.

[57] *United States v. Newman*, 441 F.2d 165 (5th Cir. 1971), 71-1 USTC ¶9329; *United States v. Nemetz*, 450 F.2d 924 (3d Cir. 1971), 71-2 USTC ¶9725; *United States v. Jones*, 84 AFTR2d 99-6830 (D.S.C. 1999).

[58] IRM 25.5.5.5. To avoid censure for unethical conduct, there must be full disclosure of the potential conflict to the witness and the witness must thereafter consent to such dual representation. See Circular 230, § 10.29.

[59] Code Sec. 7521(a); IRM 25.5.5.4.4.

affidavit) upon request, except when it is determined that its release may interfere with the development or successful prosecution of the case.[60]

¶709 THIRD-PARTY RECORDKEEPER SUMMONS

The IRS has traditionally summonsed third parties to obtain information with respect to a taxpayer. The phrase "third-party recordkeeper" includes any bank, savings and loan, or credit union, any consumer reporting agency, any person extending credit through the use of credit cards or similar devices, any broker, any attorney, any accountant, any barter exchange, and any enrolled agent. Employers are not included within the definition of third-party recordkeepers.

> **Example 7-10:** Trying to construct a bank deposit method of a taxpayer's unreported income, the IRS summonses the bank deposits at North Shore Savings & Loan. North Shore Savings & Loan is a third-party record keeper.

If the third party is a third-party recordkeeper, the IRS must provide notice to the taxpayer, who has a legal right to object to the summons issued.[61] Pursuant to certain exemptions, the IRS need not provide notice to a taxpayer of a third-party summons. These exemptions include (1) a summons served on the person with respect to whose tax liability the summons relates or any officer or employee of the person; (2) a summons served to determine whether or not records of the business transactions or affairs of an identified person have been made or kept; (3) a summons served by a criminal investigator of the IRS in connection with the investigation of an offense connected with the administration or enforcement of the revenue laws; and (4) a summons served with respect to the collection of tax.[62]

In addition to service by either handing an attested copy of the summons to a person or leaving the attested copy at the person's last and usual place of abode,[63] the IRS can also serve a third-party recordkeeper by Certified or Registered Mail at its last known address.[64]

Within twenty days after the taxpayer receives the notice, the taxpayer may then file a petition to quash the summons in the U.S. District Court. The taxpayer must serve the petition on both the IRS and the third party within the twenty-day period. The third party has the right to intervene in the proceedings, but does not have to do so. In any event, the recordkeeper will be bound by the ruling on the petition to quash.[65]

If a taxpayer files a petition to quash any third-party summons, including third-party recordkeeper summons, the statutes of limitations for assessment and for criminal prosecution are suspended for the time of the proceeding.[66] Further,

---

[60] Reg. § 601.107(b); IRM 9.4.5.8.

[61] Code Sec. 7602(c)(1). The notice must accompany a copy of the summons and be given to the taxpayer within three days of service on the third party, but not later than the twenty-third day before the date of its examination of the records. Service of the notice may occur in the same manner as the summons or mailed by certified or registered mail. Code Sec. 7609(a).

[62] Code Sec. 7609(c)(2).

[63] Code Sec. 7603(a).

[64] Code Sec. 7603(b).

[65] Code Sec. 7609(b)(2)(c).

[66] Code Sec. 7609(e). See discussion in Chapter 11, *infra.* Code Sec. 7609(e) only suspends the statute of limitations on assessment in the case of summonses issued to third-party recordkeepers. The statute of

even if the taxpayer does not attempt to quash, the statute can be suspended if the third party delays production of the records or disputes the summons. If a court does not resolve issues raised by a third-party response to the summons within six months after service of the summons, the statute is suspended beginning six months after issuance until the date the dispute is finally resolved.[67] This is unlike a regular summons action that does not toll the statute of limitations.

> **Example 7-11:** Trying to construct a bank deposit method for a taxpayer's 20X0 return filed on October 15, 20X1, the IRS summonses the bank deposits at North Shore Savings & Loan, which is a third-party record keeper. The IRS serves a summons to North Shore on January 15, 20X4, but due to issues raised by North Shore and North Shore's delay in the production of records, North Shore does not produce the records until August 1, 20X4. Because the issues were not resolved within six months after service of the summons, the October 15, 20X4 expiration of the statute of limitations is extended six months to April 15, 20X5.

Assuming that no one files a petition to quash the third-party recordkeeper summons, the IRS may begin examining the documents on the twenty-fourth day following notice to the taxpayer of the summons. The third party must begin assembling the records once it receives the original summons, so that there is no further delay once it is clear that the IRS is entitled to them. If a petition to quash is filed, the IRS can examine the records only upon order of the court or with the consent of the taxpayer.[68] Due to these burdensome requirements, the IRS often tries to obtain information from third-party recordkeepers without a summons.

> **Example 7-12:** On day one, the IRS serves a third-party recordkeeper with a summons and serves notice to the taxpayer. Unless the taxpayer (or the third-party) moves to quash by day twenty-one (twenty days after the date of notice), the IRS may begin examination pursuant to the summons on day twenty-four. On filing of the motion to quash, the IRS may not examine the records until enforcement begins and the statue of limitations on assessment (as well as collection) are suspended until the U.S. District Court rules on enforceability.

¶710 JOHN DOE SUMMONSES FOR "LISTED TRANSACTIONS" OR "TAX SHELTERS"

A John Doe Summons is any summons where the names of taxpayers are unknown and, therefore, not specifically identified.[69] The government has resorted to, and been quite successful in, using John Doe Summonses in its investigations of "listed transactions" or "tax shelters."[70] In order to serve a John

---

(Footnote Continued)

limitations may also be tolled in the case of a summons issued to a corporation if the summons is a "designated summons." A designated summons is any summons issued for the purpose of determining the amount of tax due, issued at least sixty days before the day on which the assessment period is to end and which clearly states that it is a designated summons. Code Sec. 6503(j).

[67] Code Sec. 7609(e)(2).
[68] Code Sec. 7609(d).
[69] IRM 25.5.7.2.
[70] Code Sec. 7609(f); *In Re: Does*, 93 AFTR 2d 2004-742 (John Doe Summons authorized with respect to Sidley Austin Brown & Wood).

Doe Summons, the IRS must obtain court approval and show to the Court that (1) the summons relates to the investigation of a particular person or ascertainable group or class of persons, (2) there is a reasonable basis for believing that such person or group or class of persons may fail or may have failed to comply with any provision of any Internal Revenue law, and (3) the information sought from the examination of the records or testimony (and the identity of the persons with respect to whose liabilty the summons is issued) is not readily available from other sources.[71]

> **Example 7-13:** The IRS believes that a number of U.S. citizens are not reporting income earned from deposits with a Swiss bank, which has limited activities in the United States. The IRS may try to obtain information from the Swiss bank with respect to the U.S. account holders pursuant to a John Doe Summons.

The aforementioned suspension of the statute of limitations also apply to John Doe Summonses.[72] In addition, the summoned party must notify the John Doe(s) of such suspension.[73]

¶711 POWER TO SUMMON ACCOUNTANTS' MATERIALS

The IRS has specific instructions with respect to audit workpapers, tax accrual workpapers, and tax reconciliation workpapers, which are typically prepared by accountants. These workpapers are defined as follows:

1. Audit workpapers contain information about the procedures followed, the tests performed, the information obtained, and the conclusions reached pursuant to the accountant's review of the taxpayer's financial statements, which would include taxes.

2. Tax accrual workpapers are audit workpapers, regardless of who prepares them, that relate to the tax reserve for current, deferred, and potential or contingent tax liabilities and any footnotes disclosed in tax reserves on audited financial statements.

3. Tax reconciliation workpapers are workpapers used in assembling, reconciling, and compiling financial data in preparation of a tax return such as schedules.

Although tax reconciliation workpapers have always been subject to the investigatory powers of the IRS, the IRS has the power to obtain audit workpapers and tax accrual workpapers pursuant to the Supreme Court's holding in *United States v. Arthur Young & Co.*[74] Due to the far reaching ramifications of the *Arthur Young* case, the IRS has promulgated internal guidelines to use restraint when requesting these types of materials.

No special circumstances need be shown to request tax reconciliation workpapers. In fact such workpapers are to be requested at the beginning of an examination so they can be used to trace financial information to the tax return.

---

[71] Code Sec. 7609(f).
[72] Code Sec. 7609(e).
[73] Code Sec. 7609(i)(4).
[74] 465 U.S. 805 (1984).

¶711

However, the IRS should only examine the tax accrual workpapers and audit workparers when it cannot obtain the other factual data from the taxpayer's records and then only as a collateral source of factual data to be requested with discretion and not as a matter of standard examining procedure.[75] The restraint stated by the IRS specifically applies to audit workpapers and tax accrual workpapers, as requesting these is not a routine examination procedure and must be restricted to unusual circumstances that make it necessary to have access to these workpapers to complete an examination.[76]

> **Example 7-14:** Suppose that USCo, a U.S.-based multinational company has transfer pricing transactions with numerous foreign affiliates. With respect to USCo's transfer pricing with CanCo, a Canadian company, USCo has failed to prepare the appropriate transfer pricing documentation. USCo's Big Four accounting firm discovers this during its audit and drafts a schedule for the file that calculates the potential tax liability to which USCo may be subject. Such a schedule would constitute a tax accrual workpaper that would be subject to request by the IRS pursuant to *Arthur Young*, but for their internal guidelines on restraint.

In connection with its investigation of "tax shelters," the IRS has expanded the circumstances under which it will request workpapers. More specifically, the IRS may request workpapers when examining any return which claims benefit for a transaction determined to be a "listed transaction" under the Regulations under Section 6011.[77]

The Office of Chief Counsel has promulgated procedures requiring that all summonses for audit, tax accrual, and tax reconciliation workpapers be prereviewed by Field Counsel prior to issuance.[78] If the IRS serves a summons for workpapers and later requests enforcement, the summons referral package must be reviewed by the Office of the Assistant Chief Counsel prior to referral to the Department of Justice.[79]

The limits on an agent's discretion to resort to the tax accrual workpapers do not apply when a case has been referred to the Criminal Investigation Division. Special Agents do not have any restrictions on their ability to obtain tax accrual workpapers in criminal investigations. At the first hint of criminal activity (either apparent directly from the taxpayer or its records, or indicated by the appearance of a Special Agent of the IRS) a tax practitioner should recommend that the client consult with an attorney experienced in criminal tax matters.[80]

Despite the IRS's restraint pursuant to the ramifications of *Arthur Young*, the IRS can now obtain information about uncertain tax positions through the information required on Form UTP, which comes perilously close to requesting information found on tax accrual workpapers.

---

[75] IRM 4.10.2.9.4(3).

[76] IRM 4.10.20.3.

[77] IRS Ann. 2002-63, 2002-2 CB 72, as modified by IRS Ann. 2010-9, IRB 2010-7, 408.

[78] IRM 34.6.3.1.

[79] IRM 34.6.3.1.

[80] AICPA Tax Guides and Checklists, 2000 Edition

¶712 UNCERTAIN TAX POSITIONS AND FORM UTP

In an effort to require large taxpayers to disclose uncertain tax positions, the IRS now requires the filing of Schedule UTP. Schedule UTP aids the IRS in focusing its examination resources on returns that contain specific uncertain tax positions that are of particular interest or of sufficient magnitude to warrant IRS inquiries. More specifically, the Schedule UTP requirements expand a taxpayer's obligation to self-report sensitive income tax matters on its tax returns beyond existing requirements for any tax shelters and listed transactions.

Taxpayers who must file Schedule UTP include the following:

(i) Filers of Forms 1120, 1120F, and other corporate forms;

(ii) Book value of assets equal to or in excess of $100 million for 2010 and 2011, $50 million for 2012 and 2013, and $10 million thereafter;

(iii) Corporations that receive an audited financial statement that covers all or a portion of the operations for all or a portion of the tax year; and

(iv) Corporation with one or more uncertain tax positions.

Uncertain Tax Positions are either: (i) positions for which a tax reserve must be established in the taxpayer's financial statements under FIN 48 or other accounting standards (e.g., IFRS) or (ii) any position for which a tax reserve has not been recorded because the taxpayer expects to litigate the position. For example, the taxpayer may determine that, if the IRS had full knowledge of the position, there would be a less than 50% chance of settlement and, if litigated, the taxpayer has a greater than 50% chance of prevailing.

> **Example 7-15:** USCo has a branch in foreign country F and pays foreign country F taxes. A 1990 Revenue Ruling by the IRS incorrectly states that country F's taxes are not creditable for foreign income tax purposes because, in determining the country F tax, country F does not allow deductions and, therefore, country F's tax fails the net income requirement. USCo's tax director knows that this Revenue Ruling is inapplicable because foreign country F's tax regime allows deductions and, as a result, USCo does not take a tax reserve on its 2011 financial statements with respect to the foreign tax credit position in country F. USCo's tax director realizes that if the IRS knows of USCo taking a foreign tax credit for country F taxes, USCo will be audited on this issue with less than a 50% chance of settlement (due to the existing Revenue Ruling), but if litigated, the Tax Court would agree with USCo. As a result, USCo does not have to report the foreign tax credit position in country F on a Schedule UTP.

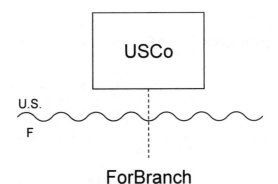

ForBranch

Example 7-16: USCo sells $10 million of widgets to ForCo, resulting in a return on sale to USCo of $500,000 (5%). USCo's tax director does not conduct a transfer pricing study, but believes that an appropriate return on sale for a company that performs the functions and assumes the risks of USCo would be $600,000 (6%). As a result, USCo's tax director books a reserve with respect to transfer pricing of $35,000 (35% of a potential $100,000 adjustment). USCo's tax director has an uncertain tax position for which USCo must file a Schedule UTP.

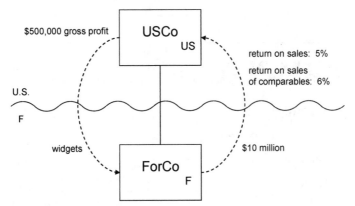

The Schedule UTP requires the corporation to rank all the tax return positions based on the U.S. federal income tax reserve recorded for the position on the return and state whether a particular UTP results in at least 10% of the total potential tax liability of all UTPs. Tax return positions includes transfer pricing and valuation positions.

The concise description of each UTP must provide "sufficient detail" so that the IRS can identify the tax position and the nature of the issue. A completed Schedule UTP is available as Exhibit 7-3, ¶723.

¶721 Exhibit 7-1

THIRD PARTY CONTACT AUTHORIZATION FORM
Internal Revenue Code Section 7602(c)

Under section 7602(c) of the Internal Revenue Code, the Internal Revenue Service (IRS) is required to provide taxpayers with reasonable advance notice that contacts with persons other than the taxpayer may be made with respect to the determination or collection of the tax liability of such taxpayer. Additionally, IRS is required to provide the taxpayer with a record of persons contacted on a periodic basis. IRS will also provide this record to the taxpayer upon request. However, IRS is not required to provide advance notice or a record of persons contacted with respect to any contacts which the taxpayer has authorized.

By signing this form, you are waiving your rights under section 7602(c) with respect to the persons you have authorized IRS to contact. Accordingly, IRS will not be required to maintain a record of these contacts. If no third party contacts are made other than those authorized by you, IRS will not be required to provide you with advance notice that contacts with third parties may be made or provide you with a record of persons contacted.

Authorization of Third Party Contact(s)

I authorize an officer or employee of the Internal Revenue Service to contact the following third person(s) with respect to the determination or collection of my tax liability.

Name(s) of Third Person(s) _____

_____

_____

I understand that in signing this form, I am waiving my rights under section 7602(c) with respect to contacts made by an officer or employee of the Internal Revenue Service with the above listed person(s).

TAXPAYER'S SIGNATURE _____ DATE _____

TAXPAYER IDENTIFICATION NUMBER _____

SPOUSE'S SIGNATURE _____ DATE _____

TAXPAYER REPRESENTATIVE _____ DATE _____

CORPORATE NAME _____ DATE _____

CORPORATE OFFICER(S) _____ DATE _____

FORM 12180 (01-1999)

¶722 Exhibit 7-2

Summons

In the matter of _____

Internal Revenue Service (Division): _____

Industry/Area (name or number): _____

Periods: _____

The Commissioner of Internal Revenue

To: _____

At: _____

You are hereby summoned and required to appear before _____
an officer of the Internal Revenue Service, to give testimony and to bring with you and to produce for examination the following books, records, papers, and other data relating to the tax liability or the collection of the tax liability or for the purpose of inquiring into any offense connected with the administration or enforcement of the internal revenue laws concerning the person identified above for the periods shown.

Do not write in this space

Business address and telephone number of IRS officer before whom you are to appear:

_____

Place and time for appearance at _____

IRS

Department of the Treasury
Internal Revenue Service

www.irs.gov

Form 2039 (Rev. 12-2001)
Catalog Number 21405J

on the _____ day of _____ , _____ at _____ o'clock _____ m.
                                          (year)
Issued under authority of the Internal Revenue Code this _____ **day of** _____ , _____ .
                                                      (year)

_____   _____
Signature of issuing officer   Title

_____   _____
Signature of approving officer *(if applicable)*   Title

Original — to be kept by IRS

Service of Summons, Notice and Recordkeeper Certificates

(Pursuant to section 7603, Internal Revenue Code)

I certify that I served the summons shown on the front of this form on:

Date	Time

How Summons Was Served

1. ❑ I certify that I handed a copy of the summons, which contained the attestation required by § 7603, to the person to whom it was directed.

2. ❑ I certify that I left a copy of the summons, which contained the attestation required by § 7603, at the last and usual place of abode of the person to whom it was directed. I left the copy with the following person (if any): _____

3. ❑ I certify that I sent a copy of the summons, which contained the attestation required by § 7603, by certified or registered mail to the last known address of the person to whom it was directed, that person being a third-party recordkeeper within the meaning of § 7603(b). I sent the summons to the following address: _____

Signature	Title

4. This certificate is made to show compliance with IRC Section 7609. This certificate does not apply to summonses served on any officer or employee of the person to whose liability the summons relates nor to summonses in aid of collection, to determine the identity of a person having a numbered account or similar arrangement, or to determine whether or not records of the business transactions or affairs of an identified person have been made or kept.

I certify that, within 3 days of serving the summons, I gave notice (Part D of Form 2039) to the person named below on the date and in the manner indicated.

Date of giving Notice: _____   Time: _____

Name of Noticee: _____

Address of Noticee (if mailed): _____

How Notice Was Given

❑ I gave notice by certified or registered mail to the last known address of the noticee.

❑ I left the notice at the last and usual place of abode of the noticee. I left the copy with the following person (if any).

❑ I gave notice by handing it to the noticee.

❑ In the absence of a last known address of the noticee, I left the notice with the person summoned.

❑ No notice is required.

Signature	Title

I certify that the period prescribed for beginning a proceeding to quash this summons has expired and that no such proceeding was instituted or that the noticee consents to the examination.

Signature	Title

Form **2039** (Rev. 12-2001)

Summons

In the matter of _____

Internal Revenue Service (Division): _____

Industry/Area (name or number): _____

Periods: _____

The Commissioner of Internal Revenue

To: _____

At: _____

You are hereby summoned and required to appear before _____
an officer of the Internal Revenue Service, to give testimony and to bring with you and to produce for examination the following books, records, papers, and other data relating to the tax liability or the collection of the tax liability or for the purpose of inquiring into any offense connected with the administration or enforcement of the internal revenue laws concerning the person identified above for the periods shown.

Attestation

I hereby certify that I have examined and compared this copy of the summons with the original and that it is a true and correct copy of the original.

_____   _____
Signature of IRS officer serving the summons   Title

Business address and telephone number of IRS officer before whom you are to appear:

_____

Place and time for appearance at _____

IRS

**Department of the Treasury
Internal Revenue Service**

www.irs.gov

Form 2039 (Rev. 12-2001)
Catalog Number 21405J

on the _____ day of _____ , _____ at _____ o'clock _____ m.
                                                    (year)
Issued under authority of the Internal Revenue Code this _____ day of _____ , _____ .
                                                                                    (year)

_____   _____
Signature of issuing officer   Title

_____   _____
Signature of approving officer *(if applicable)*   Title

Part A - to be given to person summoned

Provisions of the Internal Revenue Code

℩. 7602. Examination of books and witnesses

᠁uthority to Summon, etc. - For the purpose of ascertaining the correctness of any return, making a return where none has been made, determining the liability of any person for any internal revenue tax or the liability at law or in equity of any transferee or fiduciary of any person in respect of any internal revenue tax, or collecting any such liability, the Secretary is authorized -

    (1) To examine any books, papers, records, or other data which may be relevant or material to such inquiry.

    (2) To summon the person liable for tax or required to perform the act, or any officer or employee of such person, or any person having possession, custody, or care of books of account containing entries relating to the business of the person liable for tax or required to perform the act, or any other person the Secretary may deem proper, to appear before the Secretary at a time and place named in the summons and to produce such books, papers, records, or other data, and to give such testimony, under oath, as may be relevant or material to such inquiry; and

    (3) To take such testimony of the person concerned, under oath, as may be relevant or material to such inquiry.

(b) Purpose may include inquiry into offense. - The purposes for which the Secretary may take any action described in paragraph (1), (2), or (3) of subsection (a) include the purpose of inquiring into any offense connected with the administration or enforcement of the internal revenue laws.

(c) Notice of contact of third parties. -

    (1) General Notice. - An officer or employee of the Internal Revenue Service may not contact any person other than the taxpayer with respect to the determination or collection of such taxpayer without providing reasonable notice in advance to the taxpayer that contacts with persons other than the taxpayer may be made.

    (2) Notice of specific contacts. - The Secretary shall periodically provide to a taxpayer a record of persons contacted during such period by the Secretary with respect to the determination or collection of the tax liability of such taxpayer. Such record shall also be provided upon request of the taxpayer.

    (3) Exceptions. - This subsection shall not apply-

        (A) to any contact which the taxpayer has authorized,

        (B) if the Secretary determines for good cause shown that such notice would jeopardize collection of any tax or such notice may involve reprisal against any person, or

        (C) with respect to any pending criminal investigation.

(d) No administrative summons when there is Justice Department referral.-

    (1) Limitation of authority. - No summons may be issued under this title, and the Secretary may not begin any action under section 7604 to enforce any summons, with respect to any person if a Justice Department referral is in effect with respect to such person.

    (2) Justice Department referral in effect. - For purposes of this subsection-

        (A) In general. - A Justice Department referral is in effect with respect to any person if-

            (i) the Secretary has recommended to the Attorney General a grand jury investigation of, or the criminal prosecution of, such person for any offense connected with the administration or enforcement of the internal revenue laws or

            (ii) any request is made under section 6103(h)(3)(B) for the disclosure of any return or return information (within the meaning of section 6103(b)) relating to such person.

        (B) Termination. - A Justice Department referral shall cease to be in effect with respect to a person when-

            (i) the Attorney General notifies the Secretary, in writing, that -

                (I) he will not prosecute such person for any offense connected with the administration or enforcement of the internal revenue laws,

                (II) he will not authorize a grand jury investigation of such person with respect to such an offense, or

                (III) he will discontinue such a grand jury investigation.

            (ii) a final disposition has been made of any criminal proceeding pertaining to the enforcement of the internal revenue laws which was instituted by the Attorney General against such person, or

            (iii) the Attorney General notifies the Secretary, in writing, that he will not prosecute such person for any offense connected with the administration or enforcement of the internal revenue laws relating to the request described in subparagraph (A)(ii).

    (3) Taxable years, etc., treated separately. - For purposes of this subsection, each taxable period (or, if there is no taxable period, each taxable event) and each tax imposed by a separate chapter of this title shall be treated separately.

(e) Limitation on examination on unreported income. - The Secretary shall not use financial status or economic reality examination techniques to determine the existence of unreported income of any taxpayer unless the Secretary has a reasonable indication that there is a likelihood of such unreported income.

᠁rity to examine books and witness is also provided under sec. 6420 (e)(2) - Gasoline ᠁᠁ ᠁ on farms; sec. 6421(g)(2) - Gasoline used for certain nonhighway purposes by local transit systems, or sold for certain exempt purposes; and sec. 6427(j)(2) - Fuels not used for taxable purposes.

٭ ٭ ٭ ٭ ٭

Sec. 7603. Service of summons

(a) In general - A summons issued under section 6420(e)(2), 6421(g)(2), 6427(j)(2), or 7602 shall be served by the Secretary, by an attested copy delivered in hand to the person to whom it is directed, or left at his last and usual place of abode; and the certificate of service signed by the person serving the summons shall be evidence of the facts it states on the hearing of an application for the enforcement of the summons. When the summons requires the production of books, papers, records, or other data, it shall be sufficient if such books, papers, records, or other data are described with reasonable certainty

(b) Service by mail to third-party recordkeepers. -

    (1) In general. - A summons referred to in subsection (a) for the production of books, papers, records, or other data by a third-party recordkeeper may also be served by certified or registered mail to the last known address of such recordkeeper.

    (2) Third party record keeper. - For purposes of paragraph (1), the term *third-party recordkeeper* means -

        (A) any mutual savings bank, cooperative bank, domestic building and loan association, or other savings institution chartered and supervised as a savings and loan or similar association under Federal or State law, any bank (as defined in section 581), or any credit union (within the meaning of section 501 (c)(14)(A));

        (B) any consumer reporting agency (as defined under section 603(f) of the Fair Credit Reporting Act (15 U.S.C. 1681 a(f)));

        (C) Any person extending credit through the use of credit cards or similar devices;

        (D) any broker (as defined in section 3(a)(4) of the Securities Exchange Act of 1934 (15 U.S.C. 78c(a)(4));

        (E) any attorney;

        (F) any accountant;

        (G) any barter exchange (as defined in section 6045(c)(3));

        (H) any regulated investment company (as defined in section 851) and any agent of such regulated investment company when acting as an agent thereof;

        (I) any enrolled agent; and

        (J) any owner or developer of a computer software source code (as defined in section 7612(d)(2)). Subparagraph (J) shall apply only with respect to a summons requiring the production of the source code referred to in subparagraph (J) or the program and data described in section 7612(b)(1)(A)(ii) to which source code relates.

Sec. 7604. Enforcement of summons

(a) Jurisdiction of District Court. - If any person is summoned under the internal revenue laws to appear, to testify, or to produce books, papers, records, or other data, the United States district court for the district in which such person resides or is found shall have jurisdiction by appropriate process to compel such attendance, testimony, or production of books, papers, records, or other data.

(b) Enforcement. - Whenever any person summoned under section 6420(e)(2), 6421 (g)(2), 6427(j)(2), or 7602 neglects or refuses to obey such summons, or to produce books, papers, records, or other data, or to give testimony, as required, the Secretary may apply to the judge of the district court or to a United States Commissioner[1] for the district within which the person so summoned resides or is found for an attachment against him as for a contempt, it shall be the duty of the judge or commissioner[1] to hear the application, and, if satisfactory proof is made, to issue an attachment, directed to some proper officer, for the arrest of such person, and upon his being brought before him to proceed to a hearing of the case; and upon such hearing the judge or the United States Commissioner[1]shall have power to make such order as he shall deem proper, not inconsistent with the law for the punishment of contempts, to enforce obedience to the requirements of the summons and to punish such person for his default or disobedience.

[1] Or United States magistrate, pursuant to P L. 90-578.

٭ ٭ ٭ ٭ ٭

Sec. 7605. Time and place of examination

(a) Time and place. - The time and place of examination pursuant to the provisions of section 6420(e)(2), 6421 (g)(2), 6427(j)(2), or 7602 shall be such time and place as may be fixed by the Secretary and as are reasonable under the circumstances. In the case of a summons under authority of paragraph (2) of section 7602, or under the corresponding authority of section 6420(e)(2), 6421 (g)(2) or 6427(j)(2), the date fixed for appearance before the Secretary shall not be less than 10 days from the date of the summons.

Sec. 7610. Fees and costs for witnesses

(a) In general. - The secretary shall by regulations establish the rates and conditions under which payment may be made of -

    (1) fees and mileage to persons who are summoned to appear before the Secretary, and

    (2) reimbursement for such costs that are reasonably necessary which have been directly incurred in searching for, reproducing, or transporting books, papers, records, or other data required to be produced by summons.

(b) Exceptions. - No payment may be made under paragraph (2) of subsection (a) if -

    (1) the person with respect to whose liability the summons is issued has a proprietary interest in the books, papers, records or other data required to be produced, or

    (2) the person summoned is the person with respect to whose liability the summons is issued or an officer, employee, agent, accountant, or attorney of such person who, at the time the summons is served, is acting as such.

(c) Summons to which section applies. - This section applies with respect to any summons authorized under section 6420(e)(2, 6421 (g)(2), 6427(j)(2), or 7602.

Sec. 7210. Failure to obey summons

Any person who, being duly summoned to appear to testify, or to appear and produce books, accounts, records, memoranda or other papers, as required under sections 6420(e)(2), 6421(g)(2), 6427(j)(2), 7602, 7603, and 7604(b), neglects to appear or to produce such books, accounts, records memoranda, or other papers, shall, upon conviction thereof, be fined not more than $1,000, or imprisoned not more than 1 year, or both, together with costs of prosecution.

Notice to Third Party
Recipient of IRS Summons

As a third-party recipient of a summons, you may be entitled to receive payment for certain costs directly incurred which are reasonably necessary to search for, reproduce, or transport records in order to comply with a summons.

This payment is made only at the rates established by the Internal Revenue Service to certain persons served with a summons to produce records or information in which the taxpayer does not have an ownership interest. The taxpayer to whose liability the summons relates and the taxpayer's officer, employee, agent, accountant, or attorney are not entitled to this payment. No payment will be made for any costs which you have charged or billed to other persons.

The rate for search costs is $8.50 an hour or fraction of an hour and is limited to the total amount of personnel time spent in locating and retrieving documents or information requested by the summons. Specific salaries of such persons may not be included in search costs. In addition, search costs do not include salaries, fees, or similar costs for analysis of material or for managerial or legal advice, expertise, research, or time spent for any of these activities. If itemized separately, search costs may include the actual costs of extracting information stored by computer in the format in which it is normally produced, based on computer time and necessary supplies; however, personnel time for computer search may be paid for only at the Internal Revenue Service rate specified above.

The rate for reproduction costs for making copies or duplicates of summoned documents, transcripts, and other similar material is 20 cents for each page. Photographs, films, and other material are reimbursed at cost.

The rate for transportation costs is the same as the actual cost necessary to transport personnel to locate and retrieve summoned records or information, or costs incurred solely by the need to transport the summoned material to the place of examination.

In addition to payment for search, reproduction, and transportation costs, persons who appear before an Internal Revenue Service officer in response to a summons may request payment for authorized witness fees and mileage fees. You may make this request by contacting the Internal Revenue Service officer or by claiming these costs separately on the itemized bill or invoice as explained below.

Instructions for requesting payment

After the summons is served, your should keep an accurate record of personnel search time, computer costs, number of reproductions made, and transportation costs. Upon satisfactory compliance, you may submit an itemized bill or invoice to the Internal Revenue Service officer before whom you were summoned to appear, either in person or by mail to the address furnished by the Internal Revenue Service officer. Please write on the itemized bill or invoice the name of the taxpayer to whose liability the summons relates.

If you wish, Form 6863, Invoice and Authorization for Payment of Administrative Summons Expenses, may be used to request payment for search, reproduction, and transportation costs. Standard Form 1157, Claims for Witness Attendance Fees, Travel, and Miscellaneous Expenses, may be used to request payment for authorized witness fees and mileage fees. These forms are available from the Internal Revenue Service officer who issued the summons.

If you have any questions about the payment, please contact the Internal Revenue Service officer before whom you were summoned to appear.

Anyone submitting false claims for payment is subject to possible criminal prosecution.

Department of the Treasury
Internal Revenue Service

www.irs.gov

Form 2039 (Rev. 12-2001)
Catalog Number 21405J

Part B — to be given to person summoned

Sec. 7609. Special procedures for third-party summons

(a) Notice-

(1) In general. - If any summons to which this section applies requires the giving of testimony on or relating to, the production of any portion of records made or kept on or relating to, or the production of any computer software source code (as defined in 7612(d)(2)) with respect to, any person (other than the person summoned) who is identified in the summons, then notice of the summons shall be given to any person so identified within 3 days of the day on which such service is made, but no later than the 23rd day before the day fixed in the summons as the day upon which such records are to be examined. Such notice shall be accompanied by a copy of the summons which has been served and shall contain an explanation of the right under subsection (b)(2) to bring a proceeding to quash the summons.

(2) Sufficiency of notice. - Such notice shall be sufficient if, on or before such third day, such notice is served in the manner provided in section 7603 (relating to service of summons) upon the person entitled to notice, or is mailed by certified or registered mail to the last known address of such person, or, in the absence of a last known address, is left with the person summoned. If such notice is mailed, it shall be sufficient if mailed to the last known address of the person entitled to notice or, in the case of notice to the Secretary under section 6903 of the existence of a fiduciary relationship, to the last known address of the fiduciary of such person, even if such person or fiduciary is then deceased, under a legal disability, or no longer in existence.

(3) Nature of summons. - Any summons to which this subsection applies (and any summons in aid of collection described in subsection (c)(2)(D)) shall identify the taxpayer to whom the summons relates or the other person to whom the records pertain and shall provide such other information as will enable the person summoned to locate the records required under the summons.

(b) Right to intervene; right to proceeding to quash. -

(1) Intervention. - Notwithstanding any other law or rule of law, any person who is entitled to notice of a summons under subsection (a) shall have the right to intervene in any proceeding with respect to the enforcement of such summons under section 7604.

(2) Proceeding to quash. -

(A) In general. - Notwithstanding any other law or rule of law, any person who is entitled to notice of a summons under subsection (a) shall have the right to begin a proceeding to quash such summons not later than the 20th day after the day such notice is given in the manner provided in subsection (a)(2). In any such proceeding, the Secretary may seek to compel compliance with the summons.

(B) Requirement that notice to person summoned and to Secretary. - If any person begins a proceeding under subparagraph (A) with respect to any summons, not later than the close of the 20-day period referred to in subparagraph (A) such person shall mail by registered or certified mail a copy of the petition to the person summoned and to such office as the Secretary may direct in the notice referred to in subsection (a)(1).

(C) Intervention, etc. - Notwithstanding any other law or rule of law, the person summoned shall have the right to intervene in any proceeding under subparagraph (A). Such person shall be bound by the decision in such proceeding (whether or not the person intervenes in such proceeding).

(c) Summons to which section applies. -

(1) In general. - Except as provided in paragraph (2), this section shall apply to any summons issued under paragraph (2) of section 7602(a) or under sections 6420(e)(2), 6421(g)(2), 6427(j)(2), or 7612.

(2) Exceptions. - This section shall not apply to any summons

(A) served on the person with respect to whose liability the summons is issued, or any officer or employee of such person;

(B) issued to determine whether or not records of the business transaction or affairs of an identified person have been made or kept;

(C) issued solely to determine the identify of any person having a numbered account (or similar arrangement) with a bank or other institution described in section 7603(b)(2)(A);

(D) issued in aid of the collection of-

(i) an assessment made or a judgment rendered against the person with respect to whose liability the summons is issued, or

(ii) the liability at law or in equity of any transferee or fiduciary of any person referred to in clause (i).

(E) - (i) issued by a criminal investigator of the Internal Revenue Service in connection with the investigation of an offense connected with the administration or enforcement of the internal revenue laws, and

(ii) served on a person who is not a third-party recordkeeper (as defined in section 7603(b)), or

(F) described in subsection (f) or (g).

(3) Records. - For purposes of this section, the term records includes books, papers, and other data.

(d) Restriction on examination of records. - No examination of any records required to be produced under a summons as to which notice is required under subsection (a) may be made -

(1) before the close of the 23rd day after the day notice with respect to the summons is given in the manner provided in subsection (a)(2), or

(2) where a proceeding under subsection (b)(2)(A) was begun within the 20-day period referred to in such subsection and the requirements of subsection (b)(2)(B) have been met, except in accordance with an order of the court having jurisdiction of such proceeding or with the consent of the person beginning the proceeding to quash.

(e) Suspension of Statute of Limitations. -

(1) Subsection (b) action. - If any person takes any action as provided in subsection (b) and such person is the person with respect to whose liability the summons is issued (or is the agent, nominee, or other person acting under the direction or control of such person), then the running of any period of limitations under section 6501 (relating to the assessment and collection of tax) or under section 6531 (relating to criminal prosecutions) with respect to such person shall be suspended for the period during which a proceeding, and appeals therein, with respect to the enforcement of such summons is pending.

(2) Suspension after 6 months of service of summons. - In the absence of the resolution of the summoned party's response to the summons, the running of any period of limitations under section 6501 or under section 6531 with respect to any person with respect to whose liability the summons is issued (other than a person taking action as provided in subsection (b)) shall be suspended for the period-

(A) beginning on the date which is 6 months after the service of such summons, and

(B) ending with the final resolution of such response.

(f) Additional requirements in the case of a John Doe summons. -

Any summons described in subsection (c)(1) which does not identify the person with respect to whose liability the summons is issued may be served only after a court proceeding in which the Secretary establishes that -

(1) the summons relates to the investigation of a particular person or ascertainable group or class of persons,

(2) there is a reasonable basis for believing that such person or group or class of persons may fail or may have failed to comply with any provision of any internal revenue law, and

(3) the information sought to be obtained from the examination of the records or testimony (and the identity of the person or persons with respect to whose liability the summons is issued) is not readily available from other sources.

(g) Special exception for certain summonses. -

A summons is described in this subsection if, upon petition by the Secretary, the court determines, on the basis of the facts and circumstances alleged, that there is reasonable cause to believe the giving of notice may lead to attempts to conceal, destroy, or alter records relevant to the examination, to prevent the communication of information from other persons through intimidation, bribery, or collusion, or to flee to avoid prosecution, testifying, or production of records.

(h) Jurisdiction of district court; etc. -

(1) Jurisdiction. - The United States district court for the district within which the person to be summoned resides or is found shall have jurisdiction to hear and determine any proceedings brought under subsection (b)(2), (f), or (g). An order denying the petition shall be deemed a final order which may be appealed.

(2) Special rule for proceedings under subsections (f) and (g) . - The determinations required to be made under subsections (f) and (g) shall be made ex parte and shall be made solely on the petition and supporting affidavits.

(i) Duty of summoned party. -

(1) Recordkeeper must assemble records and be prepared to produce records- On receipt of a summons to which this section applies for the production of records, the summoned party shall proceed to assemble the records requested, or such portion thereof as the Secretary may prescribe, and shall be prepared to produce the records pursuant to the summons on the day on which the records are to be examined.

(2) Secretary may give summoned party certificate. - The Secretary may issue a certificate to the summoned party that the period prescribed for beginning a proceeding to quash a summons has expired and that no such proceeding began within such period, or that the taxpayer consents to the examination.

(3) Protection for summoned party who discloses. - Any summoned party, or agent or employee thereof, making a disclosure of records of testimony pursuant to this section in good faith reliance on the certificate of the Secretary or an order of a court requiring production of records or the giving of such testimony shall not be liable to any customer or other person for such disclosure.

(4) Notice of suspension of statute of limitations in the case of a John Doe summons. - In the case of a summons described in subsection (f) with respect to which any period of limitations has been suspended under subsection (e)(2), the summoned party shall provide notice of such suspension to any person described in subsection (f).

(j) Use of summons not required. -

Nothing in this section shall be construed to limit the Secretary's ability to obtain information, other than by summons, through formal or informal procedures authorized by sections 7601 and 7602.

Form **2039** (Rev. 12-2001)

¶723 Exhibit 7-3

SCHEDULE UTP (Form 1120) Department of the Treasury Internal Revenue Service	**Uncertain Tax Position Statement** ▶ File with Form 1120, 1120-F, 1120-L, or 1120-PC. ▶ See separate instructions.	OMB No. 1545-0123

Name of entity as shown on page 1 of tax return	**EIN of entity**

This Part I, Schedule UTP (Form 1120) is page _____ of _____ Part I pages.

Part I   **Uncertain Tax Positions for the Current Tax Year.** See instructions for how to complete columns (a) through (f). Enter, in Part III, a description for each uncertain tax position (UTP).

Check this box if the corporation was unable to obtain information from related parties sufficient to determine whether a tax position is a UTP (see instructions) ▶ ☐

(a) UTP No.	(b) Primary IRC Section (e.g., "61", "108", etc.)	(c) Timing Codes (check if Permanent, Temporary, or both)		(d) Pass-Through Entity EIN	(e) Major Tax Position	(f) Ranking of Tax Position
		P	T	-	☐	
		P	T	-	☐	
		P	T	-	☐	
		P	T	-	☐	
		P	T	-	☐	
		P	T	-	☐	
		P	T	-	☐	
		P	T	-	☐	
		P	T	-	☐	
		P	T	-	☐	
		P	T	-	☐	
		P	T	-	☐	
		P	T	-	☐	
		P	T	-	☐	
		P	T	-	☐	
		P	T	-	☐	
		P	T	-	☐	
		P	T	-	☐	
		P	T	-	☐	
		P	T	-	☐	

For Paperwork Reduction Act Notice, see the Instructions for Form 1120.   Cat. No. 54658Q   Schedule UTP (Form 1120) 2010

Schedule UTP (Form 1120) 2010   Page **2**

| Name of entity as shown on page 1 of tax return | | | | EIN of entity | | |

This Part II, Schedule UTP (Form 1120) is page _____ of _____ Part II pages.

Part II   Uncertain Tax Positions for Prior Tax Years. Do not complete for 2010.

(a) UTP No.	(b) Primary IRC Section (e.g., "61", "108", etc.)	(c) Timing Codes (check if Permanent, Temporary, or both)	(d) Pass-Through Entity EIN	(e) Major Tax Position	(f) Ranking of Tax Position	(g) Year of Tax Position

Schedule UTP (Form 1120) 2010

Schedule UTP (Form 1120) 2010 Page **3**

Name of entity as shown on page 1 of tax return	EIN of entity

This Part III, Schedule UTP (Form 1120) is page _____ of _____ Part III pages.

Part III	**Concise Descriptions of UTPs.** Indicate the corresponding UTP number from Part I, column (a). Use as many Part III pages as necessary (see instructions).

UTP No.	Concise Description of Uncertain Tax Position

Schedule UTP (Form 1120) 2010

¶724 DISCUSSION QUESTIONS

1. You are an accountant and a client of yours is under audit by the IRS. The revenue agent contacts you after she has spent some time investigating the taxpayer's records. She says that there are certain items that she has not been able to locate and she wishes to review your workpapers, retained copies of returns and files.

   (A) Do you grant her request?

   (B) Assume that the revenue agent sent you a letter stating that under Code Sec. 7602 she has the right to request, review and copy the records and that she is formally requesting them. Do you comply with her request at this point?

   (C) If you turn the records over under either of these circumstances, do you expose yourself to any potential liability to your client?

2. On September 15, 20X0, Special Agent Iris Ireland of the IRS issued a summons to Rudy Recordkeeper, a certified public accountant. The summons sought production of Recordkeeper's workpapers regarding Gilbert Giltiasin, who was then under examination. Within the time prescribed by law, Giltiasin took steps to stay compliance by Recordkeeper.

   On October 9, 20X0, a petition to quash the summons was filed with the District Court in the district in which Recordkeeper resides. On the same day, Ireland called Recordkeeper and asked him how long it would take to assemble the records if the summons was enforced. Recordkeeper estimated that it would take approximately 100 hours to put together the records. Iris Ireland asked Recordkeeper to begin assembling the records immediately so that if the summons was enforced, there would not be a long delay before he could get the records. Must Recordkeeper comply with this request?

3. Iris Ireland also wishes to review the personal records of Gilbert Giltiasin. He issues a summons properly addressed to Giltiasin and serves it by taking it to Giltiasin's house and handing it to Giltiasin's three-year-old daughter. Unfortunately, she uses it to cut out paper dolls and never gives it to her father. Later, the IRS seeks to hold Gilbert in contempt for failing to comply with the summons. Does Gilbert have a defense because the summons was improperly served?

4. Wanda Withheld is the president of Wexley's, Inc. She failed to pay over her social security and withholding taxes for the last quarter of 20X0. Wanda has acknowledged her personal liability and consented to an assessment of an amount equal to the trust fund portion of these taxes. Wanda has failed to respond to the series of notices from the IRS seeking payment of the balance due plus interest. She has also ignored the telephone calls and repeated attempts by the revenue officer to meet with her in person. The revenue officer has also sought a financial statement from Wanda, but to no avail.

Assume that you are a new revenue officer and you seek to enforce collection against Wanda. What actions, if any, are you authorized to take to discover the value and location of any assets held by Wanda which are available for collection?

5. If the Revenue Officer in Problem 4, above, issues a summons to the third-party recordkeepers, is Wexley's, Inc., entitled to notice under Code Sec. 7609?

6. Tilda Taxpayer and her CPA, I.M. Careful, prepare a comprehensive amended return but ultimately decide not file it. If the IRS issues a summons with regard to that draft document, does Tilda have to submit it?

7. USCo, a U.S. C corporation, wholly-owns ForCo, a foreign corporation. ForCo has $800,000 of accumulated e&p and accumulated foreign taxes paid of $200,000. In 20X1, ForCo distributes a dividend of $800,000 that is subject to foreign country F's withholding tax, which is based not on the gross amount of the dividend, but on the amount of the annual income of ForCo at a 10% rate for $30,000. Because of the question over the creditability of the withholding tax as a Section 903 credit for a tax in lieu of an income tax, USCo's tax director books a $30,000 reserve. Must USCo file a Schedule UTP?

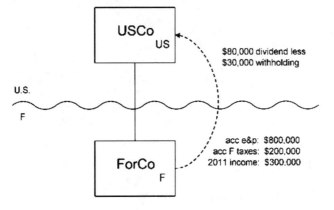

CHAPTER 8
EVIDENTIARY PRIVILEGES

¶801 INTRODUCTION

Although the IRS has broad investigatory powers, the IRS may not obtain information or documents that are subject to evidentiary privileges. The primary evidentiary privileges are the attorney-client privilege, which the Code extends on a limited basis to cover other tax practitioners, and the work product doctrine.

¶802 ATTORNEY-CLIENT PRIVILEGE

The attorney-client privilege protects confidential communication between an attorney and client for a purpose of obtaining or providing legal advice.[1] The privilege is broader than mere communications between a client and an attorney; the privilege extends to communications with non-lawyers provided the purpose of the communication is to assist the attorney in rendering legal advice to the taxpayer.

When an attorney hires an agent to assist him in a tax controversy, any work product produced by the accountant subsequent to such employment will be protected in the same manner as if it was prepared by the attorney. To aid in the protection of such information, a written engagement letter should be prepared confirming that the attorney is retaining the accountant and that the accountant will be working under the attorney's direction and control. This engagement letter is commonly known as a *Kovel Letter* (see Exhibit 8-1 at ¶811).[2] The reason for using a *Kovel Letter* is that the presence of an accountant may be necessary to "translate" a taxpayer's story to an attorney who may not be as well versed as the accountant in tax matters. The courts have held that the accountant must be "necessary, or at least highly useful" in facilitating the attorney's provision of legal advice in order to be protected by the attorney-client privilege.[3]

The privilege does not extend to communications made to the accountant prior to his retention by an attorney. It is better practice, therefore, not to hire an accountant who has previously worked on the matter, thus avoiding the stringent burden of separating what was communicated to him before and after being retained by the attorney.

> **Example 8-1:** CPA conducts Taxpayer's audit and prepares Taxpayer's return, which shows a depreciation deduction on Taxpayer's property, plant and equipment. When the IRS questions the depreciation deduction during audit, CPA begins preparing a more refined schedule and continues to work

---

[1] *Upjohn Co. v. United States*, 449 U.S. 383 (1981).

[2] *United States v. Kovel*, 296 F.2d 918 (2nd Cir. 1961) 62-1 USTC ¶9111; *In the Matter of Grand Jury Proceedings*, 220 F.3d 568 (7th Cir. 2000), 2000-2 USTC ¶50,598.

[3] *Cavallaro v. U.S.*, 284 F.3d 236 (1st Cir. 2002).

on that schedule for an Attorney that Taxpayer has retained to deal with the IRS. Assuming that the schedules were necessary to "translate" the Taxpayer's story to the Attorney, the schedules are privileged to the extent of their creation at the Attorney's direction. The attorney-client privilege does not apply to any schedules CPA prepared prior to the Attorney retaining her.

The attorney should send an engagement letter to the accountant that includes the following: (1) a recital that the attorney is hiring the accountant to assist him in rending legal advice; (2) the nature and scope of the accountant engagement; (3) acknowledgement that payment will come from the law firm (and that the ultimate client is not to be billed); (4) acknowledgement that all records, schedules, documents, etc., of the accountant-agent will be the sole property of the attorney; and (5) a recital that on completion of the assignment, all of the accountant's files will be delivered to the attorney and copies will not be retained.

To insure the communications between the client and the accountant will continue to be privileged under *Kovel,* the attorney as opposed to the accountant must act as the taxpayer's primary representative and play a visible role.

¶803 CODE SECTION 7525(a) PRIVILEGE FOR TAX PRACTITIONERS

With some exceptions, the judicially recognized attorney-client privilege statutorily extends to communications between clients and individuals who are authorized to practice before the IRS. More specifically, the same common law protections of confidentiality that apply to a communication between a taxpayer and an attorney shall also apply to a communication with respect to tax advice between a taxpayer and certain tax practitioners to the extent the communication would be considered a privileged communication if it were between a taxpayer and an attorney.[4]

The privilege only applies to tax advice between a taxpayer and a Federally Authorized Tax Practitioner (FATP), i.e., one who is authorized to practice before the IRS, but the privilege is limited.

Tax advice means advice given by a FATP with respect to a matter that is within the scope of the practitioner's authority to practice.[5] Circular 230 (see Chapter 3) defines a practitioner's authority to practice as encompassing "all matters connected with presentation to the Internal Revenue Service or any of its officers or employees relating to a client's rights, privileges or liabilities under the laws or regulations administered by the IRS."

Under Circular 230, tax advice means advice given after an event has occurred that requires presentation of information to the IRS. Since planning advice does not necessitate presenting anything to the IRS and because a tax practitioner technically does not have to be authorized to practice before the IRS

---

[4] Code Sec. 7525(a).   [5] Code Sec. 7525(a)(3).

to give planning advice, such advice would not be privileged under Code Sec. 7525(a) statute.

> **Example 8-2:** Communications regarding a corporation's value for estate tax given by a FATP is not privileged since it does not meet the narrow definition of tax advice. On the other hand, communications with respect to how to respond to an IRS inquiry regarding a corporation's value in a civil audit of that estate tax would constitute tax advice that would be privileged.

This limited privilege does not apply to criminal matters.[6]

> **Example 8-3:** The IRS audits Taxpayer for the issue of expensing versus capitalizing certain items. During the audit, Taxpayer tells her CPA that the schedule was "a little aggressive." Later, the audit evolves into a criminal investigation and at a criminal tax trial, the IRS calls CPA to the witness stand with respect to Taxpayer's comments about the expenses. Because it is a criminal trial, the limited privilege does not protect Taxpayer's comments to CPA. However, had Taxpayer made similar comments to her attorney, the comments would not be admissible due to the attorney-client privilege.

Only communications subject to the attorney-client privilege are protected communications. They must be based on facts that the taxpayer provides the practitioner for the purpose of receiving an opinion, services or assistance in some proceeding and the communication is made in confidence and by the taxpayer. The privilege applies only to advice on matters and is not applicable where the practitioner is acting in another capacity, such as a scrivener engaged to prepare a tax return.[7] The privilege is that of the taxpayer and may be waived by the taxpayer or waived by disclosure to a third party.

> **Example 8-4:** Taxpayer provides a schedule regarding the expense versus the capitalization of certain items and tells her CPA that the schedule is "a little aggressive." CPA prepares Taxpayer's return based on this schedule. The statement regarding the schedule is not privileged because it was provided in the course of preparing a return.

Limited to noncriminal proceedings before the IRS or in a federal court, the privilege does not extend to proceedings before other federal or state administrative agencies or in connection with issues arising out of transactions and lawsuits brought by third parties. Therefore, regulatory bodies other than the IRS may continue to compel the production of information pertaining to accountant/client communications.

---

[6] Code Sec. 7525(a)(2)(A) and (B).

[7] *United States v. Frederick,* 182 F.3d 496 (7th Cir. 1999), 99-1 USTC ¶ 50,465. In theory, the attorney-client privilege does not distinguish between in-house and outside counsel. *Upjohn Co. v. United States,* 449 U.S. 383 (1981), 1-1 USTC ¶ 9138; *Hartz Mountain Industries v. Comm'r,* 93 TC 521 (1989), CCH Dec. 46,126. In practice, however, courts apply greater scrutiny to privilege claims asserted by in-house attorneys. This is because only legal advice—not business advice—is protected by the privilege.

Given that in-house counsel are resolving legal issues, in a business setting, it is often difficult to divorce the legal from the business communications.

In-house tax counsel have it doubly hard. Like all in-house counsel, they must establish they have provided legal advice rather than business advice. They also have the added burden of proving that the tax advice they provided does not constitute accounting services or tax return preparation because neither is protected by the privilege.

¶803

Example 8-5: PharmCo, a pharmaceutical company, is the subject of an IRS examination of its transfer pricing practices. During the course of the examination, PharmCo's Tax Director provides an outside accountant with a schedule detailing the arm's length pricing for the license of a valuable pharmaceutical. Subsequently, the Food and Drug Administration ("FDA") independently conducts an investigation of PharmCo and summonses that schedule from the outside accountant. Because the privilege under Code Sec. 7525(a) only extends to representations before the IRS, the FDA may obtain that schedule. The FDA would not have been able to obtain that schedule were it provided to an attorney instead of an accountant.

Example 8-6: CPA annually prepares Taxpayer's federal income tax return. While seeking the tax advice of CPA, Taxpayer tells CPA that although he properly reports interest income earned from foreign bank accounts, he will never file an FBAR (TD F 90-22.1) with respect to those foreign bank accounts. Because the FBAR rules are under the purview of the Comptroller of the Currency (Title 31) instead of the Internal Revenue Code (Title 26), Taxpayer's communication to CPA does not come within the limited privilege. However, if the communication had been made to an attorney, the attorney-client privilege would apply.

The privilege does not apply to any written communication between an accountant, director, shareholder, officer, employee, agent or representative of the corporation in connection with the promotion or the direct or indirect participation of that corporation in a tax shelter.[8]

Example 8-7: Consider a promoter that hires an accountant to represent a master limited partnership, which is a tax shelter.[9] During the course of the representation, the promoter tells the accountant numerous facts with respect to the tax shelter. Because the tax shelter is under audit, the communications from the promoter to the accountant are not privileged. This shelter limitation on the privilege would not have applied had the representative been an attorney instead of an accountant. However, a similar communication to an attorney would come within the attorney-client privilege.

¶804 PRIVILEGE UNDER THE WORK-PRODUCT DOCTRINE

Generally, work product would be made up of two classes of documents. First, interviews and written statements of witnesses. Second, correspondence and memoranda in which the practitioner puts in written form his or her mental impressions and legal theories with respect to a litigated or potentially litigated matter. Although not an evidentiary privilege, work product is conditionally protected from compulsory disclosure in a tax controversy. In the rare situation that work product may be discoverable by the IRS in a tax controversy, the IRS has a significant challenge of showing absolute necessity to have the information or

---

[8] Code Sec. 7525(b); *U.S. v. BDO Seidman*, 337 F.3d 802 (7th Cir. 2003); *Valero Energy Corp. v. U.S.*, 569 F.3d 626 (7th Cir. 2009).

[9] As defined in Code Sec. 6652(d)(2)(C)(ii).

that the denial of discovery would unfairly prejudice the IRS's preparation of the case.[10]

While courts have occasionally allowed the IRS access to certain work products by the requisite showing of necessity or unfair prejudice, the Supreme Court has indicated that such showing would *never* require one to produce his mental impressions and theories of the case.[11] If an otherwise discoverable document were to contain such information, the court would have to allow such information to be redacted before completing its production.

> **Example 8-8:** Taxpayer has received a Statutory Notice of Deficiency and, as a result, must petition the Tax Court within 90 days to prevent the IRS from assessing the deficiency. Taxpayer immediately meets to present the facts to Attorney and requests Attorney to draft a memorandum evaluating the issues and the prospects for success in litigation. This memorandum puts in written form the Attorney's mental impressions and legal theories with respect to a potentially litigated matter and, therefore, is privileged under the work-product doctrine.

The work-product doctrine applies once it is reasonable to assume that litigation involving the particular issue to which the work product relates is inevitable, even if no litigation is pending at the time information is produced. In tax controversies, the work-product doctrine generally will attach when an administrative dispute with the IRS is anticipated.[12] As a result, the privilege under the work-product doctrine applies to both accountants and attorneys.

The IRS will often argue that the work-product doctrine does not apply to communications occurring before issuance of the Statutory Notice of Deficiency. However, the courts have rejected this position and extended the work-product doctrine to communications long before the IRS has issued the Statutory Notice of Deficiency. In *Bernardo v. Commissioner*,[13] the taxpayers claimed a charitable contribution deduction for their donation of a granite sculpture to a transit authority. The taxpayers received notice from the IRS Art Advisory Board with respect to potential valuation issues and, as a result, the taxpayers engaged an accountant to prepare a document supporting the taxpayer's position. Even though these documents were prepared before the IRS issued a Statutory Notice of Deficiency, the Tax Court found that these documents were protected under the work-product doctrine because the accountant prepared them in anticipation of litigation.

Communications may be privileged even before the transaction occurs as long as that communications is with respect to an unsettled area of the tax law that may almost certainly result in litigation.[14]

---

[10] The courts appear loathe to find that the IRS has surpassed this significant challenge. *P.T.& L. Construction Co. v. Comm'r*, 63 TC 404, 408 (1974); *Zaentz v. Commissioner*, 73 T.C. 469, 478 (1979).

[11] *Hickman v. Taylor*, 329 U.S. 495 (1947).

[12] *U.S. v. Adlman*, 134 F.3d 1194 (2nd Cir. 1998), 98-1 USTC ¶ 50,230.

[13] *Bernardo v. Comm'r*, 104 TC 677, 1687 (1995), CCH Dec. 50,705; Rathe v. Comm'r, 129 TC 45 (2007).

[14] *Roxworthy v. United States*, 2006-2 USTC ¶ 50,458 (6th Cir.), Nonacq. AOD 2007-04 IRB 2007-40.

Example 8-9: Taxpayer contemplates entering a listed transaction under Regulation section 1.6011-4(b)(2). Attorney advises Taxpayer that because the contemplated transaction is a listed transaction, the IRS will almost certainly examine the issue and designate the matter for litigation. Taxpayer subsequently engages Attorney to draft a memorandum evaluating the chances of prevailing on the merits at trial. Even though the IRS has not issued a Statutory Notice of Deficiency, the return has not been prepared and the Taxpayer has not even engaged in the contemplated transaction, the memorandum is still privileged under the work-product doctrine.

The work-product doctrine can only relate to information produced when it is reasonable to assume that litigation could ensue. Therefore, one cannot employ the work-product doctrine to shield information on behalf of a client when a possibility of litigation is remote or the records in question were prepared in the ordinary course of business as opposed to being prepared in preparation for litigation.[15]

Example 8-10: BizCo annually hires CPA to conduct an audit and prepare BizCo's tax return. CPA prepares workpapers to make book entries, prepare financial statements and clear audit issues. These workpapers are more routine in the ordinary course of business and are not protected by the work-product doctrine because they were not prepared in anticipation of litigation.

¶805 WAIVER OF PRIVILEGES

Voluntary disclosure to third parties of information that would otherwise be conditionally protected under the privileges discussed in this chapter by the taxpayer constitutes a waiver of the privilege.[16] Once a practitioner obtains information that is subject to the privilege, taxpayers must act to ensure that such information is kept confidential. If the taxpayer acts in a way that could be interpreted as not trying to keep the information confidential, the information may lose the privilege through waiver.

Example 8-11: After Taxpayer receives a Statutory Notice of Deficiency from the IRS, Taxpayer engages CPA to prepare a memorandum that supports the Taxpayer's position as a basis for filing a petition in Tax Court. Bank does not want to lend money to Taxpayer while Taxpayer's finances are clouded by the pending Tax Court litigation. As a result, Taxpayer, in an attempt to convince Bank that everything is fine and that Taxpayer will prevail in litigation, provides a copy of CPA's memorandum to Bank. Taxpayer has waived any opportunity to assert either the tax practitioner privilege under Code Sec. 7525(a) or the work-product doctrine.

---

[15] *Textron, Inc. v. United States,* 2009-2 USTC ¶ 50,514 (2d. Cir.).

[16] *In re Sealed case,* 676 F.2d 793 (CD cir. 1982).

¶811 Exhibit 8-1

SAMPLE "*KOVEL*-TYPE" LETTER

[DATE]

Privileged and Confidential Tax Advice Attorney-Client and Work-Product Doctrine

[NAME OF ACCOUNTANT]

[ADDRESS]

Re: Investigation Agreement

Dear Mr. Accountant:

This letter will memorialize the terms and conditions of the engagement of your accounting firm _____ (hereinafter referred to as the "Investigation Firm") by the law office of _____ (hereinafter referred to as the "Law Firm"). The Law Firm represents _____ (hereinafter referred to as the "Client"). The Investigation Firm will assist the Law Firm in connection with the rendering of legal services by the Law Firm to Client, and, in particular, with certain matters involving the examination of the correct amount of Federal and State income tax liability, as well as the location and interview of certain individuals, including, without limitation, the performance of investigative, advisory, and consulting services (collectively "investigative services") for the Law Firm. The engagement also includes all steps that are necessary to assist in the analysis, documentation, and review of the various individuals to be located and interviewed.

Investigation Firm shall undertake such examination of books, records, papers and documents, and other items as Law Firm may request, and all of the Investigation Firm's findings with respect to the services performed pursuant to this Agreement shall be submitted directly and exclusively to the Law Firm. In addition, the Investigation Firm may be called upon to participate in conferences with the Client, as well as members of the Law Firm, and to conduct or participate in meetings with other persons pursuant to instructions from the Law Firm.

The Investigation Firm shall keep the Law Firm advised of the steps that are being taken in the performance of the requested services, and the Investigation Firm and shall receive permissions from the Law Firm prior to incurring any extraordinary expenses (including, but without limitation, travel outside of the immediate area) with regard to this equipment.

It is understood that the Investigation Firm shall be compensated for their work for the Law Firm in these matters in accordance with the Investigation Firm's letter dated _____ attached as Exhibit A. It is also understood that all billings from the Investigation Firm shall be made monthly in writing and directed to the Law Firm at the above address (and not to the client). Law Firm shall make immediate payment to the Investigation Firm.

It is expressly agreed between the Investigation Firm and the Law Firm that all originals and copies of statements, records, schedules, work papers, memoranda, reports, and all other documents prepared by the Investigation Firm, incident to or in accordance with the professional services rendered to the Law Firm, shall be, and at all times remain, the property of the Law Firm and the Client and shall be considered privileged matters, not to be disclosed to any other person(s). Any and all originals and copies of statements, records, schedules, work papers, memoranda, reports, and any other documents belonging to the Client or the Law Firm which is directly or indirectly placed in the Investigation Firm's possession or which the Law Firm directs the Investigation Firm to take possession of with respect to this matter shall be given temporarily and solely for the purpose of enabling the Investigation Firm to assist the Law Firm in making legal decisions. Custody thereof shall be retained by the Investigation Firm only to the extent necessary and for the period of time necessary to perform those assignments given to the Investigation Firm. Furthermore, the statements, records, schedules, work papers, memoranda, and other documents shall at all times remain the property of the Client or the Law Firm and shall be considered privileged matters, not to be disclosed to any other person(s). All original and copies of all of the items referred to in this paragraph shall be turned over to the Client or a member of the Law Firm immediately upon either oral or written demand or the completion of this assignment. None of the foregoing material or information referred to in this paragraph shall be revealed to any third party without the advance written consent of a member of the Law Firm. In the event that the Law Firm requests the Investigation Firm to turn over all documents relating to this matter to either the Client or the Law Firm, the Investigation Firm further agrees that no photocopies or reproductions of the documents shall be retained by the Investigation Firm without express written approval of the Law Firm. The Investigation Firm shall be responsible for its compliance with the terms of this Agreement.

All oral and written communications between the Law Firm and all other persons representing or acting on behalf of the Client and the Investigation Firm, or between the Client and the investigation Firm as a result of this engagement, shall be strictly confidential and privileged and shall be safeguarded so as to protect the attorney/client privilege and work product doctrine which attached to such information and documentation.

As part of its Agreement to provide investigative services in this matter, Investigation Firm will immediately notify the Law Firm of the happening of any one of the following events: (a) the exhibition or surrender of any documents or records prepared by or submitted to Investigation Firm or someone under Investigative Firm's direction, in a manner not expressly authorized by the Law Firm; (b) a request by anyone to examine, inspect, or copy such documents or records; (c) any attempt to serve, or the actual service of, any court order, subpoena, or summons upon Investigation Firm which requires the production of any such documents or records.

¶811

If this letter accurately sets forth our understanding and agreement, please date and sign the enclosed original of this letter and return it to us for our files.

Yours very truly,

_____

Law Firm

Accepted and Agreed To:

_____

Accountant

_____

Date

¶812 DISCUSSION QUESTIONS

1. You are an accountant. A sole proprietor client of yours asks you to prepare a tax advice memorandum with regard to the prospective purchase of a business. You do so. Several years later, during an examination, an IRS agent issues a summons for said memorandum. Is there an accountant privilege for said memorandum?

   (A) Assume that the summons was instead issued by a Special Agent of the Criminal Investigation Division.

   (B) Assume that the summons was instead issued by the Labor Department (with respect to a pension issue).

2. You are an accountant. A corporate client asks you to give tax advice with respect to its recently completed corporate merger. You conclude that the merger qualifies as a tax-free reorganization and deliver your memorandum exclusively to the client. Subsequently, the client confidentially sends your memorandum to a concerned creditor. Can you and/or the client claim accountant's privilege?

3. You are an accountant. Your client, an individual, hires you to investigate the tax treatment of a particular transaction reported on a prior return (which has been prepared by another accountant). The client is concerned that the treatment was erroneous and, therefore, she might be subject to some kind of penalty. Is your tax advice memorandum privileged under either an attorney-client privilege or attorney work-product doctrine? How would your answer change if the client's attorney hires you?

4. Assume that a client is looking for tax advice from an accountant which will be privileged. Under what circumstances would it be reasonable for a client to rely upon an accountant's privilege?

CHAPTER 9
ACCESS TO INTERNAL REVENUE SERVICE INFORMATION

¶901 INFORMATION OF THE IRS

In the process of administering the Internal Revenue laws, the IRS obtains and generates a substantial amount of information. This may take the form of workpapers, memoranda, records and other documents obtained during examinations from taxpayers. This information may also include determinations, rules, procedures and legal positions developed by the IRS or its Chief Counsel. Congress has enacted specific laws to require disclosure of such information to taxpayers in appropriate situations. Superimposed on these provisions for liberal disclosure is additional legislation that attempts to protect the privacy and confidentiality of tax information furnished to the IRS. At times, these protective provisions and disclosure requirements appear to work at cross purposes.

In addition to the access to IRS information provided by specific legislation, taxpayers involved in civil tax litigation may obtain relevant information from the IRS under the pretrial discovery rules available in the courts. The Tax Court, the Court of Federal Claims and the District Courts all permit such discovery under their own rules of procedure.

¶902 THE FREEDOM OF INFORMATION ACT

The most important legislation permitting taxpayer access to IRS information is commonly known as the Freedom of Information Act (FOIA). FOIA provides that, with certain exceptions and exclusions, every government agency is required to make available to the public all information and records in its possession.[1] FOIA sets forth three methods by which certain types of information will be made available.

1. The first method requires current publication in the Federal Register of the agency's procedural and operating rules, substantive rules, general policy statements and descriptions of its organization.[2]

2. The second method requires that each agency permit inspection and copying of final opinions and orders in litigated cases, policy statements and interpretations not published in the Federal Register and administrative staff manuals that affect the public.[3] Most of the relevant informa-

---

[1] 5 U.S.C. § 552.

[2] 5 U.S.C. § 552(a)(1).

[3] 5 U.S.C. § 552(a)(2). Such material relating to the IRS is generally available in the public reading rooms at the National Office and regional offices. Copies will be mailed upon request, but such service is subject to standard fees. Reg. § 601.702(b)(3).

tion the IRS makes available or publishes is reproduced by commercial publishers and is in most tax libraries.

3. The third method for making information available to the public is probably the most significant to tax practitioners: any person may request access to any records maintained by the IRS.[4] However, various exemptions and exclusions limit the right to disclosure under FOIA (see ¶904). In addition, the restrictions relating to confidentiality of tax returns and return information under Code Sec. 6103 further limit the information the IRS is permitted to disclose.

> **Example 9-1:** After Taxpayer receives a 30-day letter, Taxpayer hires Attorney who seeks an Appeal conference. Attorney makes a FOIA request in order to see what the IRS obtained during the examination.

¶903 INFORMATION OBTAINABLE

Congress enacted Code Sec. 6110 to permit open public inspection of private letter rulings, determination letters and technical advice memoranda issued by the IRS.[5] It preempts and supersedes all requirements of FOIA to make such information available to the public.[6] More specifically, the text of any ruling, determination letter, or technical advice memorandum is available only after deletion of identifying details and confidential information regarding the taxpayer.[7] Any background information in the IRS files relating to the request for a ruling or determination will be made available only upon special request.[8] Revenue Procedure 95-15 sets forth the procedure for making requests for background file documents relating to a ruling or technical advice memorandum. No one may inspect any technical advice memorandum involving a matter that is the subject of a civil or criminal fraud investigation or a jeopardy or termination assessment until all actions relating to such investigation or assessment are completed.[9]

Taxpayers may not cite private letter rulings or determination letters as precedent in any proceeding[10] There must be deleted from such disclosures all identifying details regarding the person requesting the determination as well as all information generally exempted under FOIA.[11] On occasion, taxpayers must consider whether the business information they provide in a private letter ruling may disadvantage the taxpayer's business should competitors discover the business information.

---

[4] 5 U.S.C. §552(a)(3). See ¶907, *infra*, for procedures relating to the formal request for such information.

[5] See Chapter 16, *infra*, for discussion of procedures relating to issuance of private letter rulings and determination letters.

[6] Code Sec. 6110(l).

[7] Code Sec. 6110(c).

[8] Code Sec. 6110(e); Reg. §§301.6110-1(b) and 301.6110-5(d).

[9] Reg. §301.6110-1(b)(2).

[10] Reg. §301.6110-7(b). However, private letter rulings may be cited to avoid the substantial understatement penalty under Code Sec. 6662(d)(2)(B)(i).

[11] See ¶905.

Private letter rulings and technical advice memoranda are open to inspection and copying at the public reading rooms of the National Office of the IRS.[12] Anyone may inspect and copy determination letters the reading rooms of the local offices that issued the letters.[13] Written requests for copies of such material may be made to the IRS reading rooms holding such material for inspection.[14]

¶904 EXEMPTIONS AND EXCLUSIONS UNDER FOIA

The Freedom of Information Act provides nine specific exemptions from required disclosure.[15] Only six of these nine exemptions and two other provisions are relevant to the typical disclosure requested by a taxpayer.[16]

Internal Personnel Rules and Practices. In general, rules which only affect the conduct of IRS personnel as employees that do not relate to their conduct with respect to the public are exempted from disclosure.[17] However, if an internal personnel rule affects interests outside of the IRS, that rule must be made available to the public.[18] Major portions of the Internal Revenue Manual have been made available to the public despite this exemption.[19] Such information will be made available unless the information would assist an individual in evading the law or would endanger the safety of law enforcement agents.[20]

> **Example 9-2:** To avoid arguing by its attorneys, the IRS Chief Counsel promulgates procedures for the assignment of corner offices. Because these procedures do not relate to the conduct of the IRS attorneys with respect to the public, FOIA exempts these procedures from disclosure.

Information Exempt by Other Statute. The IRS need not disclose under FOIA if it is specifically exempted from disclosure by some other law. Such law must (1) require that the matter be withheld from the public in such a manner as to leave no discretion on the issue or (2) establish particular criteria for withholding or refers to particular matters to be withheld.[21]

> **Example 9-3:** Suppose a Homeland Security statute prohibits the disclosure of the names of potential terrorists to the public. However, Homeland Security provides the names of these potential terrorists to the IRS to obtain their last known address. The IRS may not disclose the names of the potential terrorists to the public due to the exemption from disclosure in the Homeland Security statute.

---

[12] These rulings and memoranda are now commercially published and are available in most tax libraries.

[13] Reg. § 301.6110-1(c).

[14] *Id.*

[15] 5 U.S.C. § 552(b).

[16] The three exemptions that are normally irrelevant to the usual request for tax information include (1) matters involving national security, (2) information relating to the regulation of financial institu-

tions, and (3) geological and geophysical information concerning wells.

[17] 5 U.S.C. § 552(b)(2).

[18] See *Dept. of Air Force v. Rose*, 425 U.S. 352 (1976).

[19] *Long v. IRS*, 339 F.Supp. 1266 (W.D. Wash. 1971), 72-1 USTC ¶ 9110.

[20] *Crooker v. Bureau of Alcohol, Tobacco & Firearms*, 670 F.2d 1051 (D.C. Cir. 1981).

[21] 5 U.S.C. § 552(b)(3). *Crooker v. IRS*, 75 AFTR2d 2375 (D.D.C. 1995); *Pacific Fisheries v. IRS*, 2009-2 USTC ¶ 50,510 (9th Cir.).

A taxpayer may obtain its own return and return information.[22] However, return information will not be disclosed even to the taxpayer or those authorized by the taxpayer if the IRS determines "that such disclosures would seriously impair Federal tax administration."[23] "Tax administration" is broadly defined to cover all governmental functions relating to the tax laws, including the formulation of tax policy and the assessment, collection and enforcement activities of the IRS. This restriction on disclosure denies a taxpayer access to information gathered by the Criminal Investigation Division of the IRS during an investigation of the taxpayer for criminal violations. The IRS has denied disclosure of documents and information relating to a taxpayer's own tax liability if the disclosure would prematurely reveal the scope, direction and level of the government's investigation.[24] The government contends in these situations that such early disclosure might permit the taxpayer to interfere with potential witnesses or tailor a defense to counter the information in the IRS files.[25]

Trade Secrets and Commercial or Financial Information. For tax purposes, FOIA exempts from disclosure any "trade secrets and commercial or financial information."[26] The IRS may not disclose any such data that constitutes "return information" unless Code Sec. 6103 specifically permits it. If such information was submitted to the IRS for the purpose of obtaining a private letter ruling, a determination or technical advice, Code Sec. 6110(c)(4) explicitly exempts this confidential business information from disclosure. Treasury Regulations provide specific procedures for promptly notifying a business submitter of such information that a FOIA request for this information has been made.[27] Procedures for objecting to such a request and litigating any administrative determination are also set forth in the regulation.

> **Example 9-4:** AgriCola, a soft-drink designed to quench the thirst of farmers, seeks a private letter ruling with respect to a restructuring transaction, which involves the valuation of its valuable intellectual property, such as its secret formula. The secret formula is a trade secret that is exempt from disclosure. _← internally within IRS_

Inter-Agency or Intra-Agency Memoranda or Letters. This exemption denies access to IRS memoranda and letters that relate to the IRS's deliberative or policy-making processes that would not be subject to discovery in any tax litigation.[28] The purpose of the exemption is to protect the open exchange of ideas during the deliberative process that occurs _prior_ to a final decision on a matter by the IRS. Any memoranda issued after the final decision to explain that decision, however, are not exempt.[29]

---

[22] Code Sec. 6103(c); Reg. § 301.6103(c)-1.

[23] _Id._

[24] _Youngblood v. Comm'r_, 2000-1 USTC ¶ 50,457 CD Cal 2000 (Special Agents Report); _Anderson v. United States_, 83 AFTR 2.d 99-2051 WD Tenn. 1999, checkspread shown to taxpayer during interview. However, in _Grasso v. IRS_, 785 F.2d 70 (3d Cir. 1986), 86-1 USTC ¶9263, the court affirmed an order to disclose IRS memoranda of interviews with the taxpayer

conducted during an investigation of his civil and criminal tax liability.

[25] _Holbrook v. IRS_, 914 F.Supp 314 (SD Iowa 1996).

[26] Code Secs. 6103 and 6110; 5 U.S.C. § 552(b)(4).

[27] Reg. § 601.702(h).

[28] 5 U.S.C. § 552(b)(5).

[29] _NLRB v. Sears, Roebuck & Co._, 421 U.S. 132 (1975); _Taxation With Representation Fund v. IRS_, 646 F.2d 666 (D.C. Cir. 1981), 81-1 USTC ¶ 9252 (General

Example 9-5: Three employees with the IRS Chief Counsel—George, Ken and Lisa—document their discussion regarding the use of the capital asset pricing model when drafting regulations. Because any document with respect to the discussion relates to the IRS's deliberative process, such a document is not subject to disclosure.

Medical and Personnel Files. In the interest of privacy, the IRS may not disclose medical or personnel files that would result in an unwarranted invasion of personal privacy.[30]

Example 9-6: Attorney is preparing Taxpayer's Tax Court case for trial and hears that the Agent who originally examined the return was once suspended by the IRS due to alcohol problems. Agent is listed as a potential witness for the IRS so Attorney makes a FOIA request for Agent's personnel files in order to obtain evidence to impeach Agent's credibility at trial. Agent's personnel file is not subject to disclosure.[31]

Investigatory Records and Information. FOIA exempts records or information compiled for law enforcement purposes, but only to the extent that the disclosure of such material could:

- interfere with enforcement proceedings;
- deprive a person of a fair right to trial;
- invade personal privacy;
- disclose a confidential source;
- disclose procedures for law enforcement investigations; or
- endanger the life of an individual.[32]

The IRS usually asserts this exemption when a taxpayer under criminal investigation requests disclosure of all workpapers, memoranda, records and other information gathered by the IRS during the investigation. With the exception of memoranda or records of the taxpayer's own statements, normally such investigatory information is exempt from disclosure.[33] The refusal to produce such records and information is generally based on the belief by the IRS that such disclosure would interfere with the criminal investigation, would reveal the identity of a confidential informant, or would disclose investigation or prosecution techniques and procedures.

Example 9-7: The IRS issues a Statutory Notice of Deficiency to Drug Dealer, alleging $2 million of unreported income from the sale of drugs. The IRS bases the deficiency on the statements of a confidential informer. Attorney, who represents Drug Dealer, files a FOIA request for the administrative

---

(Footnote Continued)

Counsel's memoranda and technical memoranda); *Tax Analysts v. IRS*, 117 F.3d 607 (DC Cir. 1997) (Field Service Advice Memoranda, i.e., FSAs).

[30] 5 U.S.C. § 552(b)(6).

[31] *Berger v. IRS*, 2008-2 USTC (CCH) ¶ 50,499 (3rd Cir.).

[32] 5 U.S.C. § 552(b)(7).

[33] See notes 27 and 32.

file. The IRS does not have to disclose the name of the confidential informer because it is an investigatory record.[34]

In addition to the applicability of six of the nine exemptions under FOIA, the presence of a criminal investigation or certain tax information may preclude disclosure

Ongoing Criminal Investigations. In addition to these six aforementioned exemptions, certain criminal tax records may be treated as though they were not subject to the requirements of FOIA.[35] These exclusions permit a government agency, including the IRS, to ignore requests for records and information when a response to the request would disclose that a criminal investigation is in progress, and the target of the investigation is not aware that he or she is being investigated. The IRS may also ignore requests for records relating to a confidential informant when the existence of the informant has not been officially confirmed. A response denying such requests would reveal, in substance, that there was an ongoing investigation or confidential informant.

Tax Information. In addition to the specific and general FOIA exemptions, no tax returns or return information may be disclosed to anyone unless Code Sec. 6103 specifically authorizes that disclosure.[36] The definition of return information protected from unauthorized disclosure is broad enough to include all information obtained during, or relating to, any tax examination or investigation of the taxpayer—not merely the taxpayer's identity and the information reported on tax returns.[37] Moreover, tax shelter registration applications, the fact of registration, the registration letters that the IRS sends to registrants and the tax shelter registration number all constitute "return information."[38] However, data which does not directly or indirectly identify a particular taxpayer does not constitute return information. For example, standards used by the IRS for the selection of returns for audit or data used in determining such standards need not be disclosed if the IRS determines that such disclosure will seriously impair assessment, collection or enforcement under the Internal Revenue laws.[39]

¶905 REQUESTS FOR INFORMATION

During the administrative processing of civil tax cases and the investigation of criminal tax cases, taxpayers may use FOIA to request records and information from the examination and investigation files of the IRS. Taxpayers may also specifically request other material that is not published in the Federal Register or made available at the IRS national and local offices. Nevertheless, tax practitioners will be primarily concerned with records and information obtained by the IRS during examinations and investigations of the taxpayer.

---

[34] *Educap, Inc. v. IRS*, (D.DC 2009).

[35] 5 U.S.C. § 552(c).

[36] Unauthorized disclosure is subject to criminal prosecution under Code Sec. 7216, and the injured taxpayer may file suit for civil damages under Code Sec. 7431.

[37] Code sec. 6103(b)(2).

[38] CCA 200336029.

[39] *Buckner v. IRS*, 25 F.Supp2.d 893 (1998) USDC NO. D. Ind., 98-2 ustc ¶50,640; *Coolman v. United States*, US-CT-APP-8, 2000-1 ustc ¶50,113.

Taxpayers must request records and information by writing to the disclosure officer in the appropriate office. The Statement of Procedural Rules provide the procedure to be followed and the contents of the letter.[40] More specifially, the letter (see Exhibit 9-1 at ¶911) must contain the following information:

1. A statement that the request is being made pursuant to FOIA, 5 U.S.C. §552;

2. The address of the IRS disclosure officer who will handle the request.[41]

3. A reasonable description of the records requested to enable the IRS to locate the records;

4. If the requested records contain information whose disclosure is restricted or limited, sufficient identification or authorization to establish the individual's right to disclosure, such as a notarized statement affirming identity;

5. An address of the person(s) to whom the information and notice of the action on the request should be sent;

6. A request for either inspection or copies of the requested information;

7. A statement agreeing to pay the official fees for copying and research; and[42]

8. A statement that identifies the requester as either a commercial use requester, media requester, educational institution requester, noncommercial scientific institution requester or other requester.

A tax practitioner who requests records and files relating to an examination or investigation of a taxpayer is classified as an "other requester." A representative filing a request on behalf of a taxpayer should include a properly executed Power of Attorney (Form 2848) or Tax Information Authorization (Form 8821).

In responding to the request, the disclosure officer will indicate the portions of the requested material that have been deleted or removed. A typical IRS letter responding to the request is included as Exhibit 9-2 at ¶912. Although the IRS is required by law to respond within ten working days, in most situations the disclosure officer requests additional time to locate and review the records. Such delay could be contested in court, but normally a taxpayer will permit the additional time if the request is reasonable.

As a general rule, in civil cases the IRS will typically make available all the examination files after deletion or removal of any return information relating to third parties and other information exempt from disclosure under FOIA. If the IRS can separate and delete the exempt information from the requested information, the IRS must disclose the remainder.[43]

---

[40] Reg. §601.702(c). See also, IRM Handbook 1.3.13.5.

[41] The mailing addresses of the disclosure officers who will respond to the request are set forth in Reg. §601.702(g);

[42] The fees for copying and research are set forth in Reg. §601.702(f).

[43] 5 U.S.C. § 552(b); Reg. § 601.701(b)(3)

The regulations provide specific fees for search time and copying the requested material.[44] Those who are classified as other requesters, a category into which most taxpayers' requests will fall, are not charged for the first two hours of search time or the first 100 copies. To avoid unexpectedly high fees, the request may include a dollar limit that the IRS should not exceed unless the requester is first notified of the anticipated charges. If the costs will exceed $250, the IRS may require advance payment.[45]

¶906 ADMINISTRATIVE APPEALS AND JUDICIAL REVIEW

If the IRS denies a FOIA request, the taxpayer may file an appeal with the Commissioner of Internal Revenue within thirty-five days after notice of denial.[46] The letter of appeal should be addressed to:

IRS Office
Attn: FOIA Appeals
5045 East Butler Ave.
Mail Stop 55201
Fresno, CA 93727-5136

The appeal should describe the records requested, indicate the date of the original request and the office to which it was submitted and enclose copies of both the initial request and the letter denying the request as well as provide arguments in support of the appeal. Generally, these arguments will attempt to establish that the FOIA exemptions cited for denial of the request do not apply to the records in question.

The IRS must issue a decision on such administrative appeals within twenty working days after receipt of the appeal.[47] If the appeal is either denied or partially denied or, if the IRS has not acted timely in responding to the appeal, the taxpayer may file suit in a U.S. District Court to seek judicial review.[48] The court will determine the matter *de novo* on the basis of the evidence and arguments presented to the court. In these proceedings, the IRS has the burden of proof to justify withholding the records under one or more of the FOIA exemptions.[49] The court may ask to examine the requested records *in camera* to deter-

---

[44] Reg. § 601.702(f).

[45] Reg. § 601.702(f)(4).

[46] Reg. § 601.702(c)(8).

[47] Up to an additional ten days may be allowed under certain circumstances. Reg. § 601.702(c)(9).

[48] The taxpayer may bring the action in the district where she resides or has her principal place of business, in the district where the requested records are located or in the District of Columbia. 5 U.S.C. § 552(a)(4)(B). For the U.S. District Court to have jurisdiction, the requester must show that the agency has improperly withheld agency records. *Gabel v. Comm'r*, 61 F.3d 910 (9th Cir. 1995), 95-1 USTC ¶ 50,289.

[49] When the confidentiality restrictions of Code Sec. 6103 apply, there is a split of authority among

the courts of appeals as to whether this specific Code provision supersedes the disclosure requirements of FOIA. For a discussion of these conflicting views, see *DeSalvo v. IRS*, 861 F.2d 1217 (10th Cir. 1988), 88-2 USTC ¶ 9609; *Church of Scientology v. IRS*, 792 F.2d 146 (DC Cir. 1986), *en banc aff'd* 484 US 9 (1987), 87-2 USTC ¶ 9604; *Grasso v. IRS*, 785 F.2d 70 (3rd Cir. 1986), 86-1 USTC ¶ 9263; *Long v. IRS*, 596 F.2d 362 (9th Cir. 1979), 79-1 USTC ¶ 9381; *Linsteadt v. IRS*, 729 F.2d 998 (CA 5, 1984), 84-1 USTC ¶ 9392. The minority view that Code Sec. 6103 is controlling eliminates the heavy burden of proof on the government under FOIA and merely requires the court to determine if the decision not to disclose was "arbitrary, capricious, an abuse of discretion, or otherwise not in accordance with law." 5 U.S.C. § 706(2)(A). See *Aronson v. IRS*, 973 F.2d 962 (1st Cir. 1992), 92-2 USTC ¶ 50,366.

mine the appropriateness of whether any part of them should be withheld. To avoid the judicial burden of such *in camera* inspections, the courts have frequently ordered the government to submit a detailed listing of the items withheld, which specifically describes each record and explains the exemption which is claimed to apply. This listing is known as a "*Vaughn* index," named after the case in which it was first required.[50]

¶907 THE PRIVACY ACT

The Privacy Act regulates the disclosure and management of records maintained by a government agency with respect to any individual.[51] The Privacy Act permits disclosure only for limited purposes, allows access by the individual to his or her records, requires an accounting of disclosures made by the agency to other parties, permits an individual to correct erroneous information in his or her records, and requires the agency to explain its authority and reason when requesting information. Moreover, the Privacy Act requires an agency to inform an individual, on request, about any disclosures of his records made by the agency to other parties. Finally, the Privacy Act also prevents an agency from maintaining in its files any information about an individual that is not relevant and necessary to the purpose to be accomplished by the agency.

Despite these elaborate provisions designed to protect an individual from improper government disclosure of records and permitting an individual access to such records, the Privacy Act has very little, if any, real importance in the area of taxation. The confidentiality provisions of Code Sec. 6103 have essentially preempted disclosure of "return information." Moreover, the Secretary of the Treasury has issued regulations specifically exempting from the Privacy Act all IRS records and files accumulated for purposes of examination, investigation, collection, and appeals.[52] Any meaningful access to such IRS records and information is available only under FOIA. In addition, a taxpayer may not resort to the Privacy Act in an attempt to correct any erroneous information in his or her IRS files when such information relates directly or indirectly to the existence or determination of that individual's liability under the tax laws.[53]

The Privacy Act does not impose any additional exemptions from, or restrictions on, disclosure under FOIA. If FOIA permits access to records or information, the Privacy Act specifically allows such disclosure.[54] As a result of the specific statutory provisions and regulations limiting the application of the Privacy Act, a taxpayer's request for IRS records or information under FOIA will not be affected, either favorably or unfavorably, by the access requirements or disclosure restrictions of the Privacy Act.

---

[50] *Vaughn v. Rosen*, 484 F.2d 820 (D.C. Cir. 1973). See also, *Osborn v. IRS*, 754 F.2d 195 (6th Cir. 1985), 85-1 USTC ¶9187. Indexing each document may be unnecessary in some cases, and a category by category listing may be sufficient if the categories are sufficiently distinct to enable a court to make a determination. *Vaughn v. IRS*, 936 F.2d 862 (6th Cir. 1991).

[51] 5 U.S.C. §552(a).

[52] 31 CFR §1.36 (IRS Notice of Exempt Systems). Specific procedures for making requests for nonexempt IRS records under the Privacy Act are set forth in 31 CFR, Subtitle A, Part I, Subpart C, Appendix B. See also, IRM Handbook 1.3.14.

[53] Code Sec. 7852(e).

[54] 5 U.S.C. §552(a)(b)(2).

¶908 PRETRIAL DISCOVERY

When tax cases go to trial, the taxpayer has the additional opportunity to obtain information from the IRS by resorting to the pretrial discovery rules applicable to proceedings in the Tax Court, the Court of Federal Claims and U.S. District Courts.[55] The rules generally provide that, prior to trial, a party may obtain discovery of any information that is not privileged and that is relevant to the subject matter involved in the pending action. The methods for obtaining such discovery include depositions (formal questioning of witness with opportunity to cross-examine by opposing counsel), written interrogatories (questions requiring written responses) and requests for production of documents.[56]

The government may object to discovery of IRS records and information on the ground that such matters are privileged or are not relevant to the issues in the tax case. The privileges commonly raised as objections include the attorney-client privilege, the work-product doctrine and the qualified executive privilege.[57] The courts have generally held such privileges to be inapplicable to IRS documents and information acquired or generated during the administrative stages of a tax case, with the exception of the qualified executive privilege.[58]

The qualified executive privilege protects the confidentiality of the deliberative or policy-making process of the executive branch of the government and the various agencies involved. Congress intended to incorporate this rule of privilege in the FOIA exemption from disclosure of "interagency or intraagency memoranda or letters."[59] The purpose of the privilege and the FOIA exemption is to promote the free exchange of ideas during preliminary deliberations within government agencies. Knowledge that information and memoranda relating to such deliberations might be readily accessible to the public would obviously discourage open discussion. The privilege is not absolute, however, and discovery will be permitted when the information involves purely factual material or when there is a compelling evidentiary need for such information.[60]

> **Example 9-8:** Three employees with the IRS Chief Counsel—George, Ken and Lisa—document their discussion regarding the use of the capital asset pricing model when drafting regulations. If a taxpayer's attorney sought any documentation of such debate through a production of documents request via the Tax Court Rules, the IRS may try to avoid disclosure by claiming the qualified executive privilege.

---

[55] Tax Court Rules of Practice and Procedure, Rules 70 through 90, 15 CCH STANDARD FEDERAL TAX REPORTER, ¶42,930, *et seq.*; Rules of the United States Court of Federal Claims, Rules 26 through 37, 28 U.S.C.A.; Federal Rules of Civil Procedure, Rules 26 through 37, 28 U.S.C.A.

[56] The conditions upon which depositions may be taken are far more restrictive in the Tax Court than in the other federal courts. See Tax Court Rules 74 through 85.

[57] *P.T. & L. Construction Co. v. Comm'r*, 63 TC 404 (1974), CCH Dec. 32,993; *Branerton Corp. v. Comm'r*, 64 TC 191 (1975), CCH Dec. 33,178; *Barger v. Comm'r*, 65 TC 925 (1976), CCH Dec. 33,650.

[58] *Id.*

[59] 5 U.S.C. §552(b)(5); *EPA v. Mink*, 410 U.S. 73, 86 (1973). See discussion at ¶905, *supra*.

[60] *EPA v. Mink*, 410 U.S. at 91, *supra*, note 53; cases cited *supra*, note 51. *Linsteadt v. IRS*, 729 F.2d 998 (5th Cir. 1984), 84-1 USTC ¶9392. The minority view that Code Sec. 6103 is controlling eliminates the heavy burden of proof on the government under FOIA and merely requires the court to determine if the decision not to disclose was "arbitrary, capricious, an abuse of discretion, or otherwise not in accordance with law." 5 U.S.C. §706(2)(A). See *Aronson v. IRS*, 973 F.2d 962 (1st Cir. 1992), 92-2 USTC ¶50,366.

¶911 Exhibit 9-1

FOIA Request
June 18, 2012

Disclosure Officer

Internal Revenue Service

(Address)

Re: (Taxpayer's Name)

S.S. No.:_____

Years:_____

Dear _____:

    This request for information under the Freedom of Information Act, 5 U.S.C. §552, is made by _____, attorney for the taxpayer. A Power of Attorney and Declaration accompany this request. The records requested are as follows:

    (a) All workpapers, correspondance, and other documents pertinent to the examination and investigation of the federal income tax liability of the above-named taxpayer for the years (specify years) including, but not limited to: (describe records in detail).

    (b) All statements given by the taxpayer to the Internal Revenue Service during the course of its examination, including all written statements, all oral statements recorded by any mechanical recording device, all oral statements reduced to writing by Internal Revenue Agents, whether verbatim or not, and whether or not signed by the taxpayer.

    Please copy and send to me 100% of these records in the taxpayer's file, including any records or information contained on computer software or disks.

    My return address is:

    (Attorney's Name and Address)

_____

_____

    I am authorized and agree to pay the current fee per copy for each copy obtained pursuant to this request and also the current hourly search fee. I attest under penalty of perjury that I am **not** a (a) commercial use requester, (b) media requester, (c) educational institutions requester, or (d) noncommercial scientific institution requester, but that I am an (e) other requester.

    Yours very truly,

    (Attorney for Taxpayer)

¶912 Exhibit 9-2

FOIA Reply

Internal Revenue Service
Disclosure Office

Department of the Treasury
Person to Contact:
Telephone Number:
Refer Reply to:
Date:

Dear _____:

We are replying to your Freedom of Information request of _____, regarding your client, _____. We are enclosing copies of all nonexempt documents found in their examination file. Your payment of $___ for our copying costs has been received.

Certain information was removed from the file since it is exempt from disclosure under the provisions of the Freedom of Information Act. We have listed this material below and cited the appropriate exemptions at the end of this letter.

1. The Discriminant Function (DIF) Score has been deleted from eight pages because DIF scores are solely related to internal practices and their release would reveal guidelines used in our investigations.[61]

2. Information related to years not covered by your power of attorney has been deleted.[62]

3. Confidential tax information of third-party taxpayers has been deleted.[63]

4. Information which could impair tax administration has been deleted.[64]

Since we withheld information from your client's file, your request has been partially denied. However, you may appeal this decision. We have enclosed Notice 393 which provides information concerning your appeal rights.

If you have any questions, please contact _____ at _____.

Sincerely yours,

Disclosure Officer

Enclosures

---

[61] FOIA Subsection (b)(2), (b)(7)(E), and (b)(3) with IRC Section 6103(b)(2).

[62] FOIA Subsection (b)(3) with IRC Section 6103(a).

[63] FOIA Subsection (b)(7)(C) and (b)(3) with IRC Section 6103(a).

[64] FOIA Subsection (b)(2) and (b)(7)(E) with IRC Section 6103(e)(7).

¶921 DISCUSSION QUESTIONS

1. Danny Delinquent is an American citizen who has been working for an oil company in Saudi Arabia for the past seven years. Danny has failed to file timely income tax returns for the years 2008 through 2011 under the mistaken impression that the Code Sec. 911 foreign earned income exclusion eliminated his taxable income. What he did not realize was that the exclusion is available only if he timely elects it. Danny received a Notice of Assessment in the amount of $175,000 and has asked for your help in dealing with the Revenue Officer who is pursuing collection.

   In reviewing the matter you discover that there may be doubt as to Danny's liability and, therefore, you intend to file an Offer in Compromise as soon as possible. However, you need information from the IRS files and, therefore, you filed a request pursuant to the Freedom of Information Act (FOIA). The IRS Disclosure Officer has sent you a letter asking for an additional thirty days to locate and consider releasing the requested records. The letter reads as follows:

   Dear Representative:

   We are sorry, but we must ask for additional time to locate and consider releasing the IRS records of Danny Delinquent, because we are still searching for the 2008 through 2011 records. We will make every effort to respond within thirty days from the date of this letter.

   If you agree to this extension of time, no reply to this letter is necessary. You will still have the right to file an appeal if we subsequently deny your request.

   We hope you will agree to a voluntary extension of time. If you do not agree, you have the right to consider this letter as a denial and, if you wish, immediately file an appeal. If you have any questions or need information about the status of your request, please contact the person whose name and telephone number are shown above.

   Thank you for your cooperation.

   Sincerely yours,

   Internal Revenue Service Disclosure Officer

   Do you voluntarily grant the extension to locate the records or file an appeal?

2. In January 2011, Sam Skimmer was interviewed by two special agents of the IRS in the course of a criminal tax investigation. In May 2011 Sam retained an attorney who in turn has hired you to assist him as his agent. You make a FOIA request for the Special Agents' notes and memoranda prepared during the interview. The IRS Disclosure Officer responded by providing a copy of their memoranda of the interview. However, the IRS has deleted significant portions. The IRS stated that the deleted information is exempt from disclosure since such information would impair

federal tax administration under Code Sec. 6103. Are there any grounds for appeal?

3. Attorney Larry Litigatee has been retained to represent a client in the U.S. Tax Court. As part of his pretrial discovery, Larry served the IRS with a Request for the Production of Documents under Tax Court Rule 72. Larry's request called for the production of the following documents:

   (A) Copies of a statement made by his client in the presence of an IRS special agent and revenue agent.

   (B) Copies of statements made by third parties who were interviewed by the IRS agents.

   (C) Copies of a statement made by his client to a third party concerning issues to be addressed during the trial.

   (D) Copies of all special agents' reports and revenue agents' reports concerning the case.

   Can the IRS object to the production of any of the documents? If so, why? If not, why?

CHAPTER 10
ASSESSMENT PROCEDURE

¶1001 INTRODUCTION TO ASSESSMENT

The IRS assesses tax by formally recording the taxpayer's tax liability that fixes the amount of tax payable.[1] When the IRS makes an assessment, a Service Center employee merely enters on an Assessment List the taxpayer's name, identifying number, the tax year, and the type of tax.[2] All of the amounts of tax for a particular day are summarized at the Service Center on Form 23-C "Assessment Certificate." The IRS completes the formal act of assessment when the Assessment Officer at the Service Center signs this summary list.[3]

> **Example 10-1:** Taxpayer, who resides in San Jose, California, mails his income tax return to the Fresno Service Center. After confirming that there are not any mathematical errors with respect to either the return or the check, a Service Center employee lists Taxpayer's name, the year of the return, and income tax on the Assessment List. At the end of the day, another Service Center employee prepares Form 23-C containing a summary list of all the amounts on the Assessment List for signing by the Assessment Officer. The Assessment Date is the date the Assessment Officer signs the summary list.

If an assessment is erroneous in some manner, the IRS may abate the assessment.[4]

¶1002 THE STATUTORY NOTICE OF DEFICIENCY

ignore

In addition to the normal assessment process described above, the IRS may not access any income tax until after the IRS mails a notice of deficiency by registered or certified mail to the taxpayer. The notice of deficiency is more formally referred to as a Statutory Notice of Deficiency[5] or less formally as a 90-day letter[6] (see Exhibit 4-12 at ¶432). The Statutory Notice of Deficiency is accompanied by a relevant portion of the agent's report explaining, in abbreviated form, the reasons for the proposed adjustments along with a detailed computation of the tax effect of the adjustments (see Exhibit 10-1 at ¶1021).

The term "90-day letter" stems from the taxpayer having ninety days after the mailing of the notice to file a petition for redetermination of the deficiency with the United States Tax Court.[7] During the ninety-day period and, if the

---

[1] Code Sec. 6203.

[2] Code Sec. 6201(a)(1).

[3] Code Sec. 6203; Reg. § 301.6203-1.

[4] Code Sec. 6404(a).

[5] Code Sec. 6212.

[6] The notice of deficiency is even less formally known as a "ticket to Tax Court" because it is a prerequisite of filing a petition to Tax Court.

[7] Code Sec. 6213(a).

taxpayer petitions to the Tax Court, until the decision of the Tax Court becomes final, the IRS may not assess a deficiency and may not levy or attempt to collect a deficiency. In the event the IRS makes an assessment before a decision is rendered, the Tax Court has authority to restrain the assessment and collection of tax.[8]

> **Example 10-2:** The IRS mails a Statutory Notice of Deficiency to Taxpayer on August 1. If the Taxpayer does not file a petition with the Tax Court, the IRS may assess the deficiency after October 29, which is the 90th day after the issuance of the Statutory Notice of Deficiency. If, however, Taxpayer files a petition with the Tax Court, the IRS may not assess the deficiency until the decision of the Tax Court becomes final.

The term deficiency refers to the amount of tax (income, estate, gift and certain excise taxes) determined to be due in excess of the amount shown as tax on the return.

> **Example 10-3:** Taxpayer files a return showing a tax liability of $10,000 and providing a check for that amount. During audit, the IRS determines that the actual amount of tax due is $15,000. The deficiency is five thousand dollars ($5,000), the amount determined to be due in excess of the amount shown as tax on the return.

If a taxpayer has not filed a return or if the return does not show any tax liability, then for purposes of computing the deficiency, the amount shown as tax on the return is deemed to be zero. Moreover, any amount shown as additional tax on an amended return filed after the due date of the return is treated as an amount shown on the return in computing the amount of deficiency. Therefore, any additional tax shown on an amended return may be assessed without the formal requirement of a Statutory Notice of Deficiency.[9]

> **Example 10-4:** Taxpayer filed a return showing a tax liability of $10,000 and providing a check for that amount. During the audit, Taxpayer files an amended return showing a total tax liability of $12,000 and provides a check for the additional $2,000. The amount of deficiency is $3,000, which represents the excess of the amount shown as tax.

¶1003 RESCISSION OF A STATUTORY NOTICE OF DEFICIENCY

The IRS, with the consent of the taxpayer, can rescind a Statutory Notice of Deficiency after issuance under Code Sec. 6212(d). Revenue Procedure 98-54[10] provides instructions for agreements with respect to the rescission of a Statutory Notice of Deficiency.[11] The Revenue Procedure indicates that rescission is purely discretionary with the Commissioner of the IRS and the taxpayer must consent to the rescission of the Statutory Notice of Deficiency. The Revenue Procedure suggests that the following reasons are sufficient for the IRS to rescind a Statutory Notice of Deficiency:

---

[8] Code Sec. 6213(a).
[9] Reg. § 301.6211-1(a).

[10] 1998-2 CB 531.
[11] See also IRM 4.14.1.24.

1. If the IRS issued the Statutory Notice of Deficiency due to an administrative error (e.g., for the wrong taxpayer, the wrong year or without recognizing execution of an extension of the statute);

2. If the taxpayer submits information establishing that the actual tax liability is less than that shown in the Statutory Notice of Deficiency; or

3. If the taxpayer specifically requests an Appeals Conference to enter into settlement negotiations (for this procedure to be used, the Appeals Office must confirm that the case is susceptible to settlement.)

If fewer than ninety days remain before the statute of limitations for assessment expires, the Statutory Notice of Deficiency can only be rescinded if both the taxpayer and the IRS agree to extend the statute (see Form 872, Exhibit 11-1 at ¶1131) by the taxpayer. If an unlimited extension has been entered on Form 872-A (see Form 872-A, Exhibit 11-2 at ¶1132), the IRS cannot rescind the Statutory Notice of Deficiency.[12] Finally, there is no rescission if either the taxpayer has filed a petition to the Tax Court or the period to file a petition has expired.

Form 8626, Agreement to Rescind Notice of Deficiency (see Exhibit 10-2 at ¶1022), is the form the IRS uses when a taxpayer wishes to consent to a rescission of the Statutory Notice of Deficiency. The taxpayer must first contact the office that issued the Statutory Notice of Deficiency and explain the reasons for seeking the rescission. If the taxpayer wishes an Appeals Conference, that taxpayer will be informed as to how to contact the Appeals Office to see if they concur in the request.

If the IRS and the taxpayer rescind the Statutory Notice of Deficiency, the IRS can later issue another Statutory Notice of Deficiency, and nothing prohibits the IRS from issuing another Statutory Notice of Deficiency for an amount greater than that reflected in the original. The running of the statute of limitations on assessment is suspended during the period the rescinded Statutory Notice of Deficiency's outstanding.

Example 10-5: BizCo goes out of business during the taxable year and later sends an incorrect Form W-2 to Taxpayer, one of BizCo's former employees, stating wages of $1 million when Taxpayer's actual wages were $100,000. Because BizCo is out of business, the Form W-2 was never corrected to the proper amount of wages of $100,000. Taxpayer filed a return assessing tax on $100,000 and the IRS issued a Statutory Notice of Deficiency based on wages of $1 million. Sixty (60) days after receiving the Statutory Notice of Deficiency, Taxpayer and the IRS signed a Form 8626, Agreement to Rescind Notice of Deficiency. Although this form correctly rescinds the Statutory Notice of Deficiency, the statute of limitations extends 60 days for the time that the Statutory Notice of Deficiency was outstanding.

---

[12] The rationale behind not permitting the rescission with respect to the Form 872-A is that the taxpayer could then rescind the statute of limitations before the IRS has the ability to issue a new Statutory Notice of Deficiency that corrects any defects..

¶1004 MAILING TO LAST KNOWN ADDRESS

Mailing of a Statutory Notice of Deficiency to the taxpayer's last known address is sufficient to commence the running of the ninety-day period.[13] This is the case even if the taxpayer is deceased or under a legal disability or, if a corporation, has terminated its existence. The statute does not require actual notice, only mailing to the last known address by certified or registered mail. Therefore, a notice sent by certified mail to the proper address is effective even though never actually received by the taxpayer.[14]

The taxpayer's "last known address" has been the subject of voluminous litigation. In a significant reversal of position, the Tax Court held in *Abeles v. Commissioner*[15] that a taxpayer's last known address is the address on the taxpayer's most recently filed return, unless the taxpayer has given the IRS clear and concise notification of a different address.[16] The most recently filed return is the return that the IRS Service Center has properly processed so that the address on that return is available to the agent who prepares the Statutory Notice of Deficiency with respect to the previously filed return. The address must be obtainable at such time by a computer generation of an IRS transcript using the taxpayer's Taxpayer Identification Number (TIN) (i.e, Social Security or employer identification number).

> **Example 10-6:** Brett Traitor files his income tax return with the address listed as 1265 Lombardi Avenue, Green Bay. Shortly after filing the return, Brett Traitor temporarily moves to New York before moving to Minneapolis, but never files another return and never notifies the IRS of his new address. The last known address for Brett Traitor is 1265 Lombardi Avenue, Green Bay.

A representative filing a Form 2848, Power of Attorney (see Chapter 2), may often request that the IRS send copies of correspondence to his or her office. The IRS has stated that its practice will be to treat the address of the taxpayer's attorney as the "last known address" of the taxpayer only where the Power of Attorney requires that all communications be mailed to the representative.[17] This practice does not extend to a situation where, as with the printed form of the Power of Attorney, the power merely requires that copies of communications be sent to the attorney.[18]

---

[13] Code Sec. 6212(b).

[14] *M.P. Gam v. Comm'r*, 79 TCM 1798, TC Memo. 2000-115, CCH Dec. 53,831(M).

[15] 91 TC 1019 (1988), CCH Dec. 45,203. In *Abeles*, a wife was held to have properly notified the IRS of her last known address (that of her tax advisor) by filing a separate return after the years under examination, which were for a joint return filed with her husband.

[16] Form 8822.

[17] Rev. Proc. 61-18, 1961-2 CB 550; *Honts v. Comm'r*, 70 TCM 1256, TC Memo. 1995-532, CCH Dec. 50,990(M).

[18] The Tax Court has held that receipt of a copy of a Statutory Notice of Deficiency by the taxpayer's accountant who had filed a Form 2848, Power of Attorney, did not constitute the mailing of a Statutory Notice of Deficiency to the taxpayer's last known address and, thus, that the Statutory Notice of Deficiency was not valid. See *Mulvania v. Comm'r*, 47 TCM 1187, TC Memo. 1984-98, CCH Dec. 41,026(M), *aff'd* 769 F.2d 1376 (9th Cir. 1985), 85-2 USTC ¶ 9634.

A husband and wife filing a joint Form 1040, U.S. Individual Income Tax Return, are considered to have the same address for purposes of their last known address unless either spouse has given the IRS notice of a separate residence.[19] A duplicate original Statutory Notice of Deficiency must be sent to each spouse at his or her last known address.[20]

Where a Statutory Notice of Deficiency does not contain the last known address and the Notice does not reach the taxpayer, the Tax Court lacks jurisdiction. The courts have generally held that an incorrect address will not nullify a Statutory Notice of Deficiency if in fact the taxpayer receives it without delay.[21] Even if the incorrect address causes a delay in delivery, the defect may be waived by the taxpayer's filing a timely petition with the Tax Court. No case has held a notice insufficient where it was sent by registered or certified mail to the wrong address but the taxpayer received it in due course.[22]

> **Example 10-7:** Suppose that Herman lives at 1313 Mockingbird Lane. The IRS sends a Statutory Notice of Deficiency to Herman on July 1 with the address of 3131 Mockingbird Lane. The resident at 3131 Mockingbird Lane received the Statutory Notice of Deficiency on July 5 and brought it over to Herman that day. After September 28, the 90th day following the issuance of the Statutory Notice of Deficiency on July 1, Herman files a petition with the Tax Court on October 1. Because Herman received the Statutory Notice of Deficiency without delay, even though it was not sent to his last known address, Herman failed to file a timely petition, the Tax Court should dismiss the case, and the IRS may assess the deficiency.

The filing of the petition with the Tax Court, even though untimely, may disclose the claimed defect in time to permit the IRS to issue a new Statutory Notice of Deficiency to correct the error.[23] On the other hand, if the Statutory Notice of Deficiency is ignored because of its possible defect, the taxpayer can still file a petition with the Tax Court to void it.[24] If the court finds the Statutory Notice of Deficiency was not defective and refuses to void it, the taxpayer will have foregone its right to trial on the merits and then must pay the tax, file the claim for refund and commence a suit in either the U.S. District Court or the Court of Federal Claims.

---

[19] Code Sec. 6212(b)(2); Reg. § 301.6212-1.

[20] *Monge v. Comm'r*, 93 TC 22 (1989), CCH 45,827 (Tax Court lacked jurisdiction because the IRS had notice of a separate residence for the wife and failed to send a duplicate original of the notice of deficiency to her).

[21] *Miller v. Comm'r*, 94 TC 316 (1990), CCH Dec. 46,435 (although IRS failed to send a duplicate original to the wife, the Statutory Notice of Deficiency was timely because she received actual notice of the deficiency and was not prejudiced). Also physical receipt is actual receipt and a taxpayer cannot claim he or she did not receive a Statutory Notice of Deficiency by refusing to accept delivery. *Erhard v.*

Comm'r, 87 F.3d 273 (9th Cir. 1996), 96-2 USTC ¶50,331. Also, compare *Bonty v. Comm'r*, 74 TCM 322 (1997) (21 day was not prejudicial) with *Pyo v. Comm'r*, 83 TC 626 (1984) (12 days was prejudicial).

[22] See, e.g., *Bachynsky v. Comm'r*, TC Memo. 1997-138.

[23] The statute of limitations will not be suspended if the Statutory Notice of Deficiency is held invalid. Where the Notice is mailed to an incorrect address and never delivered to the taxpayer, the Notice will be considered a nullity which will not suspend the statute. *Mulvania, supra*, note 8. See ¶1140, *supra*.

[24] *Rule v. Comm'r*, TC Memo 2009-39.

¶1005 NOTIFYING THE INTERNAL REVENUE SERVICE OF ADDRESS CHANGE

To avoid the dispute as to whether the IRS mailed a Statutory Notice of Deficiency mailed to the last known address, a taxpayer should ensure that the IRS has the current address on file. The address of record for IRS purposes is the address that appears on the gummed, peel-off label of the income tax return package which is mailed to taxpayers each year. If the address on the peel-off label is not correct, the taxpayers should correct the address. This correction serves to update the tax account so that all future correspondence will go to the current address. In situations where taxpayers have moved after the return has been filed, the IRS has developed Form 8822, Change of Address (see Exhibit 10-3 at ¶1023), for use in notifying the IRS of a new address. Form 8822 should be filed with the Internal Revenue Service Center for the old address.

> **Example 10-8:** Brett Traitor files his income tax return with the address listed as 1265 Lombardi Avenue, Green Bay. Shortly after filing the return, Brett Traitor temporarily moves to New York before moving to Minneapolis. Brett Traitor immediately files a Form 8822 with the IRS listing his new address as 900 South 5th Street, Minneapolis. Brett Traitor's last known address is now 900 South 5th Street, Minneapolis.

The recent pronouncement by the IRS regarding change of address is contained in Revenue Procedure 2010-16.[25] The IRS generally will use the address on the most recently filed and properly processed return as the address of record for all notices. However, under new regulations, the IRS may update the taxpayer's address of record using United States Postal Service's (USPS) National Change of Address Database (NCOAD).[26] If a taxpayer wishes to change the address of record, he or she must give clear and concise notification of a different address. Citing *Abeles* (discussed *supra*), the Revenue Procedure states that the address on the most recently filed and properly processed return will be considered the "last known address." A return will be considered "properly processed" after a forty-five-day processing period which begins the due day after the date of the receipt of the return by the Service Center. A taxpayer filing Form 8822, Change of Address or other clear and concise notification will be considered to have complied with the requirements and will be considered properly processed after a forty-five-day processing period beginning on the day after the date of receipt by the IRS.

> **Example 10-9:** During the taxable year, Taxpayer moves to a new address. On March 1 of the following year, Taxpayer files a return with her new address. On April 1, Taxpayer files a Form 8822 with her new address. The new address is considered the Taxpayer's last known address effective May 14, 45 days after the filing of the Form 8822. The new address on the Taxpayer's return would only become effective on May 29, which is 45 days after the due date for the return of April 15 and after May 14.

---

[25] 2010-19 IRB 664.   [26] Regulation § 301.6212-2.

¶1006 TAX COURT REVIEW

The initial paper a taxpayer files with the Tax Court is the petition.[27] The contents of a petition generally consist of six paragraphs, the first five of which are numbered.[28] The first paragraph should contain the name and address of the taxpayer along with his or her identification number (social security or employer identification) and the office of the IRS where the tax return for the period in controversy was filed. The second paragraph, which is the basis of the Tax Court's jurisdiction, must state the date of the mailing of the Statutory Notice of Deficiency, the city and state of the IRS office that issued the notice and any other proper allegations demonstrating the jurisdiction of the Court. This paragraph should refer to an attached copy of the Statutory Notice of Deficiency. The third paragraph states the type of tax in dispute (income, gift or estate) and the year or periods for which the determination was made, as well as the appropriate amount in controversy. The fourth paragraph sets forth in detail the assignment of the errors that the petitioner contends the Commissioner made rendering a determination. The fifth paragraph must contain a clear and concise statement of the facts on which the petitioner relies in support of his or her assignments of error. The final paragraph, unnumbered, is the prayer for relief and the request that the Court grant the relief sought by the petitioner.

The taxpayer or his counsel[29] must sign the petition and should have a designation of place of trial as an attachment (Official Form 4). A sample petition is included as Exhibit 10-4 at ¶ 1024.

Following the filing of the petition by the taxpayer, the IRS, through the local office of the IRS Chief Counsel, will file an answer within sixty days. If the IRS makes an affirmative allegation, such as fraud, the taxpayer must respond with a secondary pleading referred to as a reply. In the reply, the taxpayer admits or denies facts or allegations of fact affirmatively made by the Commissioner in his or her answer.

The Appeals Office possesses complete settlement jurisdiction of all docketed cases after the issuance of a Statutory Notice of Deficiency, unless it issued the Statutory Notice of Deficiency. If the examination function issued the Statutory Notice of Deficiency and there is no recommendation for criminal prosecution pending, the IRS Chief Counsel will refer the case to the Appeals Office for settlement as soon as it has filed its answer in the Tax Court. The Appeals Office has settlement jurisdiction over the case until the case is returned to the IRS Chief Counsel for preparation for trial. On the taxpayer's request, the Appeals Office

---

[27] A taxpayer has the option of not filing a petition and paying the assessed amount and then filing a claim for refund which, if denied, may be litigated in a District Court or the Court of Federal Claims. The choice of forum for litigating a tax controversy is discussed in Chapter 15, *infra*.

[28] Tax Court Rule 34(b).

[29] Tax Court Rule 200 provides that an applicant for admission to the Tax Court must establish that he or she is of good moral character and repute, and

that he or she possesses requisite qualifications to represent others in the preparation and trial of cases. An attorney can be admitted to practice by showing that he or she is a member in good standing of the Bar of the Supreme Court of the United States or the highest Court of any state, territory or the District of Columbia. An individual taxpayer may appear on his or her own behalf and, with the permission of the Tax Court, an officer of a corporation may appear on behalf of the corporation.

will grant the taxpayer a hearing and consider any case for settlement purposes where the Examination function has issued the Statutory Notice of Deficiency. Except in unusual circumstances, no hearing will occur during the 90-day period after the issuance of the Statutory Notice of Deficiency and prior to the filing of a petition with the Tax Court.

If the taxpayer and the Appeals Office reach an agreement after the taxpayer files a petition in the Tax Court, the parties will prepare and execute a stipulation of settlement. This stipulation is then filed with the Tax Court, which will enter its order in conformity with the stipulation. The taxpayer may also receive an "audit statement" setting forth the adjustments based on the settlement, a computation of the revised tax liability and the resulting deficiency or overpayment. These documents are not filed with the Tax Court and are for the information of the taxpayer only.

> **Example 10-10:** The Examination function issues Taxpayer a Statutory Notice of Deficiency so Taxpayer hires Attorney. Attorney files a petition with the Tax Court. After the IRS Chief Counsel answers the petition, the IRS Chief Counsel returns the administrative file to the local Appeals Office for a hearing.

The Tax Court has jurisdiction to order a refund if its determination results in an overpayment.[30] The Tax Court also has jurisdiction to determine whether interest on a deficiency resulting from its decision was computed correctly.[31] A taxpayer desiring a review of the interest computation must petition the Tax Court within one year of the decision. Such review is permitted, however, only if the taxpayer has paid all the assessed tax and interest.

The Tax Court will award reasonable litigation costs, including attorneys' fees, to a prevailing taxpayer who is able to establish that the position of the IRS in the proceeding was not substantially justified.[32] To recover such costs, the prevailing party must have exhausted all of the administrative remedies available within the IRS before petitioning the Tax Court. Therefore, the taxpayer must have filed a protest with the Appeals Office. The prevailing party is defined as one who has substantially prevailed either with respect to the amount in controversy or with respect to the most significant issue or set of issues.

To provide taxpayers with a simplified and relatively informal procedure for handling small tax cases, the Tax Court created the small case division. When neither the amount of the deficiency nor the amount of any claimed overpayment exceeds $50,000.00, the taxpayer may request to have the proceedings conducted under the small tax case procedure at the time of filing the petition.[33] Small case proceedings are informal, and any evidence deemed by the Court to have probative value will be admissible. A decision entered in a small case is not subject to review by any other court, nor is it treated as precedent for any other case. Cases considered under the procedures are generally referred to as "S" cases due to the presence of "S" in the docket number.

---

[30] Code Sec. 6512(b)(2).
[31] Code Sec. 7481(c).

[32] Code Sec. 7430.
[33] Code Sec. 7463(a).

¶1007 SPECIAL ASSESSMENTS

Congress has given the IRS power to take whatever measures are necessary to collect unpaid taxes. Normally, these efforts do not begin until the IRS makes an assessment. This could either be the assessment of the tax shown as due on the return or the assessment of a deficiency after an examination of the return. However, in certain instances the IRS does not have to follow the normal assessment procedures because the delay from doing so will endanger the collection of the taxes.

¶1008 JEOPARDY ASSESSMENT

If the IRS has reason to believe that the assessment or collection of a deficiency *for a year in which the filing deadline has passed* will be jeopardized by delay, by the departure of the taxpayer or by the removal of his or her assets, the IRS may make a jeopardy assessment, notwithstanding the restrictions on assessment.[34] In making such an assessment, the IRS is not bound by the requirement that a Statutory Notice of Deficiency be sent before any assessment is made or any effort to collect a tax is undertaken.

For the IRS to make a jeopardy assessment, a determination must be made that at least one of the following conditions exists:

does not count

1. The taxpayer appears to be planning to quickly depart from the United States or to conceal himself or herself; *Not from state to state*

2. The taxpayer appears to be planning to quickly place his or her property beyond the reach of the government either by removing it from the United States, by concealing it, by dissipating it or by transferring it to other persons; or

3. The taxpayer's financial solvency appears to be imperiled.[35]

Although the regulations provide only the three grounds for making jeopardy assessments that are detailed in this paragraph, the courts have generally interpreted these requirements very broadly.[36] For example, with respect to the concealment of assets, the courts generally have been willing to draw the inference of concealment of assets from any evidence of illegal activity.[37]

> **Example 10-11:** Suppose that on April 1, 2012, the IRS agent reads in the newspaper the Don Dealer is acquitted of dealing drugs for which he was arrested on December 31, 2010. The IRS agent goes to the courthouse and reviews the evidence, which reveals that during the raid of Dealer's apart-

---

[34] Code Sec. 6861(a).

[35] For purposes of determining solvency, the proposed assessment of taxes, any interest or penalty is not considered; Reg. §1.6851-1(a)(1). See also IRM 1.2.1.4.27 P-4-88.

[36] *Park v. U.S.*, 1992 WL 136622 4 (C.D. Cal. 1992), 92-1 USTC ¶50,270 (government was reasonable in concluding that taxpayer was planning to leave the country when he liquidated substantially all of his real property). But see *Modern Bookkeeping v. U.S.*,

854 F.Supp 475 (D.C. Minn. 1994), 94-2 USTC ¶50,310 (jeopardy assessment was unreasonable because the taxpayer filed corporate returns and declared distributions received in the form of precious metals).

[37] Reg. §1.8651-1(a)(1)(ii). See *Hamilton v. United States*, 81-1 USTC ¶9325 (E.D. Va. 1981), and *Prather v. United States*, 84-2 USTC ¶9730 (M.D. Pa. 1984). Such illegal activity does not include the intentional failure to report income. *Burd v. United States*, 774 F. Supp. 903 (D.N.J. 1991), 91-2 USTC ¶50,530.

ment on December 31, 2010, the police found $10 million of cocaine. The IRS agent determines that Dealer never filed a tax return for 2010 and the newspaper article discussing the trial quotes Dealer as saying he plans to leave town to spend some time in Europe after this long ordeal. A jeopardy assessment is appropriate for this previous tax year.

Jeopardy assessments concerning trust-fund recovery penalty assessments (the 100-percent penalty) employment or excise tax assessments, or income tax assessments (where there is no question as to the amount of the liability) can be initiated and processed by the Collection function. The Examination function initiates jeopardy assessments of income taxes (where liability may be in question), estate taxes and gift taxes.

Whether the jeopardy assessment is initiated by the Examination or Collection function, the recommendation must be reviewed by the jeopardy assessment coordinator in the Collection Technical Support unit, the Criminal Investigation area director, and the area office of Chief Counsel prior to issuance.[38]

A jeopardy assessment can be made for virtually any reasonable amount that the IRS desires (see Exhibit 10-5 at ¶1025). Even if the IRS has already issued a Statutory Notice of Deficiency, the IRS can make a jeopardy assessment for an amount greater than that set forth in the prior notice.[39]

After making a jeopardy assessment, the IRS can seize the taxpayer's property to satisfy the amount of the assessment, including any penalties and interest. Jeopardy assessments are made sparingly.[40]

¶1009 REMEDIES OF TAXPAYER TO A JEOPARDY ASSESSMENT

Having made a jeopardy assessment, the taxpayer receives a Notice and Demand to pay the tax, a Notice of Jeopardy Assessment and Right of Appeal, and a computation of the tax. The Notice of Jeopardy Assessment and Right of Appeal (see Exhibit 10-5 at ¶1025) is in a letter from the IRS and informs the taxpayer that he may file a protest seeking redetermination with respect to the reasonableness of the assessment and the appropriateness of the amount.

Procedures permit expedited administrative and judicial review of jeopardy and termination (see ¶1012) assessments.[41] Pursuant to this provision, within five days after the jeopardy or termination assessment, the IRS must give the taxpayer a written statement of the information on which it relies in making the assessment. Within thirty days thereafter, the taxpayer may request the IRS to review the assessment and determine whether the assessment was reasonable and the amount assessed was appropriate. Such a request for review receives immediate consideration and the results of the redetermination are provided within sixteen days from the date of the receipt of the taxpayer's request.[42]

---

[38] IRM 1.2.43.31 Order Number 219.

[39] Code Sec. 6861(c).

[40] Policy Statement P-4-88.

[41] Code Sec. 7429.

[42] Rev. Proc. 78-12, 1978-1 CB 590.

If the IRS makes an unfavorable determination or fails to make any review within the sixteen-day period, the taxpayer has ninety days to bring a civil action in the U.S. District Court to determine the reasonableness of the assessment and the appropriateness of the amount. This is to be a priority item on the court's calendar and the court must render a decision within twenty days unless the taxpayer requests an extension and establishes reasonable grounds for such additional time. The decision of the court is final and unappealable. The court may order the assessment abated in whole or in part or may require such other action as the court finds appropriate. The Tax Court has concurrent jurisdiction with the U.S. District Courts if the taxpayer files a petition for redetermination of the deficiency with the Tax Court before the IRS makes a jeopardy assessment.

In determining whether the assessment was reasonable, the court must find the IRS actions to be something more than arbitrary and capricious but not necessarily supported by substantial evidence.[43] The courts can and should consider information that was not available to the IRS at the time of the assessment to determine whether the IRS's actions were reasonable.[44]

Because of the unusual nature of a jeopardy assessment, the taxpayer has a statutory right to stay collection. The collection of a jeopardy assessment may be stayed by the taxpayer by filing a bond with the IRS. The taxpayer can file the bond at any time before actual levy is made on any property or property rights.[45] The amount of the bond must be equal to the full amount of tax, penalties and interest calculated to be due by the IRS as of the date of the jeopardy assessment. Furthermore, the bond must be conditioned on the payment of the full amount of tax, penalty and interest. The filing of the bond stays the collection of the assessment. The taxpayer then will have an opportunity to allow the Tax Court to determine whether the amount assessed is more or less than the correct amount of tax due.

If not previously sent to the taxpayer, then a Statutory Notice of Deficiency must be mailed to the taxpayer within sixty days following the jeopardy assessment.[46] The mailing of the Statutory Notice of Deficiency within this sixty-day period is necessary to make the jeopardy assessment enforceable. As is the case with a Statutory Notice of Deficiency, a taxpayer may appeal to the Tax Court. In addition to issuing a Statutory Notice of Deficiency, the IRS must also send the taxpayer a "Notice and Demand" for payment. The taxpayer must pay the full amount of the assessment within ten days after the Notice and Demand.[47]

---

[43] The general standard of review followed by the courts was articulated in *Loretto v. United States*, 440 F. Supp. 1168 (E.D. Pa. 1978), 78-1 USTC ¶9110. According to *Loretto*, the court is not to give great weight to the judgment of the IRS, but rather it should make an independent de novo determination.

[44] *See also, Golden West Holdings Trust v. United States*, 2007-1 USTC ¶50,243 (D.C. Ariz).

[45] Under Reg. §301.6863-1(a)(2)(iii), a bond may also be filed in the discretion of the IRS, after any such levy has been made and before the expiration of the period of limitations on collection.

[46] Code Sec. 6861(b).

[47] Reg. §301.6861-1(d).

¶1010 JEOPARDY LEVIES

Administrative and judicial review provisions are also available for jeopardy levies. The IRS may demand immediate payment of assessed taxes and levy on and seize any property or right to property, including wages and commissions, if collection is determined to be in jeopardy.[48] Without this jeopardy provision for an immediate levy, the IRS would not be permitted to make a levy until thirty days after notifying the taxpayer by certified or registered mail of the intention to levy.[49] The grounds for making a jeopardy levy are the same as those for a jeopardy assessment but grounds for both must be found.[50] If such a levy is contested, the burden is on the IRS to establish the reasonableness of the levy. The jeopardy levy is frequently used in conjunction with the jeopardy assessment so as to permit the IRS not only to make an immediate assessment, but also to seize or levy on property at the same time without having to wait thirty days after the issuance of a notice of intent to levy.

> **Example 10-12:** Suppose, that on April 1, 2012, the IRS agent reads in the newspaper that Don Dealer is acquitted of dealing drugs for which he was arrested on December 31, 2010. The IRS agent goes to the courthouse and reviews the evidence, which reveals that during the raid of Dealer's apartment on December 31, 2010, the police found $10 million of cocaine. The IRS agent determines that Dealer never filed a tax return for 2010 and the newspaper article discussing the trial quotes Dealer as saying he plans to leave town to spend some time in Europe after this long ordeal. In addition to a jeopardy assessment, the IRS may pursue a jeopardy levy because collection appears to be in jeopardy.

¶1011 ALTERNATIVE JEOPARDY ASSESSMENT: SECTION 6867

An alternative jeopardy assessment procedure exists.[51] Primarily aimed at the situation where law enforcement officials discover a large amount of cash and where the person holding the cash does not admit to ownership, the alternative provides a mechanism by which cash can be seized and an assessment of tax made immediately. The statute presumes that the cash represents gross income of the person in possession and that it is taxable at the highest allowable rate.[52] The IRS gives an assessment notice and statement to the person in possession that describes the information on which the IRS relies in making the assessment.

After such an assessment, the true owner can come forward and contest the assessment. In that case, the IRS will abate the original assessment, but will probably make a jeopardy assessment against the true owner. For the special assessment provision to apply, a person must be found in possession of cash or its equivalent in excess of $10,000.00 and that person must neither claim the cash or identify the person to whom it belongs. For purposes of these provisions, cash

---

[48] Code Sec. 6331(a).

[49] Code Sec. 6331(d). See Chapter 14, *infra,* for detailed discussion of the IRS right to levy.

[50] *Henderson v. Unites States,* 949 F. Supp. 473 (N.D. Tex. 1996).

[51] Code Sec. 6867.

[52] Code Sec. 6867(b)(2).

equivalence can include any foreign currency, any bearer obligation and any medium of exchange commonly used in illegal activities. The law presumes that because delay will jeopardize the collection of the tax, the IRS may immediately assess and levy on the cash.

> **Example 10-13:** Suppose that on April 1, 2012, the IRS agent reads in the newspaper the Don Dealer is acquitted of dealing drugs for which he was arrested on December 31, 2010. The IRS agent goes to the courthouse and reviews the evidence, which reveals that during the raid of Dealer's apartment on December 31, 2010, the police found $1 million in cash. The IRS agent determines that Dealer never filed a tax return for 2008 and the newspaper article discussing the trial quotes Dealer as saying he plans to leave town to spend some time in Europe after this long ordeal. An alternative jeopardy assessment is appropriate for this previous tax year with respect to the cash.

¶1012 TERMINATION ASSESSMENT

Another type of immediate assessment available to the IRS is a termination assessment. The IRS can terminate the *current or prior taxable year of the taxpayer for which the filing due date has not passed* if the IRS determines that the taxpayer is planning to act in such a manner as will prejudice or make ineffectual proceedings to collect income tax.[53] A termination assessment for the current year is based on a short taxable year ending on the date of assessment. A letter informing the taxpayer of the termination of the taxable period (see Exhibit 10-6 at ¶1026) is not a "Statutory Notice of Deficiency," and, therefore, the Tax Court does not have jurisdiction.

The circumstances under which the IRS can make a termination assessment are similar to those for a jeopardy assessment. However, the IRS can only make a termination assessment as to an income tax liability for the current or the immediately preceding taxable year. Further, the IRS cannot make a termination assessment after the due date of the taxpayer's return for the immediately preceding year. If no return has been filed, then at that point a jeopardy assessment of the delinquency could be made and immediate collection measures pursued.

> **Example 10-14:** Suppose that on April 1, 2012, the IRS agent reads in the newspaper the Don Dealer is acquitted of dealing drugs for which he was arrested on December 31, 2011. The IRS agent goes to the courthouse and reviews the evidence, which reveals that during the raid of Dealer's apartment on December 31, 2011, the police found $10 million of cocaine. Dealer's 2011 tax return has not yet been filed and the newspaper article discussing the trial quotes Dealer as saying he plans to leave town to spend some time in Europe after this long ordeal. A termination assessment is appropriate for 2011 because Dealer has not filed a return.

---

[53] Code Sec. 6851.

The Internal Revenue Manual requires that the termination assessment be based on a reasonable computation of tax liability and further requires stating the basis on which taxable income is computed (for example, source and application of funds statement or net worth computation, see Chapter 19). If appropriate, a reasonable estimate is to be made of the expenses of the taxpayer in arriving at taxable income.[54] As described in ¶1009, a taxpayer has the right to expedited administrative and judicial review of a termination assessment.

¶1013 ASSESSMENT IN BANKRUPTCY CASES

Under the Federal Bankruptcy Code, the commencement of a bankruptcy case creates a bankruptcy estate generally consisting of the debtor's property. A taxpayer's filing of bankruptcy also creates an automatic stay generally prohibiting a wide variety of acts including the collection of taxes. Nevertheless, the government has the right to audit the taxpayer, to demand the filing of tax returns, and to issue a Statutory Notice of Deficiency. The IRS can also assess tax and issue notice and demand for payment. However, the provisions of the bankruptcy law prohibit actual collection of the tax during administration of the bankruptcy case absent permission from the Bankruptcy Court.

> **Example 10-15:** The IRS issues a Statutory Notice of Deficiency to Taxpayer, who fails to file a petition within 90 days. As a result, the IRS assesses the deficiency. During the 90-day period to file a petition with the Tax Court, Taxpayer declares bankruptcy and lets the 90 days lapse without filing a petition. Although the IRS may assess the tax and issue a notice and demand for payment, the IRS may not actually collect the deficiency assessed during administration of the bankruptcy case.

The tax lien that would attach to the debtor's property by reason of an assessment made during the administration of a bankruptcy case only takes effect if (1) the tax is not be discharged in the bankruptcy case and (2) the property to which the lien would attach is transferred out of the bankruptcy estate or revested in the taxpayer.

The IRS uses a special form of a Statutory Notice of Deficiency (see Exhibit 10-7 at ¶1027) when the taxpayer is in bankruptcy proceedings. If the taxpayer wishes to petition the U.S. Tax Court, she will first have to obtain relief from the automatic stay to file the petition. However, the taxpayer has an alternative to filing a petition in the Tax Court - the taxpayer can elect to have the merits of the tax case heard in the Bankruptcy Court.

The Collection function is responsible for ascertaining the commencement of bankruptcy and receivership proceedings. Once the collection function has determined that the taxpayer has filed a bankruptcy proceeding, it determines whether the case is an "asset" or "no asset" case.

In an assets case, the Collection function contacts the Examination function to determine whether the taxpayer's returns are presently under audit. If the Examination function is not currently auditing the returns, the Examination

---

[54] IRM Handbook 4.15.2.4.1.3.2.

¶1013

function reviews the returns and, if an audit is warranted, begins auditing immediately. If an audit is not warranted, the returns will be accepted as filed. The Examination function expeditiously determines the taxpayer's liability for federal taxes in each asset case assigned for examination. After the audit, the Collection function files a proof of claim (see Exhibit 10-8 at ¶ 1028). In preparing the proof of claim, the IRS includes not only amounts the Examination function determines to be due, but also any other taxes that the taxpayer has not paid. The proof of claim describes the type of tax and also the nature of the claim as secured or unsecured and as a priority claim or a general claim. The proof of claim will include the calculation of any interest or penalties accrued before the filing of the bankruptcy petition.

A no-asset case is one in which the assets of an individual taxpayer are valued at an amount less than the cost of administration.[55] When the collection function has determined that a case is a no-asset case, usually the only action taken on it will be to freeze the account to avoid issuing notices or taking collection efforts during the period that the stay imposed by the Bankruptcy Court is in effect.

Claims of creditors in all bankruptcy proceedings generally fall into three categories: secured, priority and unsecured. Secured claims generally have specific assets to distribute to the creditors in satisfaction of their claim and, therefore, their claims are paid first in order of priority. Priority claims are entitled to priority in distribution over unsecured claims.[56] Tax claims generally are assigned to eighth priority among the priority claims. However, tax claims representing taxes incurred in the administration of the bankrupt estate can be first priority because they are treated as administrative expense claims.

> **Example 10-16:** Suppose that the IRS has filed a Notice of Federal Tax Lien against the taxpayer's real estate in the amount of $200,000. Later, during a bankruptcy proceeding, the real estate is determined to be worth only $150,000. The IRS would have a secured claim in the amount of $150,000 and a priority claim of $50,000.

The trustee is required to file a U.S. Income Tax Return for Estates and Trusts, Form 1041, covering the income and expenses of the bankruptcy estate during the period of administration. When the trustee files the final Form 1041, the trustee can request an immediate determination of any unpaid tax liability of the estate. The IRS has sixty days to notify the trustee whether it accepts the returns as filed or whether it wishes to audit the returns. If an audit is performed, any deficiency must be proposed within 180 days after the original audit request. If the trustee disagrees with the proposed deficiency, the jurisdiction of the Bankruptcy Court can be invoked to resolve the disagreement.

---

[55] IRM 5.5.1.4.1. [56] Sec. 507 of the Bankruptcy Code.

¶1014 TRUST-FUND RECOVERY PENALTY ASSESSMENT (100-PERCENT PENALTY)

The IRS in its tax collection process relies heavily on the withholding of taxes at the source by an employer. The primary responsibility for withholding is that of the employing entity and its managers. To protect against failure to discharge this duty properly, when a designated collection entity fails to perform its statutory duty to collect, truthfully account for, and pay over the amount of taxes due, those individuals who are responsible for the performance of those duties and who willfully fail to do so become personally liable for a penalty equal to 100 percent of the amount that should have been withheld and paid over.[57] The 100-percent penalty is not punitive in the conventional sense; rather, it is more in the nature of a recompense to the government for funds that should have been withheld from employees which the responsible individual has failed to remit as taxes held in trust for the IRS. Investigations concerning the penalty are conducted by the Collection function.

The two primary factors in the imposition of a 100-percent penalty are (1) the responsible person and (2) willfulness. If the person against whom the 100-percent penalty is assessed is not a "person required to collect, truthfully account for, and pay over," the individual in question is not liable for the penalty. However, even if that individual is such a responsible person, he or she must willfully fail to collect, account for, or pay over to be liable for the 100-percent penalty.

> **Example 10-17:** Suppose that a struggling company has fallen behind on its bills. The controller pays other creditors instead of tendering employment taxes to the IRS to ensure that the company's vendors continue to supply product. The controller, who is responsible for paying the company's bills, hopes that by the time the IRS discovers what has occurred, the company will have rebounded and have sufficient funds available to satisfy employment taxes. In this situation, the controller is a responsible person who would be personally liable for paying over the taxes due and, therefore, may be subject to the trust-fund recovery penalty.

Responsible Persons. The Internal Revenue Manual indicates that a responsible person may be an officer, an employee, a director or a shareholder of a corporation, or some other person[58] with sufficient control over the funds to direct disbursement of such funds. This does not preclude another person, such as a lender, from also being treated as a responsible person if that person exercises significant control over corporate operations.[59] The IRS has further

---

[57] Code Sec. 6672; This penalty only enforces personal liability for the withheld taxes; no *personal* liability will exist under Code Sec. 6672 for the corporate FICA tax or employment tax penalties and interest assessed against the corporation. See IRM 5.17.7.1.6.

[58] *In Re Thomas*, 187 B.R. 471 (Bankr. E.D. Pa. 1995), 95-2 USTC ¶50,490 (an accountant was held to be a responsible person because he had knowledge

that the company did not pay over its payroll tax and he preferred certain creditors over the government).

[59] *Merchants National Bank of Mobile v. U.S.*, 878 F.2d 1382 (11th Cir. 1989), 89-2 USTC ¶9511 (a bank was held to be a responsible person because it had the right to oversee substantially all of the corporation's significant operations).

stated that an employee who performs his or her duties under the dominion and control of others and who does not make decisions on behalf of the corporation will not be subject to the trust-fund recovery penalty.[60] In conducting the investigation to determine who is a responsible officer, the Collection Function personnel reviews the corporation's charter, by-laws and minute books. A review of the actual operation and control of the corporation is also significant. The Manual indicates that the authority to sign or co-sign checks is a significant factor to be considered; however, the fact that an employee signs corporate checks by itself is not enough to establish responsibility.[61] Sole owners of disregarded entities and partners of partnerships are also responsible persons.[62]

If the IRS cannot conclusively determine which person is responsible for withholding, collecting or paying over taxes, the IRS will look to the president, secretary and the treasurer as responsible officers. Case law has established that it is possible for more than one officer to be a responsible person for the same quarter.[63]

In most 100-percent penalty cases involving officers of corporations, the revenue officer conducting the investigation must determine which officer or officers were actually under a duty to see that the taxes were withheld, collected or paid over to the government. An analysis of the operation and control of the corporation's affairs normally will disclose which officer or officers were responsible individuals. As a tool in making this determination, a revenue officer will conduct interviews with the individuals involved. Form 4180 (see Exhibit 10-9 at ¶ 1029) is a guide used by the revenue officer in these interviews.

The courts have determined that if a person is able to exercise full authority over the financial affairs of an entity required to collect, withhold or pay over trust-fund taxes, he or she is "a responsible person" regardless of what formal title or connection he or she may have with the entity. Furthermore, even a director who is neither an officer nor an employee of the corporation may be found liable as a responsible person if the Board of Directors has the final decision on what corporate debts are to be paid.[64]

Willfulness. The term willfulness is used in the broadest sense of the term. It includes a voluntary, conscious and intentional act. The actions of the responsible person need not be malicious nor stem from bad motives or evil purposes. The mere voluntary act of preferring any creditor over the IRS is sufficient for willfully failing to pay over or collect taxes.[65] Willfulness is defined as the attitude of a person who, having a free will or choice, either intentionally disregards the law or is plainly indifferent to its requirements.[66]

---

[60] IRM 1.2.1.5.14.

[61] IRM 5.7.3.3.1.1.

[62] Reg. Secs. 1.1361-4 and 301.7701-2(c)(2).

[63] *Brown v. United States*, 591 F.2d 1136 (5th Cir. 1979), 79-1 USTC ¶ 9285.

[64] *Wood v. U.S.*, 808 F.2d 411 (5th Cir. 1987), 87-1 USTC ¶ 9165 (board member who had authority to sign checks, was active in decision making, and had control over the corporation was a responsible per-

son); but see Code Sec. 6672(e) for voluntary board members of Tax Exempt Organizations.

[65] *Purcell v. U.S.*, 1 F.3d 932 (9th Cir. 1993), 93-2 USTC ¶ 50,460 (taxpayer who had knowledge that the withholding taxes had not been paid over and consciously directed payment to other creditors was held to be willful).

[66] IRM 5.7.3.3.2. See *In re Slodov*, 436 U.S. 238 (1978), 78-1 USTC ¶ 9447, for discussion of willfulness

Procedures. Once the Collection function personnel has determined responsibility and willfulness, the IRS will make a 100-percent assessment recommendation against all those who are so identified. This is to assure that the penalty is asserted in an even-handed manner against all parties regardless of considerations such as the degree of responsibility or collectibility. Each responsible person is jointly and severally liable for the full amount of the penalty. The IRS may collect all or any part of the penalty from any one of the responsible parties. It is the policy of the IRS, however, not to collect more than the total unpaid trust-fund taxes when several responsible parties are involved.[67] A taxpayer subject to the 100-percent penalty shall, upon request, receive in writing the names of any other parties the IRS has determined to be liable for the penalty and whether the IRS has attempted to collect the penalty from such parties.[68] Furthermore, a taxpayer subject to the penalty has the right to contribution when more than one person is liable for the penalty.

> **Example 10-18:** Running into financial trouble, BizCo fails to pay its trust fund employment taxes. Revenue Officer asserts a 100-percent penalty against President, Vice-President, Treasurer, and Secretary in the amount of $100,000. Although he does not believe that he is a responsible person, Secretary pays the $100,000 to clear his name. Subsequently, Secretary files suit against President, Vice-President, and Treasurer to obtain contribution.

The factor of collectibility will be considered as a basis for nonassertion of the 100-percent penalty only in those cases where future collection potential is obviously nonexistent because of advanced age or deteriorating physical or mental condition.

The IRS assesses and collects the 100-percent penalty in the same manner as taxes.[69] Under this provision, the statute of limitations for assessment of the penalty is the same as for the assessment of the tax: three years from the time the employment tax return is deemed to have been filed. If such returns are timely filed, the returns are considered to have been filed on April fifteenth of the succeeding year.[70] The Internal Revenue Manual indicates that every effort must be made to collect the liability from the corporation before asserting the 100-percent penalty. However, if the assets of the corporation are not readily available to pay the withholding tax liability, often the potential expiration of the statute of limitations will force the IRS to assert the 100-percent even though there is a possibility that the corporation might be able to satisfy the delinquency at some point in the future. The IRS will abate the assessment against the individual to the extent that the corporation does pay withheld taxes.

> **Example 10-19:** Running into financial trouble, BizCo fails to pay its trust fund employment taxes. Revenue Officer asserts a 100-percent penalty against Secretary in the amount of $100,000. Subsequently, the corporation

---

(Footnote Continued)

when an individual acquires control of a corporation with pre-existing employment tax liabilities.

[67] IRM 1.2.1.5.14.

[68] P.L. 104-168.

[69] Code Sec. 6671.

[70] Code Sec. 6501(b)(2).

pays the trust fund employment taxes. As a result, the IRS will abate the 100-percent penalty against Secretary.

Because the payment does not constitute a voluntary payment, it must be applied in the best interests of the IRS, which in this instance would require application of the levied amount first to the corporate FICA (Federal Insurance Contributions Act) expense before any employment tax penalties and interest assessed against the corporation.

The IRS must notify the taxpayer in writing that she is subject to assessment for the 100-percent penalty at least sixty days before sending a notice and demand letter. If the initial notice is sent before the expiration of the three-year statute of limitations, the period for assessment will not expire before the later of ninety days after the mailing of such notice or if there is a timely protest, thirty days after the IRS makes a final determination with respect to such protest.[71]

When the IRS determines that an individual is a potentially responsible person, the IRS will send the individual a letter (see Exhibit 10-10 at ¶1030) advising that the penalty is being proposed. The letter requests that the taxpayer agree to the penalty by executing Form 2751, Proposed Assessment of 100-Percent Penalty (see Exhibit 10-11 at ¶1031). If the taxpayer does not agree, the taxpayer has opportunities to discuss the matter with the Collection function manager and to appeal the proposed penalty through the Appeals office. However, if there are fewer than 120 days remaining before the expiration of the statutory period for assessment, the Collection function cannot transfer the case to the Appeals Office prior to assessment unless the taxpayer executes a Form 2750, Waiver of Statutory Period (see Exhibit 10-12 at ¶1032), to extend the time for assessment.

A liability somewhat similar to that under Code Sec. 6672 exists under Code Sec. 3505(b), which provides that any lender, surety or other person who supplies funds for the account of an employer for the purpose of paying wages of the employer can be personally liable for any taxes not withheld or paid over to the IRS on those wages. However, the IRS can access such liability only if the lender has actual notice or knowledge that the withholding taxes will not be paid over. Further, this liability is limited to twenty-five percent of the amount loaned to the employer for purposes of making wage payments.

---

[71] Code Sec. 6672.

¶1021 Exhibit 10-1

Form 5278 (Rev. June 2004)	Department of the Treasury - Internal Revenue Service **Statement - Income Tax Changes**	Schedule		
1. Name(s) of taxpayer(s)	2. ☐ Notice of Deficiency ☐ Other *(specify)* ☐ Settlement computation			
	4. Form number	5. Docket number	6. Office symbols	
3. Taxpayer Identification Number		**Tax years ended**		
7. Adjustment to income				
a.				
b.				
c.				
d.				
e.				
f.				
9.				
h.				
8. Total adjustments				

9. Taxable income as shown in:
  ☐ Preliminary letter dated _____
  ☐ Notice of deficiency dated _____
  ☐ Return as filed				

10. Taxable income as revised				
11. Tax Tax method _____ Filing status _____				
12. Alternative tax, if applicable				
13. Alternative minimum tax *(Starting tax year 2000)*				
14. Corrected tax liability *(lesser of line 11 or 12 plus line 13)*				

15. Less credits   a.
             b.
             c.				

16. Balance *(line 14 less total of lines 15a - 15c)*				

17. Plus other   a.
    taxes   b.
             c.				

18. Total corrected tax liability *(line 16 plus lines 17a - 17c)*				
19. Total tax shown on return or as previously adjusted				
20. Adjustments: increase (decrease) to:				
a. Earned income credit				
b. Additional child tax credit				
c. Fuel credits / other				
21. Deficiency - Increase in tax (overassessment - decrease in tax) *(line 18 less line 19 adjusted by lines 20a - 20c)*				
22. Adjustments to prepayment credits - Increase (decrease)				
23. Balance due or (Overpayment) excluding interest and penalties *(line 21 adjusted by line 22)*				
24. Penalties and/or Additions to Tax *(listed below)*				

Catalog Number 23735U   Form **5278** (Rev. June 2004)

¶1022 Exhibit 10-2

Form **8626** (Rev. May 2001)	Department of the Treasury-Internal Revenue Service ## Agreement to Rescind Notice of Deficiency *(See instructions on reverse)*	In reply refer to: Taxpayer Identification Number

Pursuant to section 6212(d) of the Internal Revenue Code, the parties _____

_____
(Name(s))

_____ taxpayer(s) of

_____ and the Commissioner of
(Number, Street, City or Town, State, Zip Code)

Internal Revenue consents and agrees to the following:

1. The parties mutually agree to rescind the notice of deficiency issued on _____

to the above taxpayer(s) stating a deficiency in Federal _____ tax due and,
(Kind of tax)

where applicable, additions to the tax for the year(s) as follows:

Tax Year Ended	Deficiency	Penalties or Additions to Tax:	Penalties or Additions to Tax:	Penalties or Additions to Tax:

2. The parties agree that the statute of limitations has not expired as to the above tax year(s) and can be further extended at the time of this agreement or at a later date under applicable provisions of the Internal Revenue Code.

3. The parties agree that good reasons have been shown to exist for the action being taken in this agreement. The parties agree that the effect of this rescission is as if the notice of deficiency had never been issued. The parties are returned to the rights and obligations existing on the day immediately prior to the date on which the rescinded notice of deficiency was issued. Included among those rights and obligations is the right of the Commissioner or his delegate to issue a later notice of deficiency in an amount that exceeds, or is the same as, or is less than the amount previously determined, from which amount the taxpayer(s) may exercise all administrative and statutory appeal rights.

4. The taxpayers affirmatively state that at the time of signing this agreement they have not petitioned the United States Tax Court contesting the deficiencies in the notice of deficiency.

Your Signature	Date
Spouse's Signature	Date
Taxpayers' Representative	Date
Corporate Name	
Corporate Officer Title	Date
Commissioner of Internal Revenue or Delegate	Date

Catalog Number 64182H	www.irs.gov	Form **8626** (Rev. 5-2001)

Instructions

If the rescission of the notice of deficiency is for income tax for which a joint return was filed, and a joint notice of deficiency was issued both husband and wife must sign the original and copy of this form. Unless one acting under power of attorney, signs as agent for the other. The signatures must match the names as they appear on the front of this form.

If you are an attorney or agent of the taxpayer(s), you may sign this agreement provided the action is specifically authorized by a power of attorney. If a power of attorney was not previously filed, it must be included with this form.

If you are acting as a fiduciary (such as executor, administrator, trustee, etc.) and you sign this agreement, attach Form 56, *Notice Concerning Fiduciary Relationship*, unless it was previously filed.

If the taxpayer is a corporation, sign this agreement with the corporate name followed by the signature and title of the officer(s) authorized to sign.

The effective date of this agreement shall be the date on which the Commissioner or his delegate signs this form.

Catalog Number 64182H   Form **8626** (Rev. 5-2001)

¶1023 Exhibit 10-3

| Form **8822**
(Rev. January 2011)
Department of the Treasury
Internal Revenue Service | **Change of Address**
► Please type or print.
► See instructions on back.   ► Do not attach this form to your return. | OMB No. 1545-1163 |

Before you begin: If you are changing both your home and business address, use a separate Form 8822 to report each change.

| **Part I** | **Complete This Part To Change Your Home Mailing Address** |

Check **all** boxes this change affects:

1 ☐ Individual income tax returns (Forms 1040, 1040A, 1040EZ, 1040NR, etc.)
   ► If your last return was a joint return and you are now establishing a residence separate
   from the spouse with whom you filed that return, check here . . . . ► ☐

2 ☐ Gift, estate, or generation-skipping transfer tax returns (Forms 706, 709, etc.)
   ► For Forms 706 and 706-NA, enter the decedent's name and social security number below.
   ► Decedent's name   ► Social security number

| **3a** Your name (first name, initial, and last name) | **3b** Your social security number |
| **4a** Spouse's name (first name, initial, and last name) | **4b** Spouse's social security number |

5a Your prior name. See instructions.

5b Spouse's prior name. See instructions.

6a Old address (no., street, apt no., city or town, state, and ZIP code). If a P.O. box or foreign address, see instructions.

6b Spouse's old address, if different from line 6a (no., street, apt no., city or town, state, and ZIP code). If a P.O. box or foreign address, see instructions.

7 New address (no., street, apt no., city or town, state, and ZIP code). If a P.O. box or foreign address, see instructions.

| **Part II** | **Complete This Part To Change Your Business Mailing Address or Business Location** |

Check **all** boxes this change affects:

8   ☐ Employment, excise, income, and other business returns (Forms 720, 940, 940-EZ, 941, 990, 1041, 1065, 1120, etc.)
9   ☐ Employee plan returns (Forms 5500, 5500-EZ, etc.)
10 ☐ Business location

| **11a** Business name | **11b** Employer identification number |

12 Old mailing address (no., street, room or suite no., city or town, state, and ZIP code). If a P.O. box or foreign address, see instructions.

13 New mailing address (no., street, room or suite no., city or town, state, and ZIP code). If a P.O. box or foreign address, see instructions.

14 New business location, if different from mailing address (no., street, room or suite no., city or town, state, and ZIP code). If a foreign address, see instructions.

| **Part III** | **Signature** |

Daytime telephone number of person to contact (optional) ►

Sign Here

► Your signature   Date   ► If Part II completed, signature of owner, officer, or representative   Date

► If joint return, spouse's signature   Date   Title

For Privacy Act and Paperwork Reduction Act Notice, see back of form.   Cat. No. 12081V   Form **8822** (Rev. 1-2011)

Form 8822 (Rev. 1-2011)

Purpose of Form

You can use Form 8822 to notify the Internal Revenue Service if you changed your home or business mailing address or your business location. If this change also affects the mailing address for your children who filed income tax returns, complete and file a separate Form 8822 for each child. If you are a representative signing for the taxpayer, attach to Form 8822 a copy of your power of attorney.

Note. The IRS automatically updates your address of record based on any new address you provide the U.S. Postal Service (USPS). We use the information in the USPS's National Change of Address database. IRS also automatically updates your address of record when the USPS changes your address because of a new Zip Code boundary or other administrative reason. IRS notices or documents sent to a taxpayer's "last known address," are legally effective even if the taxpayer never receives it.

Changing both home and business addresses? If you are, use a separate Form 8822 to show each change.

Prior Name(s)

If you or your spouse changed your name because of marriage, divorce, etc., complete line 5. Also, be sure to notify the Social Security Administration of your new name so that it has the same name in its records that you have on your tax return. This prevents delays in processing your return and issuing refunds. It also safeguards your future social security benefits.

Addresses

Be sure to include any apartment, room, or suite number in the space provided.

P.O. Box

Enter your box number instead of your street address only if your post office does not deliver mail to your street address.

Foreign Address

Enter the information in the following order: city, province or state, and country. Follow the country's practice for entering the postal code. Please do not abbreviate the country name.

"In Care of" Address

If you receive your mail in care of a third party (such as an accountant or attorney), enter "C/O" followed by the third party's name and street address or P.O. box.

Signature

If you are completing Part I, the taxpayer, executor, donor, or an authorized representative must sign. If your last return was a joint return, your spouse must also sign (unless you have indicated by checking the box on line 1 that you are establishing a separate residence).

If you are completing Part II, an officer, owner, general partner or LLC member manager, plan administrator, fiduciary, or an authorized representative must sign. An officer is the president, vice president, treasurer, chief accounting officer, etc.

If you are a representative signing on behalf of the taxpayer, you must attach to Form 8822 a copy of your power of attorney. To do this, you can use Form 2848. The Internal Revenue Service will not complete an address change from an "unauthorized" third party.

Where To File

Send this form to the Department of the Treasury, Internal Revenue Service Center, and the address shown next that applies to you. Generally, it takes 4 to 6 weeks to process your change of address.

Note. If you checked the box on line 2, or you checked the box on both lines 1 and 2, send this form to: Cincinnati, OH 45999-0023.

Filers Who Completed Part I
(You checked the box on line 1 only)

IF your old home mailing address was in . . .	THEN use this address . . .
Florida, Georgia —Before July 1, 2011	Atlanta, GA 39901-0023
Florida, Georgia —After June 30, 2011	Kansas City, MO 64999-0023
Alabama, Kentucky, Louisiana, Mississippi, Tennessee, Texas	Austin, TX 73301-0023
Alaska, Arizona, Arkansas, California, Colorado, Hawaii, Idaho, Illinois, Indiana, Iowa, Kansas, Michigan, Minnesota, Montana, Nebraska, Nevada, New Mexico, North Dakota, Oklahoma, Oregon, South Dakota, Utah, Washington, Wisconsin, Wyoming	Fresno, CA 93888-0023
Connecticut, Delaware, District of Columbia, Maine, Maryland, Massachusetts, Missouri, New Hampshire, New Jersey, New York, North Carolina, Ohio, Pennsylvania, Rhode Island, South Carolina, Vermont, Virginia, West Virginia	Kansas City, MO 64999-0023
A foreign country, American Samoa, or Puerto Rico (or are excluding income under Internal Revenue Code section 933), or use an APO or FPO address, or file Form 2555, 2555-EZ, or 4563, or are a dual-status alien or nonpermanent resident of Guam or the Virgin Islands.	Austin, TX 73301-0023
Guam: Permanent residents	Department of Revenue and Taxation Government of Guam P.O. Box 23607 GMF, GU 96921
Virgin Islands: Permanent residents	V.I. Bureau of Internal Revenue 9601 Estate Thomas Charlotte Amalie St. Thomas, VI 00802

Filers Who Completed Part II

IF your old business address was in . . .	THEN use this address . . .
Connecticut, Delaware, District of Columbia, Georgia, Illinois, Indiana, Kentucky, Maine, Maryland, Massachusetts, Michigan, New Hampshire, New Jersey, New York, North Carolina, Ohio, Pennsylvania, Rhode Island, South Carolina, Tennessee, Vermont, Virginia, West Virginia, Wisconsin	Cincinnati, OH 45999-0023

Alabama, Alaska, Arizona, Arkansas, California, Colorado, Florida, Hawaii, Idaho, Iowa, Kansas, Louisiana, Minnesota, Mississippi, Missouri, Montana, Nebraska, Nevada, New Mexico, North Dakota, Oklahoma, Oregon, South Dakota, Texas, Utah, Washington, Wyoming, any place outside the United States	Ogden, UT 84201-0023

Privacy Act and Paperwork Reduction Act Notice. We ask for the information on this form to carry out the Internal Revenue laws of the United States. Our legal right to ask for information is Internal Revenue Code sections 6001 and 6011, which require you to file a statement with us for any tax for which you are liable. Section 6109 requires that you provide your identifying number on what you file. This is so we know who you are, and can process your form and other papers.

Generally, tax returns and return information are confidential, as required by section 6103. However, we may give the information to the Department of Justice and to other federal agencies, as provided by law. We may give it to cities, states, the District of Columbia, and U.S. commonwealths or possessions to carry out their tax laws. We may also disclose this information to other countries under a tax treaty, to federal and state agencies to enforce federal nontax criminal laws, or to federal law enforcement and intelligence agencies to combat terrorism.

The use of this form is voluntary. However, if you fail to provide the Internal Revenue Service with your current mailing address, you may not receive a notice of deficiency or a notice and demand for tax. Despite the failure to receive such notices, penalties and interest will continue to accrue on the tax deficiencies.

You are not required to provide the information requested on a form that is subject to the Paperwork Reduction Act unless the form displays a valid OMB control number. Books or records relating to a form or its instructions must be retained as long as their contents may become material in the administration of any Internal Revenue law.

The time needed to complete and file this form will vary depending on individual circumstances. The estimated burden for individual taxpayers filing this form is approved under OMB control number 1545-0074 and is included in the estimates shown in the instructions for their individual income tax return. The estimated burden for all other taxpayers who file this form is 16 minutes.

If you have comments concerning the accuracy of this time estimate or suggestions for making this form simpler, we would be happy to hear from you. You can write to the Internal Revenue Service, Tax Products Coordinating Committee, SE:W:CAR:MP:T:T:SP, 1111 Constitution Ave. NW, IR-6526, Washington, DC 20224. Do not send the form to this address. Instead, see *Where To File* on this page.

¶1024 Exhibit 10-4

UNITED STATES TAX COURT

XYZ MANUFACTURING COMPANY,	:
Petitioner,	:
	: Docket
v.	:
	: No._____
COMMISSIONER OF INTERNAL REVENUE,	:
Respondent.	:

PETITION

The above-named Petitioner, hereby petitions for redetermination of the deficiencies set forth by the Commissioner of Internal Revenue in his Notice of Deficiency dated April 21, 20X9, and as a basis for this proceeding alleges as follows:

1. Petitioner is a Wisconsin corporation presently located at 103 Favre Drive, Lambeau Lake, Wisconsin, 55555. The Petitioner's employer identification number is 39-0000000. The returns for the periods herein involved were filed with the Internal Revenue Service Center at Kansas City, Missouri.

2. The Statutory Notice of Deficiency, (a copy of which is attached and marked Exhibit A), was mailed to Petitioner under date of April 21, 20X9 by the Internal Revenue Service at Milwaukee, Wisconsin.

3. The Commissioner has determined deficiencies in income tax and penalties for the calendar 20X8, all of which are in dispute, as follows:

Tax Year	Tax	Penalties Under §6662(b)
20X8	$14,019,431	$2,803,886

4. The determination set forth in the Statutory Notice of Deficiency is based upon the following errors by the Commissioner:

   A. In determining the taxable income, the Commissioner increased the income in the amount of $40,055,518 by erroneously disallowing expenses from rental activities.

   B. In his alternative claim in which the Commissioner asserted that the sale of the lease receivable (the "Assignment" as defined below) was a financing arrangement, which increased taxable income by $27,585,814.

   C. In erroneously determining that the Petitioner was negligent or that there was a substantial understatement of tax, the Commissioner asserted a penalty under IRC §6662(b) in the amount of $2,803,886.

5. The facts upon which Petitioner relies in support of the foregoing assignments of error are as follows:

¶1024

(A) 1. Prior to May 4, 20X8, ABC Corporation (ABC) was the owner of certain construction equipment with a fair market value of $97,932,610.

     2. ABC sold construction equipment to the petitioner on May 4, 20X8, for its fair market value of $97,932,610.

     3. The purchase of the construction equipment was financed by the petitioner by borrowing $11,996,745 from the Banco Internationale, Cayman Islands—Green Bay Branch, giving promissory notes totaling $15,992,410 to ABC, and borrowing $81,940,200 from ABC.

     4. The petitioner immediately leased the construction equipment back ABC at a fair market rent pursuant to a net lease between the petitioner and ABC dated May 4, 20X8. Under the lease, the construction equipment was leased to ABC for a period of 38 to 44 months, depending on the category of construction equipment.

     5. The petitioner reasonably anticipated that the construction equipment would have a residual value at the termination of the lease of at least 20% of the construction equipment's value at the inception of the lease, and that each item of construction equipment would have a remaining useful life of approximately three years at the end of the lease term.

(B) 1. The petitioner alleges and incorporates all of the facts set forth in paragraph 5 (A) above.

     2. The assignment, referred to by the Commissioner as the sale of the lease receivable, to Kiln Leasing (Kiln) occurred on May 4, 20X8, prior to the time Kiln was part of the consolidated group. The proceeds of the assignment were paid to ABC to satisfy the ABC loan.

(C) No part of any underpayment of tax was due to negligence or substantial understatement. Underpayment of tax, if any, was due to reasonable basis and, therefore, the imposition of the penalty under Sec.6662 of the Internal Revenue Code is inappropriate.

WHEREFORE, Petitioner prays that the Court may hear this case and determine that there is no deficiency in income tax from the Petitioner.

Dated at Milwaukee, Wisconsin, this 15th day of May, 20X9.

Evil and Evil, S.C.
1234 North Main Street, Suite 100
Milwaukee, Wisconsin 55555-0000
414-555-1212

Seeno Evil
Tax Court No. ES0000
Attorney for Petitioner

Mailing Address:
P.O. Box 000000
Milwaukee, WI 55555-0000

Hearno Evil
Tax Court No. EH0000
Attorney for Petitioner

¶1025 Exhibit 10-5

IRM No. 5.1 Exhibit 5.1.4-1

Pattern Letter P-513 (Rev. 9-2008) (Reference: IRM 5.1.4.2.4)

> Taxpayer Identification Number:
> Contact Person:
> Contact Telephone Number:
> Employee Identification Number:

NOTICE OF JEOPARDY ASSESSMENT AND RIGHT OF APPEAL

Dear Taxpayer:

Under section (insert 6861, 6862, or 6867) of the Internal Revenue Code (the Code), you are notified that I have found (insert reason for asserting the jeopardy assessment) thereby tending to prejudice or render ineffectual collection of (insert type of tax) for the period ending (insert tax period). Accordingly, based on information available at this time, I have approved assessment of tax and additional amounts determined to be due as reflected in the attached computation:

Taxable Period Tax Penalty Interest

For a joint income tax assessment include the following, To ensure that you and your spouse receive this notice, we are sending a copy to each of you. Each copy contains the same information related to your joint account. Any amount you owe should be paid only once.

Under section 7429 of the Code, you are entitled to request administrative and judicial reviews of this assessment action.

For an administrative review, you must file a written proposal with the Area Director within 30 days from the date of this letter, requesting redetermination of whether or not: (1) the making of the assessment is reasonable under the circumstances, and/or (2) the amount so assessed or demanded as a result of the action is appropriate under the circumstances. A conference will be held on an expedite basis to consider your protest. Your protest will be forwarded to the area Appeals Office where a conference will be held. If you submit new information or documentation for the first time at an Appeals conference, the Appeals Office may request comment from the Area Director on such evidence or documents. Enforced collection action may proceed during any administrative appeal process unless arrangements are made regarding collection of the amount assessed. To make such arrangements, please contact (name of appropriate area official) at (appropriate telephone number).

You may pursue a judicial review of this assessment by bringing a civil suit against the United States in the U.S. District Court in the judicial district in which you reside, or in which your principal office is located. However, in order to have this action reviewed by the District Court, you must request administrative review within 30 days of the date of this letter. Such suit must be filed within 90 days after the earlier of : (1) the day the Service notifies you of its decision on your protest, or (2) the 16th day after your protest. The Court will make a determination of whether the making of the assessment is reasonable under the circumstances, and whether the amount assessed or demanded is appropriate under the circumstances. The Court's determination is final and not reviewable by any other court.

Appeal to Courts in Case of Income, Estate, Gift and Certain Excise Taxes

If an agreement is not reached with the Internal Revenue Service, a notice of deficiency is required by law to be issued within 60 days from the date of the jeopardy assessment made under section 6861 of the Code. You will then have 90 days (150 days if outside the United States) from the date the notice is mailed to file a petition with the United States Tax Court.

Appeal to Courts in Case of Other Taxes Assessed Under IRC 6862

Claim for credit of refund of taxes assessed under section 6862 of the Code may be filed in accordance with section 6511(a) of the Code for administrative and judicial review of the merits of the liability assessed. An administrative decision on the claim may be appealed to the courts under the provisions of section 7422(a) of the Code.

If you have questions about this letter, you may contact the contact person identified on the front of this letter.

Sincerely,

Area Director

¶1026 Exhibit 10-6

IRM No. 4.15 Exhibit 4.15.1-1

Date document last amended: 6-30-1999

Pattern Letter 1583

[Internal Revenue Service]	[Department of the Treasury]
[Area Director]	[Letter Date:]
[Taxpayer Identification Number:]	[Form:]
[Taxpayer year Ended and Deficiency:]	[Person to Contact:]
[Telephone Number:]	[Employee Identification Number:]
[Refer Reply to]:	[Last Date to File for Administrative Review:]

NOTICE OF TERMINATION ASSESSMENT OF INCOME TAX

Dear Taxpayer:

Under section 6851 of the Internal Revenue Code (the Code), you are notified that I have found you are attempting to place your property beyond the reach of the Government by concealing it, thereby tending to impede the collection of income tax for the 1997 taxable year.

I have found that on December 25, 1997, you were arrested by the xxxx Police Department and charged with possession of illegal narcotics paraphernalia. At the time of your arrest, $239,222 in U.S. currency was seized, which you claimed to be yours. The xxxx Police Department tested the money for traces of narcotics, which proved to be positive

A search of the Internal Revenue Service Center records indicates that you have not filed a Federal individual income tax return since 1993. Accordingly the income tax, as set forth below, is due and payable immediately.

Taxable Period	Tax
December 31, 1997	$83,626

Based on information available at this time, tax and penalty, if any, reflected in the attached computations, have been assessed.

This action does not relieve you of the responsibility for filing a return for your usual annual accounting period under section .6012 of the Code. Such return must be filed with the office of the Area Director of the area in which you reside, or the area in which your principal office is located, not with the Internal Revenue Service Center. A copy of this letter should accompany the return so that any amount collected as a result of this termination assessment will be applied against the tax finally determined to be due on your annual return or to be credited or refunded.

Under section 7429 of the Code, you are entitled to request administrative and judicial reviews of this assessment action.

For an administrative review, you may file a written protest with the Area Director within 30 days from the date of this letter, requesting a redetermination of whether or not:

1. the making of the assessment is reasonable under the circumstances, and
2. the amount so assessed or demanded as a result of the action is appropriate under the circumstances.

When feasible, a conference will be held on an expedite basis by the Area Director of Appeals Office to consider your protest.

If you submit information or documentation for the first time at an Appeals conference, the Appeals Office may request comment from the Area Director on such evidence or documents.

As indicated above, enforced collection action may proceed during any administrative appeal process unless arrangements are made regarding collection of the amount assessed. To make such arrangements, please contact [INSERT NAME OF REVENUE OFFICER] Revenue Officer, at (nnn)nnn-nnnn. [INSERT PHONE NO.]

You may request a judicial review of this assessment by bringing a civil suit against the United States in the U.S. District Court in the judicial district in which you reside or in which your principal office is located. However, in order to have this action reviewed by the District Court, you must first request administrative review explained above. A civil suit must be filed in writing within 90 days after the earlier of (1) the day the Service notifies you of its decision on your protest, or (2) the 16th day after your protest. The Court will make an early determination of the same points raised in your protest to determine whether the making of the assessment is reasonable under the circumstances and to determine whether the amount assessed or demanded as a result of the action is appropriate under the circumstances. The Court's determination is final and not reviewable by any other court.

If you have any questions about this letter, you may call or write to the contact person identified on the front of this letter. You also have the right to contact the office of the Taxpayer Advocate. Taxpayer Advocate assistance is not a substitute for established IRS procedures, and it cannot reverse legally correct tax determinations nor extend the fixed time for you to request an administrative review or bring civil suit. The Taxpayer Advocate can, however, see that a tax matter that may not have been resolved through normal channels gets prompt and proper handling. If you want Taxpayer Advocate assistance, call 1-800-nnn-nnnn.

Thank you for your cooperation.

Sincerly,

Area Director

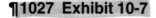

¶1027 Exhibit 10-7

Internal Revenue Service   **Department of the Treasury**

Date:

CERTIFIED / REGISTERED MAIL

Employee to Contact:

Employee Identification Number:

Contact Telephone Number:

Taxpayer Identification Number:

Notice of Deficiency			Penalties or Additions to Tax		
			IRC Section	IRC Section	IRC Section
Tax Year Ended	Type of Tax	Deficiency			

Dear

The last date to file a petition with the United States Tax Court is   if the filing of the tax court petition is not prohibited by the automatic stay imposed by the bankruptcy code. If the automatic stay was in effect on the date of this letter or comes into effect during the period from the date of this letter through   , see the description of how to calculate the last date to file a petition below.

We have determined that you owe additional tax, other amounts, or both for the tax year(s) identified above. This letter is your NOTICE OF DEFICIENCY, as required by law and permitted by Bankruptcy Code § 362(b)(9). The enclosed statement shows how we figured the deficiency. If you are a C-corporation, section 6621(c) of the Internal Revenue Code requires that we charge an interest rate two percent higher than the normal rate on large corporate underpayments of $100,000 or more.

You and/or your spouse have various options in responding to this letter. The **first** option is to agree with the amount of proposed deficiency listed above. *If you agree,* sign the enclosed waiver form and return it in the enclosed envelope addressed to the IRS. This will permit us to assess the deficiency quickly and can limit the accumulation of interest. If you choose this option, you do not need to read any further.

A **second** option is to petition the United States Tax Court by the date shown above, *if the automatic stay **was not** in effect from the date of this letter through the date shown above as the last date to file a petition.* A stay is a temporary suspension of proceedings. If we issue a notice of deficiency and the automatic stay is in effect, the automatic stay prohibits a person in bankruptcy from filing a petition with the Tax Court until the automatic stay is lifted or terminated by operation of law.

A **third** option is to request the Bankruptcy Court to lift the automatic stay under Bankruptcy Code section 362(d)(1) so that you can file a Tax Court petition while you are still in bankruptcy. *If you file a Tax Court petition while the automatic stay is still in effect, the Tax Court will dismiss your petition for lack of jurisdiction.*

Letter 1384 (Rev. 12-2004)
Catalog Number 40693N

A **fourth** option is to petition the Tax Court *after* the automatic stay is no longer in effect by operation of law. Generally, the automatic stay terminates by operation of law at the earliest of the time the bankruptcy case is closed, the time the bankruptcy case is dismissed, or in an individual Chapter 7 case or a case under Chapters 9, 11, 12 or 13, the time a discharge is granted or denied by the Bankruptcy Court.

WHEN TO FILE A PETITION

Second Option — File by the date shown above as "the last date to file a petition," *if the automatic stay was* ***never*** *in effect for the time period from the date of this letter through the date listed above as the "last date to file a petition."*

Third and Fourth Options — If the automatic **stay is in effect** as of the date of this letter and prohibits the filing of a Tax Court petition, you may file a Tax Court petition after the automatic stay is lifted by the Bankruptcy Court or when the automatic stay is no longer in effect by operation of law. If the automatic stay was in effect as of the date of this letter, then once the automatic stay is terminated you have 90 days from the date it was terminated (150 days if we mailed this letter to an address outside of the United States), plus the additional 60 day period set out in section 6213(f)(1) of the Internal Revenue Code, to file your Tax Court petition asking for a redetermination of the deficiency.

If the automatic **stay was not in effect** as of the date of this letter but you file a bankruptcy petition within the 90 day (or if applicable, 150 day) period to file a Tax Court petition but prior to filing your Tax Court petition, then once the automatic stay is terminated, you have 90 days (or if applicable, 150 days) less the number of days between the date of this letter and the date of filing the bankruptcy petition, plus the additional 60 day period set out in section 6213(f)(1), to file your Tax Court petition. However, we suggest that you file your petition as soon as possible after the Bankruptcy Court lifts the automatic stay or the automatic stay is no longer in effect.

HOW TO FILE A PETITION

If this letter is addressed to a husband and wife, both want to petition the Tax Court, **and** neither is in bankruptcy with an automatic stay in effect, you may file a joint petition that both of you must sign, or you may each file a separately signed petition.

If both spouses are in bankruptcy and the automatic stay is in effect, each spouse should request the Bankruptcy Court to lift the automatic stay before filing a Tax Court petition. If only one spouse has the automatic stay lifted, then only that spouse can file a Tax Court petition. If only one spouse is in bankruptcy and the automatic stay is in effect, the spouse in bankruptcy must request the Bankruptcy Court to lift the stay before filing a petition with the Tax Court. The spouse not in bankruptcy can file a separate petition to the Tax Court. The extension of time given the spouse in bankruptcy does not extend the time to file a petition for the spouse not in bankruptcy.

All petitions to the Tax Court for a redetermination of this deficiency must be sent to: **United States Tax Court, 400 Second Street, N.W., Washington, D.C. 20217.** Attach a copy of this letter and copies of all statements and/or schedules you received with this letter. You can get a copy of the rules for filing a petition and a petition form by writing to the Clerk of the Tax Court at the same address. If more than one tax year is shown above, you may file one petition form showing all of the years you are contesting. You may represent yourself or you may be represented by anyone admitted to practice before the Tax Court.

Letter 1384 (Rev. 12-2004)
Catalog Number 40693N

The Tax Court has a simplified procedure for cases when the amount in dispute is $50,000 or less for any one tax year. You can get information about this procedure by writing to the Tax Court at the address listed above, or from the court's internet site at www.ustaxcourt.gov. Write promptly if you intend to file a timely petition with the Tax Court.

The Court cannot consider your case if the petition is filed late. The petition is considered timely filed if the U. S. postmark date falls within the 90 (or 150) day period stated above and as extended by I.R.C. § 6213(f)(1), if applicable, and the envelope containing the petition is properly addressed to the Tax Court with the correct postage affixed. Contacting the Internal Revenue Service (IRS) for more information, or receiving other correspondence from the IRS will not change the allowable period for filing a petition with the Tax Court. If you decide not to sign and return the enclosed waiver form, and you do not file a petition with the Tax Court within the applicable time limits discussed above, the law requires us to assess the proposed deficiency and send you a request for payment.

BANKRUPTCY COURT CONSIDERATIONS AND OPTIONS

Whether you file a petition with the Tax Court, contest the deficiency in the Bankruptcy Court, or sign and return the waiver form, the IRS is authorized to file a proof of claim with the Bankruptcy Court for the deficiency, interest and additions to tax provided by law.

You have the option of filing an objection in the Bankruptcy Court to any proof of claim the IRS may file or of initiating a proceeding under section 505 of the Bankruptcy Code to determine the amount of the proposed deficiency, interest and additions to tax provided by law that are due from you. You can initiate a section 505 proceeding even if the IRS has not filed a proof of claim in your bankruptcy case. If the Bankruptcy Court or the Tax Court determines your tax liability, you can not petition the other Court to redetermine the same liability at some later date.

GETTING ANSWERS TO ANY QUESTIONS

If you have questions about this letter, you may write to or call the contact person whose name, telephone number, employee identification number and IRS address are shown on the front of this letter. If you write, please include your telephone number, the best time for us to call, and a copy of this letter to help us to identify your account. You may wish to keep the original letter for your records. If you prefer to call and the telephone number is outside your local calling area, there will be a long distance charge to you.

The contact person can access your tax information and help you to get answers. Also you have the right to contact the office of the Taxpayer Advocate. Taxpayer Advocate assistance is not a substitute for established IRS procedures such as the formal appeals process. The Taxpayer Advocate is not able to reverse legally correct tax determinations, nor extend the time fixed by law that you have to file a petition with the Tax Court. The Taxpayer Advocate can ensure that a tax matter gets prompt and proper handling when it may not have been resolved through normal channels. If you want Taxpayer Advocate assistance, please contact the Taxpayer Advocate for the IRS office that issued this notice of deficiency. For a list of Taxpayer Advocate telephone numbers and addresses, see the enclosed Notice 1214, *Helpful Contacts for Your "Notice of Deficiency"*.

Thank you for your cooperation.

Letter 1384 (Rev. 12-2004)
Catalog Number 40693N

Thank you for your cooperation.

Sincerely yours,

Commissioner
By

Enclosures:
Statement
Copy of this letter
Attachments to this letter
Waiver
Notice 1214
Envelope

Letter 1384 (Rev. 12-2004)
Catalog Number 40693N

¶1027

¶1028 Exhibit 10-8

Form **6338** (Rev. September. 1982)	Department of the Treasury — Internal Revenue Service **Proof of Claim for Internal Revenue Taxes** **(Bankruptcy Code Cases)**	Case Number
		Type of Bankruptcy Case

United States Bankruptcy Court for the _____ District of _____

In the Matter of:

	Date of Petition
	Social Security Number
	Employer Identification Number

1. The undersigned, whose business address is _____, is the agent of the Department of Treasury. Internal Revenue Service. and is authorized to make this proof of claim on behalf of the United States
2. The debtor is indebted to the United States in the sum of $ _____ as of the petition date.
3. The amount of all payments on this claim has been credited and deducted for the purpose of making this claim.
4. The ground of liability is taxes due under the internal revenue laws of the United States.

A. Secured Claims (Notice of Federal tax lien filed under internal revenue laws before petition date)

Kind of Tax	Tax Period	Date Tax Assessed	Tax Due $	Penalty to Petition Date $	Interest to Petition Date $	Notice of Tax Lien Filed: Date	Office Location

For the purposes of section 506(b) of the Bankruptcy Code. post petition interest may be payable.

B. Unsecured Priority Claims under section 507 (a) (6) of the Bankruptcy Code

Kind of Tax	Tax Period	Date Tax Assessed	Tax Due $	Interest to Petition Date $

C. Unsecured General Claims

Kind of Tax	Tax Period	Date Tax Assessed	Tax Due $	Interest to Petition Date $

Penalty to date of petition on unsecured priority claims .... $ _____
Penalty to date of petition on unsecured general claims .... $ _____

5. No note or other negotiable instrument has been received for the account or any part of it. except _____ .
6. No judgment has been rendered on this claim. except _____ .
7. This claim is not subject to any set off or counterclaim. except _____ .
8. No security interest is held. except for the secured claims listed in item 4A above and _____
9. To the extent that post petition penalties and interest are nondischargeable and remain unpaid. they may be collectible from the debtor.

Penalty for Presenting Fraudulent Claim—Fine of not more than $5,000 or imprisonment for not more than 5 years or both—Title 18, U.S.C. Section 152.	Signature	Date
	Title	Telephone Number

Part 1 — For Court (or Fiduciary, if required by local procedures)   Form 6338 (Rev. 9-82)

¶1029 Exhibit 10-9

Report of Interview with Individual Relative to Trust Fund Recovery Penalty or Personal Liability for Excise Taxes	Instructions The interviewer *must* prepare this form either in person or via telephone. *Do not* leave any information blank. Enter "N/A" if an item is not applicable.	Interview Handouts *("X" if given or explain why not in case history.)* ☐ **Notice 609**, Privacy Act Notice ☐ **Notice 784**, Could You be Personally Liable for Certain Unpaid Federal Taxes?

Type of Interview *("x" one.)*	☐ IRC 6672, Failure to collect and pay over tax from *(mmddyyyy)* _____ to _____ ☐ IRC 4103, Failure to pay excise taxes from *(mmddyyyy)* _____ to _____

Section I.   **Background Information for Person Interviewed**

1. Name	2. Social Security Number *(SSN)*
3. Address *(Street, City, State, ZIP code)*	4. Home telephone number ( ) 5. Work telephone number ( )

6. What was your job title and how were you associated with the business? *(Describe your duties and responsibilities and dates of employment.)*

7. Did you resign from your position? ☐ No ☐ Yes a. When? _____ b. Is a copy available? ☐ Yes ☐ No c. To whom was it submitted? _____	8. Do/Did you have any money invested in the business? ☐ Yes ☐ No	9. If you were listed on the company's bank signature cards, did you have your name removed from them? ☐ N/A ☐ No ☐ Yes When? _____
10. Were financial statements prepared for the business? ☐ Yes If yes, who reviewed them and where are the ☐ No statements located? _____	11. Have you ever been involved in another business that had tax problems? ☐ Yes If so, provide name of business and dates. ☐ No _____	

Section II.   **Background Information for Business Entity**
(Complete shaded items only if this is the first Form 4180 secured on the business entity.)

1. Name of Business and Employer Identification Number (EIN)	2. Business telephone number ( )
3. Address *(Street, City, State, ZIP code)*	4. Has the business ever filed bankruptcy? ☐ No Date Filed: _____ ☐ Yes Chapter: _____ Petition # _____

5. Type of Entity
☐ Partnership ☐ Corporation
☐ Sole Proprietor   Date incorporated _____
   State where incorporated _____
   Has the state ever revoked the charter?
   ☐ No ☐ Yes When? _____
	☐ Limited Liability Company (LLC)
	How is the LLC treated for tax purposes?
	☐ Disregarded Entity
	☐ Taxed as a Partnership
	☐ Taxed as a Corporation
	Has the LLC made any recent election for reclassification?
	☐ Yes If Yes, explain
	☐ No

6. Is the business still operating? ☐ Yes ☐ No When did it stop operating? _____ What happened to the assets? _____	7. Was any property of the business sold, transferred, quit-claimed, donated, or otherwise disposed of, for less than full value? ☐ No ☐ Yes *(Provide explanation.)*

8. Which banks or financial institutions did the business use for transactions such as checking, savings, loans, financing agreements, etc.?

Name	Address	Types of Transactions	Dates

Form **4180** (Rev. 7-2007)   Page 1 of 4   www.irs.gov   Department of the Treasury – Internal Revenue Service
Catalog No. 22710P

Section II. — continued   **Background Information for Business Entity**

9. Please list corporate positions below, identifying the persons who occupied them and their dates of service.

Position (e.g. President, Director)	Name	Address	Dates

10. Does the business use the Electronic Federal Tax Payment System *(EFTPS)* to make Federal Tax Deposits *(FTDs)* or payments? ☐ No ☐ Yes

To whom are the PINs or passwords assigned?

Who authorized the assignment of EFTPS PINs/passwords? *(If more than one, list dates.)*

11. Other than the EFTPS, does the business do any other banking electronically?

☐ No ☐ Yes   Where? _____

To whom are the PINs/passwords assigned?

Who authorizes changes to the PINs/passwords?

12. Does the business file Form 941 electronically?

☐ No ☐ Yes   Who is authorized to sign Form 941?

13. Does/did the business ever use a Payroll Service Provider (PSP) or Professional Employer Organization (PEO) for making deposits and/or file returns?

☐ No ☐ Yes   If yes, identify the PSP or PEO. _____

Who signed the contract? _____

Section III.   **Responsibility**

1. Please state whether you performed any of the duties / functions listed below for the business and the time periods during which you performed these duties. Please also provide the names and time periods that any other person performed these duties.

Did you...	Yes	No	Dates From	Dates To	Who else performed this duty?	Dates From	Dates To
a. Determine financial policy for the business?	☐	☐					
b. Direct or authorize payments of bills/ creditors?	☐	☐					
c. Open or close bank accounts for the business?	☐	☐					
d. Guarantee or co-sign loans?	☐	☐					
e. Sign or counter-sign checks?	☐	☐					
f. Authorize payroll?	☐	☐					
g. Authorize or make Federal Tax Deposits?	☐	☐					
h. Prepare, review, sign, transmit payroll tax returns?	☐	☐					
i. Hire/Fire?	☐	☐					

Form **4180** (Rev. 7-2007)   Page 2 of 4   www.irs.gov   Department of the Treasury – Internal Revenue Service
Catalog No. 22710P

Section IV.	Knowledge / Willfulness
1. When and how did you first become aware of the delinquent taxes?	2. What actions did you take to see that the taxes were paid?

3. Were discussions ever held by stockholders, officers, or other interested parties regarding nonpayment of the taxes? ☐ No ☐ Yes Identify who attended, dates, any decisions reached, and whether any documentation is available.	4. Who handled IRS contacts such as phone calls, correspondence, or visits by IRS personnel? When did these contacts take place, and what were the results of these contacts?

5. During the time the delinquent taxes were increasing, or at any time thereafter, were any financial obligations of the business paid?

☐ No   ☐ Yes   Which obligations were paid?

Who authorized them to be paid?

6. Were all or a portion of the payrolls met? ☐ No ☐ Yes	7. Did any person or organization provide funds to pay net corporate payroll? ☐ No ☐ Yes *(Explain in detail)*

8. Other than those previously listed, please provide the name, address, and telephone number of anyone else who may have additional knowledge about or control over the company's financial affairs.

Name	Address	Telephone Number
		( )
		( )
		( )

Section V.	Personal Liability for Excise Tax Cases
	(Complete only if Business is required to file Excise Tax Returns)

1. Are you aware of any required excise tax returns which have not been filed? ☐ No ☐ Yes *(List periods)*	2. With respect to excise taxes, were the patrons or customers informed that the tax was included in the sales price? ☐ No ☐ Yes
3. If the liability is one of the "collected" taxes *(transportation of persons or property and communications)*, was the tax collected? ☐ No ☐ Yes	4. Were you aware, during the period tax accrued, that the law required collection of the tax? ☐ No ☐ Yes

Section VI.	Signatures

I declare that I have examined the information given in this interview and to the best of my knowledge and belief, it is true, correct, and complete.

Signature of person interviewed	Date
Signature of Interviewer	Date
Date copy of completed interview form given to person interviewed ▶	

Form **4180** (Rev. 7-2007)   Page 3 of 4   www.irs.gov   Department of the Treasury – Internal Revenue Service
Catalog No. 22710P

Additional Information

¶1030 Exhibit 10-10

Letter 1153

Internal Revenue Service   **Department of the Treasury**

Date:

Number of this Letter:

Person to Contact:

Employee Number:

IRS Contact Address:

IRS Telephone Number:

Employer Identification Number:

Business Name and Address:

Dear

Our efforts to collect the federal employment or excise taxes due from the business named above have not resulted in full payment of the liability. We therefore propose to assess a penalty against you as a person required to collect, account for, and pay over withhold taxes for the above business.

Under the provisions of Internal Revenue Code section 6672, individuals who were required to collect, account for, and pay over these taxes for the business may be personally liable for a penalty if the business doesn't pay the taxes. These taxes, described in the enclosed Form 2751, consist of employment taxes you withheld (or should have withheld) from the employees' wages (and didn't pay) or excise taxes you collected (or should have collected) from patrons (and didn't pay), and are commonly referred to as "trust fund taxes."

The penalty we propose to assess against you is a personal liability called the Trust Fund Recovery Penalty. It is equal to the unpaid trust fund taxes which the business still owes the government. If you agree with this penalty for each tax period shown, please sign Part 1 of the enclosed Form 2751 and return it to us in the enclosed envelope.

If you don't agree, have additional information to support your case, and wish to try to resolve the matter informally, contact the person named at the top of this letter within ten days from the date of this letter.

You also have the right to appeal or protest this action. To preserve your appeal rights you need to mail us your written appeal within 60 days from the date of this letter (75 days if this letter is addressed to you outside the United States). The instructions below explain how to make the request.

Letter 1153 (DO) (Rev. 3-2002)
Catalog Number: 40545C

APPEALS

You may appeal your case to the local Appeals Office. Send your written appeal to the attention of the Person to Contact at the address shown at the top of this letter. The dollar amount of the proposed liability for each specific tax period you are protesting affects the form your appeal should take.

For each period you are protesting, if the proposed penalty amount is:	You should:
$25,000 or less	Send a letter listing the issues you disagree with and explain why you disagree. (Small Case Request).
More than $25,000	Submit a formal Written Protest.

One protest will suffice for all the periods listed on the enclosed Form 2751, however if any one of those periods is more than $25,000, a formal protest must be filed. Include any additional information that you want the Settlement Officer/Appeals Officer to consider. You may still appeal without additional information, but including it at this stage will help us to process your request promptly.

A SMALL CASE REQUEST should include:

1. A copy of this letter, or your name, address, social security number, and any information that will help us locate your file;

2. A statement that you want an Appeal's conference;

3. A list of the issues you disagree with and an explanation of why you disagree. Usually, penalty cases like this one involve issues of responsibility and willfulness. Willfulness means that an action was intentional, deliberate or voluntary and not an accident or mistake. Therefore, your statement should include a clear explanation of your duties and responsibilities; and specifically, your duty and authority to collect, account for, and pay the trust fund taxes. Should you disagree with how we calculated the penalty, your statement should identify the dates and amounts of payments that you believe we didn't consider and or/ any computation errors that you believe we made.

Please submit two copies of your Small Case Request.

A formal **WRITTEN PROTEST should** include the items below. Pay particular attention to item 6 and the note that follows it.

Letter 1153 (DO) (Rev. 3-2002)
Catalog Number: 40545C

¶1030

1. Your name, address, and social security number;

2.   A statement that you want a conference;

3.   A copy of this letter, or the date and number of this letter;

4.   The tax periods involved (see Form 2751);

5.   A list of the findings you disagree with;

6.   A statement of fact, signed under penalties of perjury, that explains why you disagree and why you believe you shouldn't be charged with the penalty. Include specific dates, names, amounts, and locations which support your position. Usually, penalty cases like this one involve issues of responsibility and willfulness. Willfulness means that an action was intentional, deliberate or voluntary and not an accident or mistake. Therefore, your statement should include a clear explanation of your duties and responsibilities; and specifically, your duty and authority to collect, account for, and pay the trust fund taxes. Should you disagree with how we calculated the penalty, your statement should identify the dates and amounts of payments that you believe we didn't consider and/or any computation errors you believe we made;

NOTE:

To declare that the statement in item 6 is true under penalties of perjury, you must add the following to your statement and sign it:

"Under penalties of perjury, I declare that I have examined the facts presented in this statement and any accompanying information, and, to the best of my knowledge and belief, they are true, correct, and complete."

7. If you rely on a law or other authority to support your arguments, explain what it is and how it applies.

REPRESENTATION

You may represent yourself at your conference or have someone who is qualified to practice before the Internal Revenue Service represent you. This may be your attorney, a certified public accountant, or another individual enrolled to practice before the IRS. If your representative attends a conference without you, he or she must file a power of attorney or tax information authorization before receiving or inspecting confidential tax information. Form 2848, Power of Attorney and Declaration of Representative, or Form 8821, Tax Information Authorization, may be used for this purpose. Both forms are available from any IRS office. A properly written power of attorney or authorization is acceptable.

Letter 1153 (DO) (Rev. 3-2002)
Catalog Number: 40545C

If your representative prepares and signs the protest for you, he or she must substitute a declaration stating:

1. That he or she submitted the protest and accompanying documents, and

2. Whether he or she knows personally that the facts stated in the protest and accompanying documents are true and correct.

CLAIMS FOR REFUND AND CONSIDERATION BY THE COURTS

CONSIDERATION BY THE COURTS

If you and the IRS still disagree after your conference, we will send you a bill. However, by following the procedures outlined below, you may take your case to the United States Court of Federal Claims or to your United States District Court. These courts have no connection with the IRS.

Before you can file a claim with these courts, you must pay a portion of the tax liability and file a claim for refund with the IRS, as described below.

SPECIAL BOND TO DELAY IRS COLLECTION ACTIONS FOR ANY PERIOD AS SOON AS A CLAIM FOR REFUND IS FILED

To request a delay in collection of the penalty by the IRS for any period as soon as you file a claim for refund for that period, you must do the following within 30 days of the date of the official notice of assessment and demand (the first bill) for that period:

1. Pay the tax for one employee for each period (quarter) of liability that you wish to contest, if we've based the amount of the penalty on unpaid employment taxes; or pay the tax for one transaction for each period that you wish to contest, if we've based the amount of the penalty on unpaid excise tax.

2. File a claim for a refund of the amount(s) you paid using Form(s) 843, Claim for Refund and Request for Abatement.

3. Post a bond with the IRS for one and one half times the amount of the penalty that is left after you have made the payment in Item 1.

If the IRS denies your claim when you have posted this bond, you then have 30 days to file suit in your United States District Court or the United States Court of Federal Claims before the IRS may apply the bond to your trust fund recovery penalty and the interest accruing on this debt.

Letter 1153 (DO) (Rev. 3-2002)
Catalog Number: 40545C

CLAIM FOR REFUND WITH NO SPECIAL BOND

If you do not file a special bond with a prompt claim for refund, as described above, you may still file a claim for refund following above action items 1 and 2, except these action items do not have to be taken in the first 30 days after the date of the official notice of assessment and demand for the period.

If IRS has not acted on your claim within 6 months from the date you filed it, you can file a suit for refund. You can also file a suit for refund within 2 years after IRS has disallowed your claim.

You should be aware that if IRS finds that the collection of this penalty is in jeopardy, we may take immediate action to collect it without regard to the 60-day period for submitting a protest mentioned above.

For further information about filing a suit you may contact the Clerk of your District Court or the Clerk of the United States Court of Federal Claims, 717 Madison Place, NW, Washington, D.C. 20005.

If we do not hear from you within 60 days from the date of this letter (or 75 days if this letter is addressed to you outside the United States), we will assess the penalty and begin collection action.

Sincerely yours,

Revenue Officer

Enclosures:
Form 2751
Publication 1
Envelope

Letter 1153 (DO) (Rev. 3-2002)
Catalog Number: 40545C

¶1030

¶1031 Exhibit 10-11

| Form **2751**
(Rev. 7-2002) | Department of the Treasury — Internal Revenue Service
Proposed Assessment of Trust Fund Recovery Penalty
(Sec. 6672, Internal Revenue Code, or corresponding provisions of prior internal revenue laws) |

Report of Business Taxpayer's Unpaid Tax Liability

Name and address of business

Tax Return Form Number	Tax Period Ended	Date Return Filed	Date Tax Assessed	Identifying Number	Amount Outstanding	Penalty
					$	$

Agreement to Assessment and Collection of Trust Fund Recovery Penalty

Name, address, and social security number of person responsible

I consent to the assessment and collection of the penalty shown for each period, which is equal either to the amount of federal employment taxes withheld from employees' wages or to the amount of federal excise taxes collected from patrons or members, and which was not paid over to the Government by the business named above. I waive the 60 day restriction on notice and demand set forth in Internal Revenue Code Section 6672(b).

Signature of person responsible	Date

Part 1 — Please sign and return this copy to Internal Revenue Service   www.irs.gov   Form **2751** (Rev. 7-2002)

| Form **2751**
(Rev. 7-2002) | Department of the Treasury — Internal Revenue Service
Proposed Assessment of Trust Fund Recovery Penalty
(Sec. 6672, Internal Revenue Code, or corresponding provisions of prior internal revenue laws) |

Report of Business Taxpayer's Unpaid Tax Liability

Name and address of business

Tax Return Form Number	Tax Period Ended	Date Return Filed	Date Tax Assessed	Identifying Number	Amount Outstanding	Penalty
					$	$

Agreement to Assessment and Collection of Trust Fund Recovery Penalty

Name, address, and social security number of person responsible

I consent to the assessment and collection of the penalty shown for each period, which is equal either to the amount of federal employment taxes withheld from employees' wages or to the amount of federal excise taxes collected from patrons or members, and which was not paid over to the Government by the business named above. I waive the 60 day restriction on notice and demand set forth in Internal Revenue Code Section 6672(b).

Signature of person responsible	Date

Part 2 — Please keep this copy for your records   www.irs.gov   Form **2751** (Rev. 7-2002)

Form **2751**	Department of the Treasury — Internal Revenue Service
(Rev. 7-2002)	**Proposed Assessment of Trust Fund Recovery Penalty** *(Sec. 6672, Internal Revenue Code, or corresponding provisions of prior internal revenue laws)*

Report of Business Taxpayer's Unpaid Tax Liability

Name and address of business

Tax Return Form Number	Tax Period Ended	Date Return Filed	Date Tax Assessed	Identifying Number	Amount Outstanding	Penalty
					$	$

Agreement to Assessment and Collection of Trust Fund Recovery Penalty

Name, address, and social security number of person responsible

I consent to the assessment and collection of the penalty shown for each period, which is equal either to the amount of federal employment taxes withheld from employees' wages or to the amount of federal excise taxes collected from patrons or members, and which was not paid over to the Government by the business named above. I waive the 60 day restriction on notice and demand set forth in Internal Revenue Code Section 6672(b).

Signature of person responsible	Date

Part 3 — IRS File Copy   www.irs.gov   Form **2751** (Rev. 7-2002)

¶1031

¶1032 Exhibit 10-12

	Department of the Treasury — Internal Revenue Service
Form **2750** (Rev. 5-2003)	**Waiver Extending Statutory Period for Assessment of Trust Fund Recovery Penalty** *(Section 6672, Internal Revenue Code, or corresponding provisions of prior internal revenue laws)*

1. Name and address of person potentially responsible	2. Social security number *(SSN)*
The person named above and the Area Director of Internal Revenue or the Director of Appeals agree that the penalty under Internal Revenue Code section 6672 *(applicable to the tax for the periods shown below)* may be assessed against that person on or before the date shown at the right. This agreement extends the statutory period for assessing the penalty. It *does not mean* that the person named accepts responsibility for the penalty.	3. Statutory period extended to

4.   **Taxpayer Data**

Name and Address of Employer or Collection Agency	Form Number	Tax Period Ended

Employer Identification Number *(EIN)* ▶		

Person Potentially Responsible	I understand that I have a right to refuse to sign this waiver or to limit the extension to particular issues or periods of time as set forth in I.R.C. § 6501(c)(4)(B).	
	5. Signature	6. Date

7. Name of Area Director	**or**	8. Name of Director of Appeals

9. By *(Signature and title)*	10. Date

Part 1 - IRS Copy   www.irs.gov   Form **2750** (Rev. 5-2003)

ISA
STF FED4647F.1

¶1032

¶1041 DISCUSSION QUESTIONS

1. Peter Procrastinator, who resides in Detroit, Michigan, was audited for the years 2009 and 2010. On September 13, 2012, a Statutory Notice of Deficiency was mailed to Procrastinator's last known address in Detroit. On September 14, Procrastinator traveled to Windsor, Ontario, Canada, to visit relatives. The Statutory Notice of Deficiency arrived in the United States mail at Procrastinator's home on September 17, 2012. He remained in Canada for a couple of days and returned to his residence in Detroit on the evening of September 17, 2012. When he returned, Procrastinator received the Statutory Notice of Deficiency.

   On December 31, 2012, Procrastinator sent by certified mail a petition to the United States Tax Court. The government has filed a motion to dismiss the petition, alleging that it was not filed within the 90-day period required under Code Sec. 6213. Procrastinator responds by alleging that he had 150 days to file his petition.

   Should Procrastinator's petition be dismissed for lack of jurisdiction?

2. Leroy Loser is in the scrap metal business. During the years 2012 and 2013, he "allegedly" purchased scrap from the Drill-a-Bit Manufacturing Corporation. Leroy deducted all of the "purchases" on his Schedule C for each year. However, Drill-a-Bit has not reflected any "sales" to Leroy on their returns. Following an audit of both taxpayers, the IRS disallows Leroy's purchases and increases Drill-a-Bit sales by an identical amount. Leroy receives a Statutory Notice of Deficiency for 2012 and 2013 and files a petition with the U.S. Tax Court. At the same time, Drill-a-Bit receives a Statutory Notice of Deficiency resulting from the increase on sales. Drill-a-Bit defaults on the Statutory Notice of Deficiency, pays the tax, files a claim for refund, and eventually sues for refund. It loses its case in the U.S. District Court in the area in which Leroy resides.

   Leroy now wants to dismiss his Tax Court Petition, pay the tax, and file a claim for refund and sue in the same U.S. District Court. What advice can you give him?

3. Harry Hardluck and his ex-wife, Hortense Hapless Hardluck, were divorced in 2009. Under the divorce decree, Harry was required to make payments of $600 a month (for the support of Hortense and their children). Because the decree labels these payments as alimony, Harry had deducted them on his 2010, 2011 and 2012 income tax returns. At the same time, Hortense has taken the position that these are child support payments and has not reported them as income for the years in question.

   The IRS has audited Harry and Hortense. They have issued a Statutory Notice of Deficiency to Harry disallowing the deduction claimed for alimony payments. At the same time, they have sent a Statutory Notice of Deficiency to Hortense claiming that the payments were alimony and should have been reported as income. Harry and Hortense's respective attorneys consult you as a noted tax expert in tax procedure to find out whether the IRS can actually make assessments in such an "inconsistent" fashion. What advice do you give them?

4. B.N. Krupt Company, Inc., timely filed its first quarter 2011 withholding tax return (Form 941) on April 29, 2011. On May 1, 2011, Mr. Scatterbrain, the president of the corporation, resigned. Scatterbrain normally signed all corporate checks and approved all financial transactions. No successor was appointed, but Mr. Disorganized, the vice president, and Ms. Slipshod, the treasurer, were given co-check-signing authority and together assumed Scatterbrain's financial duties. Ms. Neglectful, the corporation's sole shareholder and director, assumed the acting presidency.

Ten days before the second quarter 2011 withholding tax return (Form 941) was due, Mr. Diligent, the accounts payable clerk, prepared the Form 941 and a check for the total amount due. The check and the Form 941 were given to the treasurer, Ms. Slipshod, to be signed and forwarded to Mr. Disorganized for co-signature of the check. Because of the corporation's poor financial condition that month, Mr. Disorganized decided to sign only certain checks and failed to co-sign the tax check. Mr. Disorganized returned all of the checks to Mr. Diligent. Mr. Diligent noticed that several checks were not co-signed and adjusted his cash disbursement journal accordingly. Mr. Disorganized resigned two days prior to the due date for filing the return. No tax was paid for the second quarter. Ms. Neglectful had no knowledge of the nonpayment of the Form 941 taxes.

(A) For each person involved, state whether you think the person is liable for the 100-percent penalty under Code Sec. 6672. Why or why not?

(B) The corporation's portion of the FICA tax was also not paid. Is this amount included in the 100% penalty?

5. You are consulted by Kal Koke regarding the following situation. Kal tells you that he is an unregistered "pharmacist" dealing primarily in certain controlled substances. He explains that he has just received a termination assessment of income tax under Code Sec. 6851. The assessment resulted from a raid upon Kal's home on July 1, 2012. In that raid, $500,000 in cash was seized. As Kal explains it, the IRS determined that $500,000 constituted his gross receipts for that week. They have now made an assessment against him of income tax for the period January 1 through July 1, 2012. The IRS has computed his income to be $13,000,000 and is seeking tax of approximately $6,000,000. In addition, the IRS is holding the $500,000 seized for eventual application to the tax liability for the year.

Kal said that he objected to this assessment and that he asked for review. His grounds for review were as follows: (1) $500,000 only constituted his gross receipts for a month, not for a week and (2) the IRS failed to give any effect to his cost of goods sold, which he estimates to be approxi-

¶1041

mately $260,000 per month. The request for review of the assessment has been denied. Kal wants to know what he can do next! He is willing to pay for "successful" advice.

6. You are consulted by the court-appointed guardian of Sam Strate regarding the following situation. In 2011, Sam sold a piece of property that had a basis of $35,000 for $235,000. Under the terms of the contract of sale, Sam received $35,000 in 2012 with the balance of the proceeds being placed in escrow. The escrowee was to pay the remaining $200,000 out in four equal installments over the four years after the closing of the sale. However, the escrowee was given authority to pay the balance to Sam if Sam were to request accelerated payments and were to cite changed circumstances that would convince his nephew, the escrowee, that acceleration was warranted.

In 2014, Seymour Sharpeyes of the IRS Examination function audited Sam's return. Sharpeyes determined that Sam was in constructive receipt of the entire sale proceeds and, thus, disallowed the installment treatment claimed on the 2012 return. He sought to tax Sam upon the entire gain in 2012. At his final conference with the agent, Sam was informed that the understatement of tax would be at least $35,000.

The very evening that Sam had his final conference with the Sharpeyes, he happened to attend a cocktail party. He mentioned to one of the persons there that he had the conference with the IRS, and his acquaintance told him about the terrible things the IRS can do. He referred to something called a jeopardy assessment, which he said the IRS can use to tie up all of his property if he does not pay the tax. Sam was very nervous about this, and a week later he became so distraught that he had a nervous breakdown and was hospitalized. Because of his stay in the hospital, all correspondence from the IRS went unanswered. Finally, a guardian was appointed to look into Sam's affairs. The guardian consults you to see whether the IRS can make a jeopardy assessment of the taxes and whether they can seize all of Sam's property on the basis of the circumstances that he has described.

CHAPTER 11
STATUTE OF LIMITATIONS ON ASSESSMENT

¶1101 THE THREE YEAR STATUTE OF LIMITATIONS

In most instances, any tax due must be paid at the time of filing the return. However, if a taxpayer has either not reported all its income on the return or taken an improper deduction, the Internal Revenue Service (IRS) can examine the return and seek additional tax in the form of a deficiency. Tax policy suggests that at some point, a taxpayer should no longer have the responsibility for, and the government should no longer expend its resources in pursuing additional amounts of tax for a given year. In the legal system, this function is served by statutes of limitations—laws which specify the amount of time within which an act must be performed to be legally binding.

The Internal Revenue Code (the Code) contains a number of statutes of limitations contained in Subtitle F of the Code.[1] Many other provisions can have an effect on the statute of limitations in different circumstances.

Normally, the IRS must make any assessment of additional tax within three years of the time a return is filed.[2]

Example 11-1: Suppose Taxpayer files his 20X1 return on April 15, 20X2. The IRS has until April 15, 20X5, three years later, to assess a deficiency.

The three-year statute of limitations also applies to the filing date of amended returns.

Example 11-2: Suppose Taxpayer extends the filing date for his 20X1 return from April 15, 20X2 until October 15, 20X2 and actually files on October 15, 20X2. The IRS has until October 15, 20X5, three years after October 15, 20X2, to assess any deficiency.

A return filed prior to the due date is treated for purposes of the statute of limitations as though the return was filed on the due date.[3]

Example 11-3: Suppose Taxpayer files his 20X1 return on March 1, 20X2. The IRS has until April 15, 20X5, three years after the April 15, 20X2 due date, to assess any deficiency.

The rule deeming timely-filed returns as filed on their due date also applies to returns filed before extended due dates.

---

[1] Sections 6501 through 6533.

[2] Code Sec. 6501(a).

[3] Code Sec. 6501(b)(1).

— NOT ON EXAM

Example 11-4: Suppose Taxpayer extends the filing date for his 20X1 return from April 15, 20X2 until October 15, 20X2 and files on October 1, 20X2. The IRS has until October 15, 20X5, three years after the extended due date of October 15, 20X2, to assess any deficiency. *— WRONG*

If the return is filed after the due date, then the actual date of filing is used.[4]

— exam

Example 11-5: Suppose that without an extension, a taxpayer files his 20X1 return on May 1, 20X2. The IRS has until May 1, 20X5 to make an assessment.

The general three-year statute for assessment applies to all income tax returns, as well as estate and gift tax returns. However, a deficiency attributable to the carryback for a net operation loss, capital loss or unused tax credit may be assessed within three years of the date of filing the return for the year of the loss or credit, even though such date may be well beyond the normal statute of limitations for the years from which the loss or credit was carried.[5]

¶1102 THE SIX YEAR STATUTE OF LIMITATIONS FOR A SUBSTANTIAL OMISSION OF INCOME

If the taxpayer omits income exceeding twenty-five percent of the gross income reported on his or her return, the IRS has a six-year period to assess any additional tax. A similar rule applies to estate tax or gift tax returns where an amount is omitted that exceeds twenty-five percent of the amount of the gross estate or total gifts reported.[6]

Example 11-6: Suppose Taxpayer files its 20X1 tax return on April 15, 20X2 that contains $100,000 of gross income due to sales commissions, but fails to include the $30,000 earned from a bit role in a major motion picture. Because the omission of income exceeds twenty-five percent of the gross income reported, the statute of limitations does not expire on April 15, 20X5, but extends for a total of six-years to April 15, 20X8.

On an income tax return reflecting a trade or business, the term "gross income" refers to gross receipts (defined as the total of the amounts received or accrued from the sale of goods or services prior to reduction for the cost of such sales or services). Therefore, in determining whether there has been an omission in excess of a twenty-five percent, use the larger gross receipts figure, not the smaller gross profit figure.

Example 11-7: If a taxpayer has sales of $100,000, costs of goods of $40,000, and gross profit of $60,000, an income item of more than $25,000 must be omitted for the six-year statute to apply because gross income would actually be the gross receipts of $100,000.[7]

However, gross income from the sale of stock or other capital assets is not treated in a similar fashion. For purposes of the six-year statute, gross income

---

[4] *Burnet v. Willingham Loan & Trust Co.*, 282 U.S. 437 (1931), S.Ct., 2 ustc ¶ 655.

[5] Code Secs. 6501(h) and (j).

[6] Code Sec. 6501(e)(1) and (2).

[7] Code Sec. 6501(e)(1)(A)(i).

from the sale of stock is only the gain actually reported and not the gross proceeds of the sale.[8]

Example 11-8: Suppose on April 15, 20X2 Taxpayer files her 20X1 return that reports $100,000 of gross income from commissions. However, Taxpayer failed to report her $2,000 gain on the sale of stock for $26,000 in which she had a basis of $24,000. Because only the gain from the sale of stock constitutes gross income, only $2,000 is considered omitted and the three-year statute of limitations applies instead of the six-year statute of limitations. As a result, the statute of limitations for assessment expires on April 15, 20X5.

If the net income or loss from a flow-through entity should have been reported on a taxpayer's individual return, add her share of the gross income reported on the flow-through's tax return to the gross income reported on that individual's return to determine the amount of gross income to which the twenty-five percent test applies.[9]

Example 11-9: Suppose on April 15, 20X2 Taxpayer files its 20X1 tax return that contains $100,000 of gross income due to sales commissions, but fails to include the $26,000 earned from a chinchilla breading partnership. Because the omission of income exceeds twenty-five percent, the statute of limitations does not expire on April 15, 20X5, but extends for a total of six-years to April 15, 20X8.

The courts have interpreted the six-year statute of limitations provision to require an omission from gross income. Even if deductions are overstated such that they would produce a tax deficiency as significant as would occur with a failure to report gross income, the six-year statute of limitations will not apply.[10] Similarly, where a dealer overstates the cost basis of property sold, reducing the profit on sale, courts have applied the three-year statute of limitations, even though overstating the cost had the same effect as not reporting twenty-five percent of the gross sale proceeds.[11]

Example 11-10: Suppose on April 15, 20X2 Taxpayer filed her 20X1 return on that reported $100,000 of gross income from commissions. However, Taxpayer failed to report her $24,000 gain on the sale of stock for $26,000 in which she had a basis of $2,000 and negligently overstated trade and business expenses by $90,000. Although the $90,000 overstatement of deductions has a greater tax impact than a $24,000 of gross income, deductions do not impact the statute of limitations. Furthermore, because the actual omission of gross income was only $24,000, the three-year statute of

---

[8] ILM 200537029. See also, *CC & F W. Operations LP v. Comm'r*, 273 F.3d 402 (1st Cir. 2001).

[9] *Davenport v. Comm'r*, 48 TC 921 (1967), CCH Dec. 28,615. But See *The Connell Business Co. v. Comm'r*, TC Memo 2004-131.

[10] For instance, in Example 11-7, an overstatement of the cost of goods sold by $30,000 would understate gross profit by $30,000. Similarly, an omission of gross receipts of $30,000 would also understate gross profit by $30,000.

[11] *Colony, Inc. v. Comm'r*, 357 U.S. 28, 78 S.Ct. 1033 (1958), 58-2 USTC ¶9593. But compare *Home Concrete & Supply, LLC v. United States*, 2008-2 USTC ¶50,694 (D.C.N.C) with *Beard v. Comm'r*, 98 TCM 95 (2009) and *Salman Ranch, Ltd. v. United States*, 2009-2 USTC 50,528 (Fed. Cir.)

limitations applies, resulting in the IRS having only until April 15, 20X5 to assess a deficiency.

The rationale for this result is that claiming the deductions fully apprises the IRS of the nature of the items. If there is a substantial omission of gross income, however, the six-year statute of limitations applies to the entire deficiency irrespective of the fact that some items of the deficiency were not included in calculating the omission.[12]

> **Example 11-11:** Suppose on April 15, 20X2 Taxpayer filed her 20X1 return that reported $100,000 of gross income from commissions. However, Taxpayer failed to report her $26,000 gain on the sale of stock for $28,000 in which she had a basis of $2,000 and negligently overstated trade and business expenses by $90,000. The $26,000 omission of gross income extends the statute of limitations for the assessment of a deficiency to six years, which is April 15, 20X8. Furthermore, the IRS may examine any item on the return during that time, including the negligent overstatement of deductions.

An item is not considered omitted if its existence has been disclosed in the return, or in a statement attached to the return, in a manner that apprises the IRS of the nature and amount of the item.[13] For example, if the return discloses the existence of an item (e.g., a settlement received in litigation) but erroneously takes the position that the amount is not includible in gross income, then the six-year statute of limitations will not apply, even though the omission is more than twenty-five percent of the gross income. The taxpayer's own return must disclose the item as it is irrelevant that a return of a related taxpayer or entity may have disclosed the existence of the item.[14]

> **Example 11-12:** Suppose on April 15, 20X2 Taxpayer files its 20X1 tax return that contains $100,000 of gross income due to sales commissions, but fails to include the $26,000 earned from a partnership that conducted chinchilla breeding and properly reported all its income on its Form 1065. Because the omission of income exceeds twenty-five percent, the statute of limitations does not expire on April 15, 20X5, but extends for a total of six-years to April 15, 20X8. The fact that the partnership's Form 1065 reported the $26,000 item of income is irrelevant.

Nevertheless, with respect to smaller partnerships not subject to the unified audit procedures of TEFRA and S corporations, disclosure of an item on the partnership or S corporation return constitutes sufficient disclosure on the individual return of the partner or shareholder to avoid the six-year statutute of

---

[12] *Colestock v. Comm'r*, 102 TC 380 (1994), CCH Dec. 49,703.

[13] Code Sec. 6501(e)(1)(A)(ii); Rev. Proc. 2001-11, IRB 2001-2 applicable to any return filed on 2000 tax forms for tax years beginning in 2000. (Guidelines for adequate disclosure).

[14] See *Reuter v. Comm'r*, 51 TCM 99, TC Memo. 1985-607, CCH Dec. 42,536(M).

limitations.[15] For larger partnerships covered by the unified rules, the audit is conducted at the partnership level where special statutes of limitations apply.[16]

¶1103 THE STATUTE BEGINS TO RUN ONLY FOR A FILED RETURN

If a taxpayer never filed a return or if a taxpayer files an incomplete return, the IRS may assess the tax at any time.[17]

>   **Example 11-13:** Suppose on April 15, 20X2 Taxpayer files a Form 1040 for the taxable year 20X1 that only contains his name and address. Because Taxpayer has not filed a complete return, the IRS may assess a deficiency at any time.

A return that the IRS prepares and executes on behalf of a nonfiling taxpayer under the authority of Code Sec. 6020(b) is not treated as a return that will start the running of the statute of limitations.[18] Even if a taxpayer files a document denominated as a "return", it may not constitute a return that is sufficient to trigger the statute of limitations.

A return sufficient to start the running of the period of limitations generally must be properly signed and contain substantial information as to gross income, deductions and credits, which is the information necessary to compute tax.[19] A document described as a "tentative" return that fails to include items of gross income or any deductions or credits is not a proper return.[20] [21] The Tax Court has even held that a return which computed the taxable income was insufficient to commence the running of the statute of limitations where the taxpayer omitted his social security number, occupation and any information as to personal exemptions while the return was marked "tentative."[22]

On the other hand, the IRS has determined that a Form 1040 that lists zeroes on each line and is signed by the taxpayer without modification to the attestation statement should be treated as a return for statute of limitation purposes.[23] Alteration of the jurat on the return, however, results in document filed that does not constitute a return.[24]

---

[15] *Roschuni v. Comm'r*, 44 TC 80 (1965), CCH Dec. 27,345; *Ketchum v. United States*, 697 F.2d 466 (2d Cir. 1982), 83-1 USTC ¶9122 (S corporations); *Walker v. Comm'r*, 46 TC 630 (1966), CCH Dec. 28,080; *Rose v. Comm'r*, 24 TC 755 (1955), CCH Dec. 21,160 (partnerships).

[16] See ¶612, *supra*.

[17] Code Sec. 6501(c)(3).

[18] Code Sec. 6501(b)(3).

[19] *Zellerbach Paper Co. Helvering*, 293 US 172 (1934), 35-1 USTC ¶9003; *Florsheim Bros. Dry Goods v. United States*, 280 U.S. 453 (1930).

[20] *Chesterfield Textile Corp. v. Comm'r*, 29 TC 651 (1958), CCH Dec. 22,802. The fact that a tentative

return is properly signed, moreover, does not validate an improperly signed final return.

[21] *General Instrument Corp. v. Comm'r*, 35 TC 803 (1961), CCH Dec. 24,686.

[22] *Foutz v. Comm'r*, 24 TC 1109 (1955), CCH Dec. 21,244. A tampered Form 1040 which deleted various margin and item captions, in whole or in part, and which replaced them with language fabricated by the taxpayer, was also held not to be a valid return (for purposes of the failure to file penalty). *Beard v. Comm'r*, 82 TC 766 (1984), CCH Dec. 41,237, *aff'd per curiam*, 793 F.2d 139 (6th Cir. 1986), 86-2 USTC ¶9496.

[23] SCA 200028033.

[24] *Letscher v. United States*, DC-NY, 2000-2 USTC ¶50,723.

Example 11-14: Suppose that on April 15, 20X2, Taxpayer files a Form 1040 for 20X1 that is complete in all respect except that Taxpayer does not sign the return. Because a signature is required for a completed return, the IRS may assess a deficiency at any time.[25]

The IRS may assess a deficiency at any time if the taxpayer fails to file an information return required with respect to cross-border transactions[26] until the taxpayer files the information return. While the statute of limitations remains open, the IRS may assess a deficiency with respect to any item on the return, not just the cross-border items, unless the failure to file the information return is due to reasonable cause.

Example 11-15: Eb, a farmhand in Hooterville, inherits all the shares of a Netherlands corporation from a long-lost Dutch uncle during 20X1. On April 15, 20X2, Eb files his return for 20X1, which Mr. Haney prepared. Because Mr. Haney does not have any international tax experience, Mr. Haney fails to prepare a Form 5471 to attach to Eb's return. If Eb did not have reasonable cause to file Form 5471, the IRS may assess a deficiency with respect to any items related to the Netherlands corporation as well as Eb's farming income at any time. However, if Eb had reasonable cause to file a Form 5471, the statute of limitations with respect to Eb's farming income expires on April 15, 20X5 and with respect to items related to the Netherlands company three years after he files the Form 5471.

¶1104 FALSE OR FRAUDULENT RETURNS DO NOT START THE RUNNING OF THE STATUTE OF LIMITATIONS

When a taxpayer files a false or fraudulent return with the intent to evade tax, the IRS may assess a deficiency at any time. The government, however, has the burden of proving by clear and convincing evidence that the taxpayer intended to evade tax. The conviction of the taxpayer in a tax evasion prosecution[27] is sufficient to meet this burden of proof and collaterally estops the taxpayer from contending that he did not intend to evade tax.[28]

Example 11-16: Suppose that a basketball official intentionally inflates the amount of his expenses that the league must reimburse him so he can have additional cash without reporting additional tax. The official files his fraudulent 20X1 return on April 15, 20X2. Instead of the normal three-year statute of limitations expiring on April 15, 20X5, the IRS may make an assessment at any time.

Amending a false return has little, if any, impact on the statute of limitations. In *Badaracco v. Commissioner,*[29] the Supreme Court held that the Code does not explicitly provide for either the filing or acceptance of an amended return and

---

[25] Reg. § 1.661-1(a); *Lucas v. Pilliod Lumber Co.,* 281 U.S. 245 (1930).

[26] Code Sec. 6501(c)(8).

[27] Code Sec. 7201.

[28] *Taylor v. Comm'r,* 73 TCM 2028, TC Memo. 1997-82, CCH Dec. 51,887(M); *DiLeo v. Comm'r,* 96 TC 858, 885-886 (1991), CCH Dec. 47,423, aff'd, 959 F.2d 16 (2nd Cir. 1992), 92-1 ustc ¶50,197.

[29] *Badaracco v. Comm'r,* 464 U.S. 386 (1984), 84-1 ustc ¶9150.

that an amended return is merely a creature of administrative origin and grace. Only the original return, not an amended return, the Court said, determines which statute of limitations on assessment applies.[30] An amended return, therefore, does not trigger the three-year statute of limitations. The time to assess remains open on the basis of the fraud in the original return.

¶1105 TAX SHELTERS: LISTED TRANSACTIONS

If a taxpayer fails to include any information required to be disclosed in respect to a listed transaction,[31] the statute of limitations will not expire before one year after the earlier of 1) the date the IRS receives the required information or 2) the date that a material advisor provides the IRS with a list identifying each person to whom the advisor had acted as a material advisor.[32]

> **Example 11-17:** Suppose that a taxpayer engages in a listed transaction during 20X1 that results in significant deductions on his return. However, the taxpayer fails to disclose the listed transaction on his 20X1 return that he timely files on April 15, 20X2. Instead of the normal three-year statute of limitations for 20X1 expiring on April 15, 20X5, the three-year statute of limitations only begins to run when the IRS receives information about the listed transactions.

¶1106 GIFT OMISSION ON GIFT TAX RETURN

If a donor erroneously omits a gift from a gift tax return, the IRS may assess the tax on such gift at any time or proceed in court to collect such tax without assessment at any time. In other words, the statute of limitations does not run on omitted gifts regardless of the fact that a donor filed a gift tax return for other transfers in the same period.[33] This rule does not apply if the gift tax return discloses the transfer in a manner that adequately apprises the IRS of the nature of the omitted item.[34]

> **Example 11-18:** Kris Kringle, a benevolent gentleman, makes numerous gifts to good little boys and girls throughout 20X1 that he details on his Form 709 that he files on March 15, 20X2. The three-year statute of limitations on assessing a deficiency with respect to these gifts expires on April 15, 20X5, which is three years after the due date of April 15, 20X2. However, Kris inadvertently fails to report a gift to Madonna, who is on the naughty girls list, and the IRS may assess a gift tax deficiency at any time with respect to his gifts to her.

---

[30] Code Sec. 6501. The Court noted that other courts have consistently held that the filing of an amended return does not serve either to extend the statute of limitations on assessments and refunds or to reduce the six-year limitations period triggered by the omission of gross income in the original return.

[31] Code Sec. 6011.

[32] Code Sec. 6501(c)(10).

[33] Code Sec. 6501(c)(9) applicable to gifts made after August 5, 1997.

[34] Rev. Proc. 2000-34, IRB 2000-34, 186, provides guidance for submitting information adequate to meet the disclosure requirement.

¶1107 STATUTE OF LIMITATIONS FOR FLOW-THROUGH ENTITIES

The passthrough adjustments to an individual's reported income resulting from the IRS examination of partnerships raise an interesting question regarding the period of limitations for assessment. Does the limitations period begin to run from the filing date of the return for the passthrough entity or from the date the individual return of the shareholder or partner was filed? With respect to partnerships with more than ten partners, the statute of limitations for assessments arising from adjustments to the income of these larger passthrough entities is measured from the filing date of the entity's tax return.[35]

For partnerships with 10 or fewer partners the period of limitations is based on the partner's individual return.[36] Therefore, the statute of limitations is triggered by the filing of the return of the individual reporting the passthrough entity income and not the return of the passthrough entity.

> **Example 11-19:** Robin and Paulie become 50-50 owners of a partnership that files its Form 1065 for 20X1 on March 15, 20X2. The Form 1065 reports gross income of $100,000, but fails to report an item of $20,000. Similarly, Robin and Paulie timely file their individual returns for 20X1 on April 15, 20X2 and similarly omit their share of the $20,000 item of gross income ($10,000 each). The IRS has until April 15, 20X5 to assess a deficiency of tax for the unreported item of gross income and is not limited to the March 15 date because with less than ten owners, the triggering date is the date that the individual owners file their returns.

The statute of limitations begins to run on items that flow through from S corporation returns (Form 1120S) on the date that the individual owner files the return.[37]

¶1108 COMPUTATION OF TIME FROM THE DATE OF FILING

A return is deemed timely filed for purposes of determining the commencement of the limitations period when it is postmarked. Therefore, even if a return is actually received after the last date prescribed for filing, the return is considered as timely filed if postmarked on or before the due date.[38]

> **Example 11-20:** Suppose that Taxpayer goes to his local United States Post Office where he mails his return with a postmark of April 15, 20X2, 11:59 p.m. Although the IRS Service Center does not receive the return until April 20, 20X2, the timely-mailed return constitutes a timely-filed return and, therefore, the IRS has until April 15, 20X5 to make an assessment, not April 20, 20X5.
>
> However, if Taxpayer goes to his local United States Post Office and mails his return with a postmark of April 16, 20X2, 12:01 a.m., and the IRS

---

[35] Code Secs. 6229 and 6244.

[36] *Siben v. Comm'r*, 930 F.2d 1034 (2d Cir. 1991), 91-1 USTC ¶50,215; *Stahl v. Comm'r*, 96 TC 798 (1991), CCH Dec. 47,395.

[37] *Bufferd v. Commissioner*, 506 U.S. 523 (1993).

[38] Code Sec. 7502.

¶1107

Service Center receives the return on April 19, 20X2, the return is not timely filed. Under the Code and the Regulations, the three-year statute of limitations for the IRS to assess a deficiency does not expire until April 19, 20X5.

This rule in the Code and Regulations applies only to returns timely filed where the envelope containing the return has been properly addressed and bears the proper postage. The timely-mailing-is-timely-filing rule applies to private delivery services as well as to returns sent by the United States Postal Service.[39] In addition to the transmittal of returns by conventional means a special provision deems electronically transmitted documents as filed on the date of the electronic postmark.[40] The timely mailing is timely filing rule also applies to foreign postmarks. A return bearing an official foreign postmark dated on or before midnight as of the last date prescribed for filing, including any extensions of time, will be treated as timely filed.[41] The IRS bases this position on the general authority granted in Code Sec. 6081(a) for the IRS to "grant a reasonable extension of time for filing any return." The decision to accept a return as timely when it is mailed and officially postmarked in a foreign country is a reasonable and proper exercise of the IRS Commissioner's administrative authority.[42]

Despite the timely filing rule described in the Code and the Regulations, the Supreme Court has extended the law one step further such that the date of the postmark does not control as long as the taxpayer timely placed the document in a mailbox.[43] However, the taxpayer will have a challenge in proving that he timely mailed the document.

> **Example 11-21:** On his way home from work at approximately 6 p.m. on April 15, 20X2, Taxpayer drops his return for 20X1 in a mailbox. The local United States Post Office does not collect mail out of the box until the following morning and postmarks the return's envelope with the date April 16, 20X2 and the IRS Service Center does not receive the return until April 20, 20X2. The three-year statute of limitations begins to run on April 15, 20X2 and will expire on 20X5 assuming that the Taxpayer can prove that he timely mailed the return.

In computing the three-year period, the date that the return is actually filed is excluded. When the due date falls on a Saturday, Sunday or a legal holiday the return will be considered timely filed if it is filed on the next business day.[44] In such an instance, the statute of limitations begins to run on the actual date of filing.

---

[39] Code Sec. 7502(f). IRS designated private delivery services include: DHL Worldwide Express (DHL)-DHL "Same Day" Service and DHL USA Overnight; Federal Express (FedEx)-FedEx Priority Overnight, FedEx Standard Overnight, FedEx 2 Day, FedEx International Priority, and FedEx International First; United Parcel Service (UPS)-UPS Next Day Air, UPS Next Day Air Saver, UPS 2nd Day Air, UPS 2nd Day Air A.M., UPS Worldwide Express Plus, and UPS Worldwide Express.

[40] Reg. § 301.7502-1(d); TD 8932.

[41] ITA 200012085. But see Reg. § 301.7502-1(c)(ii); *Cespedes v. Comm'r*, 33 TC 214 (1959), CCH Dec. 23,833; *Madison v. Comm'r*, 28 TC 1301 (1957), CCH Dec. 22,596; *Electronic Automation Sys., Inc. v. Comm'r*, 35 TCM 1183, TC Memo. 1976-270, CCH Dec. 33,995(M).

[42] Code Sec. 6081(a); ITA 200012085, at p.3.

[43] *Sorrentino v. United States*, 383 F.3d 1187 (10th Cir. 2004), *cert. denied*, 126 S. Ct. 334 (2005).

[44] Code Sec. 7503.

Example 11-22: If April 15, 20X2 is a Saturday, a return filed on April 17, 20X2 , the next business day, is considered timely filed. The IRS has three years from April 17, 20X2 to assess any additional tax.[45]

This rule similarly applies to the date the statute expires.

Example 11-23: Suppose that a taxpayer, as a result of an extension, timely-files his 20X1 return on October 15, 20X2. Because the three years the IRS has to make an assessment ends on October 15, 20X5, which is a Saturday, the IRS has an extra two days until October 17, 20X5.

¶1109 REFUND CLAIMS

A claim for refund must be filed within either three years of filing the original return or two years of the time the tax was paid, whichever is later.[46] If the taxpayer did not file a return, the two year rule applies. See ¶ 1503.

¶1110 CONSENT TO EXTEND THE STATUTE OF LIMITATIONS

The taxpayer can voluntarily agree with the IRS to extend the time within which the tax may be assessed. This extension by consent, however, is not available in the case of estate tax assessments.[47]

Form 872, Consent to Extend the Time to Assess Tax (see Exhibit 11-1 at ¶1131), is the form normally used by the IRS when a taxpayer voluntarily agrees to extend to a specified date the period in which an assessment can be made. If an extension on a Form 872 is limited to specific issues, the IRS must adhere to the restrictions agreed upon in the extension.[48] Once the taxpayer and the IRS have executed a Form 872, neither side can unilaterally terminate the extended statute of limitations.

Example 11-24: Suppose that a taxpayer files his 20X1 return on April 15, 20X2. Although the three-year statute of limitations on assessment would expire on April 15, 20X5, on April 1, 20X5 the taxpayer and the IRS sign a Form 872 that extends the statute of limitation on assessment until December 31, 20X5.

A Form 872-A is a special consent form to extend the time to access tax (see Exhibit 11-2 at ¶1132). The extension will not terminate until ninety days after either (1) the IRS receives a notice of termination on Form 872-T, Notice of Termination of Special Consent to Extend the Time to Assess Tax (see Exhibit 11-3 at ¶1133) executed by the taxpayer or (2) the IRS mails the taxpayer either a Statutory Notice of Deficiency or a Form 872-T. An extension on Form 872-A can terminate only pursuant to these provisions and will not expire by operation of law simply as a result of the passage of a reasonable period of time.[49] Neither the

---

[45] *Brown v. U.S.*, 391 F.2d 653 (Ct. Cl. 1968), 68-1 USTC ¶9275.

[46] Code Sec. 6511.

[47] Code Sec. 6501(c)(4).

[48] *Ripley v. Comm'r*, 103 F.3d 332 (4th Cir. 1996), 96-2 USTC ¶60,253.

[49] *Estate of Camara v. Comm'r*, 91 TC 957 (1988), CCH Dec. 45,181; *Wall v. Comm'r*, 875 F.2d 812 (10th Cir. 1989), 89-1 USTC ¶9343.

execution of a closing agreement[50] or a letter sent by the IRS or the taxpayer terminates the statute of limitations.[51]

> **Example 11-25:** Suppose that a taxpayer timely files his 20X1 return by April 15, 20X2. Although the three-year statute of limitations on assessment would expire on April 15, 20X5, the taxpayer and the IRS execute a Form 872-A on April 1, 20X5 to extend the statute of limitation on assessment indefinitely. Once a month for the next two years, the taxpayer's attorney writes a letter to the IRS requesting termination of the statute (24 letters in total). Finally, on April 30, 20X7, the IRS issues a Statutory Notice of Deficiency. The letters the attorney wrote are irrelevant[52] and the statute of limitation on assessment expires on July 29, 20X7, which is 90 days after the issuance of the Statutory Notice of Deficiency.

The Form 872-T is the exclusive way to notify the IRS of termination of a Form 872-A.[53] The notification form, moreover, must be sent to the IRS office considering the case, and delivery to another IRS office or representative may not be sufficient to start the running of the ninety-day period following notice of termination. In *Burke v. Commissioner*,[54] the Tax Court held that delivery of a termination notice to an IRS Collection Division representative was insufficient.

Special consent forms are used by the IRS to extend the limitations period with respect to partnerships and S corporations subject to the unified audit procedures.[55] These forms are similar in effect to Forms 872 and 872-A, but are given special letter designations (e.g., 872-P). These forms extend the time to assess the individual partners or shareholders for any tax resulting from audit adjustments to partnership or S corporation items (see Exhibit 11-4 at ¶1134, Exhibit 11-5 at ¶1135, Exhibit 11-6 at ¶1136, and Exhibit 11-7 at ¶1137). Other special consent forms are available for extending the time to assess miscellaneous excise taxes (see Exhibit 11-8 at ¶1138) or to assess the tax return preparer penalty (see Exhibit 11-9 at ¶1139).

The forms for the extension of the limitations period require execution both by the taxpayer (or the taxpayer's representative) and by an authorized representative of the IRS.[56] Both parties must execute the extension prior to expiration of the time within which the assessment can be made. If the taxpayer executes the consent prior to the expiration of the statute of limitations but the IRS does not execute it until after the expiration, the extension will not be valid.

> **Example 11-26:** Suppose that Taxpayer files his 20X1 return on April 15, 20X2. Because the three-year statute of limitations would expire on April 15, 20X5, the IRS sends Taxpayer a Form 872 to extend the statute of limitations until December 31, 20X5. On April 1, 20X5, the Taxpayer signs the Form 872

---

[50] *Silverman v. Comm'r*, 105 TC 157 (1995), CCH Dec. 50,878, *aff'd* 86 F.3d 260 (1996), 96-2 USTC ¶50,327.

[51] *Grunwald v. Comm'r*, 86 TC 85 (1986), CCH Dec. 42,841; *Myers v. Comm'r*, 52 TCM 841, TC Memo. 1986-518, CCH Dec. 43,447(M), and *Aronson v. Comm'r*, 989 F.2d 105 (2nd Cir. 1993), 93-1 USTC ¶50,174.

[52] *Adler v. Comm'r*, 57 TCM 1376 (1989).

[53] Rev. Proc. 79-22; 1979-1 CB 563.

[54] 53 TCM 1279, TC Memo. 1987-325, CCH Dec. 44,015(M).

[55] Code Sec. 6221 to 6245.

[56] Reg. §301.6501(c)-1(d); IRM 1.2.2.24, Order Number 42.

and hands it to the IRS Agent. However, the IRS never signs the Form 872 until April 16, 20X5. The three-year statute of limitations was not extended and expired on April 15, 20X5.

An extension may be further extended by an additional consent properly executed before the expiration of the previously extended time to assess the tax.

> **Example 11-27:** Suppose that the taxpayer and the IRS have filed a Form 872 to extend the statute of limitations for 20X1 from April 15, 20X5 to December 31, 20X5. As late as December 31, 20X5, the IRS and the taxpayer could file another extension by executing either a Form 872 or a Form 872-A.

An extension of the statute of limitations is invalid if the consent of the taxpayer is obtained by coercion or under duress. For example, where consent was coerced by threat of seizure of property, the Tax Court treated the extension as void.[57] Similarly, where the imposition of the fraud penalty was threatened in order to secure an extension, the assessment was rejected as untimely.[58]

If, in the course of an examination, there is one issue that cannot be resolved prior to the expiration of the statute of limitations, even though all other issues have been resolved, the IRS will generally request that the taxpayer extend the statute of limitations. The taxpayer normally will be reluctant to subject the entire return to the possibility of additional assessment when only one issue remains in controversy. In such a situation, a procedure exists for the IRS to secure a restricted consent. Under such a consent, the statute of limitations will be extended only with regard to the remaining unagreed issue. Restricted consents are executed on both Form 872 and Form 872-A.[59]

¶1111 EQUITABLE ESTOPPEL

Estoppel is a broad equitable doctrine that extends into many areas of tax law and applies to both the IRS and the taxpayer. Estoppel prevents, or estops, a party from taking unfair advantage of another party's action or failure to act that has been caused by the misrepresentation or concealment of material facts by the party to be estopped.[60] Because the statute requires any extension to be in writing, there can not be no implied consent either on the part of the IRS Commissioner or on the part of the taxpayer to such an alteration.[61] Although this rule applies to both parties, most altered extension forms have been altered by taxpayers.

For example, the Tax Court in *Huene v. Commissioner*[62] found that the taxpayer's sophisticated efforts to alter a Form 872-A were "tantamount to fraud." The taxpayer had substituted his own computer generated "Form 872-M" for the Form 872-A sent to him by the IRS. The modified form, visually identical in most respects to a Form 872-A, limited his potential liability for additional tax

---

[57] *Robertson v. Comm'r*, 32 TCM 955, TC Memo. 1973-205, CCH Dec. 32,136(M).

[58] *Alfred J. Diescher*, 18 BTA 353, 358 (1929), CCH Dec. 5658.

[59] Rev. Proc. 68-31, 1969-2 CB 917; Rev. Proc. 77-6, 1977-1 CB 539.

[60] *Sangers Home For Chronic Patients v. Commissioner*, 70 T.C. 105 (1979).

[61] *Cary v. Comm'r*, 48 TC 754 (1967), CCH Dec. 28,588; *Piarulle v. Comm'r*, 80 TC 1035 (1983).

[62] 58 TCM 456, TC Memo. 1989-570, CCH Dec. 46,102(M).

to fifty dollars. The government did not discover the alteration until the statute of limitations had expired. The Tax Court concluded that the taxpayer's conduct constituted "concealment or wrongful misleading silence concerning a mistake that he knew had occurred upon the part of the government." Finding all of the elements necessary to apply the doctrine of equitable estoppel, the Tax Court held that the taxpayer was precluded from raising the statute of limitations as a defense.

Equitable estoppel can also apply against the IRS. For example, IRS alterations of a consent form after signing by the taxpayer also will invalidate the extension. This is true even though the alteration merely corrects a clerical error by the IRS in typing in the wrong year to which the consent applies and the taxpayer, knowing of the error, signs and returns the form without advising the IRS of the error.[63]

The IRS may not mislead a taxpayer into providing an extension and if it does, the IRS may be equitably estopped from relying on the improperly obtained extension.[64] In *Fredericks v. Comm'r*, a revenue agent contacted a taxpayer and asked him to extend the assessment period for the year 1977 by executing Form 872. The taxpayer had already signed a Form 872-A at the request of another agent. The current agent replied that there was no Form 872-A in his file and that the former was probably lost in the mail. The taxpayer thereafter executed a number of Forms 872. At some point, the IRS located the original Form 872-A, but did not contact the taxpayer for eight years. The IRS issued a Statutory Notice of Deficiency for the tax year 1977 to the taxpayer in July of 1992. The Third Circuit concluded that the agent's statement that the Form 872-A was not in his file, confirmed by the repeated requests for single-year extensions, constitute a false representation of fact that no Form 872-A existed. Furthermore, the IRS's silence regarding the reappearance of the Form 872-A further misled the taxpayer. On the basis, the Court of Appeals found that the taxpayer had established sufficient grounds for estoppel in that the IRS's actions amounted to affirmative misconduct.[65]

¶1112 SUSPENSION OF THE STATUTE

In addition to those exceptions discussed above that provide for a period of limitations longer than the normal three-year period, there are also situations where the running of the statute of limitations will be suspended for a stated period of time. One of the most significant of these occurs when the IRS issues a Statutory Notice of Deficiency to the taxpayer.[66] More specifically, the running of the statute of limitations on assessment is suspended after the mailing of the Statutory Notice of Deficiency during the 90 day period the IRS is prohibited from making an assessment, during the time of a Tax Court proceeding, and for 60 days thereafter so that the IRS has time to administratively make the assess-

---

[63] See *Cary v. Comm'r, supra.; Piarulle v. Comm'r*, 80 TC 1035 (1983), CCH Dec. 40,130.

[64] *Fredericks v. Comm'r*, 126 F.3d 433 (3rd Cir. 1997), 97-2 USTC ¶50,692, Acq. *rev'g* 71 TCM 2998,

TC Memo. 1996-222, CCH Dec. 51,338(M); AOD 1998-004.

[65] *Id.*

[66] Code Sec. 6212.

ment. The policies behind these suspensions are somewhat intuitive. The IRS should not be able to assess while the taxpayer has the opportunity to petition and receive a decision from the Tax Court while the IRS should have some additional time to assess tax once the Tax Court decision becomes final.

> **Example 11-28:** Suppose that a taxpayer timely files his return on April 15, 20X1. The IRS timely issues a Statutory Notice of Deficiency within the three-year statute of limitations by April 15, 20X2. If the taxpayer does not file a petition with the Tax Court, the IRS may not make an assessment for 90 days until July 14, 20X2. However, if the taxpayer files a petition with the Tax Court before the 90-day period expires on July 16, 20X2, the statute of limitations is further suspended until 60 days after the decision of the Tax Court becomes final.

The statute may also be suspended when a third-party recordkeeper (a bank, a broker, an attorney, or an accountant) receives a summons.[67] If the taxpayer begins a proceeding to quash such a summons, the IRS cannot examine the records summoned until the proceeding to quash is resolved, and the statute of limitations is suspended while the proceeding and any appeals are pending.[68]

> **Example 11-29:** Suppose that the statute of limitations for the taxpayer's 20X1 return will expire on April 15, 20X5. After issuing a third-party recordkeeper summons to the taxpayer's bank, the taxpayer moves to quash the summons on March 1, 20X5. The judicial proceeding with respect to the summons is not resolved until March 30, 20X5, resulting in extension of the statute of limitation for 30 days (the amount of time the proceeding was pending) after April 15, 20X5 until May 15, 20X5.

The statute is also suspended when a summons dispute arises between a third-party recordkeeper and the IRS. Even though the taxpayer has not sought to quash the summons, the statute against the taxpayer is suspended if the dispute is not resolved within six months of the time the summons is issued. The dispute is not considered resolved during the time any action to enforce the summons is pending. Because the taxpayer would not normally know about the dispute, the recordkeeper must notify the taxpayer of the suspension of the statute. However, the fact that the taxpayer is not notified would not prevent the suspension of the statute.

The IRS can unilaterally suspend the statute of limitations by issuing a "designated" summons to a corporation under examination.[69] A "designated" summons to a corporation is one that the IRS issues at least sixty days before the statute of limitations on assessment expires and that clearly states it is a designated summons issued under Code Sec. 6503(j). The period of limitations is suspended during the judicial enforcement period and for an additional 120 days after final resolution of the matter if the court orders compliance. If the court does not order compliance, the limitations period is suspended for only an additional 60 days. See ¶1704.

---

[67] Code Sec. 7609(b). See ¶709.
[68] Code Sec. 7609(e).
[69] Code Sec. 6503(j).

A final provision temporarily suspending the statute of limitations only applies to those situations where the taxpayer submits an amended return increasing his tax liability for a given year within sixty days of the time the assessment statute would expire for that year.[70] Under such circumstances, the IRS is given a full sixty days from receipt of the amended return to make the additional assessment, regardless of how much sooner the period of limitations otherwise would have run.

> **Example 11-30:** Suppose Taxpayer files his 20X1 return on April 15, 20X2. With the statute of limitations about to expire on April 15, 20X5, Taxpayer files an amended return for 20X1 on April 1, 20X5. In order to give time to the IRS to consider any additional information in the amended return, the statute of limitations is suspended until May 30, 20X5.

¶1113 REQUEST FOR PROMPT ASSESSMENT IN EIGHTEEN-MONTHS

The Internal Revenue Code gives estates the ability to reduce the normal three-year statute of limitations to an eighteen-month period for income tax returns.[71] This privilege can be exercised by filing Form 4810, Request for Prompt Assessment[72] (see Exhibit 11-10 at ¶1140). The estate can file the request after filing the income tax return and the request must set forth the type of tax (i.e., income, employment, excise, etc.) and the taxable period for which the prompt assessment refers. A separate request must be made for each succeeding taxable period because a request filed prior to the filing of a return has no effect.[73]

This special privilege also applies to corporations that have dissolved, are in the process of dissolution, or are contemplating dissolution on or before the expiration of the eighteen-month limitations period.[74] Form 4810 provides appropriate boxes to be checked for this purpose.

> **Example 11-31:** Suppose that a corporation dissolves on December 31 of 20X1. The corporation timely-files its final corporate income tax return by March 15, 20X2. When filing that return, the corporation may properly notify the IRS of a request for a prompt assessment within 18 months, which would be by September 15, 20X2.

A Request for Prompt Assessment filed when the normal three-year statute of limitations has less than eighteen months to run will not lengthen the normal period. Moreover, such a request does not shorten the extended assessment period in the case of fraud or in the case of a twenty-five-percent omission from gross income.[75]

---

[70] Code Sec. 6501(c)(7).

[71] Code Sec. 6501(d). With the exception of the estate tax return itself, this right also extends to all other returns required to be filed by the estate.

[72] Code Sec. 6501(d).

[73] Reg. § 301.6501(d)-1(b).

[74] Reg. § 301.6501(d)-1(a)(2) and (c).

[75] Code Sec. 6501(d).

¶1114 CONSIDERATION OF TRANSFEREE LIABILITY

If a taxpayer transfers assets for less than full and adequate consideration, the IRS may assess tax against the transferee for any tax the transferor may owe.[76] For these purposes, the statute of limitations for assessing the tax against the transferee extends until one year after the expiration of the statute of limitations for assessment against the transferor. If the transferee has further transferred the property, then an additional one-year period can be added to the statute. However, regardless of the number of transfers, the transferee's statute of limitations may not extend more than three years after the expiration of the period for assessment against the initial transferor.[77]

> **Example 11-32:** Taxpayer files his return for 20X1 on April 15, 20X2. Anticipating the receipt of a Statutory Notice of Deficiency for a large amount, Taxpayer transfers his prized real estate, BlackAcre, for $1 to Bruce on March 1, 20X5. The IRS has until April 15, 20X6, one year after the statute of limitations for Taxpayer expires on April 15, 20X5, to assess any deficiency against Bruce pursuant to a transferee liability for any tax that Taxpayer may owe with respect to 20X1.

The IRS may seek to assess transferee liability against stockholders based on the receipt of liquidating distributions. Where a liquidating corporation files a request for prompt assessment, the period of limitations against the stockholders for transferee liability expires one year after the eighteen-month period involved in the request.

Mitigation Provisions

¶1115 REOPENING A CLOSED TAX YEAR

There are occasions when fairness requires that the taxpayer or the IRS should be able to reopen a taxable year to avoid the harsh results of the statute of limitations. The mitigation provisions attempt to remedy such inequities.[78] When they apply, they allow the assessment of a deficiency or the refund of an overpayment for a year which would otherwise be barred by the statute of limitations.

These mitigation Code sections essentially permit the taxpayer or the government to correct the erroneous treatment of income, deductions or credits in a barred year in order to prevent the other party from later gaining an unfair tax benefit by taking an inconsistent position in an open year with respect to the proper year that the items belong. For example, a taxpayer who has erroneously reported an item of income in a barred year will be entitled to a refund for that year if a later determination adopts the government's position that such income should have been reported in an open year. The mitigation provisions similarly would permit the IRS to disallow a deduction and assess the tax for a barred year where a taxpayer claims the same deduction in both the barred year and an open year that is later determined to be the proper year for taking the deduction.

---

[76] Code Sec. 6901(a).
[77] Code Sec. 6901(c).

[78] Code Secs. 1311 through 1314.

¶1116 REQUIREMENTS FOR MITIGATION

Correction of the erroneous treatment of an item in a barred year is permitted only when satisfying the requirements for the mitigation provisions in the Code. Those requirements are:

1. A *determination* that finally resolves the proper treatment of the item in an open year that was incorrectly included or excluded in the barred year.[79]

2. The determination in the open year and the error in the barred year must result in the doubling inclusion, exclusion, allowance, or disallowance of the item in question or must fall within one of the other *circumstances* specifically described in the Code.[80]

3. As of the determination date, the proper adjustment would be *time barred* to either the IRS or the taxpayer (or a party related to the taxpayer) if not mitigated.

4. The circumstances must result in either:

   a. The determination of the correct treatment of the item must adopt the position of the party who would benefit from the error in the barred year and that position must be *inconsistent* with the erroneous treatment of the item in the barred year,[81] or

   b. A correction of the error was not barred by the statute of limitations at the time of the erroneous action.[82]

¶1117 A DETERMINATION FOR AN OPEN YEAR

To qualify for mitigation, a determination for an open year is essential to establish the correct treatment of the item that was erroneously excluded or included in the barred year. A "determination" is defined in Code Sec. 1313(a) to include the following:

1. A final decision or judgment by the Tax Court or any other court;

2. A closing agreement under Code Sec. 7121;[83]

3. A final disposition by the IRS of a claim for refund; and

4. A special agreement between the taxpayer and the IRS that serves as a determination for purposes of mitigation (see Exhibit 11-11 at ¶1141 (Form 2259)).

Final Decision of a Court. A decision of the Tax Court or any other court becomes final when the time for appeal expires. The rules of the various courts establish the period within which an appeal must be taken. If either party appeals, the decision or order of the Court of Appeals becomes final when the time for filing a petition for certiorari to the United States Supreme Court expires or, if filed, when such petition is denied. If certiorari is granted, the decision of

---

[79] Code Sec. 1313(a).
[80] Code Sec. 1312.
[81] Code Sec. 1311(b)(1).
[82] Code Sec. 1311(b)(2).

[83] See Chapter 13, The Appeals Office, for further discussion of closing agreements which are final determinations of tax liability binding on both the taxpayer and the IRS.

NOT ON EXAM

the Supreme Court becomes final upon issuance of the Supreme Court's mandate.

> **Example 11-33:** On April 15, 20X2, Taxpayer files a return for the taxable year 20X1. Before April 15, 20X5, the IRS timely issues a Statutory Notice of Deficiency and the Taxpayer petitions the Tax Court. On March 1, 20X7, the Tax Court enters a decision against the Taxpayer, who fails to appeal by May 29, 90-days after the date the decision is entered.[84] May 29, 20X7 is the determination date.

Closing Agreement. The IRS may enter an agreement in writing with any taxpayer that conclusively determines that taxpayer's tax liability for that particular period.[85]

Final Disposition of a Claim for Refund. The time at which the disposition of a taxpayer's claim for refund becomes final depends initially on whether the IRS has allowed or disallowed the claim.

If the IRS allows a refund claim with respect to an item that is the subject of mitigation, the disposition of the claim becomes final on the date the IRS allows the refund. Even if either the IRS denies other items included in a claim or the IRS offsets adjustments to reduce the claim, the disposition becomes final if there is a *net* refund and the IRS has allowed in full the item subject to mitigation. In the unusual situation where the IRS fully allows the item subject to mitigation, but disallows the entire refund as a result of other offsetting adjustments, the date of final disposition is the date the IRS mails the notice of disallowance to the taxpayer.[86]

If the IRS disallows a refund with respect to the item subject to mitigation, the disposition generally becomes final when the two-year period for filing a suit for refund expires, unless the taxpayer commences an earlier refund action.[87] This general rule applies even though the IRS only partially disallowed the item subject to mitigation and even though the IRS allowed other items included in the claim results in a partial refund. In the event the taxpayer files a refund suit, there is no determination until there is a final decision or judgment by the court.

> **Example 11-34:** On April 15, 20X2, Taxpayer files her return for the taxable year 20X1. During the remainder of 20X2, Taxpayer discovers some additional deductions she should have taken on her return and files a claim for refund on January 15, 20X3 for which the IRS never acts. If Taxpayer does not file a suit for a refund claim by January 15, 20X5, the disposition becomes final on January 15, 20X5. However, if she does file a suit for refund, the final disposition does not occur until there is a final decision or judgment by the court.

Different rules apply when a taxpayer does not include an item subject to mitigation in a claim for refund, but the IRS applies such item to offset or reduce

---

[84] Code Sec. 7481; IRM 35.9.1.3.1; Rule 190(a) of the Tax Court's Rules of Practice and Procedure.

[85] Code Sec. 7121; IRM 8.8; See ¶1602.

[86] Reg. § 1.1313(a)-3(b).

[87] Reg. § 1.1313(a)-3(c). See Chapter 15, Claims for Refund or Abatement, *infra*.

NOT ON EXAM

the taxpayer's claim. If the net result of the IRS's offset or reduction is a refund, the disposition becomes final upon expiration of the two-year period within which a suit for refund must be filed, unless the taxpayer institutes an earlier refund action. On the other hand, if the IRS asserts a tax deficiency as a result of applying the item subject to mitigation against the taxpayer's claim, such action does not constitute a final disposition of a claim for refund.[88] The determination of the item causing the deficiency may be obtained only by means of a final court decision, a closing agreement, or a special determination agreement.

Special Determination Agreement. A special agreement between the IRS and the taxpayer relating to the tax liability of the taxpayer will serve as a determination for purposes of mitigation.[89] Form 2259, Agreement as a Determination Pursuant to Sec. 1313(a)(4) of the Internal Revenue Code (see Exhibit 11-11 at ¶ 1141), is the form provided by the IRS for this purpose.

This special agreement permits an expeditious method of obtaining the determination required for mitigation. Although the parties agree to the amount of the income tax liability for the open taxable year, the agreement does not establish the tax liability and is not binding. The determination becomes final only when the tax liability for the open year becomes final.[90] Until such finality, the IRS and the taxpayer may attempt to change or modify the stated liability. Therefore, a taxpayer may file a claim for refund or the IRS may issue a notice of deficiency asserting a different tax liability for the open year. A subsequent determination adopting a modified tax liability for the open year will provide the basis for a change in the mitigation adjustment for the barred year. Despite the lack of finality with respect to the tax liability stated in the agreement, such an agreement does permit the immediate allowance of a refund or assessment of a deficiency.

EXAM

¶1118 QUALIFYING CIRCUMSTANCES FOR MITIGATION

The determination in the open year and the erroneous treatment of the item subject to mitigation in the barred year must involve one of the following "circumstances of adjustment" set forth in Code Sec. 1312:

1. *Double inclusion of an item of income* resulting from the including of an item of income in the open year and erroneously including the same item in the barred year (if unmitigated, favors the IRS);[91]

   Example 11-35: Taxpayer, a cash basis taxpayer, erroneously believes he receives an item of income on December 31, 20X1 and reports that on his return for 20X1 filed on April 15, 20X2. The IRS determines that Taxpayer should have included the item of income on his 20X2 return that he filed April 15, 20X3, and, therefore, the IRS issues Taxpayer a Statutory Notice of Deficiency for 20X2 on April 1, 20X6. The mitigation circumstance is Taxpayer erroneously including the item of income in both 20X1 and 20X2.

---

[88] Reg. § 1.1313(a)-3(d).
[89] Code Sec. 1313(a)(4); Reg. § 1.1313(a)-4.
[90] Reg. § 1.1313(a)-4(d).
[91] Code Sec. 1312(1).

2. *Double allowance of a deduction or credit* resulting from the allowing of a deduction or credit in the open year and erroneously allowing the same deduction or credit in the barred year (if unmitigated, favors the taxpayer);[92]

> **Example 11-36:** Business Man entertains a client on December 31, 20X1. Business Man deducts the cost of the entertainment on his 20X1 return that he files on April 15, 20X2 for which the statute of limitation expires on April 15, 20X5. Business Man's accountant discovers that the entertainment expenses were actually incurred on January 1, 20X2 and deducts those expenses on Business Man's return filed on April 15, 20X3. After April 15, 20X5, the 20X1 taxable year in which Business Man erroneously took the deductions is time-barred. The mitigation circumstance is Taxpayer erroneously deducting the expense in both 20X1 and 20X2.

3. *Double exclusion of an item of income* occurring when an item of *income is reported* in the open year and erroneously omitted in the barred year, and a subsequent determination adopts the taxpayer's position that the income was erroneously included in the open year (if unmitigated, favors the taxpayer);[93]

> **Example 11-37:** Taxpayer's accountant books an item of income in January 20X2 that should have been booked as income in 20X1. Subsequently, Taxpayer files his 20X1 return on April 15, 20X2 without the item of income, but files his 20X2 return on April 15, 20X3 with the item of income. On April 1, 20X6, before the expiration of the statute of limitations for 20X2, Taxpayer files a claim for refund for 20X2 that the IRS grants on April 15, 20X6. The mitigation circumstance is Taxpayer erroneously excluding the income in both 20X1 and 20X2.

4. *Double exclusion of an item of income* resulting when an item of *income is not reported* in either the open year or the barred year, and a subsequent determination adopts the position that the item was properly excluded from income in the open year (if unmitigated, favors the taxpayer);[94]

> **Example 11-38:** Taxpayer's accountant books an item of income in January 20X2 that should have been booked as income in 20X1. Subsequently, Taxpayer files his 20X1 return on April 15, 20X2 without the item of income. When preparing his 20X2 return that he files on April 15, 20X3, Taxpayer remembers that the item was actually earned as income in 20X1 and does not include the item on his 20X2 return. On April 15, 20X5, the date for expiration of the statute of limitations for 20X1, the item is time-barred for 20X1, the year in which it should be included. The mitigating circumstance is Taxpayer excluding the income in both 20X1 and 20X2 and 20X1 was still open when Taxpayer filed his 20X2 return.

---

[92] Code Sec. 1312(2).
[93] Code Sec. 1312(3)(A).
[94] Code Sec. 1312(3)(B).

5. *Double disallowance of a deduction or credit* occuring when the determination disallows a deduction or credit that should have been allowed, but was not allowed, in another taxable year (if unmitigated, favors the IRS);[95]

Example 11-39: Taxpayer should have deducted a business expense on his 20X1 return that he files on April 15, 20X2. Instead, Taxpayer incorrectly deducts the business expense on his 20X2 return filed on April 15, 20X3. On April 15, 20X5, the statute of limitations for 20X1 expires. On March 1, 20X5, the Taxpayer receives a Statutory Notice of Deficiency denying the deduction for 20X2 and, after filing a Tax Court petition on April 1, 20X5, Taxpayer enters a Closing Agreement with the IRS disallowing the deduction for 20X2 on February 1 20X6. At the time of the Closing Agreement, the proper year for which the Taxpayer should have taken deduction, 20X1, was closed. The mitigating circumstance is the Taxpayer not taking the deduction in either 20X1 or 20X2, and 20X1 was not time barred when Taxpayer filed his petition.

6. *Correlative deductions and inclusions for trusts or estates and legatees, beneficiaries, or heirs* are also circumstances that permit mitigation when a determination disallows, allows, includes, or excludes a deduction or item of income with respect to a trust or estate and any of their distributees, and such determination has a correlative tax effect on a barred year of the other related party or parties;[96]

7. *Correlative deductions and credits for certain related corporations* similarly permit mitigation when a determination allows or disallows a deduction or credit to a corporation and a correlative deduction or credit has been erroneously allowed or disallowed with respect to a related corporation belonging to the affiliated group;[97] or

8. *A determination of the basis of property after erroneous treatment of a prior transaction* permits mitigation and the correction of the following errors that may have occurred in barred years for a transaction on which such basis depends or in respect to any transaction that was erroneously treated as affecting such basis:[98]

   a. an erroneous inclusion in or omission from gross income,

   b. an erroneous recognition or nonrecognition of gain or loss, or

   c. an erroneous deduction of an item properly chargeable to a capital account or an erroneous charge to a capital account of an item properly deductible.[99]

   Example 11-40: During 20X1, Taxpayer enters a like-kind exchange, receiving property with a basis of $20,000 and a fair market

---

[95] Code Sec. 1312(4).
[96] Code Sec. 1312(5).
[97] Code Sec. 1312(6).
[98] Code Sec. 1312(2).

[99] This mitigating circumstance only applies to the taxpayer to whom the determination is made, the taxpayer who acquired title or from whom title was mediately or immediately acquired, and those involving gifts. Code Sec. 1312(7)(B); Reg. § 1.1312-7.

value of $100,000. Taxpayer properly does not report income from the like-kind exchange on his return filed April 15, 20X2. In 20X6, Taxpayer sells the property for $100,000, but does not report a gain by incorrectly claiming a basis of $100,000. On April 15, 20X8, the Taxpayer enters a Closing Agreement with the IRS stating that the basis of the property is $100,000. The Taxpayer has incorrectly taken a stepped-up basis to fair market value of $100,000 as a result of the 20X1 transaction without having to report any gain on the like-kind exchange. The mitigating circumstance is the determination of the basis of property after erroneous treatment of a prior transaction.

¶1119 IF NOT MITIGATED, TIME BARRED

The next requirement says that if the circumstance is not mitigated, the proper year will be time barred to either the IRS, the taxpayer, or a related party.

Time Barred. On the determination date, correction of the year is time barred by the statute of limitations.[100]

> **Example 11-41:** Business Man entertains a client on December 31, 20X1. Business Man deducts the cost of the entertainment on his 20X1 return that he files on April 15, 20X2 for which the statute of limitation expires on April 15, 20X5. Business Man's accountant discovers that the entertainment expenses were actually incurred on January 1, 20X2 and deducts those expenses on Business Man's return filed on April 15, 20X3. After April 15, 20X5, the 20X1 taxable year in which Business Man erroneously took the deductions is time-barred.

Taxpayers and Related Parties. Although the mitigation provisions are most commonly applied in order to correct errors relating to the proper year in which an item should be included or allowed, they also provide relief when the error involves the proper allocation of an item between certain related taxpayers. Mitigation is available only when one of the following relationships exists:[101]

1. Husband and wife; — MOST COMMON
2. Grantor and fiduciary;
3. Grantor and beneficiary;
4. Fiduciary and beneficiary, legatee or heir;
5. Decedent and decedent's estate;
6. Partner; or
7. Member of an affiliated group of corporations.[102]

exam

The same mitigation rules applicable to the correction of an error resulting from selection of an improper year also apply to correction of an error caused by the incorrect allocation of items between related taxpayers.[103]

---

[100] Code Sec. 1311(a).
[101] Code Sec. 1313(c).

[102] Code Sec. 1504 defines an affiliated group. Code Sec. 1313(c).
[103] Reg. § 1.1313(c)-1.

Example 11-42: Partner A deducts 100 percent of a partnership loss, while Partner B deducts none of the loss. Partner B later decides he is entitled to a deduction of fifty percent of the loss and files a claim for refund based on his share of the loss. The IRS allows the refund claim but discovers that the statute of limitations is no longer open for an assessment against Partner A to recover the tax on his erroneous deduction.

As a result, the mitigation provisions permit the IRS to open the barred year and assess tax against Partner A. The requirements for mitigation have been met. The allowance of the claim for refund by the IRS constitutes a determination. The allowance of the same fifty-percent portion of the loss to both partners would be a "double allowance of a deduction," which is qualifying circumstance number 2. Partner A's year of deduction is time barred. Finally, Partner B successfully maintained in his refund claim an inconsistent position with respect to the deduction erroneously claimed by Partner A in the barred year.

When the related taxpayer is the party seeking mitigation relief, the relationship must have been in existence at some time during the year in which the erroneous treatment occurred.[104] The relationship need not exist throughout the entire year of the error.[105] However, if such a relationship exists, the error does not have to result from a transaction relating to the relationship. For example, if one partner erroneously assigns rent income to his partner and such rent is not connected in any way to their partnership, the partner relationship in itself is sufficient to afford mitigation relief.[106]

When the government is the party attempting to open a barred year to assess tax against a related taxpayer, the time at which the relationship was in existence must meet a more stringent test. For the IRS to obtain such relief, the relationship must exist not only at some time during the year of the error, but also at the time the taxpayer first maintains the inconsistent position in a tax return, claim for refund or petition to the Tax Court.[107] If the taxpayer has not filed any of these documents, then the relationship must exist at the time the determination adopts the inconsistent position.

¶1120 EITHER AN INCONSISTENT POSITION OR NOT TIME BARRED WHEN ERRONEOUS POSITION ADVANCED

The final requirement to mitigate is that either a party would benefit by taking an inconsistent position (qualifying circumstances 1, 2, 3, 6, 7 or 8 in ¶ 1118) or that the proper year would not be time barred by the statute of limitations when the erroneous position was advanced (qualifying circumstances 4 or 5 in ¶1118).

Inconsistent Position. The party who would benefit from the error in the barred year must advance an inconsistent position for the treatment of an item in

---

[104] Code Sec. 1313(c).

[105] Reg. § 1.1313(c)-1.

[106] *Id.*

[107] Code Sec. 1311(b)(3); Reg. § 1.1311(b)-3(a). The courts are divided on whether or not an "active"

inconsistency is required for this purpose. *Yagoda v. Comm'r,* 331 F.2d 485 (2d Cir. 1964), 64-1 USTC ¶ 9448 (not required); *Estate of Weinrich v. Comm'r,* 316 F.2d 97 (9th Cir. 1963), 63-1 USTC ¶ 9420 (required).

an open year that the determination must *adopt*.[108] Regardless of what position the government or taxpayer may advance at any other time and for any other purpose, only the position that is both advanced *and* adopted in the determination controls. Consequently, a position taken by the government in a ruling or unrelated proceeding is irrelevant if the determination adopts a contrary position advanced by the government.

The inconsistent position must be that of the party who would benefit from the error in the barred year not the party who is seeking to correct the error. Therefore, if the taxpayer attempts to obtain a refund for a barred year, the IRS is the party who must have successfully advanced the inconsistent position in the open year. Conversely, if the government seeks to assess a tax in a closed year, the determination must adopt the taxpayer's inconsistent position.

The inconsistent position is always attributed to the party who successfully advanced that position. Furthermore, a party does not become the party who advanced the inconsistent position simply by agreeing to the position initially advanced by the adverse party. For example, if the government agrees to the position of the taxpayer in allowing a claim for refund, such agreement does not constitute an inconsistent position attributable to the government.

Correction Not Barred at Time of Erroneous Action. The two exceptions to the inconsistent position requirement are set forth in qualifying circumstance four (double disallowance of a deduction) and five (double inclusion of an item of income not previously taxed). Therefore, where the determination rejects the position of the government that an item of income belongs in an open year, and the taxpayer has not reported the income in either that year or the prior year where such income properly belongs, the existence of an inconsistent position is irrelevant. This is also true when the IRS is advantaged because a determination disallows a deduction or credit claimed by the taxpayer in an open year and the deduction or credit was not allowed, but should have been allowed, in a prior year.

Although these two circumstances of adjustment are excluded from the inconsistent position requirement, they must meet a different requirement for mitigation. The policy behind this requirement is that parties are considered diligent in advancing positions in good faith.

In the case of the double exclusion of an item of income never reported by the taxpayer, a determination rejecting the IRS's position that the income should be included in an open year will not permit the government to open a barred year *unless the statute of limitations with respect to the barred year was still open* at the time the government first erroneously acted in a Statutory Notice of Deficiency sent to the taxpayer.[109]

The purpose of this requirement is to prevent the government from attempting to open a barred year by manipulating the mitigation provisions whenever omitted income is discovered after the period of limitations on assessment has

---

[108] Code Sec. 1311(b)(1).   [109] Code Sec. 1311(b)(2)(A).

run. Without the special restriction, an unfounded claim by the government that the income should have been reported in an open year would force the taxpayer to take an inconsistent position. The anticipated determination rejecting the government's baseless claim would then trigger mitigation relief and permit assessment of tax on the income omitted in the barred year.

A similar restriction applies when the double disallowance of a deduction or credit is involved. If a determination disallows a deduction claimed by the taxpayer in an open year that was properly allowable in an earlier barred year, the mitigation provisions will apply if a refund for the earlier year was not barred at the time the taxpayer first maintained in writing before the IRS or before the Tax Court that it was entitled to such deduction in the open year.[110] Writings that will determine the time at which the deduction was first claimed include tax returns, claims for refund, protests and Tax Court petitions.

The purpose of this restriction with respect to double disallowances is to prevent a taxpayer from improperly using the mitigation provisions to obtain a refund for a deduction that the taxpayer belatedly discovers should have been taken in a barred year. By claiming such a deduction in a current tax return or in a claim for refund for an open year, the taxpayer would force the IRS to take an inconsistent position with respect to the proper year of deduction. In the absence of this special restriction, a subsequent determination disallowing the deduction in the open year would then permit the taxpayer to open the barred year and obtain a refund. In substance, these restrictions ensure that only those who make good-faith claims regarding the proper year for taking a deduction or reporting income are allowed relief under the mitigation statutes.

¶1121 MITIGATION ADJUSTMENT

Once the mitigation provisions apply, the parties must increase or decrease the tax liability for the barred year. With several important exceptions, the computation follows the normal procedures for determining a deficiency or overpayment of tax for an open year. The most important distinction is the requirement that the adjustment of tax in the barred year must be based solely on the erroneously treated item which is the subject of mitigation.[111] No other items that may have been incorrectly reported or treated in the barred year may be included in the computation or utilized by way of setoff or credit to reduce or increase the deficiency or overpayment.[112] Although other erroneous items in the barred year must be ignored, this does not prevent the eventual overpayment or deficiency determined under the mitigation provisions from being credited against, or offset by, overpayments or tax liabilities for other years.[113]

Two examples can illustrate how the mitigation adjustmet work.

Example 11-43: Suppose that on April 15, 20X2, the taxpayer files his 20X1 return with a casualty loss of $10,000. On April 15, 20X6, having determined that the casualty loss actually occurred in 20X2, the taxpayer

---

[110] Code Sec. 1311(b)(2)(B).
[111] Code Sec. 1314(a)(2).

[112] Code Sec. 1314(c).
[113] Reg. § 1.1314(c)-1(e).

files an amended return for 20X2 claiming a refund due to the casualty loss. On July 1, 20X6, the IRS refunds the taxpayer's tax for 20X2, based on the refund claim. However, the mitigation provisions would result in the IRS being able to issue a Statutory Notice of Deficiency for 20X1 even though the three-year statute of limitations would have been otherwise closed as of April 15, 20X5 because:

1. The allowance of a refund claim by the IRS is a determination;[114]

2. The double allowance of a deduction is qualifying circumstance number two;[115]

3. But for the mitigation provisions, the IRS would be time-barred due to the expiration of the statute of limitations for 20X1 on April 15, 20X6;[116] and

4. The taxpayer took an inconsistent position by claiming the casualty loss deduction in both 20X1 and 20X2.[117]

Example 11-44: Suppose the taxpayer files his 20X1 tax return on April 15, 20X2 that fails to report $12,000 of dividend income. On April 15, 20X5, the IRS timely issues the taxpayer a Statutory Notice of Deficiency alleging a deficiency for the $12,000 dividend that was not reported. After the Tax Court trial, the decision of the Tax Court against the IRS becomes final on May 1, 20X6. In that decision, the Tax Court accepts the taxpayer's argument that the dividend income actually constituted income in 20X2 (although the taxpayer did not report it as income in 20X2) instead of 20X1. Although the three-year statute of limitations for 20X2 had expired only 16 days earlier on April 15, 20X6, the IRS may still issue the taxpayer a Statutory Notice of Deficiency on the $12,000 dividend income for 20X2 due to the mitigation provisions because:

1. The finality of the Tax Court decision constitutes a determination;[118]

2. The double exclusion of an item not included in income constitutes qualifying circumstance number four;[119]

3. But for the mitigation provisions, the IRS would be time-barred due to the expiration of the statute of limitations for 20X1 on April 15, 20X5;[120] and

4. At the time of the erroneous action of the IRS issuing the Statutory Notice of Deficiency on April 15, 20X5, the statute of limitations for 20X1 had not been time barred.[121]

The deficiency (or overpayment of tax) resulting from the mitigation computation is subject to the same interest and penalty provisions that would apply to an open year. All tax and penalty determinations, however, are made in accordance with the tax law in effect for the year of adjustment. If the mitigation

---

[114] Code Sec. 1313(a)(3).
[115] Code Sec. 1312(2).
[116] Code Sec. 1311(a).
[117] Code Sec. 1313(b)(1).

[118] Code Sec. 1313(a)(1).
[119] Code Sec. 1312(3)(B).
[120] Code Sec. 1311(a).
[121] Code Sec. 1312(b)(1).

computation produces a net operating loss or capital loss that the taxpayer may carry back or forward to other barred years, the resulting overpayment or deficiency in those years is also allowable as a mitigation adjustment subject to assessment or refund.[122]

In order to recover the overpayment or assess the deficiency for the barred year, the normal assessment and refund procedures must be followed. Therefore, the IRS must issue a Statutory Notice of Deficiency or the taxpayer must file a refund claim unless the matter is resolved earlier by agreement or consent of the parties.

A special *one-year statute of limitations* applies to the assessment or refund of tax for the mitigation year.[123] The one-year period of limitations begins to run on the date of the determination which adopts the inconsistent position triggering the mitigation relief. Therefore, the IRS must issue its Statutory Notice of Deficiency within a one-year period. Similarly, the taxpayer must file any applicable refund claim within the same one-year period.

> **Example 11-45:** After properly applying the mitigation provisions, on April 5, 20X7, the IRS may reopen 20X1 and assess a deficiency. Pursuant to the special one-year statute of limitations, the IRS may assess that deficiency until April 5, 20X8.

¶1122 JUDICIAL MITIGATION

The courts have developed principles to permit the avoidance of the statutory bar. These equitable and judicial doctrines are discussed below.[124]

Equitable Recoupment. The underlying policy of this equitable doctrine is similar to that of the statutory mitigation provisions. That policy is to prevent a party from gaining an unfair tax benefit from the statutory bar by inconsistently treating a single transaction or item in different years or between related taxpayers.[125] The doctrine also applies when inconsistent legal theories may permit the imposition of two different taxes on the same transaction.[126] As a result, a barred income tax overpayment may offset an excise tax deficiency, and an overpaid, but barred, estate tax may apply to reduce an income tax deficiency.[127]

When such inconsistency occurs, the party who has been unfairly treated can recoup or offset an erroneous underpayment or overpayment of tax in a barred year against a claimed refund or assessment in the open year. Equitable recoupment is a defensive doctrine that affords relief only by way of offset and

---

[122] Reg. § 1.1314(a)-1 and -2.

[123] Code Sec. 1314(b).

[124] See Camilla E. Watson, *Equitable Recoupment: Revisiting an Old and Inconsistent Remedy*, 65 FORDHAM L. REV. 691 (1996).

[125] *Stone v. White*, 301 U.S. 532 (1937), 37-1 USTC ¶9303. Unpaid tax on trust income taxable to beneficiaries could be recouped by the IRS against claim for refund of income tax paid by trust on same income.

[126] Code Sec. 6214.

[127] *Bull v. United States*, 295 U.S. 247 (1935), 35-1 USTC ¶9346—estate tax overpayment could be recouped by estate against income tax on same payment reported on both the estate tax and income tax returns; Rev. Rul. 71-56, 1971-1 CB 404—estate tax overpayment attributable to an income tax deficiency of the decedent could be offset against the deficiency; Ltr. Rul. 8333007 (May 16, 1983)—overpayment of income tax could be applied against an outstanding excise tax deficiency which caused the overpayment.

only against a tax claim that itself is not time-barred.[128] It may not be used affirmatively to initiate an independent suit for the refund of a barred tax. Moreover, if the amount of the erroneous tax exceeds the tax against which recoupment is sought, the excess amount is not refundable.

> **Example 11-46:** Suppose that a corporation is denied a compensation deduction on the grounds that the amount of the compensation was not reasonable. Although the Tax Court may not have jurisdiction over employment taxes associated with that unreasonable compensation, the doctrine of equitable recoupment permits the offset of the excess employment taxes against any deficiency resulting from the denied compensation deduction.[129]

Setoff. The doctrine of setoff applies in those instances where the taxpayer files a timely claim for refund when the statute of limitations bars the government from assessing tax for the year to which the refund relates. Despite the statutory bar, this doctrine permits the government to offset against the claimed refund any adjustments for errors discovered in the refund year that are favorable to the government.[130] A return may be reaudited for the purpose of discovering such offsetting errors. Should the amount of such errors exceed the refund claimed, however, the statute of limitations bars any additional assessment.

> **Example 11-47:** Suppose a taxpayer timely files a claim for refund for 20X3 for $12,000. While reviewing the refund claim, the IRS discovers that the taxpayer had an underpayment for 20X1 in the amount of $8,000, but the statute of limitations for assessment of 20X1 has already passed. The IRS may offset the $8,000 underpayment against the $12,000 refund claim and refund only $4,000.

---

[128] In *United States v. Dalm, supra,* note 56, the Supreme Court held that the doctrine of equitable recoupment does not confer upon a court the jurisdiction necessary to hear a time-barred refund suit for the recovery of gift taxes erroneously paid on the receipt of funds that were subsequently taxed as income.

[129] *Menard, Inc. v. Comm'r,* TC Memo. 2004-207.

[130] *Lewis v. Reynolds,* 284 U.S. 281 (1932), 3 USTC ¶ 856.

¶1131 Exhibit 11-1 *EXAM

Form **872** (Rev. Dec. 2004)	Department of the Treasury-Internal Revenue Service **Consent to Extend the Time to Assess Tax**	In reply refer to:
		Taxpayer Identification Number

_____
(Name(s))

taxpayer(s) of _____

_____
(Number, Street, City or Town, State, ZIP Code)

and the Commissioner of Internal Revenue consent and agree to the following:

(1) The amount of any Federal _____ tax due on any return(s) made by or
(Kind of tax)

for the above taxpayer(s) for the period(s) ended _____

_____

may be assessed at any time on or before _____ . However, if a notice of deficiency in tax for any such
(Expiration date)

period(s) is sent to the taxpayer(s) on or before that date, then the time for assessing the tax will be further extended by the number of days the assessment was previously prohibited, plus 60 days.

(2) The taxpayer(s) may file a claim for credit or refund and the Service may credit or refund the tax within 6 months after this agreement ends.

Your Rights as a Taxpayer

You have the right to refuse to extend the period of limitations or limit this extension to a mutually agreed-upon issue(s) or mutually agreed-upon period of time. **Publication 1035**, *Extending the Tax Assessment Period*, provides a more detailed explanation of your rights and the consequences of the choices you may make. If you have not already received a Publication 1035, the publication can be obtained, free of charge, from the IRS official who requested that you sign this consent or from the IRS' web site at www.irs.gov or by calling toll free at 1-800-829-3676. Signing this consent will not deprive you of any appeal rights to which you would otherwise be entitled.

YOUR SIGNATURE HERE ➜ ....
I am aware that I have the right to refuse to sign this consent or to limit the extension to mutually agreed-upon issues and/or period of time as set forth in I.R.C. § 6501(c)(4)(B).   *(Date signed)*

SPOUSE'S SIGNATURE ➜ ....
I am aware that I have the right to refuse to sign this consent or to limit the extension to mutually agreed-upon issues and/or period of time as set forth in I.R.C. § 6501(c)(4)(B).   *(Date signed)*

TAXPAYER'S REPRESENTATIVE

SIGN HERE ➜ ....
I am aware that I have the right to refuse to sign this consent or to limit the extension to mutually agreed-upon issues and/or period of time as set forth in I.R.C. § 6501(c)(4)(B). In addition, the taxpayer(s) has been made aware of these rights.   *(Date signed)*

CORPORATE NAME ➜ ....

CORPORATE OFFICER(S) SIGN HERE ➜ ....
       (Title)   *(Date signed)*
➜ ....
       (Title)   *(Date signed)*
I (we) am aware that I (we) have the right to refuse to sign this consent or to limit the extension to mutually agreed-upon issues and/or period of time as set forth in I.R.C. § 6501(c)(4)(B).

INTERNAL REVENUE SERVICE SIGNATURE AND TITLE

....
(Division Executive Name - See instructions.)   *(Division Executive Title - see instructions)*

BY ....
       (Authorized Official Signature and Title - See instructions.)   *(Date signed)*

(Signature instructions are on the back of this form)   www.irs.gov   Catalog Number 20755I   Form **872** (Rev. 12-2004)

Instructions

If this consent is for income tax, self-employment tax, or FICA tax on tips and is made for any year(s) for which a joint return was filed, both husband and wife must sign the original and copy of this form unless one, acting under a power of attorney, signs as agent for the other. The signatures must match the names as they appear on the front of this form.

If this consent is for gift tax and the donor and the donor's spouse elected to have gifts to third persons considered as made one-half by each, both husband and wife must sign the original and copy of this form unless one, acting under a power of attorney, signs as agent for the other. The signatures must match the names as they appear on the front of this form.

If this consent is for Chapter 41, 42, or 43 taxes involving a partnership or is for a partnership return, only one authorized partner need sign.

If this consent is for Chapter 42 taxes, a separate Form 872 should be completed for each potential disqualified person, entity, or foundation manager that may be involved in a taxable transaction during the related tax year. See Revenue Ruling 75-391, 1975-2 C.B. 446.

If you are an attorney or agent of the taxpayer(s), you may sign this consent provided the action is specifically authorized by a power of attorney. If the power of attorney was not previously filed, you must include it with this form.

If you are acting as a fiduciary (such as executor, administrator, trustee, etc.) and you sign this consent, attach Form 56, Notice Concerning Fiduciary Relationship, unless it was previously filed. If the taxpayer is a corporation, sign this consent with the corporate name followed by the signature and title of the officer(s) authorized to sign.

Instructions for Internal Revenue Service Employees

Complete the Division Executive's name and title depending upon your division.

If you are in the Small Business /Self-Employed Division, enter the name and title for the appropriate division executive for your business unit (e.g., Area Director for your area; Director, Specialty Programs; Director, Compliance Campus Operations; Director, Fraud/BSA, etc.)

If you are in the Wage and Investment Division, enter the name and title for the appropriate division executive for your business unit (e.g., Area Director for your area; Director, Field Compliance Services).

If you are in the Large and Mid-Size Business Division, enter the name and title of the Director, Field Operations for your industry.

If you are in the Tax Exempt and Government Entities Division, enter the name and title for the appropriate division executive for your business unit (e.g., Director, Exempt Organizations; Director, Employee Plans; Director, Federal, State and Local Governments; Director, Indian Tribal Governments; Director, Tax Exempt Bonds).

If you are in Appeals, enter the name and title of the Chief, Appeals.

The signature and title line will be signed and dated by the appropriate authorized official within your division.

Form **872** (Rev. 12-2004)

¶1132 Exhibit 11-2

Form **872-A** (Rev. February 2005)	Department of the Treasury-Internal Revenue Service ## Special Consent to Extend the ## Time to Assess Tax	In reply refer to Taxpayer Identification Number

(Name(s))

Taxpayer(s) of _____

(Number, street, city or town, state, zip code)

and the Commissioner of Internal Revenue consent and agree as follows:

(1) The amount of any Federal _____ tax due on any return(s) made by or for the

(Kind of tax)

above taxpayer(s) for the period(s) ended _____

may be assessed on or before the 90th (ninetieth) day after: (a) the date on which a Form 872-T, _Notice of Termination of Special Consent to Extend the Time to Assess Tax,_ is received by the division operating unit of the Internal Revenue Service having jurisdiction over the taxable period(s) at the address provided in paragraph (4) below or the address designated by the division operating unit in a Form 872-U, _Change of IRS Address to Submit Notice of Termination of Special Consent to Extend the Time to Assess Tax,_ which address will supersede the address provided in paragraph (4) below; or (b) the Internal Revenue Service mails Form 872-T to the last known address of the taxpayer(s); or (c) the Internal Revenue Service mails a notice of deficiency for such period(s); except that if a notice of deficiency is sent to the taxpayer(s), the time for assessing the tax for the period(s) stated in the notice of deficiency will end 60 days after the period during which the making of an assessment is prohibited. A final adverse determination subject to declaratory judgment under sections 7428, 7476, or 7477 of the Internal Revenue Code will not terminate this agreement.

(2) This agreement ends on the earlier of expiration date determined in paragraph (1) above or the assessment date of an increase in the above tax or the overassessment date of a decrease in the above tax that reflects the final determination of tax and the final administrative appeals consideration. An assessment or overassessment for one period covered by this agreement will not end this agreement for any other period it covers. Some assessments do not reflect a final determination and appeals consideration and therefore will not terminate the agreement before the expiration date. Examples are assessments of: (a) tax under a partial agreement; (b) tax in jeopardy; (c) tax to correct mathematical or clerical errors; (d) tax reported on amended returns; and (e) advance payments. In addition, unassessed payments, such as amounts treated by the Service as cash bonds and advance payments not assessed by the Service, will not terminate this agreement before the expiration date determined in (1) above. This agreement ends on the date determined in (1) above regardless of any assessment for any period includable in a report to the Joint Committee on Taxation submitted under section 6405 of the Internal Revenue Code.

(3) This agreement will not reduce the period of time otherwise provided by law for making such assessment.

(4) This agreement may be terminated by either the taxpayer or the Internal Revenue Service with the use of Form 872-T which is available from the division operating unit of the Internal Revenue Service considering the taxpayer's case. For a termination initiated by the taxpayer to be valid, the executed Form 872-T must be delivered to one of the following addresses or the address designated by the division operating unit considering the taxpayer's case in a Form 872-U, which address will supersede the address below:

If **MAILING** Form 872-T, send to: If **HAND CARRYING** Form 872-T, deliver to:

(5) The taxpayer(s) may file a claim for credit or refund and the Service may credit or refund the tax within 6 (six) months after this agreement ends.

(Signature instructions and space for signature are on the back of this form)   www.irs.gov   Catalog Number 20760B Form **872-A** (Rev. 2-2005)

Your Rights as a Taxpayer

You have the right to refuse to extend the period of limitations or limit this extension to a mutually agreed-upon issue(s) or mutually agreed-upon period of time. Publication 1035, *Extending the Tax Assessment Period,* provides a more detailed explanation of your rights and the consequences of the choices you may make. If you have not already received a Publication 1035, you can obtain one, free of charge, from the IRS official who requested that you sign this consent or from the IRS' web site at www.irs.gov or by calling toll free at **1-800-829-3676.** Signing this consent will not deprive you of any appeal rights to which you would otherwise be entitled.

	Date signed
Your signature here I am aware that I have the right to refuse to sign this consent or to limit the extension to mutually agreed-upon issues and/or period of time as set forth in I.R.C. §6501(c)(4)(B).	
Spouse's signature I am aware that I have the right to refuse to sign this consent or to limit the extension to mutually agreed-upon issues and/or period of time as set forth in I.R.C. §6501(c)(4)(B).	Date signed
Taxpayer's Representative signature I am aware that I have the right to refuse to sign this consent or to limit the extension to mutually agreed-upon issues and/or period of time as set forth in I.R.C. §6501(c)(4)(B). In addition, the taxpayer(s) has been made aware of these rights.	Date signed

(You must also attach written authorization as stated in the instructions below.)

Corporate Officer's signature
I (we) am aware that I (we) have the right to refuse to sign this consent or to limit the extension to mutually agreed-upon issues and/or period of time as set forth in I.R.C. §6501(c)(4)(B).

Authorized Official signature and title *(see instructions)*	Date signed
Authorized Official signature and title *(see instructions)*	Date signed

INTERNAL REVENUE SERVICE SIGNATURE AND TITLE

Division Executive name *(see instructions)*	Division Executive title *(see instructions)*

BY Authorized Official signature and title *(see instructions)*	Date signed

Instructions

If this consent is for income tax, self-employment tax, or FICA tax on tips and is made for any year(s) for which a joint return was filed, both husband and wife must sign the original and copy of this form unless one, acting under a power of attorney, signs as agent for the other. The signatures must match the names as they appear on the front of this form.

If this consent is for gift tax and the donor and the donor's spouse elected to have gifts to third persons considered as made one-half by each, both husband and wife must sign the original and copy of this form unless one, acting under a power of attorney, signs as agent for the other. The signatures must match the names as they appear on the front of this form.

If this consent is for Chapter 41, 42, or 43 taxes involving a partnership, only one authorized partner need sign.

If this consent is for Chapter 42 taxes, a separate Form 872-A should be completed for each potential disqualified person or entity that may have been involved in a taxable transaction during the related tax year. See Revenue Ruling 75-391, 1975-2 C.B. 446.

If you are an attorney or agent of the taxpayer(s), you may sign this consent provided the action is specifically authorized by a power of attorney. If the power of attorney was not previously filed, you must include it with this form.

If you are acting as a fiduciary *(such as executor, administrator, trustee, etc.)* and you sign this consent, attach Form 56, *Notice Concerning Fiduciary Relationship,* unless it was previously filed.

If the taxpayer is a corporation, sign this consent with the corporate name followed by the signature and title of the officer(s) authorized to sign.

Instructions for Internal Revenue Service Employees

Complete the Division Executive's name and title depending upon your division:

- Small Business and Self-Employed Division = Area Director; Director, Specialty Programs; Director, Compliance Campus Operations, etc.
- Wage and Investment Division = Area Director; Director, Field Compliance Services.
- Large and Mid-Size Business Division = Director, Field Operations for your industry.
- Tax Exempt and Government Entities Division = Director, Exempt Organizations; Director, Employee Plans; Director, Federal, State and Local Governments; Director, Indian Tribal Governments; Director, Tax Exempt Bonds.
- Appeals = Chief, Appeals.

The appropriate authorized official within your division must sign and date the signature and title line.

Form **872-A** (Rev. 2-2005)

¶1133 Exhibit 11-3

<table>
<tr>
<td>Form 872-T
(Rev. July 2003)</td>
<td colspan="2" align="center">Department of the Treasury-Internal Revenue Service

Notice of Termination of Special Consent to
Extend the Time to Assess Tax</td>
<td>In reply refer to</td>
</tr>
<tr>
<td colspan="3">Taxpayer(s) Name(s)</td>
<td>Termination by
☐ Taxpayer
☐ Internal Revenue Service</td>
</tr>
<tr>
<td colspan="3" rowspan="2">Taxpayer(s) Address</td>
<td>Taxpayer Identification Number</td>
</tr>
<tr>
<td>Office where
Form 872-A/Form 872-IA
Originated</td>
</tr>
<tr>
<td>Kind of Tax</td>
<td colspan="2">Tax Period(s) Covered by this Notice</td>
<td>IRS Center Where Return Filed</td>
</tr>
</table>

This form is written notification of termination of:
(Check the appropriate box)

☐ Form 872-A, Special Consent to Extend the Time to Assess Tax

☐ Form 872-IA, Special Consent to Extend the Time to Assess Tax As Well As Tax Attributable to Items of a Partnership

for the kind of tax and tax period(s) indicated above. This notice of termination of consent is provided under the terms of the agreement between the taxpayer(s) named above the Commissioner of Internal Revenue dated _____.

See the back of this form for signature instructions.
Please note that signing this notice may alter the taxpayer(s) appeal rights.

YOUR SIGNATURE ➤ _____   _____
                                                                (Date signed)

SPOUSE'S SIGNATURE ➤ _____   _____
                                                                (Date signed)

TAXPAYER'S REPRESENTATIVE'S

SIGNATURE ➤ _____   _____
                                                                (Date signed)
(You must also attach written authorization as stated in the instructions on the back of this
CORPORATE NAME form)

_____

CORPORATE
OFFICER(S)   ➤ _____   _____   _____
SIGNATURE   (Name)   (Title)   (Date signed)
              ➤ _____   _____   _____
                   (Name)   (Title)   (Date signed)
              (Authorized Official Signature and Title - see instructions)

INTERNAL REVENUE SERVICE SIGNATURE AND TITLE

_____   _____
(Division Executive Name - see instructions)   (Division Executive Title - see instructions)

BY _____   _____
   (Authorized Official Signature and Title - see instructions)   (Date signed)

(Instructions are on the 2nd page of this form)   www.irs.gov   Catalog Number 20775A   Form **872-T** (Rev. 7-2003)

Instructions

This notice may be made by either the taxpayer(s) or the Commissioner of Internal Revenue. All requested information must be included when this form is completed.

Please enter; in the space provided on the front of this form, the date Form 872-A/Form 872-IA was signed for the Internal Revenue Service.

If this notice is for income tax, self-employment tax, or FICA tax on tips and is made for any year(s) for which a joint return was filed, both husband and wife must sign this form unless one, acting under a power of attorney, signs as agent for the other. The signatures must match the names as they appear on the Form 872-A/Form 872-IA.

If this notice is for gift tax and the donor and the donor's spouse elected to have gifts to third persons considered as made one-half by each, both husband and wife must sign this form unless one, acting under a power of attorney, signs as agent for the other. The signatures must match the names as they appear on the Form 872-A/Form 872-IA.

If this notice is for Chapter 41, 42, or 43 taxes involving a partnership, only one authorized partner need sign.

If you are an attorney or agent of the taxpayer(s), you may sign this notice provided the action is specifically authorized by a power of attorney. If the power of attorney was not previously filed, you must include it with this form.

If you are acting as a fiduciary (such as executor, administrator, trustee, etc.) and you sign this notice, attach Form 56, Notice Concerning Fiduciary Relationship, unless it was previously filed.

If the taxpayer is a corporation, sign this notice with the corporate name followed by the signature and title of the officer(s) authorized to sign.

Delivery Instructions: See Form 872-A, Item (4)/Form 872-IA, Item (1) for the proper address to mail or hand carry this notice. This notice must be received by the Internal Revenue office from which the Form 872-A/Form 872-IA originated unless a Form 872-U, Change of IRS Address to Submit Notice of Termination of Special Consent to Extend the Time to Access Tax has been issued by the Commissioner of Internal Revenue changing the office and address to which this form must delivered. This notice has no force or effect until it is received by the office designated by the Commissioner of Internal Revenue.

Instructions for Internal Revenue Service Employees

Complete the Division Executive's name and title depending upon your division:

Small Business and Self-Employed Division = Area Director; Director, Compliance Policy; Director, Compliance Services.

Wage and Investment Division = Area Director; Director, Field Compliance Services.

Large and Mid-Size Business Division = Director, Field Operations for your industry.

Tax Exempt and Government Entities Division = Director, Exempt Organizations; Director, Employee Plans; Director, Federal, State and Local Governments; Director, Indian Tribal Governments; Director, Tax Exempt Bonds.

Appeals = Chief, Appeals.

The appropriate authorized official within your division must sign and date the signature and title line.

Catalog Number 20775A   Form **872-T** (Rev. 7-2003)

¶1134 Exhibit 11-4

Form **872-P** (Rev. February 2005)	Department of the Treasury - Internal Revenue Service **Consent to Extend the Time to Assess** **Tax Attributable to Partnership**	In reply refer to: Partnership's Taxpayer Identification Number

_____ , a partnership of

_____
(Name)

_____ and the
(Number, street, city or town, state, and ZIP code)

Commissioner of Internal Revenue consent and agree as follows:

The Internal Revenue Service may assess any federal income tax attributable to the partnership
items of the partnership named above against any partner of the partnership for the period(s) ended

_____

at any time on or before _____

If the Internal Revenue Service mails a notice of Final Partnership Administrative Adjustment to the partnership's
Tax Matters Partner, the time for assessing the tax for the period(s) stated in the notice of Final Partnership
Administrative Adjustment will be suspended

(a) For the period, under section 6226 of the Internal Revenue Code, during which a suit may be filed in court to contest
the determinations made in the notice of Final Partnership Administrative Adjustment, and

(b) If a suit is filed during such period, until the court's decision in the case becomes final, and

(c) For one (1) year thereafter.

Your Rights as a Taxpayer

The taxpayer has the right to refuse to extend the period of limitations or limit this extension to a mutually agreed-upon issue(s) or
mutually agreed-upon period of time. **Publication 1035,** _Extending the Tax Assessment Period,_ provides a more detailed explanation
of taxpayers' rights and the consequences of the choices taxpayer(s) may make. If the taxpayer(s) has not already received a
Publication 1035, the publication can be obtained, free of charge, from the IRS official who requested that the taxpayer(s) sign this
consent or from the IRS' web site at www.irs.gov or by calling toll free at 1-800-829-3676. Signing this consent will not deprive the
taxpayer(s) of any appeal rights to which the taxpayer(s) would otherwise be entitled.

(Signature instructions and space for signature are on back of this form.) ISA	www.irs.gov	Form **872-P** (Rev. 2-2005)

STF VTLM1000.1

SIGNING THIS CONSENT WILL NOT DEPRIVE THE PARTNERSHIP OR THE PARTNERS OF ANY APPEAL RIGHTS TO WHICH THEY WOULD OTHERWISE BE ENTITLED.

Partnership _____

Name _____

Under penalties of perjury, I declare that I am not currently in bankruptcy nor have I previously been named as a debtor in a bankruptcy proceeding in which the United States could have filed a claim for income tax due with respect to any partnership taxable year covered by this consent.

Tax Matters Partner

Sign Here _____   _____
                                                                                                              (Date signed)

I am aware that I have the right to refuse to sign this consent or to limit the extension to mutually agreed-upon issues/and or period of time as set forth in I.R.C § 6501(c)(4)(B).

Authorized Person

Sign Here _____ (TIN: _____)   _____
                    (You must also attach written authorization as stated in the instructions on the back of this form.)   *(Date signed)*

I am aware that I have the right to refuse to sign this consent or to limit the extension to mutually agreed-upon issues/and or period of time as set forth in I.R.C § 6501(c)(4)(B). In addition, the taxpayer(s) has been made aware of these rights.

Internal Revenue Service Signature and Title

_____   _____
Division Executive Name - see instructions   *Division Executive title - see instructions*

By _____
            (Authorized Official Signature and Title - see instructions)

Instructions for Signing Form 872-P

1. This consent generally applies to partnership returns filed for partnership tax years beginning after September 3, 1982.

2. This consent may be signed for the partnership in the appropriate space by either:

    a. The Tax Matters Partner for the partnership for the tax year(s) covered by the consent, or

    b. Any other person having written authorization from the partnership to sign the consent (See instruction Item #4 below)

3. Bankruptcy terminates the designation of a Tax Matters Partner and removes their authority to sign this extension

    a. If the Tax Matters Partner is not an individual and a person acting in a representative capacity for the Tax Matters Partner (for example, the trustee of a trust) signs the consent, the bankruptcy declaration above the signature line applies to the bankruptcy status of the Tax Matters Partner, not the person who actually signed the consent.

    b. If the Tax Matters Partner has filed a joint return with his or her spouse for the taxable year(s) covered by the consent and the Tax Matters Partner signs the consent, the bankruptcy declaration above the signature line applies to either spouse, not just the Tax Matters Partner who actually signed the document.

4. If any person other than the Tax Matters Partner signs the consent, you must attach a copy of the written authorization from the partnership to the consent. The written authorization, which is described in Treasury Regulation 301.6229(b)-1, must:

    a. State that it is an authorization for a person other than the Tax Matters Partner to extend the assessment period with respect to all partners

    b. Identify the partnership and the authorized person by name, address, and taxpayer identification number

    c. Specify the partnership tax year(s) for which the authorization is effective, and

    d. Be signed by all persons who were general partners or member-managers at any time during the year(s) for which the authorization is effective.

Instructions for Internal Revenue Service Employees

Complete the Division Executive's name and title depending upon your division

If you are in:

*   the Small Business/Self-Employed Division, enter the name and title for the appropriate division executive for your business unit (e.g., Area Director for your area, Director, Compliance Policy, Director, Compliance Services).

*   the Wage and Investment Division, enter the name and title for the appropriate division executive for your business unit (e.g., Area Director for your area; Director, Field Compliance Services)

*   the Large and Mid-Size Business Division, enter the name and title of the Director, Field Operations for your industry

*   the Tax Exempt and Government Entities Division, enter the name and title for the appropriate division executive for your business unit (e.g., Director, Exempt Organizations; Director, Employee Plans; Director, Federal, State, and Local Governments; Director, Indian Tribal Governments; Director, Tax Exempt Bonds)

*   Appeals, enter the name and title of the appropriate Director, Appeals Operating Unit.

        The signature and title line will be signed and dated by the appropriate authorized official within your division.

www.irs.gov   Form **872-P** (Rev. 2-2005)

STF VTLM1000.2

¶1135 Exhibit 11-5

Form **872-O**	Department of the Treasury - Internal Revenue Service	In reply refer to:
Rev. February 2005	**Special Consent to Extend the Time to Assess Tax Attributable to Items of a Partnership**	Taxpayer Identification Number

_____, a partnership at

_____
(Name)

_____ and the
(Number, Street, City or Town, State, and ZIP code)

Commissioner of Internal Revenue consent and agree as follows:

(1) The Internal Revenue Service may assess any federal income tax attributable to the partnership items of the partnership named above against any partner of the partnership for the period(s) ended

_____
_____

at any time on or before the ninetieth (90th) day after:

    (a) The date on which a Form 872-N, _Notice of Termination of Special Consent to Extend the Time to Assess Tax Attributable to Partnership Items_ is received by the Internal Revenue Service at the address provided in paragraph (3) below. If the Internal Revenue Service has sent the partnership a Form 872-U, _Change of Address to Submit Notice of Termination of Special Consent to Extend the Time to Assess Tax,_ the Form 872-N must be delivered to the Internal Revenue Service at the address provided in the Form 872-U; or

    (b) The date on which the Internal Revenue Service mails Form 872-N to the Tax Matters Partner at the partnership's last known address.

(2) If the Internal Revenue Service mails a Notice of Final Partnership Administrative Adjustment to the partnership's Tax Matters Partner, the time for assessing the tax for the period(s) stated in the notice will be suspended:

    (a) For the period, under section 6226 of the Internal Revenue Code, during which a suit may be filed in court to contest the determination(s) made in the Notice of Final Partnership Administrative Adjustment, and

    (b) If a suit is filed during such period, until court's decision in the case becomes final, and

    (c) For one (1) year thereafter.

(3) This agreement will not reduce the period of time otherwise provided by law for making such assessment.

(4) The Internal Revenue Service or the partnership may terminate this agreement by using Form 872-N, which is available from the Internal Revenue Service office considering the partnership's case. For a termination initiated by the partnership to be valid, the executed Form 872-N must be delivered to one of the following addresses or the address designated by the Internal Revenue Service in a Form 872-U, which address will supersede the addresses provided below:

        If **MAILING** Form 872-N, send to: If **HAND CARRYING** Form 872-N, Deliver to:

Your Rights as a Taxpayer

The taxpayer has the right to refuse to extend the period of limitations or limit this extension to a mutually agreed-upon issue(s) or mutually agreed-upon period of time. **Publication 1035,** _**Extending the Tax Assessment Period,**_ provides a more detailed explanation of taxpayers' rights and the consequences of the choices taxpayer(s) may make. If the taxpayer(s) has not already received a Publication 1035, the publication can be obtained, free of charge, from the IRS official who requested that the taxpayer(s) sign this consent or from the IRS' web site at www.irs.gov or by calling toll free at 1-800-829-3676. Signing this consent will not deprive the taxpayer(s) of any appeal rights to which the taxpayer(s) would otherwise be entitled.

(Signature instructions and space for signature are on back of this form.)   www.irs.gov   Form **872-O** (Rev. 2-2005)
ISA
STF FED1601F.1

¶1136 Exhibit 11-6

Form **872-N** (Rev. 10-2004)	Department of the Treasury — Internal Revenue Service **Notice of Termination of Special Consent to Extend the Time to Assess Tax Attributable to Partnership Items**	In reply refer to
		Termination by ☐ Tax Matters Partner ☐ Internal Revenue Service

Partnership name	Partnership address
Partnership's Taxpayer Identification Number *(TIN)* ▶	

Tax Period(s) covered by this Notice	Internal Revenue Service Office where Form 872-O originated	Internal Revenue Service Office where Partnership return filed

This form is written notification of termination of **Form 872-O,** Special Consent to Extend the Time to Assess Tax Attributable to Partnership Items, for the tax and tax period*(s)* indicated above. This notice of termination of consent is provided under the terms of the agreement between the taxpayer*(s)* named above and the Commissioner of Internal Revenue dated _____ .

Please see the back of this form for signature instructions.
SIGNING THIS NOTICE MAY ALTER THE PARTNERSHIP'S OR PARTNER'S APPEAL RIGHTS.

Under penalties of perjury, I declare that I am not currently in bankruptcy nor have I previously been named as a debtor in a bankruptcy proceeding in which the United States could have filed a claim for income tax due with respect to any partnership taxable year covered by this consent.

**Tax Matters
Partner
Sign here** ▶ _____   _____
   (Date signed)

**Authorized
Person
Sign here** ▶ _____   _____   _____
                                (You must also attach written authorization   *(TIN)*   *(Date signed)*
                                as stated on the back of this form.)

INTERNAL REVENUE SERVICE SIGNATURE AND TITLE

_____   _____
(Division Executive Name - see instructions)   *(Division Executive Title - see instructions)*

BY _____   _____
         (Authorized Official Signature and Title - see instructions)   *(Date signed)*

(Signature instructions are on the back of this form)   www.irs.gov   Form **872-N** (Rev. 10-2004)
ISA

STF CLDB1000

¶1137 Exhibit 11-7

	Department of the Treasury-Internal Revenue Service	In reply refer to
Form **872-F** (Rev. July, 2005)	**Consent to Extend the Time to Assess Tax** **Attributable to Items of a Partnership or S Corporation** **That Have Converted Under Section 6231(b)** **of the Internal Revenue Code**	
		Taxpayer Identification Number

_____ , of
(Name(s))

_____ , a partner (shareholder)
(Number, street, city or town, state, zip code)

in _____ and the
(Name of Partnership/S Corporation)

Commissioner of Internal Revenue consent and agree as follows:

The amount of any Federal income tax with respect to the above named taxpayer(s) on any partnership (subchapter S) item(s) for the above named partnership (S corporation) that have converted by reason of one or more of the events described in subsection (b) of section 6231 of the Internal Revenue Code or any item affected by such item(s) for the partnership (S Corporation) period(s) ended _____

may be assessed at any time on or before _____

If a statutory notice of deficiency is sent to the taxpayer pursuant to section 6230(a)(2)(A)(ii) of the Code with respect to the above tax on or before that date, the running of the period of limitations provided in section 6229(f) of the Code on assessment of any tax attributable to such converted items (or any item affected by such item(s)) shall be suspended for the period during which an action may be brought in the Tax Court under section 6213 of the Code (and, if an action with respect to such notice is brought in the Tax Court during such period, until the decision of the Court in such action becomes final pursuant to section 7481 of the Code), and for 60 days thereafter.

Your Rights as a Taxpayer

You have the right to refuse to extend the period of limitations or limit this extension to a mutually agreed-upon issue(s) or mutually agreed-upon period of time. Publication 1035, *Extending the Tax Assessment Period,* provides a more detailed explanation of your rights and the consequences of the choices you may make. If you have not already received a Publication 1035, you can obtain one, free of charge, from the IRS official who requested that you sign this consent or from the IRS' web site at www.irs.gov or by calling toll free at **1-800-829-3676**. Signing this consent will not deprive you of any Appeal rights to which you would otherwise be entitled.

	Date signed
Partner's (Shareholder's) Signature I am aware that I have the right to refuse to sign this consent or to limit the extension to particular issues and/or periods of time as set forth in I.R.C. §6501(c)(4)(B).	
Spouse's Signature I am aware that I have the right to refuse to sign this consent or to limit the extension to particular issues and/or periods of time as set forth in I.R.C. §6501(c)(4)(B).	Date signed
Taxpayer's Representative Signature I am aware that I have the right to refuse to sign this consent or to limit the extension to particular issues and/or periods of time as set forth in I.R.C. §6501(c)(4)(B).	Date signed

(Attach Form 2848 - Power of Attorney and Declaration of Representative)

INTERNAL REVENUE SERVICE SIGNATURE AND TITLE

Division Executive name *(see instructions)*	Division Executive title *(see instructions)*

BY Authorized Official signature and title *(see instructions)*	Date signed

(Signature instructions are on the second page of the form)   www.irs.gov   Catalog Number 16907M   Form **872-F** (Rev. 7-2005)

Instructions

The consent can only apply to partnership (subchapter S) item(s) (or any item affected by such item(s)) that have converted to nonpartnership (subchapter S) items for partnership tax years beginning after September 3, 1982 or for S corporation tax years beginning after December 31, 1982.

The Tax Matters Partner (Person) of the partnership (S corporation) in which the items arose (or any person authorized by the partnership in writing) may not consent to extend the period of limitations for a partner (shareholder).

If this consent is made for any year(s) for which a joint return was filed, both the husband and wife must sign, unless one spouse, acting under a power of attorney, signs as agent for the other.

If you are acting as an authorized representative (attorney, CPA, enrolled actuary, or enrolled agent) of the taxpayer(s), you may sign this consent provided a valid power of attorney has been executed by the taxpayer. If the power of attorney was not previously filed, please include it with this form.

Instructions for Internal Revenue Service Employees

Complete the Division Executive's name and title depending upon your division:

- Small Business and Self-Employed Division = Area Director; Director, Examination; Director, Specialty Programs; Director, Compliance Services, etc.

- Wage and Investment Division = Area Director; Director, Field Compliance Services.

- Large and Mid-Size Business Division = Director, Field Operations for your industry.

- Tax Exempt and Government Entities Division = Director, Exempt Organizations; Director, Employee Plans; Director, Federal, State and Local Governments; Director, Indian Tribal Governments; Director, Tax Exempt Bonds.

- Appeals = Chief, Appeals.

The appropriate authorized official within your division must sign and date the signature and title line.

Form **872-F** (Rev. 7-2005)

¶1138 Exhibit 11-8

Form **872-B** (Rev. July 2003)	Department of the Treasury - Internal Revenue Service **Consent to Extend the Time to Assess** **Miscellaneous Excise Taxes**	In reply refer to: Taxpayer Identification Number

_____ , taxpayer(s)
(Name(s))

of _____ and the
(Number, Street, City or Town, State, ZIP Code)

Commissioner of Internal Revenue consent and agree to the following:

(1) The amount of liability for _____ tax, imposed on the taxpayer(s) by
(Kind)

section _____ of the _____ due for the period _____
(Internal Revenue Code, Revenue Act, etc.)

_____ may be assessed at any time on or before_____
(Expiration date)

(2) The collection provisions and limitations now in effect will also apply to any tax assessed within the extended period.

(3) The taxpayer(s) may file a claim for credit or refund and the Service may credit or refund the tax within 6 months after this agreement ends.

MAKING THIS CONSENT WILL NOT DEPRIVE THE TAXPAYER(S) OF ANY APPEAL
RIGHTS TO WHICH THEY WOULD OTHERWISE BE ENTITLED.

YOUR SIGNATURE HERE   ➤ ....
(Date signed)

TAXPAYER'S REPRESENTATIVE
SIGN HERE   ➤ ....
(Date signed)

CORPORATE
NAME   ➤ ....

CORPORATE
OFFICER(S)
SIGN HERE ➤ ....
(Title)   *(Date signed)*

➤ ....
(Title)   *(Date signed)*

INTERNAL REVENUE SERVICE SIGNATURE AND TITLE

....
(Division Executive Name - see instructions)   *(Division Executive Title - see instructions)*

BY ....
(Authorized Official Signature and Title - see instructions)   *(Date signed)*

(Signature instructions are on the back of this form)   www.irs.gov   Catalog No. 61485N   Form **872-B** (Rev. 7-2003)

Instructions

If this consent is for a partnership return, only one authorized partner need sign.

If you are an attorney or agent of the taxpayer(s), you may sign this consent provided the action is specifically authorized by a power of attorney. If the power of attorney was not previously filed, you must include it with this form.

If you are acting as a fiduciary (such as executor, administrator, trustee, etc.) and you sign this consent, attach Form 56, Notice Concerning Fiduciary Relationship, unless it was previously filed.

If the taxpayer is a corporation, sign this consent with the corporate name followed by the signature and title of the officer(s) authorized to sign.

Instructions for Internal Revenue Service Employees

Complete the Division Executive's name and title depending upon your division.

If you are in the Small Business /Self-Employed Division, enter the name and title for the appropriate division executive for your business unit (e.g., Area Director for your area; Director, Compliance Policy; Director, Compliance Services).

If you are in the Wage and Investment Division, enter the name and title for the appropriate division executive for your business unit (e.g., Area Director for your area; Director, Field Compliance Services).

If you are in the Large and Mid-Size Business Division, enter the name and title of the Director, Field Operations for your industry.

If you are in the Tax Exempt and Government Entities Division, enter the name and title for the appropriate division executive for your business unit (e.g., Director, Exempt Organizations; Director, Employee Plans; Director, Federal, State and Local Governments; Director, Indian Tribal Governments; Director, Tax Exempt Bonds).

If you are in Appeals, enter the name and title of the Chief, Appeals.

The signature and title line will be signed and dated by the appropriate authorized official within your division.

Catalog No. 61485N   Form **872-B** (Rev. 7-2003)

¶1139 Exhibit 11-9

Form **872-D** (Rev. November 2008)	Department of the Treasury - Internal Revenue Service **Consent to Extend the Time on Assessment** **of Tax Return Preparer Penalty**	In reply refer to: Taxpayer Identification Number

_____
(Name)

a tax return preparer, of _____
(Number, Street, Town or City, State, and ZIP Code)

and the Commissioner of Internal Revenue consent and agree to the following:

(1) The penalty imposed by section 6694(a) and/or 6695 of the Internal Revenue Code may be assessed against the above named tax return preparer at any time on or before _____ with respect to the tax return(s) or claim(s) for refund of the taxpayers named below.

(2) The tax return preparer may file a claim for credit or refund and the Internal Revenue Service may credit or refund the penalty(ies) within 6 months after this agreement ends.

Form number of return for which penalty is being charged	Taxpayer's name as shown on return	Taxpayer's identification number	Tax period

You have the right to refuse to extend the period of limitations or limit this extension to a mutually agreed-upon issue(s) or mutually agreed-upon period of time. Signing this consent will not deprive you of any appeal rights to which you would otherwise be entitled.

WHO MUST SIGN The consent should be signed by the preparer. An attorney or agent may sign this consent if specifically authorized by a power of attorney which, if not previously filed, must accompany this form.	_____ _____ *(Signature)* *(Date signed)* I am aware that I have the right to refuse to sign this consent or to limit the extension to mutually agreed-upon issues and/or period of time as set forth in I.R.C. § 6501(c)(4)(B).

INTERNAL REVENUE SERVICE SIGNATURE and TITLE

_____   _____
(Division Executive Name - see instructions)   *(Division Executive Title - see instructions)*

BY _____
     (Authorized Official Signature and Title - see instructions)   *(Date signed)*

(Signature instructions for Internal Revenue Service Employees are on the back of this form)   www.irs.gov   Catalog No. 61634Y   Form **872-D** (Rev.11-2008)

Instructions for Internal Revenue Service Employees

Complete the Division Executive's name and title depending upon your division.

If you are in the Small Business /Self-Employed Division, enter the name and title for the appropriate division executive for your business unit (e.g., Area Director for your area; Director, Specialty Programs; Director, Compliance Campus Operations; Director, Fraud/BSA, etc.)

If you are in the Wage and Investment Division, enter the name and title for the appropriate division executive for your business unit (e.g., Area Director for your area; Director, Field Compliance Services).

If you are in the Large and Mid-Size Business Division, enter the name and title of the Director, Field Operations for your industry.

If you are in the Tax Exempt and Government Entities Division, enter the name and title for the appropriate division executive for your business unit (e.g., Director, Exempt Organizations; Director, Employee Plans; Director, Federal, State and Local Governments; Director, Indian Tribal Governments; Director, Tax Exempt Bonds).

If you are in Appeals, enter the name and title of the Chief, Appeals.

The signature and title line will be signed and dated by the appropriate authorized official within your division.

¶1140 Exhibit 11-10

| Form **4810**
 (Rev. February 2009)
 Department of the Treasury
 Internal Revenue Service | **Request for Prompt Assessment Under
 Internal Revenue Code Section 6501(d)**
 ▶ See instructions on back. | OMB No. 1545-0430

 For IRS Use Only |

Requester's name	**Kind of tax**
	☐ Income ☐ Gift
Title	☐ Employment ☐ Excise

Number, street, and room or suite no. (If a P.O. box, see instructions.)

City, town, or post office, state, and ZIP code	Daytime phone number

Tax Returns for Which Prompt Assessment of Any Additional Tax is Requested

Form Number	Tax Period Ended	SSN/EIN on Return	Name and Address Shown on Return	Service Center Where Filed	Date Filed

If applicable, provide the name of decedent's spouse (surviving or deceased)	Spouse's social security number

If corporate income tax returns are included, check the applicable box below:

☐ Dissolution has been completed.
☐ Dissolution has begun and will be completed either before or after the 18-month period of limitation.
☐ Dissolution has not begun but will begin before the 18-month period of limitation expires and will be completed either before or after that period expires.

Attached are copies of:

☐ The returns listed above.
☐ Letters of administration or letters testamentary.
☐ Other (describe):

I request a prompt assessment of any additional tax for the kind of tax and periods shown above, as provided by Internal Revenue Code section 6501(d).

Sign Here	Under penalties of perjury, I declare that I have examined this request, including accompanying schedules and statements, and to the best of my knowledge and belief, it is true, correct, and complete. ☐ I certify that I have never been assessed any penalties for civil fraud for any federal or state tax matter nor have I been charged with, indicted for, or convicted of fraud. If you cannot certify this statement, attach a detailed statement explaining the circumstances under which you were assessed a penalty, charged with, indicted for, or convicted of fraud.

▶ Signature of requester	Date	▶ Identifying number

For Privacy Act and Paperwork Reduction Act Notice, see back of form.   Cat. No. 42022S   Form **4810** (Rev. 2-2009)

General Instructions

Section references are to the Internal Revenue Code.

Purpose of Form

Use Form 4810 to request prompt assessment of tax. Attach to your request the documentation requested on Form 4810. If you prefer to use your own format, your request must list the same information as requested on this form and include the applicable attachments. Specifically, you must verify your authority to act for the taxpayers (for example, letters testamentary or letters of administration) and provide copies of the authorizing document. Also, your request must clearly show:

● It is a request for prompt assessment under section 6501(d);

● The kind of tax and the tax periods involved;

● The name and social security number (SSN) or employer identification number (EIN) shown on the return (copies of the returns may be attached to help identify the return; write at the top of the return copy: "COPY - DO NOT PROCESS AS ORIGINAL"); and

● The date and location of the IRS office where the returns were filed.

When To File

Do not file Form 4810 requesting prompt assessment until after you file the tax returns listed on the front of this form. You must submit a separate request for prompt assessment for any tax returns filed after this Form 4810.

Where To File

Send your request to the Internal Revenue Service Center where you filed the returns for which you are requesting prompt assessment.

Privacy Act and Paperwork Reduction Act Notice. We ask for the information on this form to carry out the Internal Revenue laws of the United States. We collect this information under the authority under Internal Revenue Code section 6501(d). We need it to ensure that you are complying with these laws and to allow us to figure and collect the right amount of tax. You are not required to request prompt assessment; however, if you do so you are required to provide the information requested on this form. Failure to provide the information may delay or prevent processing your request. Section 6109 requires you to provide the requested taxpayer identification numbers.

You are not required to provide the information requested on a form that is subject to the Paperwork Reduction Act unless the form displays a valid OMB control number. Books or records relating to a form or its instructions must be retained as long as their contents may become material in the administration of any Internal Revenue law. Generally, tax returns and return information are confidential as required by section 6103. However, section 6103 allows or requires the Internal Revenue Service to disclose or give such information shown on your Form 4810 to the Department of Justice to enforce the tax laws, both civil and criminal, and to cities, states, the District of Columbia, and U.S. commonwealths or possessions. We may also disclose this information to other countries under a tax treaty, to federal and state agencies to enforce federal nontax criminal laws, or to federal law enforcement and intelligence agencies to combat terrorism.

The time needed to complete and file this form and related schedules will vary depending on individual circumstances. The estimated average times are:

Recordkeeping . . . . 5 hrs., 30 min.

Learning about the law or the form . 0 hrs., 18 min.

Preparing the form . . . . 0 hrs., 24 min.

Copying, assembling, and sending the form to the IRS . . . . 0 hrs., 0 min.

If you have comments concerning the accuracy of these time estimates or suggestions for making this request simpler, we would be happy to hear from you. You can write to the Internal Revenue Service, Tax Products Coordinating Committee, SE:W:CAR:MP:T:T:SP, 1111 Constitution Ave. NW, IR-6526, Washington, DC 20224. Do not send this tax form to the above address. Instead, see *Where To File* on this page.

¶1141 Exhibit 11-11

Form **2259** (Rev. May 1980)	Department of the Treasury — Internal Revenue Service **Agreement as a Determination Pursuant to Section 1313(a)(4)** **of the Internal Revenue Code**	
Name of Taxpayers		Taxable Year Ended
Address of Taxpayers		

We, the above-named taxpayers, and the Commissioner of Internal Revenue agree that the income tax liability for the taxable year shown above is $ This liability was established by *(to complete this statement, see Income Tax Regulations section 1.1313(a)-4(b)(1) printed on the back of this form):*

We have attached as a part of this agreement the statement required by Income Tax Regulations sections 1.1313(a)-4(b)(2) and (3) that are printed on the back of this form. This statement consists of   pages.

Upon approval of this agreement for the Commissioner of Internal Revenue, we further agree to the assessment and collection of any deficiency (increase in tax) and accept any overassessment (decrease in tax) shown below, plus interest provided by law. We understand that by signing this agreement we will not be able to contest these years in the United States Tax Court, unless additional deficiencies are determined for these years.

Taxpayers	Taxable Year Ended	Kind of Tax	Increase in Tax	Decrease in Tax

We further agree that the determination date will be the date on which this agreement is signed for the Commissioner.

Signature of Taxpayers	Date

Signature of Related Taxpayers, if any	Date

Signature for the Commissioner	Date
Title	

Note: Your agreement will not prevent you from filing a claim for refund (after you have paid the tax) if you later believe you are so entitled; nor prevent us from later determining, if necessary, that you owe additional tax; nor extend the time provided by law for either action.

If this agreement is for a year for which a joint return was filed, both husband and wife must sign unless one, acting under a power of attorney, signs as agent for the other.

If the taxpayer is a corporation, this agreement must be signed with the corporate name followed by the signatures and titles of the officers authorized to sign.

This agreement may be signed by an attorney or agent of the taxpayers, provided this action is specifically authorized by a power of attorney which, if not previously filed, must accompany this form.

(See applicable regulations on the back)   Form **2259** (Rev. 5-80)

Instructions

The original of this agreement will be associated with the return of the taxpayer to whom the determination is made. An additional executed copy will be furnished to each taxpayer involved and one will also be associated with each related tax return.

The statement required by section 1.1313(a) - 4(b)(2) and (3) of the regulations must be headed "Statement to be Attached to, and Made a Part of, Form 2259 in the Case of _____", and must be securely attached to this form.

Provisions of the Internal Revenue Code and the Regulations Issued Thereunder Covering the Preparation of an Agreement as a Determination

Code section 1313(a)(4):*Determination.* [For purposes of this part, the term "determination" means. . .] under regulations prescribed by the Secretary, an agreement for purposes of this part, signed by the Secretary and by any person, relating to the liability of such person (or the person for whom he acts) in respect of a tax under this subtitle for any taxable period.

Regulations section 1.1313(a) - 4:*Agreement pursuant to section 1313(a)(4) as a determination - -(a) In general.*

(1) A determination may take the form of an agreement made pursuant to this section. This section is intended to provide an expeditious method for obtaining an adjustment under section 1311 and for offsetting deficiencies and refunds whenever possible. The provisions of part II (section 1311 and following), subchapter Q, Chapter 1 of the Code, must be strictly complied with in any such agreement.

(2) An agreement made pursuant to this section will not, in itself, establish the tax liability for the open taxable year to which it relates, but it will state the amount of the tax, as then determined, for such open year. The tax may be the amount of tax shown on the return as filed by the taxpayer, but if any changes in the amount have been made, or if any are being made by documents executed concurrently with the execution of said agreement, such changes must be taken into account. For example, an agreement pursuant to this section may be executed concurrently with the execution of a waiver of restrictions on assessment and collection of a deficiency or acceptance of an overassessment with respect to the open taxable year, or concurrently with the execution and filing of a stipulation in a proceeding before the Tax Court of the United States, where an item which is to be the subject of an adjustment under section 1311 is disposed of by the stipulation and is not left for determination by the court.

(b) *Contents of agreement.* An agreement made pursuant to this section shall be so designated in the heading of the agreement, and it shall contain the following:

(1) A statement of the amount of the tax determined for the open taxable year to which the agreement relates, and if said liability is established or altered by a document executed concurrently with the execution of the agreement, a reference to said document.

(2) A concise statement of the material facts with respect to the item that was the subject of the error in the closed taxable year or years, and a statement of the manner in which such item was treated in computing the tax liability set forth pursuant to subparagraph (1) of this paragraph.

(3) A statement as to the amount of the adjustment ascertained pursuant to section 1.1314(a) - 1 for the taxable year with respect to which the error was made and, where applicable, a statement as to the amount of the adjustment or adjustments ascertained pursuant to section 1.1314(a) - 2 with respect to any other taxable year or years; and

(4) A waiver of restrictions on assessment and collection of any deficiencies set forth pursuant to subparagraph (3) of this paragraph.

(c) *Execution and effect of agreement.* An agreement made pursuant to this section shall be signed by the taxpayer with respect to whom the determination is made, or on the taxpayer's behalf by an agent or attorney acting pursuant to a power of attorney on file with the Internal Revenue Service. If an adjustment is to be made in a case of a related taxpayer, the agreement shall be signed also by the related taxpayer, or on the related taxpayer's behalf by an agent or attorney acting pursuant to a power of attorney on file with the Internal Revenue Service. It may be signed on behalf of the Commissioner by the district director, or such other person as is authorized by the Commissioner. When duly executed, such agreement will constitute the authority for an allowance of any refund or credit agreed to therein, and for the immediate assessment of any deficiency agreed to therein for the taxable year with respect to which the error was made, or any closed taxable year or years affected, or treated as affected, by a net operating loss deduction or capital loss carryover determined with reference to the taxable year with respect to which the error was made.

(d) *Finality of determination.* A determination made by an agreement pursuant to this section becomes final when the tax liability for the open taxable year to which the determination relates becomes final. During the period, if any, that a deficiency may be assessed or a refund or credit allowed with respect to such year, either the taxpayer or the Commissioner may properly pursue any of the procedures provided by law to secure a further modification of the tax liability for such year. For example, if the taxpayer subsequently files a claim for refund, or if the Commissioner subsequently issues a notice of deficiency with respect to such year, either may adopt a position with respect to the item that was the subject of the adjustment that is at variance with the manner in which said item was treated in the agreement. Any assessment, refund, or credit that is subsequently made with respect to the tax liability for such open taxable year, to the extent that it is based upon a revision in the treatment of the item that was the subject of the adjustment, shall constitute an alteration of revocation of the determination for the purpose of a redetermination of the adjustment pursuant to paragraph (d) of section 1.1314(b) - 1.

Form 2259 (Rev. 5-80)

¶1151 DISCUSSION QUESTIONS

1. You are dealing with a Revenue Agent in the audit of one of your clients. The Agent requests that you as the taxpayer's representative execute a Form 872, extending the statute of limitations on behalf of your client. Under what circumstances should you recommend to your clients that they do not sign a Form 872?

2. Is it more favorable for the taxpayer to sign a Form 872-A than to sign a Form 872?

3. If you are called in as a representative during an audit and you find out that your client has executed a Form 872-A, what steps, if any, should you take?

4. The taxpayer, a corporation with an April 30 fiscal year, mails its return for the year 20X0 to the Any City Service Center on July 14, 20X0. The return is received at the Service Center on July 16, 20X0. Three years later, on July 16, 20X3, the IRS mails the taxpayer a Statutory Notice of Deficiency seeking additional tax for the 20X0 year. Is the proposed assessment barred by the statute of limitations?

5. (A) If the IRS prepares a return under Code Sec. 6020(b) for an individual who has filed a return for the taxable year 20X0, when would the statute of limitations expire with respect to that return?

   (B) How can the taxpayer in (A) cause the statute of limitations to expire earlier?

6. Harry Hardluck incurred a net operating loss in 20X8 and carried it back to 20X5. In auditing the 20X8 return and its net operating loss, the year 20X5 is also examined. An error in the 2006 return is found resulting in a deficiency. Assuming that the 20X5 return was filed on April 15, 20X6, and that the 20X8 return was filed on April 15, 20X9, what is the last date the IRS can assess and collect additional tax for the 20X5 year? Explain in full.

7. Backhand Berg, an accrual basis taxpayer, is a sole proprietor operating a tennis and sporting goods store in Sportville, U.S.A. Berg reported the following items of income and expense on his federal tax return for the calendar year 20X0:

Gross Business Receipts		$200,000
Cost of Goods Sold		90,000
Gross Profit		$110,000
Expenses		
Wages	$(70,000)	
Other	(15,000)	
		(85,000)
Net Profit		$25,000
Interest Income (from bank account)		5,000
Adjusted Gross Income		$30,000

Assuming that Berg's return is filed on January 6, 20X1, on what date will the statute of limitations on assessment of tax expire in each of the following situations? Explain.

(A) An IRS audit later reveals that Berg's Cost of Goods Sold was actually $30,000.

(B) An IRS audit later reveals that Berg failed to report $60,000 in gross business receipts.

(C) Berg attached the following note to his return:

Dear Sir:

In April of 20X0, I sold certain tennis equipment to Don Deadbeat in return for his $60,000 promissory note. Since Don has a reputation as a poor credit risk, I am not going to report this amount as income until he redeems the note in 20X1.

Sincerely,

Backhand Berg

(D) An IRS audit later reveals that Berg failed to report certain dividends paid to him by the Racquet Corp. The corporation's books clearly show that Berg received $54,000 in dividend income in 20X0.

(E) Berg was on a tennis vacation in Australia during April of 20X1 and completely forgot to file a tax return for 20X0.

8. On March 12, 20X1, Understatement, Inc., a new corporation, files its first corporate income tax return for the calendar year 20X0. The return shows gross receipts of $700,000, expenses of $200,000, and no other transactions. However, Schedule L, the balance sheet to the return, shows the sole asset at the beginning of the tax year as being land with a cost of $300,000. The sole asset shown on the balance sheet at the end of the tax year is cash of $1,000,000. What the return did not disclose was that the land with a cost basis of $300,000 was sold for $500,000 cash during the year in question.

On April 1, 20X6, the IRS issues a Statutory Notice of Deficiency to assess the tax on the unreported sale of the land. The taxpayer contends that the assessment is barred by the statute of limitations under Code Sec. 6501(a). The IRS argues that the failure to report the sale of the land has resulted in a substantial omission of gross income which renders the six-year statute under Code Sec. 6501(e) applicable. The taxpayer counters with the contention that a comparison of the beginning and ending balance sheet for the corporation clearly discloses that the property had been sold and thus that there is an adequate disclosure of the income apprising the Commissioner of the nature and amount of the item omitted. Is the Statutory Notice of Deficiency valid?

¶1151

9. Brite Bros., Inc., is a consulting company which keeps its books on the cash basis method and operates on a calendar year. In 20X0, the corporation erroneously included in income the amount realized on a project completed in December 20X0. The corporation did not receive payment from the client until January 20X1. The income, however, was reported on the 20X0 corporate tax return filed on March 15, 20X1.

On August 2, 20X4, the IRS commenced an audit of Brite Bros. for the tax year 20X1. During the audit the revenue agent discovered the error and included the amount in income for 20X1. The 20X1 tax return was filed on March 15, 20X2.

(A) Can Brite Bros. file a claim for refund for the tax year 20X0? If not, what would you advise them to do?

(B) Assume there was no audit and that Brite Bros. discovered on August 2, 20X4, that they erroneously deducted the cost of certain materials in 20X0 which should have been deducted on their 20X1 return. If the corporation files a claim for refund for the 20X1 tax year, what recourse would the IRS have?

CHAPTER 12
INTEREST AND PENALTIES

¶1201 INTRODUCTION

A deficiency in tax does not result merely in an increase in tax but also in the assessment of interest. In addition, the IRS may impose various civil penalties on taxpayers for failure to correctly report the tax, file a return or pay the tax when due. Tax return preparers and tax shelter promoters also may be subject to special penalties. This chapter discusses the application of these interest and penalty provisions.

Interest

¶1202 INTEREST ON DEFICIENCIES

When the IRS assesses a deficiency, the IRS also will assess interest on the deficiency. This interest compensates the IRS for being deprived of the use of the tax revenue for the period of time that the tax was not paid and is personal interest that the taxpayer can not deduct.[1] The Code provides for interest rates that are considerably above the Federal short-term rate,[2] rendering it important to understand how interest is computed.

Interest accrues from the date the taxes are due (generally, the due date of the return) until the date of actual payment.[3] However, when a taxpayer consents to the assessment of a deficiency by executing a Form 870, Waiver of Restrictions on Assessment and Collection of Deficiency in Tax and Acceptance of Overassessment (see Exhibit 4-5 at ¶425), the interest is suspended beginning thirty days after executing the Form 870[4] until IRS sends notice and demand to the taxpayer.[5] If the taxpayer does not timely pay the assessment at that time, the accrual of interest will resume.

Example 12-1: Suppose the taxpayer filed a return for 20X0 and paid tax on April 15, 20X1. On March 1, 20X4, the taxpayer executed and filed a Form 870. After assessment, the IRS issued notice and demand for tax to the taxpayer on April 22, 20X4. Interest accrued from April 15, 20X1 through March 31, 20X4, but was suspended from April 1 through April 22.

A taxpayer who receives an extension of time to pay the tax or who agrees to an installment payment arrangement with the Collection function is not excused from paying interest. The interest continues until the time the tax is paid.

---

[1] Code Sec. 163.
[2] Code Sec. 1274(d).
[3] Code Sec. 6601(a).

[4] Code Sec. 6601(c).
[5] Code Sec. 6601(e)(2)(A).

The opportunity exists to suspend the accrual of interest on a deficiency during an administrative or Tax Court proceeding. More specifically, taxpayers can make a deposit with the IRS to suspend the running of interest on potential tax underpayments with respect to a disputable tax.[6] The disputable tax is either the taxpayer's reasonable estimate of the maximum amount of tax attributable to disputable items with a safe harbor of the amount described in any 30-day letter received by the taxpayer.[7] For example, if a taxpayer makes a deposit after receiving a Statutory Notice of Deficiency, the accrual of interest on the amount remitted is suspended from the date of payment.[8] When making the remittance, the taxpayer must provide a written statement designating the remittance as a Section 6603 deposit, while including the type of tax, tax years, and the amount of the basis of the disputable tax. If the IRS uses the deposit for a tax liability, the tax will be treated as paid on the date of deposit.[9] At any time before the IRS uses any part of the deposit for payment of tax, the taxpayer may request the return of the deposit.

> **Example 12-2:** Consider a taxpayer who receives a 30-day letter on November 1, 2010 for an adjustment that would result in a deficiency of $50,000. On November 5, the taxpayer sends the IRS $50,000 with a statement designating the amount as a deposit. After the execution of several waivers of the statute of limitations and an extended Tax Court trial, the decision of the Tax Court against the taxpayer becomes final on July 1, 2015. The IRS may not charge interest from November 5, 2010 through July 1, 2015.

In addition to interest on the unpaid taxes,[10] interest accrues on certain penalties from the due date of the return.

> **Example 12-3:** Taxpayer's federal income tax return for 20X0 is due April 15, 20X1. However, Taxpayer fails to file the return and on April 1, 20X4, the IRS issues a Statutory Notice of Deficiency to Taxpayer plus interest and a delinquency penalty for failure to file a return. Interest accrues on the delinquency penalty, as well as the deficiency, beginning April 15, 20X1, the due date for the return.

With the exception of the failure-to-file penalty, the fraud penalty and the accuracy-related penalties, all other penalties begin to accrue interest upon assessment if they are not paid within twenty-one days of the date of notice and demand if the amount is less than $100,000, otherwise, interest will begin to accrue ten days after the notice and demand.

¶1203 COMPUTATION OF INTEREST RATE

The interest rate for overpayments and underpayments of taxes is established on a quarterly basis as reported in the Internal Revenue Bulletin. The rate is

---

[6] Code Sec. 6603.
[7] Code Sec. 6603(b)(2) and (3).
[8] Rev. Proc. 2005-18, 2005-1 C.B. 798.

[9] Code Sec. 6603(a).
[10] Code Sec. 6601(e)(2).

determined in the first month of each quarter, effective for the following quarter. The rate is based on the short-term federal rate,[11] rounded to the nearest full percent and generally represents the average yield on marketable obligations of the United States that have a maturity of less than three years.[12]

With respect to deficiencies, refunds or overpayments (regardless of the taxable year generating the tax), interest payable to or by the IRS compounds daily.[13] Therefore, when the taxpayer pays only the principal portion of a tax deficiency, interest will continue to compound on the outstanding interest due.

The interest rate applicable to a deficiency or an overpayment is based on the federal short term rate plus 3 percentage points in effect during any intervening period.[14] The overpayment rate for corporations is only two percentage points above the federal short term rate. If an amount due is unpaid during a period when the interest rate changes, the new rate will apply from the date of the change. Therefore, the total amount of interest is calculated by using various rates. The changing interest rates and the daily compounding create complex computational problems. However, software programs used by the IRS and available to practitioners provide a fast and accurate means for calculating interest. For those without such resources,[15] The interest rate is the same for both overpayments and underpayments of noncorporate taxpayers.[16]

When there is an underpayment of tax for one year and an overpayment of tax for another year, the interest running on the underpayment and the overpayment may differ. To the extent that there is an overlap of an underpayment and an overpayment, the Code provides a zero rate of interest.[17] This zero percent interest rate "netting" is available for any type of tax imposed by the Code. For example, income taxes can be netted against self-employment taxes and employment taxes can be netted against excise taxes.[18]

> **Example 12-4:** Taxpayer owes a deficiency to the IRS of $10,000 for 20X1. However, the IRS owes Taxpayer a refund of $15,000 for 20X2. The $10,000 Taxpayer owes is netted against the $15,000 Taxpayer is due and, accordingly, in 20X3 interest accrues only on the net $5,000 that the IRS owes Taxpayer.

¶1204 INCREASED RATE ON LARGE CORPORATE UNDERPAYMENTS

The interest rate applicable to "large corporate underpayments" is five percent greater than the federal short term rate for underpayments.[19] Therefore, if the effective interest rate is ten percent for ordinary underpayments, a large corpo-

---

[11] Code Sec. 1274(d).

[12] Code Sec. 6621(a).

[13] Code Sec. 6622(a).

[14] Code Sec. 6621(a).

[15] Rev. Proc. 95-17, 1995-1 CB 556 provides uniform tables and procedures for the daily compounding of interest at the various rates that may apply during any period.

[16] Code Sec. 6621(a)(1).

[17] Code Sec. 6621.

[18] Rev. Proc. 2000-26, 2000-1 C.B. 1257.

[19] Code Sec. 6621(c). Similarly, the overpayment rate increases by only 0.5 of a percentage point. Code Sec. 6621(a)(1).

rate underpayment would be subject to an interest rate of fifteen percent. A "large corporate underpayment" is any underpayment of tax by a C corporation[20] that exceeds $100,000 for any taxable period.

> **Example 12-5:** Suppose that CorpA has an underpayment of $99,000 and CorpB has an underpayment of $100,000. The additional 2% on the large corporate underpayment rate applies to the entire underpayment of CorpB, which satisfies the $100,000 threshold, but does not apply at all to CorpA.

The increased interest rate for such large corporate underpayments only applies thirty days after the date on which the IRS notifies the taxpayer. With respect to those underpayments to which the deficiency procedures apply, this thirty-day period begins to run from the earlier of (1) the date on which the IRS sends a thirty-day letter proposing a deficiency or (2) the date on which the IRS sends a Statutory Notice of Deficiency. In situations where the deficiency procedures do not apply, such as the failure to pay the tax reported on the tax return, the thirty-day period is measured from the date the IRS sends a notice or letter that informs the taxpayer of the amount due or the proposed assessment of a tax. If, within the thirty-day period, the taxpayer pays the full amount shown as due, the increased interest rate will not apply.

The "underpayment threshold" of $100,000 is determined by aggregating all amounts of taxes that have not been timely paid for the taxable year involved. As a result, a late payment of a portion of the tax shown on the tax return may result in reaching the underpayment threshold.[21]

> **Example 12-6:** If a corporation is one week late in paying $60,000 of its reported tax for 2010 and is later assessed a $50,000 tax deficiency for the same year, the total underpayment of $110,000 would exceed the $100,000 "threshold" level required to trigger the increased rate of interest. In this example, if the corporation was first notified of the proposed deficiency by a thirty-day letter sent on June 1, 2012, the date on which the increased interest rate first begins to apply would be July 1, 2012.

For the purpose of determining whether this "threshold underpayment" is reached, only the tax itself is considered.[22] The Code excludes any penalties or interest in analyzing the $100,000 underpayment threshold. However, once met, the increased interest rate applies to the total underpayment, including all interest and penalties.

¶1205 ALLOCATION OF PAYMENT

When a taxpayer makes a partial payment without designating the allocation of the payment, the IRS will apply the payment, first to the tax, then to the penalties and finally to the interest for the earliest year. The IRS then applies any remaining balance in the same order to each succeeding year until the entire payment is exhausted. However, the IRS will honor any allocation designated by the tax-

---

[20] As opposed to an "S corporation," Code Sec. 6621(c)(3).

[21] See examples in Reg. § 301.6621-3.

[22] Reg. § 301.6621-3(b)(2)(ii).

payer.[23] This rule does not apply to an involuntary payment, which would include any payments resulting from levies or from court actions.

> **Example 12-7:** Suppose, for example, that a taxpayer owes the following amounts:

	Deficiency	Penalty	Interest
Year 1	$20,000	$5,000	$500
Year 2	$10,000	$2,000	$100

> The taxpayer makes a payment of $22,000 without designating the categories to which it should apply. As a result, the $22,000 will cover the $20,000 deficiency and $2,000 of the $5,000 penalty for year 1. The amounts due and owing after this payment will be as follows:

	Deficiency	Penalty	Interest
Year 1	$0	$3,000	$500
Year 2	$10,000	$2,000	$100

> If the taxpayer makes a second payment of $5,000 without designating the categories to which the payment belongs, that $5,000 will eliminate the remaining $3,000 penalty and the entire amount of interest of $500 for year 1, leaving $1,500 to reduce the $10,000 deficiency for year 2 to $8,500. The amounts then due and owing would be as follows:

	Deficiency	Penalty	Interest
Year 1	$0	$0	$0
Year 2	$8,500	$2,000	$100

¶1206 REVIEW OF INTEREST LIABILITY

The IRS does not have discretion as to when to compute interest or to excuse anyone from paying interest. If the taxpayer disagrees with the amount of interest due and is unable to convince the IRS to reassess or eliminate the interest liability, the taxpayer must pay the amount determined. The taxpayer can thereafter file a claim for refund for the amount of interest disputed. If the taxpayer is able to recover interest pursuant to a claim for refund, the taxpayer is entitled to interest from the date the liability arose (either the due date or the assessment date) to the date of judgment.

When the Tax Court has determined a deficiency, the taxpayer also may file a petition in the Tax Court to claim that excessive interest was assessed on the deficiency.[24] The Tax Court has jurisdiction to determine if either the IRS underpaid overpayment interest or the taxpayer overpaid underpayment interest.[25]

¶1207 ABATEMENT OF INTEREST DUE TO INTERNAL REVENUE SERVICE ERROR

The IRS can abate any unpaid interest on a deficiency to the extent that the interest is attributable to unreasonable errors or delays resulting from the failure

---

[23] Rev. Proc. 2002-26, 2002-1 CB 746.

[24] Code Sec. 7481(c).

[25] Code Sec. 6404(h).

of an IRS official to perform a ministerial or managerial act.[26] The abatement may be made with respect to adjustment directly to the taxpayer's return or when the tax is the result of a flow-through adjustment of a partnership item.[27] For interest to qualify,[28] no significant aspect of any error or delay may be attributable to the taxpayer. Further, the error or delay must have occurred after the IRS contacted the taxpayer in writing. Therefore, this provision cannot be used to abate interest prior to the time an audit starts.

The regulations define the scope of a "ministerial act" as one that does not involve the exercise of judgment or discretion and that occurs during the processing of a taxpayer's case after all prerequisites to the act, such as conferences and review by supervisors, have taken place. A decision concerning the proper application of federal or state law is not a ministerial act.[29] The regulations give several examples of delays in the performance of managerial and ministerial acts, including a delay in transferring an audit to the local office in which the taxpayer has moved and a delay in the issuance of a Statutory Notice of Ddeficiency after all issues in a case are agreed to and the entire review process completed.[30]

> **Example 12-8:** After Taxpayer files his 20X0 return on April 15, 20X1, the IRS begins an audit for which Taxpayer and the IRS execute a Closing Agreement on June 30, 20X1 for a deficiency of $50,000. However, the IRS loses the administrative file and does not assess the deficiency until April 1, 20X4, several years after the execution of the closing agreement. The IRS should abate the interest due to its ministerial act.

A taxpayer must file a claim for interest abatement on Form 843, Claim for Refund and Request for Abatement.

The IRS must further abate interest on any erroneous refund sent to the taxpayer up until the time the IRS demands repayment of the refund.[31] To qualify for this relief, the taxpayer cannot have caused the erroneous refund in any way. Further, no abatement of interest applies if the erroneous refund exceeds $50,000.

The Tax Court has jurisdiction over any action brought by the taxpayer to determine whether the IRS's refusal to abate the interest was an abuse of discretion. Such an action must be brought within 180 days after the mailing of the IRS's final determination not to abate the interest.

¶1208 SPECIAL RULE FOR EMPLOYMENT TAXES

While the general rule is that interest is assessed on all deficiencies in tax, under certain circumstances it may be possible to obtain an interest-free adjustment for an erroneous reporting of employment taxes. For example, if less than the correct amount of Federal Insurance Contributions Act, Railroad Retirement Tax Act or

---

[26] Code Sec. 6404.

[27] Field Service Advice 199941010 (July 2, 1999).

[28] Code Sec. 6404(e)(1).

[29] Reg. § 301.6404-2(b)(2).

[30] Reg. § 301.6404-2(c).

[31] Code Sec. 6404(e)(2).

Federal Withholding tax is paid with respect to wages or compensation, proper adjustments can be made without interest.[32]

¶1209 SUSPENSION OF INTEREST AND PENALTIES FOR FAILURE TO SEND NOTICE

Interest and penalties generally accrue during periods for which taxes are unpaid, regardless of whether the taxpayer is aware that there is an additional tax due. Prompted by a concern that accrual of interest and penalties absent prompt resolution of tax deficiencies may lead to the perception that the IRS is more concerned about collecting revenue than in resolving taxpayer's problems, Congress has suspended the accrual of interest or penalties if the IRS fails to send proper notice to the taxpayer. This suspension of interest and penalties is available only if the tax relates to timely filed returns (including extensions) by individuals with respect to income taxes.

The IRS must include the name of any penalty assessed, the Code section that authorizes the penalty, and a computation explaining the penalty shown on the notice. Moreover, the IRS may not assess a penalty unless the initial determination is approved in writing by either the immediate supervisor of the individual making the determination or a designated higher-level official. The preassessment approval rules do not apply to delinquency penalties,[33], estimated tax penalties,[34] or any other penalties automatically calculated through electronic means.

Furthermore, the statute suspends the accrual of certain interest and penalties if the IRS does not send the taxpayer a notice specifically stating the taxpayer's liability for additional taxes and the basis for the liability within one year following the date that is the later of (1) the original due date of the return, or (2) the date on which the individual taxpayer timely filed the return.[35] The suspension does not apply to the failure-to-pay penalty, the fraud penalty, on criminal penalties. Once suspended interest and penalties will resume accruing twenty-one days after the IRS sends appropriate notice. The suspension of interest rules do not apply to interest applicable to listed transactions.[36]

¶1210 THE NATURE OF PENALTIES

When a deficiency in tax results from culpable conduct on the part of the taxpayer, the IRS can impose penalties. These civil penalties are designed to deter taxpayers from understating their tax liabilities. For more flagrant violations, criminal penalties[37] exist as an additional deterrent. Some penalties and additions to tax are treated as tax and subject to the deficiency process for assessment. These include the fraud penalty (¶1211), the accuracy-related penalties (¶1212 through ¶1218), and the delinquency penalties (¶1219). The other penalties are

---

[32] Code Sec. 6205(a); Regulation § 31.6205-1.

[33] Code Sec. 6651.

[34] Code Secs. 6654 and 6655.

[35] Code Sec. 6404(g).

[36] The IRS has also issued guidance with respect to the suspension of penalties and interest for individual amended returns. Rev. Rul. 2005-4, 2005-1 C.B. 366, Prop. Reg. § 301.6404-4.

[37] See Chapter 18, *infra*.

the assessable penalties for which the IRS must merely provide notice and demand before trying to collect and include, inter alia, the preparer penalties (¶1225). The Code interchanges the phrase "addition to tax" with the term "penalty" without any legal distinction between the two.

The procedure for assessing and collecting civil penalties is the same as that used for taxes. The more significant civil penalties are described in the following paragraphs. No deduction is allowed to a taxpayer for the amount of any penalty paid.

¶1211 THE PENALTY FOR FRAUD

If any underpayment of tax is due to fraud, a penalty is imposed equal to seventy-five percent to only the portion of the underpayment due to fraud and not to the entire amount of the underpayment.[38] However, the taxpayer has the burden of proving the amount not attributable to fraud.[39] Statutory interest on the penalty accrues from the due date of the return.

A portion of the underpayment will be considered to be due to fraud where it is the result of an intent to evade tax. An underpayment that results from mere negligence or intentional disregard of rules or regulations will not subject the taxpayer to the fraud penalty. Moreover, the existence of an understatement of income, standing alone, generally will not be sufficient to justify the fraud penalty unless there is some showing of intentional wrongdoing on the part of the taxpayer.

Badges of fraud include:[40]

1. the understatement of income;
2. books and records that are inadequate;
3. the failure to file a return;
4. inconsistent explanations of behavior;
5. the concealment of income and assets;
6. the failure to cooperate with the IRS;
7. filing a false return;
8. the failure to make estimated tax payments;
9. dealing in cash; and
10. attempting to conceal the engagement of illegal activity.

Example 12-9: Suppose that Joe Scalper, who runs a Schedule C business of buying and selling tickets to major sporting events, fails to report $100,000 of income for the taxable year 2012. Although the mere underreporting of income, without any other acts, does not constitute fraud, on further review the IRS learns that Joe Scalper kept two sets of books and records (one which included the unreported income and the other which did

---

[38] Code Sec. 6663.

[39] Code Sec. 6663(b).

[40] *Bradford v. Comm'r*, 796 F.2d 303 (9th Cir. 1986) *aff'g* T.C. Memo. 1984-601.

not) that he attempted to destroy when being informed of the IRS audit. Furthermore, on audit, Joe Scalper lied to the IRS revenue agent that he did not have any books and records and that he did not have any unreported income. In this situation, the 75% fraud penalty and interest would apply to the tax due on the $100,000 underpayment attributable to fraud.

The burden of proof is on the IRS in any proceeding where fraud is an issue.[41] The IRS is required to prove that the taxpayer's conduct was fraudulent by clear and convincing evidence. However, where the taxpayer has been convicted or has entered a guilty plea to a charge of willfully attempting to evade tax,[42] the taxpayer will be collaterally estopped from denying that fraud existed and the IRS will have met its burden of proof.[43]

> **Example 12-10:** Suppose that Joe Politician is convicted of the criminal tax crime of tax evasion for failure to report and later conceal income from bribes. When the IRS proceeds civilly against Joe Politician, due to the conviction, Joe Politician will be collaterally estopped from denying that fraud existed. As a result, the IRS will have met its burden of proof for fraud.

There are two instances where the IRS does not have the burden of proving fraud even though it proposes to assess the fraud penalty. The first is where the taxpayer fails to pay the filing fee when a petition is filed in the Tax Court. The failure to pay the fee results in the Tax Court's dismissal of the petition and, accordingly, the IRS can assess the fraud penalty without the burden of proof. The second instance is where allegations of fraud are made in the answer to the taxpayer's petition in the Tax Court. If the taxpayer fails to reply to these allegations of fraud, the taxpayer is deemed to have admitted fraud. Therefore, the IRS need not prove that any portion of the understatement was due to fraud. If the petitioner files a reply denying that there was fraud, the burden of proving the existence of fraud remains with the IRS.[44]

¶1212 THE ACCURACY-RELATED PENALTY

The accuracy-related applies to includes the following violations:

1. Negligence or disregard of rules or regulations;

2. Substantial understatement of income tax;

3. Substantial valuation misstatement;

4. Substantial overstatement of pension liabilities;

---

[41] Code Sec. 7454(a).

[42] Code Sec. 7201.

[43] *Amos v. Comm'r*, 43 TC 50 (1964), *aff'd* 360 F.2d 358 (4th Cir. 1966). With respect to collateral estoppel regarding the filing of a false return. See *Charles Ray Considine v. Comm'r*, 68 TC 52 (1977), CCH Dec. 34,365 (the Tax Court held that a taxpayer was collaterally estopped to deny fraud where he had been convicted of willfully making a false return under Code Sec. 7206(1). But see *Considine v. Comm'r*, 683 F.2d 1285, 1287 (9th Cir. 1982), 82-2

USTC ¶9537 (criticized the Tax Court view); *John T. Wright v. Comm'r*, 84 TC 636 (1985), CCH Dec. 42,013 (Tax Court overruled *Considine* and held that there is no collateral estoppel where the offense charged was the filing of a false return under Code Sec. 7206(1).

[44] Tax Court Rule 123(a); *Hicks v. Comm'r*, 46 TCM 1135, TC Memo. 1983-496, CCH Dec. 40,371(M). See *Rechtzigel v. Comm'r*, 79 TC 132 (1982), CCH Dec. 39,204, *aff'd*, 703 F.2d 1063 (8th Cir. 1983), 83-1 USTC ¶9281.

5. Substantial estate or gift tax valuation understatement;

6. Disallowance of benefits for a transaction that lacks economic substance; and

7. Understatement of foreign financial assets.[45]

A uniform penalty of twenty percent applies to any portion of an underpayment of tax attributable to one or more of these accuracy-related violations.[46] The Code does not permit the overlapping or "stacking" of these penalties.[47] The twenty percent accuracy-related penalty does not apply to any portion of an underpayment on which the fraud penalty is imposed.[48]

The IRS will not impose the accuracy-related penalty if the taxpayer had reasonable cause for the underpayment and the taxpayer acted in good faith.[49] The accuracy-related penalty is not applied when taxpayers disclose that they participated in any transaction for which the accuracy-related penalty could be imposed.[50] Interest on the accuracy-related penalty and the fraud penalty is computed from the due date of the return.[51] Neither the accuracy-related penalty nor the fraud penalty may be imposed in any case where the 100-percent penalty[52] is asserted for failure to collect or pay over tax.

A uniform definition of "underpayment" applies to all accuracy-related and fraud penalties.[53] The "underpayment" is the amount by which the correct tax exceeds the tax shown on the return, plus any additional assessments not shown on the return, less the amount of any "rebates" (an abatement, credit, refund or other repayment). This is the same definition as that of a deficiency.[54] As a result, if a taxpayer files a delinquent return, the penalty for fraud or negligence will apply to the tax liability with a reduction for the tax shown on the delinquent return.

The accuracy-related and fraud penalties apply only where the taxpayer has filed a return.[55] The components of the accuracy-related penalty are discussed below.

¶1213 THE ACCURACY-RELATED PENALTY FOR NEGLIGENCE

When an underpayment of tax is due to negligence or disregard of the rules and regulations, an accuracy-related penalty of twenty percent applies.[56] The penalty applies only to the portion of the underpayment attributable to such negligence or disregard. Statutory interest on the penalty accrues from the due date of the return.

---

[45] Code Sec. 6662.

[46] However, if there is a "gross valuation misstatement" with respect to items 3, 4 and 5 above, a 40-percent penalty applies. Code Sec. 6662(h).

[47] Previously, the IRS could stack separate penalties for each of these violations for amounts approaching the fraud penalty amount without the IRS having burden of proof.

[48] Code Sec. 6662(b).

[49] Code Sec. 6664(c).

[50] Announcement 2000-2, 2002-1 C.B. 304.

[51] Code Sec. 6601(e).

[52] Code Sec. 6672.

[53] Code Sec. 6664(a).

[54] Code Sec. 6211.

[55] Code Sec. 6664(b).

[56] Code Sec. 6662(b)(1).

"Negligence" is "any failure to make a reasonable attempt to comply with the provisions of [the Code]."[57] The term "disregard" includes any "careless, reckless, or intentional disregard." If a position taken by a taxpayer "lacks a reasonable basis," the negligence penalty will apply.[58] However, a taxpayer who takes a position that is contrary to a revenue ruling or an IRS notice will not be subject to the penalty if the position has "a realistic possibility of being sustained on its merits."[59]

> **Example 12-11:** Joe Scalper is a ticket broker who buys, sells, and trades tickets to major sporting events. Joe Scalper keeps very poor books and records and fails to report any barter income because none of his competitors do, even though his CPA advised him to do so. Joe Scalper has shown a careless, reckless or intentional disregard of the rules or regulations and is subject to the accuracy-related penalty due to negligence.

The IRS may impose the negligence penalty as well as the delinquency penalty.[60]

When the IRS proposes the penalty for negligence or disregard of the rules and regulations, that determination is presumed correct and the taxpayer has the burden of proving that the penalty does not apply. In any situation where the taxpayer shows that the underpayment is due to reasonable cause and that he acted in good faith, the penalty should be abated.[61] According to the Regulations, whether the reasonable cause and good faith exception applies is a facts and circumstances determination. The Regulations state that the most important factor will be the efforts of the taxpayer in determining the correct tax liability.[62] Further, the Regulations suggest two sets of circumstances that would qualify for the exception: (1) an honest misunderstanding of fact or law that is reasonable, taking into consideration the taxpayers education and experience[63] and (2) an isolated computational error. Relying on the advice of a tax professional, in and of itself, does not necessarily demonstrate reasonable cause and good faith. However, reliance on a tax professional will qualify for the exception if the advice is based on all the pertinent facts and applicable law and does not rely on unreasonable assumptions.[64] If the taxpayer fails to disclose pertinent facts or circumstances that he or she knows or should know to be relevant, the taxpayer will not qualify for the exception.[65] Similarly, if the tax professional unreasonably relies on the representations, statements or findings of the taxpayer or any other person, the exception will not apply.

---

[57] Code Sec. 6662(c).

[58] Reg. § 1.6662-3(b)(1).

[59] Reg. § 1.6662-3(a). This is the same test applied to tax return preparers to determine whether the preparer penalty should be imposed. See Reg. § 1.6694-2(b) and ¶¶ 1225 through 1227, *infra*.

[60] Code Sec. 6651(a).

[61] Code Sec. 6664(c)(1).

[62] Reg. § 1.6664-4(b).

[63] See *U.S. v. Boyle*, 469 U.S. 241 (1985), 85-1 USTC ¶ 13,602 (relying on a tax professional for filing deadlines is not reasonable as it is a simple matter of

which a layperson should have knowledge); *Olsen v. U.S.*, 853 F.Supp. 396 (D.C. Fla. 1993) (corporate president's reliance on a CPA's misleading advice was not reasonable given that complex tax concepts were not involved).

[64] *Mauerman v. Comm'r*, 22 F.3d 1001 (10th Cir. 1994), 94-1 USTC ¶ 50,222 (reliance on advice of tax professional to deduct fees instead of capitalizing was reasonable).

[65] *Baugh v. Comm'r*, 71 TCM 2140, TC Memo. 1996-70, CCH Dec. 51,173(M) (lack of full disclosure to an accountant precluded qualifying for the reasonable cause and good faith exception).

Example 12-12: Taxpayer suggests to his Accountant that he is entitled to a large deduction due to losses that flowed-through to him for a Horse Racing Partnership. Accountant asks about the extent of Taxpayer's involvement due to the possible restriction of deductibility due to the material participation requirements. Taxpayer replied that he was extremely involved in the operation even though his sole participation encompassed drinking mint juleps at the track and squiring a trophy-wife on his arm to the paddock to find out from the jockey and the trainer if the horse was "ready to win." Because Taxpayer did not disclose pertinent facts or circumstances, Taxpayer does not have a defense to show reasonable cause to the penalty for negligence.

¶1214 THE ACCURACY-RELATED PENALTY FOR A SUBSTANTIAL UNDERSTATEMENT OF TAX

If there is a substantial understatement of tax,[66] the twenty-percent accuracy-related penalty applies. The penalty applies only to that portion of the underpayment due to "substantial understatement." To be substantial, the understatement must exceed the greater of ten percent of the tax required to be shown on the return or $5,000 for individuals (or $10,000 for C corporations).

Example 12-13: Suppose that Joe Scalper is a ticket broker who buys, sells and trades tickets to major sporting events. He fails to report $100,000 of barter income that results in additional tax to him of $35,000. Regardless of the amount of tax he originally reported on his return, the additional tax due exceeds $5,000, resulting in an accuracy-related penalty for a substantial understatement of 20% of the $35,000 for $7,000, plus interest.

The substantial understatement penalty will not be imposed if the taxpayer can show that there was reasonable cause for such understatement and that he or she acted in good faith.[67] The penalty also does not apply if either there was substantial authority for the taxpayer's treatment of the item (a greater than 50% chance of succeeding) or a statement attached to the return discloses the relevant facts with respect to such item the return.

In determining whether there is substantial authority for the taxpayer's position, the taxpayer can rely on court decisions, revenue rulings, regulations, congressional committee reports, private letter rulings, technical advice memoranda, general counsel memoranda, IRS information or press releases and other IRS announcements published in the Internal Revenue Bulletin.[68] Conclusions reached in treatises, legal periodicals, legal opinions or opinions by tax professionals are not authority. However, the authorities underlying such conclusions or opinions may provide substantial authority for the tax treatment of the item in question. The IRS must publish and annually revise, a list of positions for which the IRS believes there is not substantial authority and which affect a substantial number of taxpayers.[69]

---

[66] Code Sec. 6662(b)(2).

[67] Code Sec. 6664(c)(1); see ¶923, *infra*.

[68] Reg. § 1.6662-4(d)(3)(iii).

[69] Code Sec. 6662(d)(2)(D).

If substantial authority does not exist, but the position has a reasonable basis,[70] the substantial understatement penalty can still be avoided by adequate disclosure of the relevant facts. The IRS issues revenue procedures that set forth the circumstances under which disclosure on a return of information relating to an item is adequate.[71] This revenue procedure lists the specific items that must be identified for various itemized deductions, trade or business expenses, Schedule M-1 adjustments, foreign tax items and various other matters. If the revenue procedure does not include the questionable item as one that can be adequately disclosed on the return, disclosure must be made on Form 8275 (Exhibit 12-1 at ¶1241) or Form 8275-R (Exhibit 12-2 at ¶1242). The taxpayer must use Form 827 for disclosures relating to an item or position that is consistent with a regulation. The taxpayer must use Form 8275-R for a position contrary to a regulation.[72]

If the understatement relates to a tax shelter (an investment the principal purpose of which is the avoidance of federal income tax), then even adequate disclosure of the item will not relieve the taxpayer from the penalty. The taxpayer must have both substantial authority and a reasonable belief that the position was more likely than not to be proper.[73]

¶1215 THE ACCURACY-RELATED PENALTY FOR SUBSTANTIAL VALUATION MISSTATEMENTS

The IRS may impose penalties for substantial errors in valuing property on income, estate or gift tax returns. This penalty punishes taxpayers who overvalue property to obtain a high charitable deduction or undervalue property to reduce gift tax. There is a two-tier penalty rate structure of twenty percent and forty percent for substantial valuation errors[74]

Overvaluation on Income Tax Returns	Undervaluation on Estate and Gift Tax Returns	Penalty
200% or more, but less than 400%	50% or less, but not less than 25%	20%
400% or more	25% or less	40%

The underpayment of tax due to valuation misstatements also must meet certain threshold levels before the penalty will apply:

Type Of Valuation Misstatement	Underpayment Must Exceed
Substantial Valuation Misstatement	$5,000 ($10,000 in the case of a corporation)
Substantial Overstatement of Pension Liability	$1,000
Substantial Estate or Gift Tax Valuation Understatement	$5,000

> **Example 12-14:** Devereau, a high-net worth individual, wants to donate the Rembrandt letters to the Metropolitan Gallery and take a charitable contribution deduction. Although Devereau thinks that the letters are worth approximately $100,000, he takes a $300,000 charitable contribution deduc-

---

[70] Reg. § 1.6662-3(b)(3).
[71] Rev. Proc. 2005-75, I.R.B. 2005-50, 1137.
[72] Reg. § 1.6662-4(f).

[73] Reg. § 1.6662-4(e)(2); Reg. § 1.6662-4(g)(1).
[74] Code Sec. 6662(e), (f), (g) and (h).

tion on his return, resulting in a tax understatement of $70,000 (35% of the $200,000 difference). Because Devereau has overvalued the Rembrandt letters by more than 200% and the underpayment of tax is greater than $5,000, the $70,000 underpayment results from a valuation overstatement is subject to the accuracy-related penalty.

The valuation overstatement penalty also applies to certain valuation misstatements relating to transfer pricing adjustments.[75] Valuation questions are frequently involved in transfer pricing disputes with the IRS regarding the allocation of income, credits, deductions, or other items between commonly owned or controlled taxpayers.

In an attempt to promote more voluntary compliance with the arm's-length standard, Congress has enacted two special transfer pricing penalties: the transactional penalty and the net adjustment penalty. Both penalties equal 20% of the tax underpayment related to a transfer pricing adjustment made by the IRS.[76] The transactional penalty applies if the transfer price used by the taxpayer is 200% or more (or 50% or less) of the amount determined to be the correct amount.[77] The net adjustment penalty applies if the net increase in taxable income for a taxable year as a result of transfer pricing adjustments exceeds the lesser of $5 million or 10% of the taxpayer's gross receipts.[78] Both penalties increase to 40% of the related tax underpayment if the transfer price used by the taxpayer is 400% or more (or 25% or less) of the amount determined to be the correct amount or if the net adjustment to taxable income exceeds the lesser of $20 million or 20% of the taxpayer's gross receipts.[79]

> **Example 12-15:** Suppose that FORco is a foreign corporation that manufactures size AAA batteries. FORco sells the AAA batteries to its U.S. distribution subsidiary ("USDist") for resale in the United States. During the taxable year, FORco sells 100 million AAA batteries at $1 per battery to USDist. If the IRS determines that the arm's length price is actually 90¢ per battery, the IRS will make a total adjustment of $10 million (10¢ × 100 million) and, at a 35% rate of tax, results in an additional $3.5 million of corporate income tax to USDist. Because the net adjustment to taxable income of $10 million exceeds $5 million, USDist must pay a penalty of 20% of the additional tax of $3.5 million for a $700,000 penalty.

---

[75] P.L. 101-508, Act § 11312.
[76] Code Sec. 6662(a) and (b)(3).
[77] Code Sec. 6662(e)(1)(B)(i).

[78] Code Sec. 6662(e)(1)(B)(ii) and (e)(3)(A).
[79] Code Sec. 6662(h).

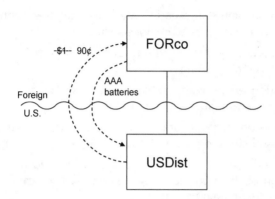

The transactional and net adjustment penalties apply automatically whenever an IRS adjustment exceeds the numerical thresholds. The only way to avoid the penalty in such cases is to satisfy certain safe-harbor requirements. For both the transactional and net adjusted penalties, the penalty is waived only if the taxpayer can demonstrate that it had reasonable cause and acted in good faith.[80] But in the case of the net adjustment penalty, the reasonable cause and good faith requirements can be met only if the taxpayer can demonstrate, through contemporaneous documentation provided to the IRS within 30 days of a request, that the taxpayer acted reasonably in selecting and applying a transfer pricing method.[81] These added requirements for avoiding the net adjustment penalty are designed to force taxpayers to develop and have waiting for the IRS all of the documentation that the IRS ordinarily would need to review in a transfer pricing examination. In addition to providing protection against the transfer pricing penalty, the documentation may also persuade the IRS that a transfer pricing adjustment is not necessary. The IRS's Large Business and International Division ("LB&I") has mandated that all LB&I agents should request documentation during audits.[82]

The principal supporting documents that a taxpayer normally must include in its contemporaneous documentation are as follows:

1. an overview of the taxpayer's business, including an analysis of the economic and legal factors that affect the pricing of its property and services,

2. a description of the organizational structure (including an organization chart) covering all related parties engaged in potentially relevant transactions,

3. any documentation explicitly required by the Regulations,

4. a description of the pricing method selected and an explanation of why that method was selected,

---

[80] Reg. § 1.6662-6(b)(3) and Reg. § 1.6664-4(a).

[81] Code Sec. 6662(e)(3)(B)(i). Documentation is considered contemporaneous if it is in existence at the time the tax return is filed. Reg. § 1.6662-6(d)(2)(iii)(A).

[82] Memorandum for LMSB Executives, Managers, and Agents, January 22, 2003.

5. a description of the alternative methods that were considered and an explanation of why they were not selected,

6. a description of the controlled transactions and any internal data used to analyze those transactions,

7. a description of the comparables used, how comparability was evaluated, and what adjustments were made,

8. an explanation of the economic analyses and projections relied on in developing the pricing method, and

9. a general index of the principal and background documents along with a description of the recordkeeping system used for cataloging and accessing those documents.[83]

¶1216 THE ACCURACY-RELATED PENALTY FOR A TRANSACTION WITHOUT ECONOMIC SUBSTANCE

A taxpayer is liable for a 20% penalty for any underpayment attributable to any disallowance of claimed tax benefits if the transaction lacks economic substance.[84] If a taxpayer does not adequately disclose the relevant facts affecting the tax treatment in the return, the penalty increases to 40%.[85] Moreover, this penalty is a strict liability penalty as the reasonable cause exception does not apply.[86]

A transaction lacks economic substance if it either (i) fails to change in a meaningful way the taxpayer's economic position[87] or (ii) the taxpayer does not have a substantial non-tax purpose for entering into the transaction.[88] Among the numerous factors that the IRS considers to determine whether a transaction has economic substance include whether (i) outside advisors promote the transaction, (ii) the transaction is highly structured, (iii) the transaction contains any unnecessary steps, (iv) the transaction is conducted with related parties at arm's length, (v) the transaction has meaningful profit potential apart from the tax benefits, and (vi) the transaction is outside the taxpayer's ordinary business operations.[89]

¶1217 THE ACCURACY-RELATED PENALTY FOR AN UNDERSTATEMENT OF FOREIGN FINANCIAL ASSETS

The accuracy related penalty on underpayments[90] includes a penalty for an undisclosed foreign financial asset understatement. An undisclosed foreign financial asset understatement includes the portion of an underpayment attributable to any transaction involving an undisclosed foreign financial asset. The penalty is 40% of the underpayment due to the lack of disclosure. Undisclosed foreign financial assets are those assets with respect to required information that the taxpayer failed to provide, pursuant to:

---

[83] Reg. § 1.6662-6(d)(2)(iii)(B).

[84] Code Sec. 6662(b)(6).

[85] Code Sec. 6662(i)(1).

[86] Code Sec. 6664(c)(2).

[87] Code Sec. 7701(o)(1)(A).

[88] Code Sec. 7701(o)(1)(B).

[89] Guidance for Examiners and Managers on the Codified Economic Substance Doctrine and Related Parties, LB&I 4-0711-015.

[90] Code Sec. 6662(b)(B)(7).

(i) Code Sec. 6038 reporting for foreign corporations and partnerships (Forms 5471, 5472 and 8865);

(ii) Code Sec. 6038B reporting for transfers to foreign persons (Forms 926, 5471 and 8865);

(iii) Code Sec. 6038D reporting for foreign financial assets held by individuals (Forms 5471 and 8865);

(iv) Code Sec. 6046A reporting for foreign partnership interests (Form 8865); and

(v) Code Sec. 6048 reporting for foreign trusts (Form 3520-A).

Example 12-16: USCo, a U.S. company, wholly-owns and, therefore, files a Form 5471 for ForSub, a foreign subsidiary. An IRS audit results in $350,000 of additional income tax attributable to $100,000 of interest earned on an unreported bank deposit by ForSub that constituted Subpart F income. USCo is subject to the accuracy-related penalty on underpayments with respect to an undisclosed foreign financial asset understatement.

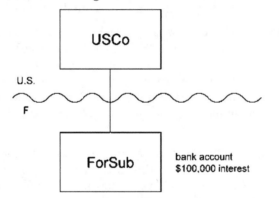

¶1218 THE ACCURACY-RELATED PENALTY FOR TAX SHELTERS

An accuracy-related penalty applies to any understatement that results from a reportable transaction.[91] A reportable transaction is a transaction where the taxpayer is required to report certain information on the tax return because the transaction is of such a nature that it has the potential for tax avoidance. So this provision applies basically to tax shelter transactions.

The penalty is 20% of the understatement, but increases to 30% if the taxpayer fails to adequately disclose the relevant facts pertaining to the transaction. The penalty does not apply if the taxpayer shows reasonable cause and acted in good faith. The reasonable cause exception applies only if the taxpayer has made adequate disclosures on the return, there was substantial authority for the position taken, and the taxpayer reasonably believed that the probability of success was more likely than not. The taxpayer is not allowed to rely on opinions pronounced by certain disqualified tax advisors (principally those with financial

---

[91] Code Sec. 6662A.

ties to the promoters) and on opinions based on unreasonable legal or factual assumptions, unreasonable reliance on the opinions of others or the failure to consider all relevant facts.

¶1219 PENALTY FOR FAILURE TO FILE OR PAY (DELINQUENCY)

There are three delinquency penalties: (1) delinquent failure to file a return, (2) delinquent failure to pay tax, and (3) delinquent failure to pay after receiving notice and demand.

Failure to file any required return may subject the taxpayer to civil penalties and possible criminal prosecution. In the case of a failure to file a return on the date prescribed, a penalty of five percent of the tax required to be shown on the return applies each month that the return is late.[92] However, this penalty cannot exceed twenty-five percent of the amount required to be shown as tax on the return. If the taxpayer can establish that the failure to file the return was due to reasonable cause and not due to willful neglect, the IRS may abate the penalty. In determining the tax required to be shown on the return, any tax paid in advance of the return is not treated as an amount subject to the penalty.[93]

> **Example 12-17:** Suppose that Taxpayer has his accountant prepare his return that shows tax due of $100,000. However, instead of filing the return and paying the tax, Taxpayer goes to the racetrack from April 1 to July 1. On July 1, Taxpayer files his return and pays the tax due. Because the return was delinquent for parts of four months—April, May, June, and July—the taxpayer owes a delinquency penalty of 20% of the $100,000 amount of tax due, which is $20,000.

The five percent penalty for each month, or part thereof, during which a delinquency continues, increase to fifteen percent per month for any failure to file due to fraud. Fraud also increases the maximum penalty of twenty-five percent for failure to file increase to seventy-five percent.

A penalty also applies to taxpayers that do not timely pay the tax shown on the return.[94] The failure to timely file a penalty equals one-half of one percent[95] of the balance for each month that the tax shown on the return is not paid, not to exceed twenty-five percent in the aggregate.

For any month in which both penalties apply, the failure to timely file penalty is reduced by the amount of the failure to timely pay penalty.[96] As a result, the maximum aggregate penalty is forty-seven and one-half percent.

> **Example 12-18:** Suppose that Taxpayer files a return on April 1 showing $100,000 of tax due. Instead of writing a check for $100,000, taxpayer goes to the racetrack where he uses the $100,000 to finance his wagering activities. After two months, Taxpayer has broken even and on June 1 sends the

---

[92] Code Sec. 6651(a)(1).

[93] Code Sec. 6651(f).

[94] Code Sec. 6651(a)(2).

[95] If an installment agreement is in effect for an individual taxpayer, the penalty is reduced to .25%. Code Sec. 6651(h).

[96] Code Sec. 6651(c)(1).

$100,000 payment to the IRS. Because Taxpayer has been delinquent in payment for parts of three months—April, May, and June—the taxpayer is subject to the failure to pay delinquency penalty of 1.5%, three months at 0.5%, or $1,500. If Taxpayer incurred the failure to file penalty (as in the previous example) and the failure to pay penalty, the $1,500 would reduce the $20,000 failure to file penalty to $18,500.

Another failure to pay penalty of one-half of one percent a month applies to additional tax deficiencies after notice and demand. The maximum penalty is twenty-five percent.[97]

¶1220 PENALTY FOR FAILURE TO DISCLOSE REPORTABLE TRANSACTIONS

A penalty applies for failing to disclose certain transactions required to be disclosed. This penalty applies all to transactions where the taxpayer is required to report information on the tax return because the transaction is of such a nature that it has the potential for tax avoidance (reportable transactions), such as tax shelter transactions. A subset of this group of reportable transactions are those transactions that the IRS has specifically identified as a tax avoidance transaction (listed transactions) and also those transactions that are substantially the same as a listed transaction.

The penalty for reportable transactions is $10,000 for individuals and $50,000 for all other taxpayers. The penalty for listed transactions is $100,000 for individuals and $200,000 for all other taxpayers. The IRS may rescind the penalty for reportable transactions that are not listed transactions if rescinding the penalty would promote compliance with the Code and effective tax administration. There is no judicial appeal of the authority to rescind the penalty.

> **Example 12-19:** Taxpayer, a U.S. individual, invests in a chinchilla breeding partnership in a manner that constitutes a reportable transaction as identified by the IRS. However, Taxpayer does not report his investment in the chinchilla breeding partnership. Taxpayer is subject to the $10,000 penalty for failure to disclose reportable transactions.

¶1221 PENALTY FOR FILING FRIVOLOUS TAX RETURNS

Two rules are designed to prevent taxpayers from filing frivolous tax returns, commonly known as protestor returns. Although protestor returns are typically caught and result in the actual amount of tax due ultimately being paid, the number of returns filed can clog the tax system and decrease the efficiency of tax administration. The policy behind these penalties is to reduce the number of protester returns.

---

[97] Code Sec. 6651(a), 6651(a)(2). If the IRS notifies the taxpayer of its intention to levy or to resort to enforced collection, the penalties under Code Secs. 6651(a)(2) and 6651(a)(3) increase to one percent per month. The penalties under Code Secs. 6651(a)(2) and 6651(a)(3) decrease to one quarter of one percent a month during the period an installment agreement is in effect. The IRS can abate these delinquent penalties if the failure to pay is due to reasonable cause.

First, in addition to any other penalties provided by law, the IRS can impose a frivolous return penalty of $500 against any individual taxpayer who, to further a frivolous position with a clear intent to impede tax administration, files a purported return that fails to contain sufficient information to determine a reasonable correct tax liability. This penalty would apply to someone who either files an incomplete return to protest the tax or claim tax protester-type deductions. This penalty can be assessed without resorting to the deficiency procedures and is immediately payable. However, taxpayers may contest the penalty in U.S. District Court by paying the amount assessed and seeking a refund. If the taxpayer contests the penalty in court, the government has the burden of proof.[98]

Second, a taxpayer may incur a $5,000 penalty by submitting a "specified frivolous submission," which occurs when any portion of a return is based on a position the IRS has identified as frivolous or reflects a desire to delay tax administration.[99]

> **Example 12-20:** Consider Peter Protestor, who files a return stating he is not subject to tax because he is a citizen of California and not the United States. Peter Protestor would be subject to the $500 penalty and, if the "state citizen" argument had been previously designated by the IRS, Peter Protestor may also be subject to the $5,000 penalty.

¶1222 FAILURE TO FILE INFORMATION RETURNS OR PROVIDE CORRECT INFORMATION

Penalties apply for failure to file information returns and for failure to include correct information on such returns.[100] Both failure to file and to provide correct information are subject to the following three-tier penalty structure:

Correction of Failure	Penalty
Within 30 days	$15 per failure ($75,000 maximum)
After 30 days, but before August 1	$30 per failure ($150,000 maximum)
After August 1	$50 per failure ($250,000 maximum)

There is a substantially higher penalty for failures due to intentional disregard of the filing or reporting requirements.

A *de minimis* exception relieves taxpayers from any penalty if they correct erroneous information on filed information returns before August 1, provided that the number of such corrected returns does not exceed the greater of ten or one-half of one percent of the total information returns the taxpayer filed.[101] In addition, if a taxpayer's average annual gross receipts for the most recent three years do not exceed $5,000,000, the maximum penalties that may be imposed during any year under the three-tier penalty structure are reduced to $25,000, $50,000 and $100,000, respectively.

---

[98] Code Sec. 6703(a).

[99] Code Sec. 6702(b)(1).

[100] Code Sec. 6721.

[101] Code Sec. 6721.

A penalty combines the failure to furnish payee statements and the penalty for failure to include correct information on such statements.[102] A $50 penalty applies to each failure to furnish a payee statement and to each failure to include correct information on such statement. The total amount of such penalties applicable during any one year is limited to $100,000.

A penalty applies for failure to supply taxpayer identification numbers. All failures to comply with the specified information reporting requirements are subject to a fifty dollar penalty. The total of all such penalties that may be imposed during any year is limited to $100,000. The failure of a transferor of a partnership interest to promptly notify the partnership of an exchange resulting in different taxpayer numbers[103] is also subject to the penalty.

An exception prohibits information reporting requirement penalties from applying if due to reasonable cause and not to willful neglect. The Code also specifically provides that if a taxpayer (or preparer) includes incorrect information on a return provided by another, that taxpayer will not be subject to the penalty if he or she had no reason to believe such information was incorrect.

The IRS may require that information returns be filed on magnetic media if at least 250 returns are required to be filed during the year.[104] Furthermore, no penalty will be imposed for failure to file on magnetic media except to the extent such failure occurs with respect to more than 250 information returns.[105]

¶1223 FAILURE TO TIMELY DEPOSIT

A penalty applies for failure to make timely deposits[106] of employment and other taxes. This penalty is designed to encourage taxpayers to make a delinquent deposit as soon as possible after the due date. The penalty rates are as follows:

Days Elapsed After Due Date	Rate
Not more than 5 days	2%
More than 5 days, but not more than 15 days	5%
More than 15 days	10%

A special fifteen-percent penalty rate further applies when the deposit is not made within ten days after the date of the first delinquency notice to the taxpayer or, if a jeopardy assessment is made, on or before the day on which the IRS gives notice and demand for payment. An exception provides relief for first-time depositors and for the first period subsequent to a change in the frequency of deposits. as well as relief for cascading penalties, which occur if a taxpayer misses a deposit early in a return period but makes succeeding deposits on time.[107]

---

[102] Code Sec. 6722.

[103] Code Sec. 6050K(c)(1).

[104] Code Sec. 6011(e).

[105] Code Sec. 6724(c).

[106] The penalty under this section also pertains to payments not made electronically when required by Code Sec. 6302(h).

[107] Code Sec 6656(e).

¶1224 PENALTY FOR ERRONEOUSLY CLAIMED REFUND OR CREDIT

A taxpayer who erroneously claims a refund or credit may be subject to a 20% penalty on the excessive amount.[108] The Code determines the excessive amount by reducing the amount of the refund or credit by (i) any amount of the refund or credit for which a reasonable basis exists and (ii) any amount subject to either the fraud penalty or the accuracy-related penalty.

¶1225 PREPARER PENALTIES

Along with those penalties that can be imposed on taxpayers who file inaccurate returns, the Code provides civil penalties for tax return preparers who prepare inaccurate returns.

A preparer penalty[109] applies where there is an understatement of a tax liability due to an unreasonable position taken on the tax return that either (a) the preparer knew or should have known of reasonably or (b) the understatement is due either to a willful attempt to understate the tax liability or to a reckless or intentional disregard of rules or regulations. The IRS can only assess the preparer penalties where the person who prepared the return is an "income tax return preparer."[110]

> **Example 12-21:** Taxpayer entertains a client at the race track. Although the admission, food and drink costs Taxpayer $100 to entertain his client, Taxpayer loses a $20,000 debt on a horse named "Cot's Chin." Taxpayer tells this to his Accountant, who prepares a tax return based on entertainment expenses of $20,100. Accountant is subject to the preparer penalty because the understatement is due to the intentional disregard of the rules and regulations.

Where the understatement results from taking an unreasonable position, the penalty is the greater of $1,000 or half the income earned by the preparer for each return or claim resulting in an understatement.[111]

If the understatement is due to a willful attempt to understate, or a reckless or intentional disregard of rules or regulations, the penalty is the greater of either $5,000 or half of the income earned by the preparer.[112]

Other penalties apply for technical violations by income tax return preparers.[113] For failure to furnish a copy of a return to a taxpayer, to retain a copy or list of returns prepared, to sign a return, to furnish the preparer's identifying number, or to file a correct information return regarding others employed to prepare returns, the penalty for each such failure is $50 and the maximum annual penalty for each type of failure is $25,000. There is a $50 penalty for failure to retain copies of the returns or a list of the names and identification numbers of taxpayers for whom such returns were prepared. A

---

[108] Code Sec. 6676.

[109] Code Sec. 6694.

[110] Code Sec. 7701(a)(36).

[111] Code Sec. 6094(a).

[112] Code Sec. 6694.

[113] Code Sec. 6695.

$500 penalty also applies to any income tax return preparer who endorses or negotiates any refund check issued to a taxpayer.

A $250 penalty applies to return preparers who make unauthorized disclosures of tax return information. Disclosures are exempt from the penalty only if they are made pursuant to either a court order, the Code or the Treasury Regulations. These exemptions include the disclosure or use of such information "for quality or peer reviews," so a return preparer may disclose tax information to another return preparer for the purpose of such reviews.[114]

¶1226 DEFINITION OF TAX RETURN PREPARER

Because the preparer penalties only apply to a "tax return preparer" as defined in Code Sec. 7701(a)(36), the statutory definition takes on great importance. The Code definition includes any person who *for compensation* prepares a substantial portion of a tax return or claim for refund. The final regulations differentiate between a signing preparer and a non-signing preparer—both of which can constitute a tax return preparer, but neither may be from the same firm.

If there is more than one preparer, the signing tax return preparer is usually the individual who signs the return and has the primary responsibility for the accuracy of the return.

> **Example 12-22:** If a senior partner of an accounting firm reviews and signs the return prepared by a junior staff member, the senior partner is the signing preparer. Because he is from the same firm, the junior staff member cannot be a preparer (signing or non-signing).

A non-signing preparer does not sign the return, but prepares all or a substantial portion of the return or a claim for refund regarding events that have occurred at the time the advice was rendered.

> **Example 12-23:** Suppose that Bob Bookkeeper is hired by a small business to conduct bookkeeping procedures. Bob takes an extremely aggressive position with respect to the sourcing of income for foreign tax credits that Bob provides to the business' CPA that prepares the business' return. The bookkeeper is a non-signing tax preparer with respect to the foreign tax credit position. However, there may not be two preparers within the same firm with respect to a position and, if Bookkeeper and CPA were part of the same accounting firm, only the preparer primarily responsible for the position is considered the preparer.[115]

With respect to a non-signing preparer, there are both a *de minimus* and an anti-abuse rule.

The *de minimus* rule provide that an individual can avoid being a non-signing preparer if he or she spends time giving advice after events have occurred that represents less than 5% of the aggregate time incurred with respect to the positions giving rise to the understatement.

---

[114] Code Sec. 7216(b).

[115] Treas. Reg. § 1.6694-1(b)(1).

Example 12-24: Suppose that an accountant assists a client with respect to a transaction and later prepares, with respect to that transaction, a portion of the client's return that the client signs. In total, the accountant spends 100 hours with respect to the client, but only 4 hours constitutes time spent preparing that portion of the return after the transaction occurred. In this matter, the accountant is not a preparer.

The anti-abuse rule states that a person who prepares a *substantial portion* of a return is a preparer.[116] The regulations indicate that providing advice with respect to an entry on a return or any portion of a return will constitute preparation of the return if the item involved is a *substantial portion* of the return.[117] Whether a portion of a return is substantial is determined by comparing that portion with the complete return on the basis of length, complexity and tax liability involved. Although a single entry on a return may be a substantial portion, specific safe harbor guidelines exempt those who prepare or give advice with respect to a portion of a tax return that has relatively nominal tax consequences.[118] For signing tax return preparers only, a portion of a return is not considered substantial if it involves gross income or deductions (or amounts on the basis of which credits are determined) that are either (1) less than $10,000, or (2) less than $400,000 and also less than twenty percent of the gross income (or adjusted gross income if the taxpayer is an individual) shown on the return or claim.

Example 12-25: Suppose that CPA takes an aggressive position on a client's return that results in a deduction of $100,000 which causes an understatement. The client shows $600,000 of gross income on his return. Although CPA signed the return, the CPA is not a tax return preparer because the $100,000 deduction was less than both $400,000 and 20% of the $600,000 gross income shown on the client's return ($150,000) and, therefore, the CPA did not prepare a substantial portion of the return.

Because of the wide sweep of the literal terms of the return preparer definition, a number of exceptions exist. For example, is an employee who types the final form of the return considered a preparer for compensation? The Code provides that such a person is not tax return preparer merely because the person furnishes typing, reproducing or other mechanical assistance.[119] A corporate employee who prepares a return for his employer (or for an officer or employee of the employer) is not considered tax return preparer so long as the corporation is one by whom he is regularly and continuously employed.[120] Also excepted from the definition is a fiduciary of an estate or trust who prepares a tax return for the estate or trust. A final exception is a person who prepares a claim for

---

[116] Code Sec. 7701(a)(36)(A).

[117] Reg. § 301.7701-15(b)(3)(ii)(A).

[118] *Id.*

[119] Code Sec. 7701(a)(36)(B)(i). Moreover, Priv. Ltr. Rul. 8416024, January 13, 1984; Priv. Ltr. Rul.

8416025, January 13, 1984. Both held that a computer tax processing firm that received computer input sheets from an insurance agency and then processed the input sheets into a completed return was not an income tax return preparer.

[120] Code Sec. 7701(a)(36)(B)(ii).

refund after an audit of the taxpayer's return has produced a deficiency determination.

¶1227 UNREASONABLE POSITIONS

If any part of an understatement is due to an unreasonable position, the tax return preparer is subject to a penalty of the greater of $1,000 or 50% of the income derived from preparing the return.[121] The reasonable basis standard is higher than a frivolous standard, but not as high as the more-likely-than-not standard. However, the more-likely-than-not standard applies to tax shelters and reportable transactions.[122]

> **Example 12-26:** Suppose that CPA takes an unreasonable position on a client's return and receives $5,000 as her fee. CPA is subject to a penalty for an understatement due to an unreasonable position of $2,500, which is 50% of her fee of $5,000.

Even if there is not a reasonable position, the IRS will not impose the penalty if there is either (1) an adequate disclosure of the questionable position on the return,[123] or (2) a showing that there was reasonable cause for the understatement and that the preparer acted in good faith. The preparer has the burden of proving both of these defenses.[124]

Proper disclosure of the questionable position will relieve the preparer from the penalty. The type of disclosure required to avoid the penalty depends on whether the preparer is a signing or nonsigning preparer. If the preparer is a signing preparer, disclosure is adequate only if made on a Form 8275 or 8275-R, whichever is appropriate, or on the tax return itself with respect to those items specifically permitted to be disclosed in such a manner by an annual revenue procedure.[125] This is the same disclosure a taxpayer is required to make in order to avoid the substantial understatement penalty.[126]

A non-signing preparer discloses in the same manner required of a signing preparer. In addition, if the nonsigning preparer gave the advice to a taxpayer, disclosure is adequate if such advice includes a statement that the position lacks substantial authority and, therefore, may be subject to the substantial understatement penalty unless properly disclosed.[127] If the non-signing preparer provided written advice, the cautionary statement to the taxpayer must be in writing. If the advice was oral, the warning regarding the potential penalty and the need for disclosure may also be oral.

When a nonsigning preparer advises another preparer with respect to a position that does not meet the reasonble basis standard, disclosure is adequate if the advice to the other preparer includes a statement that disclosure is required

---

[121] Code Sec. 6694(a).

[122] Code Sec. 894(a)(2)(C).

[123] Code Sec. 6694(a)(3).

[124] Reg. § 1.6694-2(e).

[125] Note 47, *supra,* and accompanying text.

[126] Code Sec. 6662(d) (see ¶1214).

[127] Code Sec. 6662(d); Reg. § 1.6694-2(c)(3)(ii)(A). If the questionable position relates to a tax shelter item, the taxpayer must be advised that the penalty may apply regardless of disclosure.

under Code Sec. 6694(a). As in the case of written advice to a taxpayer, the warning with respect to disclosure also must be written. An oral warning to the preparer is sufficient if the original advice was oral.[128] However, a cautious tax adviser may wish to document the fact that these required statements were made to the other preparer or to the taxpayer.

The IRS will not impose the preparer penalties under Code Sec. 6694(a) if the understatement was due to reasonable cause and the preparer acted in good faith. In making this determination, the IRS will consider all the facts and circumstances. The regulations provide some guidance concerning the factors that will be considered. These include:[129]

1. *Nature of the error causing the understatement.* The IRS will consider whether or not the error resulted from a provision that was so complex, uncommon, or highly technical that a competent preparer of returns or claims of the type at issue reasonably could have made the error. The reasonable cause and good faith exception does not apply to an error that would be apparent to the preparer from a general review of the return or claim for refund.

2. *Frequency of errors.* The IRS will consider whether or not the understatement was the result of an isolated error (such as an inadvertent mathematical or clerical error) rather than a number of errors. Although the reasonable cause and good faith exception generally applies to an isolated error, the exception does not apply if the isolated error is so obvious, flagrant or material that the preparer should have discovered it during a review of the return. Furthermore, the reasonable cause and good faith exception does not apply if there is a pattern of errors on a return or claim for refund even though any one error, in isolation, would have qualified for the reasonable cause and good faith exception.

3. *Materiality of errors.* The IRS will consider whether or not the understatement was material in relation to the correct tax liability. The reasonable cause and good faith exception generally applies if the understatement is of a relatively immaterial amount. Nevertheless, even an immaterial understatement may not qualify for the reasonable cause and good faith exception if the error or errors creating the understatement are sufficiently obvious or numerous.

4. *Preparer's normal office practice.* The IRS will consider whether or not the preparer's normal office practice, when considered together with other facts and circumstances, such as the knowledge of the preparer, indicates that the error in question would rarely occur and the normal office practice was followed in preparing the return in question. Such a normal office practice must be a system for promoting accuracy and consistency in the preparation of returns and generally would include, in the case of a signing preparer, checklists, methods for obtaining necessary informa-

---

[128] Reg. § 1.6694-2(c)(3)(ii)(B).   [129] Reg. § 1.6694-2(d).

tion from the taxpayer, a review of the prior year's return and review procedures. Notwithstanding the above, the reasonable cause and good faith exception does not apply if there is a flagrant error on a return, a pattern of errors on a return, or a repetition of the same or similar errors on numerous returns.

5. *Reliance on advice of another preparer.* The IRS will consider whether or not the preparer relied on the advice ("advice") of or schedules prepared by another preparer.[130] The reasonable cause and good faith exception applies if the preparer relied in good faith on the advice of another preparer (or a person who would be considered a preparer[131] had the advice constituted preparation of a substantial portion of the return or claim for refund) whom the relying preparer had reason to believe was competent to render such advice. A preparer is not considered to have relied in good faith if—

   i. The advice is unreasonable on its face;

   ii. The preparer knew or should have known that the other preparer was not aware of all relevant facts; or

   iii. The preparer knew or should have known (given the nature of the preparer's practice), at the time the return or claim for refund was prepared, that the advice was no longer reliable due to developments in the law since the time the advice was given.

The advice may be written or oral, but in either case the burden of establishing that the advice was received is on the preparer.[132]

¶1228 WILLFUL, RECKLESS OR INTENTIONAL CONDUCT

A more severe penalty of the greater of $10,000 or half the amount earned from preparing the return is imposed on a return preparer for any understatement on a return or refund claim that is due either to a willful attempt to understate tax or to a reckless or intentional disregard of rules or regulations.[133]

A preparer who attempts wrongfully to reduce the tax liability of a taxpayer by either disregarding information furnished to him or fabricating items or amounts on the return is subject to the penalty for a willful attempt to understate tax.[134] Therefore, if a taxpayer informs the preparer of certain items of income, but the preparer intentionally omits such income from the return, the penalty will apply.

> **Example 12-27:** The willful penalty will apply if the preparer is informed that the taxpayer has two dependents and the preparer wrongfully prepares a return that reports six dependents.[135]

---

[130] Reg. § 1.6694-1(b).
[131] Reg. § 1.6694-1(b).
[132] Reg. § 1.6694-2(d).

[133] Code Sec. 6694(b).
[134] Criminal sanctions also may apply. See Chapter 18, *infra.*
[135] Reg. § 1.6694-3(b).

In any proceeding involving the penalty, the IRS bears the burden of proving that the preparer willfully attempted to understate the tax liability.[136]

The willful preparer penalty also applies when a preparer *recklessly* or *intentionally* disregards a rule or regulation.[137] Such conduct is reckless or intentional if the preparer takes a position on a return or refund claim that is contrary to a rule or regulation and the preparer knows of, or is reckless in not knowing of, such rule or regulation.[138] A preparer is reckless if he or she makes little or no effort to determine whether a rule or regulation exists under circumstances which indicate a substantial departure from what a "reasonable preparer" would do.[139] Therefore, the failure of a preparer to research the law for rules and regulations will be judged for purposes of the penalty by a "reasonable preparer" standard of conduct.

The regulations provide that the penalty for reckless or intentional disregard of rules or regulations will not apply in three specific situations.

First, when the position taken by the preparer is contrary to a revenue ruling or notice published in the Internal Revenue Bulletin, the penalty will not be imposed if the position has a reasonable basis.[140] This is the same test applied in determining whether the preparer penalty for an unreasonable position.

Second, the penalty for reckless or intentional conduct also may be avoided by adequate disclosure of the questionable position taken on the return. Although there are some differences, the disclosure requirements are similar in most respects to the disclosure required to avoid the preparer penalty for adopting an unreasonable position.[141] However, unlike the preparer penalty for an unreasonable position, disclosure is not adequate if made only on the tax return itself with respect to those items that otherwise are permitted to be disclosed in such manner by an annual revenue procedure.[142] Only Forms 8275 and 8275-R may be used and the disclosure must identify the rule or regulation that is being challenged. Moreover, if the preparer takes a position contrary to a regulation, disclosure is adequate only if the position represents a good-faith challenge to the validity of the regulation.[143]

Third, the preparer is not subject to the penalty if a position meets the substantial authority standard and is not a reportable transaction. More specifically, the preparer can rely on court decisions, revenue rulings, regulations, congressional committee reports, private letter rulings, technical advice memoranda, general counsel memoranda, IRS informational press releases and other IRS announcements published in the Internal Revenue Bulletin.[144]

---

[136] Reg. § 1.6694-3(h).

[137] The regulations define the term "rules or regulations" to include the Internal Revenue Code, temporary or final Treasury Regulations, and revenue rulings or notices published in the Internal Revenue Bulletin. Reg. § 1.6694-3(f).

[138] Reg. § 1.6694-3(c)(1).

[139] *Id.*

[140] Reg. § 1.6694-3(c)(2).

[141] See ¶ 1239, *supra.*

[142] Note 47, *supra,* and accompanying text.

[143] Reg. § 1.6694-3(c)(2).

[144] Reg. § 1.662-4(b)(3)(iii).

The preparer has the burden of proving that he did not recklessly or intentionally disregard a rule or regulation. He also carries the burden of establishing that any challenge to the validity of a regulation was made in good faith and that any disclosure was adequate.[145]

¶1229 COMMON PRINCIPLES

Both of the preparer penalties have certain principles in common. One of the most significant relates to reliance by a preparer on the information furnished by the taxpayer. The regulations state that a preparer is not required to verify what he receives from a taxpayer and may rely on such information if he does so in good faith.[146] Therefore, the preparer is not required to audit, examine or review books and records, business operations or documents in order to independently verify such information. A preparer, however, may not ignore either the implications of the information he receives or what he actually knows. He must make reasonable inquiries if the information appears to be incorrect or incomplete. He also must ask questions to determine the existence of certain facts and circumstances required by the Code or regulations as a condition to the claiming of a deduction. The latter requirement is met with respect to travel and entertainment expenses if the preparer asks the taxpayer whether he has adequate records to substantiate such expenses and the preparer is reasonably satisfied that such records exist.

Under certain circumstances, the preparer penalties will apply not only to the individual preparer but also to the employer of the preparer or the partnership in which the preparer is a partner. The regulations state that the employer or partnership, in addition to the individual preparer, will be liable for the penalty in the following situations:

1. One or more members of the principal management (or principal officers) of the employer or the partnership participated in or knew of the conduct proscribed;

2. The employer or the partnership failed to provide reasonable and appropriate procedures for review of the position for which the penalty is imposed; or

3. The employer or the partnership disregarded these procedures in the formulation of the advice, or the preparation of the return, that included the position for which the penalty is imposed.[147]

Example 12-28: Taxpayer entertains a client at the race track. Although the admission, food and drink costs Taxpayer $100 to entertain his client, Taxpayer loses a $20,000 debt on a horse named "Cot's Chin." Taxpayer provides the $20,100 amount on his "entertainment Expense" to his Accountant. After telling this to Managing Partner, a long-time friend of Taxpayer, Accountant does not ask any questions to make reasonable in-

---

[145] Reg. § 1.6694-3(h).
[146] Reg. § 1.6694-1(e).

[147] Reg. § § 1.6694-2(a)(2) and 1.6694-3(a)(2).

quiry of such a large entertainment expenditure and prepares a tax return based on an entertainment expense of $20,100. Both Managing Partner and Accountant are subject to the preparer penalty.

There are other assessable penalties with respect to the preparation of tax returns for other persons under Section 6695. These would include, for example, failure to furnish a copy of a return to a taxpayer, a failure to sign a return, a failure to furnish an identifying number, a failure to retain a copy or list, a failure to file correct information returns, the improper negotiation of a check, and the failure to be diligent in determining eligibility for the earned income credit.

¶1230 INJUNCTION AGAINST RETURN PREPARERS

The IRS can seek an injunction against any income tax return preparer who is found to have violated certain rules of conduct.[148] Included among those rules is conduct subject to the aforementioned preparer penalties.[149] The court has juris-diction to enjoin the individual from engaging in such conduct and, if the individual has repeatedly engaged in such conduct, the court can enjoin the individual from acting as an income tax return preparer. Some courts have entered this injunction on a permanent basis.[150]

Any one of the following types of conduct constitute grounds for injunctive relief:

1. Engaging in any conduct subject to either the preparer penalties or any of the criminal penalties provided by Title 26, United States Code;

2. Misrepresenting the preparer's eligibility to practice before the IRS or otherwise misrepresenting his or her experience or education as an income tax return preparer;

3. Guaranteeing the payment of any tax refund or the allowance of any tax credit; and

4. Engaging in any other fraudulent or deceptive conduct which substan-tially interferes with the proper administration of the Internal Revenue laws.

In addition to finding one of these grounds to be present, the court must also find that injunctive relief is appropriate to prevent the recurrence of such conduct.[151]

Example 12-29: Suppose that a preparer claims to have studied account-ing at Oxford and prepared returns for Lloyd's of London. The IRS learns that the preparer actually studied at the Oxford Barber College and has prepared the returns for Lloyd's Bar and Grill in London, Kentucky. The IRS

---

[148] Code Sec. 7407.

[149] Code Secs. 6694, 6695, and 7407(b).

[150] *United States v. Owens, Jr.,* 79-2 USTC ¶9742 (C.D. Cal. 1979); *United States v. May,* 83-1 USTC

¶9220 (E.D. Mich. 1983); *United States v. Hutchinson,* 83-1 USTC ¶9322 (S.D. Cal. 1983); *United States v. Bullard,* 89-2 USTC ¶9620 (E.D. Tex. 1989), *United State v. Franchi,* 756 F, Supp. 889 (W.D. Pa. 1991).

[151] Code Sec. 7407(b)(1) and (2).

may seek an injunction with respect to the misrepresentation of experience and education.

¶1231 THE PENALTY FOR AIDING AND ABETTING AN UNDERSTATEMENT

The IRS can impose a penalty of $1,000 on any person who aids or assists in the preparation of any portion of a return, claim, affidavit or other document who knows (or has reason to believe) that such portion will be used in connection with any matter arising under the Internal Revenue laws and who knows that the use of such portion would result in an understatement of tax liability.[152] If the tax liability of a corporation is involved, the penalty increases to $10,000. This civil penalty is comparable in most respects to the criminal penalty for willfully aiding or assisting in the preparation or presentation of a false or fraudulent return or document.[153]

The scope of the aiding and abetting penalty is extremely broad. The penalty covers not only one who aids or assists, but also any person who advises or procures the preparation of a return or any portion of a return that such person knows will result in an understatement of tax. It includes advice by an attorney or accountant who knowingly counsels such a course of action. One of the purposes of the penalty is to protect taxpayers from advisors who seek to profit by leading innocent taxpayers into fraudulent conduct. The penalty will apply even if the taxpayer does not know the return is false.[154]

> **Example 12-30:** Suppose that CPA is responsible for preparing the K-1 for a partnership. CPA intentionally reports a lower amount for his friend, a partner in the partnership, so that his friend can file a return understating income. CPA is subject to the penalty for aiding and abetting an understatement.

The term "procures" includes ordering or causing a subordinate to prepare or present a false return or document. A subordinate is any other person over whose activities the person subject to the penalty has direction, supervision or control. The Code specifically provides that an individual may be a subordinate even though he is a director, officer, employee or agent of the taxpayer involved.[155]

> **Example 12-31:** If the president of a corporation instructs the comptroller to prepare false inventory sheets but does not actually prepare the inventory sheets himself, the IRS can impose the aiding and abetting penalty on the president. In fact, because the term "procures" is expanded to include knowing that a subordinate is preparing a false document and failing to prevent the subordinate from doing so, the president could be liable if he merely knew of the false inventory and did nothing to prevent it.

---

[152] Code Sec. 6701.
[153] Code Sec. 7602. See ¶1803.

[154] Code Secs. 6701(d).
[155] Code Sec. 6701(c)(2).

The person liable cannot incur more than one such penalty for each taxable period, even though there may be more than one item on the return that could be the basis for the penalty. However, the IRS may assess a separate penalty for each taxpayer whose tax liability was understated.

If the IRS assesses an aiding and abetting penalty, the IRS may not assess either the preparer penalties or the penalty for promoting abusive tax shelters. This gives the IRS discretion as to which penalty to assert when some or all of these penalties would be warranted. The IRS has the burden of proof to determine liability for the penalty in any proceeding.[156]

¶1232 PROMOTING ABUSIVE TAX SHELTERS

Another penalty is aimed at those who organize or promote abusive tax shelters.[157] To be subject to the promoter penalty under, the person must either help organize the tax shelter (partnership or other entity, any investment plan or arrangement or any other plan or arrangement) or participate, directly or indirectly, in its sale. In addition, the person must make or furnish, or cause another person to make or furnish, either a false statement as to the allowability of the tax benefits sought from the shelter or a gross valuation overstatement with respect to the shelter.

For gross valuation overstatements made or furnished, the penalty is equal to the lesser of $1,000 for each proscribed tax shelter activity or 100 percent of the gross income derived from such activity. The penalty for false statements is 50% of the gross income derived from such activity. While this penalty is not specifically aimed at return preparers, the scope of the penalty is so broad that it could apply to some activities of professional tax advisors.

In computing this penalty, each sale of an interest in a tax shelter, as well as the organization of each tax shelter plan or entity, will constitute a separate activity subject to the $1,000 penalty.

A statement concerning the tax benefits of the shelter cannot be the basis for the penalty unless the person knows or has reason to know that the statement is false. Knowledge of falsity will be presumed if facts contained in the sales materials indicate that the statement is false. However, if the sales material does not contain such information, the salesperson is not under a duty to make further inquiry. The penalty applies even though there is no reliance on the false statement by the purchasing taxpayer or no actual underpayment of tax. Thus, the penalty can be based on the offering materials alone without the necessity of auditing any returns.

> **Example 12-32:** Suppose that Joe Promoter has organized a master limited partnership in which he is selling 100 units to different purchasers. Joe (who learned everything he needed to know about tax during the two days tax was taught in his high school accounting class 20 years ago) makes the outrageous claim that each dollar invested will produce $10 of deduc-

---

[156] See ¶1234. [157] Code Sec. 6700.

tions. Joe Promoter would be subject to a penalty of $100,000 constituting $1,000 for each of the 100 units sold.

A gross valuation overstatement of the value of property or services occurs when the stated value exceeds two hundred percent of the correct valuation as finally determined. The value of the property or services involved must be directly related to the amount of some deduction or credit allowable to participants in the shelter.[158] The IRS is not required to show an intent to overstate the value in order to sustain the penalty. The IRS may waive the penalty by showing that there was a reasonable basis for the valuation and that such valuation was made in good faith.[159]

¶1233 PROCEDURAL ASPECTS OF PREPARER PENALTIES

The Internal Revenue Manual instructs examiners that during every field and office examination, the examiner is to determine if return preparer violations exist. The review of the preparer's conduct is separate from the examination of the return and no discussion of the proposed penalty is to occur in the presence of a taxpayer.[160] Generally, the examiner does not propose a preparer penalty until completion of the income tax examination.

If the examiner finds indicia of a violation, she must develop the facts to a point where she can determine if a penalty investigation should be opened. This is to be done without discussing the conduct penalty with the preparer. If the examiner concludes that the penalty should be pursued, the examiner will then discuss the case with her group manager. It is only at such time that the IRS decides whether to begin an investigation. If the examiner conducts a penalty investigation, she contacts the preparer to fully develop and document the facts and circumstances with respect to the preparation of the return. The examiner's workpapers must reflect the position of the preparer.

If the examiner decides to assert a preparer penalty, the preparer has the opportunity to agree to the assessment. The preparer formalizes the agreement (or disagreement) by executing a Form 5816, Report of Income Tax Return Preparer Penalty Case (see Exhibit 12-3 at ¶1243).

The preparer has an opportunity for an Appeals Office conference. Notice of the proposed assertion of the penalty is given in a thirty-day letter (see Exhibit 12-4 at ¶1244) from which the preparer can request an appeal. The IRS will not assess the penalty until the final determination of the Appeals Office.

If the Appeals Office rejects the preparer's contentions, the IRS sends a notice of assessment of the penalty and demand for payment to the preparer. The preparer can then pay fifteen percent of the penalty assessed within thirty days of assessment and file a claim for refund.[161] If the claim is disallowed, the preparer may file a lawsuit in the U.S. District Court.

---

[158] Code Sec. 6700(b)(1).
[159] Code Sec. 6700(b)(2).

[160] IRM 20.1.6.3.
[161] Code Sec. 6694(c).

The IRS has three years from the date the return is filed in which to assess any preparer penalty. However, in the event the penalty is for willful, reckless or intentional conduct, the Code provides that the penalty may be assessed at any time.[162]

¶1234 BURDEN OF PROOF FOR THE PREPARER PENALTIES

In any proceeding regarding a preparer penalty, the IRS bears the burden of proof in establishing that the person is liable for such penalty.[163] To contest a preparer penalty, the person assessed may pay fifteen percent of the penalty within thirty days of assessment and file a claim for refund of the amount paid. If this is done, no further proceeding or levy to collect the balance may commence until final resolution of the proceeding. If the claim is denied, the person assessed may sue in the U.S. District Court to determine liability for the penalty. However, the taxpayer must file a lawsuit within the earlier of (1) thirty days after the day of denial of the claim for refund or (2) thirty days after the expiration of six months following the day on which he filed the claim for refund. The statute of limitations on collection is suspended while the refund action is pending and, accordingly, the IRS is barred from collecting the penalty.[164]

---

[162] Code Secs. 6694(b) and 6696(d)(1).
[163] Code Sec. 6703(a).

[164] Code Sec. 6703(c).

¶1241 Exhibit 12-1

Form **8275** (Rev. August 2008) Department of the Treasury Internal Revenue Service	**Disclosure Statement** Do not use this form to disclose items or positions that are contrary to Treasury regulations. Instead, use Form 8275-R, Regulation Disclosure Statement. See separate instructions. ▶ **Attach to your tax return.**	OMB No. 1545-0889 Attachment Sequence No. **92**
Name(s) shown on return		Identifying number shown on return

Part I   **General Information** (see instructions)

	(a) Rev. Rul., Rev. Proc., etc.	(b) Item or Group of Items	(c) Detailed Description of Items	(d) Form or Schedule	(e) Line No.	(f) Amount
1						
2						
3						
4						
5						
6						

Part II   **Detailed Explanation** (see instructions)

1

2

3

4

5

6

Part III   **Information About Pass-Through Entity.** To be completed by partners, shareholders, beneficiaries, or residual interest holders.

Complete this part only if you are making adequate disclosure for a pass-through item.

Note: *A pass-through entity is a partnership, S corporation, estate, trust, regulated investment company (RIC), real estate investment trust (REIT), or real estate mortgage investment conduit (REMIC).*

1 Name, address, and ZIP code of pass-through entity	**2** Identifying number of pass-through entity
	3 Tax year of pass-through entity / / to / /
	4 Internal Revenue Service Center where the pass-through entity filed its return

For Paperwork Reduction Act Notice, see separate instructions.   Cat. No. 61935M   Form **8275** (Rev. 8-2008)

Form 8275 (Rev. 8-2008) Page **2**

Part IV	Explanations *(continued from Parts I and/or II)*

Form **8275** (Rev. 8-2008)

¶1242 Exhibit 12-2

Form **8275-R**	**Regulation Disclosure Statement**	OMB No. 1545-0889
(Rev. August 2008)	Use this form only to disclose items or positions that are contrary to Treasury regulations. For other disclosures, use Form 8275, Disclosure Statement. See separate instructions.	
Department of the Treasury Internal Revenue Service	▶ Attach to your tax return.	Attachment Sequence No. **92A**
Name(s) shown on return		Identifying number shown on return

Part I   General Information (see instructions)

	(a) Regulation Section	(b) Item or Group of Items	(c) Detailed Description of Items	(d) Form or Schedule	(e) Line No.	(f) Amount
1						
2						
3						
4						
5						
6						

Part II   Detailed Explanation (see instructions)

1

2

3

4

5

6

Part III   Information About Pass-Through Entity. To be completed by partners, shareholders, beneficiaries, or residual interest holders.

Complete this part only if you are making adequate disclosure for a pass-through item.

Note: *A pass-through entity is a partnership, S corporation, estate, trust, regulated investment company (RIC), real estate investment trust (REIT), or real estate mortgage investment conduit (REMIC).*

1 Name, address, and ZIP code of pass-through entity	2 Identifying number of pass-through entity
	3 Tax year of pass-through entity / / to / /
	4 Internal Revenue Service Center where the pass-through entity filed its return

For Paperwork Reduction Act Notice, see separate instructions.   Cat. No. 14594X   Form **8275-R** (Rev. 8-2008)

Form 8275-R (Rev. 8-2008) Page **2**

| **Part IV** | **Explanations** *(continued from Parts I and/or II)* |

Form **8275-R** (Rev. 8-2008)

¶1243 Exhibit 12-3

Form **5816** (Rev. July 2008)	Department of the Treasury — Internal Revenue Service ## Report of Tax Return Preparer Penalty Case

Name and address of preparer	Check one box below
	Preparer is:
	    Employer preparer ☐
	    Self-employed preparer ☐
	    Employee preparer ☐

Preparer's PTIN, SSN, or EIN	Examining Area/Function	Agreement ☐ Full ☐ None

Name and title of person with whom penalty was discussed	Date of report	In reply refer to:

The following information identifies the tax return or claim for which penalty is being charged:

Taxpayer's name and address	Taxpayer's social security or employer identification number	Tax period	Master file tax code

Kind of Preparer Penalty Charged	Amount
A. Understatement of tax due to unreasonable positions. IRC Sec. 6694(a)	
B. Understatement of tax due to willful or reckless conduct. IRC Sec. 6694(b)	
C. Failure to furnish a copy of the return or claim to the taxpayer by the time it was presented for taxpayer's signature. IRC Sec. 6695(a)	
D. Failure to sign return or claim. IRC Sec. 6695(b)	
E. Failure to provide preparer's social security or employer identification number on return or claim. IRC Sec. 6695(c)	
F. Failure to keep a copy or list of the returns or claims prepared. IRC Sec. 6695(d)	
G. Negotiating or endorsing a Federal income tax check issued to a taxpayer (other than the preparer). IRC Sec. 6695(f)	
H. Failure to comply with EITC Due Diligence requirements. IRC Sec. 6695(g)	
I. Disclosure or use of information, other than to prepare or assist in preparing returns. IRC Sec. 6713	
Total penalties	0.00
Other Information	Examiner's signature

- -

Note- Examiner Remove Appeals Message on Unagreed Cases

I have read the information on the back of this form that explains these penalties as they relate to tax return preparers. I agree to comply with those provisions in the future.

Consent to Assessment and Collection - I do not wish to exercise my appeal rights with the Internal Revenue Service or to contest in the United States District Court the findings in this report, therefore, I give my consent to the immediate assessment and collection of the tax return preparer penalty.

Preparer's signature	Date

PART 1   Reset Form Fields   Form **5816** (Rev. 7-2008) Catalog Number 24295B

In general, under IRC 7701(a)(36), any person who prepares for compensation, or who employs one or more persons to prepare for compensation, any return of tax or any claim for refund, is considered a tax return preparer.

A. A penalty is charged the tax return preparer for understating a taxpayer's tax liability when the understatement is due to an unreasonable belief that the position would more likely than not be sustained. The penalty is the greater of $1,000 or 50% of the income derived (or to be derived) by the preparer for the preparation of each return or claim that shows such understatement. (IRC Sec. 6694(a)).

B. The penalty for understatement of tax due to willful or reckless conduct is the greater of $5,000 or 50% of the income derived (or to be derived) by the preparer for the preparation of each return or claim that shows such understatement, less any penalty paid under IRC 6694(a). (IRC Sec. 6694(b)).

In addition to the above penalties, the penalties in C through H will be imposed. Except for G, the penalty will apply unless it can be shown that the failure to comply was due to reasonable cause and not due to willful neglect.

C. A penalty is charged the tax return preparer for not furnishing a copy of the return or claim to the taxpayer by the time it is presented for the taxpayer's signature. The penalty is $50 for each return or claim not so provided, to a maximum of $25,000, with respect to documents filed in any calendar year. (IRC Sec. 6695(a)).

D. A tax return preparer can be charged a penalty for each failure to sign a return or claim. The penalty is $50 for each return or claim not manually signed. The maximum penalty, with respect to documents filed during any calendar year, shall not exceed $25,000. (IRC Sec. 6695(b)).

E. A penalty is charged to tax return preparers for not providing their identification numbers. The penalty is $50 for each return or claim that does not show an identifying number, to a maximum of $25,000, with respect to documents filed in any calendar year. An individual preparer should use his or her PTIN or social security number. An individual who is employed by another preparer should show his or her identification number, the identification number of his or her employer and the business address where the return or claim was prepared. For this purpose, the partner in a partnership is considered an employee and should use the partnership's employer identification number. The number must be entered on the return or claim in the space provided. (IRC Sec. 6695(c)).

F. A penalty is charged the tax return preparer for not keeping a copy or list of the returns or claims prepared. These records must be kept for 3 years. The penalty is $50 for each return or claim not recorded, with a maximum penalty of $25,000 for each return period. (IRC Sec. 6695(d)).

G. A penalty is charged the tax return preparer for negotiating or endorsing a Federal income tax check issued to a taxpayer (other than the preparer). The penalty is $500 for each check. (IRC Sec. 6695(f)).

H. A penalty is charged the income tax preparer for failure to meet all four requirements of EITC Due Diligence with respect to any EITC return or claim. The penalty for failure to comply is $100 for each return or claim unless it can be shown that the failure to comply was isolated or inadvertent. (IRC Sec. 6695(g)).

I. A penalty is charged the tax return preparer if information furnished to him for, or in connection with the preparation of returns of tax is disclosed or used for any other purpose other than to prepare, or to assist in preparing returns. The penalty is $250 for each disclosure or use, to a maximum of $1,000 per person for any calendar year. (IRC Sec. 6713(a)(1) and 6713(a)(2)). Under section 7407 of the Code, the Department of Treasury may seek a court injunction against preparers to either bar them from conduct described in that section or to bar them from acting as income tax return preparers.

Form **5816** (Rev. 7-2008) Catalog Number 24295B

¶1244 Exhibit 12-4

Internal Revenue Service   **Department of the Treasury**

Taxpayer Identification Number:

Date: **Person to Contact:**

Contact Telephone Number:

Employee Identification Number:

Refer Reply to:

Last Date to Respond to this Letter:

Dear

We have enclosed a copy of our examination report explaining why we are proposing a tax return preparer penalty.

If you accept our findings, please sign and return the enclosed Form 5838, Waiver Form. If a penalty amount is due, you may want to pay it now to avoid additional interest changes. If you don't pay it now, we will send you a bill.

If you don't agree with our findings, you may request a meeting or a telephone conference with the supervisor of the person whose name is shown above. If you still do not agree with our findings, we recommend that you request a conference with our Appeals Office. You may request a conference as follows:

1.   If the total penalties shown in our report are $25,000 or less, send us a letter
       requesting Appeals consideration, indicating what you don't agree with, and the
       reasons why you don't agree.

2.   If the total penalties shown in our report are more than $25,000, you must submit
       a formal protest. The requirements for a formal protest are explained in the
       enclosed Publication 5, Your Appeal Rights and How to Prepare a Protest If You
       Don't Agree.

We have enclosed an envelope for your convenience. If we do not hear from you within 30 days, we will have to process your case based on the findings in the examination report.

We have also enclosed Publication 1, Your Rights as a Taxpayer, and Publication 594, Understanding the Collection Process, for your information.

Letter 1125 (DO) (Rev. 4-1999)
Cat. No. 13620Y

¶1244

If you have any questions, please contact the person whose name and telephone number are shown in the heading of this letter. Thank you for your cooperation.

Sincerely yours,

Enclosures:
Examination Report
Form 5838
Publication 1
Publication 5
Publication 594
Envelope

Letter 1125 (DO) (Rev. 4-1999)
Cat. No. 13620Y

¶1251 DISCUSSION QUESTIONS

1. Peter Procrastinator forgot to file his 20X3 tax return. Eventually the collection function of the IRS contacted him and after several delays, Peter was able to file a tax return early in 20X6. The return showed a liability in tax of $5,500, which Peter tendered along with the return. Peter also sent a second check which was computed to pay all of the interest due to date.

   Approximately two months later, Peter received an assessment notice from the Service Center. The notice showed an assessment of tax of $5,500, interest in the approximate amount that Peter had computed, delinquency penalties, and a substantial understatement penalty. Peter wishes to challenge the assessment of the penalties. What are his chances?

2. In August 20X5, a new corporate client retained Paula Preparer as accountant and tax return preparer. In reviewing the prior returns of the client, Paula noticed that the client had claimed substantial deductions for travel and entertainment expenses. She asked the client if the corporation had ever been audited and learned that the client had not. Paula knew that the president of the corporation spent a great deal of time traveling and promoting the business, and so in setting up their procedures for the new client, she stressed the importance of keeping adequate records for any travel and entertainment expenses. Paula also discussed the sort of recordkeeping procedures that should be followed by the bookkeeper of the corporation.

   The first fiscal year of the corporation for which Paula prepared its return was the fiscal year ending August 20X5. In reviewing the records, Paula noticed that expenses of $9,500 were claimed for travel and entertainment by the president. Because the sales of the corporation were approximately $750,000 for that year, Paula did not think that the $9,500 figure was out of line. Since Paula had spent so much time stressing the Code Sec. 274 recordkeeping requirements when the client initially retained her, she assumed that the taxpayer had followed through on her insistence of keeping adequate records. Paula did not inquire into the adequacy of the T&E records before she prepared the return.

   In 20X6, the IRS audited the corporation's return. The IRS discovered that of the $9,500, approximately $2,000 constituted personal expenditures of the president and approximately $5,500 constituted expenditures for which adequate substantiation did not exist. The IRS has disallowed $7,500 of the deduction to the corporation and is also proposing to assess a preparer penalty against Paula. Is the proposed penalty assessment justified?

3. Ned Negligent, a not overly careful accountant, has retained you for tax advice. During 20X4, in preparing tax returns for several clients, he

overlooked the mileage rules and reported deductions based on commuting mileage. The IRS audited the returns and assessed preparer penalties.

In preparing the 20X6 returns for two of his remaining clients (both of whom had been audited for 20X4 and had commuting expenses disallowed), Ned finds that one client forgot to inform him of an IRA created in 20X4 for which no deduction was taken. The refund for the IRA deduction will be greater than the tax assessed for the erroneous commuting deduction. Further, Ned finds that the other client has incurred a net operating loss that will be available for carryback to 20X3 (20X1 and 20X2 also being loss years) and totally eliminate any tax liability for that year. Can the penalty assessed for 20X4 against Ned be abated under either of these circumstances?

4. Sterling Clampett is the president and sole shareholder of Spoonful, Inc., a manufacturer of fine flatware. Sterling has always made it his job to sell the scrap silver that remains after manufacturing the flatware. The problem is that Sterling has been selling the scrap as his own, rather than on behalf of the corporation.

During their recent audit of Spoonful, Inc., the IRS has also discovered Sterling's personal silver sales. The government has enough evidence to sustain a civil fraud penalty. For the tax year 20X5, Spoonful, Inc., reported a tax of $125,500. After taking into consideration the adjustments related to the silver sales, the IRS calculated the correct tax for 20X5 to be $200,500. Sterling would like to know the maximum amount of penalties that could be imposed against the corporation due to its understatement of tax in 20X5.

5. Motoco, Inc. manufactures and designs mopeds which it sells throughout the world. In valuing its inventory for tax purposes, the corporation is subject to the uniform capitalization rules under Code Sec. 263A. Pursuant to the rules, Motoco must include not only direct costs, but also a portion of certain indirect costs in their inventory costs. The president of the corporation argues that the government is wrong in expecting the corporation to treat some of the compensation paid to its officers as inventoriable costs. Therefore, he refuses to capitalize such costs. Is the corporation subject to any penalties as a result of the failure to capitalize the indirect costs?

6. George Baily is the sole shareholder of Building and Loan, Inc. The IRS is conducting an audit and is scrutinizing withdrawals that George made from the corporation which were used to pay his personal expenses. George has argued that the withdrawals were loans that he had taken from the corporation rather than taxable income to him. He points to the fact that the withdrawals were reflected on the corporation's books and records as "Loans to Stockholders." George also attached Form W-2 to his tax return, disclosing the imputed interest income on his claimed

interest-free loan. In addition, he disclosed the interest expense associated with the claimed loans on various schedules attached to the corporation's return.

Despite George's arguments, the IRS has ultimately determined that George had no intent to repay the withdrawals and, therefore, that amounts withdrawn represent taxable income to him. The deficiencies calculated by the IRS result in a substantial understatement of income tax. George wants to know whether he can avoid any additions to tax due to the deficiencies.

7. The IRS is examining the 20X5 tax return of Sam Short. His return reported tax due in the amount of $60,000. The revenue agent has determined that Sam understated his tax for 20X5 by $22,000 and is proposing to assess the substantial understatement penalty. What arguments might Sam make that the penalty should not be imposed?

CHAPTER 13
THE APPEALS OFFICE

¶1301 INTRODUCTION

If an audit adjustment cannot be resolved at the Examination level, the Internal Revenue Service (IRS) provides a further opportunity to resolve tax controversies without litigation. This activity is conducted by the Appeals Office. As part of the IRS Restructuring and Reform Act of 1998 (The Act),[1] the IRS Appeals Office realigned itself to coordinate with the new operating divisions of the IRS. However, while the Appeals Office continues to consider cases from each of the new operating divisions of the IRS, the Appeals Office recently realigned itself a second time, as described below.

The Appeal Office is led nationwide by the Chief and Deputy Chief, Appeals.[2] The Appeals Office has both a Headquarters and a field component. "Front Office" functions performed at Headquarters include tax policy and procedure, strategic planning and measurement, business systems planning and communications. The field function is organized geographically, with eight geographic areas, each of which is led by an Area Director of Appeals who reports to an Appeals Executive in Headquarters. The purpose for the field realignment is to increase on-sight management of cases and to improve the field's ability to be flexible as workload demands change. The Area Directors of Appeals are located in Baltimore, Manhattan, Nashville, Atlanta, Chicago, Dallas, San Francisco and Laguna Niguel. In addition to Headquarters and the field areas, the Appeals Office has deployed Appeals campus teams within the areas to work mostly campus-sourced cases.

Field personnel within each area work mostly field-source cases. However, several areas have nationwide jurisdiction including: Technical Guidance; Appeals Team Case Leaders; and Processing and Tax Computation. The Technical Guidance area manages the Appeals Office Industry Specialization Program (ISP) and its Coordinated Issues Program (CIP), providing uniform methods to address abusive tax shelter issues, listed and other reportable transaction issues, and Tier I and other coordinated issues. See Chapter 5 for a more complete discussion of these types of issues. Appeals Team Case Leaders, who report directly to the Chief, Appeals, manage complex appeals of the largest taxpayers. Process and Tax Computation specialists are grouped together so that their unique needs are effectively addressed.

Finally, in contrast to Appeals Officers, Appeals Settlement Officers have an extensive background in collection issues. They concentrate their efforts in collec-

---

[1] P.L. 105-206.

[2] See *www.appealsvidoes.net* for a more extensive discussion of the Appeals Office.

tion due process hearings, offers in compromise, trust fund recovery penalties and appeals submitted within the Collection Appeal Program.

¶1302 PROTEST REQUIREMENTS

Upon receipt of a thirty-day letter from an operating division proposing a deficiency, the taxpayer may request a conference with the Appeals Office. If the total amount of proposed additional tax is under $25,000 for each year or taxable period under consideration, the taxpayer may make a small case request. The small case request should be in writing and contain a brief statement of disputed issues for Appeals Office consideration.

A formal protest is required to obtain Appeals Office review of all other proposed deficiencies, all employee plan and exempt organization cases, and of all partnership and S corporation cases.[3] The formal protest must be in writing and must include certain elements that meet the requirements of the Appeals Office (see Exhibit 13-1 at ¶1321).[4]

Exhibit 13-1 at ¶1321 is a sample protest. In particular, the protest must contain a statement of facts supporting the taxpayer's position. This statement of facts must be declared true under the penalties of perjury—this is the function of the last paragraph of the protest, where the taxpayer declares that he or she has examined the statement of facts and that, to the best of his or her knowledge and belief, they are true, correct and complete.

If the protest has been prepared by the representative and not by the taxpayer, normally it will not be possible for the representative to sign such a declaration under penalties of perjury. Instead, a declaration may be substituted which states that the representative has prepared the protest, and states whether or not he or she knows of his or her own knowledge and belief that the statement of facts is true, correct and complete. In addition, the representative may wish to go on to state that upon information and belief he or she believes the statement of facts to be true, correct and complete.

The protest is to be filed with the IRS office designated in the thirty-day letter. The protest also will be reviewed by the examining agent who made the initial determination. The administrative file will then be assembled and forwarded with all pertinent documents, including the workpapers of the auditor or revenue agent, to the Appeals Office. The appeals officer makes a preliminary review to determine whether the case should be heard by Appeals. The appeals officer is not to act as an investigator or an examining officer, and therefore, if the case requires further significant factual development, the appeals officer may return the case to the appropriate operating division.

> **Example 13-1:** An Appeals Protest contains a highly factual issue regarding whether a family's horse racing activities constitute a business or a more nondeductible hobby. This issue was included by the Revenue Agent

---

[3] Appeals has also been given jurisdiction to review certain collection actions. See Chapter 14 for details.

[4] Reg. § 601.106(a)(1).

at the very end of the exam. Virtually no factual development was accomplished. In this case the Appeals Officer may return the case to exam.

¶1303 PROCEDURE AT APPEALS

Proceedings before the Appeals Office are informal. Testimony is not taken under oath, although the Appeals Office may require matters alleged to be true to be submitted in the form of affidavits or declarations under the penalties of perjury. The taxpayer or the representative will meet with the appeals officer and informally discuss the pros and cons of the various positions taken by the taxpayer and the IRS. Under the Regulations, Appeals will follow the law and the recognized standards of legal construction in determining facts and applying the law. Appeals will determine the correct amount of the tax with strict impartiality as between the taxpayer and the Government, and without favoritism or discrimination between taxpayers.[5]

Although an appeals officer is to maintain the standard of impartiality set forth in the Regulations, he or she must, nevertheless, protect the rights of the IRS and act as an advocate on its behalf. Therefore, an appeals officer can raise a new issue or propose a new theory in support of the examining agent's proposed adjustment. However, an appeals officer generally should not do so unless the grounds for raising such new issues are substantial and the effect on the tax liability is material.[6]

> **Example 13-2:** The Appeals Officer notices that an issue the examining agent raised is also a "listed transaction" meaning an issue the IRS considers abusive. In this case, the Appeals Officer will raise new reasons upon which to disallow the transactions because the grounds for raising the new reasons are substantial and the effect on the tax liability is material.

¶1304 EX PARTE COMMUNICATIONS

The IRS Restructuring and Reconciliation Act of 1998 sought to insure an independent appeals function and prohibits ex parte communication between appeals officers and other IRS employees.[7] The IRS published Rev. Proc. 2000-43 setting out the prohibited and permitted ex parte communications.

¶1305 REVENUE PROCEDURE 2000-43

For example, Rev. Proc. 2000-43, 2000-2 CB 404, defines "ex parte communications" as:

> "communications that take place between Appeals and another Service function without the participation of the taxpayer or the taxpayer's representative (taxpayer/representative). While the legislation refers to "appeals officers," the overall intent of the ex parte provision is to ensure the independence of the entire Appeals organization. Ex parte communications between any Appeals employee, e.g., Appeals Officers, Appeals Team Case Leaders, Appeals Tax Computation Specialists, and employees of other Internal Revenue Ser-

---

[5] Reg. § 601.106(f)(1).
[6] IRM 8.6.1.6; Policy start P-8-2.

[7] Act Sec. 1001(a)(4).

vice offices are prohibited to the extent that such communications appear to compromise the independence of Appeals."

Other points made by Rev. Proc. 2000-43 include that the prohibition on *ex parte* communication includes all forms of communication whether they be oral or written or manually or computer generated communications. In addition, within the Appeals Office the prohibition does not apply, on the policy ground that Appeals needs to be free to discuss a case before it with Appeals Office specialists. Minor communications from the examination or collection functions to Appeals that are made in the process of administration of the files records and are ministerial in nature also fall outside of the prohibition. For a more complete analysis of the prohibition on *ex parte* communications, see the entire text of Rev. Proc. 2000-43.

¶1306 EARLY REFERRAL TO APPEALS

Early referral to Appeals is optional, available to any taxpayer and is intended to resolve cases more expeditiously through the operating divisions and appeals working together. The procedures are effective for requests filed after July 19, 1999.[8] Early referral may be made with respect to issues involving involuntary change of accounting methods, employment tax, employee plans, exempt organizations, as well as income tax matters.[9]

Early referral is initiated by the taxpayer with reference to any developed unagreed issue under the jurisdiction of an operating division. The operating division will continue to develop other issues that have not been referred to appeals.

Appropriate issues for early referral are limited to those issues which (1) are *fully developed* and, if resolved, can reasonably be expected to result in a quicker resolution of the entire case, and (2) both the taxpayer and the operating division agree should be referred to appeals early. Whip-saw transactions (situations produced when the government is subjected to conflicting claims of taxpayers), issues designated for litigation by the Office of Chief Counsel and those for which the taxpayer has filed a request for Competent Authority Assistance may not be referred to appeals for early resolution.

> **Example 13-3:** Consider a valuation issue that is closely tied to a second unresolved issue in a case. The taxpayer may be successful in having the valuation issued moved into early referral to Appeals, especially if the issue disposes of the second issue and can therefore close the case sooner.

In a manner similar to the formal protest, a request for early referral must be submitted in writing by the taxpayer to the team leader/group manager. The taxpayer's early referral request must contain: (1) identity of the taxpayer and the tax periods to which those issues relate; (2) each issue for which early referral is requested; and (3) the taxpayer's position with regard to the relevant early referral issue, including a brief discussion of the material facts and an analysis of the facts and law as they apply to each referral issue. The early referral request

---

[8] Code Sec. 7123.

[9] Rev. Proc. 99-28, 1999-29 IRB 109.

and any supplemental submissions (including additional documents) must include a declaration similar to the jurat required for a protest.

There is no formal taxpayer appeal of a denial of a request for early referral. If the early referral request is denied or if the team leader/group manager does not approve the early referral request with respect to any issue, the taxpayer retains the right to pursue the normal administrative appeal of any proposed deficiency relating to that issue at a later date.

In situations where the operating division concurs with the referral of an issue for early disposition, the operating division is to complete a Form 5701, Notice of Proposed Adjustment (see Chapter 5), or an equivalent form for each early referral issue approved. The operating division is then to send the notification form to the taxpayer within thirty days from the date the early referral request was accepted. The notification form is to describe the issue and explain the operating division's proposed adjustment. The taxpayer must respond in writing to each of the operating divisions' proposed adjustments set forth in the notification form. The response must contain an explanation of the taxpayer's position regarding the issues. The response is to be submitted to the team leader/group manager within thirty days (unless extended) from the date that the proposed adjustment (the notification form) is sent to the taxpayer. The procedural requirements for a statement executed under the penalties of perjury and appropriate signature similar to those used in a protest also apply to the taxpayer's response to the notification form. If a response is not received for any issue within the time provided, the taxpayer's early referral request will be considered withdrawn regarding that particular issue.

The taxpayer's written response to the notification form generally serves the same purpose as a protest to appeals. Established appeals procedures including those governing submissions and taxpayer's conferences apply to early referral issues.[10]

If an agreement is reached with respect to an early referral issue, generally a Form 906, Closing Agreement on Final Determination, covering specific matters is prepared. If early referral negotiations are unsuccessful and an agreement is not reached with respect to an early referral issue, appeals will not consider an unagreed early referral issue again if the entire case is later protested to appeals.

¶1307 SETTLEMENT AGREEMENTS

The IRS describes the "appeals mission" as one to resolve tax controversies without litigation, on a basis which is fair and impartial to both the government and the taxpayer and in a manner that will enhance voluntary compliance and public confidence in the integrity and efficiency of the IRS.[11] Thus, the appeals officer can split or trade issues where there are substantial uncertainties as to the law, the facts or both. In splitting a "legal issue," the appeals officer will ordinarily consider the hazards which would exist if the case were litigated. The appeals officer will weigh the testimony of the proposed witnesses, judge the

---

[10] Prop. Reg. § 601.106(b)(4).   [11] IRM 8.1.1.1.

trends that the court has been following in similar cases and generally try to predict the outcome of the matter if the case were actually tried.

> **Example 13-4:** Consider a case with a purely legal issue in dispute. The Appeals Officer may settle the legal issue on a percentage of the issue's value if, in the opinion of the Appeals Officer, there exist hazards to the government were it to litigate the issue.

Where a case involves concessions by both the government and the taxpayer "for purposes of settlement," and where there is substantial uncertainty as to how the courts would interpret and apply the law or what facts the court would find, a settlement is classified as a "mutual concession settlement." According to the regulations, no settlement is to be made simply on nuisance value.

Where a taxpayer and the appeals officer have reached an agreement as to some or all of the issues in controversy, generally the appeals officer will request the taxpayer to sign a Form 870, Waiver of Restrictions on Assessment and Collection of Deficiency in Tax and Acceptance of Overassessment (see Exhibit 4-5 at ¶425), the same agreement used at the district level. However, when neither party with justification is willing to concede in full the unresolved area of disagreement and a resolution of the dispute involves concessions for the purposes of settlement by both parties based on the relative strengths of the opposing positions, a "mutual concession settlement" is reached, and a Form 870-AD type of agreement is to be used.[12]

The special Appeals Form 870-AD (see Exhibit 13-2 at ¶1322) differs from the normal Form 870 in several ways. The Form 870-AD agreement contains pledges against reopening which the usual agreement does not. Furthermore, the normal Form 870 becomes effective as a Waiver of Restrictions on Assessment when *received by the IRS*, whereas the special Form 870-AD is effective only upon *acceptance by or on behalf of the Commissioner of Internal Revenue*. Finally, under Sec. 6601(c) of the Internal Revenue Code (the Code), the running of interest is suspended thirty days after a Form 870 is received, whereas with a Form 870-AD, interest is not suspended until thirty days after the agreement is executed by the government.

The finality of the Form 870-AD has been the subject of substantial litigation. The form provides that upon acceptance by or on behalf of the Commissioner,

> [T]he case shall not be reopened in the absence of fraud, malfeasance, conceal-ment or misrepresentation of material fact, [or] an important mistake in mathematical calculation . . . and no claim for refund or credit shall be filed or prosecuted for the year(s) stated . . .

Furthermore, the form states in language similar to that contained in a normal Form 870 that it *is not* a final closing agreement under Code Sec. 7121 and does not extend the statutory period of limitations on refund, assessment or collection of tax. The controversy arises where a taxpayer, after executing a Form 870-AD, pays the tax, files a claim for refund and brings suit in District Court or the Court of Federal Claims. The taxpayer takes the position that Code Sec. 7121 is the

---

[12] IRM 8.6.4.3.

exclusive method by which the IRS may enter into a final and binding agreement, and since the Form 870-AD specifically repudiates reference to this section, the taxpayer is not bound by the agreement.

¶1308 REFUND CLAIMS

Generally, the courts have held that a Form 870-AD, standing alone, is insufficient to bar a claim for refund.[13] However, other Courts have denied the taxpayer relief after the execution of a Form 870-AD on the ground of collateral estoppel.[14]

The decision whether the taxpayer should file a claim for refund after the execution of a Form 870-AD may be more a practical than a legal decision. Under Procedural Reg. §601.106(h)(2), a taxpayer may apply to reopen a case. This approval will be granted "under certain unusual circumstances favorable to the taxpayer such as retroactive legislation." Compare the following views expressed in two relatively authoritative works to see the differences in approach.

REDMAN AND QUIGGLE

As a practical matter, however, it is not frequent that a taxpayer executes an agreement in settlement of a case with the thought of awaiting the lapse of the statute of limitations on assessment by the Government and then filing a claim for refund.[33]There is a great natural reluctance of lawyers and accountants versed in tax procedure to participate in any such maneuver. This repugnance is not lessened by the knowledge that the refund claim would be routed to the same service office and probably the same individual with whom the settlement had been consummated. There seems something immoral (or better, perhaps, sneaky) in reneging upon either Form 870 or 870-AD after a settlement has been hammered out by the ardor of both parties.[34]To a different degree is a person conscience-stricken if the agreement is upset because of fraud or mistake and perhaps subsequently discovered evidence or a retroactive change in the law. This discussion was not begun to teach the reader how to renege on settlement agreements, but to inform him of (1) his chances if he should, in litigation, be faced with an agreement of which he is unaware and (2) the consequences of signing it in the first place.[15]

Footnotes

[33] One related device does not bear the same stigma of sharp practice. Taxpayers who discover errors in the Government's favor on unaudited returns may prefer to wait until just before the statute of limitations on assessment runs to file refund claims. By the time the Service has received and considered the claim, it is too late to assess a deficiency. The Service may offset the refund claim, but no more, under the doctrine of equitable overpayment. *Lewis v. Reynolds,* 284 U.S. 281 (1932).

[34] The Procedural Rulings concede that a nondocketed case closed by the Appellate Division not involving concessions by both parties (i.e., Form 870)

---

[13] *Arch Engineering Co., Inc.,* 783 F.2d 190, CA-FC, 86-1 USTC ¶9275; *D.J. Lignos,* (2nd Cir.), 71-1 USTC ¶9302; and *Uinta Livestock Corp.,* (10th Cir.), 66-1 USTC ¶9193.
[14] *M.R. Flynn,* 786 F.2d 586 (3rd Cir.), 86-1 USTC ¶9285; *Elbo Coals, Inc.,* 763 F.2d 818 (6th Cir.), 85-2 USTC ¶9454; *Stair v. United States,* 516 F.2d 560 (CA 2,

1975), 75-1 USTC ¶9463; *Kretchmar v. United States,* 91 Cl. Ct. 191 (1985); see also *McGraw-Hill, Inc. v. United States,* 90-1 USTC ¶50,053 (SD Ny. 1990); 65 FORDHAM L. REV. 691 (1996), fn. 56.
[15] *Procedure Before the Internal Revenue,* 6th Edition, American Law Institute, 1984, p. 137.

may be reopened by the taxpayer "by any appropriate means" as by the filing of a refund claim. Treasury Reg. §601.106(h)(4). At the same time the rules promise that the Service will not reopen any such case absent "fraud, malfeasance, concealment or misrepresentation of material fact, an important mistake in mathematical calculation or such other circumstances that indicates [sic] that failure to take such action would be a serious administrative omission." Treas. Reg. §601.106(h)(3).

THOMAS J. DONELLY

Where to Litigate

The split of authority therefore is quite clear. The Court of Federal Claims will enforce the Form 870-AD and similar agreements, and the courts of appeals will not. These tribunals are in conflict on both the statutory requirements and the estoppel issue. The solution is simple: if it is desired to overturn a Form 870-AD or similar agreement, do not attempt to do so in the Court of Claims.[16]

Government Should Not Be Permitted to Plead Estoppel

While the decisions of the courts of appeal have always favored the taxpayer on this issue, it is not quite clear whether the estoppel defense might ever be available to the government. If the government can show a false representation by the taxpayer, relied upon it and that it has allowed the statute of limitations to expire on further deficiencies against the taxpayer for the years involved, should the government then be allowed to interpose the defense of estoppel?

It would appear that even in this situation the government has suffered no detriment, an essential element of estoppel. The maximum burden the government might suffer as a result of permitting the taxpayer to proceed with his or her refund suit is the amount of the taxpayer's recovery. However, this may be offset in full by the government, notwithstanding the running of the statute of limitations against it. Consequently, it would appear that an estoppel argument should never prevail.

A Proposed Remedy

It is unfortunate that there is not a higher degree of finality to most of the settlements made by the Internal Revenue Service. In the great majority of cases, the "settlement" which the taxpayer considers a final disposition of his matter is in fact not what it purports to be. It is hardly good practice for the taxpayers and the Commissioner to enter into agreements which purport to legally bind them, but which in fact do not. There would seem to be little reason why the Appellate Division should not be authorized to enter into binding agreements with taxpayers. A slight change in the Code would accomplish this.

¶1309 CLOSING AGREEMENT

Some tax cases may involve matters which have a direct effect on other taxes, related taxpayers or other years. Settlement of this type of case may require an additional agreement. Sec. 7121 of the Code authorizes the Secretary to enter into an agreement in writing with any person regarding that person's tax liability for any period.

---

[16] "How Binding Are Stipulations With the Commissioner," 27 New York Univ. Inst. on Fed. Tax. 1371, at 1380-1381.

Example 13-5: WEMALE Corporation, a C corporation, involved in the sale of household products through mail order catalogs, acquired all the assets of FEMALE Corporation along with a covenant not to compete agreement from Jane Jones, the founder and sole shareholder of FEMALE. The date of the sale was 12/31/2003. The parties assigned a value of $1,500,000 to the covenant, which is the amount amortized by WEMALE under Code Sec. 197 as an intangible asset to be amortized over 15 years. Simultaneously with the sale, Ms. Jones entered into an employment contract for $4,500,000 at $1,500,000 a year for three years and an option to renew for an additional 5 years for $750,000 a year. An audit of the 2003 return of WEMALE Corporation by Internal Revenue resulted in the disallowance of the compensation of $1,500,000 to Ms. Jones as a "sham transaction". WEMALE Corporation filed a protest with Appeals and the case was settled on December 31, 2004.

- For the year 2003, the value of the covenant was agreed upon at $4,500,000 and an amortization deduction under Code Sec. 197 of $300,000 is allowed.

- For purposes of the settlement the amounts of $600,000, $500,000, and $400,000 are to be treated as compensation for the first three years of the agreement.

- No value was assigned to the option years.

WEMALE Corporation is concerned that the Internal Revenue Service may refuse to allow the increased amortization of $300,000 in later years or will attempt to disallow more of the compensation to Ms. Jones. Therefore in order to bind the Internal Revenue Service with regard to the settlement, a closing agreement was entered into. (See Exhibit 13-3 at ¶1323).

The above example illustrates the following process. While regional Appeals Offices do not have the authority in closing agreements to bind the Internal Revenue Service with regard to transactions in future years, closing agreements can characterize transactions for the years in issue so as to avoid disputes with regard to carry-over effects of the same issue in future years. It should be noted, that this closing agreement does not impact upon Ms. Jones, as she was not a party to the agreement.

A closing agreement can only be consummated pursuant to the statute. Regulation § 301.7121-1(a) provides that:

> A closing agreement may be entered into in any case in which there appears to be an advantage in having the case permanently and conclusively closed or if good and sufficient reasons are shown by the taxpayer for desiring a closing agreement and it is determined by the Commissioner that the United States will sustain no disadvantage by consummation of such an agreement.

Other examples of the use of closing agreements are where a corporate taxpayer wishes to definitely establish its tax liability to facilitate a transaction, such as the sale of its stock; a corporation in the process of liquidation or dissolution desires a closing agreement in order to wind up its affairs; or a taxpayer may wish to fulfill his or her creditors' demands for authentic evidence as to the status of that individual's tax liability.[17]

¶1310 COLLATERAL AGREEMENTS AND CLOSING AGREEMENTS DISTINGUISHED

Although in the broadest nontechnical sense, closing agreements, waivers and consents can be characterized as collateral agreements, the term as used by the IRS has reference to some matter related to a tax controversy but collateral to the amount of tax to be assessed or the amount of a refund to be received in the instant case. For example, a collateral agreement may commit a trustee or a beneficiary to use the same valuation for income tax purposes as was used for federal estate tax purposes. One important distinction between collateral agreements and closing agreements is that the collateral agreement does not purport to bind the IRS. It is a one-sided commitment. The IRS does not enter into the agreement nor does the IRS sign as a party. Furthermore, collateral agreements, unlike closing agreements, are administrative in nature and not expressly provided for by the Internal Revenue Code.

¶1311 POST-ASSESSMENT PENALTY APPEALS

The Internal Revenue Manual contains provisions for post-assessment review by the Appeals Office of certain penalties. These are generally penalties which may be immediately assessed without the usual deficiency procedures which would otherwise permit appeal to the Tax Court before assessment. A post-assessment appeal right exists for virtually any penalty that may be avoided by a showing of reasonable cause or reasonable basis.[18] Penalty Appeal consideration generally occurs after assessment of such penalties but before payment. Collection action is normally suspended during the Appeal process

The penalty appeal action generally begins with the Campus. Usually, penalties for late filing, late payment and other penalties associated with the filing of a tax return are assessed by the Campus. Taxpayers may protest the penalty charges upon receipt of the billing notice. The notice provides information on how to request elimination of the penalty when the taxpayer believes reasonable cause exists. If the Campus agrees with the taxpayer's position, it has authority to abate the penalty. If it rejects the explanation, an 854(C) Letter (see Exhibit 13-4 at ¶1324) is sent to the taxpayer explaining the reasons for denying the request and explaining how to file a written protest to the Appeals Office.[19]

A similar procedure is used when penalties are originally assessed by customer service representatives in the local offices.

---

[17] See Rev. Proc. 68-16, 1968-1 CB 770 and Rev. Proc. 94-67, 1994-2 CB 800 and Rev. Proc. 99-32, 1999-2 CB 296, for closing agreement procedures, forms, and additional examples. Closing agreement forms for the final determination of tax liability (Form 866) or the final determination of specific matters (Form 906) are available. These forms need not be used, however, provided the agreement includes the standard provisions set forth in the IRS forms.

[18] IRM 8.11.1.

[19] IRM 8.11.1.

The Appeals Office generally is required to dispose of a penalty case within ninety days of receipt of the case file.[20] The Internal Revenue Manual provides that most penalty appeals should be resolved with only written or telephone communication with the taxpayer. A conference is to be granted only upon request by the taxpayer and only when deemed necessary by the appeals officer. In general, it is only the more complex reasonable cause determinations that are to be handled by the penalty appeal procedure.[21] Each case is to be considered on its own facts, and the appeals officer can consider hazards of litigation in determining whether to abate all or part of the penalties asserted.[22]

---

[20] IRM 8.11.1.
[21] Id.

[22] IRM 8.11.1.

¶1321 Exhibit 13-1

SAMPLE PROTEST

CERTIFIED MAIL—RETURN RECEIPT REQUESTED

Internal Revenue Service
1234 Main Street
Milwaukee, WI 53201

Re: Frozen Tundra Meat Co., Inc. EIN 39–0000000

PROTEST

The above-named taxpayer hereby protests the proposed adjustments to its taxable income and corporation income taxes for the calendar years 2003, 2004, and 2005 as set forth in the report enclosed with your letter dated June 19, 2006.

The following information is submitted in support of this Protest:

1. Appeal and Request for Hearing.

It is requested that this case be transferred to the Appeals Office at Milwaukee, Wisconsin, and that a conference be arranged at a time convenient to that office.

2. Name and Address of Taxpayers.

Frozen Tundra Meat Co., Inc.
101 Lombardi Drive
Packers Grove, WI 55555-0000

3. Date and Symbol of Transmittal Letter.

Date: June 19, 2006

Person to Contact: Ira Agent

4. Tax Periods or Years Involved.

Form 1120 Corporation Income Taxes for the calendar years 2003, 2004, and 2005.

5. Unagreed Adjustments.

(a) The disallowance of auto/truck expenses in the amount of $42,150 for the year 2003.

(b) The disallowance of cost of goods sold in the amount of $56,320 for the year 2003.

(c) The additional allowance of depreciation for the calendar year 2004 in the amount of $18,052.

(d) The disallowance of officer's compensation in the amount of $1,740,906 for the year 2004.

(e) The additional allowance of depreciation in the amount of $10,831 for the year 2005.

(f) The disallowance of officer's compensation in the amount of $1,742,698 for the year 2005.

(g) The determination that the taxpayer was liable for the negligence portion of the accuracy related penalty under Section 6662(c) in the amount of $6,892 for the year 2003.

(h) The determination that the taxpayer was liable for the negligence portion of the accuracy related penalty under Section 6662(c) in the amount of $120,600 for the year 2004.

(i) The determination that the taxpayer was liable for the negligence portion of the accuracy related penalty under Section 6662(c) in the amount of $121,989 for the year 2005.

(j) The determination that, should it be finally determined that the taxpayer is not liable for the negligence portion of the accuracy related penalty for the year 2003, then in the alternative the taxpayer is liable for the substantial understatement portion of the accuracy related penalty under Section 6662(d) in the amount of $6,892 for the year 2003.

(k) The determination that, should it be finally determined that the taxpayer is not liable for the negligence portion of the accuracy related penalty for the year 2004, then in the alternative the taxpayer is liable for the substantial understatement portion of the accuracy related penalty under Section 6662(d) in the amount of $120,600 for the year 2004.

(l) The determination that, should it be finally determined that the taxpayer is not liable for the negligence portion of the accuracy related penalty for the year 2005, then in the alternative the taxpayer is liable for the substantial understatement portion of the accuracy related penalty under Section 6662(d) in the amount of $121,989 for the year 2005.

6. Facts Supporting Position.

(a) Taxpayer alleges that the auto/truck expenses paid or incurred in the amount of $42,150 for the year 2003 constituted ordinary and necessary business expenses deductible under Section 162 of the Internal Revenue Code of 1986 as Amended.

(b) Taxpayer alleges that the expenses paid or incurred in the amount of $56,320 in repairing certain trailers constituted ordinary and necessary business expenses deductible under Section 162 of the Internal Revenue Code of 1986 as Amended and did not constitute a permanent improvement or betterment made to increase the value of property.

(c) Taxpayer alleges that the additional depreciation deduction of $18,052 for 2004 is erroneous in that the taxpayer did not make a permanent improvement or betterment to a depreciable asset subject to depreciation.

(d) Taxpayer alleges that the amounts paid or incurred as compensation to officers during the year 2004 constituted an ordinary and necessary business expense deductible under Section 162 of the Internal Revenue Code of 1986 as Amended

¶1321

(e) Taxpayer alleges that the additional depreciation deduction of $10,831 for 2005 is erroneous in that the taxpayer did not make a permanent improvement or betterment to a depreciable asset subject to depreciation.

(f) Taxpayer alleges that the amounts paid or incurred as compensation to officers during the year 2005 constituted an ordinary and necessary business expense deductible under Section 162 of the Internal Revenue Code of 1986 as Amended.

(g) Taxpayer alleges that any underpayment that may have occurred for the calendar year 2003 was due to reasonable cause and not negligence or disregard of rules or regulations and that a penalty under § 6662(c) is inapplicable.

(h) Taxpayer alleges that any underpayment that may have occurred for the calendar year 2004 was due to reasonable cause and not negligence or disregard of rules or regulations and that a penalty under § 6662(c) is inapplicable.

(i) Taxpayer alleges that any underpayment that may have occurred for the calendar year 2005 was due to reasonable cause and not negligence or disregard of rules or regulations and that a penalty under § 6662(c) is inapplicable.

(j) Taxpayer alleges that there was no substantial understatement of tax for 2003. However, in the alternative, should it be finally determined that there was such understatement then and in that event, taxpayer alleges that it had reasonable cause for the underpayment and it acted in good faith.

(k) Taxpayer alleges that there was no substantial understatement of tax for 2004. However, in the alternative, should it be finally determined that there was such understatement then and in that event, taxpayer alleges that it had reasonable cause for the underpayment and it acted in good faith.

(l) Taxpayer alleges that there was no substantial understatement of tax for 2005. However, in the alternative, should it be finally determined that there was such understatement then and in that event, taxpayer alleges that it had reasonable cause for the underpayment and it acted in good faith.

7. Statement Outlining Authority.

All of the issues raised by the protest are of a factual nature and will be presented in further detail at the conference with the appeals officer.

8. Taxpayer's Representation.

(a) Seeno Evil and Hearno Evil are the representatives of the taxpayer named in the Protest. A Power of Attorney with respect to each of these years is on file with the Internal Revenue Service.

(b) Taxpayer's representatives have prepared this Protest on the basis of records and statements furnished by the taxpayer.

(c) Taxpayer's representatives have no personal knowledge of whether the statements of fact contained in this Protest are true and correct, but upon information and belief, they believe them to be true and correct.

Respectfully submitted,

Evil and Evil S.C.

Date: July 5, 2006

By_____

Seeno Evil

_____

Hearno Evil

¶1322 Exhibit 13-2

Form **870-AD** (Rev. April 1992)	Department of the Treasury—Internal Revenue Service **Offer to Waive Restrictions on Assessment and Collection of Tax** **Deficiency and to Accept Overassessment**	
Symbols	Name of Taxpayer	SSN or EIN

Under the provisions of section 6213(d) of the Internal Revenue Code of 1986 (the Code), or corresponding provisions of prior internal revenue laws, the undersigned offers to waive the restrictions provided in section 6213(a) of the Code or corresponding provisions of prior internal revenue laws, and to consent to the assessment and collection of the following deficiencies and additions to tax, if any, with interest as provided by law. The undersigned offers also to accept the following overassessments, if any, as correct. Any waiver or acceptance of an overassessment is subject to any terms and conditions stated below and on the reverse side of this form.

		Deficiencies (Overassessments) and Additions to Tax			
Year Ended	Kind of Tax	Tax			
		$	$	$	
		$	$	$	
		$	$	$	
		$	$	$	
		$	$	$	
		$	$	$	

Signature of Taxpayer		Date
Signature of Taxpayer		Date
Signature of Taxpayer's Representative		Date
Corporate Name		Date
By Corporate Officer	Title	Date

For Internal Revenue Use Only	Date Accepted for Commissioner	Signature
	Office	Title

Cat. No. 16896Q   **(See Reverse Side)**   Form **870-AD** (Rev. 4-92)

This offer must be accepted for the Commissioner of Internal Revenue and will take effect on the date it is accepted. Unless and until it is accepted, it will have no force or effect.

If this offer is accepted, the case will not be reopened by the Commissioner unless there was:

- fraud, malfeasance, concealment or misrepresentation of a material fact
- an important mistake in mathematical calculation
- a deficiency or overassessment resulting from adjustments made under Subchapters C and D of Chapter 63 concerning the tax treatment of partnership and subchapter S items determined at the partnership and corporate level
- an excessive tentative allowance of a carryback provided by law

No claim for refund or credit will be filed or prosecuted by the taxpayer for the years stated on this form, other than for amounts attributed to carrybacks provided by law.

The proper filing of this offer, when accepted, will expedite assessment and billing (or overassessment, credit or refund) by adjusting the tax liability. This offer, when executed and timely submitted, will be considered a claim for refund for the above overassessment(s), if any.

This offer may be executed by the taxpayer's attorney, certified public accountant, or agent provided this is specifically authorized by a power of attorney which, if not previously filed, must accompany this form. If this offer is signed by a person acting in a fiduciary capacity (for example: an executor, administrator, or a trustee) Form 56, Notice Concerning Fiduciary Relationship, must accompany this form, unless previously filed.

If this offer is executed for a year for which a joint return was filed, it must be signed by both spouses unless one spouse, acting under a power of attorney, signs as agent for the other.

If this offer is executed by a corporation, it must be signed with the corporate name followed by the signature and title of the officer(s) authorized to sign. If the offer is accepted, as a condition of acceptance, any signature by or for a corporate officer will be considered a representation by that person and the corporation, to induce reliance, that such signature is binding under law for the corporation to be assessed the deficiencies or receive credit or refund under this agreement. If the corporation later contests the signature as being unauthorized on its behalf, the person who signed may be subject to criminal penalties for representing that he or she had authority to sign this agreement on behalf of the corporation.

*U.S. GPO: 1992-617-016/49236

Form **870-AD** (Rev. 4-92)

¶1323 Exhibit 13-3 Not tested

CLOSING AGREEMENT ON FINAL DETERMINATION COVERING SPECIFIC MATTERS

Under section 7121 of the Internal Revenue Code, WEMALE Corporation, 123 Main Street, Milwaukee, WI 55555-0000, 39–0000000, and the Commissioner of Internal Revenue make the following agreement:

WHEREAS, the Taxpayer acquired all the assets of FEMALE Corporation (Seller) on December 31, 2003;

WHEREAS, the Taxpayer and Seller assigned a value of $1,500,000 to a covenant to compete agreement from the founder and sole shareholder (Seller Shareholder), which amount was treated by the Taxpayer as an intangible asset to be amortized over 15 years under Section 197 of the Internal Revenue Code;

WHEREAS, the Taxpayer and Seller Shareholder have entered into an employment contract whereby Taxpayer will pay Seller Shareholder $1,500,000 a year during 2004, 2005, and 2006 with Taxpayer having an option to renew at $750,000 a year for 2007 through 2011;

WHEREAS, the parties wish to determine (a) the amount to be allowed as an amortization deduction under Section 197 of the Internal Revenue Code for the year 2003 and succeeding years, (b) the amount deductible as compensation paid to Seller Shareholder for years 2004, 2005, and 2006, and (c) the treatment of payments to Seller Shareholder during the option years 2007 through 2011; and

WHEREAS, the parties have determined that the agreement set forth herein is in their best interests;

NOW, IT IS HEREBY DETERMINED AND AGREED, for Federal income tax purposes, that:

1. The amount to be amortized under Section 197 of the Internal Revenue Code by Taxpayer is $4,500,000, which consists of $1,500,000 which was paid to Seller and $900,000, $1,000,000, and $1,100,000 to be paid to Seller Shareholder during the years 2004, 2005, and 2006, respectively.

2. The amount to be allowed as deductible compensation to taxpayer for payments to Seller Shareholder for years 2004, 2005, and 2006 shall be limited to amounts paid reduced by the amounts to be treated as amounts to be amortized under Section 197 of the Internal Revenue Code as stated above.

3. Any amounts paid to Seller Shareholder by the Taxpayer in accordance with the employment contract should the renewal option be exercised for years after 2006 shall be allowed as deductible compensation.

This agreement is final and conclusive except:

(a) the matter it relates to may be reopened in event of fraud, malfeasance, or misrepresentation of material facts;

(b) it is subject to the Internal Revenue Code sections that expressly provide that effect be given to their provisions (including any stated exception for Code section 7122) notwithstanding any other law or rule of law; and

(c) if it relates to a tax period ending after the date of this agreement, it is subject to any law, enacted after this agreement date, that applies to that tax period.

By signing, the above parties certify that they have read and agree to the terms of this document.

Taxpayer (other than individual)

By _____ Date Signed _____

Title _____

Commissioner of Internal Revenue

By _____ Date Signed _____

Title _____

¶1324 Exhibit 13-4

Department of the Treasury
Internal Revenue Service
Stop 6800 (CS:TPR)
Kansas City MO 64999

In reply refer to: 0957921848
Aug. 28, 2000   LTR 854C
                200003 01 000   1
0957921848   01751

```
                Taxpayer Identification Number:  39-
                             Tax Period(s):  Mar. 31, 2000

                                      Form:  941

                          Kind of Penalty:  EFTPS
```

Dear Taxpayer:

Thank you for the inquiry dated June 20, 2000.

We are sorry, but the information submitted does not establish
reasonable cause or show due diligence. Therefore, we must deny your
request for penalty adjustment.

. Our records show that you were mandated to file electronically in
1999. Taxpayers were issued three letters informing and reminding
them of the requirement date. This is required for all tax forms.

. We will be sending you a current balance due notice in two to three
weeks.

If you want to appeal or give us more information, the following
will be helpful.

APPEALS PROCEDURES

If you have additional information and want your case to receive
further consideration by an Appeals Officer, please provide a brief
written statement of the disputed issues to the Service Center
Appeals Coordinator. It should include:

1. Your name and address;
2. Your social security number or employer identification number;
3. A statement that you want to appeal the findings;
4. A statement of facts supporting your position on the issues you
   are appealing,
5. If possible, a statement outlining the law or other authority
   on which you rely.

0957921848
Aug. 28, 2000   LTR 854C
200003 01 000   1
0957921848   01752

6. A copy of this letter.

The statement of facts, under 4 above, should be detailed and complete, including specific dates, names, amounts, and locations. It must be declared true under penalties of perjury. You may do this by adding to your statement the following signed declaration:

"Under penalties of perjury, I declare that the facts presented in my written protest, which are set out in the accompanying statement of facts, schedules, and other statements are, to the best of my knowledge and belief, true, correct, and complete."

If your authorized representative sends us the protest for you, he or she may substitute a declaration stating that he or she prepared the statement and accompanying documents and whether he or she knows that the statement and accompanying documents are true and correct.

Please send your response to:

Internal Revenue Service
Service Center Penalty Appeals Coordinator
Attn: Pete Seamans
        P.O. BOX 24551 (ADMIN.)
        KANSAS CITY MO 64999

The Service Center Appeals Coordinator will review your appeal information to determine whether the penalty should be removed or reduced. If your appeal can't be resolved immediately with the additional information, the coordinator will send your written statement to the Appeals Office serving your district.

REPRESENTATION

An attorney, certified public accountant, or person enrolled to practice before the Internal Revenue Service may represent you. To have someone represent you, attach a Form 2848, Power of Attorney and Declaration of Representative, (or similar written authorization) to your written statement.

Forms, instructions, and Treasury Department Circular 230, Regulations Governing the Practice of Attorneys, Certified Public Accountants, and Enrolled Agents Before the Internal Revenue Service, are available from any Internal Revenue Service office.

OTHER INFORMATION

                                                        0957921848
                                    Aug. 28, 2000   LTR 854C
                                            200003 01 000   1
                                        0957921848   01753

If taxes are overdue on your account, you will continue to receive
bills even if you appeal the penalty. If you decide to appeal,
you may pay the penalty to avoid further interest charges on the
penalty amount. If you appeal the penalty and the Appeals Officer
determines that you are not required to pay it, we will adjust your
account and send you a refund.

If you don't appeal, you may file a claim for refund after you pay
the penalty. If you want to take your case to court immediately, you
should request in writing that your claim for refund be immediately
rejected. Then you will be issued a notice of disallowance. You
have two years from the date of the notice of disallowance to bring
suit in the United States District Court having jurisdiction or in
the United States Claims Court.

If you have any questions, please call our Customer Service area at
1-800-829-8815 between the hours of 12:00 AM and 11:59 PM.
If you prefer, you may write to us at the address shown at the top of
the first page of this letter.

Whenever you write, please include this letter and, in the spaces
below, give us your telephone number with the hours we can reach you.
Keep a copy of this letter for your records.

Telephone Number (   )_____ Hours_____

                                    Sincerely yours,

                                    Patricia E. Manes

                                    Patricia E. Manes
                                    Chief, Taxpayer Relations Branch

Enclosures:
Copy of this letter
Envelope

¶1331 DISCUSSION QUESTIONS

1. The Appeals Office and the taxpayer reach a settlement in a tax case. A Form 870-AD is executed by the taxpayer and is accepted on behalf of the Commissioner of Internal Revenue. The taxpayer pays the tax and interest in full. The taxpayer, still believing that he deserves a better deal, comes to you and asks that you file on his behalf a claim for refund to recover the full tax and interest paid with the Form 870-AD. Should you file the claim for refund for the taxpayer?

2. Should the ethical and moral considerations of filing a claim for refund after the execution of Form 870-AD at the Appeals Office level be any different than with a Form 870 at the examination level?

3. Leroy Loser's return has been examined and the IRS has disallowed losses claimed in his chinchilla farm operation as an activity not entered into for profit. Leroy wants you to appeal the Revenue Agent's determination. He explains to you that his intention in entering into the venture was to make a profit and that it was only bad luck and poor economic conditions that caused him to show a loss for the last six years. During the entire six-year period, Leroy was also a highly paid consultant to a nationwide engineering firm.

    (A) Should Leroy attend the conference with the Appeals Officer "to help establish the profit motive?"

    (B) If not, how else can he "prove" his profit motive?

4. You have been assigned to be the mentor for Betty Beancounter, a summer intern. Betty has been asked to prepare a protest on behalf of a major client of the firm. The client received a 30-day letter from the IRS proposing a deficiency of $195,000, including interest and penalties. The proposed deficiency is based on the IRS's argument that the client should account for its manufacturing contracts on the percentage of completion method. The client argues that it is not subject to long-term contract treatment since the items they produce are not unique and normally require less than 12 months to complete.

    Both the tax and audit partners handling the client's matters have approached Betty on different occasions regarding their theory on preparing this protest. One partner believes that brevity is best. His theory is that a simple protest should be filed and then see what the appeals officer thinks before giving any more information. The other partner takes an exhaustive approach. She believes that a protest should contain all the arguments which could be presented and the case cites to support the arguments. Betty has come to you for advice in preparing the protest.

    Which theory should she adopt and why?

5. You have appealed a determination by the SB/SE that gains on various installment sales of real estate constitutes ordinary income rather than capital gain. Upon careful review of the case law, you conclude that the taxpayer has an overall 50% chance of prevailing in court. Explain how

you would present your case to the Appeals Officer. What approach would you utilize to guarantee that the SB/SE does not subsequently raise the same issue with respect to future installment payments on said sales.

CHAPTER 14

THE COLLECTION PROCESS

¶1401 INTRODUCTION

Revenue officers possess a very wide range of authority. They possess all the powers enjoyed by the Internal Revenue Service (IRS) to collect or abate delinquent accounts. They also have the authority to seize and sell property, impose and enforce major penalties for failure to comply with the revenue laws and recommend compromises of accounts for less than the balance due. A revenue officer may also make the initial recommendation whether to relieve property from the effect of federal tax liens or protect the government's interest by lawsuit or jeopardy assessment. In addition to these powers, revenue officers possess a wide range of investigative tools. However, the IRS must abide by provisions of the Fair Debt Collection Practices Act. For example, the IRS may generally not communicate with the taxpayer at an inconvenient time or place.[1]

The Internal Revenue Manual recognizes that at times taxpayers are not immediately able to pay the entire amount of tax that is due. Therefore, the manual states that installment agreements must be considered.[2] In many situations, a short-term installment agreement will be entered into, the payments made and the entire matter handled without any threats of levy on property or other enforced collection measures. The key to such a result is good communication with the revenue officer.

Generally, the initial step in the collection process is the assessment of tax against the taxpayer. The assessment may arise under various provisions of law, but usually results from a return filed by the taxpayer. Under Section 6201 of the Internal Revenue Code (the Code) and the accompanying regulations, the IRS has broad authority to assess taxes either determined by the taxpayer on a self-assessing basis or as a result of a subsequent examination of the return. However, with the exceptions noted,[3] no collection action can be taken until a tax assessment has been made.

After a return has been processed, the actual assessment of the tax itself is made by an assessment officer. The assessment officer signs a Form 23-C, Assessment Certificate. This record provides identification of the taxpayer by

---

[1] Code Sec. 6304.

[2] IRM Handbook 5.14.1.2.

[3] Under Code Sec. 6201(a)(3), the IRS has been given the authority to assess erroneous income tax prepayment credits. If the amount of income tax withheld or the amount of estimated tax paid is overstated by a taxpayer on a return or a claim for refund, the overstated amount can be automatically assessed in the same manner as a mathematical error under Code Sec. 6213(b)(1). Also, any income tax assessed against a child (to the extent the amount is attributable to income included in the gross income of the child solely by reason of Code Sec. 73(a)), if not paid by the child, may be considered as having also been properly assessed against the parents under Code Sec. 6201(c).

name and number, taxable period, the nature of the tax and the amount assessed. The "date of assessment" is the date that the Form 23-C is actually signed by the assessment officer. This date becomes particularly important in the collection process, since it establishes the beginning of the ten-year statutory period for collection and is the date on which the statutory lien arises.[4]

The first billing notice generally will come from the Internal Revenue Service Campus. The computer in the Campus will generate a notice of amount due and ask for payment within ten days. Often taxpayers will ignore the notice. They then receive a series of notices, each more threatening than the previous one. Eventually someone will contact the taxpayer, either in person or by telephone. Even at that point, the IRS will generally only ask for information as to how the taxpayer proposes to take care of the delinquency. If the taxpayer indicates that he or she cannot pay the full amount due at that time, the IRS will ask for a financial statement from which ability to pay the taxes can be determined. Often at this time, an installment arrangement will be entered into based on the payments that the financial statement indicates the taxpayer can afford.

¶1402 DOCUMENT LOCATOR NUMBER

The IRS uses a Document Locator Number (DLN) as a means to control returns and documents. A DLN is a controlled, 13-digit number assigned to every return or document that is input through the Campuses. DLNs are used to control, identify, and locate documents and appear on all notices sent to taxpayers, usually situated in the upper right-hand corner of the document.

The following is an example of a DLN, and explains how information is tracked by the specific digits contained in a DLN.

28 210-105-60025

These first two digits identify the IRS Campus; Campus codes are:

07=Atlanta	08=Andover	09=Kansas City
17=Cincinnati	18=Austin	19=Brookhaven
28=Philadelphia	29=Ogden	49=Memphis
89=Fresno[5]		

282 10-105-60025

The third digit identifies the tax class code for the documents. Some sample codes are:

    1=Withholding and FICA
    2=Individual
    3=Corporate and Partnership
    6=Fiduciary and Non-Master File (NMF)
    8=FUTA

---

[4] Code Sec. 6321.

[5] Older returns or documents have a district code rather than a Service Center or Campus code.

28210-105-60025

The fourth and fifth digits are document codes. Sample document codes are:

10=Form 1040
36=Form 1041
41=Form 941

28210-**105**-60025

The sixth through eighth digits indicate the Julian date with which the return was numbered.

28210-105-**600** 25

The ninth through eleventh digits indicate the block of 100 that contains the document.

28210-105-600**25**

The twelfth and thirteenth digits are the serial numbers—from 00 through 99—of the document with the block of 100.[6]

See Exhibit 14-1 at ¶ 1421 for a partial list of tax classes and document codes.

¶1403 CAMPUS BILLING PROCESS

The actual billing process for the IRS is done on a regional basis by the various Campuses. A taxpayer will receive a series of notices from the Campus requesting payment before a demand for payment is received. Unless unusual circumstances exist, there generally will be three notices requesting payment (see Exhibit 14-2 at ¶ 1422) before a final notice is received (see Exhibit 14-3 at ¶ 1423). The final notice is sent by certified mail and informs the taxpayer that the IRS intends to levy on his or her assets if payment is not made within thirty days.

If a balance due condition still exists on the account after the mailing of the fourth and final notice, a taxpayer's delinquent account (TDA) will be created by the Campus and transmitted to the field office. The TDA also serves as a case assignment to the revenue officer who then assumes responsibility for the account.

¶1404 TRANSCRIPTS

A taxpayer or representative may at times request a transcript or copy of the taxpayer's account maintained at the Campus to verify the balance due and to determine whether assessments and payments have been properly charged or credited to the account. Generally, the IRS will provide what is called a "literal translation transcript." This transcript must be ordered by the local office from the Campus and therefore is not immediately available. The local office has online access to a transcript with transaction codes rather than the literal translation of the codes. For a partial listing of transaction codes, see Exhibit 14-4 at ¶ 1424.

---

[6] IRS Pub. 1966, section 2.

¶1405 STATUTE OF LIMITATIONS ON COLLECTION

The IRS has ten years from the date of assessment to collect the amount of tax assessed.[7] During the period the tax may be collected by levy or by a proceeding in court.

After December 31, 1999, the IRS cannot request waivers to extend collection statute in connection with an installment agreement.[8] The collection statute will automatically expire 90 days after any period for collection agreed upon in writing at the time at which the installment agreement was entered. On the other hand, if a suit in a U.S. District Court to collect the tax is begun before the expiration of the ten-year period, and a judgment against the taxpayer is obtained, the period for collecting the tax by levy is extended until the judgment is satisfied or becomes unenforceable.

In order to insure the taxpayers are aware that they have a right to refuse to extend the limitations period for tax assessments, the IRS must notify each taxpayer of this right. More specifically, the IRS must notify the taxpayer that he or she may (1) refuse to extend the limitation period, or (2) limit the extension to particular issues or a particular period of time. These provisions are equally applicable to the assessment of additional taxes generally as well as a requested waiver of the statute of limitations entered in connection with an installment agreement. The Congressional Committee Reports accompanying the IRS Restructuring and Reform Act of 1998,[9] in relation to section 6502, provide:

> The statute of limitations on collection, however, continues to be suspended by various acts specified in Section 6503. For example, under Section 6503(b), if assets of the taxpayer are in the control or custody of any court, the statute is suspended until six months after the termination of those proceedings. Section 6503(c) provides that, if the taxpayer is outside the United States for a continuous period of six months, the statute of limitations is suspended until six months after the return of the taxpayer to the United States. Prior to December 31, 1999, the filing of an Offer in Compromise ("Offer") by the taxpayer represented an agreement between the taxpayer and the Internal Revenue Service that the statute of limitations on collection was to be suspended during the period that an Offer was pending or during the period that installments remained unpaid and for one year thereafter.[10] After December 31, 1999, the collection statute will only be suspended from the time the Offer is considered pending.[11] The term pending is the date it is determined processable, lasting until it is accepted, rejected or withdrawn, plus a 30-day period following rejection of the Offer. This period is further extended during the time a timely filed appeal of the rejection is being heard and considered.[12]

¶1406 FIELD COLLECTION PROCESS

The first step in the field collection process involves a referral of the account to one of the twenty-one automated collection system (ACS) sites, where the on-site computers determine which cases receive priority attention, monitor the case until full payment is made or until the case is referred to a field officer, and

---

[7] Code Sec. 6502(a)(1).

[8] P.L. 101-206, Act § 3461(c)(2).

[9] P.L. 105-206; section 6502 of the Code.

[10] See From 656 (Rev. March 2009).

[11] *Id.*

[12] See IRM 5.1.19.

display current information regarding the status of the account. A contact person from ACS will call the taxpayer to review sources from which payment can be made. The contact person can enter into an installment agreement or can initiate a levy action. If an installment agreement is entered into, the case will remain within ACS jurisdiction until the liability is paid or until there is a default on one of the installments. If it is not possible for ACS to contact the taxpayer, the case will be assigned to the field office.

Generally, a revenue officer assigned to the field office will attempt to contact the taxpayer for either a telephone interview or person-to-person interview. The purpose of the interview is to request full payment of the tax as well as to determine the means of payment and sources from which collection can be made if full payment is not possible.

> **Example 14-1:** When a taxpayer is requested to appear for an interview, he or she is usually asked to bring all documents necessary to resolve the tax matter. If the taxpayer alleges an inability to pay, for example, that individual will be requested to bring a copy of his or her latest income tax return as well as information necessary to establish his or her financial condition, such as earnings statements and records of outstanding debts. Revenue officers are instructed to conduct such interviews in a courteous and businesslike manner.

To aid the interview process, a number of forms have been developed for summarizing essential financial information necessary in evaluating collection cases. Generally, in smaller cases, a Form 433-A, Collection Information Statement for Individuals (see Exhibit 14-5 at ¶1425 and Exhibit 14-6 at ¶1426), is sufficient. This form provides information needed to determine how an individual taxpayer can satisfy a tax liability. It is generally used in connection with Form 433-B when the taxpayer operates a business. The Form 433-B, Collection Information Statement for Businesses (see Exhibit 14-7 at ¶1427), is used to determine how a business taxpayer can satisfy a tax liability. It includes such information as a profit and loss statement and balance sheet. In addition to these formal IRS forms, taxpayers can submit any similar forms that adequately reflect their true and complete financial condition. Each form should contain a statement to the effect that: "Under the penalties of perjury, I declare that to the best of my knowledge and belief the statement of assets, liabilities, and other information is true, correct, and complete." The taxpayer should sign and date the statement and indicate a title, if applicable.

If the taxpayer refuses to voluntarily produce financial information, the revenue officer may use the summons authority contained in Code Sec. 7602 to require the taxpayer to produce books and records. For these purposes a special summons, Form 6639 (see Exhibit 14-8 at ¶1428), is used. If the summons is to be served upon the taxpayer, the revenue officer need not obtain approval prior to issuing the summons. However, if the summons is to be issued to a third party, then supervisory approval is required.[13]

---

[13] IRM 5.1.17.8.

Following an interview with the taxpayer, the revenue officer prepares a Collection Information Statement. The information to be secured depends on the taxpayer's financial condition and the unpaid liability. For example, if the taxpayer has assets which can readily satisfy the liability, an income and expense analysis is unnecessary. The analysis of the taxpayer's financial condition should provide the revenue officer with a basis for deciding whether to secure a short-term payment agreement (sixty days or less), or whether a longer installment agreement is necessary. In analyzing the financial information submitted, the revenue officer is to determine the manner in which assets can be liquidated. If necessary, the revenue officer is to review any unencumbered assets, any equity in encumbered assets, any interests in estates or trusts and any lines of credit from which money can be secured to make payment. If such items exist, the taxpayer is advised of the possibilities of obtaining money from these sources and full payment is requested.

When this analysis does not disclose any obvious means to liquidate the liability, the taxpayer's income and expenses are to be analyzed. Take-home pay and net business income in excess of necessary living expenses are considered available for payment of the tax liability. In analyzing the taxpayer's expenses, the revenue officer is instructed to use prudent judgment in determining which are necessary or excessive living expenses. The dates that payments on loans and installment purchases terminate are noted so that additional funds can be made available to pay the tax liability. If the items on the Collection Information Statement appear overstated, understated or unusual, the taxpayer is to be asked for an explanation or substantiation.

In arriving at the value of assets, the revenue officer is to consider the forced sales value of assets. The forced sales value is the amount which would be realized as the result of a seizure and sale. The depreciated cost of the asset, its going concern value and other bases of valuation commonly relied on may not reflect the forced sales value of the assets. Because of this possibility, current sales of similar property in the locality or any recent appraisals made of the property are considered. If machinery and equipment of large size is involved, its state of depreciation or obsolescence and its movability are factors to be considered because they affect its marketability in the event of seizure.

¶1407 FEDERAL TAX LIENS

Notice of Federal Tax Lien. The IRS Restructuring and Reform Act of 1998 (the Act) requires the IRS to develop procedures whereby revenue officers generally obtain a supervisor's approval prior to issuing a Notice of Lien, serving a Notice of Levy or seizing property. Information with respect to adhering to these service procedures are to be subject to disclosure under the Freedom of Information Act. Revenue officers and supervisors are subject to disciplinary action for failure to adhere to these procedures. These procedures apply generally as of July 22, 1998, but not to the automated collection system until December 31, 2000.[14]

---

[14] Act Sec. 3421.

The IRS must notify the taxpayer within five business days after the filing of a Notice of Lien.[15] The Notice must include certain information, including the amount of the unpaid tax, the right of the person to request a hearing during the 30-day period beginning on the day after the five-day period described above and their right to an IRS hearing and Tax Court review (see Exhibit 14-9 at ¶1429 (Form Letter 3172)).

Withdrawal of Notice of Federal Tax Lien. The IRS is allowed to withdraw a notice of lien in certain circumstances.[16] A notice may be withdrawn if (1) the filing was premature or was not in accordance with administrative procedures; (2) the taxpayer entered into an installment agreement under Code Sec. 6159; (3) the withdrawal of the notice will facilitate the collection of the tax; or (4) it is in the best interests of the taxpayer and the United States as determined by the National Taxpayer Advocate. If the IRS withdraws a notice of a lien, it must file a notice of the withdrawal at each office where the notice of the lien was filed.

Filing of Federal Tax Lien. A "statutory lien" attaches to a taxpayer's property in an amount equal to the liability for the tax assessment due and owing.[17] The statutory lien arises automatically when three events occur:

1. An assessment of tax is made pursuant to Code Sec. 6203;

2. A demand for payment as prescribed in Code Sec. 6303(a) is made, unless waived by the taxpayer; and

3. The taxpayer neglects or refuses to pay the tax.

The lien attaches to all property and rights to property belonging to the taxpayer at any time during the period of the lien, including any property or rights to property acquired after the lien arises. The lien may be satisfied by payment or abatement, allowance of a claim, an audit adjustment or discharge in bankruptcy proceedings.

The statutory lien for federal taxes arises at the time the assessment is made, which is the date the summary record of assessment is signed by an assessment officer.[18] This statutory lien only gives the government a right to the taxpayer's property which is superior to that of the taxpayer. Until a Notice of Lien is filed, this statutory lien does not provide the IRS with a right to property which is superior to the rights of third parties who later acquire an interest in the property.

The form used by the IRS to file the notice of lien is Form 668, Notice of Federal Tax Lien (see Exhibit 14-10 at ¶1430). The Notice of Federal Tax Lien is required to be filed and recorded at various locations, depending upon the nature of the property affected. For example, in the case of real property, the notice is to be filed in the office within the state designated by the laws of such state for real property filings. In the case of personal property (whether tangible or intangible property), the lien notice is to be filed in the office within the state as designated by the laws of such state in which the property subject to the lien is

---

[15] Code Sec. 6320.   [17] Code Sec. 6323(j).
[16] Code Sec. 6321.   [18] Code Sec. 6322.

situated. If the state has not designated any particular office within its jurisdiction for filing, the Notice of Federal Tax Lien is to be filed in the office of the clerk of the United States District Court.

Priority of tax liens works as follows.[19] Until a lien notice has been filed, the tax lien is not valid against prior purchasers, holders of security interests, mechanic liens or judgment lien creditors. To keep the lien notice effective (if the limitation period on collection has not expired), the lien notice must be refiled within a one-year period ending ten years and thirty days after the date of the assessment.[20] Failure to refile the lien notice does not affect the validity of the lien itself. However, if a member of the "protected group" (holders of security interests, purchasers, mechanic lien creditors) acquires an interest in property subject to the tax lien after the filing of the prior lien notice but before the late refiling, that interest obtains a priority, as a result of the late refiling, to the same extent as if no tax lien notice had been filed. The tax lien will be subordinated to the interest acquired by the purchaser or other member of a protected group.

Even if the Notice of Federal Tax Lien has not been filed, the government's claim receives priority in some special cases (for example, if the taxpayer is insolvent or the estate of a decedent is insufficient to pay all the decedent's debts).[21] Furthermore, if no special rules apply, the first-in-time, first-in-right principle governs. This means that liens of equal standing have priority according to the date on which they were actually perfected.

Even though a proper Notice of Federal Tax Lien is filed, the lien is neither valid against certain purchases made nor against security interests arising after such filing.[22] These classifications are known as "super priorities" and include: (1) purchases of securities; (2) motor vehicle purchases; (3) retail purchases; (4) purchases in casual sales; (5) possessory liens; (6) real property and special assessment liens; (7) liens for small repairs and improvements of residential real property; (8) attorneys' liens; (9) certain insurance contracts; and (10) savings passbook loans. In addition to these "super priorities," certain other security interests may take priority over a filed tax lien if they result from financing agreements entered into prior to the filing of the tax lien.[23]

Discharge of Property from Federal Tax Lien. Often a taxpayer will have an opportunity to sell property or borrow against property to obtain funds to pay a delinquent tax liability. A problem created in this situation is to give clear title to the purchaser or to protect the security interest of the lender. Because the lien will attach to all property of the taxpayer, and because the lien has been filed before the contemplated transaction occurs, the transaction designed to give the taxpayer the funds needed to satisfy the tax liability can be threatened.

In such a situation, the IRS is authorized to discharge a portion of the taxpayer's property from the if either of the following circumstances exist:[24]

---

[19] Code Sec. 6323(a).
[20] Code Sec. 6323(g).
[21] 31 U.S.C. § 3713(a)(1).

[22] Code Sec. 6323(b).
[23] Code Sec. 6323(c).
[24] Code Sec. 6325(b).

1. The remaining property covered by the lien has a fair market value at least twice the unpaid tax liability plus the sum of all encumbrances that have priority over the tax lien;[25] or

2. There is paid, in part satisfaction of the liability secured by the lien, an amount determined to be not less than the value of the interest of the United States in the property to be discharged.[26]

The IRS is authorized to release a federal tax lien or discharge property from the lien if certain conditions are met.[27] The release of a tax lien operates to completely extinguish the lien, while a discharge operates only to discharge specific property from the reach of the lien. A lien can be released when an acceptable bond has been filed. The lien must be released no later than thirty days after the day on which any of these events has occurred (see Exhibit 14-11 at ¶1431 (Pub. 1450)).[28]

An administrative procedure exists whereby a third-party record owner of property against which a tax lien has been filed can obtain a certificate of discharge of the property from the lien.[29] To obtain such a discharge the owner must (1) deposit an amount of money equal to the value of the IRS's interest in the property (as determined by the IRS), or (2) furnish a bond acceptable to the IRS in a like amount. After receipt of the certificate of discharge, the record owner may bring a civil action against the United States to redetermine the value of the government's interest in the property.[30] Finally, the IRS has the authority to grant the discharge of specific property from the lien if the taxpayer agrees to have the proceeds from the sale of such property substituted for the discharged property and subject to the same lien (see Exhibit 14-12 at ¶1432 (Form 669-A) and Exhibit 14-13 at ¶1433 (Pub. 783)).[31]

The IRS is authorized to subordinate the federal tax lien to a new security interest if the proceeds of the new loan are paid over to the government, or if it believes that subordination of the tax liability will ultimately increase the amount realizable from the property in question.[32] To obtain a subordination of lien (see Exhibit 14-14 at ¶1434 (Form 669-D) and Exhibit 14-15 at ¶1435 (Pub. 784)), a written application must be submitted and must contain such information as may be required.[33]

A sale (or foreclosure) of property on which the United States has a valid tax lien does not extinguish the lien and is made subject to the lien unless notice of the sale is given to the IRS.[34] This rule is specifically extended to require notice of any forfeiture of a land contract.[35]

---

[25] Code Sec. 6325(b)(1).

[26] Code Sec. 6325(b)(2)(A).

[27] Code Sec. 6325.

[28] IRM 5.12.2.1 (05-20-2005). Under Code Sec. 7432, a taxpayer may bring a civil action for damages if the IRS knowingly or negligently fails to release a lien.

[29] Code Sec. 6325(b)(4).

[30] Code Sec. 7426(a)(4).

[31] Code Sec. 6325(b)(3).

[32] Code Sec. 6325(d).

[33] Reg. § 301.6325-1(b)(4).

[34] Code Sec. 7425(b).

[35] Code Sec. 7425(c)(4).

¶1408 ADMINISTRATIVE APPEAL OF LIENS

Taxpayers have a right to an administrative appeal if a federal tax lien has been erroneously filed on their property.[36] An appeal is permitted only if one of the following errors occurred:

1. The tax liability that gave rise to the lien was paid prior to the filing of the lien;

2. The tax liability that was the basis for the lien was assessed in violation of the deficiency procedures set forth in Code Sec. 6213;

3. The tax liability underlying the lien was assessed in violation of the Bankruptcy Code (11 U.S.C.); or

4. The statute of limitations on collection of the tax liability that gave rise to the lien expired before the lien was filed.[37]

No consideration will be given during an appeal to any questions regarding the correctness of the underlying tax deficiency.

The appeal must be made within one year after the taxpayer becomes aware of the erroneous filing. If the filing was incorrect, the IRS must expeditiously issue a certificate of release and, to the extent practicable, the certificate must be issued within fourteen days after such determination. The release must acknowledge that the filing was erroneous and was not the fault of the taxpayer. This statement is to ensure that the taxpayer's credit rating will not be affected by the erroneous filing.

The appeal must be in writing and should include a copy of the erroneous lien. It also must include the taxpayer's name, current address and identification number. The appeal should state why the lien is erroneous and, if the claim is made that the tax liability was previously paid, copies of receipts or cancelled checks showing full payment should be included.[38]

¶1409 LEVY AND SALE

A levy is defined as the power to collect taxes by distraint or seizure of the taxpayer's assets.[39] Through a levy, the IRS can attach property in the possession of third parties or payments to be made by third parties to the taxpayer. The IRS is required to give notice by certified or registered mail to the taxpayer thirty days prior to the time it levies upon any property (see Exhibit 14-16 at ¶1436).[40]

The notice of levy must describe in simple nontechnical terms:

1. The amount of unpaid tax;

2. The right to request a hearing during the 30-day period before the day of levy; and

3. The proposed action by the IRS and the taxpayer's rights with respect to:

a. the Code section relating to levy and sale;

---

[36] Code Sec. 6326.
[37] Reg. § 301.6326-1(b).
[38] Reg. § 301.6326-1(e).

[39] Code Sec. 6331(b).
[40] Code Sec. 6331(d).

¶1408

b. the procedures that apply to levy and sale of the property;

c. the administrative and judicial appeals available to the taxpayer;

d. the alternatives available which could prevent a levy, including installment agreements; and

e. the procedures relating to redemption of property and release of liens.

The appeal provisions are more fully discussed at ¶1414.

The levy authority of the IRS is far reaching. It permits a continuous attachment of the nonexempt portion of wages or salary payments due to a taxpayer, and the seizure and sale of all the taxpayer's assets except certain property that is specifically exempt by law. However, with the exception of wages, salaries and commissions, no "continuing levy" exists. The levy only reaches property held by the taxpayer or a third party at the time of the levy itself.[41]

A minimum amount of salaries and wages is exempt from levy.[42] The weekly amount of wages exempt from levy is equal to the taxpayer's standard deduction and personal exemptions for the taxable year, divided by fifty-two. If such wages or other income are received on other than a weekly basis, the exemption from levy will be determined in such a manner that the exemption will be comparable to what it would have been on a weekly basis. When a taxpayer receives a notice of levy upon his or her wages, that individual should be advised to file a statement claiming the number of exemptions from levy to which he or she is entitled. If that statement is not filed, the exemption from levy will be computed as if the taxpayer were a married individual filing a separate return claiming only one personal exemption.

A levy on salary or wages is often used by the IRS as a last resort when a delinquent taxpayer will not respond to notices or otherwise cooperate in the liquidating of a tax delinquency. Generally, when the taxpayer receives the notice of levy on wages, he or she will decide to cooperate with the IRS, file an appropriate financial statement and enter into a realistic installment arrangement. However, IRS policy is not to release the levy on the wages until at least one payment from the employer has been received. This policy can work a hardship on a taxpayer in certain circumstances.

Certain other property is exempt from levy such as wearing apparel, school-books, unemployment benefits, undelivered mail, certain railroad and service-related annuity and pension benefits, payments needed for child support, service-connected disability payments, welfare payments and job training program payments.[43] The Code further exempts books and tools of the taxpayer's trade, business or profession which, for levies issued after July 22, 1998, do not exceed

---

[41] Code Sec. 6331(b).
[42] Code Sec. 6334(d).

[43] Code Sec. 6334(a).

$3,125.00 in total value.[44] If the taxpayer is the head of a family, fuel, provisions, furniture and personal effects not exceeding $6,250.00 in value also are exempt.[45]

In order to prevent undue disruption to the occupants of any residence, the IRS may not seize any real property used as a residence by the taxpayer or any real property of the taxpayer (other than rented property) that is used as a residence by another person in order to satisfy a liability of $5,000 or less (including tax, penalties and interest).[46] In the case of the taxpayer's principal residence, the IRS may not seize the residence without written approval of a U.S. District Court Judge or Magistrate.[47]

In addition to these statutory exemptions, IRS policy as contained in the Internal Revenue Manual is to use discretion before levying on retirement income.[48]

Any person in possession of property or rights to property upon which a levy has been made shall, upon demand, surrender such property or rights to the IRS.[49] Anything which has been attached or upon which execution has been had under any judicial process need not be surrendered. Normally, the service of a levy and demand requires immediate surrender of the property or rights to property. However, as a result of numerous claims that bank account deposits seized by levy belonged to someone other than the taxpayer, Congress provided in Code Sec. 6332(c) that banks are not allowed to surrender a taxpayer's deposits until twenty-one days after service of the levy.

Any person who fails or refuses upon demand to surrender any property or rights to property subject to levy is personally liable to the United States in a sum equal to the value of the property or rights not so surrendered (not exceeding the amount of the taxes for the collection of which the levy has been made together with costs and interest). In addition, a civil penalty equal to fifty percent of the amount recoverable is provided where the holder of property fails or refuses to surrender it without reasonable cause.[50] A bona fide dispute over the amount of the property to be surrendered or the legal effectiveness of the levy itself constitutes reasonable cause.[51] When collected, the fifty-percent penalty, however, is not credited against the delinquent tax liability but is deposited as a collection of miscellaneous revenue.

The circumstances under which the IRS is required to release a levy are:[52]

1. The tax liability underlying the levy has been paid or collection of the tax has become barred by the statute of limitations;

2. Release of the levy would facilitate collection of the taxes;

3. The taxpayer has entered into an installment agreement under Code Sec. 6159 to pay the tax liability (unless such agreement provides to the

---

[44] Code Sec. 6334(a)(3). For levies issued before July 22, 1998, the exemption is not to exceed $1,250.00 in total value.

[45] Code Sec. 6334(a)(2). For levies issued before July 22, 1998, the exemption is not to exceed $2,500.00.

[46] Code Sec. 6334(a)(13)(A).

[47] Code Sec. 6334(a)(13)(B) and (e)(1).

[48] IRM 5.11.6.1.

[49] Code Sec. 6332(a).

[50] Code Sec. 6332(d)(2).

[51] Reg. §301.6332-1(b)(2).

[52] Code Sec. 6343(a).

contrary or release of the levy would jeopardize the creditor status of the IRS);

4. The IRS has determined that the levy is creating an economic hardship due to the financial condition of the taxpayer; or

5. The fair market value of the property exceeds the tax liability and release of the levy could be made without hindering the collection of the liability.

A levy will be released on the grounds of economic hardship if the levy causes the taxpayer to be unable to pay his or her "reasonable basic living expenses."[53]

A taxpayer who wishes to obtain the release of a levy must submit such request in writing to the appropriate IRS personnel.[54] The request must include the taxpayer's name, address, identification number and a statement of the grounds for release. It also should describe the property levied upon and set forth the date of the levy, the type of tax and the period for which the tax is due. The written request must normally be made more than five days prior to any scheduled sale of the property to which the levy relates. The Area Manager is required to make a determination promptly, and this generally should be within thirty days. In the case of a levy on personal property essential to the operation of a taxpayer's business, where such levy would prevent the taxpayer from carrying on his or her business, the Area Manager is required to provide an expedited determination of the taxpayer's request for release of the levy. This determination must be made within ten business days of receipt of the written request or, if later, receipt of any necessary supporting data.[55] If it is determined that release of a levy is justified, a revenue officer will issue a Form 668-D, Release of Levy/Release of Property from Levy (see Exhibit 14-17 at ¶1437).

If any property is actually seized by levy, the Area Manager is required to give the taxpayer immediate notice of the tax demanded and the description of the seized property. The IRS is also required to give notice to the taxpayer and to publish the time, place, manner and conditions for a sale of the seized property. The sale must take place not less than ten days and not more than forty days after the public notice. It must be by public auction or by public sale under sealed bids.[56] The owner of the seized property may request the IRS to sell the property within sixty days (or some longer period) after such request. The IRS must comply with the request for such early sale unless it is determined that to do so would not be in the best interest of the government.[57]

When property is seized to be sold for delinquent taxes, the IRS is required to determine a minimum bid price and also to determine whether the purchase of the property at that price by the United States is in the best interest of the government. If there are no bids at the sale that exceed the minimum bid price, and if the IRS has determined to purchase, the property will be sold to the United

---

[53] Reg. § 301.6343-1(b)(4).
[54] Reg. § 301.6343-1(c).
[55] Reg. § 301.6343-1(d).

[56] Reg. § 301.6335-1; Code Sec. 6335.
[57] Code Sec. 6335(f); see Reg. § 301.6335-1(d) for the procedural requirements for making a written request.

States at that price.[58] If the IRS determines not to purchase the property, the property can be released to the owner, although it will remain subject to the tax lien.

The taxpayer may reacquire[59] property before sale by payment of the outstanding tax liability and expenses. The taxpayer may also redeem real estate within a 180-day period after the sale by payment of the purchase price plus interest at the rate of twenty percent per annum.[60]

The IRS may return property to a taxpayer under certain circumstances.[61] These circumstances are the same as those under which a notice of a lien may be withdrawn.[62] The IRS is also required to provide a taxpayer the opportunity to appeal a levy or a seizure administratively.

¶1410 FORCED SALE AND HOMESTEAD RIGHTS OF NONDELINQUENT SPOUSE

The United States Supreme Court has held that state homestead laws do not exempt real property from a forced sale by the IRS to satisfy the delinquent tax liability of one co-owner.[63] The Court did temper the effect of this holding, however, by formally recognizing that District Courts may exercise limited discretion in ordering a sale and that the nondelinquent spouse is entitled to full compensation for the separate homestead interest of such spouse. Unfortunately, such compensation may be in monetary form and may not seem adequate to spouses required to move from their homes. The nondelinquent spouse, however, generally will have a property interest in the home and, thus, will be able to redeem the property during the 180-day period specified in Code Sec. 6337(b), assuming the spouse can obtain the financing to do so. When such spouse does redeem, he or she obtains an equity in the property up to the amount paid to redeem. Such equity will be a superior interest to the IRS lien. If both spouses redeem, the status of their equity following redemption *vis-á-vis* the tax lien is not clear.

¶1411 INNOCENT SPOUSE RELIEF

The Code substantially alters and expands the circumstances under which a person may qualify for "innocent spouse" treatment, which releases them from what otherwise would be a joint liability.[64] Generally, an "innocent spouse" election must be made within two years after collection activities begin.[65] "Inno-

---

[58] Code Sec. 6335(e)(1).

[59] Code Sec. 6337(a).

[60] Code Sec. 6337(b).

[61] Code Sec. 6343(d).

[62] See ¶1421, *supra.*

[63] *United States v. Rodgers*, 461 U.S. 677 (1983), 83-1 USTC ¶9374. Some courts have held that where state law creates an undivided interest in the house, one spouse cannot unilaterally convey his or her interest without the consent of the other, and thus the IRS may not sell the interest without consent as it steps into the shoes of the delinquent taxpayer. *Marshall v. Marshall*, 921 F.Supp. 641 (D.C. Minn.

1995), 96-1 USTC ¶50,122; *O'Hagan v. U.S.*, 1995 WL 113417 (D.C. Minn. 1994), 95-1 USTC ¶50,082; *Elfelt v. Cooper*, 168 Wis.2d 1008 (1992), 92-2 USTC ¶50,338. The Supreme Court has extended the result in *Rodgers* to recognize the ability of the IRS to levy on a joint bank account to satisfy tax delinquencies of one of the joint owners. See *United States v. National Bank of Commerce*, 472 U.S. 713 (1985), 85-2 USTC ¶9482. But see *I.R.S. v. Gaster*, 42 F.3d 787 (3rd Cir. 1994), 94-2 USTC ¶50,622. IRS could not levy a joint bank account because under state law the taxpayer could not unilaterally withdraw funds.

[64] Code Sec. 6015.

[65] Code Sec. 6015.

cent spouse" relief is now available for *all* understatements of tax (rather than only "substantial" understatements) attributable to erroneous items (rather than only *grossly* erroneous items) of the other spouse. A person seeking "innocent spouse" relief must still establish that, in signing the return, he or she did not know and had no reason to know of the understatement.[66] If the lack of knowledge is only as to the extent of the understatement, relief is available on an apportioned basis. The IRS is permitted to grant equitable relief to taxpayers who do not satisfy the stated tests.[67]

An individual may elect separation tax liability, despite having filed a joint return, if the taxpayers are (1) divorced or legally separated, or (2) have been living apart for more than one year.[68] This election must be made no later than two years after the IRS has started collection action. A request for equitable relief need not be filed within two years of the commencement of collection activity.[69]

The new "innocent spouse" provisions are applicable to any tax liability arising after July 22, 1998, and any tax liability arising on or before that date, but remaining unpaid as of July 22, 1998.

The Tax Court is granted jurisdiction to review IRS decisions regarding "innocent spouse" status and separate liability elections.[70]

¶1412 BANKRUPTCY PROCEEDINGS

A petition in bankruptcy acts as an automatic stay of any Tax Court proceeding and of any judicial or nonjudicial action for the collection of taxes. Jurisdiction to determine taxes lies with the Bankruptcy Court unless it lifts the stay. Generally, a claim for taxes is entitled to an eighth-level priority among competing claims in bankruptcy.[71] Further, if the tax is one for which an income tax return was due within three years of the date of bankruptcy filing, or if the tax was assessed within 240 days before the date of such filing, the debt is not subject to discharge in bankruptcy.[72] Discharge also is not available if the taxpayer made a fraudulent return or willfully attempted to evade the tax.

¶1413 TAXPAYER ASSISTANCE ORDERS

The National Taxpayer Advocate is now appointed by the Secretary of the Treasury. The duties of the Advocate are to (1) assist taxpayers in resolving problems with the IRS; (2) identify areas in which taxpayers have difficulty in dealing with the IRS; (3) propose changes in administrative practices of the IRS to decrease the aforementioned problems; and (4) identify potential legislation which might decrease taxpayers' problems in dealing with the IRS. In assisting taxpayers suffering significant hardships as a result of *how* the revenue laws are being enforced, the National Taxpayer Advocate may issue Taxpayer Assistance Orders.[73] Such hardships commonly occur during the collection process. The

---

[66] *Johnson v. Comm'r*, 118 T.C. 106 (2002).

[67] Code Sec. 6015(f); Rev. Proc. 2003-61, 2003-32 IRB.

[68] Code Sec. 6015(c).

[69] IRS Notice 2011-70.

[70] Code Sec. 6015(e)(1).

[71] 11 U.S.C. §507(a)(8).

[72] 11 U.S.C. §§523(a)(1) and 507(a)(8)(A). A similar rule applies where the assessment is for the Code Sec. 6672 penalty. See *United States v. Sotelo*, 436 U.S. 268 (1978), 78-1 USTC ¶9446.

[73] Code Sec. 7811.

local taxpayer advocate's office under the authority of the National Taxpayer Advocate, is primarily responsible for issuing such orders. The order may require the IRS to release levied property or stop any action, or refrain from taking further action, under *any* section of the Internal Revenue Code.

An application for a Taxpayer Assistance Order (TAO) should be made on Form 911 (see Exhibit 14-18 at ¶1438) and filed with the local National Taxpayer Advocate's office (formerly the problem resolution office) in the area where the taxpayer resides. The application may be filed by the taxpayer or the taxpayer's duly authorized representative. If filed by a representative, Form 911 should be accompanied by a Form 2848, Power of Attorney and Declaration of Representative, or other power of attorney in proper form.

An application for a TAO on Form 911, however, is not essential. National Taxpayer Advocate officers, as well as personnel in other divisions of the IRS, are directed to prepare Forms 911 on behalf of taxpayers in response to requests for assistance received by telephone, correspondence or personal contact. These informal requests for relief must meet certain basic hardship guidelines. However, if the taxpayer or the taxpayer's representative insists that the matter requires this form of special consideration by the problem resolution officer, a Form 911 will be prepared by the IRS personnel involved.

What constitutes a "significant hardship" warranting the issuance of a TAO is a very subjective determination which must be made on a case-by-case basis. Such hardship could include the exceptional emotional stress of a taxpayer in dealing with tax problems, the threat of a poor credit rating caused by erroneous enforcement action, gross disserve to a taxpayer, pending eviction, possible loss of job, significant personal emergencies or other equally serious situations. Imminent bankruptcy, failure to meet payroll and inability to buy needed prescription medication are cited as other examples of what may be considered to be significant hardships.

The regulations define "significant hardship" as a "serious privation caused or about to be caused to the taxpayer as the result of the particular manner in which the revenue laws are being administered by the Internal Revenue Service."[74] The Act now allows the National Taxpayer Advocate to issue a TAO if it is determined that the taxpayer is suffering, or is about to suffer, a significant hardship as a result of the manner in which the Internal Revenue laws are being administered by the IRS or if the taxpayer meets such other requirements as may be set forth in any future regulations.[75] Specifically, the National Taxpayer Advocate must consider among other things the following four specific facts when determining whether there is a "significant hardship" and whether a TAO should be issued:

1. Whether there is an immediate threat of adverse action;

2. Whether there has been a delay of more than 30 days in resolving the taxpayer's account problems;

---

[74] Reg. § 301.7811-1(a)(4). [75] Code Sec. 7811(a)(1).

3. Whether the taxpayer will have to pay significant costs (including fees for professional representation) if relief is not granted; or

4. Whether the taxpayer will suffer irreparable injury or a long term adverse upset if relief is not granted.

The TAO may not require any action or restraint that is not permitted by law. The order also may not be issued to contest the merits of any tax liability or as a substitute for any established administrative or judicial review procedure. A TAO may require the IRS, within a specified period of time, to take any action permitted by law which relates to collection or other tax matters to relieve a taxpayer's hardship. For example, a TAO may require the IRS to pay a refund to an eligible taxpayer who faces a hardship.

An application for a TAO filed by a taxpayer suspends the running of any statute of limitations affected by the action required by the assistance order. However, if the Form 911 is prepared by the IRS on the basis of an informal request for relief, and is not filed or signed by the taxpayer, the statute of limitations is not suspended.

The law authorizing the issuance of TAOs replaces earlier informal practices with a defined procedure for obtaining relief in certain hardship situations. It assures the taxpayer of a prompt response in accordance with strict time constraints established by the IRS for processing applications for such assistance orders.

¶1414 ADMINISTRATIVE AND JUDICIAL APPEAL AND REVIEW OF NOTICE OF LIEN OR LEVY

A person who receives a Notice of Lien or Levy[76] may, within 30 days, request a Collection Due Process Hearing (see Exhibit 14-19 at ¶1439 (Form 12153)) which is held by the IRS Office of Appeals.[77] The hearing must be conducted by an officer or employee who had no prior involvement with respect to that unpaid tax.[78] The appeals officer at the hearing must obtain verification from the IRS that the requirements of any applicable law or administrative procedure have been met. This would include but not be limited to a showing that the revenue officer recommending the collection action has verified the taxpayer's tax liability, that the estimated expenses of levy and sale will not exceed the value of the property to be seized and that the revenue officer has determined that there is sufficient equity in the property to be seized to yield net proceeds from sale to apply to the unpaid tax liability. If the seizure of assets is of a going business, the revenue officers recommending the collection action must thoroughly have considered the facts and circumstances of the case including the availability of alternative collection methods before recommending the collection action.

The taxpayer or an affected third party may raise any relevant issues at the hearing regarding the unpaid tax or proposed lien or levy including but not

---

[76] Code Sec. 6330(a).
[77] Code Sec. 6330(b)(1); Reg § 301.6330-1.

[78] However, a taxpayer may waive this requirement. Code Sec. 6330(b)(3). See CAP (Collection Appeals Program) at ¶1419, *infra*, and Exhibit 14-22 at ¶1442 (Collection Appeal Rights).

limited to appropriate spousal defenses (innocent spouse status), challenges to the appropriateness of collection actions, offers of collection alternatives which may include the posting of a bond, the substitution of other assets, an installment agreement, an Offer in Compromise, or challenges to the existence of the amount of the underlying tax liability for any tax period. The IRS Office of Appeals is to retain jurisdiction over any determination that it makes at a hearing. This includes jurisdiction to hold a further hearing as requested by the person who sought the original hearing on issues regarding (1) collection actions taken or proposed with respect to the determination and after the person has exhausted all administrative remedies, or (2) a change in circumstances with respect to such action which affects the determination.

If the hearing officer, after verifying that all the applicable laws are satisfied and considering all of the issues raised by the taxpayer, determines that the collection action balances efficient tax collection with the taxpayer's legitimate concerns, the officer may issue an order upholding the filing of the Notice of Tax Lien. For a determination made through October 16, 2006, the person subject to the Notice of Tax Lien may, within 30 days of the date of the determination, appeal to the Tax Court.[79] The Tax Court has generally upheld the IRS's action in Collection Due Process cases.[80] If a court determines that the appeal of a determination made through October 16, 2006 was to an incorrect court, a person shall have 30 days after the court determination to file an appeal with the correct court.[81]

The Chief Judge of the Tax Court may assign an appeal from a IRS determination regarding a lien or levy to be heard by a special trial judge and may authorize the special trial judge to make a decision of the court with respect to the appeal.

¶1415 ACTIONS TO ENJOIN COLLECTION

The Internal Revenue Code generally denies a taxpayer any right to interfere with the assessment or collection of taxes. Under Code Sec. 7421(a),

> [N]o suit for the purpose of restraining the assessment or collection of any tax shall be maintained in any Court by any person, whether or not such person is the person against whom such tax was assessed.

Despite the absolute nature of the statutory language used in Code Sec. 7421, the Supreme Court of the United States has ruled that an injunction against collection may be granted where "it is clear that under no circumstances can the government ultimately prevail"[82] and then only if a refund suit would be an inadequate remedy "because collection would cause irreparable injury, such as the ruination of the taxpayer's enterprise."[83]

---

[79] Code Sec. 6330(d)(1)(A).

[80] *Willis v. Comm'r*, T.C. Memo 2003-302; *Crisan v. Comm'r*, T.C. Memo 2003-318; *Van Vlaenderen v. Comm'r*, T.C. Memo 2003-346; *Goldman v. Comm'r*, T.C. Memo 2004-3.

[81] Code Sec. 6330(d)(1).

[82] *Enochs v. Williams Packing & Navigation Co., Inc.*, 370 U.S. 1 (1962), 62-2 USTC ¶9545.

[83] *Hillyer v. Comm'r*, 817 F.Supp 532 (M.D. Pa. 1993), 93-1 USTC ¶50,184. The court enjoined the sale of a lot containing the taxpayer's residence because he was unemployed and would suffer irreparable damage.

The right of taxpayers and third parties[84] to bring an action against the United States for civil damages stemming from reckless or intentional disregard of the statutory collection provisions has been expanded to include negligence on the part of a IRS employee. Claimants are required to exhaust all administrative remedies. The liability is limited to $1 million, except in the case of negligence where the limitation is $100,000.

¶1416 INSTALLMENT AGREEMENTS

Generally, when taxpayers claim inability to pay due to financial reasons, installment agreements are considered. The IRS is specifically authorized to enter into installment agreements if such agreements will facilitate collection of the tax liability.[85] Form 9465, Installment Agreement Request (see Exhibit 14-20 at ¶1440), may be attached to the return if the taxpayer cannot pay the full amount due when filing the return. However, before any installment agreements are considered, future compliance with the tax laws will be addressed, and any returns or tax due within the prescribed period of the agreement must be timely filed and timely paid.

There are a number of possible installment agreements. The IRS is required to accept the proposals of installment agreements under certain circumstances.[86] These "guaranteed installment agreements" must be accepted by the IRS if the taxpayer: (1) owes income tax only of $10,000 or less; (2) has filed and paid all tax returns during the five-year period prior to the year of the liability; (3) cannot pay the tax immediately; (4) agrees to fully pay the tax liability within three years; (5) files and pays all tax returns during the term of the agreement; and (6) did not have an installment agreement during the prior five-year period. Unlike the criteria for "streamlined agreements" (discussed below), the $10,000 limit for "guaranteed installment agreements" applies to tax only. The taxpayer may owe additional amounts in penalty and interest (both assessed and accrued) but qualify for a guaranteed installment agreement, so long as the tax alone is not greater than $10,000.

"Guaranteed installment agreements" may be granted by revenue officers. If a request for an installment agreement would require the extension of the statute of limitations, the request cannot be processed under the guaranteed installment agreement provisions.[87]

The second type of installment agreement generally calls for full payment within five years. These "streamlined installment agreements" may be approved for taxpayers where: (1) the unpaid balance of assessments is $25,000 or less; (the unpaid balance includes tax, assessed penalty and interest, and all other assessments—it does not include accrued penalty and interest); (2) the "streamlined installment agreement" must be fully paid in 60 months or prior to the CSED, whichever comes first; and (3) the taxpayer must have filed all tax returns that are due prior to entering into the agreement.

---

[84] Under Code Secs. 7433 and 7426(h).
[85] Code Sec. 6159(a).

[86] Code Sec. 6159(c).
[87] IRM 5.14..

Taxpayers may request an installment payment agreement by completing Form 9465, Installment Agreement Request (see Exhibit 14-20 at ¶1440). The IRS will normally notify the taxpayer within 30 days if the proposal is acceptable and a Form 433-D, Installment Agreement (see Exhibit 14-21 at ¶1441), will then be executed. For individuals, the penalty amount for failure to pay tax is limited to one-half the usual rates (one-fourth of one percent rather than one-half of one percent) for any month in which an installment payment agreement with the IRS is in effect.[88] This provision applies in determining additions to tax for the months beginning after December 31, 1999.

Section 3506 of the Act also requires the IRS, beginning no later than July 1, 2000, to provide every taxpayer who has an installment agreement[89] an annual statement showing the initial balance of the account at the beginning of the year, the payments made during the year and the remaining balance in the account at the end of the year.

If a taxpayer's request for an installment agreement is denied, the taxpayer will be informed of the rejection and the right to appeal it to the Office of Appeals within 30 days of the date of the rejection.[90]

Although it is the revenue officer's duty to insure that the interests of the government are protected during any extended payment period, the Act placed a number of restrictions on the IRS's ability to secure their interests. Certain levy restrictions have been imposed during the period that an installment agreement is pending and/or in effect.[91] No levy may be made on taxpayer accounts: (1) while requests for installment agreements are pending; (2) while installment agreements are in effect; (3) for 30 days after requests for installment agreements are rejected; (4) for 30 days after agreements are terminated; and (5) while an appeal of a termination or rejection of an installment agreement is pending or unresolved. Exceptions to this general rule allow a levy if a taxpayer waives the restrictions in writing or if the IRS believes that its collection is in jeopardy. If an installment agreement is pending and a levy is outstanding, the levy may be released but it is not required that the levy be released. If an installment agreement is approved and there is a levy outstanding, the levy must be released unless the installment agreement otherwise provides. For example, with the taxpayer's written consent reflected in the "additional conditions block" of Form 433-D, where a levy has attached to funds in the taxpayer's bank account and an installment agreement is prepared *before* the proceeds are received, the levy need not be released. Similarly, if a wage levy is to remain open while a taxpayer is making installment payments, such concurrence must be reflected in writing in the "additional conditions block" of Form 433-D in order to allow the levy to remain open until the liability is satisfied.

---

[88] Code Sec. 6651(h): The failure to pay penalty reduction is only applicable if the individual timely filed (including extensions) the return relating to the liability that is subject to the installment agreement.

[89] Code Sec. 6159.
[90] Code Sec. 6159(d).
[91] Code Sec. 6331(k)(2).

¶1417 AUDIT RECONSIDERATION AFTER ASSESSMENT

Often a practitioner will be consulted by a taxpayer faced with the collection of delinquent tax. In most instances, the revenue officer's job is to collect the amount of the tax shown as due. The revenue officer generally has no authority to reexamine the return and determine if the deficiency assessed was proper.

However, in those instances where the taxpayer has ignored a Statutory Notice of Deficiency or where there has been a breakdown in communications between the IRS and the taxpayer, the Internal Revenue Manual permits audits of returns after the collection process has begun. Such an audit is available to the individual only after having received a balance due notice and when one of the following conditions is present:

1. The taxpayer has not received any notification from the IRS prior to the billing;

2. The taxpayer has moved since filing the return in question; or

3. The taxpayer has not had an opportunity to submit required substantiation and now has the necessary documents or documentation.

Office audits can be obtained through employees assigned to the SB & SE (see ¶105) division who will review and evaluate information submitted by the taxpayer, including copies of the tax return and examination reports. If these employees determine that an audit should be made, the case is forwarded to a revenue agent for resolution. Collection efforts are suspended while the case is in examination.

¶1418 OFFERS IN COMPROMISE

History and Regulatory Framework

As early as 1831, the Treasury Department was authorized to compromise tax liabilities. This authority is currently vested in the Secretary of the Treasury pursuant to Code Sec. 7122,[92] and allows the IRS to enter agreements with taxpayers to settle tax liabilities for less than the full amount due. The IRS liberalized its policies on the use and acceptance of these agreements, known as "Offers in Compromise" (hereinafter "OIC") in 1992. IRS Policy Statement P-5-100 set forth the IRS's position on OIC. Later, to comply with mandate set forth the IRS Restructuring and Reform Act of 1998[93] that the IRS become more reasonable in its collection efforts, the IRS revised its Internal Revenue Manual (hereinafter "IRM") provisions that pertain to OICs.

More recently, major changes were made to OICs by the Tax Increase Prevention and Reconciliation Act of 2005 (hereinafter "TIPRA")[94] These changes have required the IRS to revise its OIC program further, and to make additional modifications to the IRM. These changes include a new mandatory application fee and mandatory payment terms for OICs, and a provision that if the IRS does not make a determination on an OIC within 24 months the OIC will be consid-

---

[92] 26 U.S.C. 7122.
[93] Pub. L. 105-206.

[94] Pub. L. 109-222.

ered accepted. TIPRA changes apply to all OICs received by the IRS on or after July 16, 2006.

Treasury Regulation 301.7122-1 authorizes the IRS to compromise tax liabilities on the following grounds, each of which will be explained below: Doubt As To Liability, Doubt As to Collectibility; and to promote Effective Tax Administration. Consistent with the regulatory authority, within the IRS, the IRS has issued Delegation Order No 5-1 (rev 2) in IRM 1.244 to delegate to the appropriate IRS personnel the authority to handle OICs. Finally, in Policy Statement p-5-100, the IRS sets forth policies covering when a liability will be compromised and why.

IRS Policy Statement P-5-100 states that the IRS "will accept an OIC when it is unlikely that the tax liability can be collected in full and the amount offered reasonably reflects collection potential. An OIC is a legitimate alternative to declaring a case as currently not collectible or as a protracted installment agreement. The goal is to achieve collection of what is potentially collectible at the earliest possible time and at the least cost to the Government."

Further, the Policy Statement states that "in cases where an OIC appears to be a viable solution to a tax delinquency, the Service employee assigned the case will discuss the compromise alternative with the taxpayer and, when necessary, assist in preparing the required forms. The taxpayer will be responsible for initiating the first specific proposal for compromise."

The Policy Statement notes that "the success of the OIC program will be assured only if taxpayers make adequate compromise proposals consistent with their ability to pay and the Service makes prompt and reasonable decisions. Taxpayers are expected to provide reasonable documentation to verify their ability to pay. The ultimate goal is a compromise that is in the best interest of both the taxpayer and the government. Acceptance of an adequate offer will also result in creating for the taxpayer an expectation of a fresh start toward compliance with all future filing and payment requirements."

Taxpayer Submission of an Offer in Compromise

As noted above, Treasury Regulation 301.7122-1 authorizes the IRS to compromise tax liabilities on the following grounds:

- Doubt As To Liability (hereinafter "DATL"). This basis for acceptance of an OIC exists where there is doubt that the underlying stated tax liability is owed;

- Doubt As To Collectibility (hereinafter "DATC"). This basis for acceptance of an OIC exists where there is doubt that the underlying tax liability can be paid in full; and

- Effective Tax Administration (hereinafter "ETA"). Traditionally, IRS personnel were instructed not to take into consideration economic or other hardship or "equity" when considering an OIC. This policy changed in 1999 and the authority for accepting an offer based upon hardship or equity was placed in the Treasury Regulation 301.7122-1 cited above. ETA offers will be accepted only in exceptional circumstances where a combination of factors or special circumstances, other than collectibles, are considered by the IRS to warrant acceptance of an offered amount. Among the factors that may warrant acceptance of an offer are age, illness, and assets of a type that liquidation would render the taxpayer penniless.[95]

Since DATL, DATC and ETA are the three bases upon which the IRS may compromise a liability, taxpayers must have one of these bases in order to submit a potentially successful OIC. Taxpayers must make clear the basis upon which their OIC is being offered, and must provide the type of documentation necessary to support the basis upon which their particular OIC is being filed.

Prior to July 16, 2006, no deposits were required when making an OIC. TIPRA made statutory changes for all OICs received on and after July 16, 2006, that require both an applicable fee, currently $150, and nonrefundable payment on the liability as part of filing each OIC. In light of TIPRA, the IRS considers the following types of OICs:

- Lump Sum Cash Agreement: Code Section 7122(c)(1)(A)(i) requires a non refundable payment of 20 percent of the offered amount, with the balance of the offered amount paid in 5 or fewer installments starting with when the notice of acceptance of the OIC is issued. Taxpayers can designate how the payment is to be applied to their outstanding tax liabilities.

- Short Term Periodic Payment: Code Section 7122(c)(1)(B) requires a nonrefundable initial proposed period payment. Periodic payments must continue to be made while the OIC is being evaluated or the IRS may consider the offer withdrawn. These agreements must be paid within 24 months from the date the IRS receives the OIC. Taxpayers can designate how the payment is to be applied to their outstanding tax liabilities.

- Deferred Periodic Payment: Code Section 7122(c)(1)(B) requires a nonrefundable initial proposed periodic payment. Periodic payments must continue while the OIC is under evaluation or the IRS may consider the offer withdrawn. These OICs must be paid within 25 months or longer, but in all events within the 10 year statute of limitations on collection. Taxpayers can designate how the payment is to be applied to their outstanding tax liabilities.

OICs are to be submitted on the most current version of From 656, Offer in Compromise.[96] The form 656 Booklet provides detailed instructions along with other forms that my be required depending on whether the OIC is being files based upon DATL, DATC or ETA. For example, a comprehensive financial statement detailing the taxpayer's assets, liabilities, income and expenses must accompany an offer that is based on DATC and ETA filings. Official forms for providing such financial information are normally used for this purpose. They are Form 433-A (Collection Information Statement for Wage Earners and Self-Employed Individuals) and Form 433-B (Collection Information Statement for Businesses). These two forms are not the ones most commonly submitted with an OIC. The $150 application fee and required payments, described above, must be

---

[95] IRM 5.8.11.   [96] IRM 5.8.1.8.1.

included, unless the taxpayer qualifies for the low-income exemption. Periodic payments are not required for an offer based on DATL.

Taxpayers must agree to all standard conditions of Form 656 and may not alter them.[97] The total liability must be clearly set forth and the monetary amount offered must also be clearly set forth and may not include amounts already paid or taken by levy.[98] The IRS expects the offer to be paid as quickly as possible with the payment dates clearly set forth and in compliance with TIPRA requirements.[99] All required signatures must be present.[100]

IRS Receipt of An Offer in Compromise

Most OICs are processed in one of two Centralized Offer In Compromise (COIC) units within the IRS, one in Brookhaven, New York and the other in Memphis Tennessee. OICs received in other parts of the IRS will generally be forwarded to the appropriate COIC. IRS field personnel who receive OICs from taxpayers with whom they are working will generally forward them to the proper COIC. Certain OICs are processed separately. Most DATL OICs, for example, are processes in a centralized DATL unit located in the Brookhaven Campus.

As an initial matter for COICs determine whether a OIC is processable and whether additional forms or information is necessary to perfect the OIC filing. Collection activity generally is suspended during the pendency of the offer if the offer is not deemed frivolous and there is not indication that the filing of the offer was solely for purposes of delaying collection or that a delay would jeopardize the government's interests.[101] For less complex OICs personnel in the COICs may work them to completion. The other COICs are sent out to various functions within the IRS, such as the collection field function, the examination function, and appeals, where the OICs are investigated and worked to completion whether that be acceptance or rejection.

In rare instances an offer may be rejected on public policy grounds even through the amount offered is otherwise acceptable. The rejection on public policy grounds is generally limited to situations where public knowledge of the accepted offer would have a seriously harmful effect on voluntary compliance with the tax laws. The Internal Revenue Manual dictates that such decisions should be rare. Rejections of this nature include cases not only of negative public reaction and undermining voluntary compliance but also cases of criminal activity involving a taxpayer submitting an offer or attempting to compromise tax liabilities arising from egregious criminal activity. The Manual, however, provides that an offer will not be rejected on public grounds solely because it might generate substantial critical public interest and/or a taxpayer who was criminally prosecuted for a tax or nontax violation.[102]

The Examination function is responsible for the investigation and processing of offers based solely on doubt as to liability. Frequently, such offers result from

---

[97] IRM 5.8.1.8.5.
[98] IRM 5.8.1.8.3.
[99] IRM 5.8.1.8.3.

[100] IRM 5.8.1.8.8.
[101] IRM 5.8.1.9.
[102] IRM 5.8.7.7.2.

the failure of the taxpayer to take advantage of opportunities to contest proposed adjustments before an assessment is made. Evidence which has not previously been submitted by the taxpayer to correct errors in the assessment will be considered by the revenue agent assigned to investigate the offer.

Collection division revenue officers have the responsibility for processing and investigating all Offers in Compromise based solely on doubt as to collectibility. They also have initial jurisdiction over offers based on doubt as to both liability anc collectibility.[103]

The IRS places Offers in Compromise into three categories: (1) cash offers, (2) short-term deferred payment offers, and (3) deferred payment offers. The amount considered acceptable for each type of offer is different. In each case, the amount of the offer must include the "quick sale value" (QSV) of the taxpayer's assets.[104] In addition, in each case the offer must also include the total amount the IRS could collect from available income of the taxpayer.[105]

Generally, the excess of the taxpayer's income over his or her expenses and current tax payment is what the IRS expects that it can collect. Expenses for housing and transportation are determined from the tables of "Collection Financial Standards" for specific geographic areas.[106] Other monthly expenses generally need to be justified on an item-by-item basis.

The Internal Revenue Manual now also included a tabled titled "Deferred Payment Offer Chart" which is based on the time remaining before the expiration of the collection statues and adjusted to reflect current IRS interest rates that are applicable to deferred payment offers of more than twenty-four months.[107]

Cash Offers. In the case of a cash offer, the offer amount must include an amount equal to forty-eight months of the "collectible amount" in addition to the quick sale value of assets. A short-term deferred payment offer requires that the offer amount will include sixty months of the "collectible amount" in addition to the quick sale value of assets, and that full payment will occur later than ninety days but within two years from acceptance.[108]

A deferred payment offer requires that the offer amount will include an amount (in addition to the quick sale value of assets) equivalent to the monthly "collectible amount" multiplied by the number of months remaining on the collection statute.[109] For deferred payment offers, a taxpayer can elect: (1) to make fully payment of the quick sale value of assets within ninety days of acceptance of the offer, and the amount the IRS could expect to collect during the lifetime of that statute; or (2) to make payment of a portion of the quick sale value of assets within ninety days of acceptance and the remainder of the quick sale value and the payment of the entire offer amount over the lifetime of the statute.

---

[103] IRM 4.18.4. Form 656 no longer allows combined OICs. Now a DATL offer must be filed on Form 656-L.

[104] Normally eighty percent of fair market value. IRM 5.8.5.4.1.

[105] IRM 5.15.1.11.

[106] See IRS website www.irs.gov.

[107] IRM Exhibit 5.19.7-10.

[108] IRM 5.8.4.3.1.

[109] IRM 5.8.4.3.1.

Generally, the manual supplement requires consideration of the filing of federal tax liens in the case of each type of Offer in Compromise and provides, that if liens are filed, they are released when the taxpayer satisfies the terms and conditions of the offer.[110] Furthermore, it also instructs IRS personnel to inform the taxpayer that interest accrues on the offered amount from the date of acceptance until it is paid in full.

The IRS is also to advise the taxpayer of his or her right to appeal any rejection of an Offer in Compromise.

¶1419 INTERNAL REVIEW WITHIN THE INTERNAL REVENUE SERVICE

Review of Offers in Compromise and Installment Agreements. The IRS must subject any proposals for an installment agreement and/or an offer in compromise that it is considering rejecting to an internal review. This IRS "self examination" must occur before communicating the rejection to the taxpayer.[111]

Appeal of Offers in Compromise and Installment Agreements. The right to appeal denials or termination of installment agreements and/or offers in compromise is a matter of right rather than administrative grace (see Exhibit 14-20 at ¶1440).[112] These appeals are governed by the Collection Appeals Program (CAP). Taxpayers who disagree with the decision of the revenue officer must first request a conference with a collection manager. If they are unable to resolve their disagreement, then consideration by the Appeals Office is made by completion of Form 9423, Collection Appeal Request (see Exhibit 14-23 at ¶1443). The appeal must be received by the collection office within:

1. Two days of the taxpayer's conference with the collection manager on appeals of liens, levies or seizures; or

2. Thirty days from the date of denial or termination of an installment agreement and/or an offer in compromise.

Decisions by the Appeals officer are binding on both the taxpayer and the IRS and are not subject to judicial review.

---

[110] IRM 5.8.4.9 and 5.19.7.3.9.2.
[111] Code Sec. 7122(d)(1).
[112] Code Secs. 6159(d) and 7122(d)(2).

¶1421 Exhibit 14-1

Partial Table of Tax Class and Document Codes

Form No.	Title	Tax Class	Doc. Code
CP2000	Proposed Changes to Income or Withholding Tax	2	54
CTR	Currency Transaction	5	15
SS-4	Application for Employer TIN	9	04
W-2	Wage and Tax Statement	5	11
W-4	Employee's Withholding Certificate	5	42
706	U.S. Estate Tax Return	5	06
709	U.S. Gift Tax Return	5	09
720	Quarterly Federal Excise Tax Return	4	20
730	Tax on Wagering	4	13
940	FUTA (Paper)	8	40
940	FUTA (Magnetic Tape)	8	39
941	FICA (Paper)	1	41
941	FICA (Magnetic Tape)	1	35
942	Employer's Quarterly Return for Household Employee	1	42
943	Employer's Annual Return for Agricultural Employee	1	43
990	Tax Exempt Organization Return	4	90
1040	U.S. Individual Income Tax Return	2	11
1040A	U.S. Individual Income Tax Return	2	09
1040X	Amended U.S. Individual Income Tax	2	11
1099-INT	Statement of Interest Income	5	92
1120	U.S. Corporation Income Tax Return	3	10
1120-S	U.S. Small Business Corporation Income Tax	3	16
1139	Corporation Application for Tentative Refund	3	84
4868	Automatic Extension of Time to File	2	17
5500	Annual Report of Employee Benefit Plan	0	37
5713	International Boycott Report	6	08
7004	Corporation Automatic Extension to File	3	04

¶1422 Exhibit 14-2

Department of the Treasury
Internal Revenue Service
KANSAS CITY MO 64999

Date of this notice: SEP. 11, 2000
Taxpayer Identifying Number   39-
Form.   941   Tax Period: JUNE 30, 2000

For assistance you may
call us at:

1-800-829-8815

..ıll

WE CHANGED YOUR RETURN -- YOU HAVE AN AMOUNT DUE IRS

     WE CHANGED YOUR EMPLOYMENT TAX RETURN FOR THE ABOVE TAX PERIOD. YOU MAY
WANT TO CHECK YOUR FIGURES AGAINST THOSE SHOWN BELOW:

```
ADJUSTED TOTAL OF FEDERAL INCOME TAX WITHHELD      $40,016.47
TAX ON SOCIAL SECURITY WAGES              46,753.27
TAX ON MEDICARE WAGES AND TIPS                    $10,934.23
ADJUSTED TOTAL OF SOCIAL SECURITY AND MEDICARE TAXES              57,799.96
TOTAL TAXES                                       $97,816.45
TOTAL TAX DEPOSITED FOR THE QUARTER               $97,717.38-
OVERPAYMENT FROM THE PREVIOUS QUARTER                   .00
OTHER CREDITS AND PAYMENTS                              .00
TOTAL CREDITS AND PAYMENTS                                        $97,717.38-
     UNDERPAYMENT                                                     $99.07
PLUS:*PENALTY                                      $.99
     *INTEREST                                    $1.03
       TOTAL AMOUNT YOU OWE                                          $101.09
```

WE MADE THE CHANGES FOR THE FOLLOWING REASON(S):
THERE WAS A DISCREPANCY IN THE AMOUNT REPORTED AS TOTAL FEDERAL TAX
DEPOSITS FOR THE QUARTER AND THE AMOUNT SHOWN ON OUR RECORDS.

THE FOLLOWING IS A LIST OF PAYMENTS WE HAVE CREDITED TO YOUR ACCOUNT FOR THE ABOVE
TAX AND TAX PERIOD.

```
DATE OF PAYMENT    AMOUNT    DATE OF PAYMENT    AMOUNT    DATE OF PAYMENT    AMOUNT
APR. 11, 2000    7,723.38   APR. 17, 2000    7,537.25   APR. 24, 2000    7,132.07
MAY  1, 2000     7,390.09   MAY  8, 2000     7,400.48   MAY 15, 2000     7,030.77
MAY 22, 2000     9,031.20   MAY 30, 2000     6,736.13   JUNE  5, 2000    7,102.16
JUNE 12, 2000    7,966.32   JUNE 19, 2000    7,130.67   JUNE 26, 2000    8,804.13
JULY  3, 2000    6,696.40   JULY 31, 2000      36.33
```

     TO AVOID ADDITIONAL FAILURE TO PAY PENALTY AND INTEREST, PLEASE ALLOW ENOUGH MAILING
TIME SO THAT WE RECEIVE YOUR PAYMENT BY OCT. 2, 2000. MAKE YOUR CHECK OR MONEY ORDER
PAYABLE TO THE UNITED STATES TREASURY. SHOW YOUR TAXPAYER IDENTIFICATION NUMBER OR
YOUR IDENTIFYING NUMBER ON YOUR PAYMENT AND MAIL IT WITH THE STUB PORTION OF THIS NOTICE.

IF YOU THINK WE MADE A MISTAKE, PLEASE CALL US AT THE NUMBER LISTED ABOVE. WHEN YOU
CALL, PLEASE HAVE YOUR PAYMENT INFORMATION AND A COPY OF YOUR TAX RETURN AVAILABLE.
THIS INFORMATION WILL HELP US FIND ANY PAYMENT YOU MADE THAT WE HAVEN'T APPLIED.

ABOUT YOUR NOTICE. YOU MAY CALL YOUR LOCAL IRS TELEPHONE NUMBER IF THE NUMBER
SHOWN ON YOUR NOTICE IS A LONG-DISTANCE CALL FOR YOU. ALL DAYS MENTIONED IN
THE PARAGRAPHS BELOW ARE CALENDAR DAYS, UNLESS SPECIFICALLY STATED OTHERWISE.

     $.99   PAYING LATE

WE CHARGED A PENALTY BECAUSE, ACCORDING TO OUR RECORDS, YOU DIDN'T PAY YOUR TAX
ON TIME. INITIALLY, THE PENALTY IS 1/2% OF THE UNPAID TAX FOR EACH MONTH OR
PART OF A MONTH YOU DIDN'T PAY YOUR TAX.

NOTE: EFFECTIVE FOR MONTHS BEGINNING AFTER DECEMBER 31, 1999, THE FAILURE TO
PAY TAX PENALTY (FTP) FOR INDIVIDUALS, WHO FILE A TAX RETURN ON OR BEFORE THE
DUE DATE (INCLUDING EXTENSIONS), IS LIMITED TO HALF THE USUAL RATE (0.25% RATHER
THAN 0.5%) FOR ANY MONTH IN WHICH AN INSTALLMENT PAYMENT AGREEMENT IS IN EFFECT.

                             PAGE 1

TIN   FORM: 941   TAX PERIOD: JUNE 30, 2000

IF WE ISSUE A NOTICE OF INTENT TO LEVY AND YOU DON'T PAY THE BALANCE DUE WITHIN
10 DAYS FROM THE DATE OF THE NOTICE, THE PENALTY INCREASES TO 1% A MONTH.
NOTE: WE WILL NOT REDUCE THE 1% FTP EVEN IF YOU FILED TIMELY AND HAVE A VALID
INSTALLMENT AGREEMENT.

THE PENALTY CAN'T BE MORE THAN 25% OF THE TAX PAID LATE. IF YOU THINK WE SHOULD
REMOVE OR REDUCE THIS PENALTY, SEE "REMOVAL OF PENALTIES - REASONABLE CAUSE."

—   REMOVAL OF PENALTIES

REASONABLE CAUSE. THE LAW LETS US REMOVE OR REDUCE THE PENALTIES WE EXPLAIN IN
—   THIS NOTICE IF YOU HAVE AN ACCEPTABLE REASON. IF YOU BELIEVE YOU HAVE AN
ACCEPTABLE REASON, YOU MAY SEND US A SIGNED STATEMENT EXPLAINING YOUR REASON. WE
WILL REVIEW IT AND LET YOU KNOW IF WE ACCEPT YOUR EXPLANATION AS REASONABLE CAUSE
TO REMOVE OR REDUCE YOUR PENALTY. THIS PROCEDURE DOESN'T APPLY TO INTEREST AND,
IN SOME CASES, WE MAY ASK YOU TO PAY THE TAX IN FULL BEFORE WE REDUCE OR REMOVE
THE PENALTY FOR PAYING LATE.

ERRONEOUS WRITTEN ADVICE FROM IRS

WE WILL ALSO REMOVE YOUR PENALTY IF:

 -YOU WROTE TO IRS AND ASKED FOR ADVICE ON A SPECIFIC ISSUE,
 -YOU GAVE IRS COMPLETE AND ACCURATE INFORMATION,
 -IRS WROTE BACK TO YOU AND GAVE YOU A SPECIFIC COURSE OF
  ACTION TO TAKE OR EXPLAINED WHAT ACTIONS NOT TO TAKE,
 -YOU FOLLOWED OUR WRITTEN ADVICE IN THE MANNER WE OUTLINED, AND
 -YOU WERE PENALIZED FOR THE WRITTEN ADVICE WE GAVE YOU.

TO HAVE THE PENALTY REMOVED BECAUSE OF ERRONEOUS WRITTEN ADVICE FROM IRS,
YOU SHOULD:

 -COMPLETE FORM 843, CLAIM FOR REFUND AND REQUEST FOR ABATEMENT,
 -REQUEST THAT IRS REMOVE THE PENALTY, AND
 -SEND FORM 843 TO THE IRS SERVICE CENTER WHERE YOU FILED YOUR
  RETURN FOR THE YEAR YOU RELIED ON ERRONEOUS ADVICE FROM THE IRS.

THE THREE DOCUMENTS YOU MUST ATTACH TO YOUR FORM 843 ARE:

 -A COPY OF YOUR ORIGINAL REQUEST FOR ADVICE FROM IRS,
 -A COPY OF THE ERRONEOUS WRITTEN ADVICE FROM IRS, AND
 -A NOTICE (IF ANY) SHOWING THE PENALTY WE CHARGED THAT
  YOU NOW WISH US TO REMOVE.

THE INTEREST RATES ON UNDERPAYMENT AND OVERPAYMENT OF TAXES ARE AS FOLLOWS:

PERIODS   PERCENTAGE RATES

PERIODS	UNDERPAYMENT	OVERPAYMENT
OCTOBER 1, 1988 THROUGH MARCH 31, 1989...................	11	10
APRIL 1, 1989 THROUGH SEPTEMBER 30, 1989.................	12	11
OCTOBER 1, 1989 THROUGH MARCH 31, 1991..................	11	10
APRIL 1, 1991 THROUGH DECEMBER 31, 1991.................	10	9
JANUARY 1, 1992 THROUGH MARCH 31, 1992..................	9	8
APRIL 1, 1992 THROUGH SEPTEMBER 30, 1992................	8	7
OCTOBER 1, 1992 THROUGH JUNE 30, 1994...................	7	6
JULY 1, 1994 THROUGH SEPTEMBER 30, 1994.................	8	7
OCTOBER 1, 1994 THROUGH MARCH 31, 1995..................	9	8
APRIL 1, 1995 THROUGH JUNE 30, 1995....................	10	9
JULY 1, 1995 THROUGH MARCH 31, 1996....................	9	8
APRIL 1, 1996 THROUGH JUNE 30, 1996....................	8	7
JULY 1, 1996 THROUGH MARCH 31, 1998....................	9	8
APRIL 1, 1998 THROUGH DECEMBER 31, 1998.................	8	7
JANUARY 1, 1999 THROUGH MARCH 31, 1999..................	7	7
APRIL 1, 1999 THROUGH MARCH 31, 2000...................	8	8
BEGINNING APRIL 1, 2000...............................	9	9

PAGE 2

¶1422

TIN   FORM: 941   TAX PERIOD: JUNE 30, 2000

BEGINNING JANUARY 1, 1999, THE INTEREST RATE WE PAY ON OVERPAYMENT OF TAXES, EXCEPT FOR CORPORATE TAXES, IS THE SAME AS THE RATE OF INTEREST WE CHARGE ON THE UNDERPAYMENT OF TAXES. THE LAW REQUIRES US TO REDETERMINE THESE INTEREST RATES QUARTERLY. FROM JANUARY 1, 1987 THROUGH DECEMBER 31, 1998, THE INTEREST RATE WE PAID ON AN OVERPAYMENT OF TAXES WAS ONE PERCENT LESS THAN THE RATE OF INTEREST WE CHARGED ON YOUR UNDERPAYMENT OF TAXES.

WE COMPOUND INTEREST DAILY EXCEPT ON LATE OR UNDERPAID ESTIMATED TAXES FOR INDIVIDUALS OR CORPORATIONS.

WE CHARGE A SPECIAL INTEREST RATE OF 120 PERCENT OF THE UNDERPAYMENT RATE IF:

- THE RETURN, NOT INCLUDING EXTENSIONS, WAS DUE BEFORE JANUARY 1, 1990,
- THE UNDERPAYMENT WAS MORE THAN $1,000, AND
- THE UNDERPAYMENT CAME FROM A TAX-MOTIVATED TRANSACTION.

WE CHARGE INTEREST ON PENALTIES FOR LATE FILING, OVER OR UNDERSTATING VALUATIONS, AND SUBSTANTIALLY UNDERSTATING THE TAX YOU OWE. ALSO, WE CHARGE INTEREST ON FRAUD AND NEGLIGENCE PENALTIES IF THE TAX RETURNS, INCLUDING EXTENSIONS, ARE DUE AFTER DECEMBER 31, 1988.

WE CONTINUE TO CHARGE INTEREST UNTIL YOU PAY THE AMOUNT YOU OWE IN FULL.

AFTER DECEMBER 31, 1990, THE LAW ALLOWS US TO CHARGE INTEREST AT THE UNDERPAYMENT RATE PLUS TWO PERCENT ON UNDERPAYMENTS OF MORE THAN $100,000 FOR LARGE CORPORATIONS.

        $1.03   INTEREST

WE CHARGED INTEREST BECAUSE, ACCORDING TO OUR RECORDS, YOU DIDN'T PAY YOUR TAX ON TIME. WE FIGURED INTEREST FROM THE DUE DATE OF YOUR RETURN (REGARDLESS OF EXTENSIONS) TO THE DATE WE RECEIVE YOUR FULL PAYMENTS OR THE DATE OF THIS NOTICE.

CORPORATE INTEREST - WE CHARGE ADDITIONAL INTEREST OF 2% BECAUSE, ACCORDING TO OUR RECORDS, YOU DIDN'T MAKE YOUR CORPORATE TAX PAYMENT WITHIN 30 DAYS AFTER THE IRS NOTIFIED YOU OF THE UNDERPAYMENT OF TAX. THIS INTEREST BEGINS ON THE 31ST DAY AFTER WE NOTIFY YOU OF THE UNDERPAYMENT ON TAX AMOUNTS YOU OWE OVER $100,000, MINUS YOUR TIMELY PAYMENTS AND CREDITS.

INTEREST REDUCED

IF WE REDUCE INTEREST THAT YOU PREVIOUSLY REPORTED AS A DEDUCTION ON YOUR TAX RETURN, YOU MUST REPORT THIS REDUCTION OF INTEREST AS INCOME ON YOUR TAX RETURN FOR THE YEAR WE REDUCE IT.

INTEREST REMOVED - ERRONEOUS REFUND

THE LAW REQUIRES US TO REMOVE INTEREST UP TO THE DATE WE REQUEST YOU TO REPAY THE ERRONEOUS REFUND WHEN:

- YOU DIDN'T CAUSE THE ERRONEOUS REFUND IN ANY WAY, AND
- THE REFUND DOESN'T EXCEED $50,000.

THE IRS MAY REMOVE OR REDUCE INTEREST ON OTHER ERRONEOUS REFUNDS BASED ON THE FACTS AND CIRCUMSTANCES INVOLVED IN EACH CASE.

ANNUAL INTEREST NETTING

EFFECTIVE JANUARY 1, 1987, THROUGH DECEMBER 31, 1998, THE INTEREST RATE WE PAID ON THE OVERPAYMENT OF TAXES WAS 1% LESS THAN THE INTEREST RATE WE CHARGED ON THE UNDERPAYMENT OF TAXES. AS OF JANUARY 1, 1999, THE OVERPAYMENT AND UNDERPAYMENT RATES OF INTEREST THAT WE PAY AND CHARGE ARE THE SAME, EXCEPT FOR CORPORATE OVERPAYMENTS. IF WE REFUND AN OVERPAYMENT WITH INTEREST AND WE HAVE TO INCREASE THE TAX AT A LATER DATE, WE GIVE SPECIAL CONSIDERATION TO THE INTEREST ON THAT ACCOUNT.

ON THE TAX INCREASE MADE AFTER THE REFUND, WE WILL CHARGE THE LOWER REFUND RATE OF INTEREST (UP TO THE AMOUNT OF THE REFUND) FOR THE SAME TIME PERIOD THAT WE PAID INTEREST ON THE OVERPAYMENT.

TIN   FORM: 941   TAX PERIOD: JUNE 30, 2000

REQUEST FOR NET INTEREST RATE OF ZERO

GENERAL RULE - IF YOU OWE INTEREST TO THE IRS ON AN UNDERPAYMENT FOR THE SAME
PERIOD OF TIME THAT THE IRS OWES YOU INTEREST ON AN OVERPAYMENT, YOU MAY BE
ENTITLED TO RECEIVE A NET INTEREST RATE OF ZERO (THE SAME RATE OF INTEREST
APPLIES TO YOUR UNDERPAYMENT AS YOUR OVERPAYMENT).

TO RECEIVE THE NET INTEREST RATE OF ZERO FOR INTEREST YOU OWED (OR PAID) THE
IRS, OR INTEREST THAT WE OWED (OR PAID) YOU BEFORE OCTOBER 1, 1998, YOU MUST
FILE A FORM 843, CLAIM FOR REFUND AND REQUEST FOR ABATEMENT. FOR MORE
INFORMATION ON THE FILING REQUIREMENTS FOR THE FORM 843, SEE REVENUE PROCEDURE
99-43, 1999-47 I.R.B. 579. REVENUE PROCEDURE 99-43 AND FORM 843 ARE AVAILABLE
ON THE WORLD WIDE WEB AT WWW.IRS.USTREAS.GOV.

TO QUALIFY FOR THE NET INTEREST RATE OF ZERO, THE PERIOD OF LIMITATION FOR
CLAIMING A REFUND OF INTEREST ON AN UNDERPAYMENT AND THE PERIOD OF LIMITATION
FOR CLAIMING ADDITIONAL INTEREST ON AN OVERPAYMENT MUST HAVE BEEN OPEN ON
JULY 22, 1998. GENERALLY, THE PERIOD OF LIMITATION FOR CLAIMING A REFUND OF
INTEREST ON AN UNDERPAYMENT IS 3 YEARS FROM THE TIME YOU FILED YOUR TAX
RETURN, OR 2 YEARS FROM THE TIME YOU PAID THE INTEREST, WHICHEVER IS LATER.
THE PERIOD OF LIMITATION TO REQUEST ADDITIONAL INTEREST ON AN OVERPAYMENT IS
6 YEARS FROM THE DATE OF THE REFUND.

YOU MUST FILE FORM 843 ON OR BEFORE THE CLOSING DATE OF THE LATER STATUE OF
LIMITATION PERIOD. MAIL FORM 843 TO:

U.S. MAIL
INTERNAL REVENUE SERVICE
NET RATE INTEREST NETTING CLAIM
P.O. BOX 9987
MAIL STOP 6800
OGDEN, UT 84409

OTHER THAN U.S. MAIL
INTERNAL REVENUE SERVICE
NET RATE INTEREST NETTING CLAIM
1160 WEST 1200 SOUTH
MAIL STOP 6800
OGDEN, UT 84201

FOR INTEREST YOU OWED THE IRS OR THAT THE IRS OWED YOU ON OR AFTER OCTOBER 1,
1998, THE IRS WILL TAKE REASONABLE STEPS TO IDENTIFY THESE PERIODS AND APPLY
THE NET INTEREST RATE OF ZERO. HOWEVER, TO ENSURE THAT YOU RECEIVE THE NET
INTEREST RATE OF ZERO FOR OVERLAPPING PERIODS, YOU SHOULD FILE A FORM 843
FOLLOWING THE PROCEDURES DESCRIBED ABOVE.

RETURN THIS PART TO US WITH YOUR CHECK OR INQUIRY
YOUR TELEPHONE NUMBER   BEST TIME TO CALL
(   )   -

AMOUNT YOU OWE......................$101.09

LESS PAYMENTS NOT INCLUDED.$_____

24   PAY ADJUSTED AMOUNT........$_____

I.I

670   00000010109

102
          INTERNAL REVENUE SERVICE
          KANSAS CITY MO   64999

200035 0709   09141-213-12192-0

¶1423 Exhibit 14-3

IRM 5.11.7-6
CP 90 (or 297) Final Notice, Notice of Intent to Levy and Notice of Right to a Hearing

Department of the Treasury
Internal Revenue Service

Notice Number: CP *[90 or 297]*
Notice Date:
[Social Security or Employer Identification]
Number:

CERTIFIED MAIL - RETURN RECEIPT

> Collection Assistance:
> xxx-xxx-xxxx
> (Asistencia en Español
> disponible)
> Caller ID: xxxxxx

Final Notice
Notice Of Intent To Levy And Notice Of Your Right To A Hearing
Please Respond Immediately

We previously asked you to pay the federal tax shown on the next page, but we haven't received your payment. This letter is your notice of our intent to levy under Internal Revenue Code (IRC) Section 6331 and your right to appeal under IRC Section 6330.

We may also file a Notice of Federal Tax Lien at any time to protect the government's interest. A lien is a public notice to your creditors that the government has a right to your current assets, including any assets you acquire after we file the lien.

If you don't pay the amount you owe, make alternative arrangements to pay, or request an appeals hearing within 30 days from the date of this letter, we may take your property, or rights to property. Property includes real estate, automobiles, business assets, bank accounts, wages, commissions, social security benefits, and other income. We've enclosed Publication 594, which has more information about our collection process; Publication 1660, which explains your appeal rights; and Form 12153, which you can use to request a Collection Due Process hearing with our Appeals Office.

To prevent collection action, please send your full payment today.

- Make your check or money order payable to United States Treasury.
- Write your *[Social Security (CP 90) or Employer Identification (CP 297)]* Number on your payment.
- Send your payment and the attached payment stub to us in the enclosed envelope. The amount you owe is shown on the next page.

If you have recently paid this tax or you can't pay it, call us immediately at the above telephone number and let us know.

The assessed balance may include tax, penalties, and interest you still owe. It also includes any credits and payments we've received since we sent our last notice to you. Penalty and interest charges continue to accrue until you pay the total amount in full. We detail these charges, known as Statutory Additions, on the following pages.

Enclosures:
Copy of this notice
Pub 594, IRS Collection Process
Pub 1660, Collection Appeal Rights
Form 12153, Request for a Collection Due Process Hearing
Envelope

CP 90 (Rev. 06-2005)

¶1424 Exhibit 14-4

IRS Transaction Codes

A transcript of a taxpayer's account with the IRS may contain numerous transaction codes. The following list will assist in interpreting such codes.

Code	Description	Code	Description
000	Establish an Account	350	Negligence Penalty
013	Name Change	351	Reversal of TC 350
014	Address Change	360	Fees and Collection Costs
150	Return Filed/Tax Assessed	361	Abatement of Fees and Collection Costs
160	Delinquent Return Penalty	420	Examination Indicator
161	Reversal of TC 160, 166	430	Estimated Tax Payment
166	Delinquent Return Penalty	459	Prior Quarter Liability
167	Reversal of TC 166	460	Extension of Time for Filing
170	Estimated Tax Penalty	470	Taxpayer Claim Pending
171	Reversal of TC 170, 176	480	Offer in Compromise Pending
176	Estimated Tax Penalty	481	Offer in Compromise Rejected
177	Reversal of TC 176	482	Offer in Compromise Withdrawn
180	Deposit (FTD) Penalty	488	Installment or Manual Billing
181	Reversal of TC 180, 186	520	IRS Litigation Instituted
186	Deposit (FTD) Penalty	550	Waiver of Extension of Collection Statute
187	Reversal of TC 186	560	Waiver of Extension of Assessment Statute
190	Interest Assessed	570	Additional Liability Pending
191	Reversal of TC 190	582	Lien Indicator
196	Interest Assessed	610	Remittance With Return
197	Reversal of TC 196	611	Remittance With Return Dishonored
270	Late Payment Penalty	612	Correction to TC 610 Error
271	Reversal of TC 270, 276	620	Installment Payment
276	Late Payment Penalty	621	Installment Payment Dishonored
277	Reversal of TC 276	622	Correction to TC 620 Error
280	Bad Check Penalty	640	Advanced Payment-Determined Deficiency
281	Reversal of TC 280, 286	641	Payment Dishonored
286	Bad Check Penalty	642	Correction to TC 640 Error
290	Additional Tax Assessed	650	Depository Receipt/FTD Credit
291	Abatement of Prior Tax	651	Invalid TC 650
294	Additional Tax/Reverses TC 295	652	Correction to TC 650
295	Tentative Allowance/Tax Decrease	660	Estimated Tax Payment
298	Additional Tax/TC 299	661	Estimated Tax Payment
299	Carryback Allow/Tax Decrease	662	Correction to TC 660
300	Additional Tax by Examination	670	Subsequent Payment
301	Abatement by Examination	671	Subsequent Payment Dishonored
308	Additional Tax by Examination	672	Correction to TC 670
309	Abatement by Examination	700	Credit Applied
320	Fraud Penalty	701	Reversal of TC 700 and 706
321	Reversal of TC 320	702	Correction to TC 700
336	Interest Assessed	706	Credit Applied
340	Interest Assessed	710	Credit From Prior Period
341	Interest Abated		

Code	Description	Code	Description
712	Correction to 710 or 716	800	Credit for Withheld Tax
716	Credit From Prior Period	806	Credit for Withheld Tax
720	Refund Payment	807	Reversal of TC 800 and 806
721	Refund Repayment Check Dishonored	820	Credit Transferred Out
730	Interest Overpayment Credit Applied	821	Reversal of TC 820 and 826
732	Correction to TC 730	826	Credit Transferred Out
736	Overpayment Interest Applied by Computer	830	Overpayment Transferred to Next Period
		832	Correction to TC 830
740	Undelivered Refund Check	836	Overpayment Transferred to Next Period
742	Correction to TC 740	840	Refund Issued
764	Earned Income Credit	841	Refund Cancelled/Credit to Account
765	Reversal of TC 764 and 768	842	Refund Deleted
766	Refundable Credit	844	Erroneous Refund Identified
767	Reversal of TC 766	846	Refund Issued
768	Earned Income Credit	850	Overpayment Interest Transfer
770	Interest Due Taxpayer	856	Overpayment Interest Transferred
772	Reversal of TC 770	960	Add Centralized Authorization
776	Interest Due Taxpayer	976	Duplicate Return
777	Reversal of TC 776	977	Amended Return Filed

Most other transaction codes append administrative data to accounts. A minus sign (–) designates a credit transaction.

¶1425 Exhibit 14-5

Form **433-A** (Rev. January 2008) Department of the Treasury Internal Revenue Service	**Collection Information Statement for Wage Earners and Self-Employed Individuals**

Wage Earners Complete Sections 1, 2, 3, and 4, including signature line on page 4. *Answer all questions or write N/A.*
Self-Employed Individuals Complete Sections 1, 2, 3, 4, 5 and 6 and signature line on page 4. *Answer all questions or write N/A.*
For Additional Information, refer to Publication 1854, "How To Prepare a Collection Information Statement"
Include attachments if additional space is needed to respond completely to any question.

Name on Internal Revenue Service (IRS) Account	Social Security Number *SSN* on IRS Account	Employer Identification Number *EIN*

Section 1: Personal Information

1a Full Name of Taxpayer and Spouse (if applicable)   1c Home Phone ( )   1d Cell Phone ( )

1b Address *(Street, City, State, ZIP code) (County of Residence)*   1e Business Phone ( )   1f Business Cell Phone ( )

2b Name, Age, and Relationship of dependent(s)

2a Marital Status: ☐Married ☐Unmarried *(Single, Divorced, Widowed)*

	Social Security No. (SSN)	Date of Birth *(mmddyyyy)*	Driver's License Number and State
3a Taxpayer			
3b Spouse			

Section 2: Employment Information
If the taxpayer or spouse is self-employed or has self-employment income, also complete Business Information in Sections 5 and 6.

Taxpayer	**Spouse**
4a Taxpayer's Employer Name	5a Spouse's Employer Name
4b Address *(Street, City, State, ZIP code)*	5b Address *(Street, City, State, ZIP code)*
4c Work Telephone Number ( ) 4d Does employer allow contact at work ☐Yes ☐No	5c Work Telephone Number ( ) 5d Does employer allow contact at work ☐Yes ☐No
4e How long with this employer *(years) (months)* 4f Occupation	5e How long with this employer *(years) (months)* 5f Occupation
4g Number of exemptions claimed on Form W-4 4h Pay Period: ☐Weekly ☐Bi-weekly ☐Monthly ☐Other	5g Number of exemptions claimed on Form W-4 5h Pay Period: ☐Weekly ☐Bi-weekly ☐Monthly ☐Other

Section 3: Other Financial Information *(Attach copies of applicable documentation.)*

6 **Is the individual or sole proprietorship party to a lawsuit** *(If yes, answer the following)*   Yes ☐ No ☐

☐ Plaintiff ☐ Defendant | Location of Filing | Represented by | Docket/Case No.

Amount of Suit $ | Possible Completion Date *(mmddyyyy)* | Subject of Suit

7 **Has the individual or sole proprietorship ever filed bankruptcy** *(If yes, answer the following)*   Yes ☐ No ☐

Date Filed *(mmddyyyy)* | Date Dismissed or Discharged *(mmddyyyy)* | Petition No. | Location

8 **Any increase/decrease in income anticipated** *(business or personal)* *(If yes, answer the following)*   Yes ☐ No ☐

Explain. *(Use attachment if needed)* | How much will it increase/decrease $ | When will it increase/decrease

9 **Is the individual or sole proprietorship a beneficiary of a trust, estate, or life insurance policy** *(If yes, answer the following)*   Yes ☐ No ☐

Place where recorded: EIN:

Name of the trust, estate, or policy | Anticipated amount to be received $ | When will the amount be received

10 **In the past 10 years, has the individual resided outside of the United States for periods of 6 months or longer** *(If yes, answer the following)*   Yes ☐ No ☐

Dates lived abroad: *from (mmddyyyy)* | To *(mmddyyyy)*

Form 433-A (Rev. 1-2008)   Page **2**

Section 4: Personal Asset Information for All Individuals

11   **Cash on Hand.** Include cash that is not in a bank.   **Total Cash on Hand** $

Personal Bank Accounts. Include all checking, online bank accounts, money market accounts, savings accounts, stored value cards (e.g., payroll cards, government benefit cards, etc.) List safe deposit boxes including location and contents.

Type of Account	Full Name & Address *(Street, City, State, ZIP code)* of Bank, Savings & Loan, Credit Union, or Financial Institution.	Account Number	**Account Balance** As of _____ mmddyyyy
12a			
			$
12b			
			$

12c   **Total Cash** *(Add lines 12a, 12b, and amounts from any attachments)* $

Investments. Include stocks, bonds, mutual funds, stock options, certificates of deposit, and retirement assets such as IRAs, Keogh, and 401(k) plans. **Include all corporations, partnerships, limited liability companies or other business entities in which the individual is an officer, director, owner, member, or otherwise has a financial interest.**

Type of Investment or Financial Interest	Full Name & Address *(Street, City, State, ZIP code)* of Company	Current Value	Loan Balance (if applicable) As of _____ mmddyyyy	**Equity** Value Minus Loan
13a				
	Phone	$	$	$
13b				
	Phone	$	$	$
13c				
	Phone	$	$	$

13d   **Total Equity** *(Add lines 13a through 13c and amounts from any attachments)* $

Available Credit. List bank issued credit cards with available credit. Full Name & Address *(Street, City, State, ZIP code)* of Credit Institution	Credit Limit	Amount Owed As of _____ mmddyyyy	**Available Credit** As of _____ mmddyyyy
14a			
Acct No.:	$	$	$
14b			
Acct No.:	$	$	$

14c   **Total Available Credit** *(Add lines 14a, 14b and amounts from any attachments)* $

15a   **Life Insurance.** Does the individual have life insurance with a cash value (Term Life insurance does not have a cash value.)
     ☐ **Yes** ☐ **No**   If **Yes** complete blocks 15b through 15f for each policy:

15b Name and Address of Insurance Company(ies):		
15c Policy Number(s)		
15d Owner of Policy		
15e Current Cash Value	$ $	$
15f Outstanding Loan Balance	$ $	$

15g   **Total Available Cash.** *(Subtract amounts on line 15f from line 15e and include amounts from any attachments)* $

Form **433-A** (Rev. 1-2008)

Form 433-A (Rev. 1-2008)   Page **3**

16   **In the past 10 years, have any assets been transferred by the individual for less than full value**   Yes ☐   No ☐
(If yes, answer the following. If no, skip to 17a)

List Asset	Value at Time of Transfer	Date Transferred *(mmddyyyy)*	To Whom or Where was it Transferred
	$		

Real Property Owned, Rented, and Leased. Include all real property and land contracts.

	Purchase/Lease Date *(mmddyyyy)*	Current Fair Market Value *(FMV)*	Current Loan Balance	Amount of Monthly Payment	Date of Final Payment *(mmddyyyy)*	**Equity** FMV Minus Loan
17a Property Description		$	$	$		$
Location *(Street, City, State, ZIP code)* and County			Lender/Lessor/Landlord Name, Address, *(Street, City, State, ZIP code)* and Phone			
17b Property Description		$	$	$		$
Location *(Street, City, State, ZIP code)* and County			Lender/Lessor/Landlord Name, Address, *(Street, City, State, ZIP code)* and Phone			

17c   **Total Equity** *(Add lines 17a, 17b and amounts from any attachments)* $

Personal Vehicles Leased and Purchased. Include boats, RVs, motorcycles, trailers, etc.

Description *(Year, Mileage, Make, Model)*		Purchase/Lease Date *(mmddyyyy)*	Current Fair Market Value *(FMV)*	Current Loan Balance	Amount of Monthly Payment	Date of Final Payment *(mmddyyyy)*	**Equity** FMV Minus Loan
18a Year	Mileage		$	$	$		$
Make	Model	Lender/Lessor Name, Address, *(Street, City, State, ZIP code)* and Phone					
18b Year	Mileage		$	$	$		$
Make	Model	Lender/Lessor Name, Address, *(Street, City, State, ZIP code)* and Phone					

18c   **Total Equity** *(Add lines 18a, 18b and amounts from any attachments)* $

Personal Assets. Include all furniture, personal effects, artwork, jewelry, collections *(coins, guns, etc.)*, antiques or other assets.

	Purchase/Lease Date *(mmddyyyy)*	Current Fair Market Value *(FMV)*	Current Loan Balance	Amount of Monthly Payment	Date of Final Payment *(mmddyyyy)*	**Equity** FMV Minus Loan
19a Property Description		$	$	$		$
Location *(Street, City, State, ZIP code)* and County			Lender/Lessor Name, Address, *(Street, City, State, ZIP code)* and Phone			
19b Property Description		$	$	$		$
Location *(Street, City, State, ZIP code)* and County			Lender/Lessor Name, Address, *(Street, City, State, ZIP code)* and Phone			

19c   **Total Equity** *(Add lines 19a, 19b and amounts from any attachments)* $

Form **433-A** (Rev. 1-2008)

Form 433-A (Rev. 1-2008)   Page **4**

If the taxpayer is self-employed, sections 5 and 6 must be completed before continuing.

Monthly Income/Expense Statement *(For additional information, refer to Publication 1854.)*

	Total Income			Total Living Expenses		IRS USE ONLY
	Source	Gross Monthly		Expense Items [5]	Actual Monthly	Allowable Expenses
20	Wages *(Taxpayer)* [1]	$	33	Food, Clothing, and Misc. [6]	$	
21	Wages *(Spouse)* [1]	$	34	Housing and Utilities [7]	$	
22	Interest - Dividends	$	35	Vehicle Ownership Costs [8]	$	
23	Net Business Income [2]	$	36	Vehicle Operating Costs [9]	$	
24	Net Rental Income [3]	$	37	Public Transportation [10]	$	
25	Distributions [4]	$	38	Health Insurance	$	
26	Pension/Social Security *(Taxpayer)*	$	39	Out of Pocket Health Care Costs [11]	$	
27	Pension/Social Security *(Spouse)*	$	40	Court Ordered Payments	$	
28	Child Support	$	41	Child/Dependent Care	$	
29	Alimony	$	42	Life insurance	$	
30	Other (Rent subsidy, Oil credit, etc.)	$	43	Taxes *(Income and FICA)*	$	
31	Other	$	44	Other Secured Debts (Attach list)	$	
32	**Total Income** *(add lines 20-31)*	$	45	**Total Living Expenses** *(add lines 33-44)*	$	

1. **Wages, salaries, pensions, and social security:** Enter gross monthly wages and/or salaries. Do not deduct withholding or allotments taken out of pay, such as insurance payments, credit union deductions, car payments, etc. To calculate the gross monthly wages and/or salaries:
   If paid weekly - multiply weekly gross wages by 4.3. Example: $425.89 x 4.3 = $1,831.33
   If paid biweekly (every 2 weeks) - multiply biweekly gross wages by 2.17. Example: $972.45 x 2.17 = $2,110.22
   If paid semimonthly (twice each month) - multiply semimonthly gross wages by 2. Example: $856.23 x 2 = $1,712.46

2. **Net Income from Business:** Enter monthly net business income. This is the amount earned after ordinary and necessary monthly business expenses are paid. **This figure is the amount from page 6, line 82.** If the net business income is a loss, enter "0". Do not enter a negative number. If this amount is more or less than previous years, attach an explanation.

3. **Net Rental Income:** Enter monthly net rental income. This is the amount earned after ordinary and necessary monthly rental expenses are paid. Do not include deductions for depreciation or depletion. If the net rental income is a loss, enter "0". Do not enter a negative number.

4. **Distributions:** Enter the total distributions from partnerships and subchapter S corporations reported on Schedule K-1, and from limited liability companies reported on Form 1040, Schedule C, D or E.

5. **Expenses not generally allowed:** We generally do not allow tuition for private schools, public or private college expenses, charitable contributions, voluntary retirement contributions, payments on unsecured debts such as credit card bills, cable television and other similar expenses. However, we may allow these expenses if it is proven that they are necessary for the health and welfare of the individual or family or for the production of income.

6. **Food, Clothing, and Misc.:** Total of clothing, food, housekeeping supplies, and personal care products for one month.

7. **Housing and Utilities:** For principal residence: Total of rent or mortgage payment. Add the average monthly expenses for the following: property taxes, home owner's or renter's insurance, maintenance, dues, fees, and utilities. Utilities include gas, electricity, water, fuel, oil, other fuels, trash collection, telephone, and cell phone.

8. **Vehicle Ownership Costs:** Total of monthly lease or purchase/loan payments.

9. **Vehicle Operating Costs:** Total of maintenance, repairs, insurance, fuel, registrations, licenses, inspections, parking, and tolls for one month.

10. **Public Transportation:** Total of monthly fares for mass transit (e.g., bus, train, ferry, taxi, etc.)

11. **Out of Pocket Health Care Costs:** Monthly total of medical services, prescription drugs and medical supplies (e.g., eyeglasses, hearing aids, etc.)

Certification: *Under penalties of perjury, I declare that to the best of my knowledge and belief this statement of assets, liabilities, and other information is true, correct, and complete.*

Taxpayer's Signature	Spouse's Signature	Date

Attachments Required for Wage Earners and Self-Employed Individuals:
Copies of the following items for the last 3 months from the date this form is submitted (check all attached items):

☐ Income - Earnings statements, pay stubs, etc. from each employer, pension/social security/other income, self employment income (commissions, invoices, sales records, etc.).

☐ Banks, Investments, and Life Insurance - Statements for all money market, brokerage, checking and savings accounts, certificates of deposit, IRA, stocks/bonds, and life insurance policies with a cash value.

☐ Assets - Statements from lenders on loans, monthly payments, payoffs, and balances for all personal and business assets. Include copies of UCC financing statements and accountant's depreciation schedules.

☐ Expenses - Bills or statements for monthly recurring expenses of utilities, rent, insurance, property taxes, phone and cell phone, insurance premiums, court orders requiring payments (child support, alimony, etc.), other out of pocket expenses.

☐ Other - credit card statements, profit and loss statements, all loan payoffs, etc.

☐ A copy of last year's Form 1040 with all attachments. Include all Schedules K-1 from Form 1120S or Form 1065, as applicable.

Form **433-A** (Rev. 1-2008)

Form 433-A (Rev. 1-2008)

Sections 5 and 6 must be completed only if the taxpayer is SELF-EMPLOYED.

Section 5: Business Information

46   Is the business a sole proprietorship (filing Schedule C)   ☐   Yes, Continue with Sections 5 and 6.   ☐   No, Complete Form 433-B.
All other business entities, including limited liability companies, partnerships or corporations, must complete Form 433-B.

47 Business Name	48 Employer Identification Number	49 Type of Business
		Federal Contractor ☐ Yes ☐ No
50 Business Website	51 Total Number of Employees	52a Average Gross Monthly Payroll
		52b Frequency of Tax Deposits

53   Does the business engage in e-Commerce (Internet sales)   ☐ Yes ☐ No

Payment Processor (e.g., PayPal, Authorize.net, Google Checkout, etc.) Name & Address (Street, City, State, ZIP code)	Payment Processor Account Number
54a	
54b	

Credit Cards Accepted by the Business.

Credit Card	Merchant Account Number	Merchant Account Provider, Name & Address (Street, City, State, ZIP code)
55a		
55b		
55c		

56   **Business Cash on Hand.** Include cash that is not in a bank.   **Total Cash on Hand** $

Business Bank Accounts. Include checking accounts, online bank accounts, money market accounts, savings accounts, and stored value cards (e.g. payroll cards, government benefit cards, etc.) *Report Personal Accounts in Section 4.*

Type of Account	Full name & Address (Street, City, State, ZIP code) of Bank, Savings & Loan, Credit Union or Financial Institution.	Account Number	Account Balance As of _____ mmddyyyy
57a			
57b			$
			$

57c   **Total Cash in Banks** *(Add lines 57a, 57b and amounts from any attachments)* $

Accounts/Notes Receivable. Include e-payment accounts receivable and factoring companies, and any bartering or online auction accounts. *(List all contracts separately, including contracts awarded, but not started.)* **Include Federal Government Contracts.**

Accounts/Notes Receivable & Address (Street, City, State, ZIP code)	Status (e.g., age, factored, other)	Date Due (mmddyyyy)	Invoice Number or Federal Government Contract Number	Amount Due
58a				
				$
58b				
				$
58c				
				$
58d				
				$

58e   **Total Outstanding Balance** *(Add lines 58a through 58d and amounts from any attachments)* $

Form **433-A** (Rev. 1-2008)

¶1425

Form 433-A (Rev. 1-2008)   Page **6**

Business Assets. Include all tools, books, machinery, equipment, inventory or other assets used in trade or business. Include Uniform Commercial Code *(UCC)* filings. Include Vehicles and Real Property owned/leased/rented by the business, if not shown in Section 4.

		Purchase/Lease/Rental Date *(mmddyyyy)*	Current Fair Market Value (FMV)	Current Loan Balance	Amount of Monthly Payment	Date of Final Payment *(mmddyyyy)*	**Equity** FMV Minus Loan
59a	Property Description		$	$	$		$
	Location *(Street, City, State, ZIP code) and County*			Lender/Lessor/Landlord Name, Address *(Street, City, State, ZIP code)* and Phone			
59b	Property Description		$	$	$		$
	Location *(Street, City, State, ZIP code) and County*			Lender/Lessor/Landlord Name, Address *(Street, City, State, ZIP code)* and Phone			

59c Total Equity *(Add lines 59a, 59b and amounts from any attachments)* $

Section 6 should be completed only if the taxpayer is SELF-EMPLOYED

Section 6: Sole Proprietorship Information *(lines 60 through 81 should reconcile with business Profit and Loss Statement)*

Accounting Method Used: ☐ Cash ☐ Accrual

Income and Expenses during the period *(mmddyyyy)* _____ to *(mmddyyyy)* _____

Total Monthly Business Income			Total Monthly Business Expenses *(Use attachments as needed.)*	
	Source	Gross Monthly		Expense Items	Actual Monthly
60	Gross Receipts	$	70	Materials Purchased [1]	$
61	Gross Rental Income	$	71	Inventory Purchased [2]	$
62	Interest	$	72	Gross Wages & Salaries	$
63	Dividends	$	73	Rent	$
64	Cash	$	74	Supplies [3]	$
	Other Income *(Specify below)*		75	Utilities/Telephone [4]	$
65		$	76	Vehicle Gasoline/Oil	$
66		$	77	Repairs & Maintenance	$
67		$	78	Insurance	$
68		$	79	Current Taxes [5]	$
			80	Other Expenses, including installment payments *(Specify)*	$
69	**Total Income** *(Add lines 60 through 68)*	$	81	**Total Expenses** *(Add lines 70 through 80)*	$
			82	**Net Business Income** *(Line 69 minus 81)* [6]	$

Enter the amount from line 82 on line 23, section 4. If line 82 is a loss, enter "0" on line 23, section 4.

Self-employed taxpayers must return to page 4 to sign the certification and include all applicable attachments.

[1] **Materials Purchased:** Materials are items directly related to the production of a product or service.

[2] **Inventory Purchased:** Goods bought for resale.

[3] **Supplies:** Supplies are items used in the business that are consumed or used up within one year. This could be the cost of books, office supplies, professional equipment, etc.

[4] **Utilities/Telephone:** Utilities include gas, electricity, water, oil, other fuels, trash collection, telephone and cell phone.

[5] **Current Taxes:** Real estate, excise, franchise, occupational, personal property, sales and employer's portion of employment taxes.

[6] **Net Business Income:** Net profit from Form 1040, Schedule C may be used if duplicated deductions are eliminated (e.g., expenses for business use of home already included in housing and utility expenses on page 4). Deductions for depreciation and depletion on Schedule C are not cash expenses and must be added back to the net income figure. In addition, interest cannot be deducted if it is already included in any other installment payments allowed.

FINANCIAL ANALYSIS OF COLLECTION POTENTIAL FOR INDIVIDUAL WAGE EARNERS AND SELF-EMPLOYED INDIVIDUALS		(IRS USE ONLY)
Cash Available *(Lines 11, 12c, 13d, 14c, 15g, 56, 57c and 58e)*	Total Cash	$
Distrainable Asset Summary *(Lines 17c, 18c, 19c, and 59c)*	Total Equity	$
Monthly Total Positive Income minus Expenses *(Line 32 minus Line 45)*	Monthly Available Cash	$

Privacy Act: The information requested on this Form is covered under Privacy Acts and Paperwork Reduction Notices which have already been provided to the taxpayer.

Form **433-A** (Rev. 1-2008)

¶1426 Exhibit 14-6

How to prepare a
Collection Information Statement (Form 433-A)

IRS

Who should use Form 433-A?

Form 433-A is used to obtain current financial information necessary for determining how a wage earner or self-employed individual can satisfy an outstanding tax liability.

You may need to complete Form 433-A:

- if you are an individual who owes income tax on Form 1040,
- if you are an individual who may be a responsible person for a Trust Fund Recovery Penalty,
- if you are an individual who may be personally responsible for a partnership liability,
- if you are an individual owner of a limited liability company that is a disregarded entity,
- or if you are an individual who is self-employed or has self-employment income. You are self-employed if you are in business for yourself, or carry on a trade or business as a sole proprietor or an independent contractor.

If you are a wage earner:

Complete Sections 1, 2, 3 and 4, including the signature line on page 4.
Include the attachments required on page 4.
Answer all questions in these sections or write N/A.
Include attachments if additional space is needed to respond completely to any question.

If you are a self-employed individual:

Complete sections 1, 2, 3, 4, 5 and 6, and the signature line on page 4.
Include the attachments required on page 4.
Answer all questions in these sections or write N/A.
Include attachments if additional space is needed to respond completely to any question.

Certification for Signature Line on page 4

This requires the taxpayer's signature. For joint income tax liabilities, both husband and wife must sign the statement.

If you do not complete the form, we will not be able to help determine the best method for you to pay the amount due. This may result in significant delay in account resolution. The areas explained in this publication are the ones we have found to be the most confusing to people completing the form.

Section 4 (Wage earners and Self-employed Individuals)

Items 12 – Personal Bank Accounts

Enter all accounts, even if there is currently no balance. Include stored value cards such as a payroll card from an employer, an electronic benefit card from a government agency, or a child support payment card. *Do not* enter bank loans.

Item 13 – Investments

Include any investment or interest you have in a business.

Item 14 – Available Credit

Enter only credit cards issued by a bank, credit union, or savings and loan *(MasterCard, Visa, overdraft protection, etc.)*

Items 17, 18 and 19 – Real Estate, Vehicles and Personal Assets

Current Fair Market Value – Indicate the amount you could sell the asset for today.
Date of Final Payment – Enter the date the loan or lease will be fully paid.

Item 17 – Real Estate

List locations of all property that you lease, own or are purchasing. If you are leasing or renting, list lessor or landlord. If you are purchasing, list lender.

Item 18 – Personal Vehicle

List all vehicles owned and leased (cars, boats, RVs, etc.) If you are leasing, list lessor. If you are purchasing, list lender.

Item 19 – Personal Assets

List other personal assets you own such as artwork, jewelry, antiques, furniture, collections (coins, guns etc.) not included in previous sections.

Section 5 (Self-employed only) Business Information/Assets

Item 54 – Payment Processor

List all third-party processors you use for business to accept credit card payments.

Item 57 – Business Bank Accounts

Enter all business bank accounts, even if there is currently no balance. Include stored value cards such as a telephone card or prepaid debit card for expenses. Do not enter bank loans.

Item 59 – Business Assets

List all other assets used in trade or business that were not included in previous sections.

Section 6 (Self-employed only) Business Income and Expenses

Complete Business Income and Expenses in Section 6 before completing Monthly Income/Expense Statement in Section 4. The business information in Section 6 should reconcile with your business profit and loss statement. See footnote 6 on page 6 if using Form 1040, Schedule C.

¶1426

Section 4 Monthly Income/Expense Statement

If only one spouse has a tax liability, but both have income, list the total household income and expenses.

TOTAL INCOME
Items 20 and 21 – Wages
Enter your *gross* monthly wages and/or salaries. Do not deduct withholding or allotments you elect to take out of you pay such as insurance, credit union deductions, car payments, etc. List these deductions in Total Living Expenses.
Item 23 – Net Business Income
Enter your monthly *net* business income from line 82 on page 6.
Item 25 – Distributions
Enter the monthly average of your distributions from Partnerships, Subchapter S Corporations or Limited Liability Companies.

TOTAL LIVING EXPENSES *(necessary)*
To be necessary, expenses must provide for the health and welfare of you and your family and/or provide for the production of income, and must be reasonable in amount. We may ask you to provide substantiation of certain expenses.
Item 33 – Standard for Food, Clothing and Misc.
Enter the total amount for this item from the chart in the next column. If you claim a higher amount for a specific expense, you must verify and substantiate that amount.
Item 34 – Housing and Utilities
Enter the monthly rent or mortgage payment for your principal residence. Add the average monthly payment for the following expenses, if they are *not* included in your rent or mortgage payments: property taxes, homeowner's or renter's insurance, necessary maintenance and repair, homeowner dues, condominium fees, and utilities.
Item 35 – Vehicle Ownership Costs
Enter your monthly lease, purchase or loan payments.
Item 36 – Vehicle Operating Costs
Enter the average monthly costs for insurance, licenses, registration fees, inspections, normal repairs and maintenance, fuel, parking and tolls.
Item 37 – Public Transportation
Enter the average monthly public transportation expenses you pay for bus, train and taxi fares and any other mass transit fares.
Item 38 – Health Insurance
Enter your monthly expense for health insurance.
Item 39 – Out-of-Pocket Health Care Costs
Enter the amount for this item from the chart in the next column. If you claim a higher amount, you must verify and substantiate the expenses.
Item 40 – Court Ordered Payments
Includes child support, alimony, etc.
Item 44 – Other Secured Debts
Enter your average monthly payments for any other secured debts. Do not duplicate mortgage or car payments entered in Items 34 or 35 above.

Total Monthly National Standards for Food, Clothing and Misc. (Section 4, Item 33)
Effective 03/01/2011

Expense	One Person	Two Persons	Three Persons	Four Persons
Food	$300	$537	$639	$757
Housekeeping supplies	$29	$66	$65	$74
Apparel & services	$86	$162	$209	$244
Personal care products & services	$32	$55	$61	$67
Miscellaneous	$87	$165	$197	$235
Total	$534	$985	$1,171	$1,377

More than four persons	Over Four Persons Amount
For each additional person, add to four-person total allowance:	$262

To calculate the allowance, please read across to the column that matches the number of persons in your family.

When you have more than four persons in your family, you need to multiply the amount of additional persons over four by the dollar amount in the "Over Four" column; then add the answer to the dollar amount in the "Four" column. For example, when you have six persons in your family, you would multiply $262 by the two members of your family over four to get $524. You then would add this $524 to the $1,377 allowed for a family of four. As a result, your allowed expenses would equal $1,901 ($524 + $1,377).

Total Monthly National Standards for Out-of-Pocket Health Care Costs
(Section 4, item 39)
Effective 03/01/2011

	Out-of-Pocket Health Care Costs
Under 65	$60
65 and Older	$144

To calculate the allowance, determine the number and age of persons in your household and multiply by the amount reflected in the chart.

For example, a family of three persons, all under 65, would be allowed $180 ($60 x 3)

Publication 1854 (Rev. 3-2011) Catalog Number 21563Q Department of the Treasury **Internal Revenue Service** www.irs.gov

¶1427 Exhibit 14-7

Form **433-B**	**Collection Information Statement for Businesses**

(Rev. January 2008)
Department of the Treasury
Internal Revenue Service

Note: *Complete all entry spaces with the current data available or "N/A" (not applicable). Failure to complete all entry spaces may result in rejection of your request or significant delay in account resolution.* **Include attachments if additional space is needed to respond completely to any question.**

Section 1: Business Information

1a Business Name _____

1b Business Street Address _____
Mailing Address _____
City _____
State _____ ZIP_____

1c County _____

1d Business Telephone (_____)

1e Type of
Business

1f Business
Website

2a Employer Identification No. (EIN) _____

2b Type of Entity *(Check appropriate box below)*
☐ Partnership ☐ Corporation ☐ Other _____
☐ Limited Liability Company (LLC) classified as a corporation
☐ Other LLC – Include number of members _____

2c Date Incorporated/Established _____
mmddyyyy

3a Number of Employees _____

3b Monthly Gross Payroll _____

3c Frequency of Tax Deposits _____

3d Is the business enrolled in Electronic Federal
Tax Payment System (EFTPS) ☐ Yes ☐ No

4 Does the business engage in e-Commerce (Internet sales) ☐ Yes ☐ No

Payment Processor (e.g., PayPal, Authorize.net, Google Checkout, etc.), Name and Address *(Street, City, State, ZIP code)*	Payment Processor Account Number
5a	
5b	

Credit cards accepted by the business

Type of Credit Card (e.g., Visa, MasterCard, etc.)	Merchant Account Number	Merchant Account Provider Name and Address *(Street, City, State, ZIP code)*
6a		Phone
6b		Phone
6c		Phone

Section 2: Business Personnel and Contacts

Partners, Officers, LLC Members, Major Shareholders, Etc.

7a Full Name _____
Title _____
Home Address _____
City _____ State _____ ZIP _____
Responsible for Depositing Payroll Taxes ☐ Yes ☐ No

Social Security Number ____ | ____ | ____
Home Telephone (_____)
Work/Cell Phone (_____)
Ownership Percentage & Shares or Interest

7b Full Name _____
Title _____
Home Address _____
City _____ State _____ ZIP _____
Responsible for Depositing Payroll Taxes ☐ Yes ☐ No

Social Security Number ____ | ____ | ____
Home Telephone (_____)
Work/Cell Phone (_____)
Ownership Percentage & Shares or Interest

7c Full Name _____
Title _____
Home Address _____
City _____ State _____ ZIP _____
Responsible for Depositing Payroll Taxes ☐ Yes ☐ No

Social Security Number ____ | ____ | ____
Home Telephone (_____)
Work/Cell Phone (_____)
Ownership Percentage & Shares or Interest

7d Full Name _____
Title _____
Home Address _____
City _____ State _____ ZIP _____
Responsible for Depositing Payroll Taxes ☐ Yes ☐ No

Social Security Number ____ | ____ | ____
Home Telephone (_____)
Work/Cell Phone (_____)
Ownership Percentage & Shares or Interest

www.irs.gov   Cat. No. 16649P   Form **433-B** (Rev. 1-2008)

Form 433-B (Rev. 1-2008)   Page **2**

Section 3: Other Financial Information *(Attach copies of all applicable documentation.)*

8 **Does the business use a Payroll Service Provider or Reporting Agent** *(If yes, answer the following)* ☐ Yes ☐ No

Name and Address *(Street, City, State, ZIP code)*	Effective dates *(mmddyyyy)*

9 **Is the business a party to a lawsuit** *(If yes, answer the following)* ☐ Yes ☐ No

☐ Plaintiff ☐ Defendant	Location of Filing	Represented by	Docket/Case No.
Amount of Suit $	Possible Completion Date *(mmddyyyy)*	Subject of Suit	

10 **Has the business ever filed bankruptcy** *(If yes, answer the following)* ☐ Yes ☐ No

Date Filed *(mmddyyyy)*	Date Dismissed or Discharged *(mmddyyyy)*	Petition No.	Location

11 Do any related parties (e.g., officers, partners, employees) have outstanding amounts owed to the business *(If yes, answer the following)* ☐ Yes ☐ No

Name and Address *(Street, City, State, ZIP code)*	Date of Loan	Current Balance As of _____ mmddyyyy	Payment Date	Payment Amount
		$		$

12 Have any assets been transferred, in the last 10 years, from this business for less than full value *(If yes, answer the following)* ☐ Yes ☐ No

List Asset	Value at Time of Transfer	Date Transferred *(mmddyyyy)*	To Whom or Where Transferred
	$		

13 Does this business have other business affiliations (e.g., subsidiary or parent companies) *(If yes, answer the following)* ☐ Yes ☐ No

Related Business Name and Address *(Street, City, State, ZIP code)*	Related Business EIN:

14 **Any increase/decrease in income anticipated** *(If yes, answer the following)* ☐ Yes ☐ No

Explain *(use attachment if needed)*	How much will it increase/decrease	When will it increase/decrease
	$	

Section 4: Business Asset and Liability Information

15 **Cash on Hand.** *Include cash that is not in the bank*   **Total Cash on Hand** | $

Business Bank Accounts. Include online bank accounts, money market accounts, savings accounts, checking accounts, and stored value cards (e.g., payroll cards, government benefit cards, etc.)
List safe deposit boxes including location and contents.

	Type of Account	Full Name and Address *(Street, City, State, ZIP code)* of Bank, Savings & Loan, Credit Union or Financial Institution.	Account Number	Account Balance As of _____ mmddyyyy
16a				$
16b				$
16c				$
16d	**Total Cash in Banks** *(Add lines 16a through 16c and amounts from any attachments)*			$

Form **433-B** (Rev. 1-2008)

¶1427

Form 433-B (Rev. 1-2008)   Page **3**

Accounts/Notes Receivable. Include e-payment accounts receivable and factoring companies, and any bartering or online auction accounts. *(List all contracts separately, including contracts awarded, but not started.)*

17   Is the business a Federal Government Contractor   ☐ Yes ☐ No   *(Include Federal Government contracts below)*

Accounts/Notes Receivable & Address *(Street, City, State, ZIP code)*	Status *(e.g., age, factored, other)*	Date Due *(mmddyyyy)*	Invoice Number or Federal Government Contract Number	**Amount Due**
18a Contact Name: Phone:				$
18b Contact Name: Phone:				$
18c Contact Name: Phone:				$
18d Contact Name: Phone:				$
18e Contact Name: Phone:				$

18f   Outstanding Balance *(Add lines 18a through 18e and amounts from any attachments)* $

Investments. List all investment assets below. Include stocks, bonds, mutual funds, stock options, and certificates of deposit.

Name of Company & Address *(Street, City, State, ZIP code)*	Used as collateral on loan	Current Value	Loan Balance	**Equity** Value Minus Loan
19a Phone:	☐ Yes ☐ No	$	$	$
19b Phone:	☐ Yes ☐ No	$	$	$

19c   Total Investments *(Add lines 19a, 19b, and amounts from any attachments)* $

Available Credit. Include all lines of credit and credit cards. Full Name & Address *(Street, City, State, ZIP code)* of Credit Institution	Credit Limit	Amount Owed As of _____ mmddyyyy	**Available Credit** As of _____ mmddyyyy
20a Account No.	$	$	$
20b Account No.	$	$	$

20c   Total Credit Available *(Add lines 20a, 20b, and amounts from any attachments)* $

Form **433-B** (Rev. 1-2008)

Real Property. Include all real property and land contracts the business owns/leases/rents.

	Purchase/Lease Date *(mmddyyyy)*	Current Fair Market Value *(FMV)*	Current Loan Balance	Amount of Monthly Payment	Date of Final Payment *(mmddyyyy)*	**Equity** FMV Minus Loan
21a Property Description		$	$	$		$
Location *(Street, City, State, ZIP code)* and County			Lender/Lessor/Landlord Name, Address *(Street, City, State, ZIP code)*, and Phone			
21b Property Description		$	$	$		$
Location *(Street, City, State, ZIP code)* and County			Lender/Lessor/Landlord Name, Address *(Street, City, State, ZIP code)*, and Phone			
21c Property Description		$	$	$		$
Location *(Street, City, State, ZIP code)* and County			Lender/Lessor/Landlord Name, Address *(Street, City, State, ZIP code)*, and Phone			
21d Property Description		$	$	$		$
Location *(Street, City, State, ZIP code)* and County			Lender/Lessor/Landlord Name, Address *(Street, City, State, ZIP code)*, and Phone			

21e Total Equity *(Add lines 21a through 21d and amounts from any attachments)* $

Vehicles, Leased and Purchased. Include boats, RVs, motorcycles, trailers, mobile homes, etc.

		Purchase/Lease Date *(mmddyyyy)*	Current Fair Market Value *(FMV)*	Current Loan Balance	Amount of Monthly Payment	Date of Final Payment *(mmddyyyy)*	**Equity** FMV Minus Loan
22a Year	Mileage		$	$	$		$
Make	Model	Lender/Lessor Name, Address, *(Street, City, State, ZIP code)* and Phone					
22b Year	Mileage		$	$	$		$
Make	Model	Lender/Lessor Name, Address, *(Street, City, State, ZIP code)* and Phone					
22c Year	Mileage		$	$	$		$
Make	Model	Lender/Lessor Name, Address, *(Street, City, State, ZIP code)* and Phone					
22d Year	Mileage		$	$	$		$
Make	Model	Lender/Lessor Name, Address, *(Street, City, State, ZIP code)* and Phone					

22e Total Equity *(Add lines 22a through 22d and amounts from any attachments)* $

Form **433-B** (Rev. 1-2008)

Business Equipment. Include all machinery, equipment, merchandise inventory, and/or other assets. Include Uniform Commercial Code (UCC) filings.

	Purchase/Lease Date *(mmddyyyy)*	Current Fair Market Value *(FMV)*	Current Loan Balance	Amount of Monthly Payment	Date of Final Payment *(mmddyyyy)*	**Equity** FMV Minus Loan
23a Asset Description		$	$	$		$
Location of asset *(Street, City, State, ZIP code)* and County			Lender/Lessor Name, Address, *(Street, City, State, ZIP code)* and Phone			
23b Asset Description		$	$	$		$
Location of asset *(Street, City, State, ZIP code)* and County			Lender/Lessor Name, Address, *(Street, City, State, ZIP code)* and Phone			
23c Asset Description		$	$	$		$
Location of asset *(Street, City, State, ZIP code)* and County			Lender/Lessor Name, Address, *(Street, City, State, ZIP code)* and Phone			
23d Asset Description		$	$	$		$
Location of asset *(Street, City, State, ZIP code)* and County			Lender/Lessor Name, Address, *(Street, City, State, ZIP code)* and Phone			

23e Total Equity *(Add lines 23a through 23d and amounts from any attachments)* $

Business Liabilities. Include notes and judgments below.

Business Liabilities	Secured/ Unsecured	Date Pledged *(mmddyyyy)*	Balance Owed	Date of Final Payment *(mmddyyyy)*	Payment Amount
24a Description:	☐ Secured ☐ Unsecured		$		$
Name Street Address City/State/ZIP code				Phone:	
24b Description:	☐ Secured ☐ Unsecured		$		$
Name Street Address City/State/ZIP code				Phone:	
24c Description:	☐ Secured ☐ Unsecured		$		$
Name Street Address City/State/ZIP code				Phone:	

24d Total Payments *(Add lines 24a through 24c and amounts from any attachments)* $

Form **433-B** (Rev. 1-2008)

Form 433-B (Rev. 1-2008)   Page **6**

Section 5: Monthly Income/Expense Statement for Business

Accounting Method Used: ☐ Cash ☐ Accrual

Income and Expenses during the period *(mmddyyyy)* _____ to *(mmddyyyy)* _____

Total Monthly Business Income			**Total Monthly Business Expenses**	
	Source	Gross Monthly		Expense Items	Actual Monthly
25	Gross Receipts from Sales/Services	$	36	Materials Purchased[1]	$
26	Gross Rental Income	$	37	Inventory Purchased[2]	$
27	Interest Income	$	38	Gross Wages & Salaries	$
28	Dividends	$	39	Rent	$
29	Cash	$	40	Supplies[3]	$
	Other Income *(Specify below)*		41	Utilities/Telephone[4]	$
30		$	42	Vehicle Gasoline/Oil	$
31		$	43	Repairs & Maintenance	$
32		$	44	Insurance	$
33		$	45	Current Taxes[5]	$
34		$	46	Other Expenses *(Specify)*	$
35	**Total Income** *(Add lines 25 through 34)*	$	47	IRS Use Only Allowable Installment Payments	$
			48	**Total Expenses** *(Add lines 36 through 47)*	$

[1] **Materials Purchased:** Materials are items directly related to the production of a product or service.

[2] **Inventory Purchased:** Goods bought for resale.

[3] **Supplies:** Supplies are items used to conduct business and are consumed or used up within one year. This could be the cost of books, office supplies, professional equipment, etc.

[4] **Utilities/Telephone:** Utilities include gas, electricity, water, oil, other fuels, trash collection, telephone and cell phone.

[5] **Current Taxes:** Real estate, state, and local income tax, excise, franchise, occupational, personal property, sales and the employer's portion of employment taxes.

Certification: *Under penalties of perjury, I declare that to the best of my knowledge and belief this statement of assets, liabilities, and other information is true, correct, and complete.*

Signature	Title	Date

Print Name of Officer, Partner or LLC Member

Attachments Required: Copies of the following items for the last 3 months from the date this form is submitted (check all attached items):

☐ Banks and Investments - Statements for all money market, brokerage, checking/savings accounts, certificates of deposit, stocks/bonds.

☐ Assets - Statements from lenders on loans, monthly payments, payoffs, and balances, for all assets. Include copies of UCC financing statements and accountant's depreciation schedules.

☐ Expenses - Bills or statements for monthly recurring expenses of utilities, rent, insurance, property taxes, telephone and cell phone, insurance premiums, court orders requiring payments, other expenses.

☐ Other - credit card statements, profit and loss statements, all loan payoffs, etc.

☐ Copy of the last income tax return filed; Form 1120, 1120S, 1065, 1040, 990, etc.

Additional information or proof may be subsequently requested.

FINANCIAL ANALYSIS OF COLLECTION POTENTIAL FOR BUSINESSES		**(IRS USE ONLY)**
Cash Available (Lines 15, 16d, 18f, 19c, and 20c)	Total Cash	$
Distrainable Asset Summary (Lines 21e, 22e, and 23e)	Total Equity	$
Monthly Income Minus Expenses (Line 35 Minus Line 48)	Monthly Available Cash	$

Privacy Act: The information requested on this Form is covered under Privacy Acts and Paperwork Reduction Notices which have already been provided to the taxpayer.

Form **433-B** (Rev. 1-2008)

¶1428 Exhibit 14-8

Form 6639
(Rev. October 1993)

Summons
Financial Records

Department of the Treasury
Internal Revenue Service

In the matter of _____

Internal Revenue District of _____ Periods _____

The Commissioner of Internal Revenue

To _____

At _____

You are hearby summoned and required to appear before _____ ,
an Internal Revenue Service (IRS) officer, to give testimony and to bring for examination the following information related
to the collection of the tax liability of the person identified above for the periods shown:

Copies of documents and records that you possess or control that concern banking matters of the taxpayer named above,
as described in the subparagraphs checked below for the periods shown:

☐   bank signature cards in effect . . . . from _____ to _____

☐   corporate resolutions in effect . . . . from _____ to _____

☐   bank statements . . . . from _____ to _____

☐   _____ cancelled checks issued by
   (NUMBER)   the taxpayer for each month
                 of the period . . . . from _____ to _____

☐   loan applications, agreements, and
     related records, including corporate
     financial statements, submitted,
     entered into, or in effect . . . . from _____ to _____

Do not write in this space

Business address and telephone number of Internal Revenue Service officer named above:

_____

Place and time for appearance:

at _____

on the _____ day of _____ , 19 _____ at _____ o'clock _____ m.

Issued under authority of the Internal Revenue Code this _____ day of _____ , 19 ____

_____   _____
Signature of Issuing Officer   Title

_____   _____
Signature of Approving Officer (If applicable)   Title

Original to be kept by IRS   Catalog No. 25004I   Form **6639** (Rev. 10-93)

¶1428

Form 6639 (Rev. 10-93)

Certificate of
Service of Summons
(Pursuant to section 7603, Internal Revenue Code)

I certify that I served the summons shown on
the front of this form on:

Date	Time

How Summons Was Served

☐ I handed an attested copy of the summons to
the person to whom it was directed.

☐ I left an attested copy of the summons
at the last and usual place of abode of
th person to whom it was directed. I
left the copy with the following
person (if any):

Signature	Title

**I certify that the copy of the summons served
contained the required certification.**

Signature	Title

Form **6639** (Rev. 10-93)

¶1429 Exhibit 14-9

Internal Revenue Service
District Director

Department of the Treasury

Date:

Social Security or Employer Identification Number:

Person to Contact:

Telephone Number:

⌐   ⌐

Notice of Federal Tax Lien Filing and Your Right to a Hearing Under IRC 6320

This letter is to inform you that we have filed a Notice of Federal Tax Lien and that you have a right to a hearing to discuss collection options and liability issues. The enclosed Publication 1660, Collection Appeal Rights, explains your right to a hearing.

The amount of the unpaid tax is:

Type of Tax	Period	Amount

In order to exercise your right to a hearing, you must file your request by _____. A copy of the request form is attached. It must be sent to

A Notice of Federal Tax Lien was filed on_____, with respect to these taxes. The total amount you owe for the period(s) includes interest and other additions such as penalties and lien fees. You must pay all of the taxes, interest and other additions in order to obtain release of the lien. Call the number above to obtain your current balance.

The lien attaches to all property you currently own and to all property you may acquire in the future. It also may damage your credit rating and hinder your ability to obtain additional credit.

We will issue a Certificate of Release of Notice of Federal Tax Lien within 30 days after you pay the debt or have us adjust it. We will release the lien within 30 days after we accept a bond that you submit, guaranteeing payment of the debt.

(over)

Letter 3172(DO) (01-1999)
Cat. No. 26767I

Procedures for requesting a certificate of release are in the enclosed Publication 14560, Request of Federal Tax Lien.

Sincerely,

Chief, Special Procedures

Enclosures:
 Publication 1660
 Publication 1450
 Form 668Y, Notice Of federal Tax Lien
 Form 12153, Request for Collection Due Process Hearing

Letter 3172(DO) (01-1999)
Cat. No. 267671

¶1430   Exhibit 14-10

Form 668 (Y) (c)	Department of the Treasury - Internal Revenue Service
(Rev. October 1999)	**Notice of Federal Tax Lien**

District	Serial Number	For Optional Use by Recording Office

As provided by sections 6321, 6322, and 6323 of the Internal Revenue Code, we are giving a notice that taxes (including interest and penalties) have been assessed against the following-named taxpayer. We have made a demand for payment of this liability, but it remains unpaid. Therefore, there is a lien in favor of the United States on all property and rights to property belonging to this taxpayer for the amount of these taxes, and additional penalties, interest, and costs that may accrue.

Name of Taxpayer

Residence

IMPORTANT RELEASE INFORMATION: For each assessment listed below, unless notice of lien is refiled by the date given in column (e), this notice shall, on the day following such date, operate as a certificate of release as defined in IRC 6325(a).

Kind of Tax (a)	Tax Period Ended (b)	Identifying Number (c)	Date of Assessment (d)	Last Day for Refiling (e)	Unpaid Balance of Assessment (f)

Place of Filing

		Total	$

This notice was prepared and signed at _____ , on this,

the _____ day of _____ , _____ .

Signature	Title

(NOTE: *Certificate of officer authorized by law to take acknowledgments is not essential to the validity of Notice of Federal Tax lien Rev. Rul. 71-466, 1971-2 C.B. 409*)

PART 1 - KEPT BY RECORDING OFFICE

Form 688 (Y) (c) (Rev. 10-99)
CAT. NO. 60025X

¶1430

¶1431 Exhibit 14-11

Instructions on How to Request a

Certificate of Release of Federal Tax Lien

Section 6325(a) of the Internal Revenue Code directs us to release a Federal Tax Lien after a tax liability becomes fully paid or legally unenforceable. We also must release a lien when we accept a bond for payment of the tax.

If we haven't released the lien within 30 days, you can ask for a Certificate of Release of Federal Tax Lien.

Requesting a Copy of the Certificate

If you have paid the tax you owed and have not received a copy of the Certificate of Release of Federal Tax Lien, you may call 1-800-913-6050. If you prefer to write, see page 2 for the address to which your request should be mailed or faxed.

The certificate you receive will not show the official recording information. For a copy of the recorded certificate, you must contact the recording office where the Certificate of Release of Federal Tax Lien was filed.

Other Requests

Requests for certificates of release for any other reason should be mailed to IRS, Attn: Technical Services Advisory Group Manager. Use Publication 4235, Technical Services Advisory Group Addresses, to determine where to mail your request.

Send your written request with any required documents to the appropriate address.

Your request must contain the following information:

1. The date of your request,
2. The name and address of the taxpayer,
3. One copy of each Notice of Federal Tax Lien you want released, and
4. Why you want us to release the lien.

If you've paid the tax, enclose a copy of either of the following:

1. An Internal Revenue receipt,
2. A canceled check, or
3. Any other acceptable proof.

Please include a telephone number with the best time for us to call you should we need additional information.

We may need to research your account to confirm you no longer have a liability. We will provide a release once we have done so.

If you have an immediate or urgent need for a Certificate of Release of Federal Tax Lien, visit or telephone your local IRS office. Be prepared to show proof of payment.

You can pay any unpaid tax with a certified check, cashier's check, or postal or bank money order to receive the certificate of release.

IRS Department of the Treasury Publication 1450 (Rev. 12-2005)
Internal Revenue Service Catalog Number 10665H
www.irs.gov

Page 1 of 2

Case Processing Address and Phone Numbers

Send your written request with any required documents to:

Internal Revenue Service
CCP - Lien Unit
P.O. Box 145595
Stop 8420G Team *(enter Team Number from list below)*
Cincinnati, Ohio 45250-5595

State	Team	Fax Number	State	Team	Fax Number
Alabama	205	859-669-3805	Pennsylvania	202	859-669-3805
Alaska	206	859-669-5152	Puerto Rico	204	859-669-4961
Arizona	206	859-669-5152	Rhode Island	203	859-669-4954
Arkansas	205	859-669-3805	South Carolina	201	859-669-3805
California	207	859-669-4954	South Dakota	206	859-669-5152
Colorado	206	859-669-5152	Tennessee	205	859-669-3805
Connecticut	203	859-669-4954	Texas	205	859-669-3805
District of Columbia	201	859-669-3805	Utah	206	859-669-5152
Delaware	201	859-669-3805	Vermont	203	859-669-4954
Florida	201	859-669-3805	Virginia	201	859-669-3805
Georgia	205	859-669-3805	Washington	206	859-669-3805
Hawaii	206	859-669-5152	West Virginia	202	859-669-5152
Idaho	206	859-669-5152	Wisconsin	206	859-669-5152
Illinois	206	859-669-5152	Wyoming	206	859-669-5152
Indiana	206	859-669-5152			
Iowa	206	859-669-5152			
Kansas	206	859-669-5152			
Kentucky	202	859-669-5152			
Louisiana	205	859-669-3805			
Maine	203	859-669-4954			
Maryland	201	859-669-3805			
Massachusetts	203	859-669-4954			
Michigan	202	859-669-5152			
Minnesota	206	859-669-5152			
Mississippi	205	859-669-3805			
Missouri	206	859-669-5152			
Montana	206	859-669-5152			
Nebraska	206	859-669-5152			
Nevada	206	859-669-5152			
New Hampshire	203	859-669-4954			
New Jersey	202	859-669-5152			
New Mexico	206	859-669-5152			
New York	203	859-669-4954			
North Carolina	201	859-669-3805			
North Dakota	206	859-669-5152			
Ohio	202	859-669-5152			
Oklahoma	205	859-669-3805			
Oregon	206	859-669-5152			

¶1431

¶1432 Exhibit 14-12

Form 669-A (Rev. August 2005)	Department of the Treasury - Internal Revenue Service **Certificate of Discharge of Property From Federal Tax Lien** *(Sec. 6325(b)(1) of the Internal Revenue Code)*

_____

Of _____ , City of _____

County of _____ , State of _____

is indebted to the United States for unpaid internal revenue tax in the sum of _____

_____ Dollars ($ _____)

as evidenced by:

Notice of Federal Tax Lien Serial Number (a)	Recording Information (b)	Date Recorded (c)	Taxpayer Identification Number (d)	Amount Shown on Lien (e)

A lien attaching to all the property of the taxpayer was filed to secure the amount owed. The notice of lien was filed

with the _____for the _____, and also with

the _____ in accordance with the applicable provisions of law.

The lien listed above is attached to certain property described as:

(Use this space for continued description of property)

Under the provisions of section 6325(b)(1) of the Internal Revenue Code, the Internal Revenue Service discharges the above described property from the lien. However, the lien remains in effect for all other property, or rights to property, to which the lien is attached.

Signature	Title	Date

(NOTE: Certificate of officer authorized by law to take acknowledgments is not essential to the validity of Discharge of Federal Tax Lien. Rev. Rul. 71-466, 1971-2, C.B. 409.)

Catalog No. 16751C   www.irs.gov   Form **669-A** (Rev. 8-2005)

¶1433 Exhibit 14-13

Instructions on how to apply for

Certificate of Discharge From Federal Tax Lien

IRS

A Certificate of Discharge under Internal Revenue Code Section 6325(b) removes the United States' lien from the property named in the certificate. Discharge of property under Internal Revenue Code Section 6325(c) subject to an Estate Tax Lien is not covered in this publication. For Estate Tax Lien discharges see instead the application and instructions found in <u>Form 4422</u>

1. Complete Form 14135, *Application for Certificate of Discharge of Federal Tax Lien* attached with this publication.

2. Mail the completed Form 14135 and the appropriate attachments to:

   IRS, Attn: Advisory Group Manager
   (Refer to **Publication 4235** <u>Collection Advisory Group Addresses</u> for the correct address. The correct address is the office assigned to the location where the property is located.)

If you have any questions, contact the applicable Advisory Office.

If you want to know how much you owe in order to pay the lien(s) in full, call 1-800-913-6050, visit the nearest Taxpayer Assistance Center, or contact the revenue officer assigned to your case.

Important!

Please submit your application at least 45 days before the transaction date that the certificate of discharge is needed. Doing so will allow sufficient time for review, determination, notification and the furnishing of any applicable documents by the transaction date.

Information Required on the Application

Section 1 - Taxpayer Information

1. Enter the name and address of the individual(s) or business as it appears on the Notice of Federal Tax Lien (NFTL). A second name line is provided if needed.

2. Enter, if known, the last 4 digits of the social security number (SSN) or full employer identification number as it appears on the NFTL.

3. Enter, if known and if applicable, the last 4 digits of any spousal SSN (secondary SSN) associated with the tax debt listed on the NFTL.

4. Provide a daytime phone number and a fax number.

Section 2 - Applicant Information

1. Check the box on the first line of Section 2 if you are both the taxpayer and the applicant. If you are not the taxpayer, attach a copy of the lien.

2. If you have checked the box indicating that you are the taxpayer **and** your information is the same as listed on the lien, enter "same as taxpayer" on the name line.

3. If you are **not** the taxpayer **or** you are the taxpayer but your information is no longer the same as the information on the Notice of Federal Tax Lien, enter your name (include any name changes), current address, daytime phone number and fax number.

4. If you are **not** the taxpayer, enter in the box next to "Name" your relationship to the taxpayer (e.g. parent, uncle, sister, no relation, etc).

Section 3 - Purchaser/Transferee/New Owner

1. Check the box on the first line of Section 3 if you are both the property owner and the applicant.

2. Enter the name of the property owner. Or enter "NA" if you have checked the box indicating you are both the applicant and the property owner, enter, "same as applicant".

3. Enter the property owner's relationship to the taxpayer (e.g. taxpayer, parent, no relation, etc.).

Section 4 - Attorney/Representative Information

This section is used to list the taxpayer's representative or a representative of a party other than the taxpayer, such as the lender, needing to receive information from the IRS. However, you do not need a representative to request discharge of the federal tax lien.

1. Check the box on the first line of Section 4 if you are attaching a Form 8821 (Tax Information Authority) or Form 2848 (Power of Attorney) with your application. If you are attaching one of these forms, please make sure it is completely filled out, signed, and dated. You must provide one of these forms if the representative represents an interest other than the taxpayer.

2. Enter the name, address, phone number, and fax number of your representative in this action. The IRS will work with you and your representative to process your application. Or enter "NA" on the name line if you are not using a representative.

3. Enter whose interest the representative represents (e.g. taxpayer, lender, title company, etc.). This allows the IRS to determine what information can be shared with the representative.

Section 5 – Lender/Finance Company Information
(Settlement/Escrow Company for Section 6325(b)(3) only)

Enter the company name, contact name, and phone number for the title or escrow company that will be used at settlement.

Section 6 – Monetary Information

1. Provide the proposed property sale amount

2. Provide the amount of proceeds the IRS can expect for application to the tax liability.

3. Enter NA for the amount of proceeds the IRS can expect, if you anticipate there will be no proceeds.

Section 7 - Basis for Discharge

Discharge of property from the federal tax lien may be granted under several Internal Revenue Code (IRC) provisions. After reviewing the discharge sections, explanations, and examples below, select the discharge section that best applies to your application. If the IRS does not agree with your selection after its review, an explanation of the decision will be provided.

Publication 783 (Rev. 6-2010)   Catalog Number 46755I   Department of the Treasury **Internal Revenue Services**   www.irs.gov

1. **6325(b)(1)** – a discharge may be issued under this provision if the value of the taxpayer's remaining property encumbered by the federal tax lien is equal to at least twice the amount of the federal tax liability secured by the lien and any encumbrance entered into before the IRS filed its public notice of the lien. If there are mortgages, state and/or local taxes, mechanics liens, etc., the amount of these debts would be added to the amount of the tax liability and multiplied by 2.

   Example

Tax liability	$15,500
Other Debts +	23,334
	38,834
X	2
	$77,668

   The property remaining subject to the lien must be at least $77,668.

2. **6325(b)(2)(A)** – a discharge may be issued under this provision when the tax liability is partially satisfied with an amount paid that is not less than the value of the United States' interest in the property being discharged. **For example**, the IRS has a lien totaling $203,000 and with the ...

   - Property selling for: $215,000
   - Minus encumbrances senior to IRS lien: $135,000
   - Minus proposed settlement costs: $ 15,000
   - The IRS lien interest equals: $ 65,000

   After the IRS receives and applies the $65,000 in partial satisfaction of the tax liability, there remains an outstanding tax debt of $138,000.

   In the case of Tenancy by Entireties property, the United States is generally paid one-half of the proceeds in partial satisfaction of the liability secured by the tax lien.

3. **6325(b)(2)(B)** - a discharge may be issued under this provision when it is determined that the government's interest in the property has no value. The debts senior to the federal tax lien are greater than the fair market value of the property or greater than the sale value of the property. Submit a copy of the proposed escrow agreement as part of the application.

4. **6325(b)(3)** – a discharge may be issued under this provision if an agreement is reached with the IRS allowing the property to be sold. Per an escrow agreement the sale proceeds must be held in a fund subject to the claims of the United States in the same manner and priority the claims had prior to the property being discharged. **For example**, there are two mortgages senior to the IRS tax lien totaling $32,000 and $5,000. The government's interest in the property is $40,000 and there are liens on the property junior to the IRS lien in the amount of $3,000, $12,000 and $2,990. The proceeds from the sale would be dispensed by paying the debts in the following sequence.

   a. $32,000
   b. $5,000
   c. $40,000
   d. $3,000
   e. 12,000
   f. $2,990

   Submit a copy of the proposed escrow agreement.

5. **6325(b)(4)** – a discharge will be issued under this provision to a third party who owns the property if a deposit is made or an acceptable bond provided equal to the government's interest in the property. **In the case of Tenancy by Entireties property,** a deposit or an acceptable bond totaling one-half the government's interest in the property must be made. If you are the property owner (but not the taxpayer, i.e., you are not responsible for the tax liability) and you make a deposit or post an acceptable bond to obtain a discharge under this section, you have 120 days to file an action in federal district court, under section 7426(a)(4), challenging the IRS' determination of the government's lien interest. **This is the exclusive remedy available to the third party for the return of the deposit or accepted bond or a portion thereof.** An administrative request for refund and a refund suit in district court is not available. The *Circular 570*, available at http://fms.treas.gov/c570/index.html contains a list of companies certified by the Secretary of the Treasury as providers of acceptable securities.

6. **6325(c)** – a discharge of property subject to an Estate Tax Lien is not covered in this publication. Please refer to Form 4422.

Section 8 - Description of Property

1. Enter a detailed description of the property to be discharged from the federal tax lien.

2. When the property is real estate include the type of property, for example, 3-bedroom house; etc. When the property is personal property include serial or vehicle numbers, as appropriate, for example, 2002 Cessna twin engine airplane, serial number AT919000000000X00; etc.

3. Provide the physical address if real estate or physical location address if personal property.

4. Check the appropriate box to indicate whether you attached a copy of the title or deed to the property.

5. If you are applying under 6325(b)(1) check the "Attached" box **and** attach copies of the titles or deeds for property remaining subject to the lien. If you are not applying under 6325(b)(1) check the "NA" box.

Section 9 - Appraisal and Valuations

1. Check the "Attached" box after "Required Appraisal" indicate whether you have attached the required appraisal by a disinterested third party. This is typically a professional appraisal providing neighborhood analysis; description of the site; description of the improvements; cost approach; comparable sales; definition of market value; certification; contingent and limiting conditions; interior and exterior photos of the property; exterior photos of comparable sales used; comparable sales location map; sketch of subject property showing room layout; flood map and qualifications of the appraiser.

2. Check the appropriate box under the "**Plus** One of the Following Additional Valuations" section to indicate which other type of property value verification is attached with your application.

   Note: For applications under IRC 6325(b)(1), valuation information described above must also be provided for property remaining subject to lien.

   Note: For property being sold at public auction, provide the date and place of the sale, the proposed amount for which the property will be sold, and a statement that the United States will be paid in the proper priority from the proceeds.

Section 10 - Federal Tax Liens

This section is important when the applicant and the taxpayer are different. If the applicant and the taxpayer are the same, this section may be skipped.

1. Check the "attached" box if you have attached copies of the liens with your application.

2. If you checked the "no" box list the System Lien Identification Number (SLID) found in the top right hand box of the lien document, if available. If you do not have the number(s) enter "unknown" in the first box.

Section 11 - Sales Contract/Purchase Agreement

1. Check the box indicating whether the proposed sales contract or purchase agreement is attached.

2. If you checked the "no" box, describe how the taxpayer named on the lien will be divested of their interest in the property or why they have no interest in the property.

Section 12 - Title Report

1. Check the box indicating whether the title report is attached.

2. If you checked the "no" box, use the space provided to list any encumbrances (liens or claims) against the property that came into existence before the United States' lien interest or which have priority over the lien. Include name and address of holder; description of encumbrance, e.g., mortgage, state lien, etc.; date of agreement; original amount and interest rate; amount due at time of application; and family relationship of the holder, if applicable.

3. Attach a separate sheet with the information in item # 2 above if there is not enough space provided on the form.

Section 13 - Closing Statement

1. Check the box indicating whether the proposed closing statement is attached. This statement is often referred to as a HUD-1.

2. If you checked the "no" box, use the space provided to itemize all proposed costs, commissions, and expenses of any transfer or sale associated with property.

3. Attach a separate sheet with the information in item # 2 above if there is not enough space provided on the form.

Section 14 - Additional Information

1. Check the box indicating whether you are attaching other documents relevant to the discharge application. This could include affidavits or court documents.

2. Check the "no" box if you do not have any additional documentation.

Section 15 - Escrow Agreement

1. Check the box indicating whether you are attaching a draft escrow agreement. This is only applicable if you are applying under 6325(b)(3).

2. An escrow agreement must specify type of account, name and depositary for account, conditions under which payment will be made, cost of escrow, and the name and address of any party identified as part of the escrow agreement.

Section 16 - Waiver

This section applies only if you are:

- The property owner, but
- Not liable for the tax debt (*i.e. not named on the lien*), and
- Applying under 6325(b)(2)(A).

By checking the "Waive" box you are waiving the option to have the payment treated as a deposit under section 6325(b)(4) which has the accompanying right to request a return of funds and to bring an action under section 7426(a)(4).

If you check the "no" box, your application will automatically be considered under 6325(b)(4) which provides for return of deposited funds and a court challenge under 7426(b)(4).

Section 17 - Declaration

The applicant or their authorized Power of Attorney signs the application form. You must sign your application under penalties of perjury attesting to having examined the application, accompanying schedules or documents, exhibits, affidavits, and statements and declaring to the best of your knowledge and belief that it is true, correct and complete.

Frequently Asked Questions

Q1: When do I make a payment?

The Internal Revenue Code section under which the certificate of discharge will be issued or granted determines the details regarding making a payment.

- Discharge under **6325(b)(1)** or **6325(b)(2)(B)** does not require a payment.
- Discharge under **6325(b)(2)(A)** requires a payment, but do not send a payment with the application. The Advisory Group Manager will notify you, after determining the amount due, when to send payment.

NOTE: If a **mortgage foreclosure** is anticipated, the application is made under section 6325(b)(2)(A) or 6325(b)(2)(B). A determination will be made that either an amount is required for discharge or the United States' interest is valueless.

In the case of foreclosure you will receive, within 30 days of the receipt of a complete and approved application, a conditional commitment letter for a certificate of discharge.

NOTE: Relocation Expenses - If a discharge under 6325(b)(2)(A) or 6325(b)(2)(B) is issued and if the sale is of the principal residence, the *taxpayer* may be eligible for a relocation expense allowance because of an inability to pay. The relocation expense allowance is subject to limitations. To apply for the allowance complete and submit Form 12451, "Request for Relocation Expense Allowance" with the application for discharge.

- Discharge under **6325(b)(3)** requires a payment, but do not send a payment with the application. First, the draft escrow agreement must be submitted.

  Second, the Advisory Group Manager approves the escrow agent selected by the applicant; any reasonable expenses submitted as incurred in connection with the sale of the property; the claim amounts and priorities, and the distribution timing of the fund.

  Third, the agreement is finalized and contains signatures of all parties involved including Advisory Group Manager prior to the discharge being issued.

Publication 783 (Rev. 6-2010)   Catalog Number 46755I   Department of the Treasury **Internal Revenue Services**   www.irs.gov

Note: The escrow account must be funded before payment of any claim or lien through money paid by the applicant or from the sale proceeds.

- Discharge under **6325(b)(4)** requires a bond or deposit but do not send one with the application. The Advisory Group manager must first determine the amount of bond or deposit needed for the discharge and determine that the bond company, if applicable, is from the approved list.

Q2: What is an acceptable form of payment?

Make payments in cash or by the following types of checks: certified; cashiers; or treasurer's check. The check must be drawn on any bank or trust company incorporated under the laws of the United States, or of any state, or possession of the United States. Payment can also be made using a United States postal, bank, express or telegraph money order.

Important! If you pay by personal check, issuance of the certificate of discharge will be delayed until the bank honors the check.

Q3: Who makes the decision to issue a Certificate of Discharge?

In all cases Advisory staff will review and verify the information provided, determine whether a certificate of discharge should be issued, and contact you with any questions. Advisory may contact you, your representative, or any person relative to the transaction for additional information.

The Advisory Group Manager has the responsibility to review and approve the determination and let you know the outcome. If approved, you will receive a conditional commitment letter.

Q4: When will I receive the Certificate of Discharge?

The Internal Revenue Code under which the certificate of discharge will be issued or granted and the time at which you are divested of your interest in the property determines when you will receive the certificate.

- Under **6325(b)(1)** you will receive the certificate when it is determined the remaining property meets the criteria of the provision.
- Under **6325(b)(2)(A)** you will receive the certificate after IRS receives payment of the agreed upon amount in partial satisfaction of the tax liability, proof that the taxpayer has been divested of title, and receipt of a copy of the final settlement statement.
- Under **6325(b)(2)(B)** you will receive the certificate when it is determined that the government's interest in the property is valueless, the IRS has received proof that the taxpayer has been divested of title, and a copy of the final settlement statement.

NOTE: Under provisions **6325(b)(2)(A)** and **6325(b)(2)(B)** at the conclusion of a mortgage foreclosure the certificate will be issued in accordance with the terms of the conditional commitment letter. Also see, Publication 487, *How to Prepare an Application Requesting the United States to Release Its Right to Redeem Property Secured by a Federal Tax Lien.*

- Under **6325(b)(3)** you will receive the certificate when the amount of the government's interest in the property has been placed in the approved escrow account.
- Under **6325(b)(4)** you will receive the certificate when the amount equal to the government's interest in the property is received or an approved bond has been posted.

Q5: What happens if my application is denied?

If your application is denied, you will receive Form 9423, Collection Appeal Request and Publication 1660, Collection Appeal Rights, with an explanation of why your application was denied.

Privacy and Paperwork Reduction Act Notice

The Privacy act of 1974 says that when we ask you for information about yourself, we must first tell you our legal right to ask for the information, why we are asking for it, and how it will be used. We must also tell you what could happen if you do not provide it and whether or not you must respond under the law.

We ask for the information on this form to carry out the Internal Revenue laws of the United States. This information requested on this form is needed to process your application and to determine whether the federal tax lien can be discharged. You are not required to apply for discharge; however, if you want the federal tax lien to be discharged, you are required to provide the information requested on this form. Section 6109 requires you to provide the requested identification numbers. Failure to provide this information may delay or prevent processing your application; providing any false information may subject you to penalties.

The time needed to complete and file this form will vary depending on individual circumstances. The estimated burden for individuals filing this form is approved under OMB control number 1545-2174. The estimated burden for those who file this form is shown below.

- Recordkeeping 2 hr., 45 min.
- Learning about the law or the form 2 hr.
- Preparing the form 1 hr., 30 min.
- Copying, assembling, and sending the form to the IRS 85 min.

Routine uses of this information include giving it to the Department of Justice for civil and criminal litigation, and to cities, states, the District of Columbia, and United States commonwealths and possessions for use in administering their tax laws. Advisory may contact you, your representative, or any person relative to the transaction for additional information. We may also disclose this information to other countries under a tax treaty, to federal and state agencies to enforce federal nontax criminal laws, or to federal law enforcement and intelligence agencies to combat terrorism.

Publication 783 (Rev. 6-2010)   Catalog Number 46755I   Department of the Treasury **Internal Revenue Services**   www.irs.gov

Form **14135** (June 2010)	Department of the Treasury — Internal Revenue Service **Application for Certificate of Discharge of Property from Federal Tax Lien**	OMB No. 1545-2174

Complete the entire application. Enter NA *(not applicable)*, when appropriate. Attachments and exhibits should be included as necessary. Additional information may be requested of you or a third party to clarify the details of the transaction(s).

1. Taxpayer Information *(Individual or Business named on the notice of lien)*:

Name *(Individual First, Middle Initial, Last)* or *(Business)* as it appears on lien	Primary Social Security Number *(last 4 digits only)*
Name Continuation *(Individual First, Middle Initial, Last)* or *(Business d/b/a)*	Secondary Social Security Number *(last 4 digits only)*
Address *(Number, Street, P.O. Box)*	Employer Identification Number

City	State	ZIP Code
Telephone Number *(with area code)*	Fax Number *(with area code)*	

2. Applicant Information: ☐ Check if also the Taxpayer *(If not the taxpayer, attach copy of lien. See Sec.10)*

Name *(First, Middle Initial, Last)*	Relationship to taxpayer
Address *(Number, Street, P.O. Box)*	

City	State	ZIP Code
Telephone Number *(with area code)*	Fax Number *(with area code)*	

3. Purchase/Transferee/New Owner   ☐ Check if also the Applicant

	Relationship to taxpayer

4. Attorney/Representative Information   **Attached:** Form 8821 or Power of Attorney Form 2848   ☐ Yes   ☐ No

Name *(First, Middle Initial, Last)*	Interest Represented *(e.g. taxpayer, lender, etc.)*
Address *(Number, Street, P.O. Box)*	

City	State	ZIP Code
Telephone Number *(with area code)*	Fax Number *(with area code)*	

5. Lender/Finance Company Information - or *(Settlement/Escrow Company* for applications under Section 6325(b)(3) only)

Company Name	Contact Name	Contact Phone Number

Catalog Number 54727S   www.irs.gov   Form **14135** (Rev. 06-2010)

6. Monetary Information

Proposed sales price	
Expected proceeds to be paid to the United States in exchange for the certificate of discharge *(Enter NA if no proceeds are anticipated)*	

7. Basis for Discharge: Check the box below that best addresses what you would like the United States to consider in your application for discharge. *(Publication 783 has additional descriptions of the Internal Revenue Code sections listed below.)*

☐ 6325(d)(1) Value of property remaining attached by the lien(s) is at least double the liability of the federal tax lien(s) plus other encumbrances senior to the lien(s)

☐ 6325(b)(2)(A) The United States receives an amount not less than the value of the United States' interest.
*(**Note**: If you are applying under 6325(b)(2)(A) and are the property owner but not the taxpayer, see also section 16.)*

☐ 6325(b)(2)(B) Interest of the United States in the property to be discharged has no value.

☐ 6325(b)(3) Proceeds from property sale held in escrow subject to the liens and claims of the United States.

☐ 6325(b)(4) Deposit made or bond furnished in an amount equal to the value of the United States' interest.
*(**Note**: This selection provides a remedy under 7426(a)(4) for return of deposit but is exclusively for a property owner not named as the taxpayer on the lien)*

8. Description of property *(for example, 3 bedroom rental house; 2002 Cessna twin engine airplane, serial number AT919000000000X00; etc.):*

Address of real property *(If this is personal property, list the address where the property is located):*

Address *(Number, Street, P.O. Box)*

City	State	ZIP Code

FOR REAL ESTATE: a legible copy of the deed or title showing the legal description is required	☐ Attached ☐ NA
FOR Discharge Requests under Section 6325(b)(1): copy of deed(s) or title(s) for property remaining subject to the Federal Tax Lien is required	☐ Attached ☐ NA

9. Appraisal and Valuations

REQUIRED APPRAISAL Professional appraisal completed by a disinterested third party	☐ Attached
PLUS ONE OF THE FOLLOWING ADDITIONAL VALUATIONS:	
County valuation of property *(real property)*	☐ Attached
Informal valuation of property by disinterested third party	☐ Attached
Proposed selling price *(for property being sold at auction)*	☐ Attached
Other: _____	☐ Attached

AND for applications under Section 6325(b)(1), valuation information (of the type described above in this section) must also be provided for property remaining subject to the lien.

10. Copy of Federal Tax Lien(s) *(Complete if applicant and taxpayer differ)* ☐ Attached   ☐ No

OR list the lien number(s) found near the top right corner on the lien document(s) *(if known)*

11. Copy of the sales contract/purchase agreement *(if available)* ☐ Attached   ☐ No

OR

Describe how and when the taxpayer will be divested of his/her interest in the property:

12. Copy of a current title report ☐ Attached   ☐ No

OR

List encumbrances senior to the Federal Tax Lien. Include name and address of holder; description of encumbrance, e.g., mortgage, state lien, etc.; date of agreement; original loan amount and interest rate; amount due at time of application; and family relationship, if applicable *(Attach additional sheets as needed)*:

13. Copy of proposed closing statement *(aka HUD-1)* ☐ Attached   ☐ No

OR

Itemize all proposed costs, commissions, and expenses of any transfer or sale associated with property *(Attach additional sheets as needed)*:

14. Additional information that may have a bearing on this request, such as pending litigation, explanations of unusual situations, etc., is attached for consideration ☐ Attached   ☐ No

15. Escrow Agreement *(For applications under IRC 6325(b)(3))* ☐ Attached   ☐ No
Escrow agreement must specify type of account, name and depositary for account, conditions under which payment will be made, cost of escrow, name and address of any party identified as part of escrow agreement, and signatures of all parties involved including Advisory Group Manager. Terms for agreement must be reached before discharge approved.

16. WAIVER *(For applications made by third parties under IRC 6325(b)(2))*
If you are applying as an owner of the property and you are not the taxpayer, to have this application considered under section 6325(b)(2), you must waive the rights that would be available if the application were made under section 6325(b)(4). If you choose not to waive these rights, the application will be treated as one made under 6325(b)(4) and any payment will be treated like a deposit under that section. Please check the appropriate box.

I understand that an application and payment made under section 6325(b)(2) does not provide the judicial remedy available under section 7426(a)(4). In making such an application / payment, I waive the option to have the payment treated as a deposit under section 6325(b)(4) and the right to request a return of funds and to bring an action under section 7426(a)(4). ☐ Waive   ☐ No

17. Declaration
Under penalties of perjury, I declare that I have examined this application, including any accompanying schedules, exhibits, affidavits, and statements and to the best of my knowledge and belief it is true, correct and complete.

_____   _____
Signature/Title   Date

_____   _____
Signature/Title   Date

Catalog Number 54727S   www.irs.gov   Form **14135** (Rev. 06-2010)

¶1434 Exhibit 14-14

Form **669-D** (September 2008)	Department of the Treasury — Internal Revenue Service **Certificate of Subordination of Property From Federal Tax Lien** *(Sec. 6325(d)(1) and/or Sec. 6325(d)(2) of the Internal Revenue Code)*

Of _____ , City of _____ ,

County of _____ , State of _____ ,

is indebted to the United States for unpaid internal revenue tax in the sum of _____

_____ Dollars ($ _____)

as evidenced by:

Notice of Federal Tax Lien Serial Number (a)	Recording Information (b)	Date Recorded (c)	Taxpayer Identification Number (d)	Amount Shown on Lien (e)

A lien attaching to all the property of the taxpayer was filed to secure the amount owed. The notice of lien was filed

with the _____ for the _____ , and also with

the _____ in accordance with the applicable provisions of law.

The lien listed above is attached to certain property described as:

NOTE: Always include the address of real property or a descriptive narrative of personal property in this section when using "See Attachment" and a more detailed description is being attached.

Under the provisions of Internal Revenue code section 6325(d)(1) and/or section 6325(d)(2), the Internal Revenue

Service subordinates the lien on the property described above to _____ .

However, the lien remains in effect for all other property, or rights to property, to which the lien is attached.

Signature	Title	Date

(NOTE: Certificate of officer authorized by law to take acknowledgments is not essential to the validity of Discharge of Federal Tax Lien. Rev. Rul. 71-466, 1971-2, C.B. 409.)

Catalog Number 16754J   www.irs.gov   Form **669-D** (Rev. 09-2008)

¶1435 Exhibit 14-15

Instructions on how to apply for a
Certificate of Subordination of Federal Tax Lien

IRS

A Certificate of Subordination under Internal Revenue Code Section 6325(d)(1) and 6325(d)(2) allows a named creditor to move their junior creditor position ahead of the United States' position for the property named in the certificate. For *How to Apply for a Certificate of Subordination of Federal Estate Tax Lien* Under Section 6325(d)(3) of the Internal Revenue Code use <u>Publication 1153</u>.

1. Complete Form 14134, *Application for Certificate of Subordination of Federal Tax Lien* attached with this publication.

2. Mail the completed Form 14134 and the appropriate attachments to:
   IRS, Attn: Advisory Group Manager
   (Refer to **Publication 4235**, *Collection Advisory Group Addresses* for the correct address. The correct address is the office assigned to the location where the property is located.)

If you have any questions, contact the applicable Advisory Office.

If you want to know how much you owe in order to pay the lien(s) in full, call 1-800-913-6050, visit the nearest Taxpayer Assistance Center, or contact the revenue officer assigned to your case.

Important!

Please submit your application at least 45 days before the transaction date that the certificate of subordination is needed. Doing so will allow sufficient time for review, determination, notification and the furnishing of any applicable documents by the transaction date.

Information Required on the Application

Section 1 - Taxpayer Information

1. Enter the name and address of the individual(s) or business as it appears on the Notice(s) of Federal Tax Lien (NFTL). A second name line is provided if needed.

2. Enter, if known, the last 4 digits of the social security number (SSN) or full employer identification number as it appears on the NFTL.

3. Enter, if known and if applicable, the last 4 digits of any spousal SSN (secondary SSN) associated with the tax debt listed on the NFTL.

4. Provide a daytime phone number and a fax number.

Section 2 - Applicant Information

1. Check the box on the first line of Section 2 if you are both the taxpayer and the applicant. If you are not the taxpayer, attach a copy of the lien.

2. If you have checked the box indicating that you are the taxpayer **and** your information is the same as listed on the lien, enter "same as taxpayer" on the name line.

3. If you are **not** the taxpayer **or** you are the taxpayer but your information is no longer the same as the informa-

tion on the Notice of Federal Tax Lien, enter your name (include any name changes), current address, daytime phone number and fax number.

4. If you are **not** the taxpayer, enter in the box next to "Name" your relationship to the taxpayer (e.g. parent, uncle, sister, no relation, etc.).

Section 3 - Property Owner

1. Check the box on the first line of Section 3 if you are both the property owner and the applicant.

2. Enter the name of the property owner. **Or** if you have checked the box indicating you are both the applicant and the property owner, enter, "same as applicant".

3. Enter the property owner's relationship to the taxpayer (e.g. taxpayer, parent, no relation, etc.).

Section 4 - Attorney/Representative Information

This section is used to list the taxpayer's representative or a representative of a party other than the taxpayer, such as the lender, needing to receive information from the IRS. However, you do not need a representative to request subordination of the federal tax lien.

1. Check the box on the first line of Section 4 if you are attaching a Form 8821 (Tax Information Authority) or Form 2848 (Power of Attorney) with your application. If you are attaching one of these forms, please make sure it is completely filled out, signed, and dated. You must provide one of these forms if the representative represents an interest other than the taxpayer.

2. Enter the name, address, phone number, and fax number of your representative in this action. The IRS will work with you and your representative to process your application. **Or** enter "NA" on the name line if you are not using a representative.

3. Enter whose interest the representative represents (e.g. taxpayer, lender, title company, etc.). This allows the IRS to determine what information can be shared with the representative.

Section 5 - Lender/Finance Company Information

1. Enter the company name, contact name, phone number, and fax number for the lender you are requesting the United States subordinate its interest to.

2. Enter the type of transaction. For example, a loan consolidation or refinance often prompts a subordination request.

Section 6 - Monetary Information

1. Enter the amount of your existing or outstanding financing.

2. Enter the amount of new financing you are seeking.

3. Enter the amount anticipated being paid toward the United States' interest (For applications requested under 6325(d)(1) only).

Publication 784 (Rev. 6-2010)   Catalog Number 46756T   Department of the Treasury **Internal Revenue Services**   www.irs.gov

Section 7 - Basis for Subordination

A subordination may be granted under Internal Revenue Code (IRC) 6325(d)(1) or 6325(d)(2). Review the information below and select the section which best applies to your subordination request. If the IRS does not agree with your selection after its review, an explanation of the decision will be provided.

6325(d)(1) - a subordination may be issued under this section if you pay an amount equal to the lien or interest to which the certificate subordinates the lien of the United States. The following example uses an 80% loan to value and a 3% closing cost to financing ratio.

Example:

	Current/New	Original
Fair Market Value	$200,000	N/A
Refinance	$160,000	$145,000
Closing Costs	$ 4,800	N/A
United States Interest	$ 10,200	N/A

In this example the United States' interest is the equity you obtain from your refinanced loan after paying off the existing loan of $145,000 and paying the closing costs to obtain the loan. ($200,000 property value x 80% loan to value = $160,000 refinance loan amount. $160,000 - $145,000 loan payoff = $15,000 potential equity. $160,000 x 3% = $4800 closing costs to obtain the loan. $15,000 potential equity - $4,800 closing costs = $10,200) The IRS would ask for $10,200 in return for the United States subordinating its interest to the refinanced loan. The lien remains on the property but the refinanced loan has priority over the lien.

4. **6325(d)(2)** – a subordination may be issued under this section if the IRS determines that the issuance of the certificate will increase the amount the government realizes and make collection of the tax liability easier. This might involve a refinance to a lower interest rate which would, if the subordination were granted, allow a larger monthly repayment rate on the tax liability. Or the situation might be more complex. For example, AAA Auto Sales currently pays the IRS $2000 per month on a $120,000 tax debt. Their inventory needs replenishing but their wholesaler is reluctant to provide added inventory because of the federal tax lien. AAA requests subordination and provides the IRS with documentation that an inventory replenishment of 500 cars could allow them to increase their monthly payment to $3000 as well as increase their pay back rate to bi-weekly. In this example the United States' interest would be second on the new inventory, if the subordination is granted.

For applications under section 6325(d)(2), **complete** and **attach** a signed and dated statement describing how the amount the United States may ultimately realize through this subordination will increase and how collection will be facilitated by the subordination.

5. **6325(d)(3)** - Questions and applications for this section refer to Publication 1153 for instructions.

Section 8 - Description of Property

1. Enter a detailed description of the collateral you will use for the loan or other financing. This is the collateral on which you want the lien interest subordinated to the loan or financing. If this is real estate, you must provide the legal description.

2. When the property is real estate include the type of property. For example, 3-bedroom house; etc. When the property is personal property include serial or vehicle numbers, as appropriate. For example, 2002 Cessna twin engine airplane, serial number AT919000000000X00; etc.

3. Provide the property's physical address if it is real estate or provide the physical address where the property is located, if it is personal property.

4. Check the appropriate box to indicate whether you attached a copy of the title or deed to the property.

Section 9 - Appraisal and Valuations

1. Check the "Attached" box after "Appraisal" to indicate whether you have attached an appraisal completed by a disinterested third party. This is typically a professional appraisal providing neighborhood analysis; description of the site; description of the improvements; cost approach; comparable sales; definition of market value; certification; contingent and limiting conditions; interior and exterior photos of the property; exterior photos of comparable sales used; comparable sales location map; sketch of subject property showing room layout; flood map and qualifications of the appraiser. **This type of appraisal is not required for a certificate of subordination.**

2. Check the appropriate box under the "**Or** One of the Following Valuations" section to indicate which type of property value verification is attached with your application.

Section 10 - Federal Tax Liens

This section is important when the applicant and the taxpayer are different. If the applicant and the taxpayer are the same, this section may be skipped.

1. Check the "Attached" box if you have attached copies of the lien(s) with your application.

2. If you checked the "no" box list the System Lien Identification Number (SLID) found in the top right hand box of the lien document, if available. If you do not have the numbers enter "unknown" in the first box.

Section 11 - Proposed loan agreement

1. Check the "attached" box if you have attached the proposed mortgage contract **and** describe how subordination is in the best interests of the United States

2. If you checked the "no" box, describe how subordination is in the best interests of the United States.

Section 12 - Current title report

1. Check the "attached" box if you attached the title report. This is required for subordination.

2. If you checked the "no" box **and** the title report is not attached, use the space provided to list any encumbrances (liens or claims) against the property and whether those encumbrances are senior to the United States' lien interest. Include the name and address of the holder; description of the encumbrance, e.g., mortgage, state lien, etc.; date of agreement; original loan amount and interest rate; amount due at time of application; and family relationship, if applicable.

3. If any mortgages listed on your title report are home equity lines of credit (HELOCs), the NFTL takes priority over advances made via the HELOC on the 46th day after the NFTL is filed. This means any advances made to you more than 46 days after the NFTL is filed, were made subject to the NFTL. The advances need to be included in the equity interest to which the United States attaches. To make an accurate value determination and to avoid processing delays with your application, provide documentation on any HELOC advances from the 46th day after the NFTL was filed, through the date you submit your application, and include expected advances through the date the certificate will be issued.

4. Attach a separate sheet titled "Section 12" with the information in item # 2 and # 3 above if there is not enough space provided on the form.

Section 13 - Proposed closing statement

1. Check the "attached" box if you attached the proposed closing statement. This statement is often referred to as a HUD-1.

2. If you checked the "no" box **and** you did not attach the proposed closing statement, use the space provided to itemize all proposed costs, commissions, and expenses to refinance the property.

3. Attach a separate sheet titled "Section 13" with the information in item # 2 above if there is not enough space provided on the form.

Section 14 - Additional Information

1. Check the "attached" box if you have attached other documents relevant to the subordination application. This could include affidavits or court documents.

2. Check the "no" box if you do not have any additional documentation.

Section 15 - Declaration

The applicant or their authorized Power of Attorney signs the application form. You must sign your application under penalties of perjury attesting to having examined the application, accompanying schedules or documents, exhibits, affidavits, and statements and declaring to the best of your knowledge and belief that the application is true, correct and complete.

Frequently Asked Questions

Q1: When do I make a payment?

The Internal Revenue Code section under which the certificate of subordination will be issued or granted determines the details regarding making a payment.

- Subordination under **6325(d)(1)** requires a payment, but do not send a payment with the application. The Advisory Group Manager will notify you after determining the amount due and when to send payment.
- Subordination under **6325(d)(2)** does not require a payment.

Q2: What is an acceptable form of payment?

Make payments in cash or by the following types of checks: certified; cashiers; or treasurer's check. The check must be drawn on any bank or trust company incorporated under the laws of the United States, or of any state, or possession of the United States. Payment can also be made using a United States postal, bank, express or telegraph money order.

Important! If you pay by personal check, issuance of the certificate of subordination will be delayed until the bank honors the check.

Q3: Who makes the decision to issue a Certificate of Subordination?

In all cases Advisory staff will review and verify the information provided, determine whether a certificate of subordination should be issued, and contact you with any questions. Advisory may contact you, your representative, or any person relative to the transaction for additional information.

The Advisory Group Manager has the responsibility to review and approve the determination and let you know the outcome. If approved, you will receive a conditional commitment letter.

Q4: When will I receive the Certificate of Subordination?

The Internal Revenue Code under which the certificate of subordination will be issued or granted determines when you will receive the certificate.

- Under **6325(d)(1)**, you will receive the certificate upon receipt of the amount determined to be the interest of the United States in the property subject to the federal tax lien.
- Under **6325(d)(2)**, you will receive the certificate after your application has been investigated and the information verified. The Advisory Group Manager will notify you of the decision and provide you with a projected date for mailing the certificate of subordination.

Publication 784 (Rev. 6-2010)   Catalog Number 46756T   Department of the Treasury **Internal Revenue Services**   www.irs.gov

Q5: What happens if my application is denied?

If your application is denied, you will receive **Form 9423,** *Collection Appeal Request* and **Publication 1660,** *Collection Appeal Rights*, with an explanation of why your application was denied.

Privacy and Paperwork Reduction Act Notice

The Privacy act of 1974 says that when we ask you for information about yourself, we must first tell you our legal right to ask for the information, why we are asking for it, and how it will be used. We must also tell you what could happen if you do not provide it and whether or not you must respond under the law.

We ask for the information on this form to carry out the Internal Revenue laws of the United States. This information requested on this form is needed to process your application and to determine whether the federal tax lien can be discharged. You are not required to apply for discharge; however, if you want the federal tax lien to be discharged, you are required to provide the information requested on this form. Section 6109 requires you to provide the requested identification numbers. Failure to provide this information

may delay or prevent processing your application; providing any false information may subject you to penalties.

The time needed to complete and file this form will vary depending on individual circumstances. The estimated burden for individuals filing this form is approved under OMB control number 1545-2174. The estimated burden for those who file this form is shown below.

- Recordkeeping 2 hr., 45 min.
- Learning about the law or the form 2 hr.
- Preparing the form 1 hr., 30 min.
- Copying, assembling, and sending the form to the IRS 85 min.

Routine uses of this information include giving it to the Department of Justice for civil and criminal litigation, and to cities, states, the District of Columbia, and United States commonwealths and possessions for use in administering their tax laws. Advisory may contact you, your representative, or any person relative to the transaction for additional information. We may also disclose this information to other countries under a tax treaty, to federal and state agencies to enforce federal nontax criminal laws, or to federal law enforcement and intelligence agencies to combat terrorism.

Form **14134** (June 2010)	Department of the Treasury — Internal Revenue Service **Application for Certificate of Subordination of Federal Tax Lien**	OMB No. 1545-2174

Complete the entire application. Enter NA *(not applicable)*, when appropriate. Attachments and exhibits should be included as necessary. Additional information may be requested to clarify the details of the transaction(s).

1. Taxpayer Information *(Individual or Business named on the notice of lien)*

Name *(Individual First, Middle Initial, Last)* or *(Business)* as it appears on lien	Primary Social Security Number *(last 4 digits only)*
Name Continuation *(Individual First, Middle Initial, Last)* or *(Business d/b/a)*	Secondary Social Security Number *(last 4 digits only)*
Address *(Number, Street, P.O. Box)*	Employer Identification Number

City	State	ZIP Code

Telephone Number *(with area code)*	Fax Number *(with area code)*

2. Applicant Information   ☐ Check if also the Taxpayer *(If not the taxpayer, attach copy of lien. See Sec.10)*

Name *(First, Middle Initial, Last)*	Relationship to taxpayer

Address *(Number, Street, P.O. Box)*

City	State	ZIP Code

Telephone Number *(with area code)*	Fax Number *(with area code)*

3. Property Owner   ☐ Check if also the Applicant

Relationship to Taxpayer

4. Attorney/Representative Information   **Attached:** Form 8821 or Power of Attorney Form 2848   ☐ Yes   ☐ No

Name *(First, Middle Initial, Last)*	Interest Represented *(e.g. taxpayer, lender, etc.)*

Address *(Number, Street, P.O. Box)*

City	State	ZIP Code

Telephone Number *(with area code)*	Fax Number *(with area code)*

5. Lending/Finance Company

Company Name	Contact Name	Contact Phone Number

Type of transaction *(For example, loan consolidation, refinance, etc)*

Catalog Number 54726H	www.irs.gov	Form **14134** (Rev. 06-2010)

6. Monetary Information

Amount of existing loan *(if refinancing)*	
Amount of new loan	
Amount to be paid to the United States *(6325(d)(1) applications only)*	

7. Basis for Subordination: Check the box below that best addresses what you would like the United States to consider in your application for subordination. *(Publication 784 has additional descriptions of the Internal Revenue Code sections listed below.)*

☐ 6325(d)(1)   the United States will receive an amount equal to the lien or interest to which the certificate of subordination is issued *(provide amount in Section 6 above)*

☐ 6325(d)(2)   the issuance of the certificate of subordination will increase the government's interest and make collection of the tax liability easier. *(**Complete and attach a signed and dated statement describing how the amount the United States may ultimately realize will increase and how collection will be facilitated by the subordination.**)*

Statement   ☐ Attached   ☐ NA

8. Description of property *(For example, 3 bedroom rental house; 2002 Cessna twin engine airplane, serial number AT919000000000X00; etc.):*

Address of real property *(If this is personal property list the address where the property is located)*:
Address *(Number, Street, P.O. Box)*

City	State	ZIP Code

Real Estate: Legible copy of deed or title showing legal description	☐ Attached ☐ NA	

9. Appraisal and Valuations

Appraisal: (Professional appraisal completed by a disinterested third party but it is not required for a subordination)	☐ Attached
OR ONE OF THE FOLLOWING VALUATIONS:	
County valuation of property *(real property)*	☐ Attached
Informal valuation of property by disinterested third party	☐ Attached
Proposed selling price *(for property being sold at auction)*	☐ Attached
Other: _____	☐ Attached

10. Copy of Federal Tax Lien(s) *(Complete if applicant and taxpayer differ)*   ☐ Attached   ☐ No

OR list the lien number(s) found near the top right corner on the lien document(s) *(if known)*

11. Copy of the proposed loan agreement *(if available)*   ☐ Attached   ☐ No

AND

Describe how subordination is in the best interests of the United States:

12. Copy of a current title report *(required for subordination)*   ☐ Attached   ☐ No

OR

List encumbrances with seniority over the Federal Tax Lien. Include name and address of the holder; description of the encumbrance, e.g., mortgage, state lien, etc.; date of agreement; original loan amount and interest rate; amount due at time of application; and family relationship, if applicable. Include any home equity line of credit (HELOCs) advances beginning the 46th day after the NFTL was filed, through the date you submit your application, and include expected advances through the date the certificate will be issued. *(Attach additional sheets as needed)*:

13. Copy of proposed closing statement *(aka HUD-1)*   ☐ Attached   ☐ No

OR

Itemize all proposed costs, commissions, and expenses of any transfer or sale associated with property *(Attach additional sheets as needed)*:

14. Additional information that may have a bearing on this request, such as pending litigation, explanations of unusual situations, etc., is attached for consideration   ☐ Yes   ☐ No

15. Declaration

Under penalties of perjury, I declare that I have examined this application, including any accompanying schedules, exhibits, affidavits, and statements and to the best of my knowledge and belief it is true, correct and complete.

_____   _____
       Signature/Title   Date

_____   _____
       Signature/Title   Date

Section 7 - Basis for Subordination

A subordination may be granted under Internal Revenue Code (IRC) 6325(d)(1) or 6325(d)(2). Review the information below and select the section which best applies to your subordination request. If the IRS does not agree with your selection after its review, an explanation of the decision will be provided.

6325(d)(1) - a subordination may be issued under this section if you pay an amount equal to the lien or interest to which the certificate subordinates the lien of the United States. The following example uses an 80% loan to value and a 3% closing cost to financing ratio.

Example:

	Current/New	Original
Fair Market Value	$200,000	N/A
Refinance	$160,000	$145,000
Closing Costs	$ 4,800	N/A
United States Interest	$ 10,200	N/A

In this example the United States' interest is the equity you obtain from your refinanced loan after paying off the existing loan of $145,000 and paying the closing costs to obtain the loan. ($200,000 property value x 80% loan to value ratio = $160,000 refinance loan amount. $160,000 - $145,000 loan payoff = $15,000 potential equity. $160,000 x 3% = $4800 closing costs to obtain the loan. $15,000 potential equity - $4,800 closing costs = $10,200) The IRS would ask for $10,200 in return for the United States subordinating its interest to the refinanced loan. The lien remains on the property but the refinanced loan has priority over the lien.

4. **6325(d)(2)** – a subordination may be issued under this section if the IRS determines that the issuance of the certificate will increase the amount the government realizes and make collection of the tax liability easier. This might involve a refinance to a lower interest rate which would, if the subordination were granted, allow a larger monthly repayment rate on the tax liability. Or the situation might be more complex. For example, AAA Auto Sales currently pays the IRS $2000 per month on a $120,000 tax debt. Their inventory needs replenishing but their wholesaler is reluctant to provide added inventory because of the federal tax lien. AAA requests subordination and provides the IRS with documentation that an inventory replenishment of 500 cars could allow them to increase their monthly payment to $3000 as well as increase their pay back rate to bi-weekly. In this example the United States' interest would be second on the new inventory, if the subordination is granted.

For applications under section 6325(d)(2), **complete** and **attach** a signed and dated statement describing how the amount the United States may ultimately realize through this subordination will increase and how collection will be facilitated by the subordination.

5. **6325(d)(3)** - Questions and applications for this section refer to Publication 1153 for instructions.

Section 8 - Description of Property

1. Enter a detailed description of the collateral you will use for the loan or other financing. This is the collateral on which you want the lien interest subordinated to the loan or financing. If this is real estate, you must provide the legal description.

2. When the property is real estate include the type of property. For example, 3-bedroom house; etc. When the property is personal property include serial or vehicle numbers, as appropriate. For example, 2002 Cessna twin engine airplane, serial number AT91900000000X00; etc.

3. Provide the property's physical address if it is real estate or provide the physical address where the property is located, if it is personal property.

4. Check the appropriate box to indicate whether you attached a copy of the title or deed to the property.

Section 9 - Appraisal and Valuations

1. Check the "Attached" box after "Appraisal" to indicate whether you have attached an appraisal completed by a disinterested third party. This is typically a professional appraisal providing neighborhood analysis; description of the site; description of the improvements; cost approach; comparable sales; definition of market value; certification; contingent and limiting conditions; interior and exterior photos of the property; exterior photos of comparable sales used; comparable sales location map; sketch of subject property showing room layout; flood map and qualifications of the appraiser. **This type of appraisal is not required for a certificate of subordination.**

2. Check the appropriate box under the "**Or** One of the Following Valuations" section to indicate which type of property value verification is attached with your application.

Section 10 - Federal Tax Liens

This section is important when the applicant and the taxpayer are different. If the applicant and the taxpayer are the same, this section may be skipped.

1. Check the "Attached" box if you have attached copies of the lien(s) with your application.

2. If you checked the "no" box list the System Lien Identification Number (SLID) found in the top right hand box of the lien document, if available. If you do not have the numbers enter "unknown" in the first box.

Section 11 - Proposed loan agreement

1. Check the "attached" box if you have attached the proposed mortgage contract **and** describe how subordination is in the best interests of the United States

2. If you checked the "no" box, describe how subordination is in the best interests of the United States.

¶1436 Exhibit 14-16

Form **668-A(c)(DO)** (Rev. July 2002)	Department of the Treasury – Internal Revenue Service **Notice of Levy**

DATE:

REPLY TO:

TELEPHONE NUMBER
OF IRS OFFICE:

NAME AND ADDRESS OF TAXPAYER:

TO:

IDENTIFYING NUMBER(S):

THIS ISN'T A BILL FOR TAXES YOU OWE. THIS IS A NOTICE OF LEVY WE ARE USING TO COLLECT MONEY OWED BY THE TAXPAYER NAMED ABOVE.

Kind of Tax	Tax Period Ended	Unpaid Balance of Assessment	Statutory Additions	Total

THIS LEVY WON'T ATTACH FUNDS IN IRAs, SELF-EMPLOYED INDIVIDUALS' RETIREMENT PLANS, OR ANY OTHER RETIREMENT PLANS IN YOUR POSSESSION OR CONTROL, UNLESS IT IS SIGNED IN THE BLOCK TO THE RIGHT. ⟶

Total Amount Due ▶

We figured the interest and late payment penalty to _____

The Internal Revenue Code provides that there is a lien for the amount that is owed. Although we have given the notice and demand required by the Code, the amount owed hasn't been paid. This levy requires you to turn over to us this person's property and rights to property *(such as money, credits, and bank deposits)* that you have or which you are already obligated to pay this person. However, don't send us more than the "Total Amount Due."

Money in banks, credit unions, savings and loans, and similar institutions described in section 408(n) of the Internal Revenue Code <u>must be held for 21 calendar days</u> from the day you receive this levy before you send us the money. Include any interest the person earns during the 21 days. Turn over any other money, property, credits, etc. that you have or are already obligated to pay the taxpayer, when you would have paid it if this person asked for payment.

Make a reasonable effort to identify all property and rights to property belonging to this person. At a minimum, search your records using the taxpayer's name, address, and identifying number(s) shown on this form. Don't offset money this person owes you without contacting us at the telephone number shown above for instructions. You may not subtract a processing fee from the amount you send us.

To respond to this levy —
1. Make your check or money order payable to **United States Treasury**.
2. Write the taxpayer's name, identifying number(s), kind of tax and tax period shown on this form, and "LEVY PROCEEDS" on your check or money order *(not on a detachable stub.)*.
3. Complete the back of Part 3 of this form and mail it to us with your payment in the enclosed envelope.
4. Keep Part 1 of this form for your records and give the taxpayer Part 2 within 2 days.

If you don't owe any money to the taxpayer, please complete the back of Part 3, and mail that part back to us in the enclosed envelope.

Signature of Service Representative	Title

¶1437 Exhibit 14-17

Form **668-D** (Rev. December 2001)	Department of the Treasury — Internal Revenue Service **Release of Levy/Release of Property from Levy**
To	Taxpayer(s)
	Identifying Number(s)

A notice of levy was served on you and demand was made for the surrender of:

☐ all property, rights to property, money, credits and bank deposits of the taxpayer(s) named above, except as provided in 6332(c) of the Internal Revenue Code—"Special Rule For Banks." See the back of this form regarding this exception.

☐ wages, salary and other income, now owed to or becoming payable to the taxpayer(s) named above.

The box checked below applies to the levy we served on you.

Release of Levy

☐ Under the provisions of Internal Revenue Code section 6343, all property, rights to property, money, credits, and bank deposits of the taxpayer(s) named above are released from the levy.

☐ Under the provisions of Internal Revenue Code section 6343, all wages, salary and other income now owed to or becoming payable to the taxpayer(s) named above are released from the levy.

Release of Property from Levy

☐ Under the provisions of Internal Revenue Code section 6343, all property, rights to property, money, credits, and bank deposits greater than $ _____ are released from the levy. The levy now attaches only to this amount.

☐ The last payment we received from you was $ _____ dated _____ . The amount the taxpayer still owes is $ _____ . When this amount is paid to the Internal Revenue Service, the levy is released. If you sent us a payment after the last payment date shown, subtract that from the amount you send now.

☐ Under the provisions of Internal Revenue Code section 6343, all wages, salary and other income ☐ **greater than**
☐ **less than** $ _____ each _____ now owed to or becoming payable to the taxpayer(s) named above are released from the levy.

Dated at _____

(Place)   (Date)

Signature	Telephone Number	Title

Part 1— To Addressee   Cat. No. 20450C   www.irs.gov   Form **668-D** (Rev. 12-2001)

Excerpts from the Internal Revenue Code

Sec. 6332 Surrender of Property Subject to Levy

(c) **Special Rule for Banks.**—Any bank *(as defined in section 408(n))* shall surrender *(subject to an attachment or execution under judicial process)* any deposits *(including interest thereon)* in such bank only after 21 days after service of levy.

* * * * * * *

Sec. 6343. Authority to Release Levy and Return Property

(a) **Release of Levy and Notice of Release.**—

(1) **In general.**—Under regulations prescribed by the Secretary, the Secretary shall release the levy upon all, or part of, the property or rights to property levied upon and shall promptly notify the person upon whom such levy was made *(if any)* that such levy has been released if—

(A) the liability for which such levy was made is satisfied or becomes unenforceable by reason of lapse of time,

(B) release of such levy will facilitate the collection of such liability,

(C) the taxpayer has entered into an agreement under section 6159 to satisfy such liability by means of installment payments, unless such agreement provides otherwise,

(D) the Secretary has determined that such levy is creating an economic hardship due to the financial condition of the taxpayer, or

(E) the fair market value of the property exceeds such liability and release of the levy on a part of such property could be made without hindering the collection of such liability.

For purposes of subparagraph (C), the Secretary is not required to release such levy if such release would jeopardize the secured creditor status of the Secretary.

(2) **Expedited determination of certain business property.**—In the case of any tangible personal property essential in carrying on the trade or business of the taxpayer, the Secretary shall provide for an expedited determination under paragraph (1) if levy on such tangible personal property would prevent the taxpayer from carrying on such trade or business.

(3) **Subsequent levy.**—The release of levy on any property under paragraph (1) shall not prevent any subsequent levy on such property.

(b) **Return of property.**—

If the Secretary determines that property has been wrongfully levied upon, it shall be lawful for the Secretary to return . . . an amount equal to the amount of money levied upon . . . any time before the expiration of 9 months from the date of such levy . . . .

(d) **Return of Property in Certain Cases.**—If—

(1) any property has been levied upon, and

(2) the Secretary determines that—

(A) the levy on such property was premature or otherwise not in accordance with administrative procedures of the Secretary,

(B) the taxpayer has entered into an agreement under section 6159 to satisfy the tax liability for which the levy was imposed by means of installment payments, unless such agreement provides otherwise,

(C) the return of such property will facilitate the collection of the tax liability, or

(D) with the consent of the taxpayer or the Taxpayer Advocate, the return of such property would be in the best interests of the taxpayer (as determined by the Taxpayer Advocate) and the United States,

the provisions of subsection (b) shall apply in the same manner as if such property had been wrongly levied upon, except that no interest shall be allowed . . . .

Form **668-D** (Rev. 12-2001)

¶1438 Exhibit 14-18

OMB No. 1545-1504

Department of the Treasury - Internal Revenue Service

Request for Taxpayer Advocate Service Assistance
(And Application for Taxpayer Assistance Order)

Form **911**
(Rev. 5-2011)

Section I – Taxpayer Information *(See Pages 3 and 4 for Form 911 Filing Requirements and Instructions for Completing this Form.)*

1a. Your name as shown on tax return	1b. Taxpayer Identifying Number (SSN, ITIN, EIN)
2a. Spouse's name as shown on tax return *(if applicable)*	2b. Spouse's Taxpayer Identifying Number (SSN, ITIN)

3a. Your current street address *(Number, Street, & Apt. Number)*

3b. City	3c. State *(or Foreign Country)*	3d. ZIP code

4. Fax number *(if applicable)*	5. Email address
6. Tax form(s)	7. Tax period(s)

8. Person to contact	9a. Daytime phone number	9b. ☐ Check here if you consent to have confidential information about your tax issue left on your answering machine or voice message at this number.
10. Best time to call	☐ Check if Cell Phone	

11. Indicate the special communication needs you require *(if applicable)*

☐ TTY/TDD Line   ☐ Interpreter - Specify language other than English *(including sign language)*
☐ Other *(please specify)*

12a. Please describe the tax issue you are experiencing and any difficulties it may be creating
(If more space is needed, attach additional sheets.)

12b. Please describe the relief/assistance you are requesting *(If more space is needed, attach additional sheets.)*

I understand that Taxpayer Advocate Service employees may contact third parties in order to respond to this request and I authorize such contacts to be made. Further, by authorizing the Taxpayer Advocate Service to contact third parties, I understand that I will not receive notice, pursuant to section 7602(c) of the Internal Revenue Code, of third parties contacted in connection with this request.

13a. Signature of Taxpayer or Corporate Officer, and title, if applicable	13b. Date signed
14a. Signature of spouse	14b. Date signed

Section II – Representative Information *(Attach Form 2848 if not already on file with the IRS.)*

1. Name of authorized representative	2. Centralized Authorization File (CAF) number
3. Current mailing address	4. Daytime phone number ☐ Check if Cell Phone
	5. Fax number

6. Signature of representative	7. Date signed

Catalog Number 16965S	www.irs.gov	Form **911** (Rev. 5-2011)

Section III – Initiating Employee Information *(Section III is to be completed by the IRS only)*

Taxpayer name			Taxpayer Identifying Number *(TIN)*	
1. Name of employee	2. Phone number	3a. Function	3b. Operating division	4. Organization code no.

5. How identified and received *(Check the appropriate box)*	6. IRS received date

IRS Function identified issue as meeting Taxpayer Advocate Service (TAS) criteria

☐ (r) Functional referral (Function identified taxpayer issue as meeting TAS criteria).

☐ (x) Congressional correspondence/inquiry not addressed to TAS but referred for TAS handling.

     Name of Senator/Representative _____

Taxpayer or Representative requested TAS assistance

☐ (n) Taxpayer or representative called into a National Taxpayer Advocate (NTA) Toll-Free site.

☐ (s) Functional referral (taxpayer or representative specifically requested TAS assistance).

7. TAS criteria *(Check the appropriate box. NOTE: Checkbox 9 is for TAS Use Only)*

☐ (1) The taxpayer is experiencing economic harm or is about to suffer economic harm.

☐ (2) The taxpayer is facing an immediate threat of adverse action.

☐ (3) The taxpayer will incur significant costs if relief is not granted (including fees for professional representation).

☐ (4) The taxpayer will suffer irreparable injury or long-term adverse impact if relief is not granted.

     (if any items 1-4 are checked, complete Question 9 below)

☐ (5) The taxpayer has experienced a delay of more than 30 days to resolve a tax account problem.

☐ (6) The taxpayer did not receive a response or resolution to their problem or inquiry by the date promised.

☐ (7) A system or procedure has either failed to operate as intended, or failed to resolve the taxpayer's problem or dispute within the IRS.

☐ (8) The manner in which the tax laws are being administered raise considerations of equity, or have impaired or will impair the taxpayer's rights.

☐ (9) The NTA determines compelling public policy warrants assistance to an individual or group of taxpayers **(TAS Use Only)**

8. What action(s) did you take to help resolve the issue? *(This block MUST be completed by the initiating employee)*
If you were unable to resolve the issue, state the reason why (if applicable)

9. Provide a description of the Taxpayer's situation, and where appropriate, explain the circumstances that are creating the economic burden and how the Taxpayer could be adversely affected if the requested assistance is not provided
(This block MUST be completed by the initiating employee)

10. How did the taxpayer learn about the Taxpayer Advocate Service

☐ IRS Forms or Publications   ☐ Media   ☐ IRS Employee   ☐ Other *(please specify)* _____

Catalog Number 16965S	**Page 2**	www.irs.gov	Form **911** (Rev. 5-2011)

Instructions for completing Form 911 (Rev. 5-2011)

Form 911 Filing Requirements

When to Use this Form: The Taxpayer Advocate Service (TAS) is your voice at the IRS. TAS may be able to help you if you're experiencing a problem with the IRS and:

- Your problem with the IRS is causing financial difficulties for you, your family or your business;
- You face (or you business is facing) an immediate threat of adverse action; or
- You have tried repeatedly to contact the IRS, but no one has responded, or the IRS has not responded by the date promised.

If an IRS office will not give you the help you've asked for or will not help you in time to avoid harm, you may submit this form. The Taxpayer Advocate Service will generally ask the IRS to stop certain activities while your request for assistance is pending (for example, lien filings, levies, and seizures).

Where to Send this Form:

- **The quickest method is Fax.** TAS has at least one office in every state, the District of Columbia, and Puerto Rico. Submit this request to the Taxpayer Advocate office in the state or city where you reside. You can find the fax number in the government listings in your local telephone directory, on our website at www.irs.gov/advocate, or in Publication 1546, Taxpayer Advocate Service - Your Voice at the IRS.
- **You also can mail this form.** You can find the mailing address and phone number (voice) of your local Taxpayer Advocate office in your phone book, on our website, and in Pub. 1546, or get this information by calling our toll-free number: 1-877-777-4778.
- **Are you sending the form from overseas?** Fax it to 1-787-622-8933 or mail it to: Taxpayer Advocate Service, Internal Revenue Service, PO Box 193479, San Juan, Puerto Rico 00919-3479.
- Please be sure to fill out the form completely and submit it to the Taxpayer Advocate office nearest you so we can work your issue as soon as possible.

What Happens Next?

If you do not hear from us within one week of submitting Form 911, please call the TAS office where you sent your request. You can find the number at www.irs.gov/advocate.

Important Notes: Please be aware that by submitting this form, you are authorizing the Taxpayer Advocate Service to contact third parties as necessary to respond to your request, and you may not receive further notice about these contacts. For more information see IRC 7602(c).

Caution: The Taxpayer Advocate Service will not consider frivolous arguments raised on this form. You can find examples of frivolous arguments in Publication 2105, Why do I have to Pay Taxes? If you use this form to raise frivolous arguments, you may be subject to a penalty of $5,000.

Paperwork Reduction Act Notice: We ask for the information on this form to carry out the Internal Revenue laws of the United States. Your response is voluntary. You are not required to provide the information requested on a form that is subject to the Paperwork Reduction Act unless the form displays a valid OMB control number. Books or records relating to a form or its instructions must be retained as long as their contents may become material in the administration of any Internal Revenue law. Generally, tax returns and return information are confidential, as required by Code section 6103. Although the time needed to complete this form may vary depending on individual circumstances, the estimated average time is 30 minutes.

Should you have comments concerning the accuracy of this time estimate or suggestions for making this form simpler, please write to: **Internal Revenue Service**, Tax Products Coordinating Committee, Room 6406, 1111 Constitution Ave. NW, Washington, DC 20224.

Instructions for Section I

1a. Enter your name as shown on the tax return that relates to this request for assistance.

1b. Enter your Taxpayer Identifying Number. If you are an individual this will be either a Social Security Number (SSN) or Individual Taxpayer Identification Number (ITIN). If you are a business entity this will be your Employer Identification Number (EIN) (e.g. a partnership, corporation, trust or self-employed individual with employees).

2a. Enter your spouse's name (if applicable) if this request relates to a jointly filed return.

2b. Enter your spouse's Taxpayer Identifying Number (SSN or ITIN) if this request relates to a jointly filed return.

3a-d. Enter your current mailing address, including street number and name, city, state, or foreign country, and zip code.

4. Enter your fax number, including the area code.

5. Enter your e-mail address. We will only use this to contact you if we are unable to reach you by telephone and your issue appears to be time sensitive. We will not, however, use your e-mail address to discuss the specifics of your case.

6. Enter the number of the Federal tax return or form that relates to this request. For example, an individual taxpayer with an income tax issue would enter Form 1040.

7. Enter the quarterly, annual, or other tax period that relates to this request. For example, if this request involves an income tax issue, enter the calendar or fiscal year, if an employment tax issue, enter the calendar quarter.

Instructions for Section I
continue on the next page ▶

¶1438

Instructions for Section I - *(Continued from Page 3)*

8. Enter the name of the individual we should contact. For partnerships, corporations, trusts, etc., enter the name of the individual authorized to act on the entity's behalf. If the contact person is not the taxpayer or other authorized individual, please see the Instructions for Section II.

9a. Enter your daytime telephone number, including the area code. If this is a cell phone number, please check the box.

9b. If you have an answering machine or voice mail at this number and you consent to the Taxpayer Advocate Service leaving confidential information about your tax issue at this number, please check the box. You are not obligated to have information about your tax issue left at this number. If other individuals have access to the answering machine or the voice mail and you do not wish for them to receive any confidential information about your tax issue, please do not check the box.

10. Indicate the best time to call you. Please specify A.M. or P.M. hours.

11. Indicate any special communication needs you require (such as sign language). Specify any language other than English.

12a. Please describe the tax issue you are experiencing and any difficulties it may be creating. Specify the actions that the IRS has taken (or not taken) to resolve the issue. If the issue involves an IRS delay of more than 30 days in resolving your issue, indicate the date you first contacted the IRS for assistance in resolving your issue.

12b. Please describe the relief/assistance you are requesting. Specify the action that you want taken and that you believe necessary to resolve the issue. Furnish any documentation that you believe would assist us in resolving the issue.

13-14. If this is a joint assistance request, both spouses must sign in the appropriate blocks and enter the date the request was signed. If only one spouse is requesting assistance, only the requesting spouse must sign the request. If this request is being submitted for another individual, only a person authorized and empowered to act on that individual's behalf should sign the request. Requests for corporations must be signed by an officer and include the officer's title.

Note: The signing of this request allows the IRS by law to suspend any applicable statutory periods of limitation relating to the assessment or collection of taxes. However, it does not suspend any applicable periods for you to perform acts related to assessment or collection, such as petitioning the Tax Court for redetermination of a deficiency or requesting a Collection Due Process hearing.

Instructions for Section II

Taxpayers: If you wish to have a representative act on your behalf, you must give him/her power of attorney or tax information authorization for the tax return(s) and period(s) involved. For additional information see Form 2848, Power of Attorney and Declaration of Representative, or Form 8821, Tax Information Authorization, and the accompanying instructions. Information can also be found in Publication 1546, Taxpayer Advocate Service-Your Voice at the IRS.

Representatives: If you are an authorized representative submitting this request on behalf of the taxpayer identified in Section I, complete Blocks 1 through 7 of Section II. Attach a copy of Form 2848, Form 8821, or other power of attorney. Enter your Centralized Authorization File (CAF) number in Block 2 of Section II. The CAF number is the unique number that the IRS assigns to a representative after Form 2848 or Form 8821 is filed with an IRS office.

Note: Form 8821 does not authorize your appointee to advocate your position with respect to the Federal tax laws; to execute waivers, consents, or closing agreements; or to otherwise represent you before the IRS. Form 8821 does authorize anyone you designate to inspect and/or receive your confidential tax information in any office of the IRS, for the type of tax and tax periods you list on Form 8821

Instructions for Section III   (For IRS Use Only) *Please complete this section in its entirety.*

Enter the taxpayer's name and taxpayer identification number from the first page of this form.

1. Enter your name.
2. Enter your phone number.
3a. Enter your Function (e.g., ACS, Collection, Examination, Customer Service, etc.).
3b. Enter your Operating Division (W&I, SB/SE, LS&I, or TE/GE).
4. Enter the Organization code number for your office (e.g., 18 for AUSC, 95 for Los Angeles).
5. Check the appropriate box that best reflects how the need for TAS assistance was identified. For example, did taxpayer or representative call or write to an IRS function or the Taxpayer Advocate Service (TAS).
6. Enter the date the taxpayer or representative called or visited an IRS office to request TAS assistance. Or enter the date when the IRS received the Congressional correspondence/inquiry or a written request for TAS assistance from the taxpayer or representative. If the IRS identified the taxpayer's issue as meeting TAS criteria, enter the date this determination was made.
7. Check the box that best describes the reason TAS assistance is requested. Box 9 is for TAS Use Only.
8. State the action(s) you took to help resolve the taxpayer's issue. State the reason(s) that prevented you from resolving the taxpayer's issue. For example, levy proceeds cannot be returned because they were already applied to a valid liability; an overpayment cannot be refunded because the statutory period for issuing a refund expired; or current law precludes a specific interest abatement.
9. Provide a description of the taxpayer's situation, and where appropriate, explain the circumstances that are creating the economic burden and how the taxpayer could be adversely affected if the requested assistance is not provided.
10. Ask the taxpayer how he or she learned about the Taxpayer Advocate Service and indicate the response here.

¶1439 Exhibit 14-19

Request for a Collection Due Process or Equivalent Hearing

Use this form to request a Collection Due Process (CDP) or equivalent hearing with the IRS Office of Appeals if you have been issued one of the following lien or levy notices:

- Notice of Federal Tax Lien Filing and Your Right to a Hearing under IRC 6320,
- Notice of Intent to Levy and Notice of Your Right to a Hearing,
- Notice of Jeopardy Levy and Right of Appeal,
- Notice of Levy on Your State Tax Refund,
- Notice of Levy and Notice of Your Right to a Hearing.

Complete this form and send it to the address shown on your lien or levy notice. Include a copy of your lien or levy notice to ensure proper handling of your request.

Call the phone number on the notice or 1-800-829-1040 if you are not sure about the correct address or if you want to fax your request.

You can find a section explaining the deadline for requesting a Collection Due Process hearing in this form's instructions. If you've missed the deadline for requesting a CDP hearing, you must check line 6 (Equivalent Hearing) to request an equivalent hearing.

1. Taxpayer Name: (Taxpayer 1) _____

   Taxpayer Identification Number _____

   Current Address _____

   City _____ State _____ Zip Code _____

2. Telephone Number and Best Time to Call During Normal Business Hours

   Home ( ) ____ - _____ _____ ☐ am. ☐ pm.
   Work ( ) ____ - _____ _____ ☐ am. ☐ pm.
   Cell ( ) _____ ☐ am. ☐ pm.

3. Taxpayer Name: (Taxpayer 2) _____

   Taxpayer Identification Number _____

   Current Address _____
   (If Different from Address Above) City _____ State _____ Zip Code _____

4. Telephone Number and Best Time to Call During Normal Business Hours

   Home ( ) ____ - _____ _____ ☐ am. ☐ pm.
   Work ( ) ____ - _____ _____ ☐ am. ☐ pm.
   Cell ( ) ____ - ☐ am. ☐ pm.

5. Tax Information as Shown on the Lien or Levy Notice (*If possible, attach a copy of the notice*)

Type of Tax (Income, Employment, Excise, etc. or Civil Penalty)	Tax Form Number (1040, 941, 720, etc)	Tax Period or Periods

Form **12153** (Rev. 3-2011)   Catalog Number 26685D   www.irs.gov   Department of the Treasury - **Internal Revenue Service**

¶1439

Request for a Collection Due Process or Equivalent Hearing

5. Basis for Hearing Request (Both boxes can be checked if you have received both a lien and levy notice)

    ☐ Filed Notice of Federal Tax Lien   ☐ Proposed Levy or Actual Levy

6. Equivalent Hearing (See the instructions for more information on Equivalent Hearings)

    ☐ I would like an Equivalent Hearing - I would like a hearing equivalent to a CDP Hearing if my request for a CDP hearing does not meet the requirements for a timely CDP Hearing.

7. Check the most appropriate box for the reason you disagree with the filing of the lien or the levy. **See page 4 of this form for examples.** You can add more pages if you don't have enough space.

If, during your CDP Hearing, you think you would like to discuss a Collection Alternative to the action proposed by the Collection function it is recommended you submit a completed Form 433A (Individual) and/or Form 433B (Business), as appropriate, with this form. See www.irs.gov for copies of the forms.

Collection Alternative ☐ Installment Agreement ☐ Offer in Compromise ☐ I Cannot Pay Balance

| Lien | | ☐ Subordination | ☐ Discharge | ☐ Withdrawal |

Please explain:

| My Spouse Is Responsible | ☐ Innocent Spouse Relief (Please attach Form 8857, *Request for Innocent Spouse Relief*, to your request.) |

Other (*For examples, see page 4*)   ☐

Reason (*You must provide a reason for the dispute or your request for a CDP hearing will not be honored. Use as much space as you need to explain the reason for your request. Attach extra pages if* necessary*.*):

8. Signatures

I understand the CDP hearing and any subsequent judicial review will suspend the statutory period of limitations for collection action. I also understand my representative or I must sign and date this request before the IRS Office of Appeals can accept it. If you are signing as an officer of a company add your title (*president, secretary, etc.*) behind your signature.

SIGN HERE

Taxpayer 1's Signature	Date
Taxpayer 2's Signature (*if a joint request, both must sign*)	Date

☐ I request my CDP hearing be held with my authorized representative (*attach a copy of Form 2848*)

Authorized Representative's Signature	Authorized Representative's Name	Telephone Number

IRS Use Only

IRS Employee (Print)	Employee Telephone Number	IRS Received Date

Form **12153** (Rev. 3-2011)   Catalog Number 26685D   www.irs.gov   Department of the Treasury - **Internal Revenue Service**

Information You Need To Know When Requesting A Collection Due Process Hearing

What Is the Deadline for Requesting a Timely Collection Due Process (CDP) Hearing?

- Your request for a CDP hearing about a Federal Tax Lien filing must be postmarked by the date indicated in the *Notice of Federal Tax Lien Filing and Your Right to a Hearing under IRC 6320* (lien notice).

- Your request for a CDP hearing about a levy must be postmarked within 30 days after the date of the *Notice of Intent to Levy and Notice of Your Right to a Hearing* (levy notice) or Notice of Your Right to a Hearing After an Actual Levy.

Your timely request for a CDP hearing will prohibit levy action in most cases. A timely request for CDP hearing will also suspend the 10-year period we have, by law, to collect your taxes. Both the prohibition on levy and the suspension of the 10-year period will last until the determination the IRS Office of Appeals makes about your disagreement is final. The amount of time the suspension is in effect will be added to the time remaining in the 10-year period. For example, if the 10-year period is suspended for six months, the time left in the period we have to collect taxes will be extended by six months.

You can go to court to appeal the CDP determination the IRS Office of Appeals makes about your disagreement.

What Is an Equivalent Hearing?

If you still want a hearing with the IRS Office of Appeals after the deadline for requesting a timely CDP hearing has passed, you can use this form to request an equivalent hearing. You must check the Equivalent Hearing box on line 6 of the form to request an equivalent hearing. **An equivalent hearing request does not prohibit levy or suspend the 10-year period for collecting your taxes; also, you cannot go to court to appeal the IRS Office of Appeals' decision about your disagreement.** You must request an equivalent hearing within the following timeframe:

- Lien Notice-- one year plus five business days from the filing date of the Notice of Federal Tax Lien.

- Levy Notice-- one year from the date of the levy notice.

- Your request for a CDP levy hearing, whether timely or Equivalent, does not prohibit the Service from filing a Notice of Federal Tax Lien.

Where Should You File Your CDP or Equivalent Hearing Request?

File your request by mail at the address on your lien notice or levy notice. You may also fax your request. Call the telephone number on the lien or levy notice to ask for the fax number. **Do not send your CDP or equivalent hearing request directly to the IRS Office of Appeals, it must be sent to the address on the lien or levy notice. If you send your request directly to Appeals it may result in your request not being considered a timely request. Depending upon your issue the originating function may contact you in an attempt to resolve the issue(s) raised in your request prior to forwarding your request to Appeals.**

Where Can You Get Help?

You can call the telephone number on the lien or levy notice with your questions about requesting a hearing. The contact person listed on the notice or other representative can access your tax information and answer your questions.

In addition, you may qualify for representation by a low-income taxpayer clinic for free or nominal charge. Our Publication 4134, Low Income Taxpayer Clinic List, provides information on clinics in your area.

If you are experiencing economic harm, the Taxpayer Advocate Service (TAS) may be able to help you resolve your problems with the IRS. TAS cannot extend the time you have to request a CDP or equivalent hearing. See Publication 594, *The IRS Collection Process*, or visit www.irs.gov/advocate/index-html. You also can call 1-877-777-4778 for TAS assistance.

Note– The IRS Office of Appeals will not consider frivolous requests. You can find examples of frivolous reasons for requesting a hearing or disagreeing with a tax assessment in Publication 2105, *Why do I have to Pay Taxes?*, or at www.irs.gov by typing "frivolous" into the search engine.

> You can get copies of tax forms, schedules, instructions, publications, and notices at www.irs.gov, at your local IRS office, or by calling toll-free *1-800-TAX-FORM (829-3676)*.

Form **12153** (Rev. 3-2011)   Catalog Number 26685D   www.irs.gov   Department of the Treasury - **Internal Revenue Service**

Information You Need To Know When Requesting A Collection Due Process Hearing

What Are Examples of Reasons for Requesting a Hearing?

You will have to explain your reason for requesting a hearing when you make your request. Below are examples of reasons for requesting a hearing.

You want a collection alternative-- "I would like to propose a different way to pay the money I owe." Common collection alternatives include:

- Full payment-- you pay your taxes by personal check, cashier's check, money order, or credit card.
- Installment Agreement-- you pay your taxes fully or partially by making monthly payments.
- Offer in Compromise-- you offer to make a payment or payments to settle your tax liability for less than the full amount you owe.

"I cannot pay my taxes." Some possible reasons why you cannot pay your taxes are: (1) you have a terminal illness or excessive medical bills; (2) your only source of income is Social Security payments, welfare payments, or unemployment benefit payments; (3) you are unemployed with little or no income; (4) you have reasonable expenses exceeding your income; or (5) you have some other hardship condition. The IRS Office of Appeals may consider freezing collection action until your circumstances improve. Penalty and interest will continue to accrue on the unpaid balance.

You want action taken about the filing of the tax lien against your property-- You can get a Federal Tax Lien released if you pay your taxes in full. You also may request a lien subordination, discharge, or withdrawal. See www.irs.gov for more information.

When you request **lien subordination**, you are asking the IRS to make a Federal Tax Lien secondary to a non-IRS lien. For example, you may ask for a subordination of the Federal Tax Lien to get a refinancing mortgage on your house or other real property you own. You would ask to make the Federal Tax Lien secondary to the mortgage, even though the mortgage came after the tax lien filing. The IRS Office of Appeals would consider lien subordination, in this example, if you used the mortgage proceeds to pay your taxes.

When you request a **lien discharge**, you are asking the IRS to remove a Federal Tax Lien from a specific property. For example, you may ask for a discharge of the Federal Tax Lien in order to sell your house if you use all of the sale proceeds to pay your taxes even though the sale proceeds will not fully pay all of the tax you owe.

When you request a **lien withdrawal**, you are asking the IRS to remove the Notice of Federal Tax Lien (NFTL) information from public records because you believe the NFTL should not have been filed. For example, you may ask for a withdrawal of the filing of the NFTL if you believe the IRS filed the NFTL prematurely or did not follow procedures, or you have entered into an installment agreement and the installment agreement does not provide for the filing of the NFTL. A withdrawal does not remove the lien from your IRS records.

Your spouse is responsible-- "My spouse (or former spouse) is responsible for all or part of the tax liability." You may believe that your spouse or former spouse is the only one responsible for all or a part of the tax liability. If this is the case, you are requesting a hearing so you can receive relief as an innocent spouse. You should complete and attach Form 8857, *Request for Innocent Spouse Relief*, to your hearing request.

Other Reasons-- "I am not liable for (I don't owe) all or part of the taxes." You can raise a disagreement about the amount you owe only if you did not receive a deficiency notice for the liability (a notice explaining why you owe taxes-it gives you the right to challenge in court, within a specific timeframe, the additional tax the IRS says you owe), or if you have not had another prior opportunity to disagree with the amount you owe.

"I do not believe I should be responsible for penalties." The IRS Office of Appeals may remove all or part of the penalties if you have a reasonable cause for not paying or not filing on time. See Notice 746, Information About Your Notice, Penalty and Interest for what is reasonable cause for removing penalties.

"I have already paid all or part of my taxes." You disagree with the amount the IRS says you haven't paid if you think you have not received credit for payments you have already made.

> See Publication 594, *The IRS Collection Process*, for more information on the following topics:
> Installment Agreements and Offers in Compromise; Lien Subordination, Discharge, and Withdrawal;
> Innocent Spouse Relief; Temporarily Delay Collection; and belief that tax bill is wrong.

Form **12153** (Rev. 3-2011)   Catalog Number 26685D   www.irs.gov   Department of the Treasury - **Internal Revenue Service**

¶1440 Exhibit 14-20

Form **9465** (Rev. December 2009) Department of the Treasury Internal Revenue Service	**Installment Agreement Request** ► If you are filing this form with your tax return, attach it to the front of the return. Otherwise, see instructions.	OMB No. 1545-0074

Caution: *Do not file this form if you are currently making payments on an installment agreement or can pay your balance due in full within 120 days. Instead, call 1-800-829-1040. If you are in bankruptcy or we have accepted your offer-in-compromise, see* **Bankruptcy or offer-in-compromise** *on page 2.*

This request is for Form(s) (for example, Form 1040) ► _____ and for tax year(s) (for example, 2008 and 2009) ► _____

1
Your first name and initial	Last name	Your social security number
If a joint return, spouse's first name and initial	Last name	Spouse's social security number

Current address (number and street). If you have a P.O. box and no home delivery, enter your box number. | Apt. number

City, town or post office, state, and ZIP code. If a foreign address, enter city, province or state, and country. Follow the country's practice for entering the postal code.

2 If this address is new since you filed your last tax return, check here . . . . ► ☐

3 _____ Your home phone number | Best time for us to call

4 _____ Your work phone number | Ext. | Best time for us to call

5 Name of your bank or other financial institution:

Address

City, state, and ZIP code

6 Your employer's name:

Address

City, state, and ZIP code

7 Enter the total amount you owe as shown on your tax return(s) (or notice(s)) . . . . | **7** |
8 Enter the amount of any payment you are making with your tax return(s) (or notice(s)). See instructions | **8** |
9 Enter the amount you can pay each month. **Make your payments as large as possible to limit interest and penalty charges.** The charges will continue until you pay in full . . . . | **9** |
10 Enter the day you want to make your payment each month. **Do not** enter a day later than the 28th ► _____
11 If you want to make your payments by electronic funds withdrawal from your checking account, see the instructions and fill in lines 11a and 11b. This is the most convenient way to make your payments and it will ensure that they are made on time.

► **a** Routing number ☐☐☐☐☐☐☐☐☐

► **b** Account number ☐☐☐☐☐☐☐☐☐☐☐☐☐☐☐☐☐

I authorize the U.S. Treasury and its designated Financial Agent to initiate a monthly ACH electronic funds withdrawal entry to the financial institution account indicated for payments of my federal taxes owed, and the financial institution to debit the entry to this account. This authorization is to remain in full force and effect until I notify the U.S. Treasury Financial Agent to terminate the authorization. To revoke payment, I must contact the U.S. Treasury Financial Agent at **1-800-829-1040** no later than 10 business days prior to the payment (settlement) date. I also authorize the financial institutions involved in the processing of the electronic payments of taxes to receive confidential information necessary to answer inquiries and resolve issues related to the payments.

Your signature	Date	Spouse's signature. If a joint return, **both** must sign.	Date

General Instructions

Section references are to the Internal Revenue Code.

Purpose of Form

Use Form 9465 to request a monthly installment plan if you cannot pay the full amount you owe shown on your tax return (or on a notice we sent you). Generally, you can have up to 60 months to pay. In certain circumstances, you can have longer to pay or your agreement can be approved for an amount that is less than the amount of tax you owe. However, before requesting an installment agreement, you should consider other less costly alternatives, such as getting a bank loan or using available credit on a credit card. If you have any questions about this request, call 1-800-829-1040.

Do not use Form 9465 if:

● You can pay the full amount you owe within 120 days (see page 2), or

● You want to request an online payment agreement. See *Applying online for a payment agreement* on page 2.

Guaranteed installment agreement. Your request for an installment agreement cannot be turned down if the tax you owe is not more than $10,000 and all three of the following apply.

● During the past 5 tax years, you (and your spouse if filing a joint return) have timely filed all income tax returns and paid any income tax due, and have not entered into an installment agreement for payment of income tax.

● The IRS determines that you cannot pay the tax owed in full when it is due and you give the IRS any information needed to make that determination.

● You agree to pay the full amount you owe within 3 years and to comply with the tax laws while the agreement is in effect.

For Privacy Act and Paperwork Reduction Act Notice, see page 3. | Cat. No. 14842Y | Form **9465** (Rev. 12-2009)

Form 9465 (Rev. 12-2009)   Page **2**

 A Notice of Federal Tax Lien may be filed to protect the government's interests until you pay in full.

Can you pay in full within 120 days? If you can pay the full amount you owe within 120 days, call 1-800-829-1040 to establish your request to pay in full. If you can do this, you can avoid paying the fee to set up an installment agreement. Instead of calling, you can apply online.

Applying online for a payment agreement. Instead of filing Form 9465, you can apply online for a payment agreement. To do that, go to *www.irs.gov*, use the pull-down menu under "I need to . . ." and select "Set Up a Payment Plan."

Bankruptcy or offer-in-compromise. If you are in bankruptcy or we have accepted your offer-in-compromise, do not file this form. Instead, call 1-800-829-1040 to get the number of your local IRS Insolvency function for bankruptcy or Technical Support function for offer-in-compromise.

How the Installment Agreement Works

We will usually let you know within 30 days after we receive your request whether it is approved or denied. However, if this request is for tax due on a return you filed after March 31, it may take us longer than 30 days to reply. If we approve your request, we will send you a notice detailing the terms of your agreement and requesting a fee of $105 ($52 if you make your payments by electronic funds withdrawal). However, you may qualify to pay a reduced fee of $43 if your income is below a certain level. The IRS will let you know whether you qualify for the reduced fee. If the IRS does not say you qualify for the reduced fee, you can request the reduced fee using Form 13844, Application For Reduced User Fee For Installment Agreements.

You will also be charged interest and may be charged a late payment penalty on any tax not paid by its due date, even if your request to pay in installments is granted. Interest and any applicable penalties will be charged until the balance is paid in full. To limit interest and penalty charges, file your return on time and pay as much of the tax as possible with your return (or notice). All payments received will be applied to your account in the best interests of the United States.

By approving your request, we agree to let you pay the tax you owe in monthly installments instead of immediately paying the amount in full. In return, you agree to make your monthly payments on time. You also agree to meet all your future tax liabilities. This means that you must have enough withholding or estimated tax payments so that your tax liability for future years is paid in full when you timely file your return. Your request for an installment agreement will be denied if all required tax returns have not been filed. Any refund due you in a future year will be applied against the amount you owe. If your refund is applied to your balance, you are still required to make your regular monthly installment payment.

Payment methods. You can make your payments by check, money order, credit card, or one of the other payment methods shown next. The fee for each payment method is also shown.

Payment method	Applicable fee
Check, money order, or credit card	$105
Electronic funds withdrawal	$ 52
Payroll deduction installment agreement	$105

For details on how to pay, see your tax return instructions, visit *www.irs.gov*, or call 1-800-829-1040.

After we receive each payment, we will send you a notice showing the remaining amount you owe, and the due date and amount of your next payment. But if you choose to have your payments automatically withdrawn from your checking account, you will not receive a notice. Your bank statement is

your record of payment. We will also send you an annual statement showing the amount you owed at the beginning of the year, all payments made during the year, and the amount you owe at the end of the year.

If you do not make your payments on time or do not pay any balance due on a return you file later, you will be in default on your agreement and we may take enforcement actions, such as the filing of a Notice of Federal Tax Lien or an IRS levy action, to collect the entire amount that you owe. To ensure that your payments are made timely, you should consider making them by electronic funds withdrawal (see the instructions for lines 11a and 11b on page 3).

Requests to modify or terminate an installment agreement. After an installment agreement is approved, you may submit a request to modify or terminate an installment agreement. This request will not suspend the statute of limitations on collection. While the IRS considers your request to modify or terminate the installment agreement, you must comply with the existing agreement.

 An installment agreement may be terminated if you provide materially incomplete or inaccurate information in response to an IRS request for a financial update.

For additional information on the IRS collection process, see Pub. 594, The IRS Collection Process.

Where To File

Attach Form 9465 to the front of your return and send it to the address shown in your tax return booklet. If you have already filed your return or you are filing this form in response to a notice, file Form 9465 by itself with the Internal Revenue Service Center at the address below that applies to you. No street address is needed.

IF you live in . . .	THEN use this address . . .
Florida, Georgia, North Carolina, South Carolina	Department of the Treasury Internal Revenue Service Center Atlanta, GA 39901
Alabama, Kentucky, Louisiana, Mississippi, Tennessee, Texas	Department of the Treasury Internal Revenue Service Center Austin, TX 73301
Alaska, Arizona, California, Colorado, Hawaii, Idaho, Illinois, Indiana, Iowa, Kansas, Michigan, Minnesota, Montana, Nebraska, Nevada, New Mexico, North Dakota, Oklahoma, Oregon, South Dakota, Utah, Washington, Wisconsin, Wyoming	Department of the Treasury Internal Revenue Service Center Fresno, CA 93888
Arkansas, Connecticut, Delaware, District of Columbia, Maine, Maryland, Massachusetts, Missouri, New Hampshire, New Jersey, New York, Ohio, Pennsylvania, Rhode Island, Vermont, Virginia, West Virginia	Department of the Treasury Internal Revenue Service Center Kansas City, MO 64999
A foreign country, American Samoa, or Puerto Rico (or are excluding income under Internal Revenue Code section 933), or use an APO or FPO address, or file Form 2555, 2555-EZ, or 4563, or are a dual-status alien or nonpermanent resident of Guam or the Virgin Islands*	Department of the Treasury Internal Revenue Service Center Austin, TX 73301

* Permanent residents of Guam or the Virgin Islands cannot use Form 9465.

Form 9465 (Rev. 12-2009)

Specific Instructions

Line 1

If you are making this request for a joint tax return, show the names and social security numbers (SSNs) in the same order as on your tax return.

Line 7

Enter the total amount you owe as shown on your tax return (or notice).

 If the total amount you owe is more than $25,000 (including any amounts you owe from prior years), complete and attach Form 433-F, Collection Information Statement. You can get Form 433-F by visiting the IRS website at www.irs.gov.

Line 8

Even if you cannot pay the full amount you owe now, you should pay as much as possible to limit penalty and interest charges. If you are filing this form with your tax return, make the payment with your return. For details on how to pay, see your tax return instructions.

If you are filing this form by itself, such as in response to a notice, attach a check or money order payable to the "United States Treasury." Do not send cash. Be sure to include:

• Your name, address, SSN, and daytime phone number.

• The tax year and tax return (for example, "2009 Form 1040") for which you are making this request.

Line 9

You should try to make your payments large enough so that your balance due will be paid off as quickly as possible without causing you a financial burden.

Line 10

You can choose the day of each month your payment is due. This can be on or after the 1st of the month, but no later than the 28th of the month. For example, if your rent or mortgage payment is due on the 1st of the month, you may want to make your installment payments on the 15th. When we approve your request, we will tell you the month and day that your first payment is due.

If we have not replied by the date you chose for your first payment, you can send the first payment to the Internal Revenue Service Center at the address shown on page 2 that applies to you. See the instructions for line 8 above for details on what to write on your payment.

Lines 11a and 11b

 Making your payments by electronic funds withdrawal will help ensure that your payments are made timely and that you are not in default of this agreement.

To pay by electronic funds withdrawal from your checking account at a bank or other financial institution (such as mutual fund, brokerage firm, or credit union), fill in lines 11a and 11b. Check with your financial institution to make sure that an electronic funds withdrawal is allowed and to get the correct routing and account numbers.

Note. We will send you a bill for the first payment and the fee. You must send us your first payment. All other payments will be electronically withdrawn.

Line 11a. The routing number must be nine digits. The first two digits of the routing number must be 01 through 12 or 21 through 32. Use a check to verify the routing number. On the sample check on this page, the routing number is 250250025. But if your check is payable through a financial institution

different from the one at which you have your checking account, do not use the routing number on that check. Instead, contact your financial institution for the correct routing number.

Line 11b. The account number can be up to 17 characters (both numbers and letters). Include hyphens but omit spaces and special symbols. Enter the number from left to right and leave any unused boxes blank. On the sample check below, the account number is 20202086. Do not include the check number.

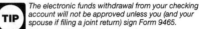 *The electronic funds withdrawal from your checking account will not be approved unless you (and your spouse if filing a joint return) sign Form 9465.*

Sample Check—Lines 11a and 11b

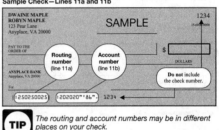

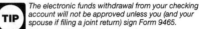 *The routing and account numbers may be in different places on your check.*

Privacy Act and Paperwork Reduction Act Notice. Our legal right to ask for the information on this form is sections 6001, 6011, 6012(a), 6109, and 6159 and their regulations. We will use the information to process your request for an installment agreement. The reason we need your name and social security number is to secure proper identification. We require this information to gain access to the tax information in our files and properly respond to your request. You are not required to request an installment agreement. If you do request an installment agreement, you are required to provide the information requested on this form. Failure to provide this information may prevent processing your request; providing false information may subject you to fines or penalties.

You are not required to provide the information requested on a form that is subject to the Paperwork Reduction Act unless the form displays a valid OMB control number. Books or records relating to a form or its instructions must be retained as long as their contents may become material in the administration of any Internal Revenue law. Generally, tax returns and return information are confidential, as required by section 6103. However, we may give this information to the Department of Justice for civil and criminal litigation, and to cities, states, and the District of Columbia to carry out their tax laws. We may also disclose this information to other countries under a tax treaty, to federal and state agencies to enforce federal nontax criminal laws, or to federal law enforcement and intelligence agencies to combat terrorism.

The average time and expenses required to complete and file this form will vary depending on individual circumstances. For the estimated averages, see the instructions for your income tax return.

If you have suggestions for making this form simpler, we would be happy to hear from you. See the instructions for your income tax return.

¶1441 Exhibit 14-21

Form **433-D**
(Rev. April 2010)

Department of the Treasury — Internal Revenue Service
Installment Agreement
(See Instructions on the back of this page)

Name and address of taxpayer(s)

Social security or employer identification number
(Taxpayer)   *(Spouse)*

Your telephone numbers *(including area code)*
(Home)   *(Work, cell or business)*

For assistance, call: **1-800-829-0115** *(Business),* or
1-800-829-8374 *(Individual – Self-Employed/Business Owners),* or
1-800-829-0922 *(Individuals – Wage Earners)*

☐ Submit a new Form W-4 to your employer to increase your withholding.

Or write:_____
(City, State, and ZIP Code)

Employer *(Name, address, and telephone number)*_____

Financial Institution *(Name and address)*_____

Kinds of taxes *(Form numbers)*	Tax periods	Amount owed as of _____ $

I / We agree to pay the federal taxes shown above, PLUS PENALTIES AND INTEREST PROVIDED BY LAW, as follows:

$_____ on _____ and $_____ on the _____ of each month thereafter

I / We also agree to increase or decrease the above installment payment as follows:

Date of increase *(or decrease)*	Amount of increase *(or decrease)*	New installment payment amount

The terms of this agreement are provided on the back of this page. Please review them thoroughly.

☐ Please initial this box after you've reviewed all terms and any additional conditions.

Additional Conditions / Terms *(To be completed by IRS)*

Note: Internal Revenue Service employees may contact third parties in order to process and maintain this agreement.

DIRECT DEBIT—Attach a voided check or complete this part only if you choose to make payments by direct debit. Read the instructions on the back of this page.

a. Routing number: ☐☐☐☐☐☐☐☐☐

b. Account number: ☐☐☐☐☐☐☐☐☐☐☐☐☐☐☐☐☐

I authorize the U.S. Treasury and its designated Financial Agent to initiate a monthly ACH debit *(electronic withdrawal)* entry to the financial institution account indicated for payments of my Federal taxes owed, and the financial institution to debit the entry to this account. This authorization is to remain in full force and effect until I notify the U.S. Treasury Financial Agent to terminate the authorization. To revoke payment, I must contact the U.S. Treasury Financial Agent at the applicable toll free number listed above no later than 14 business days prior to the payment *(settlement)* date. I also authorize the financial institutions involved in the processing of the electronic payments of taxes to receive confidential information necessary to answer inquiries and resolve issues related to the payments.

Your signature	Title *(if Corporate Officer or Partner)*	Date

Spouse's signature *(if a joint liability)*		Date

Agreement examined or approved by *(Signature, title, function)*		Date

FOR IRS USE ONLY

AGREEMENT LOCATOR NUMBER: ___ ___ ___ ___
Check the appropriate boxes:

☐ RSI "1" no further review   ☐ AI "0" Not a PPIA
☐ RSI "5" PPIA IMF 2 year review   ☐ AI "1" Field Asset PPIA
☐ RSI "6" PPIA BMF 2 year review   ☐ AI "2" All other PPIAs
Agreement Review Cycle:__ __ __ __ __ __   Earliest CSED:_____
☐ Check box if pre-assessed modules included
Originator's ID #:_____   Originator Code:_____
Name: _____   Title: _____

A NOTICE OF FEDERAL TAX LIEN *(Check one box below.)*

☐ HAS ALREADY BEEN FILED
☐ WILL BE FILED IMMEDIATELY
☐ WILL BE FILED WHEN TAX IS ASSESSED
☐ MAY BE FILED IF THIS AGREEMENT DEFAULTS

Part 1— IRS Copy

Catalog No. 16644M   www.irs.gov   Form **433-D** (Rev. 4-2010)

Reset Form Fields

AGREEMENT LOCATOR NUMBER DESIGNATIONS

XX Position (the first two numbers) denotes either the Initiator or Type of Agreement. The XX values are:

00	Form 433-D initiated by AO on an ACS case
01	Customer Service Toll-free initiated agreements
02	AO Field Territory (revenue officer) initiated agreements
03	Direct Debit agreements initiated by any function
06	Exam initiated agreements
07	Submission Processing initiated agreements
08	Agreements initiated by other functions
11	Form 2159 agreement initiated by AO, ACS or Customer Service
12	AO or ACS agreement with multiple conditions
20	Status 22/24 accounts – Call Site/CSCO
90	CSCO initiated agreements – other than status 22 or 26
91	Form 2159 agreement initiated by CSCO
92	CSCO agreement with multiple conditions
99	Up to 120 days extensions *(NOT FOR FIELD)*

YY Position (the second two numbers) denotes Conditions Affecting the Agreement. The YY values are:

08	Continuous Wage Levy (from ACS and RO)
09	All other conditions
12	Partial Pay Installment Agreement (PPIA) all functions
15	In Business Trust Fund (IBTF) monitoring required for all functions
27	Restricted Interest/Penalty condition present
32	Unassessed modules to be included in agreement
36	Streamlined agreements, less than 60 months, up to $25,000
41	BMF in Business Deferral Level (CSCO USE ONLY)
53	Report Currently Not Collectible (CNC) if agreement defaults
63	Cross-reference TIN (Status 63)
66	File lien in event of default
70	Secondary TP responsible for Joint Liability
80	Review and revise payment amount
99	Up to 120 days extensions *(NOT FOR FIELD)*

When an agreement has more than one condition, use either 12 or 92 in the "XX" position and assign the primary condition (YY) based on the following priorities:

#1-63, #2-12, #3-53, or #4-32

The remaining multiple conditions will be input as a history item on IDRS.

INSTALLMENT AGREEMENT ORIGINATOR CODES

20	Collection field function regular agreement
21	Collection field function streamlined agreement
30	Reserved
31	Reserved
50	Field assistance counter – regular agreement
51	Field assistance counter – streamlined agreement
60	Examination regular agreement
61	Examination streamlined agreement
70	Toll-free regular agreement
71	Toll-free streamlined agreement
72	Paper regular agreement CSCO
73	Paper streamlined agreement CSCO
74	Voice Response Unit (system generated)
75	Automated Collection Branch regular
76	Automated Collection Branch streamlined
77	Automated Collection Branch Voice Response Unit regular (system generated)
78	Automated Collection Branch Voice Response Unit streamlined (system generated)
80	Other function regular agreement
81	Other function-streamlined agreement
82	Electronic Installment Agreement (e-IA) - AM
83	Electronic Installment Agreement (e-IA) - ACS
90-91	Reserved for vendors – all streamlined agreements

Form **433-D**
(Rev. April 2010)

Department of the Treasury — Internal Revenue Service
Installment Agreement
(See Instructions on the back of this page)

Name and address of taxpayer(s)

Social security or employer identification number
(Taxpayer)   *(Spouse)*

Your telephone numbers *(including area code)*
(Home)   *(Work, cell or business)*

For assistance, call: **1-800-829-0115** *(Business)*, or
         1-800-829-8374 *(Individual – Self-Employed/Business Owners)*, or
         1-800-829-0922 *(Individuals – Wage Earners)*

☐ Submit a new Form W-4 to your employer to increase your withholding.

Or write:_____
         (City, State, and ZIP Code)

Employer *(Name, address, and telephone number)*_____

Financial Institution *(Name and address)* _____

Kinds of taxes *(Form numbers)*	Tax periods	Amount owed as of _____ $

I / We agree to pay the federal taxes shown above, PLUS PENALTIES AND INTEREST PROVIDED BY LAW, as follows:

$_____ on _____ and $_____ on the _____ of each month thereafter

I / We also agree to increase or decrease the above installment payment as follows:

Date of increase *(or decrease)*	Amount of increase *(or decrease)*	New installment payment amount

The terms of this agreement are provided on the back of this page. Please review them thoroughly.

☐ Please initial this box after you've reviewed all terms and any additional conditions.

Additional Conditions / Terms *(To be completed by IRS)*	**Note:** Internal Revenue Service employees may contact third parties in order to process and maintain this agreement.

DIRECT DEBIT—Attach a voided check or complete this part only if you choose to make payments by direct debit. Read the instructions on the back of this page.

a. Routing number: ☐☐☐☐☐☐☐☐☐

b. Account number: ☐☐☐☐☐☐☐☐☐☐☐☐☐☐☐☐☐

I authorize the U.S. Treasury and its designated Financial Agent to initiate a monthly ACH debit *(electronic withdrawal)* entry to the financial institution account indicated for payments of my Federal taxes owed, and the financial institution to debit the entry to this account. This authorization is to remain in full force and effect until I notify the U.S. Treasury Financial Agent to terminate the authorization. To revoke payment, I must contact the U.S. Treasury Financial Agent at the applicable toll free number listed above no later than 14 business days prior to the payment *(settlement)* date. I also authorize the financial institutions involved in the processing of the electronic payments of taxes to receive confidential information necessary to answer inquiries and resolve issues related to the payments.

Your signature	Title *(If Corporate Officer or Partner)*	Date
Spouse's signature *(if a joint liability)*		Date
Agreement examined or approved by *(Signature, title, function)*		Date

FOR IRS USE ONLY

AGREEMENT LOCATOR NUMBER: ____ ____ ____ ____
Check the appropriate boxes:

☐ RSI "1" no further review   ☐ AI "0" Not a PPIA
☐ RSI "5" PPIA IMF 2 year review   ☐ AI "1" Field Asset PPIA
☐ RSI "6" PPIA BMF 2 year review   ☐ AI "2" All other PPIAs
Agreement Review Cycle: __ __ __ __ __   Earliest CSED:_____
☐ Check box if pre-assessed modules included
Originator's ID #:_____ Originator Code:_____
Name: _____ Title: _____

A NOTICE OF FEDERAL TAX LIEN *(Check one box below.)*

☐ HAS ALREADY BEEN FILED
☐ WILL BE FILED IMMEDIATELY
☐ WILL BE FILED WHEN TAX IS ASSESSED
☐ MAY BE FILED IF THIS AGREEMENT DEFAULTS

Part 2 — Financial Institution Copy *(Direct Debit only)*   Catalog No. 16644M   www.irs.gov   Form **433-D** (Rev. 4-2010)

¶1441

Form **433-D**
(Rev. April 2010)

Department of the Treasury — Internal Revenue Service
Installment Agreement
(See Instructions on the back of this page)

Name and address of taxpayer(s)

Social security or employer identification number
(Taxpayer)   *(Spouse)*

Your telephone numbers *(including area code)*
(Home)   *(Work, cell or business)*

For assistance, call: **1-800-829-0115** *(Business)*, or
    1-800-829-8374 *(Individual – Self-Employed/Business Owners)*, or
    1-800-829-0922 *(Individuals – Wage Earners)*

☐ Submit a new Form W-4 to your employer to increase your withholding.

Or write:_____
(City, State, and ZIP Code)

Employer *(Name, address, and telephone number)*_____

Financial Institution *(Name and address)*_____

Kinds of taxes *(Form numbers)*	Tax periods	Amount owed as of _____
		$

I / We agree to pay the federal taxes shown above, PLUS PENALTIES AND INTEREST PROVIDED BY LAW, as follows:

$_____ on _____ and $_____ on the _____ of each month thereafter
I / We also agree to increase or decrease the above installment payment as follows:

Date of increase *(or decrease)*	Amount of increase *(or decrease)*	New installment payment amount

The terms of this agreement are provided on the back of this page. Please review them thoroughly.

☐ Please initial this box after you've reviewed all terms and any additional conditions.

Additional Conditions / Terms *(To be completed by IRS)*	Note: Internal Revenue Service employees may contact third parties in order to process and maintain this agreement.

DIRECT DEBIT—Attach a voided check or complete this part only if you choose to make payments by direct debit. Read the instructions on the back of this page.

a. Routing number: ☐☐☐☐☐☐☐☐☐

b. Account number: ☐☐☐☐☐☐☐☐☐☐☐☐☐☐☐☐☐

I authorize the U.S. Treasury and its designated Financial Agent to initiate a monthly ACH debit *(electronic withdrawal)* entry to the financial institution account indicated for payments of my Federal taxes owed, and the financial institution to debit the entry to this account. This authorization is to remain in full force and effect until I notify the U.S. Treasury Financial Agent to terminate the authorization. To revoke payment, I must contact the U.S. Treasury Financial Agent at the applicable toll free number listed above no later than 14 business days prior to the payment *(settlement)* date. I also authorize the financial institutions involved in the processing of the electronic payments of taxes to receive confidential information necessary to answer inquiries and resolve issues related to the payments.

Your signature	Title *(If Corporate Officer or Partner)*	Date
Spouse's signature *(if a joint liability)*		Date
Agreement examined or approved by *(Signature, title, function)*		Date

FOR IRS USE ONLY

AGREEMENT LOCATOR NUMBER: ___ ___ ___ ___
Check the appropriate boxes:

☐ RSI "1" no further review   ☐ AI "0" Not a PPIA
☐ RSI "5" PPIA IMF 2 year review   ☐ AI "1" Field Asset PPIA
☐ RSI "6" PPIA BMF 2 year review   ☐ AI "2" All other PPIAs
Agreement Review Cycle: ___ ___ ___ ___ ___   Earliest CSED:_____
☐ Check box if pre-assessed modules included
Originator's ID #:_____ Originator Code:_____
Name: _____ Title: _____

A NOTICE OF FEDERAL TAX LIEN *(Check one box below.)*

☐ HAS ALREADY BEEN FILED
☐ WILL BE FILED IMMEDIATELY
☐ WILL BE FILED WHEN TAX IS ASSESSED
☐ MAY BE FILED IF THIS AGREEMENT DEFAULTS

Part 3 — Taxpayer's Copy   Catalog No. 16644M   www.irs.gov   Form **433-D** (Rev. 4-2010)

¶1441

INSTRUCTIONS TO TAXPAYER

If not already completed by an IRS employee, please fill in the information in the spaces provided on the front of this form for:

- Your name *(include spouse's name if a joint return)* and current address;
- Your social security number and/or employer identification number *(whichever applies to your tax liability)*;
- Your home and work, cell or business telephone numbers;
- The complete name, address and phone number of your employer and your financial institution;
- The amount you can pay now as a partial payment;
- The amount you can pay each month *(or the amount determined by IRS personnel)*; and
- The date you prefer to make this payment *(This must be the same day for each month, from the 1st to the 28th)*. We must receive your payment by this date. If you elect the direct debit option, this is the day you want your payment electronically withdrawn from your financial institution account.

Review the terms of this agreement.
When you've completed this agreement form, please sign and date it. Then, return Part 1 to IRS at the address on the letter that came with it or the address shown in the "For assistance" box on the front of the form.

Terms of this agreement

By completing and submitting this agreement, you *(the taxpayer)* agree to the following terms:
- This agreement will remain in effect until your liabilities *(including penalties and interest)* are paid in full, the statutory period for collection has expired, or the agreement is terminated.
- You will make each payment so that we *(IRS)* receive it by the monthly due date stated on the front of this form. *If you cannot make a scheduled payment, contact us immediately.*
- This agreement is based on your current financial condition. We may modify or terminate the agreement if our information shows that your ability to pay has significantly changed. You must provide updated financial information when requested.
- While this agreement is in effect, you must file all federal tax returns and pay any *(federal)* taxes you owe on time.
- We will apply your federal tax refunds or overpayments *(if any)* to the amount you owe until it is fully paid or the statutory period for collection has expired.
- You must pay a $105 user fee, which we have authority to deduct from your first payment(s) *($52 fee for DDIA)*.
- If you default on your installment agreement, you must pay a $45 reinstatement fee if we reinstate the agreement. We have the authority to deduct this fee from your first payment(s) after the agreement is reinstated.
- We will apply all payments on this agreement in the best interests of the United States.
- **We can terminate your installment agreement if:**
  - You do not make monthly installment payments as agreed.
  - You do not pay any other federal tax debt when due.
  - You do not provide financial information when requested.
- If we terminate your agreement, we may collect the entire amount you owe by levy on your income, bank accounts or other assets, or by seizing your property.
- We may terminate this agreement at any time if we find that collection of the tax is in jeopardy.
- This agreement may require managerial approval. We'll notify you when we approve or don't approve the agreement.
- We may file a Federal Tax lien if one has not been filed previously.

HOW TO PAY BY DIRECT DEBIT

Instead of sending us a check, you can pay by direct debit *(electronic withdrawal)* from your checking account at a financial institution *(such as a bank, mutual fund, brokerage firm, or credit union)*. To do so, fill in Lines a, b, and c. Contact your financial institution to make sure that a direct debit is allowed and to get the correct routing and account numbers.

Line a. The first two digits of the routing number must be 01 through 12 or 21 through 32. Don't use a deposit slip to verify the number because it may contain internal routing numbers that are not part of the actual routing number.

Line b. The account number can be up to 17 characters. Include hyphens but omit spaces and special symbols. Enter the number from left to right and leave any unused boxes blank.

NOTE: *We will bill you for the first payment and the user fee.* **You must make the first payment by mail.** All other payments will be electronically withdrawn on the same day each month from your account. IRS won't send you a reminder about this.

CHECKLIST FOR MAKING INSTALLMENT PAYMENTS:

1. Write your social security or employer identification number on each payment.
2. Make your check or money order payable to "*United States Treasury.*"
3. Make each payment in an amount at least equal to the amount specified in this agreement.
4. Don't double one payment and skip the next without contacting us first.
5. Enclose a copy of the reminder notice, if you received one, with each payment using the envelope provided.
6. If you didn't receive an envelope, call the number below.

This agreement will not affect your liability *(if any)* for backup withholding under Public Law 98-67, the Interest and Dividend Compliance Act of 1983.

QUESTIONS? — If you have **any** questions about the direct debit process or completing this form, please call the applicable telephone number below for assistance.

     1-800-829-0115 *(Business)*
     1-800-829-8374 *(Individuals – Self-Employed / Business Owners)*
     1-800-829-0922 *(Individuals – Wage Earners)*

Catalog No. 16644M   Form **433-D** (Rev. 4-2010)

¶1442 Exhibit 14-22

Collection Appeal Rights

You may appeal many IRS collection actions to the IRS Office of Appeals (Appeals). The Office of Appeals is separate from and independent of the IRS Collection office that initiated the collection action. We ensure and protect our independence by adhering to a strict policy of no ex parte communication with the IRS Collection office about the accuracy of the facts or the merits of your case without providing you an opportunity to participate at that meeting. Revenue Procedure 2000-43 has more information about Appeals' mandatory independence and ex parte communication and is available at www.IRS.gov. The two main procedures are **Collection Due Process** and **Collection Appeals Program**. Other procedures are described on page four of this publication and at www.IRS.gov.

Collection Due Process (CDP) is available if you receive one of the following notices:
- *Notice of Federal Tax Lien Filing and Your Right to a Hearing under IRC 6320*
- *Final Notice - Notice of Intent to Levy and Notice of Your Right to a Hearing*
- *Notice of Jeopardy Levy and Right of Appeal*
- *Notice of Levy on Your State Tax Refund – Notice of Your Right to a Hearing*
- *Notice of Levy and Notice of Right to a Hearing with respect to a Disqualified Employment Tax Levy*

Collection Appeals Program (CAP) is available for the following actions:
- *Before or after the IRS files a Notice of Federal Tax Lien*
- *Before or after the IRS levies or seizes your property*
- *Termination, or proposed termination, of an installment agreement*
- *Rejection of an installment agreement*

CAP is generally quicker and is available for a broader range of collection actions. However, you cannot go to court if you disagree with the CAP decision. CAP procedures are described on pages three and four of this publication.

You may represent yourself at CDP, CAP and other Appeals proceedings. Or, you may be represented by an attorney, certified public accountant, or a person enrolled to practice before the IRS. Also, you may be represented by a member of your immediate family, or in the case of a business, by regular full-time employees, general partners or bona fide officers.

A Low Income Tax Clinic (LITC) may represent you if you qualify. Most LITCs provide representation before the IRS or in court on audits, tax collection disputes, and other issues for free or for a small fee. Some clinics can provide multilingual information about taxpayer rights and responsibilities. Publication 4134, *Low Income Taxpayer Clinic List*, provides information on clinics in your area and is available at your local IRS office, by calling 1-800-829-3676, or from www.IRS.gov.

If you want your representative to contact us or appear without you and to receive and inspect confidential material, you must file a properly completed Form 2848, *Power of Attorney and Declaration of Representative*. You may also authorize an individual to receive or inspect confidential material but not represent you before the IRS, by filing a Form 8821, *Tax Information Authorization*. These forms are available at your local IRS office, by calling 1-800-829-3676, or from www.IRS.gov.

HEARING AVAILABLE UNDER COLLECTION DUE PROCESS (CDP)
For Lien and Levy Notices

By law, you have the right to a CDP hearing by Appeals for these collection actions:
- The first time a Notice of Federal Tax Lien is filed for a tax and period.
- Before the first levy on your property for a tax and period.
- After levy on your state tax refund.
- After levy when collection is in jeopardy.

You may contest the CDP determination in the United States Tax Court.

Lien Notice: The IRS is required to notify you the first time a Notice of Federal Tax Lien is filed for each tax and period. The IRS must notify you within 5 business days after the lien filing. This notice may be mailed, given to you, or left at your home or office. You then have 30 days, after that 5-day period, to request a hearing with Appeals. The lien notice you receive will indicate the date this 30-day period expires.

Levy Notice: For each tax and period, the IRS is required to notify you the first time it intends to collect a tax liability by taking your property or rights to property.

The IRS does this by issuing you a levy notice. The IRS can't levy or seize your property within 30 days from the date this notice is mailed, given to you, or left at your home or office. During that 30-day period, you may request a hearing with Appeals. There are three exceptions to issuing this notice before levy:

1. When collection of the tax is in jeopardy.
2. When IRS levies your state tax refund.
3. When the criteria for a Disqualified Employment Tax Levy is met.

You may request a hearing after the levy action in these instances.

If your request for a CDP hearing is not timely, you may request an equivalent hearing. To receive an equivalent hearing, your request must be postmarked on or before the end of the one-year period after the date of the levy notice or on or before the end of the one-year period plus 5 business days after the filing date of the Notice of Federal Tax Lien.

How do you request a CDP or equivalent hearing with the Office of Appeals?

Complete Form 12153, *Request for a Collection Due Process or Equivalent Hearing*, or other written request with the same information and send it to the address shown on your lien or levy notice. To request an equivalent hearing, you must check the Equivalent Hearing box on line 6 of Form 12153, or if you don't use Form 12513 write that you want an equivalent hearing if the CDP hearing request is late. If you received both a lien and a levy notice, you may appeal both actions by checking the boxes on line 5 of Form 12153 or if you don't use Form 12153, you may appeal both actions in one written request. You must identify your alternatives to, or your reasons for disagreeing with, the lien filing or the levy action. Alternatives or reasons for disagreeing may include:

- Collection alternatives such as installment agreement or offer in compromise.

- Subordination or discharge of lien.

- Withdrawal of Notice of Federal Tax Lien.

- Appropriate spousal defenses.

- The existence or amount of the tax, but only if you did not receive a notice of deficiency or did not otherwise have an opportunity to dispute the tax liability.

- Collection of the tax liability is causing or will cause an economic or other hardship.

You may not raise an issue that was raised and considered at a prior administrative or judicial hearing, if you, or your representative, participated meaningfully in the prior hearing or proceeding.

Form 12153 is available at your local IRS Office, by calling 1-800-829-3676, or from www.IRS.gov. Include a copy of your lien and/or levy notice. List all taxes and tax periods for which you are requesting a hearing. You are entitled to only one hearing relating to a lien notice and one hearing relating to a levy notice, for each taxable period. In general, the IRS will deny a hearing request that makes arguments identified by the IRS as frivolous or that is made to delay collection.

To preserve your right to go to court, you must request a CDP hearing within the time period provided by law. Your request for a CDP hearing must be sent to the address on the lien or levy notice and postmarked on or before the date shown in the lien notice or on or before the 30th day after the date of the levy notice.

Before you formally appeal a lien or levy notice by sending us Form 12153, you may be able to work out a solution with the Collection office that sent the notice. To do so, call the telephone number on the lien or levy notice and explain to the IRS employee listed on the notice or other representative why you disagree with the action. If a telephone number is not shown on the notice, you can call 1-800-829-1040. This contact, however, does NOT extend the 30-day period to make a written request for a CDP hearing.

What will happen when you request a CDP or equivalent hearing with the Office of Appeals?

After you request a hearing, you may still discuss your concerns with the Collection office that sent the lien or levy notice. If you are able to resolve the issues with that office, you may withdraw your request for a hearing. If you are unable to, or do not choose to, resolve the issues with the Collection office, your case will be forwarded immediately to Appeals.

Appeals will contact you to schedule a conference. Your hearing will consist of an in-person or telephone conference and one or more written or oral communications.

Unless the IRS has reason to believe that collection of the tax is in jeopardy, levy action is not permitted for the subject tax and periods during the 30 days after the levy notice and during the timely requested CDP hearing. Normally, there will be no levy action during the period you have to request a hearing from a lien notice and during the CDP hearing.

If your request for a CDP hearing is timely, the 10-year period the IRS has to collect your taxes will be suspended until the date the determination becomes final or you withdraw your request for a hearing in writing.

At the conclusion of the CDP hearing, Appeals will issue a determination letter. If you don't agree with Appeals' determination, you may request judicial review of the determination by petitioning the United States Tax Court within the time period provided for in the Appeals' determination letter.

Appeals will retain jurisdiction over its determination. You may return to Appeals if you believe that the Collection function did not carry out Appeals' determination as it was stated or if there is a change in your circumstances that affects Appeals' determination. However, you must first try to work with Collection to resolve the problem.

If your request for a CDP hearing is not timely and you request an equivalent hearing, the law does not prohibit collection action and the collection statute is not suspended. Furthermore, you cannot go to court if you disagree with Appeals' decision.

| HEARING AVAILABLE UNDER COLLECTION APPEALS PROGRAM (CAP) |
| For Liens, Levies, Seizures and Installment Agreements |

The CAP procedure is available under more circumstances than Collection Due Process (CDP). Unlike CDP, you may not challenge in CAP the existence or amount of your tax liability. You also cannot proceed to court if you don't agree with Appeals' decision in your CAP case. Collection actions you may appeal under CAP are:

Notice of Federal Tax Lien. You may appeal the proposed filing of a Notice of Federal Tax Lien (NFTL) or the actual filing of an NFTL at the first and each subsequent filing of the NFTL. You are entitled to a CDP hearing after the first filing of an NFTL. See the preceding information regarding **Hearing Available under Collection Due Process.** You may also appeal denied requests to withdraw a NFTL, and denied discharges, subordinations, and non-attachments of a lien.

Notice of Levy. You may appeal before or after the IRS places a levy on your wages, bank account or other property. You may also have additional CDP appeal rights. See the preceding information regarding **Hearing Available under Collection Due Process**. Once the levy proceeds have been sent to the IRS, you may also appeal the denial by the IRS of your request to have levied property returned to you.

Seizure of Property. You may appeal before or after the IRS makes a seizure but before the property is sold.

Rejection or Termination of Installment Agreement. You may appeal when the IRS rejects your request for an installment agreement. You may also appeal when the IRS proposes to terminate or terminates your installment agreement.

How do you appeal a lien or levy action if your only collection contact has been a notice or telephone call?

1. Call the IRS at the telephone number shown on your notice. Be prepared to explain which action(s) you disagree with and why you disagree. You must also offer a solution to your tax problem.

2. If you can't reach an agreement with the employee, tell the employee that you want to appeal his or her decision. The employee must honor your request and will refer you to a manager. The manager will either speak with you then or will return your call within 24 hours.

3. Explain to the manager which action(s) you disagree with and why. The manager will make a decision on the case. If you don't agree with the manager's decision, your case will be forwarded to Appeals for review. You do not have to submit the appeal request in writing.

How do you appeal a lien, levy or seizure action if you have been contacted by a Revenue Officer?

1. If you disagree with the decision of the Revenue Officer, you must first request a conference with the Collection manager.

2. If you do not resolve your disagreement with the Collection manager, you may submit a written request for Appeals consideration, preferably by completing Form 9423, *Collection Appeal Request*. This form is available at your local IRS office, by calling 1-800-829-3676, or from www.IRS.gov. Check the action(s) you disagree with and explain why you disagree. You must also offer a solution to resolve your tax problem.

3. Submit the Form 9423 to that Collection office.

4. If you request an appeal after the IRS makes a seizure, you must appeal to the Collection manager within 10 business days after the Notice of Seizure is given to you or left at your home or business.

5. You should let the Revenue Officer or manager know within 2 business days of your conference with the Collection manager if you want to appeal under CAP or the IRS will resume collection action. Your Form 9423 must be postmarked within 3 business days after the date of your conference with the Collection manager in order to prevent the resumption of collection action.

How do you appeal the denial by the IRS of your request to release or return levied or seized property, if you believed the property was wrongfully levied or seized?

1. If you do not agree with the denial of the request to release or return wrongfully levied/seized property or its value, you must first request a conference with the manager of the Advisory Group denying your request.

2. Call the telephone number on the letter denying your request and explain that you want a conference with the Advisory Group manager.

3. If you do not resolve your disagreement with the Advisory Group manager, you must submit a written request for Appeals consideration, preferably on Form 9423, *Collection Appeal Request*. This form is available at your local IRS office, by calling 1-800-829-3676, or from www.IRS.gov. Check the action you disagree with and explain why you disagree.

4. Submit the completed Form 9423 to the Advisory Group office that denied your request to release or return of wrongfully levied/seized property or its value.

¶1442

How do you appeal the rejection of a proposed installment agreement?

1. Call the telephone number shown on the letter rejecting your proposed installment agreement and explain that you want to appeal the rejection. Your appeal need not be in writing unless the rejection letter was sent by a Revenue Officer, in which case your request for an appeal must be in writing, preferably using Form 9423, *Collection Appeal Request*. While a conference is recommended, you need not have a conference with a Collection manager before appealing the rejection of a proposed installment agreement.

2. Your request for an appeal of the rejection of a proposed installment agreement must be made on or before the 30th day after the date of the rejection letter (the mailing of a written request, including a Form 9423, must be postmarked on or before such day).

How do you appeal the termination of an installment agreement?

1. Call the telephone number shown on the notice that indicates that the IRS intends to terminate your installment agreement. If you are unable to resolve the matter, then explain that you want to appeal the termination. Your appeal need not be in writing unless the notice of intent to terminate your installment agreement was sent by a Revenue Officer, in which case your request for an appeal must be in writing, preferably using Form 9423, *Collection Appeal Request*. While a conference is recommended, you need not have a conference with a Collection manager before appealing the termination of an installment agreement.

2. You will have 76 days from the date of the notice of intent to terminate in which to request an appeal. Unless you appeal within 30 days after the date of the notice, or cure your default of the installment agreement, the installment agreement will terminate automatically on the 46th day after the date of the notice. After the 46th day, and the termination of your agreement, your right to appeal will continue for an additional 30 days. Accordingly, your request must be made on or before the 76th day after the date of the notice of intent to terminate (the mailing of a written request, including a Form 9423, must be postmarked on or before such 76th day).

What will happen when you appeal your case?

Lien, Levy and Seizure: Normally, the IRS will not take any action to collect the tax for the tax periods Appeals is considering, unless the IRS believes the collection of the tax is at risk or you are a business meeting the criteria for a Disqualified Employment Tax Levy.

Installment Agreements: *IMPORTANT* - The IRS can't levy until 30 days after the rejection or termination of your agreement. If you appeal within the 30-day period, the IRS will be prohibited from levying until your appeal is completed unless the IRS believes the collection of the tax is in jeopardy.

Once Appeals makes a decision regarding your case, that decision is binding on both you and the IRS. You cannot obtain judicial review of Appeals' decision following a CAP hearing.

Note: Providing false information, failure to provide all pertinent information or fraud will void Appeals' decision.

APPEAL OF OTHER COLLECTION ACTIONS

You may also appeal other collection actions:

- Rejected Offer in Compromise
- Proposed Trust Fund Recovery Penalty
- Denied Trust Fund Recovery Penalty Claim
- Denied request to abate penalties (i.e., late payment, late filing, or deposit penalties)

To dispute a penalty in Appeals, follow the protest requirements in Publication 5, *Your Appeal Rights and How To Prepare A Protest If You Don't Agree*. Also, the correspondence you receive on these types of cases will explain where you should send your protest.

Help if you are experiencing economic harm...

If you are experiencing economic harm or are seeking help in resolving a tax problem that has not been resolved through normal channels or believe an IRS system or procedure is not working, as it should, you may be eligible for Taxpayer Advocate Service (TAS) assistance. You can reach TAS by calling the TAS toll-free case intake line at 1-877-777-4778 or TTY/TTD 1-800-829-4059. TAS cannot extend the time you have to request a CDP, equivalent or CAP hearing. The timeframes for requesting these hearings are explained in this publication.

IRS

Publication 1660 (Rev. 06-2011) Catalog Number 14376Z Department of the Treasury - **Internal Revenue Service** www.irs.gov

¶1443 Exhibit 14-23

Collection Appeal Request

1. Taxpayer's Name	2. Representative: (Form 2848, Power of Attorney Attached)	

3. SSN/EIN	4. Taxpayer's Business Phone	5. Taxpayer's Home Phone	6. Representative's Phone

7. Taxpayer's Street Address

8. City	9. State	10. Zip Code

11. Type of Tax (Tax Form)	12. Tax Periods Being Appealed	13. Tax Due

Collection Action(s) Appealed

14. Please Check the Collection Action(s) You're Appealing:

☐ Federal Tax Lien   ☐ Denial of Installment Agreement

☐ Levy or Notice of Levy   ☐ Termination of Installment Agreement

☐ Seizure

Explanation

15. Please explain why you disagree with the collection action(s) you checked above and explain how you would resolve your tax problem. Attach additional pages if needed. Attach copies of any documents that you think will support your position.

Under penalties of perjury, I declare that I have examined this request and the attached documents, and to the best of my knowledge and belief, they are true, correct and complete. A submission by a representative, other than the taxpayer, is based on all information of which preparer has any knowledge.

16. Taxpayer's or Authorized Representative's Signature	17. Date

18. Collection Manager's Signature	19. Date Received

Form **9423** (Rev. 01-1999)   Catalog Number 141691   **(Over)**   Department of the Treasury – Internal Revenue Service

¶1443

Collection Appeal Rights

FOR LIENS, LEVIES, SEIZURES, AND DENIAL OR TERMINATION OF INSTALLMENT AGREEMENT

You may appeal a Notice of Federal Tax Lien, levy, seizure, or denial or termination of an installment agreement under these procedures. However, if you request an appeal after IRS makes a seizure, you must appeal to the Collection manager within 10 business days after the Notice of Seizure is provided to you or left at your home or business.

How to Appeal If You Disagree With One of These Actions

1. If you disagree with the decision of the Revenue Officer, and wish to appeal, you must first request a conference with a Collection manager.

2. If you do not resolve your disagreement with the Collection manager, you may request Appeals consideration by completing Form 9423, Collection Appeal Request.

3. On the Form 9423, check the Collection action(s) you disagree with and explain why you disagree. You must also explain your solution to resolve your tax problem. **THE COLLECTION OFFICE MUST RECEIVE YOUR REQUEST FOR AN APPEAL WITHIN 2 DAYS OF YOUR CONFERENCE WITH THE COLLECTION MANAGER OR WE WILL RESUME COLLECTION ACTION.**

What will happen when you appeal your case

Normally, we will stop the collection action(s) you disagree with until your appeal is settled, unless we have reason to believe that collection of the amount owed is at risk.

You may have a representative

You may represent yourself at your Appeals conference or you may be represented by an attorney, certified public accountant, or a person enrolled to practice before the IRS. If you want your representative to appear without you, you must provide a properly completed Form 2848, Power of Attorney and Declaration of Representative. You can obtain Form 2848 from your local IRS office or by calling 1-800-829-3676.

Decision on the appeal

Once the Appeals Officer makes a decision on your case, that decision is binding on both you and the IRS. This means that both you and the IRS are required to accept the decision and live up to its terms.

Note: Providing false information, failing to provide all pertinent information, or fraud will void Appeal's decision.

¶1451 DISCUSSION QUESTIONS

1. Oscar Oppressed consults you regarding his tax problems. Oscar tells you that he has not paid the $20,000 balance due on his 2008 income tax return. He had sent some information to the Collection function of the IRS showing them that he had no money aside from the wages he earned as a janitor at the local packing plant. Oscar mailed in the information approximately six months ago and heard nothing further until he went to pick up his paycheck last Friday. The paymaster informed him that they had received a levy and had paid over the amount of his check to the IRS.

   (A) Is the levy proper?

   (B) Can the IRS take Oscar's entire check or must they leave something for Oscar and his three minor children to live on?

2. Bill and Betty Bankrupt have received a notice of seizure on their home. Title to the home is jointly held, and they have owned it for five years. They give you the following information regarding the home:

Fair market value	$165,000
Mortgage	$125,000
Equity	$40,000

   Bill and Betty want to know what will happen to the mortgage if the house is sold and they want to know whether the IRS will pay off the first mortgage for them. They also want to know whether the IRS can levy on their joint equity in the house or only on Bill's equity.

   In answering this question, assume that the tax being collected by the seizure is as follows:

   (A) The assessment is $45,000, representing the balance due on their joint 2005 and 2006 federal income tax returns.

   (B) The assessment is $45,000 and represents the balance due on Bill's separate returns for 2007 and 2008. Bill had filed using the married filing separate status because the marriage was on the rocks at the time. The time to elect to file a joint return has not yet expired, and filing jointly would save them approximately $3,000.

   (C) The assessment is $45,000 resulting from an audit of their 2007 and 2008 income tax return. The auditor found that Betty had not reported approximately $40,000 of gross receipts each year resulting from her real estate business. Bill did not know how successful Betty's real estate business was, and he never saw any of the money because Betty was always reinvesting it in new properties. The assessment was made jointly against Bill and Betty.

3. Carl Cashflow consults you regarding a tax lien in the amount of $25,000 for delinquent employment taxes of his corporation. Carl tells you that his sole asset is his residence, and he gives you the following information:

Fair market value	$125,000
Mortgage	$115,000
Equity	$10,000

Carl is paying $800 per month on the mortgage, and he finds that this is more than he can afford. He has an offer to purchase his home for $125,000. He would like to buy a condominium for $75,000 after he sells his home, but he needs $7,500 for a down payment. He figures buying the condominium will bring his monthly housing payment to $550.

(A) Can anything be done to prevent the IRS from levying on the proceeds of the sale of the house?

(B) What can you suggest to Carl to get the IRS to go along with this arrangement?

4. Daryl Deadbeat owes the IRS $75,000 for delinquent income taxes. He owns real property with appraised equities of $85,000. The IRS seizes the properties and sets a minimum bid price of $75,000. Because no one trusts Daryl not to start legal hassles if they buy the properties, no one shows up to bid. Finally, the United States buys the properties at the minimum bid price and credits Daryl's account as being paid in full. All tax liens are released at the time of sale.

Seven months after the sale, the United States receives an offer to purchase the properties. Because oil has been discovered on one of the parcels, the offer is in the amount of $150,000. Obviously the offer is accepted and the transaction closes. Does the IRS have to share the profit on the sale with Daryl?

5. David Developer owes approximately $250,000 in employment taxes. David owns a large tract of land which has been subdivided into 100 lots. Liens were filed by the IRS in 2005 which attached to his interest in the land. It is now 2009, and David's subdivision has become a prime location. He has a purchaser who will buy one lot for $50,000, but he needs to get the lien released. He is afraid that the buyer's attorney will not let the buyer go ahead unless you can assure him that title will not be clouded by the lien.

(A) Will the IRS have a lien on title in the hands of the purchaser? Will the purchaser have priority over the IRS? If the purchaser gets a mortgage to buy the property, which lien is in first place?

(B) Can anything be done to improve the situation?

6. Danny Disorganized is the sole shareholder of Envigrow, Inc., a corporation which markets environmentally safe lawn products. The IRS has completed an audit of Envigrow's 2007 tax return, which was filed on March 15, 2008. The revenue agent disallowed a majority of the deductions taken for travel and entertainment due to Danny's inability to substantiate the expenses. Apparently, Danny misplaced the box which contained the travel and entertainment records. As a result, Danny

consented to the adjustments and the corporation was assessed an additional tax of $55,000 in February 2009.

In May 2009, as the corporation was completing its move to a new high-rise on Milwaukee's skyline, Danny found the box containing the 2007 travel and entertainment records. Since the time has past to file a claim for refund, Danny would like to know what, if anything, he can do to suspend collection efforts and abate the additional assessment?

7. Sam Spendthrift just completed the bankruptcy filing of Belly-Up, Inc., the most recent of his failed ventures. Sam was left with tax claims in the amount of $200,000, consisting of trust fund employment taxes which are nondischargeable in bankruptcy. Since his current job at Paupers, Inc., only pays minimum wage, he plans to pay off the debt by taking out a $200,000 loan. All Sam has to do is convince his wealthy uncle, Milton Megabucks, to co-sign for the loan. Milton calculates, however, that a 15-year loan at 9% would cost approximately $365,000. Knowing Sam's earning capabilities, Milton figures that there must be a cheaper way out.

To fully analyze the situation, Milton has asked Sam to compile a financial statement detailing any additional assets and liabilities. Sam came up with the following:

Assets
1998 Pinto Wagon	$700
Baseball card collection	$1,000
Cash in bank	$500

Liabilities
University of Wisconsin student loans	$15,000
Credit card debt	$2,500
Unpaid rent	$1,200

Unfortunately, Milton has not found it in his heart to grant Sam any right to his estate. He is a bit disappointed that, at 33 years old, all Sam has managed to do is increase his negative net worth.

What can Milton and Sam do to abate the tax claim? What factors would the IRS consider in evaluating any proposals by Sam?

8. Felisha Fitness is the sole shareholder of LaSpa, Inc., a corporation which operates three health clubs. As of January 2009, LaSpa, Inc., owed approximately $150,000 in corporate income taxes which were assessed in February 2008 for the tax years 2004 and 2005. The corporation has always filed its tax returns on a timely basis. Felisha has failed to respond to the assessment and demands for payment by the IRS due to the fact that business has been slow and she has been inundated with other bills. As a consequence, the IRS filed a tax lien which attached to all of the exercise equipment owned by LaSpa, Inc. On April 1, 2009, the IRS seized the equipment, intending to proceed with a tax sale. Is there anything Felisha can do to block the IRS's sale of the equipment? In the

event that Felisha is unable to pay any of the taxes, can any portion of the assessment be discharged?

9. Owen Ozelot has received a Notice of Intent to Levy with respect to his unpaid income tax liability of $100,000. Owen comes to you and asks what his options are.

CHAPTER 15
CLAIMS FOR REFUND

¶1501 INTRODUCTION

When an audit results in a tax deficiency, the taxpayer can either contest the liability in the United States Tax Court or pay the deficiency and file a claim for refund. If the claim for refund is disallowed by the Internal Revenue Service (IRS) or if a period of six months from the date of filing passes without any action being taken, the taxpayer may then bring suit to recover the overpayment of tax in either the United States District Court or the United States Court of Federal Claims.[1] This alternative procedure can be employed at any stage of the audit process: when the agent first proposes the deficiency, after an appeals conference or after a formal notice of deficiency.

Execution of Refund Claim

¶1502 GOVERNMENT NOTICE

A claim for refund puts the government on notice that the taxpayer believes tax has been overpaid and describes the grounds for the claim. The filing of the claim gives the IRS an opportunity to examine the taxpayer's contention and to determine whether there has been an overpayment. The filing of a claim for refund is also a prerequisite to bringing a legal action for a refund of any taxes alleged to have been overpaid.[2]

The IRS has prescribed forms to be used in seeking a refund of tax. While it is not absolutely necessary to use such forms, some courts have rejected informal claims which failed to contain the requisite elements of a Claim for Refund. For example, where the taxpayer failed to provide the IRS sufficient indication that a refund was being sought, courts have held that the statutory elements of a Claim for Refund had not been met.[3] While not all courts have been this strict in testing the sufficiency of an informal claim for refund, a cautious practitioner will generally utilize the prescribed forms to avoid unnecessary litigation.

The three principal Claim for Refund forms are included at the end of this chapter. Form 1040X (see Exhibit 15-1 at ¶1521) is used to claim a refund of individual income taxes. Form 1120X (see Exhibit 15-2 at ¶1522) is used to claim a refund of an overpayment of corporate income tax. Finally, Form 843 (see Exhibit 15-3 at ¶1523) is used to claim a refund of any tax other than income tax. Form 843 can be used to claim a refund of estate tax, gift tax, excise tax or employment taxes and to claim refunds of penalties and interest.

---

[1] Code Sec. 6532(a).
[2] Code Sec. 7422(a).

[3] *BCS Financial Corp. v. U.S.*, 118 F.3d 522 (7th Cir. 1997), 97-2 USTC ¶50,514; *Pala, Inc. v. U.S.*, 234 F.3d 873 (5th Cir. 2000), 2000-2 USTC ¶50,864.

¶1502

A number of cases have established certain requirements which must be met for a valid refund claim:

1. The claim must be in writing;
2. The claim must be signed by the person entitled to recover the overpayment;
3. The claim must demand that the overpayment be refunded;
4. The claim must specify the grounds upon which it is based; and
5. The statement of the grounds and facts upon which the refund of a claim is based must be verified by a written declaration made under the penalties of perjury.[4]

The courts will only allow the taxpayer to bring suit to recover a refund of taxes *on a ground which has been raised in the claim for refund*.[5] Thus, considerable care should be taken to assure that all grounds have been stated in the claim for refund that is filed so that all possible theories for recovery have been presented.

> **Example 15-1:** In preparing her administrative claim for refund on Form 1040X, Valerie thought of three reasons why her request should be granted, and included all three with her claim for refund. The IRS rejected Valerie's claim and so she brought suit in the local United States District Court. In her suit she added a fourth ground upon which her refund should be granted. That ground was ignored by the court since it had been included in her administrative claims for refund.

Because of the limitations on the time in which a refund claim must be filed (see ¶1503, below), it may be important to document when a claim was filed. While the IRS keeps records of all returns and claims it receives, the burden of proof to show actual filing is on the taxpayer. If for some reason the claim was not delivered to the IRS, the taxpayer may not be able to prove filing unless the claim was sent by certified or registered mail. For this reason, all claims for refund should be filed either by physical delivery, with the taxpayer or representative obtaining a receipted copy of the claim, or by mailing certified or registered mail. Failure to do so can deny the taxpayer the right to recover on the refund claim.[6]

Statute of Limitations on Refund Claim

¶1503 FILING PERIODS

A claim for credit or refund must be filed within three years of the time the return was filed or within two years of the time the tax was paid, whichever period ends later.[7] If no return was filed, then the claim for refund must be made

---

[4] Reg. § 301.6402-2(b)(1).

[5] *Boyles v. U.S.*, 2000-1 USTC ¶50,243; *Parma v. U.S.*, 45 Fed. Cl. 124 (1999), 99-2 USTC ¶50,919.

[6] For examples, see *Miller v. United States*, 784 F.2d 728 (6th Cir. 1986), 86-1 USTC ¶9261; and *Wiggins v. United States*, (D. Md. 1986), 87-1 USTC ¶9180.

[7] Code Sec. 6511. There are exceptions to this general rule. One example of this is an overpayment resulting from the deduction for a bad debt or a worthless security. In such case, a claim for refund may be filed at any time within seven years from the date on which the return was due. Code Sec. 6511(d)(1). Other examples include net operating loss or capital loss carrybacks and unused tax credit

within two years of the time the tax is paid. For tax years ending after August 5, 1997, the Tax Court, which has authority to order refunds in cases under its jurisdiction, can do so for taxes paid less than three years before a notice of deficiency is issued if the taxpayer has not filed a tax return on the date when the notice of deficiency is issued.[8] If the taxpayer files a return prior to the due date, or if the tax itself is paid prior to the due date, for purposes of the statute of limitations the return is treated as filed and the tax is treated as paid on "the last possible day." However, "the last possible day" for this purpose does not include any extensions of time to file the return.[9]

exam

The rule regarding early payment of the tax often comes into play when the taxpayer's wages are subject to withholding or estimated tax payments are made. Any tax deducted and withheld by the taxpayer's employer will be deemed to be paid against the taxpayer's income tax liability on the fifteenth day of the fourth month following the close of that taxable year.[10] In addition, any payments towards a taxpayer's estimated income tax are considered paid on the last day prescribed for filing the return for the taxable year for which the estimates are being made.

> **Example 15-2:** The taxpayer is entitled to a refund of income taxes for the taxable year ending December 31, 2004. The taxpayer requests that this amount be applied toward estimated income tax payments to be made during 2005. In addition, the taxpayer makes other estimated tax payments during 2005, and the wages made during that year are subject to withholding under the requirements of Code Secs. 3401 through 3404. The taxpayer's return is due on April 17, 2006. Under Code Sec. 6513, all of the payments credited against the taxpayer's income tax liability (including the refund of the 2004 overpayment) are considered to be made on April 17, 2006.

If the taxpayer consents to extend the period in which the IRS may assess any tax (generally by a Form 872, Consent to Extend Time to Assess Tax (see Exhibit 10-2 at ¶1032)), the time within which the taxpayer may file a claim for refund is also extended for an additional six months from the date that the extension expires.[11]

The mitigation provisions of Code Secs. 1311 through 1314 also may apply to permit a refund which would otherwise be barred by the statute of limitations. These and other judicially created mitigation provisions are discussed in Chapter 10 beginning at ¶1010.

(Footnote Continued)

carrybacks where the time for a claim for refund resulting from such carrybacks begins to run from the taxable year in which the net operating loss, capital loss or unused tax credit arose. Code Sec. 6511(d)(2) and (4). The United States Supreme Court has held that courts cannot toll the statute of limitations of refund claims for nonstatutory, equitable reasons. *United States v. Brockamp*, 117 S.Ct. 849 (1996), 97-1 USTC ¶50,216.

[8] Code Sec. 6512(b)(3). Taxpayer Relief Act of 1997, P.L. 105-34, Act §1282. For tax years ending before August 5, 1997, where no return was filed, the Tax Court has jurisdiction to order refunds for taxes paid within two years before a notice of deficiency is issued. *Comm'r v. Lundy*, 116 S.Ct. 647 (1996), 96-1 USTC ¶50,035.

[9] Code Sec. 6513(a).

[10] Code Sec. 6513(b)(1).

[11] Code Sec. 6511(c)(1).

Amount Recoverable

¶1504 TWO OR THREE-YEAR STATUTE

To determine the amount that can be recovered through a refund claim, it is important first to determine under which statute of limitations the taxpayer is filing. If the claim is filed within three years from the date the return was filed, the amount refundable cannot exceed the total tax paid within the three years plus any extension period that was granted for filing the return.

> **Example 15-3:** If the return was due on April 15, 2002, but an extension to August 15, 2002, was obtained and the original return was filed on August 15, 2002, then the claim for refund must be filed by August 15, 2005. The amount which the taxpayer can seek through a claim for refund will include all payments of tax made during the calendar year 2001, plus any payments made through August 15, 2005.

On the other hand, if the claim for refund is filed under the two-year statute of limitations, then the amount recoverable is limited to the tax paid during the two years immediately preceding the filing of the claim.

> **Example 15-4:** Taxpayer files a 2001 return on April 15, 2002, and pays a tax of $3,000 at that time. In June 2004, an audit is performed which results in a deficiency of $2,000, which he pays. Upon reviewing the return, taxpayer discovers that he forgot to claim $2,500 in tax credit for 2001. If he files a claim for refund on April 15, 2005, he can recover $2,500. However, if he does not file until April 16, 2005, he can only recover $2,000, the amount paid within two years of filing. Code Sec. 7503 allows returns filed after the due date to be deemed as filed on the due date. A claim for refund of tax on the return must be filed within three years of the due date.[12]

Interest on Refund Claims

¶1505 OVERPAYMENT OF TAX

The IRS is to pay interest on any overpayment of any Internal Revenue tax.[13] Where an overpayment is refunded, the interest is to be computed from the date of the overpayment to a date preceding the date of the refund check by no more than thirty days. Normally the tax would be considered to be overpaid from the due date of the return. However, if a return has been filed late, the due date of the return is ignored and interest is only computed from the day on which the return is actually filed.[14]

If a refund results from the carryback of a net operating loss or a capital loss, interest runs only from the day on which the return generating the loss is filed.[15]

If a taxpayer is entitled to a refund of income tax which has been withheld or paid in the form of estimated tax payments during the year, no interest is required to be paid on that refund if the overpayment is refunded within forty-

---

[12] *Hannahs v. U.S.*, W. Dist. Tenn., 95-1 USTC ¶50,111.

[13] Code Sec. 6611.

[14] Code Sec. 6611(b)(3).

[15] Code Sec. 6611(f)(1).

five days of the due date of the return or the day on which the return is actually filed, whichever is later.

Procedure on Refund Claims

¶1506 CLAIM PROCESSING

Under most circumstances a claim for refund will be filed with the Campus serving the state in which the tax was paid. The claims are recorded at the Campus, reviewed and assigned for examination at the field level if that is warranted. The review of the claim for refund at the Service Center level is conducted to determine a number of issues:

1. Whether the claim was timely filed;

2. Whether the claim is based on the alleged unconstitutionality of the Internal Revenue laws;

3. Whether the taxpayer has waived the right to a refund in having the IRS compromise a tax liability;

4. Whether the claim for refund covers a taxable year which was the subject of a closing agreement under Code Sec. 7121 or in which the tax liability was compromised under Code Sec. 7122; or

5. Whether the claim for refund relates to a return closed on the basis of a final order of the Tax Court or other court.

If any of these circumstances are found, the Service Center will generally issue a letter to the taxpayer (see Exhibit 15-4 at ¶1524) which advises the taxpayer that no consideration can be given to the claim.[16] In addition, if the claim is one which the taxpayer has requested be withdrawn, or if it is one for which the taxpayer has requested in writing that a statutory notice of claim disallowance be immediately issued, then the certified notice of claim disallowance will be issued (see Exhibit 15-5 at ¶1525).[17] If the claim for refund does not fit into any of these classifications, it will be referred to an examiner for further review.

Often when the claim for refund is assigned to an examiner, it is returned to the same agent who originally examined the return. If the claim for refund refers to a deficiency in which the Appeals Office had previously acquired jurisdiction, the concurrence of the Appeals Office in any modification of the item is required. If the closing of the matter with the Appeals Office involved the execution of a Form 870-AD, Offer to Waive Restrictions on Assessment and Collection of Tax Deficiency and to Accept Overassessment (see Chapter 12 and Exhibit 12-2 at ¶1222), then the claim for refund and the case file are generally forwarded to the Appeals Office for any further action.[18] If the only issue in dispute is identical or similar to an issue pending in a case before the Tax Court or any other court, the case will be placed in a suspense file until the court case is resolved.[19]

---

[16] See Publication 556, Examination of Returns, Appeal Rights and Claims for Refund (Rev. May 2008) at page 15.

[17] Id. and See IRM 4.90.7.5.2.

[18] IRM 8.7.7.13.

[19] IRM Handbook 4.8.2.10.1.

After the claim for refund is reviewed, if the examiner determines that the claim should not be allowed, a report will be sent to the taxpayer proposing disallowance of the claim (see Exhibit 15-6 at ¶1526). That report will propose either partial disallowance or full disallowance and will also seek the execution of a Form 2297, Waiver of Statutory Notification of Claim Disallowance (see Exhibit 15-7 at ¶1527). In addition, the taxpayer is given the opportunity to appeal the proposed disallowance of the claim and to request a hearing with the Appeals Office.

If the Form 2297 is not secured from the taxpayer, then a certified notice of disallowance will be issued to the taxpayer. The issuance of the certified notice of claim disallowance or the execution of the waiver of statutory notification of claim disallowance is a significant event because it begins the two-year statute of limitations under which any suit for refund based on the claim must be brought.[20] Unless either a waiver has been executed or a notice of disallowance has been received, the taxpayer must wait until at least six months after the filing of the claim for refund before filing a suit for refund.[21]

If the examining agent decides to allow the claim after reviewing it, normally the taxpayer will receive a check representing the overpayment from the Department of the Treasury. In some instances, the taxpayer will receive a Form 4356 (see Exhibit 15-9 at ¶1529), which states that the overpayment may be applied to unpaid taxes.[22]

If a claim for refund is allowed which would produce a refund or credit of tax in excess of $2,000,000,[23] a final decision on such refund ismade only after referral of the facts and the IRS's recommendation to the Joint Committee on Taxation.[24] It is only after the Joint Committee finishes its review that a refund can be issued to the taxpayer.

Miscellaneous

¶1507 FORMS

If a taxpayer has a carryback resulting from a net operating loss, a capital loss or an unused general business credit, the taxpayer may file a Form 1045, Application for Tentative Refund (see Exhibit 15-10 at ¶1530). Corporations apply for a tentative refund of these amounts by filing Form 1139, Corporation Application for Tentative Refund (see Exhibit 15-11 at ¶1531). Also, corporations expecting refunds from carryback claims may extend the time to pay their income tax for the preceding year by filing Form 1138, Extension of Time for Payment of Taxes by a Corporation Expecting a Net Operating Loss Carryback (see Exhibit 15-12 at ¶1532). Code Sec. 6411 authorizes the Secretary of the Treasury to refund the excess tax within a period of ninety days from the date of filing of the application

---

[20] Code Sec. 6532(a). With the concurrence of the IRS, the two year period during which a suit can be filed can be extended with the filing of a Form 907 (Exhibit 15-8 at ¶1528).

[21] Code Sec. 6532(a)(1).

[22] Because Code Sec. 6402(a) allows the Treasury to credit the overpayment against any other liabilities of the taxpayer.

[23] Amount was increased from $1,000,000 on December 21, 2000.

[24] Code Sec. 6405(a).

for tentative carryback adjustment. If the Commissioner finds that the information presented in Form 1045 or Form 1139 is incomplete or inaccurate, he or she has the authority not to allow the tentative refund. In such a case, a formal claim for refund should be filed to protect the right of the taxpayer to recover the excess payment. The tentative application is not a claim for refund, and if the application is disallowed, no suit may be maintained to recover the tax unless a formal claim has been filed.[25] In addition, the filing of the application does not constitute the filing of a claim for refund for purposes of determining if a claim was timely filed within the statute of limitations.[26]

Form 1310, Statement of Person Claiming Refund Due a Deceased Taxpayer (see Exhibit 15-13 at ¶1533), is generally used by a decedent's spouse or personal representative to claim a refund of tax owed to the decedent.

One other claim for refund with which the practitioner should be familiar is Form 6118, Claim for Refund of Income Tax Return Preparer Penalties (see Exhibit 15-14 at ¶1534). This form is used when a preparer penalty has been assessed against an income tax return preparer which the preparer wishes to litigate (see Chapter 9, *supra*).

¶1508 CHOICE OF JUDICIAL FORUM

When contested adjustments to tax are the result of an IRS examination, a taxpayer has a choice of three judicial forums in which to litigate the tax controversy. As discussed in Chapter 13, the taxpayer may challenge a proposed deficiency by filing a petition in the Tax Court without first paying the tax. In the alternative, the taxpayer may pay the assessed deficiency, file a claim for refund and then file suit in either the United States District Court or the United States Court of Federal Claims.

In choosing the court in which to litigate, consideration should be given to the controlling legal precedents in each of the forums as well as the procedural differences that exist. One important factor, of course, is the ability of the taxpayer to pay the full amount of the assessed deficiency before filing suit. If financial problems exist, the only forum realistically open to the taxpayer may be the Tax Court. If a jury trial appears to offer advantages, the District Court would be the only appropriate forum. Trial by jury is not available in either the Tax Court or Court of Federal Claims.

> **Example 15-5:** Dan Persistent was audited and the IRS determined a deficiency of $200,000, much more than Dan can afford. The core issue involves amortization of customer lists and Dan's federal circuit court has held favorably on this issue. Therefore, Dan files suit in the U.S. Tax Court knowing that court will look to the laws of Dan's federal circuit and knowing that Dan will not have to pay the deficiency in order to litigate his issue.

The IRS has the right to assert additional deficiencies after a petition is filed in the Tax Court, whereas new adjustments to taxable income may be utilized by

---

[25] Code Sec. 6411(a).　　　　[26] Reg. § 1.6411-1(b)(2).

the government in defending a refund suit only by way of setoff against the amount of the claimed refund. If a taxpayer is concerned that the IRS may raise new issues that would increase the deficiency proposed in the statutory notice, the Tax Court should be avoided as the litigating forum. However, in such a situation it should be kept in mind that the filing of a claim for refund does not prevent the IRS from attempting to assess an additional deficiency on newly discovered adjustments if the statute of limitations on assessment has not expired. To reduce this possibility, if the assessment period is still open, it may be advisable not to file the claim for refund too soon.

Settlement negotiations in the Tax Court are the responsibility of the Appeals Office and Area Counsel. Settlement discussion and trial in the District Court and Court of Federal Claims are handled by attorneys from the Tax Division of the Department of Justice. Pretrial discovery is available to both parties in all three of the forums, but is more limited in the Tax Court (see ¶ 1113). The need for, or fear of, extensive discovery may influence a taxpayer's choice of forum.

¶1509 PREREQUISITES FOR LEGAL ACTION

No suit for the recovery of any Internal Revenue tax shall be maintained until after a claim for refund has been filed with the IRS.[27] The taxpayer may only recover in a suit for refund on a ground which was presented in the claim for refund. The Code also provides that no suit may be commenced within six months of the time the claim is filed unless the claim has been disallowed during that period of time.

In addition, no suit shall be filed after two years from the time of mailing by certified mail or registered mail of a notice of disallowance to the taxpayer.[28] If the taxpayer has waived the requirement of mailing the notice of disallowance, then the two-year limitations period begins with the execution of the waiver on Form 2297, Waiver of Statutory Notification of Claim Disallowance (see Exhibit 15-7 at ¶ 1527).

The taxpayer also can be barred from filing a suit for refund by undertaking other proceedings. For example, if a timely petition to the Tax Court was filed, then the Tax Court acquires exclusive jurisdiction for that taxable year, and under most circumstances a suit for refund regarding that year cannot be prosecuted.[29] In addition, if the taxpayer previously filed a suit to recover any tax alleged to have been erroneously assessed, any finding that the taxpayer was not entitled to recover in that proceeding will be binding in any later refund action under the doctrine of *res judicata*.

¶1510 PAYMENT OF TAX IN FULL

An additional prerequisite for a suit for refund is that the entire tax must be paid in full prior to the time that the claim for refund is filed. Failure to pay the entire

---

[27] Code Sec. 7422.

[28] Code Sec. 6532(a).

[29] Code Sec. 7422(e).

amount of tax can result in a dismissal of the case for lack of jurisdiction, as illustrated by the landmark case of *Flora v. United States*.[30]

However, the Court of Appeals for the Federal Circuit has ruled that the full payment rule of *Flora* does not require the taxpayer to pay interest or penalties before filing a claim for refund.[31]

¶1511 PARTIAL PAYMENT OF TAX

The "full payment" rule enunciated in *Flora* remains binding in all income, gift, or estate tax cases. However, the rule of *Flora* does not apply to a responsible officer assessment.[32] The 100-percent penalty tax is classified as an excise tax and, therefore, is "divisible." The essential theory of divisibility is that any assessment of a divisible tax is considered to consist of the assessment of a separate tax liability for each separate tax transaction or event. Therefore, to meet the full payment rule and the jurisdictional prerequisite for a tax refund suit[33] as to these taxes, the taxpayer need not pay the full amount assessed for the taxable period but only the tax due with respect to one allegedly taxable transaction or event.[34]

> **Example 15-6:** For example, assume that the IRS has made an assessment under Code Sec. 6672 of $75,000 covering the first, second and third quarters of 2000. If a taxpayer makes a token payment representing a divisible portion of that assessment, he or she may file a claim for refund and then file a refund suit. Generally, the divisible portion of a Code Sec. 6672 penalty assessment is the amount of tax to be withheld for one employee for one quarter. However, making an arbitrary payment of $50 or $100 may not be sufficient to meet the judicial jurisdiction test.

[30] 362 U.S. 145 (1960), 80 S.Ct. 630, 60-1 USTC ¶9347.

[31] *Shore v. U.S.*, 9 F.3d 1524 (Fed. Cir. 1993), 93-2 USTC ¶50,623.

[32] Code Sec. 6672.

[33] *Flora v. U.S., supra* note 24; IRM Handbook 5.7.7.7; *Steele v. U.S.*, 280 F.2d 89 (9th Cir. 1960), 60-2 USTC ¶9573; *Magone v. U.S.*, 902 F.2d 192 (2nd Cir. 1990), 90-1 USTC ¶50,253.

[34] *ACT Restoration, Inc. v. U.S.*, 99-2 USTC ¶50,911.

¶1521 Exhibit 15-1

Form **1040X** (Rev. December 2010)	Department of the Treasury—Internal Revenue Service **Amended U.S. Individual Income Tax Return** ▶ See separate instructions.	OMB No. 1545-0074

This return is for calendar year ☐ 2010 ☐ 2009 ☐ 2008 ☐ 2007
Other year. Enter one: calendar year [   ] **or** fiscal year (month and year ended): [   ]

Your first name and middle initial	Your last name	**Your social security number**
If a joint return, your spouse's first name and middle initial	Your spouse's last name	**Your spouse's social security number**
Your current home address (number and street). If you have a P.O. box, see page 5 of instructions.	Apt. no.	Your phone number
Your city, town or post office, state, and ZIP code. If you have a foreign address, see page 5 of instructions.		

Amended return filing status. You must check one box even if you are not changing your filing status.
Caution. You cannot change your filing status from joint to separate returns after the due date.

☐ Single ☐ Married filing jointly ☐ Married filing separately
☐ Qualifying widow(er) ☐ Head of household (If the qualifying person is a child but not your dependent, see page 5 of instructions.)

Use Part III on the back to explain any changes		**A. Original amount** or as previously adjusted (see page 6)	**B. Net change—** amount of increase or (decrease)— explain in Part III	**C. Correct amount**
Income and Deductions				
1	Adjusted gross income (see page 6 of instructions). If net operating loss (NOL) carryback is included, check here . . . . ▶ ☐ **1**			
2	Itemized deductions or standard deduction (see page 7 of instructions) **2**			
3	Subtract line 2 from line 1 . . . . **3**			
4	Exemptions. **If changing, complete Part I on the back and enter the amount from line 30** (see page 7 of instructions) **4**			
5	Taxable income. Subtract line 4 from line 3 . . . . **5**			
Tax Liability				
6	Tax (see page 8 of instructions). Enter method used to figure tax: **6**			
7	Credits (see page 8 of instructions). If general business credit carryback is included, check here . . . . ▶ ☐ **7**			
8	Subtract line 7 from line 6. If the result is zero or less, enter -0- . . . **8**			
9	Other taxes (see page 8 of instructions) **9**			
10	Total tax. Add lines 8 and 9 . . . . **10**			
Payments				
11	Federal income tax withheld and excess social security and tier 1 RRTA tax withheld **(if changing,** see page 8 of instructions) **11**			
12	Estimated tax payments, including amount applied from prior year's return (see page 9 of instructions) **12**			
13	Earned income credit (EIC) (see page 9 of instructions) **13**			
14	Refundable credits from ☐ Schedule M or Form(s) ☐ 2439 ☐ 4136 ☐ 5405 ☐ 8801 ☐ 8812 ☐ 8839 ☐ 8863 ☐ 8885 or ☐ other (specify): [ ] **14**			
15	Total amount paid with request for extension of time to file, tax paid with original return, and additional tax paid after return was filed (see page 10 of instructions) **15**			
16	Total payments. Add lines 11 through 15 . . . . **16**			
Refund or Amount You Owe *(Note. Allow 8–12 weeks to process Form 1040X.)*				
17	Overpayment, if any, as shown on original return or as previously adjusted by the IRS (see page 10 of instructions) **17**			
18	Subtract line 17 from line 16 (If less than zero, see page 10 of instructions) **18**			
19	**Amount you owe.** If line 10, column C, is more than line 18, enter the difference (see page 10 of instructions) **19**			
20	If line 10, column C, is less than line 18, enter the difference. This is the amount **overpaid** on this return **20**			
21	Amount of line 20 you want **refunded to you** **21**			
22	Amount of line 20 you want **applied to your** (enter year): [ ] **estimated tax** **22**			

Complete and sign this form on Page 2.

For Paperwork Reduction Act Notice, see page 11 of instructions. Cat. No. 11360L Form **1040X** (Rev. 12-2010)

Form 1040X (Rev. 12-2010) Page **2**

Part I Exemptions

Complete this part **only** if you are:

- Increasing or decreasing the number of exemptions (personal and dependents) claimed on line 6d of the return you are amending, or
- Increasing or decreasing the exemption amount for housing individuals displaced by a Midwestern disaster in 2008 or 2009.

See *Form 1040 or Form 1040A instructions and page 11 of Form 1040X instructions.*		**A. Original number** of exemptions or amount reported or as previously adjusted	**B. Net change**	**C. Correct number or amount**
23	Yourself and spouse. **Caution.** *If someone can claim you as a dependent, you cannot claim an exemption for yourself* **23**			
24	Your dependent children who lived with you **24**			
25	Your dependent children who did not live with you due to divorce or separation **25**			
26	Other dependents **26**			
27	Total number of exemptions. Add lines 23 through 26 . . . . . . **27**			
28	Multiply the number of exemptions claimed on line 27 by the exemption amount shown in the instructions for line 28 for the year you are amending (see page 11 of instructions) **28**			
29	If you are claiming an exemption amount for housing individuals displaced by a Midwestern disaster, enter the amount from Form 8914, line 2 for 2008, or line 6 for 2009 . . . . **29**			
30	Add lines 28 and 29. Enter the result here and on line 4 on page 1 of this form **30**			

31 List **ALL** dependents (children and others) claimed on this amended return. If more than 4 dependents, see page 11 of instructions.

(a) First name	Last name	**(b)** Dependent's social security number	**(c)** Dependent's relationship to you	**(d)** Check box if qualifying child for child tax credit (see page 11 of instructions)
				☐
				☐
				☐
				☐

Part II Presidential Election Campaign Fund

Checking below will not increase your tax or reduce your refund.

☐ Check here if you did not previously want $3 to go to the fund, but now do.

☐ Check here if this is a joint return and your spouse did not previously want $3 to go to the fund, but now does.

Part III Explanation of changes. In the space provided below, tell us why you are filing Form 1040X.

► Attach any supporting documents and new or changed forms and schedules.

Sign Here

Remember to keep a copy of this form for your records.

Under penalties of perjury, I declare that I have filed an original return and that I have examined this amended return, including accompanying schedules and statements, and to the best of my knowledge and belief, this amended return is true, correct, and complete. Declaration of preparer (other than taxpayer) is based on all information about which the preparer has any knowledge.

►		►	
Your signature	Date	Spouse's signature. If a joint return, **both** must sign.	Date

Paid Preparer Use Only

►			
Preparer's signature	Date	Firm's name (or yours if self-employed)	
Print/type preparer's name		Firm's address and ZIP code	
PTIN	☐ Check if self-employed	Phone number	EIN

For forms and publications, visit IRS.gov. Form **1040X** (Rev. 12-2010)

¶1522 Exhibit 15-2

Form **1120X**	Amended U.S. Corporation	OMB No. 1545-0132
(Rev. January 2011) Department of the Treasury Internal Revenue Service	**Income Tax Return**	**For tax year ending** ▶ _____ (Enter month and year.)

Please Type or Print	Name		Employer identification number
	Number, street, and room or suite no. (If a P.O. box, see instructions.)		
	City or town, state, and ZIP code		Telephone number (optional)

Enter name and address used on original return (If same as above, write "Same.")

Internal Revenue Service Center
where original return was filed ▶

Fill in applicable items and use Part II on the back to explain any changes

Part I **Income and Deductions** (see instructions)		**(a)** As originally reported or as previously adjusted	**(b)** Net change — increase or (decrease) — explain in Part II	**(c)** Correct amount
1	Total income	**1**			
2	Total deductions	**2**			
3	Taxable income. Subtract line 2 from line 1	**3**			
4	Total tax	**4**			

Payments and Credits (see instructions)

5a	Overpayment in prior year allowed as a credit . . .	**5a**	
b	Estimated tax payments	**5b**	
c	Refund applied for on Form 4466	**5c**	
d	Subtract line 5c from the sum of lines 5a and 5b . .	**5d**	
e	Tax deposited with Form 7004	**5e**	
f	Credit from Form 2439	**5f**	
g	Credit for federal tax on fuels and other refundable credits	**5g**	
6	Tax deposited or paid with (or after) the filing of the original return	**6**	
7	Add lines 5d through 6, column (c)	**7**	
8	Overpayment, if any, as shown on original return or as later adjusted	**8**	
9	Subtract line 8 from line 7	**9**	

Tax Due or Overpayment (see instructions)

10	**Tax due.** Subtract line 9 from line 4, column (c). If paying by check, make it payable to the **"United States Treasury"** . . . . ▶	**10**	
11	**Overpayment.** Subtract line 4, column (c), from line 9 . . . . ▶	**11**	
12	Enter the amount of line 11 you want: **Credited to 20** **Estimated tax** ▶ **Refunded** ▶	**12**	

Sign Here	Under penalties of perjury, I declare that I have filed an original return and that I have examined this amended return, including accompanying schedules and statements, and to the best of my knowledge and belief, this amended return is true, correct, and complete. Declaration of preparer (other than taxpayer) is based on all information of which preparer has any knowledge.		
	▶ Signature of officer Date	▶ Title	

Paid Preparer Use Only	Print/Type preparer's name	Preparer's signature	Date	Check ☐ if self-employed	PTIN
	Firm's name ▶			Firm's EIN ▶	
	Firm's address ▶			Phone no.	

For Paperwork Reduction Act Notice, see instructions.   Cat. No. 11530Z   Form **1120X** (Rev. 1-2011)

Form 1120X (Rev. 1-2011)   Page **2**

Part II   **Explanation of Changes to Items in Part I** (Enter the line number from page 1 for the items you are changing, and give the reason for each change. Show any computation in detail. Also, see **What To Attach** in the instructions.)

If the change is due to a net operating loss carryback, a capital loss carryback, or a general business credit carryback, see **Carryback Claims** in the instructions, and check here   . . . . ▶ ☐

Form **1120X** (Rev. 1-2011)

What's New

Beginning in 2010, certain eligible small business credits are carried back five years. If Form 1120-X is used to claim the carryback of any such unused credit, see *Carryback of an eligible small business credit (ESBC)*, below.

General Instructions

Section references are to the Internal Revenue Code unless otherwise noted.

Purpose of Form

Use Form 1120X to:

• Correct a Form 1120 (or Form 1120-A, if applicable) as originally filed, or as later adjusted by an amended return, a claim for refund, or an examination, or

• Make certain elections after the prescribed deadline (see Regulations sections 301.9100-1 through 3).

Do not use Form 1120X to...	Instead, use . . .
Apply for a quick refund of estimated tax	**Form 4466,** Corporation Application for Quick Refund of Overpayment of Estimated Tax
Obtain a tentative refund of taxes due to: • A net operating loss (NOL) carryback • A net capital loss carryback • An unused general business credit carryback • A claim of right adjustment under section 1341(b)(1)	**Form 1139,** Corporation Application for Tentative Refund **Note.** Use Form 1139 only if 1 year or less has passed since the tax year in which the carryback or adjustment occurred. Otherwise, use Form 1120X.
Request IRS approval for a change in accounting method	**Form 3115,** Application for Change in Accounting Method

When To File

File Form 1120X only after the corporation has filed its original return. Generally, Form 1120X must be filed within 3 years after the date the corporation filed its original return or within 2 years after the date the corporation paid the tax (if filing a claim for a refund), whichever is later. A return filed before the due date is considered filed on the due date. A Form 1120X based on an NOL carryback, a capital loss carryback, or general business credit carryback generally must be filed within 3 years after the due date (including extensions) of the return for the tax year of the NOL, capital loss, or unused credit. A Form 1120X based on a bad debt or worthless security must be filed within 7 years after the due date of the return for the tax year in which the debt or security became worthless. See section 6511 for more details and other special rules.

Note. It often takes 3 to 4 months to process Form 1120X.

Private delivery services. See the instructions for the corporation's income tax return for information on certain private delivery services designated by the IRS to meet the "timely mailing as timely filing/paying" rule for tax returns and payments.

Caution: *Private delivery services cannot deliver items to P.O. boxes. Use the U.S. Postal Service to send any item to an IRS P.O. box address.*

What To Attach

If the corrected amount involves an item of income, deduction, or credit that must be supported with a schedule, statement, or form, attach the appropriate schedule, statement, or form to Form 1120X. Include the corporation's name and employer identification number on any attachments. See the instructions for Form 1120 or 1120-A (if applicable) for the tax year of the claim for a list of forms that may be required.

In addition, if the corporation requests that the IRS electronically deposit a refund of $1 million or more, attach Form 8302, Electronic Deposit of Tax Refund of $1 Million or More.

Tax Shelters

If the corporation's return is being amended for a tax year in which the corporation participated in a "reportable transaction," attach Form 8886, Reportable Transaction Disclosure Statement. If a reportable transaction results in a loss or credit carried back to a prior tax year, attach Form 8886 for the carryback years.

If the corporation's return is being amended to include any item (loss, credit, deduction, other tax benefit, or income) from an interest in a tax shelter required to be registered, attach any applicable Forms 8271, Investor Reporting of Tax Shelter Registration Number, due or required to be filed before August 3, 2007.

Carryback Claims

If Form 1120X is used as a carryback claim, attach copies of Form 1120, (or Form 1120-A, if applicable), pages 1 and the tax computation page, for both the year the loss or credit originated and for the carryback year. Also attach any other forms, schedules, or statements that are necessary to support the claim, including a statement that shows all adjustments required to figure any NOL that was carried back. At the top of the forms or schedules attached, write "Copy Only—Do Not Process."

Carryback of an eligible small business credit (ESBC). If the corporation is an eligible small business (as defined in section 38(c)(5)(B)) and is using Form 1120X to claim a carryback of an unused ESBC, enter "SBJA 2012" at the top of Form 1120X. For details and special rules regarding an ESBC, see the Instructions for Form 3800.

Information on Income, Deductions, Tax Computation, etc.

For information on income, deductions, tax computation, etc., see the instructions for the tax return for the tax year being amended.

Caution: *Deductions for such items as charitable contributions and the dividends-received deduction may have to be refigured because of changes made to items of income or expense.*

Where To File

File this form at the applicable Internal Revenue Service Center where the corporation filed its original return.

Specific Instructions

Tax Year

In the space above the employer identification number, enter the ending month and year of the calendar or fiscal year for the tax return being amended.

Address

If the post office does not deliver mail to the street address and the corporation has a P.O. box, show the box number instead of the street address.

If the corporation receives its mail in care of a third party (such as an accountant or an attorney), enter on the street address line "C/O" followed by the third party's name and street address or P.O. box.

Column (a)

Enter the amounts from the corporation's return as originally filed or as it was later amended. If the return was changed or audited by the IRS, enter the amounts as adjusted.

Column (b)

Enter the net increase or net decrease for each line being changed. Use parentheses around all amounts that are decreases. Explain the increase or decrease in Part II.

Column (c)

Note. Amounts entered on lines 1 through 4 in column (c) must equal the amounts that would be entered on the applicable lines of the tax return if all adjustments and corrections were taken into account.

Lines 1 and 2. Add the increase in column (b) to the amount in column (a) or subtract the column (b) decrease from column (a). Enter the result in column (c). For an item that did not change, enter the amount from column (a) in column (c).

Line 4. Figure the new amount of tax using the taxable income on line 3, column (c). Use Schedule J, Form 1120 (or Part I, Form 1120-A, if applicable) of the original return to make the necessary tax computation.

Line 5e. Enter the amount of tax deposited with Form 7004, Application for Automatic Extension of Time To File Certain Business Income Tax, Information, and Other Returns.

Line 5g. Include on line 5g any write-in credits or payments, such as the credit for tax on ozone-depleting chemicals or backup withholding.

Line 8. Enter the amount from the "Overpayment" line of the original return, even if the corporation chose to credit all or part of this amount to the next year's estimated tax. This amount must be considered in preparing Form 1120X because any refund due from the original return will be refunded separately (or credited to estimated tax) from any additional refund claimed on Form 1120X. If the original return was changed by the IRS and the result was an additional overpayment of tax, also include that amount on line 8.

Line 10. Tax due. If the corporation does not use electronic funds transfers, including the Electronic Federal Tax Payment System (EFTPS), enclose a check with this form and make it payable to the "United States Treasury."

Line 11. Overpayment. If the corporation is entitled to a refund larger than the amount claimed on the original return, line 11 will show only the additional amount of overpayment. This additional amount will be refunded separately from the amount claimed on the original return. The IRS will figure any interest due and include it in the refund.

Line 12. Enter the amount, if any, to be applied to the estimated tax for the next tax period. Also, enter that tax period. No interest will be paid on this amount. The election to apply part or all of the overpayment to the next year's estimated tax is irrevocable.

Who Must Sign

The return must be signed and dated by:

• The president, vice president, treasurer, assistant treasurer, chief accounting officer, or

• Any other corporate officer (such as tax officer) authorized to sign.

If a return is filed on behalf of a corporation by a receiver, trustee, or assignee, the fiduciary must sign the return, instead of the corporate officer. A return signed by a receiver or trustee in bankruptcy on behalf of a corporation must be filed with a copy of the order or instructions of the court authorizing signing of the return.

If an employee of the corporation completes Form 1120X, the paid preparer's space should remain blank. Anyone who prepares Form 1120X but does not charge the corporation should not complete that section. Generally, anyone who is paid to prepare the return must sign it and fill in the "Paid Preparer Use Only" area. See the Instructions for Forms 1120 for more information.

Note. A paid preparer may sign original or amended returns by rubber stamp, mechanical device, or computer software program.

Paperwork Reduction Act Notice. We ask for the information on this form to carry out the Internal Revenue laws of the United States. You are required to give us the information. We need it to ensure that you are complying with these laws and to allow us to figure and collect the right amount of tax.

You are not required to provide the information requested on a form that is subject to the Paperwork Reduction Act unless the form displays a valid OMB control number. Books or records relating to a form or its instructions must be retained as long as their contents may become material in the administration of any Internal Revenue law. Generally, tax returns and return information are confidential, as required by section 6103.

The time needed to complete and file this form will vary depending on individual circumstances. The estimated average time is:

Recordkeeping	12 hrs., 40 min.
Learning about the law or the form	1 hr., 19 min.
Preparing the form	3 hrs., 27 min.
Copying, assembling, and sending the form to the IRS	32 min.

If you have comments concerning the accuracy of these time estimates or suggestions for making this form simpler, we would be happy to hear from you. You can write to the Internal Revenue Service, Tax Products Coordinating Committee, SE:W:CAR:MP:T:T:SP, 1111 Constitution Ave. NW, IR-6526, Washington, DC 20224. Do not send the form to this address. Instead, see *Where To File* on page 3.

¶1523 Exhibit 15-3

Form **843**	**Claim for Refund and Request for Abatement**	
(Rev. August 2011) Department of the Treasury Internal Revenue Service	▶ See separate instructions.	OMB No. 1545-0024

Use Form 843 if your claim or request involves:

- **(a)** a refund of one of the taxes (other than income taxes or an employer's claim for FICA tax, RRTA tax, or income tax withholding) or a fee, shown on line 3,
- **(b)** an abatement of FUTA tax or certain excise taxes, or
- **(c)** a refund or abatement of interest, penalties, or additions to tax for one of the reasons shown on line 5a.

Do not use Form 843 if your claim or request involves:

- **(a)** an overpayment of income taxes or an employer's claim for FICA tax, RRTA tax, or income tax withholding (use the appropriate amended tax return),
- **(b)** a refund of excise taxes based on the nontaxable use or sale of fuels, or
- **(c)** an overpayment of excise taxes reported on Form(s) 11-C, 720, 730, or 2290.

Name(s)	Your social security number
Address (number, street, and room or suite no.)	Spouse's social security number
City or town, state, and ZIP code	Employer identification number (EIN)
Name and address shown on return if different from above	Daytime telephone number

1   **Period.** Prepare a separate Form 843 for each tax period or fee year.
From _____ to _____

2   **Amount** to be refunded or abated:
$ _____

3   **Type of tax or fee.** Indicate the type of tax or fee to be refunded or abated or to which the interest, penalty, or addition to tax is related.
☐ Employment   ☐ Estate   ☐ Gift   ☐ Excise   ☐ Income   ☐ Fee

4   **Type of penalty.** If the claim or request involves a penalty, enter the Internal Revenue Code section on which the penalty is based (see instructions). IRC section:

5a   **Interest, penalties, and additions to tax.** Check the box that indicates your reason for the request for refund or abatement. (If none apply, go to line 6.)
☐ Interest was assessed as a result of IRS errors or delays.
☐ A penalty or addition to tax was the result of erroneous written advice from the IRS.
☐ Reasonable cause or other reason allowed under the law (other than erroneous written advice) can be shown for not assessing a penalty or addition to tax.

b   Date(s) of payment(s) ▶ _____

6   **Original return.** Indicate the type of fee or return, if any, filed to which the tax, interest, penalty, or addition to tax relates.
☐ 706   ☐ 709   ☐ 940   ☐ 941   ☐ 943   ☐ 945
☐ 990-PF   ☐ 1040   ☐ 1120   ☐ 4720   ☐ Other (specify) ▶

7   **Explanation.** Explain why you believe this claim or request should be allowed and show the computation of the amount shown on line 2. If you need more space, attach additional sheets.

Signature. If you are filing Form 843 to request a refund or abatement relating to a joint return, both you and your spouse must sign the claim. Claims filed by corporations must be signed by a corporate officer authorized to sign, and the officer's title must be shown.

Under penalties of perjury, I declare that I have examined this claim, including accompanying schedules and statements, and, to the best of my knowledge and belief, it is true, correct, and complete. Declaration of preparer (other than taxpayer) is based on all information of which preparer has any knowledge.

_____
Signature (Title, if applicable. Claims by corporations must be signed by an officer.)   Date

_____
Signature (spouse, if joint return)   Date

Paid Preparer Use Only	Print/Type preparer's name	Preparer's signature	Date	Check ☐ if self-employed	PTIN
	Firm's name ▶			Firm's EIN ▶	
	Firm's address ▶			Phone no.	

For Privacy Act and Paperwork Reduction Act Notice, see separate instructions.   Cat. No. 10180R   Form **843** (Rev. 8-2011)

¶1524 Exhibit 15-4

Internal Revenue Service	**Department of the Treasury**

Taxpayer Identification Number:

Date:

Form:

Document Locator Number:

Tax Period(s) Ended:

Amount of Claim:

Date Claim Received:

Person to Contact:

Contact Telephone Number:

Employee Identification Number:

Refer Reply to:

CERTIFIED MAIL

Dear

We have reviewed your claim for a refund, and we cannot consider it for the reason checked below.

☐ It was received after the deadline for filing.

☐ As consideration in a previous settlement, you waived your right to claim the refund.

☐ It is based upon your failure or refusal to comply with tax laws because of moral, religious, political, constitutional, conscientious, or similar grounds. The Internal Revenue Service does not have the authority to consider such grounds in administering the tax laws.

☐ This matter has already been settled under the terms of a Closing Agreement we made for the tax period in question, according to section 7121 of the Internal Revenue Code.

☐ This matter was disposed of by a final order of the United States Tax Court or other court.

☐ This matter was settled in your favor in an earlier determination of your liability.

Letter 916(DO) (Rev. 4-1999)
Catalog Number 62367A

This letter is your legal notice that we cannot consider your claim.

If you want to bring suit or proceedings for the recovery of any tax, penalties, or other moneys for which this disallowance notice is issued, you may do so by filing such a suit with the United States District Court having jurisdiction, or the United States Claims Court. The law permits you do this within 2 years from the mailing date of this letter.

We have enclosed Publication 1, *Your Rights as a Taxpayer,* Publication 5, *Your Appeal Rights and How to Prepare a Protest If You Don't Agree,* and Publication 556, *Examination of Returns, Appeal Rights, and Claims for Refund,* for your information.

If you have any questions, please contact the person whose name and telephone number are shown in the heading of this letter. Thank you for your cooperation.

                                        Sincerely yours,

Enclosures:
Publication 1
Publication 5
Publication 556

¶1525 Exhibit 15-5

Internal Revenue Service	**Department of the Treasury**

Taxpayer Identification Number:

Kind of Tax:

Tax Period(s) Ended

Amount of Claim:

Date Claim Received:

Date: **Person to Contact:**

Contact Telephone Number:

Employee Identification Number:

Dear

We are sorry, but we cannot allow your claim for an adjustment to your tax, for the reasons stated below. This letter is your legal notice that we have fully disallowed your claim.

If you wish to bring suit or proceedings for the recovery of any tax, penalties, or other moneys for which this disallowance notice is issued, you may do so by filing suit with the United States District Court having jurisdiction, or the United States Claims Court. The law permits you to do this within 2 years from the mailing date of this letter. However, if you signed a *Waiver of Statutory Notification of Claim Disallowance,* Form 2297, the period for bringing suit began to run on the date you filed the waiver.

We have enclosed Publication 5, *Your Appeal Rights and How to Prepare a Protest If You Don't Agree,* and Publication 594, *The IRS Collection Process,* if additional tax is due.

(over)   **Letter 906 (DO) (Rev. 6-2000)**
                                            Cat. No. 14978B

¶1525

If you have any questions, please contact the person whose name and telephone number are shown in the heading of this letter. Thank you for your cooperation.

Sincerely yours,

Enclosures:
Publication 5
☐ Publication 594

Reasons for disallowance:

Letter 906 (DO) (Rev. 6-2000)
Cat. No. 14978B

¶1526 Exhibit 15-6

Internal Revenue Service   **Department of the Treasury**

Taxpayer Identification Number:

Form:

Date:

Tax Period(s) Ended and Claim Amount:

Date Claim Received:

Person to Contact:

Contact Telephone Number:

Employee Identification Number:

Last date to Respond to this Letter:

Dear

We examined your claim and propose:

☐   Partial disallowance, as shown in the enclosed examination report. If you accept our findings, please sign and return the enclosed Form 2297, *Waiver Form* and Form 3363, *Acceptance Form.*

☐   Full disallowance, as shown in the enclosed examination report or at the end of this letter. If you accept our findings, please sign and return the enclosed Form 2297, *Waiver Form* and Form 3363, *Acceptance Form.*

☐   Full disallowance with additional tax due, as shown in the enclosed examination report. If you accept our findings, please sign and return the enclosed Form 2297, *Waiver Form* and the examination report.

Note: If your claim involves a joint return, both taxpayers must sign the form(s).

If you are a "C" Corporation filer, Section 6621(c) of the Internal Revenue Code provides for an interest rate 2% higher than the standard interest rate on deficiencies of $100,000 or more.

If you don't agree with our findings, you may request a meeting or telephone conference with the supervisor of the person identified in the heading of this letter. If you still don't agree with our findings, we recommend that you request a conference with our Appeals Office. If you request a conference, we will forward your request to the Appeals Office and they will contact you to schedule an appointment.

Letter 569 (DO) (Rev. 9-2000)
Catalog Number 40248G

If the proposed change to tax is:

- $25,000 or less for *each* referenced tax period; you may send us a letter requesting Appeals consideration, indicating what you don't agree with and the reasons why you don't agree.

- More than $25,000 for *any* referenced tax period; you must submit a formal protest.

The requirements for filing a formal protest are explained in the enclosed Publication 3498, *The Examination Process.* Publication 3498 also includes information on your *Rights as a Taxpayer* and the *IRS Collection Process.*

If you don't respond by the date shown in the heading of this letter, we will process your case based on the adjustments shown in the enclosed examination report or the explanations given at the end of this letter.

If you have any questions, please contact the person whose name and telephone number are shown in the heading of this letter. Thank you for your cooperation.

Sincerely yours,

Enclosures:
☐ Examination Report
Form 2297
☐ Form 3363
Publication 3498
Envelope

Letter 569 (DO) (Rev. 9-2000)
Catalog Number 40248G

Reason for Disallowance:

Letter 569 (DO) (Rev. 9-2000)
Catalog Number 40248G

¶1527 Exhibit 15-7

Form **2297** (Rev. March 1982)	Department of the Treasury — Internal Revenue Service **Waiver of Statutory Notification** **of Claim Disallowance**

I, _____ of _____
                   (Name, SSN or EIN)   *(Number, Street, City or Town, State, ZIP Code)*

waive the requirement under Internal Revenue Code section 6532(a)(1) that a notice of claim disallowance be sent to me by certified or registered mail for the claims for credit or refund shown in column (d), below.

    I understand that the filing of this waiver is irrevocable and it will begin the 2-year period for filing suit for refund of the claims disallowed as if the notice of disallowance had been sent by certified or registered mail.

Claims

(a) Taxable Period Ended	(b) Kind of Tax	(c) Amount of Claim	(d) Amount of Claim Disallowed

| If you file this waiver for a joint return, both you and your spouse must sign the original and duplicate of this form. Sign your name exactly as it appears on the return. If you are acting under power of attorney for your spouse, you may sign as agent for him or her.
    For an agent or attorney acting under a power of attorney, a power of attorney must be sent with this form if not previously filed.
    For a partnership with excise or employment tax liability, all partners must sign. However, one partner may sign with appropriate evidence of authorization to act for the partnership.
    For a person acting in a fiduciary capacity (executor, administrator, trustee), file Form 56, Notice Concerning Fiduciary Relationship with this form if not previously filed.
    For a corporation, enter the name of the corporation followed by the signature and title of the officer(s) authorized to sign. | Your Signature ──▶ _____
                                  (Date signed)
Spouse's Signature If A Joint Return Was Filed ──▶ _____
                                  (Date signed)
Taxpayer's Representative Sign Here ──▶ _____
                                  (Date signed)
Partnership/ Corporate Name: _____
_____
Partners/ Corporate Officers Sign Here _____
_____
     (Title)   *(Date signed)*
_____
     (Title)   *(Date signed)* |

NOTE - Filing this waiver within 6 months from the date the claim was filed will not permit filing a suit for refund before the 6-month period has elapsed unless a decision is made by the Service within that time disallowing the claims.

Form **2297** (Rev. 3-82)

¶1528 Exhibit 15-8

Form **907** (Revised January 2001)	Department of the Treasury - Internal Revenue Service **Agreement to Extend the Time to Bring Suit**	In reply refer to: Taxpayer Identification Number

_____, taxpayer(s) of
(Name(s))

_____
(Number, street, city or town, State, ZIP code)

and the Commissioner of Internal Revenue agree that the taxpayer(s) may bring suit to recover the taxes described below, on or before

_____ .
(Expiration date)

Claims for the amounts shown below have been timely filed by the taxpayer(s), and these claims have been disallowed in whole or in part. A notice of disallowance has been mailed to the taxpayer(s) by certified or registered mail, unless the taxpayer(s) waived the requirement that the notice be issued.

	Period Ended	Kind of Tax	Amount of Tax	Date Notice of Disallowance Mailed or Waiver Filed
Refund Credit				

IMPORTANT:

You must submit with this agreement a statement of the issues involved in the claims for refund or credit of the taxes listed above.

You may request in writing that the claims be reopened and reconsidered at any time before the expiration date shown.
You should state the particular circumstances on which you base the request. Please identify the claims in the request by stating the amounts claimed, the periods involved, and the date and symbols appearing on the letter in which notice of disallowance was given, or the date the waiver (Form 2297) was filed. Attach a copy of this agreement to your request.

This agreement will not be effective until the appropriate Internal Revenue Service official signs this form on behalf of the Commissioner of Internal Revenue. You should therefore be prepared to protect your interests by bringing suit, if desired, at any time before this agreement is signed.
If the appropriate Internal Revenue Service official signs this agreement on behalf of the Commissioner of Internal Revenue , the final decision in any case now in litigation does not bind that official in the disposition, of the issues on the taxes covered by this agreement.

YOUR SIGNATURE HERE ➤ _____   _____
(Date signed)

SPOUSE'S SIGNATURE ➤ _____   _____
(Date signed)

TAXPAYER'S REPRESENTATIVE

SIGN HERE ➤ _____   _____
(Date signed)

**CORPORATE
NAME** ➤ _____

**CORPORATE
OFFICER(S)
SIGN HERE** ➤ _____   _____   _____
(Title)   (Date signed)

➤ _____   _____   _____
(Title)   (Date signed)

INTERNAL REVENUE SERVICE SIGNATURE AND TITLE

_____   _____
(Division Executive Name - see instructions)   (Division Executive Title - see instructions)

BY _____   _____
(Authorized Official Signature and Title - see instructions)   (Date signed)

(Signature instructions are on the back of this form)	www.irs.gov	Catalog Number 16963W	Form **907** (Rev. 1-2001)

Instructions

If this agreement is for any year(s) you filed a joint return, both husband and wife must sign the original and copy of this form unless one, acting under a power of attorney, signs as agent for the other. The signatures must match the names as they appear on this form.

If you are an attorney or agent of the taxpayer(s), you may sign this agreement provided the action is specifically authorized by a power of attorney. If you didn't previously file the power of attorney, please include it with this form.

If you are acting as a fiduciary (such as executor, administrator, trustee, etc.) and you sign this agreement, also attach a completed Form 56, Notice Concerning Fiduciary Relationship, if you haven't already filed one.

If the taxpayer is a corporation, sign this agreement with the corporate name followed by the signature and title of the officer(s) authorized to sign.

Instructions for Internal Revenue Service Employees

Complete the Division Executive's name and title depending upon your division.

If you are in the Small Business /Self-Employed Division, enter the name and title for the appropriate division executive for your business unit (e.g., Area Director for your area; Director, Compliance Policy; Director, Compliance Services).

If you are in the Wage and Investment Division, enter the name and title for the appropriate division executive for your business unit (e.g., Area Director for your area; Director, Field Compliance Services).

If you are in the Large and Mid-Size Business Division, enter the name and title of the Director, Field Operations for your industry.

If you are in the Tax Exempt and Government Entities Division, enter the name and title for the appropriate division executive for your business unit (e.g., Director, Exempt Organizations; Director, Employee Plans; Director, Federal, State and Local Governments; Director, Indian Tribal Governments; Director, Tax Exempt Bonds).

If you are in Appeals, enter the name and title of the appropriate Director, Appeals Operating Unit.

The signature and title line will be signed and dated by the appropriate authorized official within your division.

Catalog Number 16963W   Form **907** (Rev. 1-2001)

¶1529 Exhibit 15-9

Department of the Treasury
Internal Revenue Service

If you have any questions, refer to this information:

Date of This Notice:
Taxpayer Identifying Number:
Document Locator Number:
Form   Tax Period:

Call:

or

Write: Chief, Service Center Collection Branch
Internal Revenue Service Center

Delay in Processing Your Refund

This copy is for your records.

We are sorry, but there is a delay in processing your overpayment for the above tax period because we must check to make sure you do not owe other Federal taxes. This will take about 6 to 8 weeks.   Your Overpaid Tax Shown on Return. $ _____

If you owe other Federal taxes, all or part of your overpaid taxes may be applied to those taxes. We will let you know how the overpaid tax is applied. If you requested a refund and do not owe other Federal taxes, a check will be sent to you for the amount you overpaid. Any interest due you will be included in the check.

No further action is required of you, but if you have any questions you can call or write us -- see the information in the upper right corner. To make sure that IRS employees give courteous responses and correct information to taxpayers, a second employee sometimes listens in on telephone calls.

Form 4356 (Part 1) (Rev. 5-93)

¶1530 Exhibit 15-10

Form **1045**	**Application for Tentative Refund**	OMB No. 1545-0098
Department of the Treasury Internal Revenue Service	▶ See separate instructions. ▶ Do not attach to your income tax return—mail in a separate envelope. ▶ For use by individuals, estates, or trusts.	**2010**

Type or print	Name(s) shown on return	Social security or employer identification number
	Number, street, and apt. or suite no. If a P.O. box, see instructions.	Spouse's social security number (SSN)
	City, town or post office, state, and ZIP code. If a foreign address, see instructions.	Daytime phone number ( )

1 This application is filed to carry back:	**a** Net operating loss (NOL) (Sch. A, line 25, page 2) $	**b** Unused general business credit $	**c** Net section 1256 contracts loss $

2a For the calendar year 2010, or other tax year beginning , 2010, and ending , 20	**b** Date tax return was filed

3 If this application is for an unused credit created by another carryback, enter year of first carryback ▶ ....

4 If you filed a joint return (or separate return) for some, but not all, of the tax years involved in figuring the carryback, list the years and specify whether joint (J) or separate (S) return for each ▶ ....

5 If SSN for carryback year is different from above, enter **a** SSN ▶ .... and **b** Year(s) ▶ ....

6 If you changed your accounting period, give date permission to change was granted ▶ ....

7 Have you filed a petition in Tax Court for the year(s) to which the carryback is to be applied? . . . . . ☐ Yes ☐ No

8 Is any part of the decrease in tax due to a loss or credit resulting from a reportable transaction required to be disclosed on Form 8886, Reportable Transaction Disclosure Statement? . . . . ☐ Yes ☐ No

9 If you are carrying back an NOL or net section 1256 contracts loss, did this cause the release of foreign tax credits or the release of other credits due to the release of the foreign tax credit (see instructions)? . . . . ☐ Yes ☐ No

Computation of Decrease in Tax (see instructions) **Note:** *If 1a and 1c are blank, skip lines 10 through 15.*	_____ preceding tax year ended ▶		_____ preceding tax year ended ▶		_____ preceding tax year ended ▶	
	Before carryback	After carryback	Before carryback	After carryback	Before carryback	After carryback
10 NOL deduction after carryback (see instructions)						
11 Adjusted gross income						
12 Deductions (see instructions) . . .						
13 Subtract line 12 from line 11 . . .						
14 Exemptions (see instructions) . . .						
15 Taxable income. Line 13 minus line 14						
16 Income tax. See instructions and attach an explanation						
17 Alternative minimum tax						
18 Add lines 16 and 17						
19 General business credit (see instructions)						
20 Other credits. Identify						
21 Total credits. Add lines 19 and 20 .						
22 Subtract line 21 from line 18 . . .						
23 Self-employment tax						
24 Other taxes						
25 Total tax. Add lines 22 through 24 .						
26 Enter the amount from the "After carryback" column on line 25 for each year						
27 Decrease in tax. Line 25 minus line 26						
28 Overpayment of tax due to a claim of right adjustment under section 1341(b)(1) (attach computation) . .						

Sign Here
Keep a copy of this application for your records.

Under penalties of perjury, I declare that I have examined this application and accompanying schedules and statements, and to the best of my knowledge and belief, they are true, correct, and complete.

▶ Your signature	Date
▶ Spouse's signature. If Form 1045 is filed jointly, **both** must sign.	Date

Paid Preparer Use Only	Print/Type preparer's name	Preparer's signature	Date	Check ☐ if self-employed	PTIN
	Firm's name ▶			Firm's EIN ▶	
	Firm's address ▶			Phone no.	

For Disclosure, Privacy Act, and Paperwork Reduction Act Notice, see instructions.   Cat. No. 10670A   Form **1045** (2010)

Schedule A—NOL (see instructions)

1	Enter the amount from your 2010 Form 1040, line 41, or Form 1040NR, line 39. Estates and trusts, enter taxable income increased by the total of the charitable deduction, income distribution deduction, and exemption amount	**1**
2	Nonbusiness capital losses before limitation. Enter as a positive number	**2**
3	Nonbusiness capital gains (without regard to any section 1202 exclusion)	**3**
4	If line 2 is more than line 3, enter the difference; otherwise, enter -0-	**4**
5	If line 3 is more than line 2, enter the difference; otherwise, enter -0- **5**	
6	Nonbusiness deductions (see instructions)	**6**
7	Nonbusiness income other than capital gains (see instructions) **7**	
8	Add lines 5 and 7	**8**
9	If line 6 is more than line 8, enter the difference; otherwise, enter -0-	**9**
10	If line 8 is more than line 6, enter the difference; otherwise, enter -0-. **But do not enter more than line 5** **10**	
11	Business capital losses before limitation. Enter as a positive number	**11**
12	Business capital gains (without regard to any section 1202 exclusion) **12**	
13	Add lines 10 and 12	**13**
14	Subtract line 13 from line 11. If zero or less, enter -0-	**14**
15	Add lines 4 and 14	**15**
16	Enter the loss, if any, from line 16 of your 2010 Schedule D (Form 1040). (Estates and trusts, enter the loss, if any, from line 15, column (3), of Schedule D (Form 1041).) Enter as a positive number. If you do not have a loss on that line (and do not have a section 1202 exclusion), skip lines 16 through 21 and enter on line 22 the amount from line 15	**16**
17	Section 1202 exclusion. Enter as a positive number	**17**
18	Subtract line 17 from line 16. If zero or less, enter -0-	**18**
19	Enter the loss, if any, from line 21 of your 2010 Schedule D (Form 1040). (Estates and trusts, enter the loss, if any, from line 16 of Schedule D (Form 1041).) Enter as a positive number	**19**
20	If line 18 is more than line 19, enter the difference; otherwise, enter -0-	**20**
21	If line 19 is more than line 18, enter the difference; otherwise, enter -0-	**21**
22	Subtract line 20 from line 15. If zero or less, enter -0-	**22**
23	Domestic production activities deduction from your 2010 Form 1040, line 35, or Form 1040NR, line 34 (or included on Form 1041, line 15a)	**23**
24	NOL deduction for losses from other years. Enter as a positive number	**24**
25	**NOL.** Combine lines 1, 9, 17, and 21 through 24. If the result is less than zero, enter it here and on page 1, line 1a. If the result is zero or more, you **do not** have an NOL	**25**

Form **1045** (2010)

Form 1045 (2010)   Page **3**

Schedule B—NOL Carryover (see instructions)

Complete one column before going to the next column. Start with the earliest carryback year.	_____ preceding tax year ended ▶		_____ preceding tax year ended ▶		_____ preceding tax year ended ▶	
1 **NOL deduction** (see instructions). Enter as a positive number						
2 Taxable income before 2010 NOL carryback (see instructions). Estates and trusts, increase this amount by the sum of the charitable deduction and income distribution deduction .						
3 Net capital loss deduction (see instructions)						
4 Section 1202 exclusion. Enter as a positive number						
5 Domestic production activities deduction						
6 Adjustment to adjusted gross income (see instructions)						
7 Adjustment to itemized deductions (see instructions)						
8 Individuals, enter deduction for exemptions (minus any amount on Form 8914, line 6, for 2006 and 2009; line 2 for 2005 and 2008). Estates and trusts, enter exemption amount						
9 Modified taxable income. Combine lines 2 through 8. If zero or less, enter -0-						
10 **NOL carryover** (see instructions). .						
Adjustment to Itemized Deductions (Individuals Only) Complete lines 11 through 38 for the carryback year(s) for which you itemized deductions **only** if line 3, 4, or 5 above is more than zero.						
11 Adjusted gross income before 2010 NOL carryback						
12 Add lines 3 through 6 above . . .						
13 Modified adjusted gross income. Add lines 11 and 12						
14 Medical expenses from Sch. A (Form 1040), line 4 (or as previously adjusted)						
15 Medical expenses from Sch. A (Form 1040), line 1 (or as previously adjusted)						
16 Multiply line 13 by 7.5% (.075) . .						
17 Subtract line 16 from line 15. If zero or less, enter -0-						
18 Subtract line 17 from line 14 . . .						
19 Mortgage insurance premiums from Sch. A (Form 1040), line 13 (or as previously adjusted)						
20 Refigured mortgage insurance premiums (see instructions) . . .						
21 Subtract line 20 from line 19 . . .						

Form **1045** (2010)

Schedule B—NOL Carryover *(Continued)*

Complete one column before going to the next column. Start with the earliest carryback year.	_____ preceding tax year ended ▶		_____ preceding tax year ended ▶		_____ preceding tax year ended ▶	
22	Modified adjusted gross income from line 13 on page 3 of the form .					
23	Enter as a positive number any NOL carryback from a year before 2010 that was deducted to figure line 11 on page 3 of the form					
24	Add lines 22 and 23					
25	Charitable contributions from Sch. A (Form 1040), line 19 (line 18 for 2000 through 2006), or Sch. A (Form 1040NR), line 7 (or as previously adjusted)					
26	Refigured charitable contributions (see instructions)					
27	Subtract line 26 from line 25 . . .					
28	Casualty and theft losses from Form 4684, line 21 (line 23 for 2008; line 18 for 2000 through 2004 and 2007; line 20 for 2005 and 2006)					
29	Casualty and theft losses from Form 4684, line 18 (line 21 for 2008; line 16 for 2000 through 2004 and 2007) . .					
30	Multiply line 22 by 10% (.10) . . .					
31	Subtract line 30 from line 29. If zero or less, enter -0-					
32	Subtract line 31 from line 28 . . .					
33	Miscellaneous itemized deductions from Sch. A (Form 1040), line 27 (line 26 for 2000 through 2006), or Sch. A (Form 1040NR), line 15 (or as previously adjusted) . . .					
34	Miscellaneous itemized deductions from Sch. A (Form 1040), line 24 (line 23 for 2000 through 2006), or Sch. A (Form 1040NR), line 12 (or as previously adjusted) . . .					
35	Multiply line 22 by 2% (.02) . . .					
36	Subtract line 35 from line 34. If zero or less, enter -0-					
37	Subtract line 36 from line 33 . . .					
38	Complete the worksheet in the instructions if line 22 is **more than** the applicable amount shown below (more than one-half that amount if married filing separately for that year). • $128,950 for 2000. • $132,950 for 2001. • $137,300 for 2002. • $139,500 for 2003. • $142,700 for 2004. • $145,950 for 2005. • $150,500 for 2006. • $156,400 for 2007. • $159,950 for 2008. • $166,800 for 2009. Otherwise, combine lines 18, 21, 27, 32, and 37; enter the result here and on line 7 (page 3)					

Form **1045** (2010)

¶1531 Exhibit 15-11

Form **1139**	**Corporation Application for Tentative Refund**	
(Rev. August 2006) Department of the Treasury Internal Revenue Service	▶ See separate instructions. ▶ **Do not file with the corporation's income tax return—file separately.**	OMB No. 1545-0582

Name	Employer identification number
Number, street, and room or suite no. If a P.O. box, see instructions.	Date of incorporation
City or town, state, and ZIP code	Daytime phone number ( )

1	Reason(s) for filing. See instructions— attach computation	**a** Net operating loss (NOL) . . ▶	$	**c** Unused general business credit ▶	$
		b Net capital loss . . . . . ▶	$	**d** Other . . . ▶	$

2	Return for year of loss, unused credit, or overpayment under section 1341(b)(1) ▶	**a** Tax year ended	**b** Date tax return filed	**c** Service center where filed

3   If this application is for an unused credit created by another carryback, enter ending date for the tax year of the first carryback. ▶.....................

4   Did a loss result in the release of a foreign tax credit, or is the corporation carrying back a general business credit that
was released because of the release of a foreign tax credit (see instructions)? If "Yes," the corporation must file an
amended return to carry back the released credits. . . . . ☐ Yes ☐ No

5a   Was a consolidated return filed for any carryback year or did the corporation join a consolidated group (see instructions)? ☐ Yes ☐ No

  b   If "Yes," enter the tax year ending date and the name of the common parent and its EIN, if different from above (see instructions) ▶.......

6a   If Form 1138 has been filed, was an extension of time granted for filing the return for the tax year of the NOL? . . ☐ Yes ☐ No

  b   If "Yes," enter the date to which extension was granted ▶.................... **c** Enter the date Form 1138 was filed. ▶..........

  d   Unpaid tax for which Form 1138 is in effect. . . . . ▶ $.................

7   If the corporation changed its accounting period, enter the date permission to change was granted . . . . ▶.................

8   If this is an application for a dissolved corporation, enter date of dissolution . . . . ▶.................

9   Has the corporation filed a petition in Tax Court for the year or years to which the carryback is to be applied? . . ☐ Yes ☐ No

10   Does this application include a loss or credit from a tax shelter required to be registered? If "Yes," attach Form(s) 8271 ☐ Yes ☐ No

Computation of Decrease in Tax See instructions. Note: *If only filing for an unused general business credit (line 1c), skip lines 11 through 15.*	.... preceding tax year ended ▶........		.... preceding tax year ended ▶........		.... preceding tax year ended ▶........	
	(a) Before carryback	**(b)**After carryback	**(c)**Before carryback	**(d)**After carryback	**(e)**Before carryback	**(f)**After carryback
11 Taxable income from tax return . . .						
12 **Capital loss carryback (see instructions)**						
13 Subtract line 12 from line 11						
14 **NOL deduction (see instructions)** . .						
15 Taxable income. Subtract line 14 from line 13						
16 **Income tax**						
17 Alternative minimum tax						
18 Add lines 16 and 17						
19 General business credit (see instructions)						
20 Other credits (see instructions) . .						
21 Total credits. Add lines 19 and 20 . .						
22 Subtract line 21 from line 18						
23 Personal holding company tax (Sch. PH (Form 1120))						
24 Other taxes (see instructions)						
25 Total tax liability. Add lines 22 through 24						
26 Enter amount from "After carryback" column on line 25 for each year . . .						
27 **Decrease in tax.** Subtract line 26 from line 25						

28   Overpayment of tax due to a claim of right adjustment under section 1341(b)(1) (attach computation) . . . . . .

**Sign
Here**

Keep a copy of
this application
for your records.

Under penalties of perjury, I declare that I have examined this application and accompanying schedules and statements, and to the best of my
knowledge and belief, they are true, correct, and complete.

▶ _____ ▶ _____ ▶ _____
Signature of officer   Date   Title

Preparer Other Than Taxpayer	Name ▶	Date
	Address ▶	

For Paperwork Reduction Act Notice, see separate instructions.   Cat. No. 11170F   Form **1139** (Rev. 8-2006)

¶1532 Exhibit 15-12

Form **1138** (Rev. December 2005) Department of the Treasury Internal Revenue Service	**Extension of Time for Payment of Taxes by a** **Corporation Expecting a Net Operating Loss Carryback** (Under Section 6164 of the Internal Revenue Code)	OMB No. 1545-0135

Name		Employer identification number

Number, street, and room or suite no. If a P.O. box, see instructions.

City or town, state, and ZIP code

1	Ending date of the tax year of the expected net operating loss (NOL)	2 Amount of expected NOL $

3 Reduction of previously determined tax attributable to the expected NOL carryback
(see instructions—attach schedule) . . . . ▶ $

4 Ending date of the tax year immediately preceding the tax year of the expected NOL

5 Give the reasons, facts, and circumstances that cause the corporation to expect an NOL.

6 Amount for which payment is to be extended:

a Enter the total tax shown on the return, plus any amount assessed as a deficiency, interest, or penalty (see instructions)	**6a**	
b Enter amounts from line 6a that were already paid or were required to have been paid, plus refunds, credits, and abatements (see instructions)	**6b**	
c Subtract line 6b from line 6a. Do not enter more than the amount on line 3 above. This is the amount of tax for which the time for payment is extended	**6c**	

Sign
Here

Under penalties of perjury, I declare that I have examined this form, including any accompanying schedules and statements, and to the best of my knowledge and belief it is true, correct, and complete.

Keep a copy of
this form for
your records.

▶ _____
Signature of officer

▶ _____
Date

▶ _____
Title

For Paperwork Reduction Act Notice, see instructions.   Cat. No. 17250W   Form **1138** (Rev. 12-2005)

General Instructions

Section references are to the Internal Revenue Code.

Purpose of form. A corporation that expects a net operating loss (NOL) in the current tax year can file Form 1138 to extend the time for payment of tax for the immediately preceding tax year. This includes extending the time for payment of a tax deficiency. The payment of tax that can be postponed cannot exceed the expected overpayment from the carryback of the NOL.

Only payments of tax that are required to be paid after the filing of Form 1138 are eligible for extension. Do not file this form if all the required payments have been paid or were required to have been paid.

If the corporation previously filed Form 1138 and later finds information that will change the amount of the expected NOL, the corporation can file a revised Form 1138. If the amount of the NOL is increased based on the new information, the corporation can postpone the payment of a larger amount of tax as long as the larger amount has not yet been paid or is not yet required to be paid. If the amount of the NOL is reduced because of the new information, the corporation must pay the tax to the extent that the amount of tax postponed on the original filing exceeds the amount of tax postponed on the revised filing.

When and where to file. File Form 1138 after the start of the tax year of the expected NOL but before the tax of the preceding tax year is required to be paid. Generally, file Form 1138 with the Internal Revenue Service Center where the corporation files its income tax return.

A corporation can file Form 1138 separately or with Form 7004, Application for Automatic 6-Month Extension of Time To File Certain Business Income Tax, Information, and Other Returns. If Form 1138 and Form 7004 are filed together, Form 1138 will reduce or eliminate the amount of tax to be deposited when Form 7004 is filed. If Form 1138 is filed with Form 7004, then file Form 1138 with the Internal Revenue Service Center at the applicable address where the corporation files Form 7004.

Period of extension. In general, the extension for paying the tax expires at the end of the month in which the return for the tax year of the expected NOL is required to be filed (including extensions).

The corporation can further extend the time for payment by filing Form 1139, Corporation Application for Tentative Refund, before the period of extension ends. See the instructions for Form 1139. The period will be further extended until the date the IRS informs the corporation that it has allowed or disallowed the application in whole or in part.

Termination of extension. The IRS can terminate the extension if it believes that any part of the form contains erroneous or unreasonable information. The IRS can also terminate the extension if it believes it may not be able to collect the tax.

Interest. Interest is charged on postponed amounts from the dates that the payments would normally be due. The interest is figured at the underpayment rate specified in section 6621.

Specific Instructions

Address. Include the suite, room, or other unit number after the street address. If the Post Office does not deliver mail to the street address and the corporation has a P.O. box, show the box number instead.

If the corporation receives its mail in care of a third party (such as an accountant or attorney), enter on the street address line "C/O" followed by the third party's name and street address or P.O. box.

If your address is outside the United States or its possessions or territories, fill in the line for "City or town, state, and ZIP code" in the following order: city, province or state, and country. Follow the foreign country's practice for entering the postal code, if any. Do not abbreviate the country name.

Line 2. The amount of the expected NOL must be based on all of the facts relating to the operation of the corporation. Consider the following items when estimating the amount of the expected NOL:

1. The number and dollar amounts of the corporation's Government contracts that have been canceled,

2. Profit and loss statements, and

3. Other factors peculiar to the corporation's operations.

See section 172, Pub. 542, Corporations, and Pub. 536, Net Operating Losses for Individuals, Estates, and Trusts, to help determine the amount of the expected NOL. Limitations apply to (a) the amount of taxable income of a new loss corporation for any tax year ending after an ownership change that may be offset by any pre-change NOLs and (b) the use of preacquisition losses of one corporation to offset recognized built-in gains of another corporation. See sections 382 and 384 for details.

Line 3. Enter the reduction of previously determined tax attributable to the carryback, for tax years before the tax year of the NOL. Previously determined tax is generally:

1. The amount shown on the return, plus any amounts assessed as deficiencies before Form 1138 is filed, minus

2. Any abatements, credits, or refunds allowed or made before Form 1138 is filed.

See section 1314(a).

Attach a schedule showing how the reduction was figured. See the instructions for the corporate income tax return for information on figuring the NOL deduction and recomputing the tax.

Line 6a. For the year shown on line 4, enter on line 6a the total of:

1. The total tax shown on the return, plus

2. Any amount assessed as a deficiency (or as interest or a penalty) prior to the filing of this Form 1138.

Line 6b. Enter the total of the following:

1. The amount of tax paid or required to be paid before the date this form is filed. This includes any amount assessed as a deficiency or as interest or a penalty if this form is filed more than 21 calendar days after notice and demand for payment was made (more than 10 business days if the amount for which the notice and demand for payment was made equals or exceeds $100,000). An amount of tax for which the corporation has received an extension of time to pay (under section 6161) is not considered required to be paid before the end of the extension, plus

2. The amount of refunds, credits, and abatements made before the date this form is filed.

Paperwork Reduction Act Notice. We ask for the information on this form to carry out the Internal Revenue laws of the United States. You are required to give us the information. We need it to ensure that you are complying with these laws and to allow us to figure and collect the right amount of tax.

You are not required to provide the information requested on a form that is subject to the Paperwork Reduction Act unless the form displays a valid OMB control number. Books or records relating to a form or its instructions must be retained as long as their contents may become material in the administration of any Internal Revenue law. Generally, tax returns and return information are confidential, as required by section 6103.

The time needed to complete and file this form will vary depending on individual circumstances. The estimated average time is:

Recordkeeping	3 hr., 21 min.
Learning about the law or the form	42 min.
Preparing and sending the form to the IRS	47 min.

If you have comments concerning the accuracy of these time estimates or suggestions for making this form simpler, we would be happy to hear from you. You can write to the Internal Revenue Service, Tax Products Coordinating Committee, SE:W:CAR:MP:T:T:SP, 1111 Constitution Ave. NW, IR-6406, Washington, DC 20224. Do not send Form 1138 to this office. Instead, see *When and where to file*, above.

¶1533 Exhibit 15-13

Form **1310** (Rev. November 2005) Department of the Treasury Internal Revenue Service	**Statement of Person Claiming Refund Due a Deceased Taxpayer** ▶ See instructions below and on back.	OMB No. 1545-0074 Attachment Sequence No. **87**

Tax year decedent was due a refund:

Calendar year _____ , or other tax year beginning _____ , 20 ___ , and ending _____ , 20 ___

Please print or type	Name of decedent	Date of death / /	Decedent's social security number
	Name of person claiming refund		Your social security number
	Home address (number and street). If you have a P.O. box, see instructions.		Apt. no.
	City, town or post office, state, and ZIP code. If you have a foreign address, see instructions.		

Part I   **Check the box that applies to you.** Check only one box. **Be sure to complete Part III below.**

A ☐ Surviving spouse requesting reissuance of a refund check (see instructions).

B ☐ Court-appointed or certified personal representative (defined below). Attach a court certificate showing your appointment, unless previously filed (see instructions).

C ☐ Person, **other** than A or B, claiming refund for the decedent's estate (see instructions). Also, complete Part II.

Part II   **Complete this part only if you checked the box on line C above.**

		Yes	No
1	Did the decedent leave a will?		
2a	Has a court appointed a personal representative for the estate of the decedent?		
b	If you answered **"No"** to 2a, will one be appointed?		
	If you answered **"Yes"** to 2a or 2b, the personal representative must file for the refund.		
3	As the person claiming the refund for the decedent's estate, will you pay out the refund according to the laws of the state where the decedent was a legal resident?		
	If you answered **"No"** to 3, a refund cannot be made until you submit a court certificate showing your appointment as personal representative or other evidence that you are entitled under state law to receive the refund.		

Part III   **Signature and verification. All filers must complete this part.**

I request a refund of taxes overpaid by or on behalf of the decedent. Under penalties of perjury, I declare that I have examined this claim, and to the best of my knowledge and belief, it is true, correct, and complete.

Signature of person claiming refund ▶ _____   Date ▶ _____

General Instructions

Purpose of Form

Use Form 1310 to claim a refund on behalf of a deceased taxpayer.

Who Must File

If you are claiming a refund on behalf of a deceased taxpayer, you must file Form 1310 unless either of the following applies:

● You are a surviving spouse filing an original or amended joint return with the decedent, or

● You are a personal representative (defined on this page) filing an original Form 1040, Form 1040A, Form 1040EZ, or Form 1040NR for the decedent and a court certificate showing your appointment is attached to the return.

Example. Assume Mr. Green died on January 4 before filing his tax return. On April 3 of the same year, you were appointed by the court as the personal representative for Mr. Green's estate and you file Form 1040 for Mr. Green. You do not need to file Form 1310 to claim the refund on Mr. Green's

tax return. However, you must attach to his return a copy of the court certificate showing your appointment.

Where To File

If you checked the box on line A, you can return the joint-name check with Form 1310 to your local IRS office or the Internal Revenue Service Center where you filed your return. If you checked the box on line B or line C, then:

● Follow the instructions for the form to which you are attaching Form 1310, or

● Send it to the same Internal Revenue Service Center where the original return was filed if you are filing Form 1310 separately. If the original return was filed electronically, mail Form 1310 to the Internal Revenue Service Center designated for the address shown on Form 1310 above. See the instructions for the original return for the address.

Personal Representative

For purposes of this form, a personal representative is the executor or administrator of the decedent's estate, as appointed or certified by the court. A copy of the decedent's

For Privacy Act and Paperwork Reduction Act Notice, see page 2.   Cat. No. 11566B   Form **1310** (Rev. 11-2005)

¶1533

will cannot be accepted as evidence that you are the personal representative.

Additional Information

For more details, see *Death of a Taxpayer* in the index to the Form 1040, Form 1040A, or Form 1040EZ instructions, or get Pub. 559, Survivors, Executors, and Administrators.

Specific Instructions

P.O. Box

Enter your box number only if your post office does not deliver mail to your home.

Foreign Address

If your address is outside the United States or its possessions or territories, enter the information in the following order: City, province or state, and country. Follow the country's practice for entering the postal code. Do not abbreviate the country name.

Line A

Check the box on line A if you received a refund check in your name and your deceased spouse's name. You can return the joint-name check with Form 1310 to your local IRS office or the Internal Revenue Service Center where you filed your return. A new check will be issued in your name and mailed to you.

Line B

Check the box on line B only if you are the decedent's court-appointed personal representative claiming a refund for the decedent on Form 1040X, Amended U.S. Individual Income Tax Return, or Form 843, Claim for Refund and Request for Abatement. You must attach a copy of the court certificate showing your appointment. But if you have already sent the court certificate to the IRS, complete Form 1310 and write "Certificate Previously Filed" at the bottom of the form.

Line C

Check the box on line C if you are not a surviving spouse claiming a refund based on a joint return and there is no court-appointed personal representative. You must also complete Part II. If you check the box on line C, you must have proof of death.

The proof of death is a copy of either of the following:

• The death certificate, or

• The formal notification from the appropriate government office (for example, Department of Defense) informing the next of kin of the decedent's death.

Do not attach the death certificate or other proof of death to Form 1310. Instead, keep it for your records and provide it if requested.

Example. Your father died on August 25. You are his sole survivor. Your father did not have a will and the court did not appoint a personal representative for his estate. Your father is entitled to a $300 refund. To get the refund, you must complete and attach Form 1310 to your father's final return. You should check the box on Form 1310, line C, answer all the questions in Part II, and sign your name in Part III. You must also keep a copy of the death certificate or other proof of death for your records.

Lines 1–3

If you checked the box on line C, you must complete lines 1 through 3.

Privacy Act and Paperwork Reduction Act Notice

We ask for the information on this form to carry out the Internal Revenue laws of the United States. This information will be used to determine your eligibility pursuant to Internal Revenue Code section 6012 to claim the refund due the decedent. Code section 6109 requires you to provide your social security number and that of the decedent. You are not required to claim the refund due the decedent, but if you do so, you must provide the information requested on this form. Failure to provide this information may delay or prevent processing of your claim. Providing false or fraudulent information may subject you to penalties. Routine uses of this information include providing it to the Department of Justice for use in civil and criminal litigation, to the Social Security Administration for the administration of Social Security programs, and to cities, states, and the District of Columbia for the administration of their tax laws. We may also disclose this information to other countries under a tax treaty, to federal and state agencies to enforce federal nontax criminal laws, or to federal law enforcement and intelligence agencies to combat terrorism.

You are not required to provide the information requested on a form unless the form displays a valid OMB control number. Books or records relating to a form or its instructions must be retained as long as their contents may become material in the administration of any Internal Revenue law. Generally, tax returns and return information are confidential, as required by Code section 6103.

The average time and expenses required to complete and file this form will vary depending on individual circumstances. For the estimated averages, see the instructions for your income tax return.

If you have suggestions for making this form simpler, we would be happy to hear from you. See the instructions for your income tax return.

¶1534 Exhibit 15-14

Form **6118** (Rev. August 2009) Department of the Treasury Internal Revenue Service	**Claim for Refund of Tax Return Preparer and Promoter Penalties** ▶ For Penalties Assessed Under IRC Sections 6694, 6695, 6700, and 6701. ▶ See instructions on page 2. OMB No. 1545-0240

Print or Type

Name of preparer or promoter	Identifying number See instructions.
Address to which statement(s) of notice and demand were mailed	
City, town or post office, state, and ZIP code	IRS office that sent statement(s)
Address of preparer shown on return(s) for which penalties were assessed (if different from above)	

Type of Penalty. Enter letter in column (c) below.

A Understatements due to unreasonable positions—section 6694(a)

B Willful or reckless conduct (intentional disregard of rules and regulations)—section 6694(b)

C Failure to furnish copy of return or claim for refund to taxpayer—section 6695(a)

D Failure to sign return or claim for refund—section 6695(b)

E Failure to furnish identifying number—section 6695(c)

F Failure to retain copy or list—section 6695(d)

G Failure to file a record of return preparers—section 6695(e)(1)

H Failure to include an item in the required record of return preparers—section 6695(e)(2)

I Negotiation of check—section 6695(f)

J Failure to exercise due diligence in determining eligibility for, and/or amount of, the earned income credit—section 6695(g)

K Promoting abusive tax shelters, etc.—section 6700

L Aiding and abetting understatement of tax liability—section 6701

M Other (specify) (see instructions)

Identification of Penalties. Enter the information from your statement.

	(a) Statement document locator number (DLN)	(b) Date of statement	(c) Type of penalty	(d) Name(s) of taxpayer(s)
1				
2				
3				
4				
5				
6				
7				
8				
9				
10				
11				
12				

	(e) Taxpayer's identification number	(f) Form number	(g) Tax year	(h) Amount assessed	(i) Amount paid	(j) Date paid (mo., day, yr.)
1						
2						
3						
4						
5						
6						
7						
8						
9						
10						
11						
12						

Amount of Claim. Enter the total of column (i), lines 1 through 12 . . . ▶

Sign Here   Under penalties of perjury, I declare that I have examined this claim, including accompanying schedules and statements, and to the best of my knowledge and belief, it is true, correct, and complete.

▶ Signature   ▶ Date

For Privacy Act and Paperwork Reduction Act Notice, see back of form.   Cat. No. 24415J   Form **6118** (Rev. 8-2009)

General Instructions

Section references are to the Internal Revenue Code unless otherwise noted.

Purpose of Form

Use Form 6118 if you are a tax return preparer or a promoter and want to claim a refund of preparer or promoter penalties you paid but that you believe were incorrectly charged.

Claims for More Than One Penalty

If you are claiming a refund for more than one of the penalties listed, you may be able to combine some of the penalties on one Form 6118. Follow the chart below for combining the penalties. See *Type of Penalty* on the form for the list of penalties.

IF you were billed...	THEN combine penalties...
On the same statement	G and H only
On separate statements but by the same IRS office or service center	C, D, E, and F only Note. Be sure to group the penalties from each statement together.

You cannot combine:

- Penalties from different IRS offices or service centers. See *Where and When To File* below.

- Penalties A, B, I, J, K, L, and M. You must file a separate Form 6118 for each of these even if you were charged for two or more of the same type.

- Penalties K and L. You must file a separate Form 6118 for each of these even if you were charged with both. Only columns (b), (c) and (g) through (j) need to be completed for penalties under sections 6700 and 6701.

Where and When To File

File Form 6118 with the IRS service center or IRS office that sent you the statement(s). If you were assessed a penalty under section 6700, 6701, or 6694, you may file a claim for refund upon paying 15% of the penalty if you do so within 30 days from the date of notice and demand. Otherwise, your claim under sections 6700 and 6701 must be filed within 2 years from the date you paid the penalty in full. Your claim under sections 6694 and 6695 must be filed within 3 years from the date you paid the penalty in full.

Specific Instructions

Identifying Number

If you are self-employed or employed by another preparer or promoter, enter your social security number. If you are the employer of other preparers or promoters, enter your employer identification number.

Type of Penalty

For item M (other penalties), enter the name of the penalty and the corresponding Internal Revenue Code section.

Additional Information

You may want to attach a copy of the penalty statements to your claim. In addition to completing the form, you must give your reasons for claiming a refund for each penalty listed. Identify each penalty by its line number and write your explanation in the space below.

For additional information about refunds of preparer penalties, see Regulations section 1.6696-1.

Privacy Act and Paperwork Reduction Act Notice. We ask for the information on this form to carry out the Internal Revenue laws of the United States. Subtitle F, Procedure and Administration, allows for additions to tax, additional amounts, and assessable penalties. This form is used by return preparers to make a claim for refund of any overpaid penalty amount. Section 6696 requires the return preparer to provide the requested information including his taxpayer identification number (SSN or EIN) within the prescribed time for filing a claim for refund.

You are not required to provide the information requested on a form that is subject to the Paperwork Reduction Act unless the form displays a valid OMB control number. Books or records relating to a form or its instructions must be retained as long as their contents may become material in the administration of any Internal Revenue law.

Generally, tax returns and return information are confidential, as required by section 6103. However, section 6103 allows or requires the Internal Revenue Service to disclose or give the information shown on your return to others as described in the Code. For example, we may disclose your tax information to the Department of Justice for civil and criminal litigation, and to cities, states, and the District of Columbia, and U.S. commonwealths and possessions for use in administering their tax laws. We may also disclose this information to other countries under a tax treaty, to federal and state agencies to enforce federal nontax criminal laws, or to federal law enforcement and intelligence agencies to combat terrorism.

The time needed to complete and file this form will vary depending on individual circumstances. The estimated average time is: Recordkeeping, 6 min.; Learning about the law or the form, 19 min.; Preparing the form, 22 min.; and Copying, assembling, and sending the form to the IRS, 20 min.

If you have comments concerning the accuracy of these time estimates or suggestions for making this form simpler, we would be happy to hear from you. You can write to the Internal Revenue Service, Tax Products Coordinating Committee, SE:W:CAR:MP:T:T:SP, 1111 Constitution Ave. NW, IR-6526, Washington, DC 20224. Do not send this form to this address. Instead, see *Where and When To File* above.

Reasons for claiming refund. Attach additional sheets if more space is needed. Write your name and Identifying number on each sheet.

¶1541 DISCUSSION QUESTIONS

1. Paul Perplexed's 2007 income tax return was audited in January 2009. An assessment was made and the tax, interest and penalties were paid by Paul on August 2, 2009. On August 13, 2009, Paul filed a Form 1040X—Claim for Refund to recover the full amount that he had paid.

   Paul consults you today to see what further action he can take to get his money back. He has lived at the same address for the entire period since he filed his claim for refund and he has never received any correspondence from the IRS either allowing or disallowing the claim for refund.

   (A) What is the last date on which Paul can successfully bring a lawsuit against the IRS to recover his taxes, penalties and interest paid in 2007?

   (B) What is the earliest date on which a law suit could have been brought on the claim?

2. Following an audit of his 2008 income tax return, an assessment was made against Charlie Cheapskate as a result of the disallowance of certain deductions. In addition to the tax, interest and a negligence penalty were also assessed. Charlie wishes to dispute the propriety of this assessment and he consults you regarding the most economical way in which to do it. He has heard that the deduction challenged has been consistently allowed by the Court of Federal Claims and consistently disallowed by the Tax Court. Charlie tells you that he only has enough money to pay the tax. He cannot pay the interest and penalty. Charlie wants to know whether he can take his case to the Court of Federal Claims.

3. Steve Skimmer operates a tavern which has been very successful over the years. For 2005, 2006, and 2007, Steve reported taxable income of $12,000 from the operation of the tavern in each year. Steve's returns have been audited and, because of the inadequacy of the books and records, the agent has used the net worth method to determine his income. The agent has found the following information:

Date	Net Worth
12/31/05	$175,000
12/31/06	$220,000
12/31/07	$255,000

   Because the agent has not discovered, nor has Steve offered, any explanations for the increase in his net worth, the agent has made an assessment taxing Steve on the difference between his reported taxable income and the increase in net worth for each of the years. The assessments are as follows:

Year	Tax	Interest	Penalty	Total
2006	$11,550.00	$3,000.00	$7,275.00	$21,825.00
2007	8,050.00	2,200.00	5,075.00	15,375.00
2008	11,000.00	1,700.00	6,350.00	19,050.00

¶1541

Steve receives the assessment notice on October 15, 2009. He wishes to dispute the adjustments, but he does not have the cash available to pay all of the assessments. He wants to know whether he can just pay the tax, interest and penalties for just one year and then file a claim for refund and sue for recovery. He has a maximum of $22,000 available excluding any fees you may charge. What is your advice? Why? Explain in full.

4. Amanda Amendor filed her 2006, 2007, and 2008 income tax returns with the Central West Internal Revenue Service Center. In preparing those returns, Amanda omitted significant amounts of her gross income. In 2009, Amanda filed amended returns showing the correct gross income. She also computed the additional tax for the three years. Because Amanda was nervous about filing the amended returns, she sent a check to the IRS for the amount of the tax and asked that they send her a statement for the interest to the date of payment.

When the returns were received at the Service Center, Susie Suspicious thought that they looked suspect. She referred the returns to Criminal Investigation (CI) at the Service Center, and CI eventually referred the case for a criminal investigation. Because of the pending criminal investigation, Amanda's amended returns were not processed. Rather, the following letter was sent to Amanda Amendor:

November 4, 2009

Dear Ms. Amendor:

We received your amended returns for the years shown above. We are not assessing additional tax at this time, pending a final determination of your tax liability.

We will accept the payment you sent with your returns as a cash bond. Acceptance of the payment as a cash bond means that (1) interest charges will stop, at the date the payment was received, on that part of any assessment later satisfied by the payment; (2) the payment is not subject to a claim for credit or refund as an overpayment of tax, penalties, or interest; and (3) interest will not be paid to you on any of the payment returned to you if it is more than any additional tax, penalties, or interest later assessed.

If these conditions are not satisfactory to you and you would like us to return your payment, please sign the statement at the end of this letter and send it to us within 30 days. An addressed envelope is enclosed for your convenience. The copy of this letter is for your records.

Thank you for your cooperation.

Sincerely yours,

I.M. Evilminded, Chief Criminal Investigation

Amanda now wishes to hire expert legal and accounting help to represent her in the criminal investigation. However, she has no cash available to retain anyone, and she wishes she had not sent the check to the IRS. She consults with you to see whether she can get her money back from the IRS even though the 30 days in the letter have passed. What advice do you give her? See Rev. Proc. 2005-18, 2005-1 CB 798.

5. On September 16, 2005, the estate tax return for Paul Postmortem was filed with the IRS. On December 30, 2006, an assessment of additional estate tax in the amount of $300,000 was made by the IRS. This assessment resulted from the IRS including in the gross estate a gift in the amount of $1,500,000 which was determined to be a transfer with a retained life estate. The additional estate tax resulting from the inclusion of the gift in the gross estate was actually $500,000, but the estate was given a credit under Code Sec. 2012 for the $200,000 of gift tax paid at the time of the filing of the gift tax return. The $300,000 plus interest was paid by the estate on January 2, 2007.

On October 3, 2008, the estate filed a claim for refund on an amended return, alleging that the gift was not a transfer with a retained life interest and also seeking a refund of estate taxes for the allowance of additional administrative expenses. The amount of the claim for refund was $325,000. Assume that the estate is correct on the merits and that it is entitled to a recovery of the $300,000 of estate tax from the inclusion of the gift and the $25,000 of estate tax resulting from the allowance of the administration expenses. Is the recovery limited to $300,000, the amount of estate tax paid within two years of the filing of the claim?

6. Correcto Corp.'s 2007 income tax return is audited by the IRS. In 2009, the corporation pays an assessment of $100,000 of additional tax resulting from the disallowance of travel and entertainment expenses. Three weeks later the corporation files a claim for refund seeking a refund of $100,000 resulting from the denial of deductions for ordinary and necessary business expenses deductible under Code Secs. 161 through 169. The claim for refund is denied and a lawsuit is filed. After the suit is filed, the accountant determines that the substantiation for the travel and entertainment expenses in fact was insufficient, but also determines that the depreciation deduction for the corporation should have been $300,000 greater than the amount claimed on the return. Because the agent had disallowed $300,000 in travel and entertainment, the accountant is of the opinion that the claim for refund should be allowed. The government opposes the suit for refund. Who wins?

7. Brian Brinksmanship consults you regarding the following situation. Brian's 2006 income tax return was due on April 15, 2007. Because the information was not available, no return was filed on that date. Instead, Brian filed a request for extension and tendered the sum of $5,000 in payment of the tax anticipated to be due. On October 17, 2007, the extension ran out, but still no return was filed. On that date, Brian tendered another $5,000 towards the eventual tax liability. On November 15, 2007, the return was finally filed. At that time, an additional

¶1541

$5,000 in tax was paid. Finally, the return was audited during 2008 and on November 1, 2008, a deficiency of $5,000 was also paid.

Brian consults you on October 2, 2009. In reviewing his records, you discover that a tax credit for 2006 in the amount of $20,000 has not been claimed. You inform Brian of this and suggest that he file a claim for refund. Brian wants to hold off until the very last possible date to file a claim for refund because he knows that interest on the refund is presently higher than market rates of interest. Brian instructs you to prepare the claim for refund and hold it until the very last day on which it can be filed. He tells you to play it safe, but to get him every possible bit of interest that you can. On which day should the claim for refund be filed?

8. NOL Corporation filed its 2006 tax return on March 15, 2007, reporting a loss of $100,000. The corporate accountant simply chose to use the loss to offset income earned in 2007 rather than carry the loss back to years 2004 and 2005.

   The IRS is currently auditing the 2006 tax return. On May 11, 2010, the Revenue Agent proposed to disallow the loss carried forward to 2007 because the taxpayer did not make an affirmative election to forego the carryback. See Code Sec. 172(b)(3). Is there anything the accountant can do to preserve the use of the net operating loss that was carried forward? Would your answer change if the revenue agent proposed to disallow the carryforward loss on March 13, 2010?

CHAPTER 16

PRIVATE LETTER RULINGS AND DETERMINATION LETTERS

¶1601 GUIDANCE THE INTERNAL REVENUE SERVICE ISSUES

Because of the inherent complexity of the Internal Revenue laws and the time lag between the completion of a transaction and any examination of it by the IRS, the IRS has made it a practice to answer inquiries of individuals and organizations as to their status for tax purposes and as to the tax effects of their acts or transactions. The inquiries are submitted by means of letters to the IRS, and the IRS responses to these inquiries—in the form of letters—are known as rulings.[1]

The IRS issues private letter rulings, often refereed to as rulings, whenever appropriate for sound tax administration. To this end, the IRS has published rules and guidelines as to how to request a ruling and when the IRS may or may not issue a ruling. Assuming the IRS continues its long standing practice, the first eight Revenue Procedures issued every year relate to rulings and technical advice. They are as follows:

1. Procedure for requesting letter rulings and determination letters;[2]

2. Procedures for requesting technical advice;[3]

3. Domestic issues for which the IRS will not rule;[4]

4. Procedures for requesting rulings, information letters, etc., on matters relating to sections of the Code currently under the jurisdiction of the Commissioner, Tax Exempt and Government Entities Division;[5]

5. Procedures for requesting technical advice for matters under the jurisdiction of the Commissioner, Tax Exempt and Government Entities Division;[6]

6. Procedures for requesting determination letters on the qualified status of employee plans;[7]

7. International issues for which the IRS will not rule;[8] and

8. User fees and guidance for employee plans and exempt organization requests for rulings, determination letters, etc.[9]

---

[1] These rulings are also known within the tax profession as private rulings or private letter rulings because they are issued to specific taxpayers as opposed to the general public.

[2] Rev. Proc. 2011-1, IRB 2011-1, 1, whose table of contents is printed in part as Exhibit 16-1 at ¶1621.

[3] Rev. Proc. 2011-2, IRB 2011-1, 90.

[4] Rev. Proc. 2011-3, IRB 2011-1, 111.

[5] Rev. Proc. 2011-4, IRB 2011-1, 123.

[6] Rev. Proc. 2011-5, IRB 2011-1, 165.

[7] Rev. Proc. 2011-6, IRB 2011-1, 195.

[8] Rev. Proc. 2011-7, IRB 2011-1, 233.

[9] Rev. Proc. 2011-8, IRB 2011-1, 237.

The IRS has issued a list of topics on which it will not issue rulings or determination letters.[10] There are four categories of topics on the list:

1. Issues involving inherently factual matters;[11]

2. Issues where rulings and determination letters will "not ordinarily" be issued. "Not ordinarily" means the taxpayer must demonstrate unique and compelling reasons to justify a ruling in these areas;[12]

3. Issues where the IRS is temporarily not issuing advance rulings and determinations because the matters are under extensive study;[13] and

4. Issues where the IRS will not ordinarily issue rulings because the IRS has provided automatic approval procedures for these matters.[14]

Pursuant to the Freedom of Information Act, the IRS must disclose private letter rulings.[15] Moreover, the IRS must delete any identifying information from a ruling before published. A taxpayer may state what deletions she proposes in a document submitted with a ruling request.[16] See ¶ 1605.

¶1602 DEFINITION

Rulings. A "ruling" is a written statement issued to a taxpayer or a taxpayer's authorized representative by an Associate Chief Counsel of the IRS.[17] The Associate Chief Counsel interprets and applies the tax laws to a specific set of facts provided in a ruling request. Rulings are issued under the general supervision of the Associate Chief Counsels (which include Corporate, Financial Institutions & Products, Income Tax & Accounting, International, Passthrough & Special Industries, Procedure & Administration, and Division Counsel/Associate Chief Counsel—Tax Exempt and Government Entities) who can redelegate authority to the technical advisors of the corporation tax division and the individual tax division in their respective areas.[18] Issues under the jurisdiction of the various Associate Chief Counsels are listed in Section 3 of Rev. Proc. 2011-1 (see Exhibit 16-1 at ¶ 1621).

> **Example 16-1:** Taxpayer is uncertain whether a new tax imposed by the country of Chad is considered a foreign income tax for purposes of taking the foreign tax credit. Taxpayer seeks a private letter ruling from the Associate Chief Counsel (International).

In income, gift and private foundation tax matters, the Associate Chief Counsel issues rulings on prospective transactions and on completed transactions before the return is filed. However, the IRS will not ordinarily issue a ruling if the identical issue exists in a return of the taxpayer for a prior year that is under examination by a field office or which is being considered by any Appeals Office.[19]

---

[10] Rev. Proc. 2011-3, IRB 2011-1, Sec. 2.

[11] *Id.*, Sec. 3.

[12] *Id.*, Sec. 4.

[13] *Id.*, Sec. 5.

[14] *Id.*, Sec. 6.

[15] Code Sec. 6110.

[16] Reg. § 601.201(e)(5).

[17] Reg. § 301.6110-2(d).

[18] Rev. Proc 2011-1, IRB 2011-1, Sec. 3.

[19] Rev. Proc. 2011-1, IRB 2011-1, Sec. 6.01(1).

In estate tax matters, the Associate Chief Counsel issues rulings with respect to transactions affecting the estate tax of a decedent before the estate tax return is filed. No rulings will be issued after the estate tax return has been filed unless the ruling request was submitted prior to the filing of the return, nor will one be issued on the application of the estate tax to property or the estate of a living person. Practical problems can arise from this position of the Associate Chief Counsel because of the relatively short time following a decedent's death before the due date of the estate tax return and the time period it takes to prepare, review and have the Associate Chief Counsel process a ruling request. In the event an estate seeks an estate tax ruling, special attention should be given to obtaining any necessary extensions for filing the estate tax return in order to avoid incurring a penalty.[20]

The Associate Chief Counsel will rule on prospective and completed transactions either before or after the return is filed. However, the Associate Chief Counsel will not ordinarily rule on an issue if it knows an identical issue is before any field office (including Appeals) in connection with an examination or audit of the liability of the same taxpayer for the same or a prior period.[21]

> **Example 16-2:** Taxpayer takes a foreign tax credit for a new tax paid to the country of Chad in 20X1 and 20X2. While the IRS audits Taxpayer for 20X1 and 20X2 during 20X3, Taxpayer files for a private letter ruling request with the Associate Chief Counsel (International), seeking a ruling that the Chad tax is considered a foreign income tax for purposes of taking the foreign tax credit. Because this issue is under audit for the same taxpayer for a prior year, the Associate Chief Counsel (International) will not rule on the tax's creditability.

The IRS will not rule on requests of business, trade or industrial associations or other similar groups relating to the application of the tax laws to members of the group. However, rulings may be issued to groups or associations relating to their own tax status or liability, provided the issue is not before any field office (including Appeals) in connection with an examination or audit of the liability of the same taxpayer for the same or a prior period.[22]

> **Example 16-3:** The National Organization For Office Furniture Dealers is uncertain how certain depreciation rules will apply to office furniture in use. Although the Organization may not seek a ruling with respect to how the depreciation rules apply to its members' office furniture, the Organization may seek a ruling with respect to how the depreciation rules would apply to its own office furniture.

When new tax laws are enacted, pending the adoption of regulations, the IRS will consider certain conditions before issuing a ruling:

1. If an inquiry presents an issue on which the answer seems to be clear from an application of the provisions of the statute to the facts described, the IRS will issue its ruling pursuant to its usual procedures;

---

[20] See Rev. Proc. 2011-1, IRB 2011-1, Sec. 5.06.   [22] *Id.*, Sec. 6.05.

[21] *Id.*, Sec. 6.01.

2. If an inquiry presents an issue on which the answer seems reasonably certain, but not entirely free from doubt, the IRS will issue a ruling only if the taxpayer can establish that a business emergency requires a ruling or that unusual hardship will result from failure to obtain a ruling;

3. If an inquiry presents an issue that cannot be reasonably resolved prior to the issuance of regulations, the IRS will not issue a ruling ; or

4. In any case in which the taxpayer believes that a business emergency exists or that an unusual hardship will result from failure to obtain a ruling, the taxpayer should submit with the request a separate letter setting forth the facts necessary for the IRS to make a determination regarding the emergency or hardship. The IRS will not deem a "business emergency" to result from circumstances within the control of the taxpayer.[23]

Determination Letters. The IRS also issues determination letters to taxpayers. A "determination letter" is a written statement issued by a Director of an operating division of the IRS in response to a written inquiry by an individual or an organization and applies the principles and precedents previously announced by the Associate Chief Counsel to the particular facts involved. A Director issues a determination letter only where the IRS can make a determination on the basis of clearly established rules set forth in the Code, a Treasury decision or a regulation, or by a ruling, opinion or court decision published in the Internal Revenue Bulletin. Where the IRS cannot make such a determination, perhaps because the question involves a novel issue or because the matter is excluded from the Director's jurisdiction, the IRS will not issue a determination letter.[24]

The IRS also issues determination letters with respect to the qualification of an organization for exempt status under Code Sec. 501(c)(3). Organizations seeking exempt status under Code Sec. 501 must apply for a determination letter from the Exempt Organizations (EO) Determination Office, Kentucky.[25] Organizations seeking exempt status under Code Sec. 501(c)(3), which encompasses organizations to which contributions qualify for the charitable donation deduction,[26] apply for a determination letter on Form 1023, while organizations seeking exempt status under some other subsection of Code Sec. 501(c) apply by means of Form 1024. The IRS issues both of these forms as booklets and request that the applicant supply detailed factual and financial data along with documentation to show that the organization operates within the law.

Example 16-4: The National Association of Overzealous Suburban Little League Parents seeks tax exempt status so its contributions will qualify for a charitable donation deduction. The Association will have to file a Form 1023.

The IRS also issues determination letters to applicants with respect to the qualification of their retirement plans (including pension and profit-sharing

---

[23] Statement of Procedural Rules, Reg. § 601.201(b)(5).

[24] Rev. Proc. 2011-1, IRB 2011-1, Sec. 6.

[25] The procedures for seeking determination letters as to exempt status are set forth in Rev. Proc. 2011-8, IRB 2011-1.

[26] Code Sec. 170.

¶1602

plans) under Code Sec. 401. Applications in this instance are made on Form 5300, Application for Determination for Employee Benefit Plan. Determination letters regarding retirement plans are issued by the Employee Plans (EP) Determination Office.[27]

In income, gift and private foundation tax matters, operating division Directors issue determination letters regarding completed transactions that affect returns over which they have audit jurisdiction, but only if the answer to the question presented is covered specifically by a statute, Treasury Decision or regulation, or covered specifically by a ruling, opinion or court decision published in the Internal Revenue Bulletin. The Director will not usually issue a determination letter with respect to a question that involves a return to be filed by the taxpayer if the identical question is involved in a return or returns the taxpayer already filed. With few exceptions, Directors may not issue determination letters as to the tax consequences of prospective or proposed transactions, with certain exceptions to be discussed later in this portion of the chapter.

In estate and gift tax matters, Directors issue determination letters regarding estate tax returns of decedents that their offices will audit, but only if the answers to the questions presented are specifically covered by the same kinds of authority mentioned in the preceding paragraph. Directors will not issue determination letters relating to matters involving the application of the estate tax to the property or the estate of a living person.[28]

In employment and excise tax matters, Directors issue determination letters to taxpayers who have filed or who are required to file returns over which the Directors have audit jurisdiction, but only if the answers to the questions presented are covered specifically by the previously mentioned authorities. Because of the impact of these taxes on the business operation of the taxpayer and because of special problems of administration both to the IRS and to the taxpayer, Directors may take appropriate action in regard to such requests, whether they relate to completed or prospective transactions or returns previously filed or to be filed.[29]

In spite of the areas mentioned in the preceding paragraphs, a Director will not issue a determination letter in response to an inquiry where the following circumstances are present:

1. It appears that the taxpayer has directed a similar inquiry to the Associate Chief Counsel;

2. An identical issue involving the same taxpayer is pending in a case before the Appeals Office;

3. The determination letter is requested by an industry, trade association or similar group; or

4. The request involves an industry-wide problem.[30]

---

[27] Rev. Proc. 2011-6, IRB 2011-1.
[28] Rev. Proc. 2011-1, IRB 2011-1, Sec. 12.02.

[29] *Id.* at Sec. 12.04.
[30] Statement of Procedural Rules, Reg. §601.201(c)(4).

Under no circumstances will the Director issue a determination letter unless the inquiry is with regard to a taxpayer who has filed or must file returns over which that Director's office has audit jurisdiction.[31] Also, a Director will not issue a determination letter on an employment tax question when the specific question involved has been or is being considered by the central office of the Social Security Administration or the Railroad Retirement Board.[32]

Other Guidance. "Opinion letters" are written statements issued by the Director of EP Rulings and Agreements as to the acceptability of the form of a master or prototype plan and any related trust or custodian account.[33] An "information letter" is a statement issued by a Director that does no more than call attention to a well-established interpretation or principle of tax law, without applying it to a specific set of facts. The IRS may issue an information letter when a ruling request seeks general information, or when it does not meet all the requirements for a ruling or determination letter and the IRS believes that such general information will assist the requester.[34]

A "revenue ruling," as opposed to a private letter ruling, is an official interpretation that the IRS publishes in the Internal Revenue Bulletin. Drafted by an Associate Chief Counsel, revenue rulings are published for the information and guidance of taxpayers, IRS officials and others concerned.[35]

A "closing agreement" is an agreement entered between the IRS and a taxpayer with respect to a specific issue or issues.[36] A closing agreement is based on a ruling that the Commissioner has signed and that indicates that a closing agreement will be entered into on the basis of the holding of the ruling. A closing agreement is final and conclusive except on a showing of fraud, malfeasance or misrepresentation of material fact. It is used where it is advantageous to have the matter permanently and conclusively closed or where a taxpayer can show good and sufficient reasons for an agreement and the government will sustain no disadvantage by its consummation. In certain cases, the IRS may require taxpayers to enter into a closing agreement as a condition to the issuance of a ruling.[37] The IRS will not enter a closing agreement where it is requested on behalf of more than 25 taxpayers. However, in cases where the issue and holding are identical as to all of the taxpayers and the number of taxpayers exceeds 25, the IRS can enter a mass closing agreement with the taxpayer who is authorized by the others to represent the entire group.[38]

The Associate Chief Counsel issues technical advice in the form of a memorandum to a Director, in connection with the examination of a return or consideration of a claim for refund or credit. The memorandum gives advice or guidance as to the interpretation and proper application of statutes and regulations to a specific set of facts. It is furnished as a means of assisting IRS personnel in closing cases and establishing and maintaining consistent holdings throughout

---

[31] Rev. Proc. 2011-1, IRB 2011-1, Sec. 12.

[32] *Id* at Sec. 6.14.

[33] Code Secs. 401 and 501(a). Rev. Proc. 2011-4, IRB 2011-1, Sec. 3.05.

[34] Rev. Proc. 2011-1, IRB 2011-1, Sec. 2.04.

[35] Code Sec. 7805.

[36] Code Sec. 7121.

[37] For examples, see Rev. Proc. 78-15, 1978-2 CB 488, and Rev. Proc. 85-44, 1985-2 CB 504.

[38] Rev. Proc. 2011-1, IRB 2011-1, Sec. 2.02.

the nation. Seeking technical advice from the Associate Chief Counsel is discretionary with a Director. A Director may request technical advice on any technical or procedural question that develops during the audit of a return or claim for refund of a taxpayer. In addition, while the case is under the jurisdiction of a Director, a taxpayer (or representative) may request referral of an issue to the Associate Chief Counsel for technical advice on the grounds that either a lack of uniformity exists as to the disposition of the issue or that the issue is so unusual or complex as to warrant consideration by the Associate Chief Counsel.[39]

¶1603 USER FEES FOR RULING REQUESTS

Rulings, opinion letters, determination letters, and similar services incur user fees that vary, taking into account the average time needed for, and difficulty of complying with, requests in each category. Such fees are to be paid in advance.[40]

Rev. Proc. 2011-1 provides guidance regarding user fees, which must accompany all requests for rulings, determination letters or opinion letters. The fees range from $275 to $50,000, depending on the type of ruling sought.[41] If the taxpayer does not pay the fee, the IRS will return the entire file. In general, the IRS will not refund the user fee unless the IRS declines to rule on all issues for which a ruling is requested. The IRS will not refund a user fee for a withdrawn request.

¶1604 REQUIREMENTS FOR RULING AND DETERMINATION REQUESTS

Each request for a ruling or determination letter must contain a complete statement of all relevant facts relating to the transaction. Such facts include (1) names, addresses and taxpayer identification numbers of all interested parties; (2) a full and precise statement of the business reasons for the transaction; and (3) a carefully detailed description of the transaction.[42] (The term "all interested parties" does not require the listing of all shareholders of a widely held corporation or all employees under a qualified plan.)[43]

If a taxpayer advances various contentions, that individual must furnish an explanation of the grounds for the stated contentions, together with a statement from relevant authorities in support of his views.[44] Even if the taxpayer does not urge a particular contention with regard to a proposed or prospective transaction, the taxpayer must suggest the tax results of the proposed action and furnish a statement from relevant authorities to support such views.

The taxpayer must also submit true copies of all contracts, wills, deeds, instruments and other documents involved in the transaction must be submitted with the request. Taxpayer's must also submit relevant documents and not

---

[39] Rev. Proc. 2011-3, IRB 2011-1.

[40] Code Sec. 7528.

[41] Rev. Proc. 2011-1 IRB 2011-1, App. A.

[42] *Id.* at 7.01(1).

[43] As a rule of thumb, the practitioner can assume that the listing of all shareholders or employees is not required if more than 25 taxpayers are involved.

[44] Rev. Proc. 2011-1, IRB 2011-1, Sec. 7.01(1), (3) and (8).

merely incorporate them by reference.[45] The documents must accompany an analysis of their bearing on the issue or issues and specify the pertinent provisions.

When it is necessary to submit documents with a ruling request, the taxpayer shall not submit the original documents, because they will become part of the IRS file and cannot be returned to the taxpayer. If the request is with respect to a corporate distribution, reorganization or other similar or related transaction, the taxpayer would submit the corporate balance sheet closest to the date of the transaction. If the request relates to the prospective transaction, the taxpayer should submit the most recent balance sheet.[46]

The request must also contain a statement of whether, to the best of the knowledge of the taxpayer or the taxpayer's representative, the identical issue is being considered by any IRS field office, including Appeals, in connection with an active examination or audit of a tax return of the taxpayer already filed. The taxpayer or a representative should indicate in writing when filing the request if he or she desires a discussion of the issues involved, so that a conference may be arranged at that stage of consideration when it will be most helpful.

A taxpayer must submit a request for a ruling or determination letter in duplicate. However, if (1) the request presents more than one issue or (2) the taxpayer requests a closing agreement with respect to the issue presented, then the taxpayer must submit the original and two copies.

A specific declaration must accompany the request in the following form:[47]

> Under penalties of perjury, I declare that I have examined this request, including accompanying documents, and to the best of my knowledge and belief, the request contains all the relevant facts relating to the request, and such facts are true, correct and complete.

The declaration must be signed by the person or persons making the request, not by the requester's representative.[48]

See Exhibit 16-2 at ¶1622 for a sample format of a private letter ruling request.[49]

The IRS grants priority treatment of a ruling request only in rare cases. To obtain such approval a taxpayer must submit an independent request for priority treatment and demonstrate that the need for priority treatment is beyond the control of the requesting taxpayer.[50]

¶1605 DISCLOSURE OF REQUESTS

To assist the IRS in deleting identifying information[51] from the text of rulings and determination letters, requests for rulings and determination letters must include as a separate document either a statement of the deletions the taxpayer proposes

---

[45] *Id* at Sec. 7.01(2).

[46] *Id*.

[47] *Id* at Sec. 7.02(1).

[48] Reg. § 601.201(e)(1); Rev. Proc. 2011-1, 2011-1, 1, Sec. 7.01(15)(b).

[49] Rev. Proc. 2011-1, IRB 2011-1, Appendix B.

[50] *Id* at Sec. 7.02(4).

[51] Code Sec. 6110(c); *Id.* at Sec. 7.01(11).

by the requester or a statement that no information other than names, addresses and taxpayer identification numbers need be deleted. If additional deletions are proposed, the taxpayer should specify the statutory basis for the deletion. When proposing additional deletions, the taxpayer should submit a copy of the request which indicates, by use of brackets, the material which the taxpayer proposes to delete. The statement of proposed deletions should not be referred to anywhere in the request. Prior to issuing the ruling or determination letter, the taxpayer may submit additional statements to be deleted.

> **Example 16-5:** Dr. Jaye, a pharmaceutical company, creates a drug design to help basketball players creatively slam dunk a basketball. Dr. Jaye seeks a ruling with respect to the tax implications of the license of this intangible. To protect its business, Dr. Jaye seeks a deletion with respect to the secret formula of the drug.

Generally, prior to issuing the ruling or determination letter, the Associate Chief Counsel or Director informs the taxpayer of any material likely to appear in the ruling or determination letter that the taxpayer proposed to delete but which the IRS determines should be included. The taxpayer may then submit further information, arguments or other material to support deletion within twenty days. The IRS attempts to resolve all disagreements with respect to proposed deletions prior to issuing the ruling or determination letter. The taxpayer does not have any right to a conference to resolve disagreements concerning material to be deleted from the text of the ruling or determination letter, but deletions may be considered at any other conference scheduled with respect to the ruling request. Exhibit 16-3 at ¶1623 is a sample of how a ruling letter appears after deletions.

¶1606 TWO-PART PRIVATE LETTER RULINGS

To expedite prospective transactions, the Associate Chief Counsel provides an alternative procedure for the issuance of rulings.[52] The taxpayer submits a summary statement of the facts considered to control the issue, in addition to the complete statement of facts required for the ruling request. If the IRS agrees with the taxpayer's summary statement of the facts, the IRS will use the statement as a basis for the ruling. The IRS bases the ruling on the facts in the summary statement.

This procedure is elective with the taxpayer and the taxpayer's rights and responsibilities are the same as under the normal procedure. Under this procedure, the IRS reserves the right to rule on the basis of a more complete statement of facts it considers controlling and to seek further information in developing facts and restating them for ruling purposes. The two-part ruling request procedure does not apply if it is inconsistent with other procedures applicable to specific situations, such as requests for permission to change an accounting method or rulings on employment tax status.

---

[52] *Id* at Sec. 7.02(3).

¶1607 FAULTY REQUESTS

The IRS acknowledges any request for a ruling or determination letter that does not comply with all of the requirements and delineates the missing requirements. If a request lacks essential information, the IRS advises the taxpayer that the request will be closed if the IRS does not receive information within 21 days. If the IRS receives the information after closing the request, the IRS will reopen the request treat it as a new request as of the date of the receipt of the essential information. Because the Associate Chief Counsel processes ruling requests on a first-come, first-served basis, delay in providing essential information within the 21-day period can result in substantial and possibly disastrous delay of receipt of a ruling.[53]

¶1608 ASSOCIATE CHIEF COUNSEL CONFERENCES

A taxpayer is entitled, as a matter of right, to only one conference with respect to a ruling request with the Associate Chief Counsel. If the IRS deems it helpful in deciding the case or when it appears the IRS will issue an adverse ruling, the IRS may schedule a conference.[54]

The conference is usually held after the Associate Chief Counsel has had an opportunity to study the case so that there can be a free and open discussion of the issues. Because a taxpayer has no right to appeal the action of an Associate Chief Counsel, unless special circumstances are present, there is no real advantage to requesting a conference before the IRS has a chance to study the case.[55]

¶1609 WITHDRAWALS OF RULING REQUESTS

A taxpayer may withdraw a request for a ruling or a determination letter at any time prior to the signing of the letter by the IRS. When the request is withdrawn, the Associate Chief Counsel may furnish its views to the Director whose office has or will have audit jurisdiction of the return. The Director can consider the information submitted in a subsequent audit or examination of the taxpayer's return. Even though a request is withdrawn, all correspondence and exhibits are retained by the IRS, which will not return them to the taxpayer. Before requesting a ruling, the taxpayer should consider the potential for referral of a withdrawn request to a Director.[56]

> **Example 16-6:** Taxpayer is uncertain whether a new tax imposed by the country of Chad is considered a foreign income tax for purposes of taking the foreign tax credit. Taxpayer seeks a private letter ruling from the Associate Chief Counsel (International). Taxpayer subsequently withdraws the ruling request and takes a credit for the Chad taxes paid. The IRS may use the information that Taxpayer submitted in the ruling request during a subsequent audit of the creditability of the Chad taxes.

---

[53] *Id.* at Sec. 8.02.(2).
[54] *Id* at Sec. 10.

[55] *Id* at Sec. 10.
[56] *Id* at Sec. 8.06.

¶1607

¶1610 EFFECT OF PRIVATE LETTER RULINGS

The effect of a ruling is very limited: one taxpayer may not rely on a ruling issued to another and a ruling with respect to a particular transaction represents a holding of the IRS only on that transaction.[57]

> **Example 16-7:** Taxpayer obtains a private letter ruling from the IRS that a foreign tax paid to Chad is a creditable foreign income tax. A U.S. competitor of Taxpayer who also operates in Chad seeks to similarly take a foreign tax credit for the Chad tax. Although the ruling is guidance as to how the IRS may rule, the U.S. competitor may not rely on that ruling.

If the ruling is later found to be in error or no longer in accord with the position of the IRS, the ruling will not afford the taxpayer any protection with respect to a similar transaction in the same or subsequent year. However, if a ruling relates to a continuing action or a series of actions, the ruling will control until specifically withdrawn or until the IRS issues applicable regulations or revenue rulings are issued. A ruling, except to the extent that it is incorporated in a closing agreement, may be revoked or modified at any time. If the IRS revokes or modifies a ruling, the revocation or modification applies to all open years under the statutes, unless the Commissioner exercises discretionary authority to limit the retroactive effect of the revocation or modification.[58]

In determining a taxpayer's liability, the examiner ascertains whether the taxpayer has properly applied any ruling previously issued. An examiner will determine whether the representations on which the ruling was based reflected an accurate statement of the material facts and whether the taxpayer substantially conducted the transaction as proposed. If, in the course of determining tax liability, the examiner concludes that a ruling previously issued to the taxpayer should be modified or revoked, the findings and recommendations of that examiner are forwarded to the Associate Chief Counsel for consideration prior to further action. The reference to the Associate Chief Counsel is treated as a request for technical advice (see discussion, *supra*). Otherwise, the Examiner should apply the ruling in its determination of the taxpayer's liability.[59]

The IRS may modify or revoke a ruling found to be in error or not in accord with its current views. The IRS may modify or revoke the ruling by notifying the taxpayer to whom it originally issued the ruling or by issuing a revenue ruling or other statement published in the Internal Revenue Bulletin.[60] Except in rare or unusual circumstances, the IRS would not retroactively apply the ruling with respect to the taxpayer to whom the ruling was originally issued or to a taxpayer whose tax liability was directly involved in that ruling, if five circumstances are present:[61]

---

[57] *Id* at Secs. 11.01 and 11.02.

[58] Code Sec. 7805(b).

[59] For an example affecting many taxpayers as the result of the retroactive revocation of a ruling based upon a determination that the taxpayer had not complied with its representations, see *Heverly v. Comm'r*, 621 F.2d 1227 (1980), 80-1 USTC ¶9322, and

Chapman v. Comm'r, 618 F.2d 856 (1980), 80-1 USTC ¶9330, involving International Telephone and Telegraph Corporation's acquisition of Hartford Insurance Company.

[60] Rev. Proc. 2011-1, IRB 2011-1, Sec. 11.04.

[61] *Id* at Secs. 11.05 and 11.06.

1. There has not been misstatement or omission of material facts;

2. The facts subsequently developed are not materially different from the facts on which the IRS based the ruling;

3. The applicable law has not changed;

4. The IRS originally issued the ruling with respect to a prospective or proposed transaction; and

5. The taxpayer directly involved in a ruling acted in good faith in reliance on the ruling and the retroactive revocation would be to his or her detriment.[62]

When the IRS revokes a ruling retroactively,[63] the notice to that taxpayer, except in fraud cases, sets forth the grounds for revocation and the reasons supporting retroactivity. For completed transactions, taxpayers are not afforded the protection against retroactive revocation available in the case of proposed transactions. As a result it is generally better to obtain a ruling for a proposed transaction than for a completed transaction.

¶1611 EFFECT OF DETERMINATION LETTERS

A determination letter issued by a Director has the same effect as a ruling on the examination of the return of the taxpayer who received the determination letter. A Director may not limit the retroactive effect of the modification or revocation of a determination letter.[64] However, if a Director believes it is necessary to limit the retroactive effect of a modification or revocation, the Director must refer the matter to the Associate Chief Counsel for approval.[65]

---

[62] § 601.201(l)(5) of the Statement of Procedural Rules.

[63] See, for example, IRS Ltr. Rul. 8506003 (Nov. 1, 1984), in which the IRS revoked a ruling with retroactive effect for omission of a material fact in failing

to disclose that most of the taxpayer's business was conducted with a parent corporation.

[64] Rev. Proc. 2011-1, IRB 2011-1, Sec. 13.

[65] Id at Sec. 14.

¶1621 Exhibit 16-1

Revenue Procedure 2011-1 IRB

TABLE OF CONTENTS

SECTION 5. UNDER WHAT CIRCUMSTANCES DO THE ASSOCIATE OFFICES ISSUE LETTER RULINGS?

.01 In income and gift tax matters

.02 Special relief for late S corporation and related elections in lieu of letter ruling process

.03 A § 301.9100 request for extension of time for making an election or for other relief

.04 Determinations under § 999(d)

.05 In matters involving § 367

.06 In estate tax matters

.07 In matters involving additional estate tax under § 2032A(c)

.08 In matters involving qualified domestic trusts under § 2056A

.09 In generation-skipping transfer tax matters

.10 In employment and excise tax matters

.11 In administrative provisions matters

.12 In Indian tribal government matters

.13 On constructive sales price under § 4216(b) or § 4218(c)

.14 May be issued before the issuance of a regulation or other published guidance

SECTION 6. UNDER WHAT CIRCUMSTANCES DOES THE SERVICE NOT ISSUE LETTER RULINGS OR DETERMINATION LETTERS?

.01 Ordinarily not if the request involves an issue under examination, or consideration, or in litigation

.02 Ordinarily not in certain areas because of factual nature of the problem or for other reasons

.03 Ordinarily not on part of an integrated transaction

.04 Ordinarily not on which of two entities is a common law employer

.05 Ordinarily not to business associations or groups

.06 Ordinarily not where the request does not address the tax status, liability, or reporting obligations of the requester

.07 Ordinarily not to foreign governments

.08 Ordinarily not on federal tax consequences of proposed legislation

.09 Ordinarily not before issuance of a regulation or other published guidance

.10 Not on frivolous issues

.11 No "comfort" letter rulings

.12 Not on alternative plans or hypothetical situations

.13 Not on property conversion after return filed

.14 Circumstances under which determination letters are not issued by a Director

SECTION 7. WHAT ARE THE GENERAL INSTRUCTIONS FOR REQUESTING LETTER RULINGS AND DETERMINATION LETTERS?

.01 Documents and information required in all requests

(1) Complete statement of facts and other information

(2) Copies of all contracts, wills, deeds, agreements, instruments, other documents, and foreign laws

(3) Analysis of material facts

(4) Statement regarding whether same issue is in an earlier return

(5) Statement regarding whether same or similar issue was previously ruled on or whether a request involving it was submitted or is currently pending

(6) Statement regarding interpretation of a substantive provision of an income or estate tax treaty

(7) Letter from Bureau of Indian Affairs relating to a letter ruling requests

(8) Statement of supporting authorities

(9) Statement of contrary authorities

(10) Statement identifying pending legislation

(11) Statement identifying information to be deleted from copy of letter ruling or determination letter for public inspection

(12) Signature by taxpayer or authorized representative

(13) Authorized representatives

(14) Power of attorney and declaration of representative

(15) Penalties of perjury statement

(16) Number of copies of request to be submitted

(17) Sample format for a letter ruling request

(18) Checklist for letter ruling requests

.02 Additional procedural information required with request

(1) To request separate letter rulings for multiple issues in a single situation

(2) Power of attorney used to indicate recipient of a copy or copies of a letter ruling or a determination letter

(3) To request a particular conclusion on a proposed transaction

(4) To request expedited handling

(5) Taxpayer requests to receive any document related to the letter ruling request fax

(6) To request a conference

.03 Address to which to send request for letter ruling or determination letter

(1) Request for letter ruling

(2) Request for determinations letter

.04 Pending letter ruling requests

.05 When to attach letter ruling or determination letter to return

.06 How to check on status of request for letter ruling or determination letter

.07 Request for letter ruling or determination letter may be withdrawn or Associate office may decline to issue letter ruling

SECTION 8. HOW DOES THE ASSOCIATE OFFICE HANDLE LETTER RULING REQUESTS?

.01 Docket, Records, and User Fee Branch receives, initially controls and refers the request to the appropriate Associate office

.02 Branch representative of the Associate office contacts taxpayer within 21 days calendar days

.03 Determines if transaction can be modified to obtain favorable letter ruling

.04 Are not bound by informal opinion expressed

.05 May request additional information

(1) Additional information must be submitted within 21 days calendar days

(2) Extension of reply period if justified and approved

(3) Letter ruling request closed if the taxpayer does not submit additional information

(4) Penalties of perjury statement

(5) Faxing request and additional information

(6) Address to send additional information

(7) Identifying information

(8) Number of copies

.06 Near the completion of the ruling process, advises the taxpayer of conclusions and, if the Associate office will rule adversely, offers the taxpayer the opportunity to withdraw the letter ruling request

¶1621

.07 May request draft of proposed letter ruling near the completion of the ruling process

.08 Issues separate letter rulings for substantially identical letter rulings, but generally issues a single letter ruling for related § 301.9100 letter rulings

.09 Sends a copy of the letter ruling to appropriate Service official

SECTION 9. WHAT ARE THE SPECIFIC AND ADDITIONAL PROCEDURES FOR A REQUEST FOR A CHANGE IN ACCOUNTING METHOD FROM THE ASSOCIATE OFFICES?

.01 Automatic and advance consent change in accounting method requests

(1) Automatic change in method of accounting under Rev. Proc. 2008-52, 2008-2 C.B. 587, as amplified, clarified, and modified by Rev. Proc. 2009-39, 2009-2 C.B. 371 ((or any successor), or other automatic change request procedures

(2) Advance consent change in method of accounting under Rev. Proc. 97-27, 1997-1 C.B. 680, as amplified and modified by Rev. Proc. 2002-19, 2002-1 C.B. 696, as amplified and clarified by Rev. Proc. 2002-54, 2002-2 C.B. 432, as modified by Rev. Proc. 2007-67, 2007-2 C.B. 1072, and as clarified and modified by Rev. Proc. 2009-39

.02 Ordinarily only one change in accounting method on a Form 3115 and a separate Form 3115 for each taxpayer and for each separate and distinct trade or business

.03 Information required with Form 3115

(1) Facts and other information requested on Form 3115 and in applicable revenue procedures

(2) Statement of contrary authorities

(3) Copies of all contracts, agreements, and other documents

(4) Analysis of material facts

(5) Information regarding whether same issue is in an earlier return

(6) Statement regarding prior requests for a change in accounting method and other pending requests

(7) Statement identifying pending legislation

(8) Authorized representatives

(9) Power of attorney and declaration of representative

(10) Tax information authorization

(11) Penalties of perjury statement

.04 Additional procedural information required in certain circumstances

    (1) Recipients of original and copy of change in accounting method correspondence

    (2) To request expedited handling

    (3) To receive the change in accounting method letter ruling or any other correspondence related to Form 3115 by fax

    (4) To request a conference

.05 Associate office address for Forms 3115

.06 A Form 3115 must not be submitted by fax

.07 Form 3115 controlled and referred to the appropriate Associate office

.08 Additional information required

    (1) Incomplete Form 3115

    (2) Request for extension of reply period

    (3) Penalties of perjury statement

    (4) Identifying information

    (5) Faxing information request and additional information

    (6) Address to send additional information

    (7) If taxpayer does not timely submit additional information

.09 Circumstances in which the taxpayer must notify the Associate office

.10 Determines if proposed accounting method can be modified to obtain favorable letter ruling

.11 Near the completion of processing the Form 3115, advises the taxpayer if the Associate office will rule adversely and offers the taxpayer the opportunity to withdraw Form 3115

.12 Advance consent Form 3115 may be withdrawn or Associate office may decline to issue a change in accounting method letter ruling

.13 How to check status of a pending Form 3115

.14 Is not bound by informal opinion expressed

.15 Single letter ruling issued to a taxpayer or consolidated group for qualifying identical change in method of accounting

.16 Letter ruling ordinarily not issued for one of two or more interrelated items or submethods

.17 Consent Agreement

.18 A copy of the change in accounting method letter ruling to appropriate Service official

¶1621

.19 Consent to change an accounting method may be relied on subject to limitations

.20 Change in accounting method letter ruling will not apply to another taxpayer

.21 Associate office discretion to permit requested change in method of accounting

.22 List of automatic change in method of accounting request procedures

.23 Other sections of this revenue procedure that are applicable to a Form 3115

SECTION 10. HOW ARE CONFERENCES FOR LETTER RULINGS SCHEDULED?

.01 Schedules a conference if requested by taxpayer

.02 Permits taxpayer one conference of right

.03 Disallows verbatim recording of conferences

.04 Makes tentative recommendations on substantive issues

.05 May offer additional conferences

.06 Requires written confirmation of information presented at conference

.07 May schedule a pre-submission conference

.08 May schedule a conference to be held by telephone

SECTION 11. WHAT EFFECT WILL A LETTER RULING HAVE?

.01 May be relied on subject to limitations

.02 Will not apply to another taxpayer

.03 Will be used by a field office in examining the taxpayer's return

.04 May be revoked or modified if found to be in error or there has been a change in law

.05 Letter ruling revoked or modified based on material change in facts applied retroactively

.06 Not otherwise generally revoked or modified retroactively

.07 Retroactive effect of revocation or modification applied to a particular transaction

.08 Retroactive effect of revocation or modification applied to a continuing action or series of actions

.09 Generally not retroactively revoked or modified if related to sale or lease subject to excise tax

.10 May be retroactively revoked or modified when transaction is entered into before the issuance of the letter ruling

.11 Taxpayer may request that retroactivity be limited

> (1) Request for relief under §7805(b) must be made in required format

> (2) Taxpayer may request a conference on application of §7805(b)

SECTION 12. UNDER WHAT CIRCUMSTANCES DO DIRECTORS ISSUE DETERMINATION LETTERS?

.01 In income and gift tax matters

.02 In estate tax matters

.03 In generation-skipping transfer tax matters

.04 In employment and excise tax matters

.05 Requests concerning income, estate, or gift tax returns

.06 Review of determination letters

SECTION 13. WHAT EFFECT WILL A DETERMINATION LETTER HAVE?

.01 Has same effect as a letter ruling

.02 Taxpayer may request that retroactive effect of revocation or modification be limited

> (1) Request for relief under §7805(b) must be made in required format

> (2) Taxpayer may request a conference on application of §7805(b)

SECTION 14. UNDER WHAT CIRCUMSTANCES ARE MATTERS REFERRED BETWEEN A DIRECTOR AND AN ASSOCIATE OFFICE?

.01 Requests for determination letters

.02 No-rule areas

.03 Requests for letter rulings

.04 Letter ruling request mistakenly sent to a Director

SECTION 15. WHAT ARE THE USER FEE REQUIREMENTS FOR REQUESTS FOR LETTER RULINGS AND DETERMINATION LETTERS?

.01 Legislation authorizing user fees

.02 Requests to which a user fee applies

.03 Requests to which a user fee does not apply

.04 Exemptions from the user fee requirements

.05 Fee schedule

.06 Applicable user fee for a request involving multiple offices, fee categories, issues, transactions, or entities

¶1621

¶1622 Exhibit 16-2

December 31, 20X2

Internal Revenue Service

Associate Chief Counsel (Corporate)

PO Box 7604

Ben Franklin Station

Washington, DC 20044

To Whom it May Concern:

 On behalf of the USSub, Inc. ("USSub") a certain ruling set forth below is requested on the Federal income tax consequences of the proposed transaction described in this request.

<u>Statement of Facts</u>

1. The taxpayer is USSub (EIN: XX-XXXXXXX), which is located at 4747 Maryland Avenue, Shorewood, Wisconsin, 53211.

2. It our understanding that USSub is under the jurisdiction of the Large and Mid-Size Business Division.

3. The transaction is occuring to save German federal income taxes.

4. Mr. Post and Mr. Office own a German partnership that owns Holding GmbH, a German entity. Holding GmbH owns USSub, a U.S. C corporation incorporated in Wisconsin. For German tax planning purposes, Holding GmbH has contributed USSub to a new German entity, Betieligungsgesessschaft mbH ("mbH"). The mbH will form a U.S. LLC ("LLC") to own 1% of USSub. The mbH and the LLC will convert USSub into a limited partnership with the mbH being a 99% limited partner and the LLC being a 1% general partner. The mbH and the LLC will check-the-box for USSub to be a C corporation under the entity classification rules. This transaction is depicted as follows:

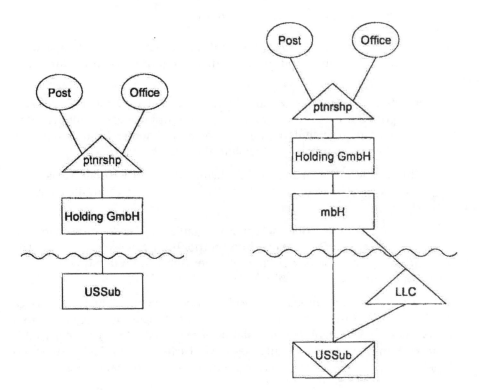

Ruling Requested

We respectfully request you rule that the conversation under state law of USSub to a limited partnership under Wisconsin's conversion statute along with the election for treatment as a C corporation will constitute a reorganization within the meaning of I.R.C. § 368(a)(1)(F) of the Code.

Rev. Proc. 2002-3 Section 3.01(30) states that the Service will not rule on a Type F reorganization "unless the Service determines that there is a significant issue that must be resolved in order to decide those matters." Furthermore, Announcement 2001-25 states that a significant issue is an issue of law that meets the following three tests: (i) the issue is not clearly and adequately addressed by a statute, regulation, decision of a court, tax treaty, revenue ruling, revenue procedure, notice, or other authority published in the Internal Revenue Bulletin; (ii) the resolution of the issue is not essentially free from doubt; and (iii) the issue is legally significant and germane to determine the major tax consequences of the transaction. This ruling request satisfies all three criteria. First, the issue is not clearly and adequately addressed in any of the previously mentioned authority. Second, although the taxpayer believes that a ruling is appropriate, the newness of the entity classification regulations may create some question. Finally, the issue is legally significant and germane because if the transaction does not qualify as a Type F reorganization, the taxpayer may incur gain.

¶1622

Supporting Authorities

USSub is a Wisconsin C Corporation that sells products in the industry. Its assets are primarily comprised of machinery, equipment, inventory and receivables.

Under Wisconsin Statutes section 180.1161, effective October 1, 20X2, a Wisconsin corporation may convert to another form of business entity provided it satisfies various requirements within that section. Another form of business entity in Wisconsin is the limited partnership. Wis. Stat. § 179.01.

By virtue of the fact that the LLC is disregarded entity under Treas. Reg. § 301.7701-2, mbH will continue to hold 100% of USSub throughout the course of the transaction.

I.R.C. § 368(a)(1)(F) describes a Type F reorganization as "a mere change in entity, form, or place of organization of one corporation, however affected." The mbH will make a check-the-box election on a Form 8832, to retain C corporation treatment for the limited partnership. Treas. Reg. § 301.7701-2.

The instant facts are almost identical to those contained in Field Service Advice 200237017. In that Field Service Advice, a C corporation converted to a limited partnership pursuant to a state statute. The owners of the entity elected C corporation status such that the entity was never treated as a limited partnership for Federal tax purposes. The Service concluded that this transaction may be treated as a F reorganization.

Unlike the other types of reorganizations, the F reorganization requirements are not specifically elucidated in the regulations under section 368. As a practical matter, the essence of the test for qualification as an F reorganization is that nothing else occurred except for the change in identity, form, or place of organization.

Changes in the form of business organizations have qualified as a Type F reorganization. For example, a change in form of organization from a corporation to a business trust that is taxable as a corporation has been approved as an F reorganization. Rev. Rul. 67-376, 1967-2 C.B. 142; Rev. Rul. 70-241, 1970-1 C.B. 84.

In addition to satisfying the Code, this F reorganization satisfies several judicially created doctrines; (i) business purpose, (ii) continuity of interest and (iii) continuity of business enterprise.

1. Business Purpose, The business purpose doctrine, which was established in *Gregory v. Helvering*, 293 U.S. 465 (1985), requires that the transaction have a bona fide business purpose other than the avoidance of tax. As a limited partnership, USSub would combine with the mbH and Holding GmbH as a tax unit for German tax purposes. As a tax unit, income in some of the entities can be offset by losses in other entities for German tax purposes. Furthermore, distribution from a member of the unit, such as USSub, would not result in income to the unit. In contrast, a distribution from an entity legally formed as a corporation would result in

income in Germany. As a result, it is beneficial for mbH to own an interest in a limited partnership as opposed to shares of a C corporation.

In Rev. Rul. 89-101, 1989-2 C.B. 67, the service ruled that foreign tax savings are a valid business purpose. The foreign tax savings in this matter do not impact U.S. federal taxes or the U.S. foreign tax credit in any way. The Service has also privately ruled that taxation implications in a foreign country constitute a valid business purpose. PLR 9437009.

2. Continuity of Interest. The continuity of interest doctrine requires that the former shareholders of the acquiring corporation acquire a substantial continuing proprietary interest in the acquired corporation. The purpose of the continuity of interest requirement is to prevent transactions resembling sales from qualifying for non-recognition treatment as a reorganization. Treas. Reg. § 1.368-1(e)(1)(i).

Those regulations specify that a proprietary interest is preserved if shares in the former entity are exchanged for shares in the new entity. In this matter, continuity of interest exists because the shares in USSub will be replaced by the partnership interests (treated as shares under the check-the-box rules) in USSub. Furthermore, special related person rules specify that there is not a continuity of interest when consideration other than a proprietary interest is used in the exchange. Treas. Reg. § 1.368-1(e)(2). In this matter, although the parties are all related persons, there is no other such consideration being used.

3. Continuity of Business Enterprise. The continuity of business enterprise is satisfied as long as the acquiring corporation in a reorganization either (a) continues the acquired's historic business or (b) uses a significant portion of the acquired historic business assets in a business. In this matter, both tests are satisfied because USSub will continue to operate the same and only business of selling products in the same industry that it had previously conducted. USSub's assets of machinery, equipment, inventory and receivables will continue to be used in the products business in the same manner as before the transaction. Treas. Reg. § 1.368-1(d)(1)(3). Here, the business and assets are essentially unchanged. *Davant v. Commissioner*, 366 F.2d 874 (5th Cir. 1966, *cert. denied*, 36 U.S. 1022 (1967).

Representations

Pursuant to Rev. Proc. 77-37, as amplified by Rev. Proc. 86-42, section 7.07, the taxpayer makes the following representations.

1. The fair market value of USSub will be the same before and after the transaction.

2. There is no plan or intention by the original owners of USSub that own 1% or more of the stock and, to the best of the knowledge of management of USSub, there is not plan or intention on the part of the remaining owners of USSub to sell, exchanges or otherwise dispose of any of the interests of USSub received in the transaction.

¶1622

3. Immediately following consummation of the transaction, the owners of USSub will be the same as before the transaction.

4. USSub has no plan or intention to issue additional interests following the transaction.

5. Immediately following consummation of the transaction, USSub will possess the same assets and liabilities as those possessed by USSub immediately prior to the transaction. No assets will be distributed and there will not be any dissenting shareholders.

6. At the time of the transaction, USSub will not have any outstanding warrants, options, convertible securites, or any other type of right pursuant to which any person could acquire ownership.

7. USSub has no plan or intention to reacquire any of its interests issued in this transaction.

8. After the transaction, USSub has no plan or intention to sell or otherwise dispose of any of the assets it owned before the transaction, except for dispositions made in the ordinary course of business.

9. The liabilities of USSub assumed in the transaction plus the liabilities, if any, to which the transferred assets are subject were incurred by USSub in the ordinary course of its business and are associated with its assets.

10. Following the transaction, USSub will continue its historic business and use a significant portion of its historic business assets in the business of selling products.

11. The owners of USSub will pay their respective expenses, if any, incurred in connection with the transaction.

12. USSub is not under the jurisdiction of a court or Title 11 or similar case within the meaning of section 368(a)(3)(A) of the Internal Revenue Code.

Declarations

To the best of knowledge of the taxpayer and its representative, the issue on which a ruling is requested is not on a return of the taxpayer (or related taxpayer) that (i) is under examination by any office of the IRS; (ii) has been examined in the Statute of Limitations on assessment or refund has not expired or a closing has not been entered into with an IRS office; (iii) is under consideration by an Appeals Office in connection with their return for a prior period and the Statute of Limitations on assessment or refund has not expired or a closing agreement has not been entered into by an Appeals Office; or (iv) is pending in litigation. Also, to the best of the knowledge of both the taxpayer and its representative, none of the issues involved in this ruling request has been the subject of a ruling to the taxpayer.

A Power of Attorney (Form 2848) in favor of the undersigned is enclosed. If additional information is required or would be helpful, please telephone me at (414) 555-8135.

¶1622

If there is any question about the issuance of a favorable ruling, a conference is hereby requested.

In the event a ruling is issued, a statement of proposed deletions is enclosed.

Yours very truly,

Tony F. Miller

Power of Attorney

Verifications

Statement of Proposed Deletions

¶1623 Exhibit 16-3

Internal Revenue Service	Department of the Treasury
Number: 200335019	Washington, DC 20224
Release Date: 8/29/20X3	Person to Contact:
Index Number: 368.06-00	Telephone Number:
	Refer Reply to: CC:CORP:1-PLR-105939-03
	Date: May 27, 20X3

Oldco   =

ForeignCO =

ForeignSub =

State X   =

Country Z =

Date 1   =

Dear _____ :

We respond to your letter dated December 31, 20X2, requesting rulings on the federal income tax consequences of a proposed transaction. Additional information was received in a letter dated March 11, 20X3. The information submitted in your request and in subsequent correspondence is summarized below.

Oldco is a State X corporation. Until Date 1, ForeignCo wholly owned Oldco.

For valid business purposes, ForeignCo wishes to convert Oldco into a limited partnership under State X law, which will continue to be taxable as a corporation for federal income tax purposes. To accomplish this intent, on Date 1, ForeignCo contributed Oldco to new Country Z ("ForeignSub"). ForeignSub then will form an LLC, which will be disregarded as an entity separate from its owner under Treas. Reg. § 301.7701-2 ("LLC"), and ForeignCo will contribute a 1% interest in Oldco to LLC. ForeignSub will cause Oldco to be converted into a limited partnership ("Newco") pursuant to State X's conversion statute with ForeignSub being a 99% limited partner and LLC being a 1% general partner for purposes of State X law ("the Conversion").

Newco will elect under Reg. § 301.7701-3 to be treated as a C corporation for federal tax purposes, effective the date of the Conversion.

Section 3.01(29) of Rev. Proc. 2003-3, 2003-1 IRB 113, 114, provides that the Service will not rule on the qualification under 368(a)(1)(F) unless the Service determines that there is a significant issue that is not clearly and adequately addressed by published authority. Oldco has made the following representations in connection with addressing the significant issue of whether the Conversion of Oldco into a limited partnership that elects corporate entity classification constitutes a reorganization under section 368(a)(1)(F).

    (a) Contribution of the shares of Oldco to ForeignSub constitutes a valid 351 transaction that is undertaken for a valid business purpose.

¶1623

(b) There is no plan or intention by the ForeignSub to Sell, exchange, or otherwise dispose of any of the interests of Newco received in the Conversion.

(c) Immediately following consummation of the Conversion, for federal tax purposes, ForeignSub will own all of the membership interests in Newco and will own such membership interests in NewCo solely by reason of its ownership of Oldco immediately prior to the Conversion

(d) Newco has no plan or intention to issue additional interests following the Conversion

(e) Immediately following consummation of the Conversion, Newco will possess the same assets and liabilities as those possessed by Oldco immediately prior to the Conversion. No assets will be distributed and there will be no dissenting shareholders.

(f) At the time of the Conversion, Oldco will not have outstanding any warrants, options, convertible securities, or any other type of right pursuant to which any person could acquire stock in Oldco.

(g) Newco has no plan or intention to reacquire any of its interests issued in the Conversion.

(h) Newco has no plan or intention to sell or otherwise dispose of any of the assets of Oldco acquired in the Conversion, except for dispositions made in the ordinary course of business

(i) Following the Conversion, Newco will continue the historic business of Oldco or use a significant portion of Oldco's business assets in a business.

(j) ForeignSub will pay its expenses, if any, incurred in connection with the Conversion

(k) Oldco is not under the jurisdiction of a court in a Title 11 or similar case within the meaning of section 368(a)(3)(A) of the Internal Revenue Code.

(l) Newco's election under the Reg. § 301.771-3 to be treated as an association taxable as a corporation will be effective as of the date of the Conversion such that Newco will never exist as a partnership for federal tax purposes.

Thus, based solely on the information submitted and the representations set forth above, we hold as follows:

1. The conversion of Oldco into Newco pursuant to State X Law and Newco's election to be treated as an association taxable as a corporation for federal tax purposes effective as of the date of conversion qualifies as a reorganization under section 368(a)(1)(F), even though it is a step in a larger transaction that includes a series of steps. See Rev. Rul. 96-29, 1996-1 C.B. 50. Shareholder will not recognize any gain or loss on the deemed exchange of its Equity Interest in Oldco for an Equity Interest in Newco (§ 354(a)(1)).

¶1623

2. Oldco will not recognize any gain or loss on the exchange (§§ 361(a) and 357(a)). The basis of the assets of Oldco in the hands of Newco will be the same as the basis of such assets in the hands of Oldco immediately prior to the proposed transaction (§ 362(b)). The holding period of the Oldco assets held by Newco will include the period during which such assets were held by Oldco (§ 1223(2)).

3. The basis of the equity interest in Newco received by ForeignSub will be the same as the basis of the shares of Oldco surrendered in exchange therefor (§ 358(a)(1)). The holding period of the equity interest in Newco to be received by ForeignSub will include the period during which the shares of Oldco surrendered therefor were held, provided that the shares are held as capital assets on the date of the exchange (§ 1223(1)).

We express no opinion as to the federal income tax treatment of the proposed transaction under other provisions of the Code and regulations or the tax treatment of any conditions existing at the time of, or effects resulting from, the proposed transaction that are not specifically covered by the above rulings.

It is important that a copy of this letter be attached to the federal income tax returns of the taxpayers involved for the taxable year in which the transaction covered by this letter is consummated.

This ruling is directed only to the taxpayer(s) requesting it. Section 6110(k)(3) of the Code provides that it may not be used or cited as precedent.

In accordance with the Power of Attorney on file with this office, a copy of this letter is being sent to your authorized representative.

The rulings contained in this letter are based upon information and representations submitted by the taxpayer and accompanied by a penalty of perjury statement executed by an appropriate party. While this office had not verified any of the material submitted in support of the request for rulings, it is subject to verification on examination.

Sincerely yours

———————

Senior Counsel, Branch 1
Offic of Associate Chief Counsel
(Corporate)

¶1631 DISCUSSION QUESTIONS

1. Tom Taxpayer meets with his CPA about a potential transaction. At the meeting Tom Taxpayer presents the CPA with a private letter ruling that is directly on point to his potential transaction. Can Tom Taxpayer rely on the private letter ruling if he is later audited with respect to the return filed for the year in which he enters the transaction? How would your answer change if Tom Taxpayer provided a Revenue Ruling directly on point?

2. J.P. Foster engages you to pursue a private letter ruling with respect to a transaction he is contemplating entering. After some consultation with the IRS Associate Chief Counsel, it appears that J.P. will not receive a favorable ruling. What do you advise J.P. with respect to his compliance requirements?

CHAPTER 17
INTERNATIONAL TAX PRACTICE AND PROCEDURE

¶1701 INTRODUCTION

As the major economies of the world have become global in nature, the frequency and complexity of cross-border transactions have increased significantly. While many of the same procedural issues present in audits of domestic businesses are germane, there are other unique problems facing U.S.-based multinationals (outbound investment) as well as U.S. subsidiaries of foreign parent companies (inbound investment).

¶1702 ORGANIZATION OF THE INTERNAL REVENUE SERVICE INTERNATIONAL OFFICES

The Office of the Director, International, in Washington, D.C., now only functions as the U.S. Competent Authority.[1] The International Examiners are assigned to the industry groups within the Large Business and International (LB&I) Division.[2]

¶1703 INTERNATIONAL EXAMINATIONS

Given the extraordinary complexity of the international provisions of the Internal Revenue Code, the importance and involvement of the International Examiner has increased in multinational corporation audits. Recognizing this, the IRS has retrained many of its domestic agents as International Examiners. Whereas previously International Examiners were located only in large metropolitan areas, many audits of corporations in rural areas with international operations now have International Examiners assigned to their audits.

The International Examiners are crucial in any audit involving international issues. Because the international examiners are involved in a complex and sophisticated tax administration, they are specially trained to deal with issues involving controlled foreign corporations, cross-border transfers and reorganizations, transfer pricing, foreign tax credit issues, export benefits, and withholding taxes.[3] Although the International Examiners are assigned to the LB&I Division, they may receive referrals from the Small Business/Self-Employed (SB/SE) Division when international issues arise.[4]

Due to the increased emphasis by the Internal Revenue Service on intercompany transfer pricing, IRS economists are also becoming involved in the audit

---

[1] IRM 4.60.3.1.6. *See* ¶1706.
[2] IRM 4.60.4.
[3] IRM 4.60.4.7.
[4] IRM Exhibits 4.60.5-1 and 4.60.5-2.

process. Their role is to identify potential transfer pricing issues early in the examination process as well as assist in gathering factual information in support of the IRS's position.

LB&I has recently initiated an Industry Issue Focus strategy to coordinate greater national control and consistency over important issues that range across industry lines.[5] Pursuant to this initiative, the International Examiners will identify potential compliance issues through the normal course of an audit. Certain issues are designated as Tier I, II, or III depending on their prevalence across industry lines and their compliance risk. For each issue designated as either a Tier I issue (high strategic importance), a Tier II issue (significant compliance risk), or a Tier III issue (industry risk), the IRS will form an issue management team comprised of personnel from Chief Counsel, Appeals, and other functional areas. This team will provide instructions to the Examiners on how to handle the respective issues. The IRS has announced on its website the Tier I and Tier II issues, but has not designated any issues as Tier III issues. International-oriented Tier I issues include:

(i) § 936 exit strategies—these issues focus on the outbound transfer and transfer pricing issues related to the offshore migration of intangibles from formerly tax-favored Puerto Rican corporations;

(ii) domestic production deduction Code Sec. 199—these issues focus on the allocation of expenses, such as compensation, to and away from qualified production activities income;

(iii) foreign earnings repatriation—these issues focus on the since-repealed one-time dividends received deduction from foreign corporations that expired after September 30, 2006;

(iv) foreign tax credit generators—these issues focus on financial services industry transactions whereby taxpayers eliminate U.S. tax by generating a foreign tax that improperly results in a credit when the underlying business transaction would not ordinarily be subject to foreign tax;

(v) international hybrid instrument transactions—these issues focus on the inconsistent treatment of financial instruments as either debt in the United States and equity in a foreign country or equity in the United States and debt in a foreign country;

(vi) cost-sharing arrangements with buy-in payments—these issues focus on cost-sharing arrangements under the transfer pricing rules when moving intangibles offshore, including the amount of any buy-in payment by a new participant to an existing participant for previously-existing intangibles and the measurement of reasonably anticipated benefits; and

(vii) reporting and withholding on U.S.-source fixed, determinable, annual, or periodic income—these issues focus on the compliance of U.S. withholding agents who make these payments.

---

[5] IRM 4.51.5.

¶1703

International-oriented Tier II issues include:

   (i) cost-sharing stock-based compensation—these issues involve the allocation and amount of compensation as a cost to be shared; and

   (ii) extraterritorial income exclusion effective date and transition rules—these issues focus on an export benefit that Congress has phased out.

The IRS has not announced any international-oriented Tier III issues.

¶1704 IRS PROCEDURAL TOOLS

The primary authority for recordkeeping requirements of an entity potentially liable for U.S. tax is Code Sec. 6001 and the related Regulations. The IRS also has the specific authority to examine any books, papers, records, or other data that may be relevant or material to ascertaining the correctness of any return, determining the tax liability of any person, or collecting any tax. Since most taxpayers and other individuals voluntarily produce records and answer questions when requested to do so by the IRS, this authority in itself is normally sufficient to obtain the necessary information.

One of the largest problems for foreign owned U.S. taxpayers is that most foreign corporations do not have records that are in a usable format. Records are often stated in foreign currency and prepared in foreign languages. Therefore, the U.S. taxpayer must spend a large amount of time and money translating and explaining the documents to the IRS.

The case of *Nissei Sangyo America, Ltd. v. U.S.*[6] dealt with this problem. *Nissei* involved the audit of a U.S. subsidiary of a Japanese parent. In response to an IRS summons, the U.S. subsidiary and its Japanese parent randomly selected documents relating to the issue under examination and provided full translations. In addition, they translated the subject matter headings or titles of 1,441 pages of Japanese correspondence and prepared English translation keys for the travel expense authorization forms. The IRS demanded that all documents described in the summonses be translated into English, which the taxapayer estimated would cost from $850,000 to $1.5 million. The court held that the IRS could not compel the translation of documents that were not relevant to the tax liability or that the IRS already had in its possession.[7] Although this case involved a response to an IRS summons, the translation issue may arise in any type of response to an IRS method to obtain documents.

Information Document Requests. An Information Document Request (IDR) is designed to request information or documents from taxpayers when there are voluminous records to be examined, or when it is desirable to document requests. Requested on Form 4564 (a copy of which is reproduced in the Appendix to this Chapter), an IDR provides the IRS a convenient means to request informa-

---

[6] DC Ill., 95-2 USTC ¶50,327. The internal procedures of the IRS require the IRS to request documents, review them and then specify the documents to be translated. Reg. § 1.6038A-3(b)(3)

[7] *See* the general summons standard of *M. Powell*, SCt, 64-2 USTC ¶9858, 379 US 48, *infra*.

tion and simultaneously yields a permanent record of what was requested, received, and returned to the taxpayer.

In addition to this authority, an International Examiner can employ several procedural tools to obtain information beyond that obtained via IDRs. These include on site inspection, summons, designated summons, formal document requests, Code Secs. 6038A and 6038, and exchanges of information under treaties.

On-site Inspections. In addition to IDRs, International Examiners appear to have taken an increased interest in foreign site visits and plant tours.[8] While IRS budget constraints and internal administrative requirements may occasionally affect the number or duration of such visits, taxpayers should expect such requests and prepare to respond. The taxpayer should remember that it is a request, not an order, and that any request may be negotiated in terms of choosing the facility to visit (the taxpayer may want to substitute a domestic plant for a foreign plant), the duration of the visit, the timing of the visit, and the number of IRS employees involved. Careful planning of any such trip may result in an opportunity to present, in effect, key facts supporting the taxpayer's position. The taxpayer should prepare the plant personnel for the visit. The taxpayer may consider pre-screening the tour to determine if the plant's operations cover processes or procedures relevant to the audit cycle and pre-interviewing all involved personnel to sensitize them to the potential issues. International Examiners have the following instructions for plant tours:[9]

   (i) Obtain information about departmental cost sheets or schedules.

  (ii) Learn the training requirements of each type of production employee.

 (iii) Obtain any records regarding sales to all customers.

 (iv) Ascertain the extent of product development performed at the plant.

  (v) Interview plant employees. Plant interviews will bring a sense of reality to the case. Interviews should flush out the employee's ability to alter the production process and the technical training each production employee received.

 (vi) If the company is a controlled foreign corporation, determine how and to whom it sells its products.

(vii) Obtain all company manuals regarding the operations of the plant.

(viii) Obtain all job descriptions prior to the plant tour.

 (ix) Obtain all annual evaluations of the employees to be interviewed.

  (x) Obtain all company "programmer" manuals. This manual offers guidance to the programmer to construct and translate the program.

The Summons Power. An IRS summons may be used only for the purposes set forth in Code Sec. 7602. These purposes are the verification, determination

---

[8] I.R.M. 4.46.3.10.2 through 4.46.3.10.5.

[9] *IRS International Continuing Professional Education materials*, Chicago, Illinois, May 2005; *see also* IRM Exhibit 4.61.3-1.

and collection of the tax liability of any person. The IRS also has specific authorization to issue summonses for the purpose of investigating any criminal tax offense.[10] See ¶703.

Designated Summonses. If, after issuing a summons, the IRS does not obtain the desired information, the IRS may consider issuing a designated summons.[11]

A designated summons tolls the running of the statute of limitations during the period in which judicial enforcement proceeding is pending and for either 30 or 120 days thereafter, depending on whether or not the court orders compliance with the summons. The legislative history indicates Congress was concerned that taxpayers made a practice of responding slowly to IRS requests for information without extending the statute of limitations. Congress did not intend to extend the statute of limitations in a large number of cases, but to encourage taxpayers to provide requested information on a timely basis by realizing that the IRS had this tool available. In addition to satisfying the standards of summons enforcement, the internal procedures the IRS personnel have to follow to issue a designated summons are a major impediment to their issuance. Both the LB&I Division Commissioner and Division Counsel-LB&I[12] must approve a summons, which must be issued at least 60 days before the expiration of the statute of limitations.[13]

> **Example 17-1:** A distributor of computers, USAco is a subsidiary of ASIAco. USAco buys computers from ASIAco and resells them in the United States. The IRS's International Examiner conducts a transfer pricing audit of USAco. After USAco fails to respond to the International Examiner's IDR requesting all agreements between USAco and ASIAco, just over 60 days remain on the statute of limitations. USAco will not sign a consent to extend the statute of limitations. Concerned about the possibility that the statute of limitations will expire, the International Examiner issues a designated summons for the agreements. The designated summons tolls the statute of limitations during enforcement proceedings and for a short time thereafter.[14]

---

[10] Code Sec. 7602(b).
[11] Code Sec. 6503(j).
[12] Prop. Reg. § 301.6503(j)-1(c)(1)(i).

[13] Code Sec. 6503(j)(2)(A).
[14] *Derr*, CA-9, 92-2 USTC ¶ 50,369.

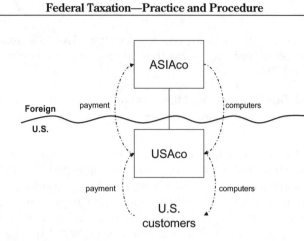

Formal Document Requests. If, through IDRs, the IRS is unable to gather the foreign information it considers necessary to conduct its examination, the IRS may issue a formal document request (FDR). The FDR is not intended to be used as a routine tool at the beginning of an examination, but instead as a mechanism for securing information that could not be obtained through normal IDRs. The rare use of the FDR is indicated by the fact that the IRS does not have a specific form for the FDR. Instead, the IRS will issue a Form 4564 entitled "Information Document Request" with the typed notation "Formal Document Request" (see Exhibit 17-1 at ¶1711). The FDR must be mailed by registered or certified mail and provide:

(i) The time and place for the production of the documentation;

(ii) A statement of the reason the documentation previously produced (if any) is not sufficient;

(iii) A description of the documentation sought; and

(iv) The consequences to the taxpayer of the failure to produce the documentation described in subparagraph (iii).[15]

If the taxpayer does not furnish the requested information within 90 days of the mailing of the FDR, the taxpayer will be prevented from later introducing the requested documentation. Foreign-based documentation is "any documentation which is outside the United States and which may be relevant or material to the tax treatment of the examined item."[16] Therefore, the IRS has broad authority to request virtually any relevant information as long as the request satisfies the standards above.[17] The purpose of the FDR procedure is to discourage taxpayers from delaying or refusing disclosure of certain foreign-based documentation. To avoid the later exclusion of documents, the taxpayer must substantially comply with the FDR. The FDR is not intended to be used as a routine beginning to an examination, but instead as a mechanism for securing information that the IRS could not obtain through normal request procedures.[18]

---

[15] Code Sec. 982(c)(1).

[16] Code Sec. 982(d).

[17] *Yujuico*, ND Cal, 93-1 USTC ¶50,097.

[18] *See* Joint Committee on Taxation, General Explanation of the Tax Equity and Fiscal Responsibil-

Whether there has been substantial compliance with an FDR will depend on all the facts and circumstances.[19] For example, if the taxpayer submits nine out of ten requested items and the court believes the missing item is the most substantial, the taxpayer could be found to have failed to comply substantially with the FDR. Accordingly, the court could prohibit the taxpayer from later introducing the missing documentation.

Any taxpayer that receives an FDR has the right to begin proceedings to quash the request within ninety days after the IRS mailed the FDR. The standard for quashing a FDR is the same *Powell* standard for quashing a summons.[20] Moreover, the taxpayer may contend, for example, that the information requested is irrelevant, that the requested information is available in the United States, or that reasonable cause exists for the failure to produce or delay in producing the information.

Reasonable cause does not exist where a foreign jurisdiction would impose a civil or criminal penalty on the taxpayer for disclosing the requested documentation.[21] In a proceeding to quash, the IRS has the burden of proof to show the relevance and materiality of the information requested. During the period that a proceeding to quash or any appeal from that proceeding is pending, the statute of limitations is suspended.[22]

The legislative history specifies that three factors should be considered in determining whether there is reasonable cause for failure to furnish the requested documentation. These factors are: (i) whether the request is reasonable in scope; (ii) whether the requested documents are available within the United States; and (iii) the reasonableness of the requested place of production within the United States.[23]

An example of an unreasonable scope may be a request "for all the books and records and all the supporting documents for all the entries made in such books or records" for a particular foreign entity that is controlled by a taxpayer. However, a request for the general ledger, an analysis of an account, and supporting documents for a particular transaction of such a foreign entity would be reasonable in scope. Moreover, the place of production of records is generally at the taxpayer's place of business or the International Examiner's office. Requesting the production of records in New York City by a taxpayer that is residing in and engages in a trade or business in Los Angeles would be considered unreasonable. The key to the reasonableness of the place for production is that such a place should be mutually convenient to both the taxpayer and the IRS.

(Footnote Continued)

ity Act of 1982, HR 4961, 97th Cong., 2d Sess. 246-247.

[19] *See Good Karma, LLC v. United States*, N.D. IL, 2008-2 USTC ¶ 50,646.

[20] *See* ¶ 706. *See also Yujuico v. United States*, N.D. Cal, 93-1 USTC ¶ 50,097.

[21] Code Sec. 982(e).

[22] Code Sec. 982(e).

[23] Conference Committee Report on P.L. 97-248, The Tax Equity and Fiscal Responsibility Act of 1982.

Code Sec. 6038A and 6038. Congressional perception that foreign-owned U.S. subsidiaries were not paying their proper share of U.S. tax and the inability of the IRS to obtain foreign-based documentation caused Congress to expand greatly the application of Code Sec. 6038A. The section places the reporting burden for intercompany transactions on the 25 percent or greater foreign-owned corporation with a U.S. subsidiary. The U.S. subsidiary, the "reporting corporation," must furnish certain information annually and maintain records necessary to determine the correctness of the intercompany transactions. In addition, the reporting corporation must furnish the required information by filing Form 5472 on an annual basis.

Reg. § 1.6038A-3(a)(1) provides that "[a] reporting corporation must keep the permanent books of account or records as required by section 6001 that are sufficient to establish the correctness of the federal income tax return of the corporation, including information, documents, or records ('records') to the extent they may be relevant to determine the correct U.S. tax treatment of transactions with related parties." Such records may include, for example, cost data, if appropriate, to determine the profit or loss from the transfer pricing of intercompany transactions.

Failure to maintain or timely furnish the required information may result in a penalty of $10,000 for each taxable year in which the failure occurs for each related party.[24] If any failure continues for more than ninety days after notice of the failure to the reporting corporation, the IRS can impose an additional penalty of $10,000 per thirty-day period while the failure continues. The IRS can assess additional penalties if the taxpayer fails to maintain records after the ninety-day notification.[25]

More specifically, Code Sec. 6038A(e) allows the IRS to reduce the cost of goods sold when a taxpayer does not obtain its foreign parent's permission to be an agent for the request of certain documents. Within thirty days after a request by the IRS, a foreign-related party must appoint the reporting corporation as its limited agent for service of a summons. Failure to appoint such an agent can result in penalties for noncompliance.[26] In such a case, the LB&I Industry Director in her sole discretion shall determine the amount of the relevant deduction or the cost to the reporting corporation.

The IRS is prepared to adhere to Code Sec. 6038A(e) as shown in *Asat, Inc. v. Commissioner*.[27] In *Asat*, the Tax Court literally applied Code Sec. 6038A(e) against the taxpayer, upholding the IRS's reduction to the cost of goods sold. Adhering to the legislative history, the Tax Court further found irrelevant that the foreign parent during the year in issue was not the parent at the time of the audit.

> **Example 17-2:** A distributor of toy dolls, USAco is a subsidiary of ASIAco. USAco buys toy dolls from ASIAco and resells them in the United States. The IRS's International Examiner conducts a transfer pricing audit of USAco. Wanting to obtain documents from ASIAco, the International Exam-

---

[24] Reg. § 1.6038A-4(a)(1).
[25] *Id.* Reg. § 1.6038A-4(d)(1).

[26] *Id.* Reg. § 1.6038A-5.
[27] 108 TC 147, Dec. 51,966.

iner requests that ASIAco appoint USAco as its agent for service of a summons. If ASIAco neither appoints USAco as its agent nor provides the pricing data to the International Examiner, the IRS can reduce USAco's cost of goods sold to $0.

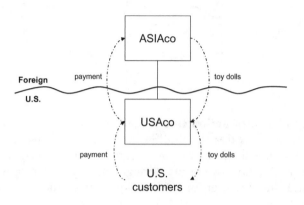

Although there is not the same perception that U.S.-owners of foreign subsidiaries are not paying their proper share of U.S. tax, Code Sec. 6038 places a reporting burden for intercompany transactions on a U.S. owner of a controlled foreign corporation. This information is reported by the U.S. owner filing Form 5471 on an annual basis.

As with Code Sec. 6038A, the failure to maintain or timely furnish the Code Sec. 6038 information may result in a penalty of $10,000 for each taxable year in which the failure occurs.[28] If any failure continues for more than 90 days after notice of the failure, the IRS can impose an additional penalty of $10,000 per 30-day period while the failure continues. The IRS can assess additional penalties if the U.S. owner fails to maintain records after receiving notification. The IRS can further reduce any foreign tax credits taken by the U.S. owner by 10%.[29]

> **Example 17-3:** Uncle Sam, a U.S. citizen, inherits all the shares of FSub, a controlled foreign corporation that is incorporated in Country F. During the taxable year, FSub pays a gross dividend of $100,000, which is reduced by the $10,000 withholding tax imposed by Country F. Although Uncle Sam takes a $10,000 direct foreign tax credit on his return, he never files a Form 5471 for FSub. The IRS can reduce Uncle Sam's foreign tax credit by $1,000.

---

[28] Code Sec. 6038(b).   [29] Code Sec. 6038(c).

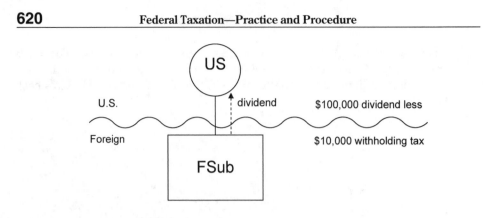

Exchanges Of Information Under Treaties. Under the exchange of information provisions of a tax treaty, the IRS can generally request information from a foreign country that is either in the foreign country's possession or available under the respective tax laws of that foreign country. These provisions generally do not require the exchange of information that would disclose any trade or business secret.

The IRS exercises discretion and judgment in both requesting and furnishing of information. In general, the IRS will not request information from another country unless: (i) there is a good reason to believe that the information is necessary to determine the tax liability of a specific taxpayer; (ii) the information is not otherwise available to the IRS; and (iii) the IRS is reasonably sure that requested information is in the possession of, or available to, the foreign government from whom the information is being requested.

> **Example 17-4:** A distributor of "Crazylegs" sports shoes, USAco is a subsidiary of ASIAco. USAco buys the sports shoes from ASIAco and resells them in the United States. The IRS's International Examiner conducts a transfer pricing audit of USAco. After USAco fails to respond to the International Examiner's IDR requesting all agreements between USAco and ASIAco, the International Examiner requests the information from ASIA country's tax authority pursuant to the exchange of information provision in the U.S.-ASIA tax treaty.

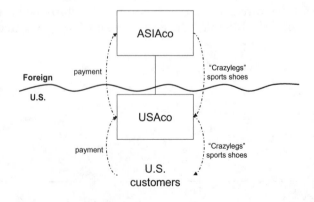

The IRS's internal guidelines require that information sought from a foreign government must specifically describe the information desired and the reason why the information is necessary.[30]

¶1705 CONCLUSION OF AN EXAMINATION

At the conclusion of the examination, the International Examiner will prepare a report summarizing the findings for incorporation into the revenue agent's report. Any disputed issues from the International Examiner's report may be pursued with the Appeals Office along with other domestic issues raised during the examination. Many of the larger Appeals Offices have Appeal Officers who specialize in international tax issues.

¶1706 COMPETENT AUTHORITY PROCEDURE

If the taxpayer has been unable to agree with the IRS on an adjustment that results in double taxation, the taxpayer may seek relief through the Competent Authority Procedure. An integral part of all U.S. Income Tax Treaties is a mutual agreement procedure which provides a mechanism for relief from double taxation. The Office of the Director International acts as the U.S. Competent Authority. The Competent Authority's primary objective is to make a reasonable effort to resolve double taxation cases and situations in which U.S. taxpayers have been denied benefits provided for by a treaty.[31] The taxpayer may request the Competent Authority Procedure when the actions of the United States, the treaty country or both will result in taxation that is contrary to provisions of an applicable tax treaty. Revenue Procedure 2006-54[32] explains how to request assistance of the U.S. Competent Authority in resolving conflicts between treaty partners. To the extent a treaty partner proposes an adjustment that appears inconsistent with a treaty provision or would result in double taxation, assistance via the Competent Authority Procedure should be sought as soon as is practical after the issue is developed by the treaty country (Revenue Procedure 2006-54's index, which details specific procedures, is reproduced in ¶1712 as Exhibit 17-2).

The opportunities to resolve disputes via the Competent Authority Procedure have increased from the traditional process, referred to as the Mutual Agreement Procedure to include the Simultaneous Appeals Procedure and the Accelerated Competent Authority Procedure. All these methods have the potential to resolve disputes of international tax issues in a manner that avoids litigation.

Mutual Agreement Procedure. The Mutual Agreement Procedure (MAP) treaty articles generally apply when the actions of the U.S. or foreign income tax authorities result in taxation not in accordance with the provisions of the applicable treaty.[33] Distribution, apportionment, or allocation under transfer pricing rules may subject a taxpayer to U.S. federal taxation on income that the taxpayer had attributed to a foreign country. Without an offsetting decrease in income

---

[30] IRM 4.60.1.2.4.2.
[31] IRM 4.60.2.1.

[32] Rev. Proc. 2006-54, IRB 2006-49.
[33] *Id.* at §4.01. A small case procedure also exists *Id.* at §5.01.

reported to the foreign country, the taxpayer may be subject to double taxation of the same income.

　　Example 17-5: A widget distributor, USAco is a subsidiary of ASIAco. USAco buys widgets from ASIAco for $100 and resells them in the United States for $105. The IRS argues that the arm's length price from ASIAco to USAco should be $90 and makes an assessment. Because $10 of income (the difference between the $100 ASIAco charged and the $90 the IRS believes is arm's length) is taxed by both the IRS and ASIA's tax administration, USAco and ASIAco can request relief from their respective competent authorities. The competent authorities will negotiate with each other to determine who will tax the $10.

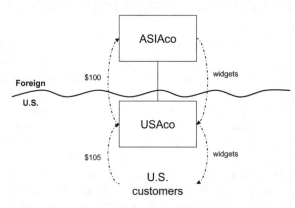

　　Simultaneous Appeals Procedure. Under the Simultaneous Appeals Procedure (SAP), taxpayers may seek simultaneous Appeals and Competent Authority consideration of an issue.[34] This procedure allows taxpayers to obtain Appeals involvement in a manner consistent with the ensuing Competent Authority Procedure and should reduce the time required to resolve disputes by allowing taxpayers more proactive involvement in the process. By informally approaching the Competent Authority before submitting a formal request, the Competent Authority effectively becomes the taxpayer's advocate. SAP further opens the possibility of developing strategies to explore the view likely to be taken by the other country.

　　Taxpayers may request SAP with the Competent Authority in three situations:

　　(i) After Examination has proposed an adjustment with respect to an issue that the taxpayer wishes to submit to the Competent Authority;[35]

　　(ii) After Examination has issued a 30-day letter, the taxpayer can file a protest, sever the issue, and seek Competent Authority assistance while other issues remain at Appeals;[36] or

---

[34] *Id.* at § 8.01.
[35] *Id.* at § 8.02(1)(a).
[36] *Id.* at § 8.02(1)(b).

(iii) After the taxpayer is at Appeals, the taxpayer can request Competent Authority assistance on an issue.[37]

The taxpayer also can request SAP with Appeals after making a Competent Authority request.[38] Generally, the U.S. Competent Authority will deny the request if the U.S. position paper has already been communicated to the foreign Competent Authority. The U.S. Competent Authority also can request the procedure.[39]

SAP is a two-part process. First, the Appeals representative will prepare an Appeals Case Memorandum (ACM) on the issue. Appeals will share the ACM with the Competent Authority representative, but not with the taxpayer. The ACM is a tentative resolution that the U.S. Competent Authority considers in preparing the U.S. position paper for presentation to the foreign Competent Authority.[40] Second, the U.S. Competent Authority prepares and presents the U.S. position paper to the foreign Competent Authority. The U.S. Competent Authority meets with the taxpayer to discuss the technical issue to be presented to the foreign Competent Authority and the Appeals representative may be asked to participate. If either the Competent Authorities fail to agree or if the taxpayer does not accept the mutual agreement reached, the taxpayer can refer the issue to Appeals for further consideration.[41]

Accelerated Competent Authority Procedure. The Accelerated Competent Authority Procedure (ACAP) shortens the time required to complete a case.[42] A taxpayer requesting ACAP assistance with respect to an issue raised by the IRS may request that the Competent Authority resolves the issue for subsequent tax years ending prior to the date of the request for the assistance.[43] In such a request, the taxpayer must agree that the inspection of the books and/or records under the ACAP will not preclude or impede a later examination or inspection for any period covered in the request; and the IRS need not comply with any procedural restrictions before beginning such an examination or inspection. The U.S. Competent Authority will contact the appropriate LB&I Industry Director to determine whether the issue should be resolved for subsequent tax years. If the Director consents, the U.S. Competent Authority will present the request to the foreign Competent Authority.[44]

¶1707 OFFSHORE INITIATIVE

Although international examinations are primarily conducted within the LB&I Division, the SB/SE Division is responsible for offshore initiatives with respect to individuals. More specifically, the SB/SE Division has jurisdiction for the Report of Foreign Bank and Financial Accounts on TD F 90-22.1 (FBAR), a completed sample of which is reproduced in the Appendix to this chapter. As a result of the

---

[37] *Id.* at §8.02(1)(c).
[38] *Id.* at §8.02(2).
[39] *Id.* at §8.01.
[40] This situation is analogous to the APA process. The Appeals representative will be a team chief,

international specialist, or Appeals officer with international experience.
[41] *Id.* at §8.07.
[42] *Id.* at §7.06.
[43] *Id.*
[44] *Id.*

Bank Secrecy Act, the Treasury Department has authority to seek information with respect to U.S. persons that control foreign bank accounts.[45] The Treasury Department has delegated this authority for enforcement of these FBAR filings to the IRS.

Potential FBAR Filers

Any U.S. person with either a financial interest in or signatory authority over a foreign bank account aggregating more than $10,000 at any time during the year must report that account on an FBAR. A foreign bank account does not include an account with a U.S. branch of a foreign bank or a foreign branch of a U.S. bank.[46]

The definition of a U.S. person includes a U.S. citizen, U.S. resident, U.S. partnership, U.S. corporation, U.S. estate, and U.S. trust.[47]

> **Example 17-6:** Bob, a U.S. citizen, is on special assignment during the winter at his condominium in Mexico. For his convenience, Bob opens an account at the Last National Bank of Mexico. At its peak, the account balance is $15,000, but on December 31 the balance is only $8,000. Because its highest balance is above $10,000, Bob must file an FBAR.

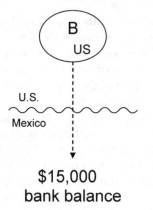

The law aggregates multiple accounts to determine whether they meet the $10,000 threshold.

> **Example 17-7:** Bob, a U.S. citizen, is on special assignment during the winter at his condominium in Mexico. Bob has two bank accounts in Mexico. The first, at the Hacienda Local Bank, has a peak balance of $2,500 and a year-end balance of $55. The second, at the Last National Bank of Mexico, has a peak balance of $8,000 and a year-end balance of $3,000. Because the aggregate of the peak balances exceed $10,000 ($2,500 plus $8,000 is $10,500), Bob must file an FBAR for the two accounts.

---

[45] 31 C.F.R. § 103.56(g).
[46] 31 C.F.R.§ 103(o). C.F.R. § 103.24.

[47] 31 C.F.R. § 103.11(z) and (n)(n); IRS Announcement 2010-16, 2010-11 I.R.B. 450.

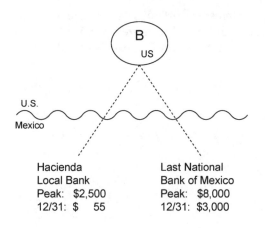

A U.S. person also has to file an FBAR if he or she owns more than 50% of a foreign corporation that has a foreign bank account in excess of $10,000.[48]

Example 17-8: Betsy Ross wholly-owns a European subsidiary called Flag Europa. Flag Europa has a bank account with a dollar equivalence at the Brinker Bank of the Netherlands. Betsy Ross must file an FBAR with respect to Flag Europa's account at the Brinker Bank of the Netherlands.

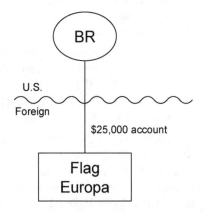

In addition to being U.S. persons that must file FBARs, flow-through[49] entities, such as U.S. partnerships and U.S. S corporations, may result in a U.S. individual having to file an FBAR. More specifically, the U.S. individual must file an FBAR when indirectly owning more than 50% of a foreign corporation.

Example 17-9: Uncle Sam, a U.S. citizen, is the only U.S. person owning a share (60%) of a U.S. limited partnership. The U.S. limited partnership owns 90% of a foreign corporation (ForCo). Because Uncle Sam's indirect ownership (his interest in the U.S. limited partnership times the U.S. limited

---

[48] *FBAR Questions and Answers* issued by the IRS on October 22, 2007.

[49] *FBAR Questions and Answers* issued by the IRS on October 22, 2007.

partnership's interest in ForCo) is 54%, Uncle Sam's ownership exceeds 50%. Both Uncle Sam and the U.S. limited partnership must file an FBAR for any foreign bank accounts of ForCo in excess of $10,000.

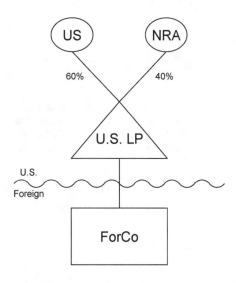

A financial account is more than just a bank account. More specifically, the definition of a financial account includes securities, securities derivatives, mutual funds, deficit cards, and prepaid credit accounts.[50]

The FBAR is due June 30th[51] for accounts held the prior taxable year and may not be extended. Also unlike a federal tax return, the FBAR is sent to the IRS Computing Center in Detroit, not the IRS Service Center with which the U.S. person files a return. The various due dates for filing and the different locations may cause confusion for some taxpayers.

> **Example 17-10:** Johnny, a U.S. citizen, has $20,000 in a bank account with the First Bank of Italy. Each year, Johnny files his Form 1040 and his FBAR by April 15. This year, due to some late information from various partnerships in which Johnny owns interests, Johnny extends his tax return and files both his Form 1040 and his FBAR by October 15. Although Johnny's income tax return is timely filed, the FBAR, which had to have been filed by June 30 and for which extension is not allowed, is late.

Failure to file FBARs may result in either civil or criminal penalties. Civil penalties depend on whether the failure to file was non-willful or willful. A non-willful failure to file results in a penalty that may not exceed $10,000[52] and a trade or business that is merely negligent in failing to file an FBAR incurs a $500

---

[50] IRS News Release 2007-15.

[51] Timely mailing is not timely filing as Code Sec. 7502(a)(1), which permits timely mailing as timely filing, only applies to filings related to Title 26 of the U.S. Code (the Internal Revenue Code) and the FBAR filing is a Title 31 requirement.

[52] 31 USC section 5321(a)(5)(B). Reasonable cause may be difficult to obtain if the taxpayer files a Form 1040 that inquires about foreign bank accounts and directs the taxpayer to an instruction describing the FBAR.

penalty.[53] A willful failure to file can result in a penalty of the greater of $100,000 or half of the balance in the account on June 30 when the FBAR was due.[54]

The normal three-year statute of limitations for income tax cases do not apply to FBAR matters. Instead, the statute of limitations on assessment of civil penalties is six years from the June 30 date that the FBAR was due.[55]

The IRS may also pursue criminal penalties for willful failure to file an FBAR. Those criminal penalties can result in a fine of up to $250,000 and five years of imprisonment.[56]

---

[53] 31 USC section 5321(a)(6)(A).
[54] 31 USC section 5321(a)(5)(C).

[55] 31 USC section 5321(b)(1).
[56] 31 USC section 5322(a).

¶1711 Exhibit 17-1

FORMAL DOCUMENT REQUEST

Form **4564** (Rev. September 2006)	Department of the Treasury — Internal Revenue Service Information Document Request	Request Number

To: (Name of Taxpayer and Company Division or Branch)	Subject	
	SAIN number	Submitted to:
	Dates of Previous Requests (mmddyyyy)	

Please return Part 2 with listed documents to requester identified below

Description of documents requested

Information Due By_____	At Next Appointment ☐	Mail in ☐

From:	Name and Title of Requester	Employee ID number	Date (mmddyyyy)
	Office Location		Telephone Number ( )

Catalog Number 23145K www.irs.gov	Part 1 - Taxpayer's File Copy	Form **4564** (Rev. 9-2006)

¶1712 Exhibit 17-2

Rev. Proc. 2006-54

SECTION 1. PURPOSE AND BACKGROUND

.01 Purpose

.02 Background

.03 Changes

SECTION 2. SCOPE

.01 In General

.02 Requests for Assistance

.03 General Process

.04 Failure to Request Assistance

SECTION 3. GENERAL CONDITIONS UNDER WHICH THIS PROCEDURE APPLIES

.01 General

.02 Requirements of a Treaty

.03 Applicable Standards in Allocation Cases

.04 Who Can File Requests for Assistance

.05 Closed Cases

.06 Foreign Initiated Competent Authority Request

.07 Requests Relating to Residence Issues

.08 Determinations Regarding Limitation on Benefits

SECTION 4. PROCEDURES FOR REQUESTING COMPETENT AUTHORITY ASSISTANCE

.01 Time for Filing

.02 Place of Filing

.03 Additional Filing

.04 Form of Request

.05 Information Required

.06 Other Dispute Resolution Programs

.07 Other Documentation

.08 Updates

.09 Conferences

SECTION 5. SMALL CASE PROCEDURE FOR REQUESTING COMPETENT AUTHORITY ASSISTANCE

.01 General

.02 Small Case Standards

.03 Small Case Filing Procedure

¶1712

¶1721 DISCUSSION QUESTIONS

1. Your client, State-Side Corporation, is a wholly owned U.S. subsidiary of Overseas, a large foreign conglomerate. State-Side purchases all its inventory from Overseas as well as paying Overseas a substantial management fee. You have asked State-Side on several occasions for documentation to support the intercompany charges but with no success. You don't believe the intracorporate pricing is tax motivated. The IRS has recently notified State-Side of an examination by the IRS, which has assigned an International Examiner. As an independent public accountant, what course of action, if any, would you recommend that State-Side take?

2. Rust Belt Manufacturing Company's founder and chief executive officer takes pride in the fact that the company has always concluded its IRS examinations within three months of its initial meeting with the Appeals office. However, this is the Company's first examination by an International Examiner. The amount of income potentially subjected to double taxation (U.S. and foreign tax) is in excess of $500,000. As the one (and only) person in the tax department of Rust Belt, you have been asked to prepare a list of the advantages and disadvantages of pursuing competent authority relief.

3. The controller of Little Swiss, a subsidiary located in Geneva, has not responded to any requests for information as part of an IRS examination of Big Swiss, Inc., its U.S. parent. The controller in Geneva claims it would violate Swiss secrecy laws to disclose the information sought by the IRS. Does the controller have any legal basis for not providing this information to the IRS? Explain in full.

4. As a newly trained International Examiner, you have recently been assigned to your first examination. The examination is of Mega Corporation, a publicly held company with 30 foreign subsidiaries. Mega employs 60 full-time tax professionals. How would you approach the examination?

5. Corrugated U.S.A., is a corporation that manufactures machinery used in the paper industry. Corrugated International, a wholly owned subsidiary of Corrugated U.S.A., is located in Zurich, Switzerland. The IRS conducts an audit of Corrugated U.S.A. and, in connection with an examination of intercompany transfers between Corrugated U.S.A. and Corrugated International, the IRS has asked to see the books of Corrugated International. In the absence of voluntary compliance, the IRS issues a summons to Corrugated U.S.A., requesting the books and records of Corrugated International. Corrugated U.S.A., contends that the IRS is precluded from using a summons to gather information on Corrugated International since the business records are held in Switzerland. Must Corrugated U.S.A., comply with the summons?

6. George Washington, a U.S. citizen, has a $20,000 bank account (the U.S. equivalent of British Pounds) in Redcoat Bank of England. George

Washington must file a TD F 90-22.1 with the Treasury Department in Detroit by June 30 of the following calendar year.

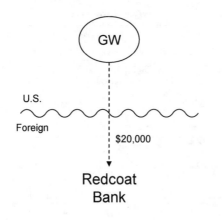

TD F 90-22.1 (Rev. November 2011) Department of the Treasury	**REPORT OF FOREIGN BANK** **AND FINANCIAL ACCOUNTS**	OMB No. 1545-2038

		1 This Report is for Calendar Year Ended 12/31
Do not use previous editions of **this form**	**Do NOT file with your Federal Tax Return**	__ __ __ __ Amended ☐

Part I   Filer Information

2   Type of Filer

  a ☐ Individual   **b** ☐ Partnership   **c** ☐ Corporation   **d** ☐ Consolidated   **e** ☐ Fiduciary or Other—Enter type _____

3   U.S. Taxpayer Identification Number
 	
If filer has no U.S. Identification
Number complete Item 4.
	4 Foreign identification (Complete only if item 3 is not applicable.)
	  a Type: ☐ Passport ☐ Other _____
	
	  b Number **c** Country of Issue
		5 Individual's Date of Birth
		MM/DD/YYYY

6 Last Name or Organization Name	**7** First Name	**8** Middle Initial

9   Address (Number, Street, and Apt. or Suite No.)

10 City	**11** State	**12** Zip/Postal Code	**13** Country

14   Does the filer have a financial interest in 25 or more financial accounts?

  ☐ Yes   If "Yes" enter total number of accounts _____

  (If "Yes" is checked, do not complete Part II or Part III, but retain records of this information)

  ☐ No

Part II   Information on Financial Account(s) Owned Separately

15 Maximum value of account during calendar year reported	**16** Type of account **a** ☐ Bank **b** ☐ Securities **c** ☐ Other—Enter type below

17   Name of Financial Institution in which account is held

18 Account number or other designation	**19** Mailing Address (Number, Street, Suite Number) of financial institution in which account is held

20 City	**21** State, if known	**22** Zip/Postal Code, if known	**23** Country

Signature

44 Filer Signature	**45** Filer Title, if not reporting a personal account	**46** Date (MM/DD/YYYY)

File this form with: U.S. Department of the Treasury, P.O. Box 32621, Detroit, MI 48232-0621

This form should be used to report a financial interest in, signature authority, or other authority over one or more financial accounts in foreign countries, as required by the Department of the Treasury Regulations 31 CFR 1010.350 (formerly 31 CFR 103.24). No report is required if the aggregate value of the accounts did not exceed $10,000. **See Instructions For Definitions.**

PRIVACY ACT AND PAPERWORK REDUCTION ACT NOTICE

Pursuant to the requirements of Public Law 93-579 (Privacy Act of 1974), notice is hereby given that the authority to collect information on TD F 90-22.1 in accordance with 5 USC 552a (e) is Public Law 91-508; 31 USC 5314; 5 USC 301; 31 CFR 1010.350 (formerly 31 CFR 103.24).

The principal purpose for collecting the information is to assure maintenance of reports where such reports or records have a high degree of usefulness in criminal, tax, or regulatory investigations or proceedings. The information collected may be provided to those officers and employees of any constituent unit of the Department of the Treasury who have a need for the records in the performance of their duties. The records may be referred to any other department or agency of the United States upon the request of the head of such department or agency for use in a criminal, tax, or regulatory investigation or proceeding. The information collected may also be provided to appropriate state, local, and foreign law enforcement and regulatory personnel in the performance of their official duties. Disclosure of this information is mandatory. Civil and criminal penalties, including in certain circumstances a fine of not more than $500,000 and imprisonment of not more than five years, are provided for failure to file a report, supply information, and for filing a false or fraudulent report. Disclosure of the Social Security number is mandatory. The authority to collect is 31 CFR 1010.350 (formerly 31 CFR 103.24) . The Social Security number will be used as a means to identify the individual who files the report.

The estimated average burden associated with this collection of information is 75 minutes per respondent or record keeper, depending on individual circumstances. Comments regarding the accuracy of this burden estimate, and suggestions for reducing the burden should be directed to the Internal Revenue Service, Bank Secrecy Act Policy, 5000 Ellin Road C-3-242, Lanham MD 20706.

Cat. No. 12996D   Form **TD F 90-22.1** (Rev. 3-2011)

Part II *Continued*—Information on Financial Account(s) Owned Separately				Form TD F 90-22.1

Complete a Separate Block for Each Account Owned Separately

Page Number

___ of ___

This side can be copied as many times as necessary in order to provide information on all accounts.

1 Filing for calendar year	3–4 Check appropriate Identification Number		6 Last Name or Organization Name
___ ___ ___ ___	☐ Taxpayer Identification Number ☐ Foreign Identification Number Enter identification number here:		

15 Maximum value of account during calendar year reported		16 Type of account a ☐ Bank b ☐ Securities c ☐ Other—Enter type below
17 Name of Financial Institution in which account is held		
18 Account number or other designation	19 Mailing Address (Number, Street, Suite Number) of financial institution in which account is held	
20 City	21 State, if known	22 Zip/Postal Code, if known 23 Country

15 Maximum value of account during calendar year reported		16 Type of account a ☐ Bank b ☐ Securities c ☐ Other—Enter type below
17 Name of Financial Institution in which account is held		
18 Account number or other designation	19 Mailing Address (Number, Street, Suite Number) of financial institution in which account is held	
20 City	21 State, if known	22 Zip/Postal Code, if known 23 Country

15 Maximum value of account during calendar year reported		16 Type of account a ☐ Bank b ☐ Securities c ☐ Other—Enter type below
17 Name of Financial Institution in which account is held		
18 Account number or other designation	19 Mailing Address (Number, Street, Suite Number) of financial institution in which account is held	
20 City	21 State, if known	22 Zip/Postal Code, if known 23 Country

15 Maximum value of account during calendar year reported		16 Type of account a ☐ Bank b ☐ Securities c ☐ Other—Enter type below
17 Name of Financial Institution in which account is held		
18 Account number or other designation	19 Mailing Address (Number, Street, Suite Number) of financial institution in which account is held	
20 City	21 State, if known	22 Zip/Postal Code, if known 23 Country

15 Maximum value of account during calendar year reported		16 Type of account a ☐ Bank b ☐ Securities c ☐ Other—Enter type below
17 Name of Financial Institution in which account is held		
18 Account number or other designation	19 Mailing Address (Number, Street, Suite Number) of financial institution in which account is held	
20 City	21 State, if known	22 Zip/Postal Code, if known 23 Country

15 Maximum value of account during calendar year reported		16 Type of account a ☐ Bank b ☐ Securities c ☐ Other—Enter type below
17 Name of Financial Institution in which account is held		
18 Account number or other designation	19 Mailing Address (Number, Street, Suite Number) of financial institution in which account is held	
20 City	21 State, if known	22 Zip/Postal Code, if known 23 Country

Form **TD F 90-22.1** (Rev. 3-2011)

¶1721

Part III Information on Financial Account(s) Owned Jointly	Form TD F 90-22.1

Complete a Separate Block for Each Account Owned Jointly

This side can be copied as many times as necessary in order to provide information on all accounts.

Page Number
____ of ____

1 Filing for calendar year ____ ____ ____ ____	3-4 Check appropriate Identification Number ☐ Taxpayer Identification Number ☐ Foreign Identification Number Enter identification number here:	6 Last Name or Organization Name

15 Maximum value of account during calendar year reported	16 Type of account a ☐ Bank b ☐ Securities c ☐ Other—Enter type below
17 Name of Financial Institution in which account is held	

18 Account number or other designation	19 Mailing Address (Number, Street, Suite Number) of financial institution in which account is held

20 City	21 State, if known	22 Zip/Postal Code, if known	23 Country

24 Number of joint owners for this account	25 Taxpayer Identification Number of principal joint owner, if known. See instructions.

26 Last Name or Organization Name of principal joint owner	27 First Name of principal joint owner, if known	28 Middle initial, if known

29 Address (Number, Street, Suite or Apartment) of principal joint owner, if known

30 City, if known	31 State, if known	32 Zip/Postal Code, if known	33 Country, if known

15 Maximum value of account during calendar year reported	16 Type of account a ☐ Bank b ☐ Securities c ☐ Other—Enter type below
17 Name of Financial Institution in which account is held	

18 Account number or other designation	19 Mailing Address (Number, Street, Suite Number) of financial institution in which account is held

20 City	21 State, if known	22 Zip/Postal Code, if known	23 Country

24 Number of joint owners for this account	25 Taxpayer Identification Number of principal joint owner, if known. See instructions.

26 Last Name or Organization Name of principal joint owner	27 First Name of principal joint owner, if known	28 Middle initial, if known

29 Address (Number, Street, Suite or Apartment) of principal joint owner, if known

30 City, if known	31 State, if known	32 Zip/Postal Code, if known	33 Country, if known

15 Maximum value of account during calendar year reported	16 Type of account a ☐ Bank b ☐ Securities c ☐ Other—Enter type below
17 Name of Financial Institution in which account is held	

18 Account number or other designation	19 Mailing Address (Number, Street, Suite Number) of financial institution in which account is held

20 City	21 State, if known	22 Zip/Postal Code, if known	23 Country

24 Number of joint owners for this account	25 Taxpayer Identification Number of principal joint owner, if known. See instructions.

26 Last Name or Organization Name of principal joint owner	27 First Name of principal joint owner, if known	28 Middle initial, if known

29 Address (Number, Street, Suite or Apartment) of principal joint owner, if known

30 City, if known	31 State, if known	32 Zip/Postal Code, if known	33 Country, if known

Form **TD F 90-22.1** (Rev. 3-2011)

¶1721

Part IV Information on Financial Account(s) Where Filer has Signature Authority but No Financial Interest in the Account(s)			Form TD F 90-22.1 Page Number
Complete a Separate Block for Each Account			____ of ____
This side can be copied as many times as necessary in order to provide information on all accounts.			

1 Filing for calendar year ____ ____ ____ ____	3–4 Check appropriate Identification Number ☐ Taxpayer Identification Number ☐ Foreign Identification Number Enter identification number here:	6 Last Name or Organization Name

15 Maximum value of account during calendar year reported	16 Type of account **a** ☐ Bank **b** ☐ Securities **c** ☐ Other—Enter type below

17 Name of Financial Institution in which account is held			

18 Account number or other designation	19 Mailing Address (Number, Street, Suite Number) of financial institution in which account is held		

20 City	21 State, if known	22 Zip/Postal Code, if known	23 Country

34 Last Name or Organization Name of Account Owner	35 Taxpayer Identification Number of Account Owner

36 First Name	37 Middle initial	38 Address (Number, Street, and Apt. or Suite No.)

39 City	40 State	41 Zip/Postal Code	42 Country

43 Filer's Title with this Owner

15 Maximum value of account during calendar year reported	16 Type of account **a** ☐ Bank **b** ☐ Securities **c** ☐ Other—Enter type below

17 Name of Financial Institution in which account is held			

18 Account number or other designation	19 Mailing Address (Number, Street, Suite Number) of financial institution in which account is held		

20 City	21 State, if known	22 Zip/Postal Code, if known	23 Country

34 Last Name or Organization Name of Account Owner	35 Taxpayer Identification Number of Account Owner

36 First Name	37 Middle initial	38 Address (Number, Street, and Apt. or Suite No.)

39 City	40 State	41 Zip/Postal Code	42 Country

43 Filer's Title with this Owner

15 Maximum value of account during calendar year reported	16 Type of account **a** ☐ Bank **b** ☐ Securities **c** ☐ Other—Enter type below

17 Name of Financial Institution in which account is held			

18 Account number or other designation	19 Mailing Address (Number, Street, Suite Number) of financial institution in which account is held		

20 City	21 State, if known	22 Zip/Postal Code, if known	23 Country

34 Last Name or Organization Name of Account Owner	35 Taxpayer Identification Number of Account Owner

36 First Name	37 Middle initial	38 Address (Number, Street, and Apt. or Suite No.)

39 City	40 State	41 Zip/Postal Code	42 Country

43 Filer's Title with this Owner

Form **TD F 90-22.1** (Rev. 3-2011)

Part V Information on Financial Account(s) Where the Filer is Filing a Consolidated Report	Form TD F 90-22.1
	Page Number

Complete a Separate Block for Each Account

This side can be copied as many times as necessary in order to provide information on all accounts.

_____ of _____

1 Filing for calendar year	3–4 Check appropriate Identification Number	6 Last Name or Organization Name
____ ____ ____ ____	☐ Taxpayer Identification Number ☐ Foreign Identification Number Enter identification number here:	

15 Maximum value of account during calendar year reported	16 Type of account **a** ☐ Bank **b** ☐ Securities **c** ☐ Other—Enter type below

17 Name of Financial Institution in which account is held

18 Account number or other designation	19 Mailing Address (Number, Street, Suite Number) of financial institution in which account is held

20 City	21 State, if known	22 Zip/Postal Code, if known	23 Country

34 Corporate Name of Account Owner	35 Taxpayer Identification Number of Account Owner

38 Address (Number, Street, and Apt. or Suite No.)

39 City	40 State	41 Zip/Postal Code	42 Country

15 Maximum value of account during calendar year reported	16 Type of account **a** ☐ Bank **b** ☐ Securities **c** ☐ Other—Enter type below

17 Name of Financial Institution in which account is held

18 Account number or other designation	19 Mailing Address (Number, Street, Suite Number) of financial institution in which account is held

20 City	21 State, if known	22 Zip/Postal Code, if known	23 Country

34 Corporate Name of Account Owner	35 Taxpayer Identification Number of Account Owner

38 Address (Number, Street, and Apt. or Suite No.)

39 City	40 State	41 Zip/Postal Code	42 Country

15 Maximum value of account during calendar year reported	16 Type of account **a** ☐ Bank **b** ☐ Securities **c** ☐ Other—Enter type below

17 Name of Financial Institution in which account is held

18 Account number or other designation	19 Mailing Address (Number, Street, Suite Number) of financial institution in which account is held

20 City	21 State, if known	22 Zip/Postal Code, if known	23 Country

34 Corporate Name of Account Owner	35 Taxpayer Identification Number of Account Owner

38 Address (Number, Street, and Apt. or Suite No.)

39 City	40 State	41 Zip/Postal Code	42 Country

Form **TD F 90-22.1** (Rev. 3-2011)

CHAPTER 18
CRIMINAL TAX PROCEDURE

¶1801 INTRODUCTION TO CRIMINAL TAX INVESTIGATIONS

Our system of taxation is based on the concept of voluntary compliance with the Internal Revenue laws. To encourage compliance and deter taxpayers from violating the law, the Criminal Investigation Division (CID) personnel of the IRS investigates and recommends prosecution of those who commit tax offenses. The specially trained field agents who conduct these criminal investigations hold the title of "Special Agent."

Information from various sources may prompt a criminal tax investigation. A routine examination by a revenue agent may disclose indications of fraud. A disgruntled employee, spurned lover, estranged wife, business associate, neighbor or acquaintance may furnish incriminating information to CID. Newspaper articles and other news reports may reveal activity that suggests possible tax evasion. Information obtained during a routine audit or criminal investigation of one taxpayer may implicate another taxpayer. Information returns filed with the IRS, such as Forms 1099 and W-2, may disclose unreported income. Reports of currency transactions in excess of $10,000 which must be filed with the IRS also may provide a basis for initiating a criminal investigation.[1]

¶1802 STATUTORY OFFENSES

Most statutues under which the IRS may prosecute tax crimes are found in the Code. However, the IRS may also charge some broadly defined crimes such as conspiracy, which is in the Criminal Code, Title 18 of the United States Code. In addition, Title 31 of the United States Code contains the criminal penalties enforced by CID for violating the currency and other reporting requirements of the Bank Secrecy Act.

¶1803 CRIMES UNDER THE INTERNAL REVENUE CODE

The principal offenses under the Internal Revenue Code are contained in Code Secs. 7201 through 7207. These criminal statutes seek to punish only those who "willfully" violate the law. The Supreme Court has defined the term "willfully" to mean "a voluntary, intentional violation of a known legal duty."[2] Under this definition, ignorance of the tax law or a misunderstanding of that law is a valid defense to any of these tax charges regardless of how objectively unreasonable

---

[1] Banks and other financial institutions must report currency transactions in excess of $10,000 on Form FinCen 104. See 31 U.S.C. §5313 and 31 CFR §103.22. Any person engaged in a trade or business who receives more than $10,000 in currency also must report the transaction on Form 8300, Code Sec. 6050I.

[2] *United States v. Pomponio*, 429 U.S. 10, 12 (1976), 76-2 USTC ¶9695, quoting *United States v. Bishop*, 412 U.S. 346, 360 (1973), 73-1 USTC ¶9459.

such a claim may appear.[3] However, the jury or judge weighs the credibility of testimony that a defendant believed in good faith that he or she was not violating the tax laws.[4]

Tax Evasion. Code Sec. 7201 provides that "any person who *willfully* attempts in any manner to evade the payment or evasion of any tax" is guilty of a felony. To convict anyone of tax evasion, the government must prove three elements: (1) a tax deficiency, (2) an affirmative act constituting an evasion or attempted evasion of the tax, and (3) willfulness.[5] The government may prove understatement of tax either by the specific-item method or by one of the indirect methods of reconstructing income discussed in Chapter 19, *infra*. With the specific-item method, the government attempts to prove that the taxpayer intentionally omitted individual items of income or falsely reported specific expenses.

An affirmative act constituting an attempt to evade or defeat a tax is any conduct, "the likely effect of which would be to mislead or conceal."[6] Filing a false or fraudulent tax return is the affirmative act most frequently cited as the basis for an evasion charge.

> **Example 18-1:** Governor receives payoffs to sell liquor licenses to a favored campaign contributor. Instead of reporting the payoffs as ordinary income on his return, Governor reports the payoffs as the receipt of proceeds from the sale of partnership interests that would constitute lightly-taxed capital gain income. Governor's filing the return is an affirmative act to willfully evade tax that created a tax deficiency. Therefore, Governor is guilty of tax evasion.

Other examples of an affirmative act include: (1) keeping a double set of books, (2) making false entries or alterations, (3) making false invoices or documents, (4) destroying books or records, (5) concealing assets or covering up sources of income (6) lying to the IRS personnel, and (7) handling one's affairs to avoid making the usual records in such transactions.[7]

Mere failure to file a return does not constitute an affirmative act.

> **Example 18-2:** Suppose that a drug dealer earns $10 million of income during the taxable year but never files an income tax return. After his conviction for dealing drugs, an IRS agent interviews him with respect to the unfiled return and the drug dealer states that he earned $10 million, but that he never filed a return. Although the drug dealer may be convicted of the misdemeanor for failure to file a return (see below), the drug dealer has not

---

[3] See *Cheek v. United States,* 498 U.S. 192 (1991), 91-1 USTC ¶50,012. The defendant in *Cheek* testified that he believed his wages did not constitute taxable income and did not have to be reported. See *Ratzlaf v. United States,* 510 U.S. 135 (1994), 94-1 USTC ¶50,015. The Government must prove that the defendant acted with knowledge that his conduct was unlawful. *Cf. Bryan v. United States,* 524 U.S. 184 (1998). In *Bryan* the Court distinguished *Cheeks* and *Ratzlaf* by explaining that the highly technical stat-

utes of those cases carved out an exception from the traditional rule that ignorance of the law is no excuse.

[4] *Id.*

[5] See *Sansone v. United States,* 380 U.S. 343, 351 (1965), 65-1 USTC ¶9307; *United States v. Eaken,* 17 F.3d 203 (7th Cir. 1994), 94-1 USTC ¶50,098.

[6] *Spies v. United States,* 317 U.S. 492, 499 (1943), 43-1 USTC ¶9243.

[7] *Id.*

committed an affirmative act necessary for a tax evasion conviction. However, if the drug dealer lies and says he did not earn any income during that taxable year, the lie constitutes the affirmative act necessary for a tax evasion conviction.

In evasion cases, "willfulness" is the element most frequently contested.[8] As previously discussed, the government must prove the taxpayer intentionally, not inadvertently, understated his or her taxes and knew that to do so was wrong. Unless the taxpayer has admitted wrongdoing, "willfulness" is normally proved by means of circumstantial evidence. Proof of substantial understatements over a period of years is one example of the circumstantial evidence to show willfulness.

There appears to be some controversy with respect to whether there is a fourth element to tax evasion—a substantial tax due and owing. Although the Supreme Court has recognized the split of the U.S. Circuit Court of Appeals, the Supreme Court has not chosen to address the issue.[9]

The maximum sentence under Code Sec. 7201 cannot exceed five years of imprisonment and a fine of either $100,000 for individuals or $500,000 for corporations.[10] Technically, each count of an indictment charging tax evasion subjects the defendant to the maximum term of imprisonment and fine. Therefore, an individual taxpayer charged with evasion over a three-year period could be sentenced to a maximum term of imprisonment for 15 years and a maximum fine of $300,000. As a practical matter, however, the Federal Sentencing Guidelines that Congress established provide narrow parameters within which to sentence and fine a defendant.[11] The Guidelines have increased the average sentence of imprisonment imposed on tax offenders. The mandatory term of imprisonment for tax evasion falls within a narrow range and is based on the tax loss determined for the years under investigation and the criminal history of the defendant.[12]

False Return. Code Sec. 7206(1) imposes criminal sanctions on any person who *willfully* signs "any return . . . or other document verified by a written declaration that it is made under the penalties of perjury . . . which [the signer] does not believe to be true and correct as to every material matter." To convict anyone of filing a false return, the government must prove four elements: (1) the signing of a return, statement, or other document, (2) under penalties of perjury, (3) that the signer did not believe to be true in every respect, and (4) with willfulness.

The IRS frequently recommends a false return charge when it appears that the IRS may have difficulty proving a tax deficiency or understatement for tax evasion. Unlike tax evasion, a false return charge does not require proof that tax

---

[8] *U.S. v. Pomponio*, 429 U.S. 10 (1976).

[9] *Boulware v. United States*, 128 S.Ct. 1168 (2008).

[10] Maximum fines for all felonies have been established at not more than $250,000 for individuals and $500,000 for organizations. 18 U.S.C. § 3571.

[11] *Id.* §§ 3551-3586. For specific guidelines, see the *Federal Sentencing Guidelines* published annually in Title 18 of the United States Code.

[12] See *United States Sentencing Commission Guidelines Manual*, §§ 2T1.1, 2T1.4, 2T1.6, 2T1.9 and 2T4.1.

was understated. The government only has to prove that the taxpayer falsified one "material" item on the tax return. If a taxpayer has understated gross business receipts, but has offsetting unreported deductions as a potential defense to tax evasion, the government may simply resort to a false return charge rather than an evasion charge to avoid the doubt raised by such a defense. Proof of the intentionally false gross receipts would be sufficient for a false return conviction.

The materiality of a false item on the return depends on whether a return is true and correct for examination purposes.[13] Obviously, substantial amounts of gross income or deductions falsely reported on a tax return would be material. Moreover, the false description of illegal kickbacks as miscellaneous interest income is material and may be prosecuted even though there is not a deficiency.[14]

> **Example 18-3:** Suppose that the CEO of a Fortune 500 company has his return prepared by Conrad The Idiot, who learned everything he knows about tax during the two days tax was covered in his eleventh grade accounting class before he dropped out of school. When the two review the prepared return, the CEO realizes he is not entitled to the $400,000 deduction for the total cost of his summer home. Conrad replies that the CEO should just sign the return and send it in, which the CEO does. The CEO has filed a false return.

The maximum sentence for subscribing to a false return or other document is three years imprisonment and a fine of $100,000 for individuals or $500,000 for corporations. For all practical purposes, however, the Federal Sentencing Guidelines will control the actual prison term and fine for this felony.

Aiding or Assisting. The aiding or assisting crime under Codes Sec. 7206(2) prosecutes those who *willfully*, assist with the preparation of a false return with respect to any material matter. To convict anyone of this felony, the government must prove four elements: (1) aiding or assisting with respect to the preparation of any tax-related document, (2) falsity (and knowing it was false), (3) materiality, and (4) willfulness. This provision is primarily directed at accountants, attorneys and others who prepare false returns or provide advice or information for tax return purposes that is knowingly false. The government is not required to prove that the taxpayer filing the false return or other document was aware of or consented to the fraud. The maximum term of imprisonment and maximum fine for aiding or assisting are the same as those for filing a false return, and the Federal Sentencing Guidelines will control the actual sentence imposed.

> **Example 18-4:** Suppose that a preparer prepares a return for his client that intentionally understates income and overstates deductions. The preparer has committed the crime of aiding or assisting.

Failure to File. Code Sec. 7203 contains the crime for those who *willfully* fail to file returns.[15] To convict anyone of this crime, the government must prove four

---

[13] *United States v. Nicolaoce*, 83 AFTR2d 2821 (4th Cir. 1999).

[14] See *United States v. Hedman*, 630 F.2d 1184 (7th Cir. 1980), *cert. denied*, 450 U.S. 965 (1981).

[15] Code Sec. 7203 also punishes willful failure to pay taxes, maintain records or supply information, but is rarely used for these purposes. If any Code

elements: (1) failure to file a return, (2) by a person under a legal duty to do so, (3) at a time required by law, and (4) willfulness. This is a misdemeanor, a lesser crime, which recognizes that the failure to act should be punished less severely than an affirmative act of fraud. However, if the failure to file is accompanied by some affirmative act that is intended to mislead or conceal, such as the submission to an employer of a false Form W-4 claiming tax-exempt status, the failure to file together with such affirmative act can be charged as an attempt to evade tax under Code Sec. 7201.

> **Example 18-5:** Suppose that a drug dealer earns $10 million of income during the taxable year but never files an income tax return. After his conviction for dealing drugs, an IRS agent interviews him with respect to the unfiled return and the drug dealer states that he earned $10 million, but that he never filed a return. The drug dealer may be convicted of the misdemeanor under Code Sec. 7203 for failure to file a return.

The maximum sentence for failure to file is one year of imprisonment and a fine of $25,000 for individuals and $100,000 for corporations.[16] Because each yearly failure to file a return constitutes a separate charge, the maximum sentence is cumulative for anyone who has willfully failed to file over a period of years. As a practical matter, however, the Federal Sentencing Guidelines will control the term of imprisonment and the amount of fine within narrow limits which are normally well below the statutory maximum. The tax loss is the amount of the additional tax that the taxpayer should have reported on the unfiled returns. The sentence imposed under the Guidelines may therefore increase with the increase in the number of years returns were not filed.

Altered or False Documents. Code Sec. 7207 imposes liability on anyone who *willfully* submits or delivers to the IRS any document knowing it to be fraudulent or false as to any material matter. To convict anyone of this misdemeanor, the government must prove five elements: (1) tender a document to the IRS, (2) falsity, (3) knowledge of the falsity, (4) willfulness, and (5) materiality. This offense is a misdemeanor punishable by a maximum term of imprisonment for one year and a maximum fine of $10,000 for individuals or $50,000 for corporations. The Federal Sentencing Guidelines, however, will determine the actual sentence to be imposed.

The government has limited use of this misdemeanor charge to cases involving fraudulently altered documents, such as invoices and checks, submitted by taxpayers to IRS agents for the purpose of improperly gaining some tax benefit.

> **Example 18-6:** Taxpayer alters a cancelled check submitted to support a charitable contribution by raising the amount on the check from $50 to $500. Taxpayer has committed the crime of providing a false document.

(Footnote Continued)

Sec. 6050I willful violation occurs, the Code Sec. 7203 sentence is increased to five years.

[16] The maximum fine for all misdemeanors authorizing a maximum sentence of more than six months but not more than one year has been established at $100,000 for individuals and $200,000 for organizations. 18 U.S.C. §§ 3559(a)(6), 3571(b)(5) and (c)(5).

Other Code Offenses. Code Sec. 7204 is aimed at employers who *willfully* file false Forms W-2 or fail to furnish such forms to their employees. Code Sec. 7205 represents the converse of Code Sec. 7204 and penalizes employees who willfully submit false Forms W-4 or fail to submit such forms to their employers. Both crimes are misdemeanors punishable by a maximum of one year in prison and a maximum fine of $1,000. The actual sentence will be determined under the Federal Sentencing Guidelines.

Other criminal provisions punish the willful failure to collect or pay over tax by persons responsible for withholding and paying over employment taxes (a felony under Code Sec. 7202), failure to obey a summons (a misdemeanor under Code Sec. 7210), attempts to interfere with the administration of the Internal Revenue laws (a felony under Code Sec. 7212), unauthorized disclosure of information (a felony under Code Sec. 7213), and disclosure or use of information by preparers of returns (a misdemeanor under Code Sec. 7216).

Lesser-Included Offenses. When requesting a jury instruction for a felony, such as tax evasion, the defendant or the government may request a jury instruction that provides a lesser-included offense, such as the misdemeanor for failure to file a return. The defendant may seek such an instruction to give the court the opportunity to impose a misdemeanor instead of a felony. The government may seek such a jury instruction if it believes that its tax evasion case is not strong. A lesser-included offense instruction is only appropriate when the greater offense charged requires the court to find a disputed factual element that is not required for conviction of the lesser-included offense.[17]

Federal Sentencing Guidelines. As noted in the description of the previous tax crimes, the Code states a maximum sentence, but the courts will impose a sentence pursuant to the Federal Sentencing Guidelines. Those Guidelines require sentencing of a specific number of months in prison pursuant to a Sentencing Table (see Exhibit 18-1 at ¶ 1821). Those guidelines determine a range of months of imprisonment based on both a criminal history (see Exhibit 18-2, ¶ 1822) and an offense level based on the amount of tax lost (see Exhibit 18-3, ¶ 1823). The court can increase the base offense level due to specific offense characteristics and reduce the base offense level due to the acceptance of responsibility (see Exhibit 18-4, ¶ 1824).

> **Example 18-7:** Schemer pleads guilty to tax evasion that results in a loss to the federal government of $50,000 of tax. Schemer does not have any criminal history, Schemer did not exhibit any specific offense characteristics nor did he accept responsibility for his actions. With a base offense level of 14 and zero criminal history points, the recommended sentence is imprisonment of 15 to 21 months.

Voluntary Disclosure Practice. It is currently the practice of the IRS that a voluntary disclosure will be considered along with all other factors in the investigation when determining whether to recommend criminal prosecution.

---

[17] *Sansone v. United States*, 380 U.S. 343 (1965).

¶1803

A voluntary disclosure will not guarantee immunity from prosecution, yet a voluntary disclosure may result in a no prosecution recommendation. However, since the IRS application of the voluntary disclosure practice does not automatically result in immunity from criminal prosecution, taxpayers should be advised that they cannot rely on the fact that others may not have been prosecuted. A voluntary disclosure occurs when the communication is:

(a) truthful;

(b) timely;

(c) complete;

(d) when the taxpayer shows a willingness to cooperate (and does in fact cooperate) with the IRS in determining his or her correct tax liability.

A disclosure is timely if it is received before:

(a) The IRS has initiated an inquiry that is likely to lead to the taxpayer, and the taxpayer is reasonably thought to be aware of that investigative activity.

(b) Some event known by the taxpayer occurs that would be likely to cause an audit into the taxpayer's liabilities.[18]

¶1804 OFFENSES UNDER THE CRIMINAL CODE

The Criminal Code contains several offenses which are frequently charged in tax prosecutions. These crimes involve conspiracies, false statements, false claims and money laundering and are in Title 18 of the United States Code.

Conspiracy. Any two or more persons who conspire against the United States shall be guilty of a felony punishable by a maximum term of imprisonment for five years and/or a fine.[19] To convict anyone of this felony, the government must prove four elements: (1) the defendant and at least one other person agree to either defraud or commit an offense against the United States, (2) the defendant knew the unlawful purpose of the agreement, (3) the defendant joined in it willfully, with the intent to further the unlawful purpose, and (4) one of the conspirators, during the conspiracy, knowingly committed at least one overt act in an effort to accomplish the conspiracy The maximum fine for conspiracy is $250,000 for individuals and $500,000 for corporations. The Federal Sentencing Guidelines set the term of imprisonment and fine to be imposed for conspiracies committed.

The conspiracy statute is extremely broad in its coverage. In tax cases where two or more persons agree to commit an offense under the Internal Revenue Code, such as tax evasion, they may be prosecuted for the conspiracy as well as the underlying tax crime. The government must prove not only an agreement but also at least one "overt act" in furtherance of the conspiracy. The overt act need not be illegal in itself and circumstantial evidence may prove the agreement. Government prosecutors favor the conspiracy charge because it permits trying

---

[18] IRM 9.5.11.9.   [19] 18 U.S.C. §371.

number of defendants at the same time and allows the widest possible latitude in the offering of evidence.

> **Example 18-8:** Suppose that a client engages a preparer to prepare a return that intentionally understates income and overstates deductions. Preparer agrees and prepares such a return that the client files. Both client and preparer are guilty of conspiracy to commit tax evasion.

This charge also punishes conspiracies to defraud the United States or any of its agencies in any manner and for any purpose. To conspire to defraud the United States means to interfere with or obstruct one of its lawful governmental functions by deceit, craft or trickery, or by means that are dishonest.[20] In tax cases, the government will prosecute a conspiracy to defraud "by impeding, obstructing and defeating the lawful functions of the Department of the Treasury in the collection of the revenue, to wit, income taxes."[21] This extremely broad charge encompasses all forms of deceitful actions that interfere with the administration of the tax laws.

False Statements. Any person who knowingly and willfully makes a false statement to the United States shall be guilty of a felony punishable by a maximum term of imprisonment for five years.[22] The maximum fine is $250,000 for individuals and $500,000 for organizations. As in all other cases involving federal crimes, the Federal Sentencing Guidelines control the actual sentence and fine imposed. To convict anyone of this felony, the government must prove four elements: (1) the defendant made a false statement to the United States, (2) the defendant intentionally made the statement, knowing it was false, (3) the defendant made the false statement to mislead the government, and (4) the statement was material.

The false statements offense applies not only to false written statements or documents submitted to an IRS agent, but also to any false oral statements made to such agents. Such statements do not have to be made under oath or under the penalties of perjury. False oral statements made to a revenue agent during seemingly informal discussions can be the basis for prosecution.

> **Example 18-9:** Suppose that a son rents a room at his mother's house and deducts the rent as a business expense for his office. When auditing the son, a revenue agent meets with the son's mother who lies that the son used the room exclusively for business purposes, when she knows that her son took the room for personal use. The son's mother has committed the crime of knowingly and willfully making a false statement.

---

[20] See *Hammerschmidt v. United States*, 265 U.S. 182 (1924).

[21] *United States v. Klein*, 247 F.2d 908, 915 (2d Cir. 1957), 57-2 USTC ¶ 9912. This case provided the genesis for the term "Klein Conspiracy," which has become the generic term for a conspiracy to frustrate the government, particularly the IRS, in its lawful information-gathering function. See *United States v.*

Alston, 77 F.3d 713, 717 n. 13 (3d Cir. 1996). The Second Circuit has held that the *Klein* indictment language is not legally required in indictments for conspiracy to defraud if the essential nature of the fraud is alleged. See *United States v. Helmsley*, 941 F.2d 71 (2d Cir. 1991), 91-2 USTC ¶ 50,455, *cert. denied*, 502 U.S. 1091 (1992).

[22] 18 U.S.C. § 1001.

¶1804

False Claims. Anyone who knowingly makes a false claim against the United States shall be guilty of a felony.[23] To convict anyone of this felony, the government must prove three elements: (1) the defendant knowingly made a false claim, (2) against the United States, and (3) the defendant knew the claim was false. The principal use of this section in tax cases is the prosecution of fraudulent refund claims.

> **Example 18-10:** Suppose that Bowie timely files a tax return with a tax payment of $50,000. Bowie decides he needs money to invest in chinchilla breeding and files a false refund claim that creates erroneous overstated deductions that result in a refund of $20,000. Bowie has committed the crime of making a false claim.

Mail Fraud and Wire Fraud. It is a crime to conduct any scheme to defraud through use of the U.S. mail or transmit any information by wire, radio or television for the purpose of executing such scheme.[24] This law enables the prosecution of all types of fraud, particularly those that are not covered by any specific federal law. The elements of U.S. mail or interstate wire transmissions were added to create the necessary federal jurisdictional nexus to the power to regulate foreign and interstate commerce.[25]

To convict anyone of mail fraud, the government must prove three elements: (1) the defendant knowingly created a scheme to defraud, (2) the defendant acted with specific intent to commit fraud, and (3) the defendant posted something through the mail for purposes of carrying out a scheme. To convict anyone of wire fraud, the government must also prove three elements: (1) the defendant knowingly created a scheme to defraud, (2) the defendant acted with specific intent to commit fraud, and (3) the defendant used interstate wire communication facilities to carry out the scheme.

Mail and wire fraud charges are often asserted in tax prosecutions of fraudulent schemes involving tax shelters, charitable contributions, money laundering and investment securities. There is some doubt that such charges may be used in a straightforward tax evasion case where the mail fraud is based solely on the mailing of a false return.[26]

Money Laundering. It is a crime to conceal, launder and use money derived from unlawful activities.[27] These money laundering sanctions contain very severe criminal penalties and forfeiture provisions. The Federal Sentencing Guidelines impose equally harsh penalties. Anyone may be subject to prosecution who attempts to launder or deposit funds that are known to have come from specified unlawful activities,[28] which excludes tax crimes. However, the attempt to laun-

---

[23] 18 U.S.C. § 287.

[24] 18 U.S.C. § § 1341 and 1343.

[25] *U.S. v. Dale*, 991 F.2d 819 (D.C. Cir. 1993) cert. denied 510 U.S. 906.

[26] Compare *United States v. Henderson*, 386 F. Supp. 1048 (S.D.N.Y. 1974), 74-2 USTC ¶ 9807 (charge dismissed), with *United States v. Miller*, 545 F.2d 1204 (9th Cir. 1976), 76-2 USTC ¶ 9809 (charge sus-

tained), *cert. denied*, 430 U.S. 930 (1977); and *United States v. Weatherspoon*, 581 F.2d 595 (7th Cir. 1978). The denial of certiorari in *Miller* should lend support to the government's use of mail fraud charges in tax evasion cases.

[27] 18 U.S.C. § § 1956 and 1957.

[28] See 18 U.S.C. § 1957(f)(1), which excludes from the crime of engaging in a "monetary transaction," in which illicit funds are received or deposited,

¶1804

der or conceal income from such illicit activities often relates to the commission of tax offenses, such as tax evasion, false returns or the failure to file.

Perjury. It is a crime to lie under oath.[29] A conviction can result in up to five years of imprisonment. To convict anyone of perjury, the government must prove four elements: (1) the defendant made an oral or written statement, (2) under oath or penalties of perjury, (3) knowing it to be false, and (4) as to any material matter.

> **Example 18-11:** Suppose that the CEO of a Fortune 500 company has his return prepared by Conrad The Idiot, who learned everything he knows about tax during the two days tax was covered in his eleventh grade accounting class before he dropped out of school. When the two review the prepared return, the CEO realizes he is not entitled to the $400,000 deduction for the total cost of his summer home. Conrad replies that the CEO should just sign the return and send it in, which the CEO does. The CEO has committed perjury.

¶1805 CRIMES UNDER THE BANK SECRECY ACT

The final group of tax-related offenses includes violations of the Bank Secrecy Act[30] The regulations under the Bank Secrecy Act[31] require financial institutions to file a report on Form 4790, whenever a person engages in a currency transaction of more than $10,000.[32] Banks and other financial institutions must also file a Suspicious Activity Report for transactions of $5,000 or more in "suspicious" circumstances as delineated by the Treasury Department on Form TD F 90-22, 47.[33]

In addition, any person who has an interest in a foreign financial account must disclose it on his or her income tax return. CID has jurisdiction over offenses under the Bank Secrecy Act. This offshore initiative is more fully described in ¶1708.

Closely related to the currency reporting requirements of the Bank Secrecy Act is the provision of Code Sec. 6050I that requires any person engaged in a trade or business who receives more than $10,000 in currency to report the transaction to the IRS. These reports are to be filed on Form 8300, Report of Cash Payments Over $10,000 Received in a Trade or Business. Willful failure to file

---

(Footnote Continued)

money received by an attorney for the representation of a defendant in a criminal case. However, if the transaction was undertaken with the knowledge that it was designed to launder the money or avoid any currency reporting requirements, the attorney could be found guilty of the offense of money laundering under 18 U.S.C. § 1956.

[29] 18 U.S.C. § 1621.

[30] Title 31 of the United States Code.

[31] 31 CFR §§ 103.22–103.28, 103.32, as amended 1987, 1989, 1994 and 1996.

[32] Section 5324 of Title 31 of the United States Code proscribes attempts to structure transactions

to avoid the reporting requirements. 31 U.S.C. § 5324 (West Supp. 2009). See also *Ratzlaf v. United States*, 510 U.S. 135 (1994), 94-1 USTC ¶ 50,015. The *Ratzlaf* court required the prosecution to prove that a defendant knew it was a crime to structure transactions to avoid the currency reporting requirements. Congress, however, later added to Code Sec. 5324 an express provision criminalizing simple violation of the statute, thus eliminating the willfulness requirement. See Money Laundering Suppression Act of 1994, P.L. 103-325, Title IV, §§ 411(a), 413(a)(2), 108 Stat. 2253, 2254.

[33] See 31 CFR § 103.21 (2009).

such currency transaction reports is specifically punishable as a felony.[34] The maximum term of imprisonment for such violations is five years, and the maximum fine is $25,000 for individuals or $100,000 for corporations. The Federal Sentencing Guidelines will determine the actual sentence length.

¶1806 STATUTE OF LIMITATIONS

The Internal Revenue Code contains a separate statute of limitations for criminal prosecution of tax offenses. Code Sec. 6531 provides that prosecution of the principal tax offenses under the Code must commence within six years of the commission of the offense. The six-year limitation period also applies to conspiracies to evade tax or to defraud the United States. The running of the statute of limitations is suspended during the time the person to be charged is either outside the United States or a fugitive from justice. A criminal action commences for purposes of complying with the limitations period when the grand jury returns an indictment or the government files an information with the court.

The criminal statute of limitations begins to run at the time the offense is committed or completed. The limitation period for failure to file runs from the due date or extended due date of the return. For the crime of subscribing to a false return, the six-year period is measured from the date the return is considered filed. The same rule applies to the offense of aiding or assisting in the preparation of a false return. The crime of submitting false documents is committed at the time the taxpayer submits the document to the government.

If the act of filing a false return is the basis for a tax evasion prosecution, the statute of limitations will begin to run from the date the tax return is deemed filed. However, when affirmative acts constituting attempts to evade tax occur after the return is filed, the six-year limitations period is measured from the date of those subsequent acts.[35] Altering records or making false statements to a revenue agent filing after a return are examples of acts that may extend the statute of limitations for tax evasion.[36]

> **Example 18-12:** Suppose that an individual earns $200,000 of income in 2010, but she does not file an income tax return, which would have been due on April 15, 2011. The six year statute of limitations to pursue a failure to file prosecution would be April 15, 2017. However, if the IRS interviews her on November 1, 2016 and she lies that she did not earn $200,000 of income in 2010, the statute of limitations for a tax evasion prosecution would extend six years from the date of that lie to November 1, 2022.

With the exception of conspiracy, the tax-related offenses found in the U.S. Criminal Code are subject to a five-year statute of limitations.[37] The six-year

---

[34] Code Sec. 7203.

[35] See *United States v. Beacon Brass Co.*, 344 U.S. 43 (1952), 52-2 USTC ¶9528; see also *United States v. Hunerlach*, 197 F.3d 1059 (11th Cir. 1999), 99-2 USTC ¶51,009, holding that the statute of limitations for willful evasion of payment of tax also begins to run from the last affirmative act of evasion, even if the act occurs past six years from the date the tax was due.

[36] *United States v. Ferris*, 807 F.2d 269 (1st Cir. 1986), 86-2 USTC ¶9844, *cert. denied*, 480 U.S. 950 (1987).

[37] See 18 U.S.C. § 3282 (2009).

period of limitations for conspiracy begins to run on the date the taxpayer conducts the last overt act in furtherance of the conspiracy.[38]

¶1807 REVENUE AGENT REFERRALS TO THE CRIMINAL INVESTIGATION DIVISION

Revenue agents follow special procedures, outlined in the Internal Revenue Manual, in handling audits of returns when indications of possible tax fraud exist.[39] If there is *only a suspicion* of fraud, called the "first indication of fraud," the revenue agent will attempt to gather more information concerning the suspected fraud during the course of the examination. The revenue agent will ask the taxpayer, the return preparer or any other involved party for an explanation of the issues that form the basis of the suspicion of fraud and will ask questions to determine the taxpayer's intent. If the examination convinces the revenue agent that there is a "firm indication of fraud," she will suspend auditing activities at the earliest opportunity without disclosing the reason to the taxpayer, the practitioner or employees.[40]

The determination of whether a firm indication of fraud exists is a factual one.[41] The revenue agent usually makes the determination after consulting with the group/team manager and/or an Examination Fraud Coordinator. If the reviewer concurs in the fraud determination, the revenue agent will then refer the case to CID. During this fraud evaluation process, the agent is instructed not to solicit an agreement from the taxpayer or to solicit and obtain delinquent returns prior to the submission of a fraud referral.[42]

If CID concurs that there are indications of possible fraud, CID will accept the case and assign a Special Agent. The Special Agent will then attempt to develop information sufficient to determine whether to recommend criminal prosecution.

¶1808 THE CRIMINAL INVESTIGATION

Criminal investigations receive classification as either numbered or unnumbered. Before a Special Agent determines whether grounds exist for a full-scale investigation, the case is unnumbered. If the case warrants a full-scale investigation, the IRS will assign a number and will refer to it thereafter as a numbered case. The Special Agent will continue the investigation of a numbered case until sufficient evidence is developed to recommend whether or not to prosecute the taxpayer. Normally both a Special Agent and a revenue agent, who assists in examining records, interviewing witnesses, and other matters, jointly conduct a full-scale investigation. The Special Agent, however, is in charge of the investigation.[43]

The Special Agent normally makes initial contact with the taxpayer without giving the taxpayer prior notice. The surprise visit is an important element in an

---

[38] Title 18 of the U.S. Code.

[39] IRM 25.1.2.

[40] IRM 25.1.3.2.

[41] Compare *Kontny v. U.S.*, 2001-1 USTC ¶50,197 (7th Cir. 2001), with *McKee v. U.S.*, 192 3d 535 (7th Cir. 1999), 99-2 USTC ¶50,867.

[42] IRM 25.1.2.

[43] IRM 25.1.4.3.

attempt to obtain spontaneous responses from the taxpayer that often provide the critical admissions or statements necessary for a successful prosecution. The Special Agent is always accompanied by another agent, who may at some later time appear as a corroborating witness.

At the initial meeting, the Special Agent must identify herself as such, produce credentials, and inform the taxpayer that one of a Special Agent's functions is to investigate the possibility of criminal violations of the Internal Revenue laws and related offenses.[44] The Special Agent must give a *Miranda*-type warning to inform the taxpayer that under the Fifth Amendment, she cannot be compelled to answer any questions or submit any information that might tend to be self-incriminating.[45] The taxpayer further learns of the right to the assistance of an attorney before responding.[46] This warning is not a constitutional requirement, however, because the taxpayer is not in a custodial setting.[47] Nevertheless, failure to give the warning, accompanied by affirmative efforts to mislead or deceive the taxpayer into believing that the investigation is not criminal in nature, but merely a routine civil examination, may be grounds for suppression of evidence obtained at the initial meeting.[48]

To establish an understatement of taxable income, the Special Agent will use either a specific item method or an indirect method of proof. The specific item method requires the agent to obtain evidence from books, records, documents and third parties that directly proves that specific items of income were not reported or that specific items of expense were falsely reported.[49] The indirect methods of proof, discussed in Chapter 19, *infra*, require the Special Agent to reconstruct taxable income by a thorough analysis of the taxpayer's financial affairs during the period under investigation. For example, the Special Agent will analyze the taxpayer's returns for at least five years preceding and all years subsequent to the starting point to furnish additional support for the use of a net-worth method of proof.[50]

The Special Agent can issue an administrative summonses to compel any person to give testimony or to produce records or documents (see discussion in Chapter 7, *supra*) under threat of or pursuant to court order. In certain circumstances, a Special Agent may also obtain a search warrant to seize records, documents and other evidence. To obtain a warrant, however, the Special Agent must first prepare to establish to the satisfaction of a Federal Magistrate Judge that there is probable cause to believe that a tax crime has been committed and that she will find evidence of such crime on the premises to be searched.[51] When

---

[44] IRM 9.4.5.11.3.1.

[45] The *Special Agent's Handbook* requires agents to inform taxpayers of constitutional rights in noncustodial interviews. *Id.*

[46] *Id.*, subsection 9384.2(2) (Rev. 9-16-93); HB 9781 §§342.132 (Rev. 10-19-92) and 342.16 (Rev. 4-9-84).

[47] *Stansbury v. California*, 511 U.S. 318 (1994); *Beckwith v. United States*, 425 U.S. 341 (1976), 76-1 USTC ¶9352.

[48] See *United States v. Serlin*, 707 F.2d 953 (7th Cir. 1983), 83-1 USTC ¶9368; *United States v. Tweel*, 550 F.2d 297 (5th Cir. 1977), 77-1 USTC ¶9330.

[49] IRM 9.5.9.2.1.

[50] *Id.*, subsection 9327(4) (Rev. 9-16-93). See Chapter 19, *infra*, on net-worth method. IRM 9.5.9.5.

[51] U.S. Const., Amend. IV; FED. R. CRIM. P. 41(e).

the investigation begins, there may not be sufficient evidence to establish such probable cause. The Special Agent may request a search warrant to prevent destruction or concealment of incriminating records. The Special Agent may also resort to a search warrant to seize personal or business records from a taxpayer that the Fifth Amendment would otherwise protect from compulsory production if a summons were to be used.[52]

A criminal tax investigation is a very slow and deliberate process. An investigation that continues for more than a year is common. A criminal tax investigation that continues for two or more years is not unusual.

¶1809 THE SPECIAL AGENT'S REPORT

On completing the investigation, the Special Agent will prepare a detailed Special Agent's Report (SAR) summarizing the findings, the supporting evidence and a recommendation regarding prosecution. If the Special Agent determines that no criminal violation has occurred or that a prosecution would not be successful, the Special Agent will discuss the findings with her manager and request approval from the Special Agent in Charge to close the case without prosecution.[53] When CID declines a criminal prosecution, the taxpayer will receive a letter from the IRS informing the taxpayer that he is no longer the subject of a criminal investigation, but that CID may re-enter the case if additional information becomes available to warrant such action (see Exhibit 18-5 at ¶1825).[54] If the Special Agent recommends prosecution, the supervisory Special Agent and the Special Agent in Charge will review the case. The taxpayer is then notified by letter that CID has recommended prosecution and CID is forwarding the case to the local Chief Counsel office for a review of the sufficiency of the evidence and a meeting with the taxpayer and/or his attorney.[55] Approval by Chief Counsel will result in further forwarding of the case to the United States Department of Justice, Tax Division, Criminal Section in Washington, D.C., for review.

¶1810 CONFERENCE OPPORTUNITIES

A case forwarded to the Tax Division of the Department of Justice for final review is conducted by a Justice attorney who is very experienced in criminal tax cases. Should the taxpayer request, in writing, a conference at this point, the request must be in writing, and the conference will be held in Washington, D.C. The Justice attorney will not consider plea bargaining at this conference. The Justice Department conference probably provides the best opportunity for convincing the government to decline prosecution. It should be noted, however, that if the government's case is shown to have weaknesses, the Justice attorney may simply forward the case to the United States Attorney with an authorization for a grand jury investigation to bolster the case with additional evidence.

If it does not decline prosecution, the Justice Department will refer the case to the appropriate U.S. Attorney for prosecution. The taxpayer may request a

---

[52] See *Andresen v. Maryland*, 427 U.S. 463 (1976).
[53] IRM 9.5.1.3.3.
[54] IRM 9.5.1.3.3.1.
[55] IRM 31.4.2.6.

conference before indictment to discuss the merits of the case or to enter into plea negotiations. The Justice attorney may refer the cas to the U.S. Attorney with or without discretion to prosecute. Prosecution is very rarely declined at this stage.

¶1811 EARLY PLEA PROCEDURE

If the taxpayer wishes to enter a guilty plea in the criminal proceedings, the referral to the Department of Justice is unnecessary. This early plea procedure is not available to any taxpayer that is either accused of tax crimes relating to income from illegal sources or not represented by counsel.[56] Under this procedure the taxpayer can enter into plea discussions while the case is still under investigation.[57]

Entering this early plea procedure will not have any effect on any civil tax liability. The IRS will simultaneously refer the case to both the U.S. Attorney for plea discussions and the Department of Justice.

Under the early plea procedure, any plea must include the most significant violation involved (the major count policy). Moreover, the IRS will consider the totality of the fraud conducted by the taxpayer in any plea discussions.[58]

¶1812 GRAND JURY INVESTIGATIONS

If either the administrative investigation process cannot develop the relevant facts within a reasonable period of time or it appears that coordination with an ongoing grand jury investigation would be more efficient, the CID may refer the matter to the Justice Department and request that a grand jury conduct a criminal tax investigation.[59] A case that is factually complex and involves numerous witnesses, some of whom are uncooperative, will be an appropriate candidate for a grand jury. The U.S. Attorney, as well as the Criminal Division and Tax Division of the Department of Justice, may also initiate a grand jury investigation of tax crimes.

The procedures involved in a grand jury investigation differ substantially from those in an administrative investigation conducted by the CID. The U.S. Attorney's office may designate the Special Agents assigned to the grand jury investigation as agents of the grand jury. The service of a grand jury subpoena can compel the testimony of witnesses and the production of records. A Special Agent cannot use an IRS summons after a grand jury investigation is commences.[60] Instead, a grand jury can issue a subpoena that is not restricted by either the waiting periods or the lengthy legal process required for an administrative summons.[61] Although a witness may file motion to quash a subpoena, the witness may not appeal any denial of that motion. To further contest and appeal the validity of the grand jury subpoena, the witness must refuse to testify or produce documents and then be held in contempt. A witness may not wish to

---

[56] IRM 9.6.2.2.

[57] Id.

[58] Id.

[59] IRM 9.5.2.2.

[60] Code Secs. 7605(a) and 7609.

[61] See Id. §§7605(a) (2009) and 7609 (West Supp. 2009).

face the harsh reality of confinement or other contempt penalties while waiting for an appeal to be heard.[62]

¶1813 CONSTITUTIONAL RIGHTS

The most important constitutional rights available to a taxpayer under criminal investigation are in the Fifth Amendment privilege against self-incrimination and the Fourth Amendment protection from unreasonable searches and seizures. The most significant of these in tax investigations is the taxpayer's Fifth Amendment right not to be compelled to testify or produce personal records if doing so might tend to be self-incriminating.

Privilege Against Self-Incrimination. A taxpayer or any witness may claim the Fifth Amendment privilege and refuse to testify or answer any questions with respect to any matters that may tend to be incriminating. A Fifth Amendment claim is also available with respect to a taxpayer's individual, personal or business records, provided the business records are those of a sole proprietorship.[63] Records of corporations and partnerships, however, are not protected by the privilege against self-incrimination.[64] Instead, the custodian of corporate records must produce the records even though she is the target of the investigation and the production of the records might be self-incriminating.[65]

The U.S. Supreme Court has held that the privilege protects a person only against being incriminated by her own compelled testimonial communication.[66] The privilege may protect from compulsory production the taxpayer's personal books and records, not because of the incriminating contents of such voluntarily prepared records, but because the act of production itself has communicative aspects that might tend to incriminate. By producing the records, the individual is being compelled to testify, in effect, that the records exist. The courts will balance this communicative production concept against a need for required records, which are not privileged

Example 18-13: Taxpayer leaves important records in the possession of his Accountant. Pursuant to a Grand Jury investigation, the Grand Jury subpoenas the Accountant for any records existing with respect to that transaction. Taxpayer cannot assert the Fifth Amendment privilege to prevent Accountant from producing those records. However, had Taxpayer retained those records for the transactions, Taxpayer could try to assert the Fifth Amendment privilege against compelled communication under the theory that Taxpayer would be communicating the existence of those records by producing those records.

---

[62] Information obtained during a grand jury tax investigation cannot be disclosed for use in the civil tax audit, but may be obtainable for a trial. See *United States v. Baggot*, 463 U.S. 476 (1983), 83-2 USTC ¶9438; *United States v. Sells Engineering, Inc.*, 463 U.S. 418 (1983); FED. R. CRIM. P. 6(e)(2)

[63] See *United States v. Doe*, 465 U.S. 605 (1984).

[64] See *Braswell v. United States*, 487 U.S. 99 (1988), 88-2 USTC ¶9546; *Bellis v. United States*, 417 U.S. 85

(1974). In *Bellis*, the Supreme Court suggested that the privilege might apply to partnership records in a case involving a "small family partnership" or if there were some other pre-existing relationship of confidentiality among the partners.

[65] See *Braswell v. United States*, 487 U.S. 99 (1988), 88-2 USTC ¶9546.

[66] See *Fisher v. United States*, 425 U.S. 391 (1976), 76-1 USTC ¶9353.

Unreasonable Searches and Seizures. The Fourth Amendment protects "persons, houses, papers, and effects" against unreasonable searches and seizures. A search and seizure is presumed to be unreasonable unless the government first obtains a search warrant from a U.S. Magistrate Judge on a showing of probable cause. As previously discussed, search warrants are occasionally used by the CID to seize a taxpayer's records.

If an IRS agent surreptitiously searches through a taxpayer's desk drawers or cabinets while conducting an examination at the taxpayer's office, such a search is illegal. The court will suppress any information obtained in such a search as evidence in any subsequent criminal proceeding under the "exclusionary rule." An illegal search and seizure also occurs if an investigating agent directs an employee of the taxpayer to take records secretly from the taxpayer's place of business.[67]

¶1814 PRIVILEGED COMMUNICATIONS

The attorney-client privilege provides a taxpayer under investigation with the assurance that his attorney cannot disclose whatever the taxpayer discusses in confidence with his attorney unless the taxpayer waives the privilege. The privilege applies only if:[68]

1. The asserted holder of the privilege is or sought to become a client;

2. The person to whom the communication was made (a) is a member of the bar of a court or a bar member's subordinate and (b) is acting as an attorney in connection with this communication;

3. The communication relates to a fact told to the attorney (a) by the client (b) without the presence of strangers (c) for the purpose of securing primarily either (i) an opinion on law or (ii) legal services or (iii) assistance in some legal proceeding, and not (d) for the purpose of committing a crime or tort; and

4. The client has claimed and not waived privilege.[69]

Example 18-14: Suppose that a Special Agent approached a taxpayer with respect to a CID investigation. The taxpayer says he wants to talk with an attorney and the taxpayer does have an initial meeting with an attorney. At that initial meeting, the taxpayer tells the attorney all of the facts with respect to the year that is the subject of the CID investigation. At the close of this initial meeting, the attorney realizes that due to his representation of a business colleague of the taxpayer, the attorney has a conflict of interest and cannot represent the taxpayer. Subsequently, the taxpayer meets with a second attorney and hires him. All of the information the taxpayer told the first attorney is privileged because it was told while seeking to become a client.

---

[67] See *United States v. Feffer*, 831 F.2d 734 (7th Cir. 1987), 87-2 USTC ¶9614.

[68] For a full discussion on privileged communications see Chapter 8, *supra*.

[69] *United States v. United Shoe Mach. Corp.*, 89 F.Supp 357 (D. Mass. 1950). See *Bernardo v. Comm'r*, 104 TC 677 (1995), CCH Dec. 50,705. See also Chapter 8 on attorney-client privilege and work product.

If an attorney is acting in some other capacity, such as a tax return preparer or business adviser, communications to the attorney are not privileged.[70] Also, the privilege does not normally protect information regarding the fee arrangement and the fee paid. When an attorney engages an accountant to assist in representing a taxpayer during a criminal investigation, the privilege applies to any confidential communications to the accountant while she assists the attorney.[71] In the case of a corporate or organizational taxpayer, the privilege will extend to all officers and employees who have information related to the matter under investigation.[72]

Confidential communications between husband and wife are also privileged. In addition to the protection offered by this privilege, the law also recognizes the right of either spouse not to be compelled to testify against the other.[73] The testimonial privilege belongs to the spouse who is called to testify. Therefore, if a wife chooses to testify against her husband, she may do so. However, the husband would be able to claim a privilege with respect to any communications with his wife that he made in confidence during their marriage.[74]

¶1815 PRACTICAL CONSIDERATIONS AND ADVICE

The taxpayer under criminal investigation should not speak to the Special Agent without the presence and advice of an attorney. The taxpayer should retain an attorney with whom the taxpayer can discuss the matter confidentially with the knowledge that whatever he or she tells the attorney is subject to the attorney-client privilege. If the attorney is present at the meeting with the Special Agent, the attorney should refuse to submit the taxpayer to questioning or furnish records or documents until the attorney has had an opportunity to explore the matter fully.

The taxpayer should not discuss pending tax problems with anyone else, including a personal accountant, close friends, or relatives. Privileges do not protect anything said to these individuals. If these individuals are subsequently questioned by a Special Agent, they may face the dilemma of choosing between lying or disclosing what may be harmful information. The taxpayer should retrieve any personal business records in the hands of an accountant or any other third party as soon as possible. Unless such records are in the possession of the taxpayer, they are not protected by the privilege against self-incrimination.

The general rule is that cooperation in a criminal tax investigation rarely helps the taxpayer and frequently provides the evidence necessary to make a

---

[70] See *United States v. Davis*, 636 F.2d 1028 (5th Cir. 1981), 81-1 USTC ¶9193, *cert. denied*, 454 U.S. 862 (1981); *United States v. El Paso Co.*, 81-2 USTC ¶9819 (SD Tex. 1981), *aff'd* 682 F.2d 530 (5th Cir. 1982) *cert. denied* 104 S.Ct 1927 (1984). *Canaday v. United States*, 354 F.2d 849 (8th Cir. 1966), 66-1 USTC ¶9192.

[71] See *United States v. Kovel*, 296 F.2d 918 (2d Cir. 1961), 62-1 USTC ¶9111. But *cf. U.S. v. Adlman*, 68 F.3d 1495 (2d Cir. 1995), 95-2 USTC ¶50,579 (tax opinion memorandum prepared by outside accounting firm not protected by attorney-client privilege because accounting firm not hired to provide legal advice).

[72] See *Upjohn Co. v. United States*, 449 U.S. 383 (1981), 81-1 USTC ¶9138, *In re Sealed Case*, 737 F.2d 94 (D.C. Cir. 1984).

[73] See *Trammel v. United States*, 445 U.S. 40 (1980).

[74] *Pereira v. United States*, 347 U.S. 1 (1954).

¶1815

case. Whether or not the taxpayer cooperates, the Special Agent will not recommend prosecution unless there is sufficient evidence of an intentional violation of the Internal Revenue laws. It may be appropriate to cooperate when it is certain that the Special Agent will obtain the material from other sources.

The Special Agent routinely advises the taxpayer that cooperation in providing information will avoid the time and embarrassment involved in contacting the taxpayer's friends, customers and business associates to obtain the requested information. The Special Agent will not inform the taxpayer, however, that all of the information submitted by the taxpayer will have to be verified by contacting the very same people the taxpayer did not want contacted in the first place. Moreover, such cooperation may provide the Special Agent with more leads and more persons to contact than otherwise she would have developed.

Hasty decisions should not be made with respect to cooperation, even partial cooperation. The golden rule in criminal tax investigations applies to the question of cooperation, "when in doubt, don't."

¶1816 THE ACCOUNTANT'S ROLE

The taxpayer's accountant should be alert to the danger of discussing or allowing the taxpayer to personally discuss anything regarding the tax matter under investigation. Under current law, there is no accountant-client privilege in criminal cases to protect the accountant from disclosing what the taxpayer has disclosed. Often the initial contact by the Special Agent will cause the taxpayer to go to the accountant and confess all.

If necessary to assist the attorney in developing the case, the attorney should engage the accountant to preserve the attorney-client privilege. The same accountant who prepared the tax returns for the taxpayer or did the regular accounting for the taxpayer generally is the wrong choice to do the work required in the criminal case. Although the regular accountant may have historical background, it may be difficult to sort out what was learned during this period of time from what the accountant previously learned during the tax return preparation or routine accounting work. The latter information would not be privileged.[75]

¶1817 ATTEMPTS TO SETTLE

In many cases, where a taxpayer is under investigation and has admitted an understatement of tax to a practitioner, the taxpayer may attempt to file an amended return disclosing any omitted income. The practitioner should be aware that filing an amended return after a criminal investigation has begun will be of little effect in terminating the investigation because the Special Agent is concerned primarily with determining whether there has been a criminal violation. Instead the Special Agent may treat the filing of an amended return as evidence of a violation and the government may use the amended return to show there has been an understatement of the taxpayer's income in any trial of the

---

[75] See note 68, *supra.*

criminal case. For this reason, no amended return should be filed nor should any offer to pay additional tax be communicated to the Special Agent during the criminal investigation.

Prior to an investigation, a taxpayer who has failed to file returns or omitted income may consider voluntarily submitting amended returns. The IRS has an informal policy of not prosecuting taxpayers who come forward to report under-statements if the reporting is truly voluntary.[76]

---

[76] IRM 9.5.11.9.

¶1817

¶1821 Exhibit 18-1

SENTENCING TABLE
(in months of imprisonment)

	Offense Level	I (0 or 1)	II (2 or 3)	III (4, 5, 6)	IV (7, 8, 9)	V (10, 11, 12)	VI (13 or more)
		Criminal History Category (Criminal History Points)					
Zone A	1	0-6	0-6	0-6	0-6	0-6	0-6
	2	0-6	0-6	0-6	0-6	0-6	1-7
	3	0-6	0-6	0-6	0-6	2-8	3-9
	4	0-6	0-6	0-6	2-8	4-10	6-12
	5	0-6	0-6	1-7	4-10	6-12	9-15
	6	0-6	1-7	2-8	6-12	9-15	12-18
Zone B	7	0-6	2-8	4-10	8-14	12-18	15-21
	8	0-6	4-10	6-12	10-16	15-21	18-24
	9	4-10	6-12	8-14	12-18	18-24	21-27
	10	6-12	8-14	10-16	15-21	21-27	24-30
Zone C	11	8-14	10-16	12-18	18-24	24-30	27-33
	12	10-16	12-18	15-21	21-27	27-33	30-37
	13	12-18	15-21	18-24	24-30	30-37	33-41
	14	15-21	18-24	21-27	27-33	33-41	37-46
	15	18-24	21-27	24-30	30-37	37-46	41-51
	16	21-27	24-30	27-33	33-41	41-51	46-57
	17	24-30	27-33	30-37	37-46	46-57	51-63
	18	27-33	30-37	33-41	41-51	51-63	57-71
	19	30-37	33-41	37-46	46-57	57-71	63-78
	20	33-41	37-46	41-51	51-63	63-78	70-87
	21	37-46	41-51	46-57	57-71	70-87	77-96
	22	41-51	46-57	51-63	63-78	77-96	84-105
	23	46-57	51-63	57-71	70-87	84-105	92-115
	24	51-63	57-71	63-78	77-96	92-115	100-125
	25	57-71	63-78	70-87	84-105	100-125	110-137
	26	63-78	70-87	78-97	92-115	110-137	120-150
Zone D	27	70-87	78-97	87-108	100-125	120-150	130-162
	28	78-97	87-108	97-121	110-137	130-162	140-175
	29	87-108	97-121	108-135	121-151	140-175	151-188
	30	97-121	108-135	121-151	135-168	151-188	168-210
	31	108-135	121-151	135-168	151-188	168-210	188-235
	32	121-151	135-168	151-188	168-210	188-235	210-262
	33	135-168	151-188	168-210	188-235	210-262	235-293
	34	151-188	168-210	188-235	210-262	235-293	262-327
	35	168-210	188-235	210-262	235-293	262-327	292-365
	36	188-235	210-262	235-293	262-327	292-365	324-405
	37	210-262	235-293	262-327	292-365	324-405	360-life
	38	235-293	262-327	292-365	324-405	360-life	360-life
	39	262-327	292-365	324-405	360-life	360-life	360-life
	40	292-365	324-405	360-life	360-life	360-life	360-life
	41	324-405	360-life	360-life	360-life	360-life	360-life
	42	360-life	360-life	360-life	360-life	360-life	360-life
	43	life	life	life	life	life	life

¶1822   Exhibit 18-2

2010 FEDERAL SENTENCING GUIDELINES MANUAL

CHAPTER FOUR - CRIMINAL HISTORY AND CRIMINAL LIVELIHOOD

PART A - CRIMINAL HISTORY

Introductory Commentary

The Comprehensive Crime Control Act sets forth four purposes of sentencing. (See 18 U.S.C. § 3553(a)(2).) A defendant's record of past criminal conduct is directly relevant to those purposes. A defendant with a record of prior criminal behavior is more culpable than a first offender and thus deserving of greater punishment. General deterrence of criminal conduct dictates that a clear message be sent to society that repeated criminal behavior will aggravate the need for punishment with each recurrence. To protect the public from further crimes of the particular defendant, the likelihood of recidivism and future criminal behavior must be considered. Repeated criminal behavior is an indicator of a limited likelihood of successful rehabilitation.

The specific factors included in §4A1.1 and §4A1.3 are consistent with the extant empirical research assessing correlates of recidivism and patterns of career criminal behavior. While empirical research has shown that other factors are correlated highly with the likelihood of recidivism, e.g., age and drug abuse, for policy reasons they were not included here at this time. The Commission has made no definitive judgment as to the reliability of the existing data. However, the Commission will review additional data insofar as they become available in the future.

<u>Historical Note</u>: Effective November 1, 1987.

§4A1.1.   <u>Criminal History Category</u>

The total points from subsections (a) through (e) determine the criminal history category in the Sentencing Table in Chapter Five, Part A.

(a)   Add 3 points for each prior sentence of imprisonment exceeding one year and one month.

(b)   Add 2 points for each prior sentence of imprisonment of at least sixty days not counted in (a).

(c)   Add 1 point for each prior sentence not counted in (a) or (b), up to a total of 4 points for this subsection.

(d)   Add 2 points if the defendant committed the instant offense while under any criminal justice sentence, including probation, parole, supervised release, imprisonment, work release, or escape status.

(e)   Add 1 point for each prior sentence resulting from a conviction of a crime of violence that did not receive any points under (a), (b), or (c) above because such sentence was counted as a single sentence, up to a total of 3 points for this subsection.

Commentary

The total criminal history points from §4A1.1 determine the criminal history category (I-VI) in the Sentencing Table in Chapter Five, Part A. The definitions and instructions in §4A1.2 govern the computation of the criminal history points. Therefore, §§4A1.1 and 4A1.2 must be read together. The following notes highlight the interaction of §§4A1.1 and 4A1.2.

Application Notes:

1.   *§4A1.1(a).—Three points are added for each prior sentence of imprisonment exceeding one year and one month. There is no limit to the number of points that may be counted under this subsection. The term "prior sentence" is defined at §4A1.2(a). The term "sentence of imprisonment" is defined at §4A1.2(b). Where a prior sentence of imprisonment resulted from a revocation of probation, parole, or a similar form of release, see §4A1.2(k).*

Certain prior sentences are not counted or are counted only under certain conditions:

> *A sentence imposed more than fifteen years prior to the defendant's commencement of the instant offense is not counted unless the defendant's incarceration extended into this fifteen-year period. See §4A1.2(e).*

> *A sentence imposed for an offense committed prior to the defendant's eighteenth birthday is counted under this subsection only if it resulted from an adult conviction. See §4A1.2(d).*

> *A sentence for a foreign conviction, a conviction that has been expunged, or an invalid conviction is not counted. See §4A1.2 (h) and (j) and the Commentary to §4A1.2.*

2.   *§4A1.1(b).—Two points are added for each prior sentence of imprisonment of at least sixty days not counted in §4A1.1(a). There is no limit to the number of points that may be counted under this subsection. The term "prior sentence" is defined at §4A1.2(a). The term "sentence of imprisonment" is defined at §4A1.2(b). Where a prior sentence of imprisonment resulted from a revocation of probation, parole, or a similar form of release, see §4A1.2(k).*

Certain prior sentences are not counted or are counted only under certain conditions:

> *A sentence imposed more than ten years prior to the defendant's commencement of the instant offense is not counted. See §4A1.2(e).*

> *An adult or juvenile sentence imposed for an offense committed prior to the defendant's eighteenth birthday is counted only if confinement resulting from such sentence extended into the five-year period preceding the defendant's commencement of the instant offense. See §4A1.2(d).*

Sentences for certain specified non-felony offenses are never counted. See §4A1.2(c)(2).

A sentence for a foreign conviction or a tribal court conviction, an expunged conviction, or an invalid conviction is not counted. See §4A1.2(h), (i), (j), and the Commentary to §4A1.2.

A military sentence is counted only if imposed by a general or special court martial. See §4A1.2(g).

3.   §4A1.1(c).—One point is added for each prior sentence not counted under §4A1.1(a) or (b). A maximum of four points may be counted under this subsection. The term "prior sentence" is defined at §4A1.2(a).

Certain prior sentences are not counted or are counted only under certain conditions:

A sentence imposed more than ten years prior to the defendant's commencement of the instant offense is not counted. See §4A1.2(e).

An adult or juvenile sentence imposed for an offense committed prior to the defendant's eighteenth birthday is counted only if imposed within five years of the defendant's commencement of the current offense. See §4A1.2(d).

Sentences for certain specified non-felony offenses are counted only if they meet certain requirements. See §4A1.2(c)(1).

Sentences for certain specified non-felony offenses are never counted. See §4A1.2(c)(2).

A diversionary disposition is counted only where there is a finding or admission of guilt in a judicial proceeding. See §4A1.2 (f).

A sentence for a foreign conviction, a tribal court conviction, an expunged conviction, or an invalid conviction, is not counted. See §4A1.2(h), (i), (j), and the Commentary to §4A1.2.

A military sentence is counted only if imposed by a general or special court martial. See §4A1.2(g).

4.   §4A1.1(d).—Two points are added if the defendant committed any part of the instant offense (i.e., any relevant conduct) while under any criminal justice sentence, including probation, parole, supervised release, imprisonment, work release, or escape status. Failure to report for service of a sentence of imprisonment is to be treated as an escape from such sentence. See §4A1.2(n). For the purposes of this subsection, a "criminal justice sentence" means a sentence countable under §4A1.2 (Definitions and Instructions for Computing Criminal History) having a custodial or supervisory component, although active supervision is not required for this subsection to apply. For example, a term of unsupervised probation would be included; but a sentence to pay a fine, by itself, would not be included. A defendant who commits the instant offense while a violation warrant from a prior sentence is outstanding (e.g., a probation, parole, or supervised release violation warrant) shall be deemed to be under a criminal justice sentence for the purposes of this provision if that sentence is otherwise countable, even if that sentence would have expired absent such warrant. See §4A1.2(m).

5.   §4A1.1(e).—In a case in which the defendant received two or more prior sentences as a result of convictions for crimes of violence that are counted as a single sentence (see §4A1.2(a)(2)), one point is added under §4A1.1(e) for each such sentence that did not result in any additional points under §4A1.1(a), (b), or (c). A total of up to 3 points may be added under §4A1.1(e). For purposes of this guideline, "crime of violence" has the meaning given that term in §4B1.2(a). See §4A1.2(p).

For example, a defendant's criminal history includes two robbery convictions for offenses committed on different occasions. The sentences for these offenses were imposed on the same day and are counted as a single prior sentence. See §4A1.2(a)(2). If the defendant received a five-year sentence of imprisonment for one robbery and a four-year sentence of imprisonment for the other robbery (consecutively or concurrently), a total of 3 points is added under §4A1.1(a). An additional point is added under §4A1.1(e) because the second sentence did not result in any additional point(s) (under §4A1.1(a), (b), or (c)). In contrast, if the defendant received a one-year sentence of imprisonment for one robbery and a nine-month consecutive sentence of imprisonment for the other robbery, a total of 3 points also is added under §4A1.1(a) (a one-year sentence of imprisonment and a consecutive nine-month sentence of imprisonment are treated as a combined one-year-nine-month sentence of imprisonment). But no additional point is added under §4A1.1(e) because the sentence for the second robbery already resulted in an additional point under §4A1.1(a). Without the second sentence, the defendant would only have received two points under §4A1.1(b) for the one-year sentence of imprisonment.

Background. Prior convictions may represent convictions in the federal system, fifty state systems, the District of Columbia, territories, and foreign, tribal, and military courts. There are jurisdictional variations in offense definitions, sentencing structures, and manner of sentence pronouncement. To minimize problems with imperfect measures of past crime seriousness, criminal history categories are based on the maximum term imposed in previous sentences rather than on other measures, such as whether the conviction was designated a felony or misdemeanor. In recognition of the imperfection of this measure however, §4A1.3 authorizes the court to depart from the otherwise applicable criminal history category in certain circumstances.

Subsections (a), (b), and (c) of §4A1.1 distinguish confinement sentences longer than one year and one month, shorter confinement sentences of at least sixty days, and all other sentences, such as confinement sentences of less than sixty days, probation, fines, and residency in a halfway house.

Section 4A1.1(d) adds two points if the defendant was under a criminal justice sentence during any part of the instant offense.

Historical Note: Effective November 1, 1987. Amended effective November 1, 1989 (see Appendix C, amendments 259-261); November 1, 1991 (see Appendix C, amendments 381 and 382); October 27, 2003 (see Appendix C, amendment 651); November 1, 2007 (see Appendix C, amendment 709); November 1, 2010 (see Appendix C, amendment 742).

(EFFECTIVE November 1, 2010)

¶1823 Exhibit 18-3

2010 FEDERAL SENTENCING GUIDELINES MANUAL

CHAPTER TWO - OFFENSE CONDUCT

PART T - OFFENSES INVOLVING TAXATION

4.   TAX TABLE

§2T4.1.   Tax Table

	Tax Loss (Apply the Greatest)	Offense Level
(A)	$2,000 or less	6
(B)	More than $2,000	8
(C)	More than $5,000	10
(D)	More than $12,500	12
(E)	More than $30,000	14
(F)	More than $80,000	16
(G)	More than $200,000	18
(H)	More than $400,000	20
(I)	More than $1,000,000	22
(J)	More than $2,500,000	24
(K)	More than $7,000,000	26
(L)	More than $20,000,000	28
(M)	More than $50,000,000	30
(N)	More than $100,000,000	32
(O)	More than $200,000,000	34
(P)	More than $400,000,000	36.

Historical Note: Effective November 1, 1987. Amended effective November 1, 1989 (see Appendix C, amendment 237); November 1, 1993 (see Appendix C, amendment 491); November 1, 2001 (see Appendix C, amendment 617); January 25, 2003 (see Appendix C, amendment 647); November 1, 2003 (see Appendix C, 653).

(EFFECTIVE November 1, 2010)

United States Sentencing Commission

¶1824 Exhibit 18-4

2010 FEDERAL SENTENCING GUIDELINES MANUAL

CHAPTER TWO - OFFENSE CONDUCT

PART T - OFFENSES INVOLVING TAXATION

1.   INCOME TAXES, EMPLOYMENT TAXES, ESTATE TAXES, GIFT TAXES, AND EXCISE TAXES (OTHER THAN ALCOHOL, TOBACCO, AND CUSTOMS TAXES)

Historical Note: Effective November 1, 1987. Amended effective November 1, 1993 (see Appendix C, amendment 491).

Introductory Commentary

The criminal tax laws are designed to protect the public interest in preserving the integrity of the nation's tax system. Criminal tax prosecutions serve to punish the violator and promote respect for the tax laws. Because of the limited number of criminal tax prosecutions relative to the estimated incidence of such violations, deterring others from violating the tax laws is a primary consideration underlying these guidelines. Recognition that the sentence for a criminal tax case will be commensurate with the gravity of the offense should act as a deterrent to would-be violators.

Historical Note: Effective November 1, 1987.

§2T1.1.   Tax Evasion; Willful Failure to File Return, Supply Information, or Pay Tax; Fraudulent or False Returns, Statements, or Other Documents

  (a)   Base Offense Level:

   (1)   Level from §2T4.1 (Tax Table) corresponding to the tax loss; or

   (2)   **6**, if there is no tax loss.

  (b)   Specific Offense Characteristics

   (1)   If the defendant failed to report or to correctly identify the source of income exceeding $10,000 in any year from criminal activity, increase by **2** levels. If the resulting offense level is less than level **12**, increase to level **12**.

   (2)   If the offense involved sophisticated means, increase by **2** levels. If the resulting offense level is less than level **12**, increase to level **12**.

  (c)   Special Instructions

  For the purposes of this guideline --

   (1)   If the offense involved tax evasion or a fraudulent or false return, statement, or other document, the tax loss is the total amount of loss that was the object of the offense (*i.e.*, the loss that would have resulted had the offense been successfully completed).

   Notes:

   (A)   If the offense involved filing a tax return in which gross income was underreported, the tax loss shall be treated as equal to 28% of the unreported gross income (34% if the taxpayer is a corporation) plus 100% of any false credits claimed against tax, unless a more accurate determination of the tax loss can be made.

   (B)   If the offense involved improperly claiming a deduction or an exemption, the tax loss shall be treated as equal to 28% of the amount of the improperly claimed deduction or exemption (34% if the taxpayer is a corporation) plus 100% of any false credits claimed against tax, unless a more accurate determination of the tax loss can be made.

   (C)   If the offense involved improperly claiming a deduction to provide a basis for tax evasion in the future, the tax loss shall be treated as equal to 28% of the amount of the improperly claimed deduction (34% if the taxpayer is a corporation) plus 100% of any false credits claimed against tax, unless a more accurate determination of the tax loss can be made.

   (D)   If the offense involved (i) conduct described in subdivision (A), (B), or (C) of these Notes; and (ii) both individual and corporate tax returns, the tax loss is the aggregate tax loss from the offenses added together.

   (2)   If the offense involved failure to file a tax return, the tax loss is the amount of tax that the taxpayer owed and did not pay.

   Notes:

(A)   If the offense involved failure to file a tax return, the tax loss shall be treated as equal to 20% of the gross income (25% if the taxpayer is a corporation) less any tax withheld or otherwise paid, unless a more accurate determination of the tax loss can be made.

(B)   If the offense involved (i) conduct described in subdivision (A) of these Notes; and (ii) both individual and corporate tax returns, the tax loss is the aggregate tax loss from the offenses added together.

(3)   If the offense involved willful failure to pay tax, the tax loss is the amount of tax that the taxpayer owed and did not pay.

(4)   If the offense involved improperly claiming a refund to which the claimant was not entitled, the tax loss is the amount of the claimed refund to which the claimant was not entitled.

(5)   The tax loss is not reduced by any payment of the tax subsequent to the commission of the offense.

Commentary

Statutory Provisions: 26 U.S.C. §§ 7201, 7203 (other than a violation based upon 26 U.S.C. § 6050I), 7206 (other than a violation based upon 26 U.S.C. § 6050I or § 7206(2)), and 7207. For additional statutory provision(s), see Appendix A (Statutory Index).

Application Notes:

1.   "Tax loss" is defined in subsection (c). The tax loss does not include interest or penalties, except in willful evasion of payment cases under 26 U.S.C. § 7201 and willful failure to pay cases under 26 U.S.C. § 7203. Although the definition of tax loss corresponds to what is commonly called the "criminal figures," its amount is to be determined by the same rules applicable in determining any other sentencing factor. In some instances, such as when indirect methods of proof are used, the amount of the tax loss may be uncertain; the guidelines contemplate that the court will simply make a reasonable estimate based on the available facts.

Notes under subsections (c)(1) and (c)(2) address certain situations in income tax cases in which the tax loss may not be reasonably ascertainable. In these situations, the "presumptions" set forth are to be used unless the government or defense provides sufficient information for a more accurate assessment of the tax loss. In cases involving other types of taxes, the presumptions in the notes under subsections (c)(1) and (c)(2) do not apply.

Example 1: A defendant files a tax return reporting income of $40,000 when his income was actually $90,000. Under Note (A) to subsection (c)(1), the tax loss is treated as $14,000 ($90,000 of actual gross income minus $40,000 of reported gross income = $50,000 x 28%) unless sufficient information is available to make a more accurate assessment of the tax loss.

Example 2: A defendant files a tax return reporting income of $60,000 when his income was actually $130,000. In addition, the defendant claims $10,000 in false tax credits. Under Note (A) to subsection (c)(1), the tax loss is treated as $29,600 ($130,000 of actual gross income minus $60,000 of reported gross income = $70,000 x 28% = $19,600, plus $10,000 of false tax credits) unless sufficient information is available to make a more accurate assessment of the tax loss.

Example 3: A defendant fails to file a tax return for a year in which his salary was $24,000, and $2,600 in income tax was withheld by his employer. Under the note to subsection (c)(2), the tax loss is treated as $2,200 ($24,000 of gross income x 20% = $4,800, minus $2,600 of tax withheld) unless sufficient information is available to make a more accurate assessment of the tax loss.

In determining the tax loss attributable to the offense, the court should use as many methods set forth in subsection (c) and this commentary as are necessary given the circumstances of the particular case. If none of the methods of determining the tax loss set forth fit the circumstances of the particular case, the court should use any method of determining the tax loss that appears appropriate to reasonably calculate the loss that would have resulted had the offense been successfully completed.

2.   In determining the total tax loss attributable to the offense (see §1B1.3(a)(2)), all conduct violating the tax laws should be considered as part of the same course of conduct or common scheme or plan unless the evidence demonstrates that the conduct is clearly unrelated. The following examples are illustrative of conduct that is part of the same course of conduct or common scheme or plan: (a) there is a continuing pattern of violations of the tax laws by the defendant; (b) the defendant uses a consistent method to evade or camouflage income, e.g., backdating documents or using off-shore accounts; (c) the violations involve the same or a related series of transactions; (d) the violation in each instance involves a false or inflated claim of a similar deduction or credit; and (e) the violation in each instance involves a failure to report or an understatement of a specific source of income, e.g., interest from savings accounts or income from a particular business activity. These examples are not intended to be exhaustive.

3.   "Criminal activity" means any conduct constituting a criminal offense under federal, state, local, or foreign law.

4.   Sophisticated Means Enhancement.— For purposes of subsection (b)(2), "sophisticated means" means especially complex or especially intricate offense conduct pertaining to the execution or concealment of an offense. Conduct such as hiding assets or transactions, or both, through the use of fictitious entities, corporate shells, or offshore financial accounts ordinarily indicates sophisticated means.

5.   A "credit claimed against tax" is an item that reduces the amount of tax directly. In contrast, a "deduction" is an item that reduces the amount of taxable income.

6.   "Gross income," for the purposes of this section, has the same meaning as it has in 26 U.S.C. § 61 and 26 C.F.R. § 1.61.

7.   If the offense involved both individual and corporate tax returns, the tax loss is the aggregate tax loss from the individual tax offense and the corporate tax offense added together. Accordingly, in a case in which a defendant fails to report income derived from a corporation on both the defendant's individual tax return and the defendant's corporate tax return, the tax loss is the sum of (A) the unreported or diverted amount multiplied by (i) 28%; or (ii) the tax rate for the individual tax offense, if sufficient information is available to make a more accurate assessment of that tax rate; and (B) the unreported or diverted amount multiplied by (i) 34%; or (ii) the tax rate for the corporate tax offense, if sufficient information is available to make a more accurate assessment of that tax rate. For example, the defendant, the sole owner of a Subchapter C corporation, fraudulently understates the corporation's income in the amount of $100,000 on the corporation's tax return, diverts the funds to the defendant's own use, and does not report these funds on the defendant's individual tax *return. For purposes of this example, assume the use of 34% with respect to the corporate tax loss and the use of 28% with respect to the individual tax loss. The tax loss attributable to the defendant's corporate tax return is $34,000 ($100,000 multiplied by 34%). The tax loss attributable to the defendant's individual tax return is $28,000 ($100,000 multiplied by 28%). The tax loss for the offenses are added together to equal $62,000 ($34,000 + $28,000).*

<u>*Background.*</u> *This guideline relies most heavily on the amount of loss that was the object of the offense. Tax offenses, in and of themselves, are serious offenses; however, a greater tax loss is obviously more harmful to the treasury and more serious than a smaller one with otherwise similar characteristics. Furthermore, as the potential benefit from the offense increases, the sanction necessary to deter also increases.*

Under pre-guidelines practice, roughly half of all tax evaders were sentenced to probation without imprisonment, while the other half received sentences that required them to serve an average prison term of twelve months. This guideline is intended to reduce disparity in sentencing for tax offenses and to somewhat increase average sentence length. As a result, the number of purely probationary sentences will be reduced. The Commission believes that any additional costs of imprisonment that may be incurred as a result of the increase in the average term of imprisonment for tax offenses are inconsequential in relation to the potential increase in revenue. According to estimates current at the time this guideline was originally developed (1987), income taxes are underpaid by approximately $90 billion annually. Guideline sentences should result in small increases in the average length of imprisonment for most tax cases that involve less than $100,000 in tax loss. The increase is expected to be somewhat larger for cases involving more taxes.

Failure to report criminally derived income is included as a factor for deterrence purposes. Criminally derived income is generally difficult to establish, so that the tax loss in such cases will tend to be substantially understated. An enhancement for offenders who violate the tax laws as part of a pattern of criminal activity from which they derive a substantial portion of their income also serves to implement the mandate of 28 U.S.C. § 994(i)(2).

Although tax offenses always involve some planning, unusually sophisticated efforts to conceal the offense decrease the likelihood of detection and therefore warrant an additional sanction for deterrence purposes.

The guideline does not make a distinction for an employee who prepares fraudulent returns on behalf of his employer. The adjustments in Chapter Three, Part B (Role in the Offense) should be used to make appropriate distinctions.

<u>Historical Note</u>: Effective November 1, 1987. Amended effective November 1, 1989 (<u>see</u> Appendix C, amendments 219-223); November 1, 1990 (<u>see</u> Appendix C, amendment 343); November 1, 1992 (<u>see</u> Appendix C, amendment 468); November 1, 1993 (<u>see</u> Appendix C, amendment 491); November 1, 1998 (<u>see</u> Appendix C, amendment 577); November 1, 2001 (<u>see</u> Appendix C, amendment 617); November 1, 2002 (<u>see</u> Appendix C, amendment 646).

(EFFECTIVE November 1, 2010)

United States Sentencing Commission

¶1825 Exhibit 18-5

[Internal Revenue Service]   Department of the Treasury
Criminal Investigation   Enter Address
                                                    Enter City, State Zip
                                                    Person to Contact:
                                                    Telephone Number:
                                                    Refer Reply to:
                                                    Date:

Certified Mail

Return Receipt Requested

Dear ____:

You are no longer the subject of a criminal investigation by our office regarding your Federal tax liabilities for 20X0 and 20X1. However, this does not preclude re-entry by Criminal Investigation into this matter.

The matter is presently in the SB/SE Division for further consideration. If you have any questions, please contact the person whose name and telephone number are shown above.

Sincerely yours,

Special Agent in Charge

¶1831 DISCUSSION QUESTIONS

1. You are an accountant representing Harry Holesale, who operates a retail hardware store in your area. You have prepared Harry's 2010 tax return, and Harry has now come to you because his 2008, 2009 and 2010 returns are scheduled for office examination. Harry asks you to represent him at the audit regarding all three years.

   In preparation for the audit appointment, you perform a preliminary T-account on the 2010 year. You are surprised to discover that the cash expenditures exceed sources of income by some $45,000. A close inspection of the return, which you prepared, discloses that the gross profit percentage reflected in the return is 15%. You have recently worked with other clients in the retail hardware business, and you know their gross profit percentage is generally closer to 35% to 37%. You then review Harry's prior returns and find that in 2008 the gross profit percentage was 14.8% and that for 2009 it was 15.3%. The preliminary T-account of these three years shows a potential understatement of over $100,000.

   Aside from any ethical considerations, what do you do in this situation? Consider the following alternatives:

   (A) Call Harry and grill him until he gives you a satisfactory explanation regarding the apparent understatement:

       (1) If Harry has a convincing explanation that the understatement was the result of an innocent error, do you prepare amended returns? Or is it better to go to the office examination appointment and not divulge the understatement until the auditor finds it?

       (2) If Harry admits that he was cheating on his returns, do you prepare amended returns in that situation?

   (B) Do not ask Harry for any explanation; rather, you prepare amended returns based on the T-account, insist that Harry sign them without review, and then file them with the examiner at the beginning of your appointment. You're hoping that your "voluntary disclosure" of the unreported income will deter the examiner from asking for any further explanation.

   (C) Without asking Harry for any explanation, strongly suggest that he seek competent legal advice and help him find a tax attorney.

   (D) Hire a tax attorney as your agent to interview Harry and get his explanation for the understatement, and then have the attorney report back to you with the results.

2. Freddy Fearful did not file his 2002 federal income tax return because he did not have the cash available to pay the balance due. When the time came to file his 2003 return, Freddy had sufficient cash to pay his 2003 taxes, but he was afraid to file the 2003 return because he figured that if he filed for 2003, the IRS would find out that he did not file in 2002. From 2004 through 2007, Freddy continued not to file even though he

was entitled to a sizable refund in each of those years. In 2008 and 2009, Freddy was not entitled to any refund, but again he did not file even though he had the cash available to pay the current tax.

You are a Special Agent for the IRS's CID and are assigned to investigate Freddy for the years 2005 through 2010. Does the pattern of conduct described above constitute the "willful" failure to file an income tax return proscribed by Code Sec. 7203?

3. Ronny Refundable is under investigation by CID personnel of the IRS. Ronny is an accountant who prepares approximately 1,500 returns a year. Of the returns that he prepares for individuals, 95% produce a refund. Ronny accomplishes this by utilizing pre-prepared schedules showing itemized deductions, employee business expenses, and child care credits. It is Ronny's boast that by a careful combination of his schedules he can produce a refund for virtually any taxpayer in any tax bracket, unless the taxpayer happens to be subject to the alternative minimum tax. While those of Ronny's clients who have been audited have not fared well, Ronny points out to potential clients that fewer than two percent of taxpayers nationwide get audited and so the odds are good that they won't get caught.

You are the Special Agent in Charge for Ronny's office. Would you recommend prosecution in his case? What sections of the Internal Revenue Code or other statutes have been violated by Ronny in his fictitious deduction and credit scheme?

4. Assume that you are Adele Accurate, an accountant, and that one of your clients is under criminal investigation. In accordance with the guidelines provided by the ABA and AICPA, you refer the client to an attorney familiar with criminal tax matters. You have prepared the client's returns for the past three years. The attorney retains you to make an analysis of the income and expenses of the client. Assume that you prepare a report for the attorney which discloses an understatement of income in excess of $35,000 for each year.

(A) Is your report protected within the attorney-client privilege?

(B) What practical problems does your retention cause?

5. Priscilla Persistent, a revenue agent, is auditing C&C Bar and Grill. The bar and grill is a business operated by the husband and wife team of Clyde and Cindy Social. The business has no other employees. Clyde and Cindy deposit their "receipts" into their personal joint checking account. For tax purposes, however, the business files a Form 1065— Return of Partnership Income.

(A) Priscilla Persistent issued a summons to the taxpayers requesting the books and records of the business. Can Clyde and Cindy invoke their Fifth Amendment privilege against self-incrimination?

(B) Would your answer change if the business run by Clyde and Cindy had several locations, numerous employees and substantial assets, and the business maintained a bank account in the partnership name?

(C) What rights, if any, would Clyde and Cindy have if Priscilla issued a summons to their bank for copies of their records?

(D) Would your answer to (C) change if a "grand jury investigation" had been commenced?

CHAPTER 19

INDIRECT METHODS OF PROVING INCOME

¶1901 INTRODUCTION

Conventional audit techniques employed by the Internal Revenue Service (IRS) are at times inadequate to prove that a taxpayer has failed to report all of the taxpayer's taxable income. Where conventional audit techniques prove unproductive, the government may resort to one or more indirect methods for detecting unreported income. The most common special methods are: (1) the cash transaction ("T" account) method, (2) the net worth method, (3) the source and application of funds (or cash expenditures) method and (4) the bank deposits method.[1]

The IRS in the past had increased its efforts to find unreported income with an emphasis on small businesses by using "Economic Reality Examination Audit Techniques." These audit techniques focused on the taxpayer's lifestyle, standard of living and other elements unrelated to the tax return, such as education, vacations, children's schools, automobiles, large assets, cash payments and cash on hand. Taxpayers under examination were also asked to submit a Statement Of Annual Estimated Personal And Family Expenses (see Exhibit 19-1 at ¶1941). As a result of public criticism with regard to the intrusive nature of financial status audits, Code Sec. 7602(e) was enacted and provides that "[t]he Secretary shall not use financial status or economic reality examination techniques to determine the existence of unreported income of any taxpayer unless the Secretary has a reasonable indication that there is a likelihood of such unreported income."[2]

¶1902 UTILIZATION

The revenue agent normally does not approach a typical examination intending to use an indirect method of proof. However, if books and records are missing or unavailable for any reason, the agent usually has no alternative but to reconstruct income by one of the accepted indirect methods. The same course of action may be necessary where the books and records are obviously incomplete or inaccurate. Even where the books and records appear to be complete, correct and internally consistent, suspicions raised by recurring large business losses, unrealistically low income for the nature of the business, informants' tips as to omitted income, bank deposits greatly in excess of reported gross receipts, or a lifestyle

---

[1] See IRM 4.10.4.2.8 et seq.

[2] Field Service Advice 200101030 (see Exhibit 19-2 at ¶1942).

inconsistent with reported income may cause the agent to resort to an indirect method of proof.[3]

The special agent in a criminal investigation will normally employ an indirect method where the nature of the taxpayer's business virtually precludes the development of direct evidence of specific items of omitted income or where business records have been withheld or are otherwise unavailable. Businesses involving both large numbers of customers, patients, or clients, and numerous sales or receipts, usually do not lend themselves to direct proof of omitted income. However, proof of some specific omissions may be used to bolster an indirect method case or to establish a likely source of unreported income.

Technical Aspects of the Formulas

¶1903 BASIC PRINCIPLES

Before discussing in detail the technical formulas employed in each of the indirect methods of proof, it is important to consider certain basic principles common to all. Burden-of-proof problems will be reserved for later consideration.

¶1904 GATHERING AND ANALYZING THE FACTUAL DATA

Regardless of the indirect method used, accuracy of result is wholly dependent on success in obtaining all facts relating to the taxpayer's financial affairs. Any one of the indirect methods can produce a precise reconstruction of income provided all facts are precisely known. Some facts, however, such as cash on hand and personal currency expenditures, usually will not be known with certainty and will require estimates which may distort the reconstructed income.

Once the examining agent obtains basic records and documents, the agent will determine whether the taxpayer's financial picture is complete and accurate. All substantial deposits in checking and savings accounts will be examined to determine the source of the funds. This inquiry may reveal the existence of previously undisclosed assets, loans or nontaxable income. For the same reason, the agent must determine the source of funds used in the acquisition of assets or payment of loans. If the source is not identifiable, the agent will explore the possibility of a prior cash accumulation.

Checks and savings account withdrawals will be examined for possible asset acquisitions, personal expenditures, or loan payments that may have been previously overlooked. The disposition of proceeds from loans or the sale of assets will be similarly traced. The possibility of cash accumulation or unidentified cash expenditures will be considered where the proceeds cannot be readily traced.

---

[3] When the results of a preliminary analysis suggest the need for further inquiry, the IRS will most commonly use the cash expenditures method. The IRS believes taxpayers easily understand this method. In those cases the IRS takes to court, it uses the net worth method most frequently to prove underreporting of income. See generally Gormley and Porcano, *Reconstruction of Income by the Internal Revenue Service*, TAXES, THE TAX MAGAZINE, vol. 77, No. 4, April 1999, p. 34. See generally Robert Carney, John Gardner and Kenneth Winter, *Indirect Methods of Income Reconstruction*, TAX ADVISOR 536 (August 1992).

The importance of examining tax returns as an investigative tool cannot be overemphasized. Much of the information required for the reconstruction of income can be found within the returns themselves. Equally important, the returns frequently furnish leads to other essential information, such as investments and loans. Tax returns for a number of years before the period under audit will also be examined. They occasionally reveal assets or liabilities that have been overlooked in the current years. In addition, they may evidence sufficient income to support the taxpayer's claim of a prior cash accumulation.

The examination of the underlying records and documents in a reconstruction-of-income case is a specialized accounting task. It is extremely time-consuming, and the integrity of the results is dependent upon the skill of the individual conducting the examination.

¶1905 THE CONSISTENCY PRINCIPLE

The consistency principle requires that, in reconstructing income, every transaction of the taxpayer, reported or not, be accorded the same tax consequences as it was, or would have been, accorded on the tax return. The importance of this principle should be apparent. It must be kept in mind continually when any transaction is examined for its effect on the formulae being used to prove income indirectly.

Indirect methods of proof are not methods of accounting,[4] and therefore, are not controlled by provisions of the Internal Revenue Code relating to accounting methods.[5] They are techniques used to determine whether income has been fully reported. As a result, the formulae for reconstructing income are not rigidly fixed but must be adjusted to conform to, or be consistent with, the methods of accounting used in the taxpayer's books and tax returns. If the taxpayer is properly reporting on a cash, accrual or hybrid method, reconstruction of income must properly reflect the taxpayer's method. The precise manner in which income is reconstructed will be discussed below.

The tax laws are replete with examples of special tax or accounting treatment accorded to various sales, exchanges and other transactions which might otherwise generate immediate and fully taxable income. To the extent that reconstruction of income involves such special transactions, consistent treatment must be accorded to these transactions by appropriate adjustments in the reconstruction formula. Examples of these special situations include (1) installment sales, (2) involuntary conversions, (3) nontaxable corporate distributions to stockholders which reduce basis of stock, and (4) like-kind exchanges.

---

[4] See *Holland v. United States*, 348 U.S. 121 (1954), 54-2 USTC ¶9714.

[5] The provisions relating to methods of accounting are found in Internal Revenue Code Sec. 446 which appears to provide authority to permit the use of indirect methods to compute taxable income. Code Sec. 446(b) states that "if no method of accounting has been regularly used by the taxpayer,

or if the method used does not clearly reflect income, the computation of taxable income shall be made under such method as, in the opinion of the Secretary, does clearly reflect income." See also Treas. Reg. § 1.446-1(a)(2) ("[N]o method of accounting is acceptable unless, in the opinion of the Commissioner, it clearly reflects income"). See generally Carney, Gardner and Winter, *supra*, note 3.

The Cash T-Account Method

¶1906 A SIMPLIFIED AUDITING TECHNIQUE

The cash transaction or T-account method is a simplified auditing technique used to make a preliminary verification of reported income. As its name implies, this method concentrates solely on those transactions which involve the generation or the use of cash. The term "cash" in this method includes currency, checks, or any other medium used to convey or transfer funds. The cash transaction method excludes from its formula all transactions, whether taxable or nontaxable, which do not result in the receipt or the payment of cash.

The cash T-account method utilizes a formula and format suggested by its name (see Exhibit 19-3 at ¶1943). On the left-hand (debit) side of the "T" are listed the sources of cash for the year under audit. On the right-hand (credit) side are listed the expenditures or applications of cash. The goal of the cash transaction method is to determine whether a taxpayer has used and accumulated more cash than has been received from all reported taxable and nontaxable sources, in other words, the use and accumulation of cash for which there is no ready explanation. If a discrepancy appears, it is presumed to constitute an understatement of taxable income.

The starting point for the T-account analysis is the tax return itself. All transactions on the return are carefully examined to determine their effect on cash. Sources of cash on the return include wages, dividends and interest, and all gross receipts from the operation of a business, farm or rental property. The gross selling price of all assets on the capital gains schedule is included as a source of cash, but only to the extent that cash payment, and not a security instrument or other property, was received. Other items on the tax return are examined to determine their potential as a source of cash, and the taxpayer's financial transactions not reflected on the return are thoroughly explored. Additional sources of cash include tax refunds, loans and other nontaxable income, such as gifts, inheritances, insurance proceeds and personal injury settlements.

The tax return also will disclose many cash expenditures which must be included on the credit side of the T-account. Business purchases, excluding any adjustment for inventory changes, are included as cash expenditures. Similarly, all business expenses, with the exception of depreciation (a noncash item), are added to the credits. Any additional expenses appearing on other schedules or portions of the return are included as credits. Care will be taken to exclude all noncash deductions such as depreciation and amortization. Cash expenditures found outside the return include payments on loans, purchases of assets, investments in securities and all personal expenses (see Exhibit 19-1 at ¶1941).

¶1907 CASH ON HAND AND IN BANKS

On the T-account, the IRS accords special treatment to cash on hand and to checking and savings accounts. Cash on hand at the beginning of the year is included as a debit representing accumulated cash. Establishing the amount of

¶1906

cash on hand presents a serious problem if the results of the T-Account analysis are to be accurate.

Checking and savings account balances at the beginning and end of the year are included on the T-account as debits and credits, respectively. The opening balances provide sources of cash and the closing balances represent cash accumulations. The bank balances should be adjusted and reconciled to account for outstanding checks and deposits in transit.

Example 19-1: John Davis received net wages of $21,500 in 2010. His bank statements and savings account passbook showed the following balances:

	12/31/09	12/31/10
Checking Account	$1,300	$2,800
Savings Account	1,500	4,600

A reconciliation of his checking account indicated checks outstanding in the amount of $400 at the end of 2009, and $700 at the end of 2010. A check in the amount of $500 received on December 28, 2010, for the sale of a boat was not deposited in his account until January 2, 2011. John had cash on hand in the amount of $500 at the end of 2009, and $1,200 at the end of 2010. His personal living expenses totaled $23,000. The cash transaction method would disclose the following:

Cash on hand			Cash on hand	
12/31/09	$500		12/31/10	$1,200
Checking account			Checking account	
12/31/09	900		12/31/10	2,100
Savings account			Savings account	
12/31/09	1,500		12/31/10	4,600
Sale of boat	500		Deposit in transit	500
Net wages	21,500		Personal expenses	23,000
Total	$24,900		Total	$31,400
Understatement				
(Unexplained cash)	6,500			
Total	$31,400			

¶1908 ACCOUNTS RECEIVABLE AND PAYABLE

Adjustments are required on the T-account to eliminate the effect of trade accounts receivable that have been included in the gross sales of a business reporting on the accrual basis. Such adjustments convert the reported sales to the cash basis required by the cash transaction method. On the T-account, this is accomplished by including the balance of trade receivables at the beginning of the year as a debit and the balance at the end of the year as a credit.

A related T-account adjustment is made to eliminate the accounts payable included in the purchases and expenses of a business on the accrual basis. In this situation, however, the accounts payable at the end of the year are added to the

¶1908

debit side, while the payables at the beginning of the year are listed on the credit side.

The cash transaction method conceals the cause of the reconstructed understatement. Although on the surface the unexplained excess cash may appear to be unreported gross receipts, the discrepancy may just as well arise from inflated or overstated business expenses. The T-account formula assumes that the reported expenses are correct and that cash was paid out in the amount indicated by such expenses. The overstatement of any expenses for which cash was not actually paid creates unexplained excess cash. The same discrepancy results when personal expenses are deducted erroneously as business expenses and the examining agent duplicates such expenses on the T-account by also including them as personal expenses.

¶1909 T-ACCOUNT EXAMPLE

The following example illustrates the basic operation of the T-account method and shows how the method can disclose an understatement of gross income. Particular attention should be paid to the exclusion of noncash items having no effect on the T-account analysis.

Example 19-2: Paula Hanson reports her business income and expenses on the accrual basis. Selected balance sheet items for the business and schedules for her 2010 return showed the following:

SCHEDULE A (Itemized Deductions)

Taxes	$2,000
Interest on Mortgage	1,200
Cash Contributions	800
Medical Expenses (before limitation deduction)	1,500
Theft Loss (Value of jewelry—not reimbursed by insurance—before $100 exclusion and limitation)	10,200

In addition to the itemized deductions above, Ms. Hanson had other personal living expenses totaling $28,500 for 2010.

SCHEDULE B

Gross Dividends	$4,200
Interest Income	1,500

SCHEDULE C

Income

Gross Sales	$180,000	
Cost of Goods Sold (Schedule C-1)	100,000	
Gross Profit		$80,000

Deductions

Depreciation	$4,000	
Taxes	1,500	
Rent	2,000	
Repairs	500	
Insurance	900	
Amortization	700	

Salaries	8,000	
Interest	400	
Legal Fees	800	
Other...	200	
Total Expenses		19,000
Net Profit		$61,000

SCHEDULE C-1

Inventory at 1/1/10........................	$20,000
Purchases.....................................	130,000
Total	$150,000
Inventory at 12/31/10	50,000
Cost of Goods Sold	$100,000

The depreciation schedule on Schedule C included equipment purchased in 2010 at a cost of $2,500.

MISCELLANEOUS	12/31/09	12/31/10
Trade Accounts Receivable	$15,000	$23,000
Trade Accounts Payable	8,000	10,000
Accrued Expenses	2,500	1,800

SCHEDULE D

Stock	Date Acquired	Date Sold	Gross Sales Price	Cost	Gain or (Loss)
Stock X.............	5-03-09	2-07-10	$15,000	$11,000	$4,000
Stock Y.............	6-20-10	7-15-10	5,000	4,000	1,000
Stock Z.............	9-02-92	8-04-10	2,000	5,000	(3,000)

Ms. Hanson also acquired an additional $52,000 of stock in 2010 which did not appear on Schedule D.

SCHEDULE E

Total Amount of Rents	Depreciation	Other Expenses	Net Rent Income
$6,000	$4,000	$3,000	($1,000)

Additional investigation revealed that Ms. Hanson bought a personal car in May 2010 for $9,200. In 2010, she also borrowed $7,000 from a bank and $3,000 from a friend. No part of either loan was repaid in 2010. A one-year bank loan in the amount of $4,000 came due in 2010 and was refinanced by a new one-year loan from the bank in the amount of $9,000. No part of the new loan was repaid before the end of 2010. Ms. Hanson also received a gift of $3,000 from her parents during 2010.

Ms. Hanson's personal checking account had a reconciled balance of $4,000 at the end of 2009, and $1,500 at the end of 2010. Her savings account balance increased from $2,500 at the end of 2009 to $6,000 at the end of 2010. She had $1,000 in cash on hand at the end of 2009, but none at the end of 2010. In the same year, she also inherited, and still holds, a parcel of land worth $10,000. In 2010, Ms. Hanson received a refund of income taxes from the State in the amount of $1,200.

On the basis of the foregoing facts, the cash transaction analysis would disclose the following:

Cash Transaction (T) Account[6]

Debits		*Credits*	
Cash on Hand (12/31/09)	$1,000	Cash on Hand (12/31/10)	$-0-
Bank Account (12/31/09)	4,000	Bank Account (12/31/10)	1,500
Savings Account (12/31/09)	2,500	Savings Account (12/31/10)	6,000
Schedule D—Stock Sales	22,000	Schedule D—Cost of Stocks	4,000
Bank Loans—Proceeds	16,000	Other Securities Acquired	52,000
Personal Loan—Proceeds	3,000	Bank Loan Repayment	4,000
Schedule C—Gross Sales	180,000	Schedule C—Purchases	130,000
Schedule B—Dividends	4,200	Expenses	14,300
Interest	1,500	Equipment Acquired	2,500
Schedule E—Rental Income	6,000	Schedule E—Rental Expenses . . .	3,000
Gift Received	3,000	Auto Acquired	9,200
Inheritance (noncash)	-0-	Itemized Deductions (cash)	5,500
State Tax Refund	1,200	Stolen Jewelry (noncash)	-0-
*Accounts Receivable (12/31/09) .	15,000	Other Personal Living Expenses .	28,500
*Accounts Payable (12/31/10) . . .	10,000	*Accounts Receivable (12/31/10)	23,000
*Accrued Expenses (12/31/10) . . .	1,800		
Total	$271,200	*Accounts Payable (12/31/09) . .	8,000
Understatement		*Accrued Expenses (12/31/09) . .	$2,500
(Unexplained Cash)	22,800		
Total	$294,000	Total	$294,000

The Net Worth Method

¶1910 RECONSTRUCTION OF INCOME

The net worth method is one of the most commonly employed techniques for reconstructing taxable income in both civil and criminal income tax cases. It is premised on the accounting formula that an increase in net worth plus nondeductible expenditures and losses, minus nontaxable receipts, equals adjusted gross income. Appropriate adjustments are then made to arrive at taxable income. If the annual income thus reconstructed exceeds reported income, the discrepancy is presumed to be current unreported income, and deficiencies are determined accordingly.[7]

---

[6] The asterisked (*) items are included only for a business reporting on the accrual basis.

[7] Taxpayers may also use the net worth method defensively to disprove an IRS assertion of defi-

ciency. See *Whittington v. Comm'r*, 64 TCM 1618, TC Memo. 1992-732, CCH Dec. 48,714(M), aff'd, 22 F.3d 1099 (11th Cir. 1994) (although taxpayer's efforts failed, he was allowed to use net worth method as defense to IRS assertion).

Net worth is simply a taxpayer's assets less liabilities.[8] In a net worth computation, the assets and liabilities existing at the beginning and end of each year under audit must be determined. Assets are included in net worth at their cost basis, not their market value.

Example 19-3: Joe Hernandez purchased a lot in January 2009 for $25,000. On December 31, 2010, the lot had a fair market value of $30,000. The net worth computation, using the cost basis of the lot, would be as follows:

	12/31/09	12/31/10
Assets (Lot at Cost)	$25,000	$25,000
Liabilities	-0-	-0-
Net Worth	$25,000	$25,000
Net Worth 12/31/09		25,000
Net Worth Increase		-0-

¶1911 CASH ON HAND

Cash on hand is currency carried by a taxpayer or kept at a place of business, at home, in a safe deposit box or anywhere else. This item has generated more controversy than any other. When unexplained discrepancies appear between reported and reconstructed income, the taxpayer will frequently claim that before the years in question he or she had accumulated a "cash hoard" which was deposited or used for other purposes during the audit years.[9] If believed, the story explains the nontaxable cause of the alleged understatement.

To foreclose the success of a "cash hoard" explanation, the Internal Revenue Manual instructs agents to obtain at the earliest possible time the taxpayer's best recollection and estimate of cash on hand at the beginning of the period under audit and at the end of each subsequent year covered by the examination.[10] The taxpayer will be carefully questioned on this matter and is to be made to understand precisely the meaning of the questions asked.

A taxpayer's statement to the agent, whether oral or written, regarding cash on hand creates a difficult, if not insurmountable, obstacle to later attempts to establish the existence of a larger cash hoard. Even though the taxpayer may have made estimates under the assumption that admitting a larger accumulation of cash would raise the agent's suspicions or that such a hoard would adversely affect the tax liability for the years under audit, nothing but the most credible and direct evidence of the cash hoard will overcome the initial statement.

---

[8] A format for the net worth calculation formula can be found in Gormley and Porcano, *supra*, note 3.

[9] See, e.g., *Gorman v. Comm'r*, 69 TCM 2924, TC Memo. 1995-268, CCH Dec. 50,700(M) (lumber company's income, as reconstructed by Internal Revenue Service, was reduced in part by cash hoard); *American Valmar Internatoinal, Ltd. v. Comm'r*, 76 TCM 911, TC Memo. 1998-419, CCH Dec. 52,968(M), aff'd 229 F3d 98 (2nd Cir. 2000), 2000-2 USTC ¶50,781 (cash-hoard defesnse of overseas funds successful; used cash-hoard defense to IRS income reconstruction).

[10] See IRM 4.10.4.3.

Cash-hoard defenses have been notoriously unsuccessful over the years. In many cases, failure results from an inherently incredible story. Others fail for lack of corroborating evidence or as a result of overwhelming contradictory proof by the government. Nevertheless, the cash-hoard issue should be carefully explored whenever an indirect method of proof appears relevant.

Example 19-4: For 2010, John Coe reported a net profit from his business in the amount of $25,000. He had cash in banks totaling $15,000 at the end of 2009, and $25,000 at the end of 2010. He bought a parcel of land for $35,000 in 2010. He claims to have had a $20,000 cash hoard in his basement safe at the end of 2009, which he deposited into his bank accounts. He also states that he no longer had any cash hoarded at the end of 2010. If his cash-hoard claim is disregarded, a net worth computation would show the following:

Assets	12/31/09	12/31/10
Cash in Banks	$15,000	$25,000
Land	-0-	35,000
Total Assets	$15,000	$60,000
Liabilities	-0-	-0-
Net Worth	$15,000	$60,000
Net Worth 12/31/09		15,000
Net Worth Increase		$45,000
Adjusted Gross Income Reported		25,000
Understatement of Income		$20,000

If his claim is accepted, the net worth determination would disclose no understatement of income, as follows:

Assets	12/31/09	12/31/10
Cash on Hand	$20,000	-0-
Cash in Banks	15,000	25,000
Land	-0-	35,000
Total Assets	$35,000	$60,000
Liabilities	-0-	-0-
Net Worth	$35,000	$60,000
Net Worth 12/31/09		35,000
Net Worth Increase		$25,000
Adjusted Gross Income Reported		25,000
Understatement of Income		$ -0-

¶1912 CASH IN BANKS

Cash in banks includes money on deposit in checking and savings accounts and certificates of deposit. For net worth purposes, the year end balances shown on the checking account bank statements must be adjusted by subtracting the checks outstanding at the end of the year. Outstanding checks are those written near the end of the year which do not clear the bank until the following year.

Deposits in transit are equivalent to cash on hand and may be shown on the net worth statement as either additional cash on hand or as a separate asset item. To determine the amount of deposits in transit at the end of each year, a careful inspection must be made of deposits occurring near the beginning of the following year. Both savings and checking account deposits should be examined. The deposits early in the year should be compared with the cash receipts journal or other record of business receipts to determine when such amounts were received and recorded. Other transactions near the end of the year which generate funds should also be examined to determine whether the proceeds were received but not deposited before the end of the year. Sales of assets and loans from banks or others are typical examples of such transactions.

Example 19-5: Acme Enterprises reported a net profit of $140,000 in 2010. The company's bank statements showed unreconciled balances of $30,000 at the end of 2009, and $190,000 at the end of 2010. A reconciliation of the bank account balances disclosed checks outstanding in the amount of $10,000 at the end of 2009, and $30,000 at the end of 2010. The failure to adjust the bank account balances in a net worth determination would artificially produce the following understatement of income:

Assets	12/31/09	12/31/10
Cash in Banks (per bank statements)	$30,000	$190,000
Liabilities	-0-	-0-
Net Worth	$30,000	$190,000
Net Worth 12/31/09		30,000
Net Worth Increase		$160,000
Adjusted Gross Income Reported		140,000
Apparent Understatement of Income		$20,000

When the bank account balances are adjusted for checks outstanding, the net worth method would disclose that income is fully reported, as follows:

Assets	12/31/09	12/31/10
Cash in Banks (Reconciled for checks outstanding)	$20,000	$160,000
Liabilities	-0-	-0-
Net Worth	$20,000	$160,000
Net Worth 12/31/09		20,000
Net Worth Increase		$140,000
Adjusted Gross Income Reported		140,000
Understatement of Income		-0-

Example 19-6: Alice Green reported a net profit of $28,000 from her business in 2010. She had received a check in the amount of $25,000 from a

¶1912

customer on December 29, 2009, which she did not deposit until January 3, 2010. Her bank account balances, reconciled for checks outstanding, were $10,000 at the end of 2009, and $63,000 at the end of 2010. Failure to adjust the net worth computation for the deposit in transit would produce the following understatement:

Assets	12/31/09	12/31/10
Cash in Banks	$10,000	$63,000
Liabilities	-0-	-0-
Net Worth	$10,000	$63,000
Net Worth 12/31/09		10,000
Net Worth Increase		$53,000
Adjusted Gross Income Reported		28,000
Apparent Understatement of Income		$25,000

When the deposit in transit is properly included in the net worth, the computations would disclose no understatement, as follows:

Assets	12/31/09	12/31/10
Cash in Banks	$10,000	$63,000
Deposit in Transit	25,000	-0-
Total Assets	$35,000	$63,000
Liabilities	-0-	-0-
Net Worth	$35,000	$63,000
Net Worth 12/31/09		35,000
Net Worth Increase		$28,000
Adjusted Gross Income Reported		28,000
Understatement of Income		-0-

¶1913 LOANS AND ACCOUNTS RECEIVABLE

Accounts receivable of a taxpayer's business are included in the net worth statement only when the business income is reported on the accrual basis. All other loans and personal accounts receivable are included in the net worth. Such receivables generally represent funds which have been loaned to others or which constitute proceeds from sales of assets. In either situation, the receivables merely replace the cash or asset which otherwise would have remained in the net worth. Included among such receivables are personal loans, land contracts, mortgages and installment sale contracts. The amount due on each loan or receivable must be determined at the end of each year.

Example 19-7: Morris Allen reported a $38,000 net profit from his business in 2010. Assume that $13,000 was omitted from reported sales as a result of inadvertent bookkeeping errors. The business was on the accrual basis and had trade accounts receivable in the amount of $27,000 at the end of 2010. At the end of 2009, his business receivables totaled $15,000. In 2010, he loaned $25,000 to his brother, none of which was repaid before the end of the year. He also sold a parcel of land in March 2010 for $15,000. The land had been acquired in October 2009 at a cost of $10,000. The purchaser paid $10,000 to Mr. Allen in 2010 and gave him a note for the balance which remained unpaid at the end of 2010. Mr. Allen reported a gain on the sale in the amount of $5,000. Cash in banks totaled $5,000 at the end of 2009, and $29,000 at the end of 2010. A net worth reconstruction of income would disclose the following:

Assets	12/31/09	12/31/10
Cash in Banks	$5,000	$29,000
Accounts Receivable	15,000	27,000
Personal Loan Receivable	-0-	25,000
Note Receivable	-0-	5,000
Land	10,000	-0-
Total Assets	$30,000	$86,000
Liabilities	-0-	-0-
Net Worth	$30,000	$86,000
Net Worth 12/31/09		30,000
Net Worth Increase		$56,000
Adjusted Gross Income Reported		43,000
Understatement of Income		$13,000

¶1914 INVENTORY

The amount of the business inventory at the end of each year is normally obtained from the tax returns. However, if the taxpayer can establish that the inventory was in error, the corrected value should be included in the net worth. The same is true if the examining agent determines that the reported inventory is incorrect. In a criminal prosecution, any increase in taxable income caused by such correction will be excluded from the unreported taxable income if the error was the result of inadvertence or negligence. The adjustment is considered merely technical and not attributable to fraud.

Example 19-8: The Nye Sales Company reported a net profit of $62,000 for 2010. Schedule C of the tax return disclosed opening and closing inventories of $90,000 and $135,000, respectively. An examining revenue agent discovered that several inventory sheets, totaling $32,000, had been inadvertently overlooked in preparing the closing inventory for 2010. Cash in banks totaled $8,000 at the end of 2009 and $25,000 at the end of 2010. The agent's net worth determination would appear as follows:

Assets	12/31/09	12/31/10
Cash in Banks	$8,000	$25,000
Inventory (Corrected)	90,000	167,000
Total Assets	$98,000	$192,000
Liabilities	-0-	-0-

Net Worth	$98,000	$192,000
Net Worth 12/31/09		98,000
Net Worth Increase		$94,000
Adjusted Gross Income Reported		62,000
Understatement of Income		$32,000

The entire understatement in this example is attributable to the inadvertent inventory error. These errors must be eliminated from the net worth understatement when evaluating civil and criminal fraud potential. It also should be apparent that such inventory corrections will affect the income of a subsequent or prior year (depending upon whether an opening or closing inventory is adjusted).

¶1915 OTHER ASSETS

Other assets such as stock, bonds, brokerage account balances, real estate, furniture, fixtures, equipment, automobiles and trucks are included in net worth at their cost basis. Although most information regarding business assets can be obtained from the tax returns, the costs and dates of acquisition and sale are be verified from the underlying records.

Care is taken to assure that all assets are included at their proper cost and in the year to which they belong. Purchase and sale documents will serve to verify the correct dates and amounts. If an asset is purchased near the end of the year, but payment is delayed for any reason until the next year, a proper account payable must be included in the net worth of the year of acquisition. All sales and purchases near the end of the year are scrutinized to determine that the attendant proceeds and payments are properly treated and do not cause a shift or distortion of income.

¶1916 ACCOUNTS AND NOTES PAYABLE

Trade accounts payable, representing purchases that enter into cost of goods sold, and accrued deductible expenses are included in the net worth statement only when business income is reported on the accrual basis. Other loans and payables, both business and personal, are always added to the taxpayer's liabilities on the net worth statement. Such liabilities include amounts due on personal and bank loans, mortgages, land contracts and installment contracts.

¶1917 RESERVE FOR DEPRECIATION

The reserve for depreciation represents the accumulation of allowances for depreciation which were deducted or deductible in the current and prior years. Depreciation information normally can be obtained directly from the tax return. The increase in the depreciation reserve for each year represents the depreciation deducted for that year. Although the reserve is included as a liability in the net worth method, it could more accurately be shown as a reduction of the basis of the asset to which it applies. Its inclusion in net worth actually reflects an annual decrease in the basis of the assets. It serves to offset the depreciation deduction on the tax return which does not require the expenditure of funds and which would not otherwise be taken into proper account in the net worth determination.

> **Example 19-9:** Janet Eng started a business in 2010. She reported a net profit of $22,000 from the business for 2010. In determining the net profit, a deduction of $7,000 was taken for depreciation. Cash in banks increased from nothing at the end of 2009 to $29,000 at the end of 2010. Since depreciation is a noncash deduction, failure to reflect the annual charges in the reserve for depreciation on the net worth statement would create an artificial and erroneous understatement. The net worth computation, with and without the depreciation reserve, discloses the following:

	With Reserve		Without Reserve	
	12/31/09	12/31/10	12/31/09	12/31/10
Assets (Cash in Banks)	-0-	$29,000	-0-	$29,000
Liabilities (Reserve for Depreciation)	-0-	7,000	-0-	-0-
Net Worth	-0-	$22,000	-0-	$29,000
Net Worth 12/31/09		-0-		-0-
Net Worth Increase		$22,000		$29,000
Adjusted Gross Income Reported		22,000		22,000
Understatement of Income		-0-	(Incorrect)	$7,000

¶1918 OTHER LIABILITIES

Occasionally the liability section of the net worth computation is used for items of deferred or unrealized income which will be taxable over a period of years. Such items are not truly liabilities but are included as such to offset that part of an asset which represents deferred or unrealized income. An installment sale, for example, results in the acquisition of a receivable for the balance due on the sale. Part of the receivable represents gain to be reported in later years when payments are made. As a liability, the deferred income account reduces the receivable by the amount necessary to eliminate the deferred gain that otherwise would be improperly incorporated in the net worth computation.

¶1919 NONDEDUCTIBLE EXPENDITURES AND LOSSES

Each year the taxpayer's net worth will either increase or decrease. This annual net worth change must then be further increased and decreased by certain items commonly referred to as "below the line" adjustments. The adjustments added to the annual change in net worth are "nondeductible expenditures and losses." These adjustments include all expenditures which are not deductible in arriving at adjusted gross income. Since itemized deductions are deductible only from adjusted gross income, they are also included in the nondeductible expenses added to the net worth change. A later allowance for itemized deductions is made in the final step of the net worth computation to arrive at taxable income.

All nondeductible losses must also be added to the annual net worth change. Such losses include that portion of a capital loss in excess of the $3,000 limit and losses incurred on the sale of personal assets. The addition of these losses prevents the distortion of reconstructed income caused by the excessive decrease in net worth when the assets sold are eliminated at their full cost basis.

Gifts to relatives and others are nondeductible items which must be added to the net worth change. The personal gift of an asset other than cash is included as a below-the-line addition in an amount equal to the basis at which the asset was included in the net worth. If a reserve for depreciation is associated with the asset, the amount of the gift for adjustment purposes is the cost basis of the asset reduced by the reserve. The reason for this treatment is that the decrease in the net worth caused by removal of the asset must be offset by the addition of the gift. Otherwise, such net worth decrease would artificially reduce the reconstructed income.

The amount of personal living expenses is always controversial. Many of these expenses are paid in cash, and estimates are frequently required. Much of the problem is usually resolved in a routine audit through the cooperation of the taxpayer with the agent's requests for information. Sometimes an agent will use estimates of living expenses based on published statistics of the average cost of living for families of various sizes in different income ranges. Usually, however, the agent will establish as many of the personal expenses as possible from the taxpayer's checks and then either estimate the cash items or ask the taxpayer to do so. In criminal cases, the special agent normally will exclude all estimates and include only living expenses which can be documented by cancelled checks or other records.

Example 19-10: During 2010, John Connors sold his personal car for $2,500. He had purchased the car in 2005 for $6,000. In March 2010, he sold 500 shares of stock for $10,000. He had acquired the stock in December 2005 for $22,000. On January 11, 2010, he gave his nephew a truck that had been used solely in his business. The truck cost $9,000 in 2007. Depreciation totaling $6,500 had been previously deducted on the truck at the time of the gift. John paid the following personal expenses in 2010:

Food	$3,000
Real Estate Taxes on Home	2,500
Repairs to Home	300
Utilities	900
Personal Auto Expenses	1,800
Vacations	1,100
Department Store Purchases	1,700
Interest on Home Mortgage	2,000
Charitable Contributions	500
Life Insurance Premiums	1,500
Medical Bills	600
Entertainment	900
Other	300
Total	$17,100

For 2010, John reported adjusted gross income of $19,000. The balances in his bank accounts were $1,500 at the end of 2009 and $18,900 at the end of 2010. Assuming that John correctly reported his income for 2010, the net worth computation would appear as follows:

Assets	12/31/09	12/31/10
Cash in Banks	$1,500	$18,900
Personal Auto	6,000	-0-
Truck	9,000	-0-
Stock	22,000	-0-
Total Assets...............................	$38,500	$18,900
Liabilities		
Reserve for Depreciation (Truck)	6,500	-0-
Net Worth.................................	$32,000	$18,900
Net Worth 12/31/10		$18,900
Net Worth 12/31/09		(32,000)
Net Worth Increase (Decrease)		($13,100)
Plus: Nondeductible Expenses and Losses		
Gift of Truck		2,500
Loss on Sale of Car		3,500
Loss on Stock in Excess of $3,000		9,000
Personal Living Expenses		17,100
Reconstructed Adjusted Gross Income		$19,000
Reported Adjusted Gross Income		$19,000
Understatement of Income		-0-

¶1920 NONTAXABLE RECEIPTS AND LOSS CARRYOVERS AND CARRYBACKS

Another group of below-the-line adjustments which are subtracted from, rather than added to, the annual net worth changes includes all nontaxable receipts and the tax return deductions allowed for carryover and carryback losses. The subtraction of the nontaxable receipts serves to offset the increase in net worth caused by such receipts. The adjustment for the loss carryover and carryback deductions recognizes that the actual economic impact of such losses occurred in other years. To compensate for the failure to reflect the losses in the net worth for the year of the deduction, the losses are subtracted as special below-the-line adjustments. Deductions allowed for net operating loss carryovers and carrybacks, as well as capital loss carryovers, are examples of such adjustments.

Nontaxable receipts include gifts, inheritances, tax-exempt interest, federal income tax refunds, nontaxable pensions, dividends on life insurance, proceeds from surrender of life insurance policies, personal injury settlements and all nontaxable gains. A common example of such gains is the nonrecognized gain on sale of a personal residence.

Example 19-11: During 2010, Mabel Moss received a gift of $6,000 in cash from her mother. She also received an inheritance of $12,000 from her favorite aunt. She had invested in municipal bonds, and in 2010 received interest of $8,000 on such bonds. She owned $90,000 of such bonds at the end of 2009, and $110,000 at the end of 2010. She withdrew her life insurance dividends of $1,500 in 2010. A personal injury action she had instituted in 2000 was settled, and she received $15,000 in 2010. She sold her home in which she had lived for the past 10 years for $110,000 in 2010. She realized a gain of $40,000. On her 2010 tax return, she deducted a net operating loss carryover of $5,000. Her cash in banks increased from $12,500 at the end of 2009 to $15,000 at the end of 2010. In 2010, she invested $150,000 in a partnership venture. She reported adjusted gross income of $15,000 for 2010. Assuming she correctly reported for 2010, a net worth reconstruction of income would show the following:

Assets	12/31/09	12/31/10
Cash in Banks	$12,500	$15,000
Municipal Bonds	90,000	110,000
Interest in Partnership	-0-	150,000
Home	70,000	-0-
Total Assets	$172,500	$275,000
Liabilities	-0-	-0-
Net Worth	$172,500	$275,000
Net Worth 12/31/09		172,500
Net Worth Increase		$102,500

Less: Nontaxable Receipts and Loss Carryovers and Carrybacks

	Amount	
Gift from Mother	$6,000	
Inheritance	12,000	
Interest on Municipal Bonds	8,000	
Life Insurance Dividends	1,500	
Personal Injury Settlement	15,000	
Nontaxable Gain on Home	40,000	
Net Operating Loss Carryover	5,000	
Total		$87,500
Reconstructed Adjusted Gross Income		$15,000
Adjusted Gross Income Reported		15,000
Understatement of Income		-0-

¶1921 ADJUSTMENTS TO ARRIVE AT TAXABLE INCOME

The adjusted gross income determined by adding and subtracting the foregoing items must be further adjusted to arrive at taxable income. These final adjustments, involving the itemized deductions and personal exemptions, are treated in the same manner as they would be on the income tax return and follow the same method of computation in arriving at taxable income.

¶1921

Example 19-12: Harvey and Marisa Kluge filed a joint return for 2010. Both were under age 65 and had two dependent children, ages 8 and 10. For 2010, they reported the following itemized deductions:

Interest on Home Mortgage	$3,800
Taxes	2,300
Contributions	800
Medical Expenses (in excess of limitations)	275
Total Itemized Deductions	$7,175

The adjustment to the adjusted gross income determined by the net worth method would appear as follows:

	2010
Adjusted Gross Income as Reconstructed by the Net Worth Method	$34,000
Adjustments to Arrive at Taxable Income	
Itemized Deductions	$7,175
Balance	$26,825
Exemptions	11,200
Taxable Income Reconstructed	$15,625

Source and Application of Funds Method

¶1922 VARIATION OF NET WORTH METHOD

The source and application of funds method, or the expenditures method, is merely an accounting variation of the net worth method using a different format.[11] Net worth may be converted to the source and application of funds by extracting from the net worth statement the annual increases and decreases in the assets and liabilities. The increases in assets and decreases in liabilities are treated as applications of funds. The decreases in assets and increases in liabilities represent sources of funds. The nondeductible expenses and losses in the net worth method are included as applications of funds, while the nontaxable receipts and loss carryovers and carrybacks become sources of funds.

The accounting formula for the source and application of funds method is quite simple. The total of all the sources of funds is subtracted from the total of all applications of funds to arrive at adjusted gross income. To determine taxable income, the normal adjustments are then made for itemized deductions and personal exemptions. Comparing reconstructed taxable income with reported taxable income will disclose any understatement.

The format of this method eliminates those assets and liabilities which have not changed during the period involved by including only changes in assets and liabilities. Those items in the net worth which remain constant over the period in question are not essential to the computation and are excluded. In those cases

---

[11] Use of this method will be upheld where a taxpayer fails to produce evidence to refute the IRS's computations. See *Flood v. Commissioner*, 81 TCM 1175, TC Memo. 2001-39, CCH Dec. 54,247(M).

involving a considerable number of unchanging assets and liabilities, the source and application of funds method offers a clearer and more concise presentation of the essential facts.

Example 19-13: Except for the format and the elimination of nonchanging assets and liabilities, the source and application of funds method is identical to the net worth method. The conversion of the following net worth statement to a source and application of funds analysis serves to demonstrate this similarity.

Net Worth

Assets	12/31/09	12/31/10	
Cash on Hand	$3,000	$2,500	
Bank Accounts	1,750	2,975	
Accounts Receivable	7,500	6,200	
Merchandise Inventory	3,220	4,780	
Stocks	4,000	18,000	
Bonds	2,750	2,750	
Equipment	4,175	10,745	
Automobile	2,500	2,500	
Furniture and Fixtures	8,000	8,000	
Residence	50,000	50,000	
Total Assets	$86,895	$108,450	
Liabilities			
Accounts Payable	$2,900	$1,900	
Loans Payable	5,000	7,750	
Reserve for Depreciation	1,225	2,075	
Total Liabilities	$9,125	$11,725	
Net Worth	$77,770	$96,725	
Net Worth 12/31/09		($77,770)	
Net Worth Increase		$18,955	
Plus: Nondeductible Expenditures and Losses			
Income Taxes Paid		$4,200	
Personal Living Expenses		16,500	
Life Insurance Premiums		1,720	
Gift to Third Party		2,100	
Loss on Sale of Personal Auto		3,800	
Net Worth Increase Plus Nondeductible Expenditures			$47,275
Less: Nontaxable Receipts			
Gifts from Third Parties		($925)	
Inheritances		(11,700)	
Net Operating Loss Carryover Deducted in 2010		(2,100)	
Total Nontaxable Receipts			($14,725)
Adjusted Gross Income			$32,550
Less: Standard Deduction			(7,350)

¶1922

Less: Nontaxable Receipts

Balance..	$25,200
Less: Exemptions	(5,600)
Taxable Income	$19,600
Less: Taxable Income Reported	($8,025)
Unreported Taxable Income	$11,575

SOURCE AND APPLICATION OF FUNDS

Application of Funds

Bank Accounts	$1,225	
Merchandise Inventory......................	1,560	
Stocks.....................................	14,000	
Equipment	6,570	
Accounts Payable	1,000	
Income Taxes Paid	4,200	
Personal Living Expenses	16,500	
Life Insurance Premiums	1,720	
Gift to Third Party	2,100	
Loss on Sale of Personal Auto	3,800	
Total		$52,675

Sources of Funds

Cash on Hand	$500	
Accounts Receivable	1,300	
Loans Payable	2,750	
Increase in Depreciation Reserve	850	
Gifts from Third Parties	925	
Inheritance	11,700	
Net Operating Loss Carryover Deduction in 2010	2,100	
Total		($20,125)

Adjusted Gross Income	$32,550
Less: Standard Deduction	(7,350)
Balance...	$25,200
Less: Exemptions	(5,600)
Taxable Income (Reconstructed)	$19,600
Less: Taxable Income Reported	(8,025)
Unreported Taxable Income	$11,575

Bank Deposit Method

¶1923 GROSS RECEIPTS RECONSTRUCTED

The bank deposit method employs a distinct accounting technique. Unlike the other methods, it is an attempt to reconstruct gross taxable receipts rather than adjusted gross income. It directs primary attention to the taxpayer's bank deposits on the premise that such deposits normally represent current taxable receipts. Before this method can be used, it must be shown that the taxpayer was engaged in a business or some other activity capable of producing income and that regular, periodic deposits were made in the taxpayer's bank accounts.

There are two principal variations of the bank deposit method. The more basic concentrates solely on the bank deposits and, after eliminating identifiable, nontaxable items, arrives at reconstructed gross income. The formula most commonly in use, however, is the bank deposit and expenditures method. This method adds all expenditures of currency to the bank deposits on the theory that such expenditures represent the use of current taxable receipts that have not been deposited.

The bank deposit and expenditures method proceeds on the theory that total deposits, plus currency expenditures, less nontaxable receipts, equals corrected gross income. The deductions and other items not incorporated in the determination of the gross income are then included in the computation to arrive at taxable income.

¶1924 TOTAL DEPOSITS

Total deposits include all funds deposited in checking, savings and brokerage accounts. Allowance for nontaxable items is made in a separate computation. Total deposits must be reconciled for deposits in transit by examining deposits made early in the year under audit and those made in the first months of the following year. Deposits relating to prior years' receipts, but belatedly deposited in the current year, should be deducted from total deposits. Conversely, receipts in the current year deposited in the following year should be added.

> **Example 19-14:** Marcus Horn deposited $35,000 into his checking account and $7,000 into his savings account during 2010. He received dividends of $5,000 and net wages of $37,000 in 2010. He received a dividend check of $500 at the end of 2009 which he was not able to deposit in his savings account until January 3, 2010. Two salary checks, each in the amount of $2,500, were received by him in December 2010 but were not deposited until January 2011. If the deposits in transit are ignored, there appears to be no understatement of income. By incorporating the proper adjustments for these items, the total deposits method would disclose the following:

Deposits in 2010—Checking Account	$35,000	
Plus: Current Year's Receipts Deposited in Following Year	5,000	
Reconciled Bank Deposits		$40,000
Deposits in 2010—Savings Account	$7,000	
Less: Previous Year's Receipts Deposited in Current Year	(500)	
Reconciled Savings Deposits		6,500
Total Reconciled Deposits		$46,500
Gross Receipts Reported		(42,000)
Understatement of Income		$4,500

¶1925 CURRENCY EXPENDITURES

Currency expenditures made for any purpose are added to the total deposits on the assumption that such items represent undeposited taxable receipts. Sources of nontaxable currency that may account for these expenditures are separately deducted later as part of the nontaxable receipts.

An analysis of checks will disclose what business and personal expenditures may have been made with currency.[12] One auditing approach simplifies the problem by accepting as correct all business expenses deducted on the tax return. All business checks issued are then subtracted from the total of business expenses to arrive at a balance of the expenses that were presumably paid by currency. Depreciation, amortization and other noncash business deductions are eliminated from this computation.

Currency may be used for a variety of purposes other than routine business and personal expenses. Investments, acquisitions of assets, loans to others, payments on loans and gifts to others may all involve currency as a medium of payment. These transactions are carefully examined to determine the source of funds. Cash on hand that is found to exist at the end of the year also will be added to the deposits.

> **Example 19-15:** For 2010, Theresa Fall reported business expenses on Schedule C, excluding depreciation, totaling $48,000. Her checks for business expenses totaled $42,000 in 2010. The business reported on the cash method of accounting, and Schedule C disclosed $78,000 of gross receipts for 2010. During 2010, she deposited $70,000 in her checking account and made the following payments in currency:
>
> | | |
> |---|---:|
> | Funds to Broker | $3,000 |
> | Loan to Sister | 2,000 |
> | Purchase of Boat | 800 |
> | Groceries | 2,500 |
> | Entertainment | 3,200 |

Ms. Fall had accumulated $4,500 in cash on hand at the end of 2010. She had no cash on hand at the beginning of the year. A deposits and expenditures analysis would disclose the following:

Total Deposits		$70,000
Currency Expenditures (and Accumulation)		
Business Expenses	$6,000	
Personal Items	11,500	
Cash Accumulated	4,500	
Total Currency Expenditures		$22,000
Gross Receipts from Business (Reconstructed)		$92,000
Gross Receipts from Business Reported		(78,000)
Understatement of Income		$14,000

---

[12] See *McGee v. Comm'r*, TC Memo. 2000-308, CCH Dec. 54,067(M) (IRS analysis of bank deposits and cash expenditures demonstrated understatement of income).

¶1926 NONTAXABLE DEPOSITS AND RECEIPTS

The sum of the total deposits and currency expenditures must be reduced by various nontaxable deposits and receipts. Transfers of funds between checking, savings and brokerage accounts provide the most common examples of nontaxable deposits. A withdrawal from a savings account may be deposited in a checking account or a check may be written for deposit to a savings account. Such transfers are eliminated to avoid duplication of deposited amounts.

Checks written to cash or withdrawals of cash from savings accounts are also deducted. Such items generate currency which is assumed to have been deposited or used for other purposes. Other items which must be eliminated include checks deposited and returned by the bank for insufficient funds, prior year's receipts deposited in the current year, transfers resulting from check kiting, and all other items of nontaxable income. Inheritances, gifts, loans, life insurance proceeds and receipts from the sale of assets are examples of nontaxable items which should be deducted. Cash on hand at the beginning of the year is another source that serves to offset the total deposits and currency expenditures.

Example 19-16: Assume that Ms. Fall in the previous example had the following additional transactions during 2010:

Deposits to Savings Account	$8,000
Savings Account Withdrawals Deposited in Checking Account	3,000
Checks Written for Deposits to Savings Account	5,000
Checks Written to Cash	2,500
Customer Checks Deposited but Returned for Insufficient Funds	1,800
Cash Inheritance	8,000
Cash Gifts Received	1,700

On the basis of the above, the deposits analysis would appear as follows:

Total Deposits (Checking and Savings)		$78,000
Currency Expenditures (and Accumulations)		22,000
Total Deposits and Expenditures		$100,000
Less: Nontaxable Receipts		
Transfers from Savings to Checking	$3,000	
Transfers from Checking to Savings	5,000	
Checks to Cash	1,800	
Cash Inheritance	8,000	
Cash Gifts Received	1,700	
Total Nontaxable Receipts		($22,000)
Gross Business Receipts (Reconstructed)		$78,000
Gross Business Receipts Reported		(78,000)
Understatement of Income		-0-

¶1926

¶1927 ACCRUAL BASIS ADJUSTMENTS

Accounts receivable require special adjustments for a business on the accrual method of accounting. Deposits are adjusted to exclude receivables at the end of the preceding year, and receivables at the end of the current year are added. This will conform the deposit method computation of gross income to the taxpayer's accrual basis of accounting.

Adjustments for accounts payable and accrued expenses are only required for an accrual basis business when the indirect method of computing business currency expenses is employed. In these instances, the total expenses and purchases shown on the return must be converted to a cash basis by subtracting the payables and accruals at the end of the year from the total expenses. This total is then increased by the payables and accrued expenses at the end of the preceding year. When checks written during the year are subtracted from the adjusted total, the balance of expenses is presumed to represent currency expenditures.

Example 19-17: Assume that Ms. Fall in the previous example reported on the accrual method of accounting with selected balance sheet items as follows:

	12/31/09	12/31/10
Trade Accounts Receivable	$9,000	$14,000
Accrued Expenses	2,800	4,700

The total deposits of $78,000 must be adjusted for the increase in accounts receivable, as follows:

Total Deposits		$78,000
Accounts Receivable 12/31/10	$14,000	
Accounts Receivable 12/31/09	9,000	
Add: Net Increase in Receivables		5,000
Adjusted Total Deposits		$83,000

The business expenses paid by currency would have to be determined as follows:

Schedule C Expenses (Less Depreciation)		$48,000
Accrued Expenses (12/31/10)	$4,700	
Accrued Expenses (12/31/09)	2,800	
Less: Increase in Accrued Expenses		(1,900)
Schedule C Expenses Paid in 2010		$46,100
Checks for Business Expenses		(42,000)
Business Expenses Paid by Currency		$4,100

Burden of Proof

¶1928 INDIRECT PROOF

The burden of proof in civil and criminal tax proceedings plays a prominent role in cases employing indirect proof of income. In criminal evasion cases, the government must carry the burden of proving the essential elements of the tax crime beyond a reasonable doubt. In civil cases, proof of fraud must be by clear and convincing evidence. Despite the difference in expression, however, the practical distinction between the two burdens is virtually nonexistent.

In ordinary civil cases, the government will have the burden of proof by a preponderance of the evidence if certain conditions are met.[13] In those cases in which such conditions are not met, the government's determinations continue to be presumed correct until the taxpayer establishes by a preponderance of the evidence that such findings are in error. However, in situations involving deficiencies subject to assessment under the special six-year statute of limitations,[14] the government must prove by a preponderance of the evidence that the taxpayer has omitted twenty-five percent of gross income.

¶1929 CRIMINAL EVASION AND CIVIL FRAUD

When the government uses indirect methods to establish unreported income, courts have recognized potential infirmities in such circumstantial evidence, including its tendency to shift the burden of persuasion to the taxpayer. In criminal cases, courts have established various safeguards to correct these problems and have extended them to the civil fraud field.

The landmark Supreme Court opinion, *Holland v. United States,*[15] established basic safeguards which determine the government's burden in net worth cases. Over the years, other decisions have developed and refined these protective rules, applying them to the source and application of funds method, and partially adopting them in bank deposit cases.

The *Holland* Court devised three prerequisites the government must meet in a criminal net worth case. First, the government must establish an opening net worth "with reasonable certainty" to serve as an accurate starting point. Second, there must be proof of a likely source of current taxable income which could reasonably be found to give rise to the net worth increase. Third, the government must investigate relevant leads offered by the taxpayer to explain the net worth discrepancies, provided that such leads are reasonably susceptible to being checked. A subsequent Supreme Court opinion, clarifying *Holland,* held that the government need not prove a likely source of income if it has negated all nontaxable sources of income.[16]

In bank deposit cases, the government must show that the taxpayer was engaged in a business or other activity capable of producing income and made

---

[13] See discussion ¶410, *supra.*
[14] Code Sec. 6501(ce).

[15] 348 U.S. 121 (1954), 54-2 USTC ¶9714.
[16] See *United States v. Massei,* 355 U.S. 595 (1958), 58-1 USTC ¶9326 (per curiam).

¶1928

regular and periodic bank deposits indicative of a regular business practice.[17] The government must also establish that it made an adequate effort to exclude all nonincome items.[18] Although proof of opening net worth is not required to corroborate the deposits method,[19] the government must establish with reasonable certainty the amount of cash on hand at the beginning of the period.[20] The obligation of the government to investigate relevant leads, which originated in *Holland,* is not imposed in bank deposit cases.

¶1930 NONFRAUD CIVIL CASES

In ordinary civil tax proceedings not involving fraud, the government will have the burden of proof if certain conditions are met.[21] If those conditions are not met, the taxpayer has the burden of showing that the Commissioner's reconstruction of income is erroneous. In any event, the protective rules relating to criminal and civil fraud cases are not generally applicable.[22] However, in the special case involving the six-year statute of limitations on assessment, the full panoply of safeguards will attach to the government's burden of proving a twenty-five percent omission of gross income by the net worth method.[23]

In those cases in which the burden of proof is not shifted to the government, the presumption of correctness which attaches to the government's reconstruction of income may be destroyed by evidence of inherent defects which establish that the determination is seriously in error and that it is arbitrary, speculative or unreasonable.[24] In such cases, once the taxpayer has discredited the method of reconstructing income, even though unable to prove the correct amounts that may be involved, the burden of proof with respect to these amounts shifts to the government.[25] The reconstruction may then be rejected in its entirety, or the court may view the evidence as sufficient to permit an amount to be estimated.[26]

---

[17] See *Gleckman v. United States,* 80 F.2d 394 (8th Cir. 1935), 35-2 USTC ¶9645.

[18] See *United States v. Morse,* 491 F.2d 149 (1st Cir. 1974), 74-1 USTC ¶9228.

[19] See *United States v. Stein,* 437 F.2d 775 (7th Cir. 1971), 71-1 USTC ¶9209, *cert. denied,* 403 U.S. 905 (1971), 71-1 USTC ¶9209.

[20] See *United States v. Slutsky,* 487 F.2d 832 (2d Cir. 1973), 75-1 USTC ¶9430, *cert. denied,* 416 U.S. 937, *reh'g denied,* 416 U.S. 1000 (1974).

[21] See ¶410, *supra.*

[22] See *Tunnel v. Comm'r,* 74 TC 44 (1980), CCH Dec. 36,881, aff'd, 663 F.2d 527 (5th Cir. 1981), 81-2 USTC ¶9823.

[23] See *Cox v. Comm'r,* 50 TCM 317, TC Memo. 1985-324, CCH Dec. 42,200(M).

[24] See *Powell v. Comm'r,* 18 TCM 170, TC Memo. 1959-36, CCH Dec. 23,472(M).

[25] See *Helvering v. Taylor,* 293 U.S. 507 (1935), 35-1 USTC ¶9044; *Welch v. Comm'r,* 297 F.2d 309 (4th Cir. 1961), 62-1 USTC ¶9157; *Llorente v. Comm'r,* 74 TC 260 (1980), CCH Dec. 36,955, modified, 649 F.2d 152 (2nd Cir. 1981), 81-1 USTC ¶9446; *Powell v. Comm'r,* 18 TCM 170, TC Memo. 1959-36, CCH Dec. 23,472(M).

[26] See *Llorente v. Comm'r,* 74 TC 260 (1980), CCH Dec. 36,955, modified, 649 F.2d 152 (2nd Cir. 1981), 81-1 USTC ¶9446.

Records for Examination

¶1931 SOURCES OF FINANCIAL DATA

The following checklist may prove useful in gathering the financial records essential to an analysis of income by an indirect method of proof:

1. Tax returns (income and gift);
2. Business journals, ledgers, financial statements and audit reports;
3. Bank statements, cancelled checks, check stubs and duplicate deposit tickets;
4. Savings account passbooks or transcripts of accounts; certificates of deposit;
5. Financial statements submitted to banks or others;
6. Stock and bond confirmations, brokerage statements and informal records of security transactions maintained by taxpayer;
7. Records of loans payable, including notes, installment loan contracts, land contracts, mortgages and transcripts of bank loan accounts (liability ledger cards);
8. Records of loans receivable, including notes, installment contracts, mortgages and land contracts;
9. Closing statements for real estate transactions;
10. Safe-deposit box entry record;
11. Copies of cashier's checks;
12. Tax return worksheets;
13. Personal records of financial transactions; and
14. Invoices or statements relating to purchase of automobiles, furniture and other substantial assets.

¶1941 Exhibit 19-1

Form **4822** (Rev. 6-83)	Department of the Treasury - Internal Revenue Service **STATEMENT OF ANNUAL ESTIMATED PERSONAL AND FAMILY EXPENSES**				
TAXPAYER'S NAME AND ADDRESS					TAX YEAR ENDED

	ITEM	BY CASH	BY CHECK	TOTAL	REMARKS
1. PERSONAL EXPENSES	Groceries and outside meals				
	Clothing				
	Laundry and dry cleaning				
	Barber, beauty shop, and cosmetics				
	Education (tuition, room, board, books, etc.)				
	Recreation, entertainment, vacations				
	Dues (clubs, lodge, etc.)				
	Gifts and allowances				
	Life and accident insurance				
	Federal taxes (income, FICA, etc.)				
2. HOUSEHOLD EXPENSES	Rent				
	Mortgage payments (including interest)				
	Utilities (electricity, gas, telephone, water, etc.)				
	Domestic help				
	Home insurance				
	Repairs and improvements				
	Child care				
3. AUTO EXPENSES	Gasoline, oil, grease, wash				
	Tires, batteries, repairs, tags				
	Insurance				
	Auto payments (including interest)				
	Lease of auto				
4. DEDUCTIBLE ITEMS	Contributions				
	Medical Expenses — Insurance				
	Drugs				
	Doctors, hospitals, etc.				
	Taxes — Real estate (not included in 2. above)				
	Personal property				
	Income (State and local)				
	Interest (not included in 2. and 3. above)				
	Miscellaneous — Alimony				
	Union dues				
5. PERSONAL ASSETS ETC	Stocks and bonds				
	Furniture, appliances, jewelry				
	Loans to others				
	Boat				
	TOTALS ▶				

Form **4822** (Rev. 6-83)

¶1942 Exhibit 19-2

Field Service Advice 200101030, October 25, 2000

Uniform Issue List Information:

UIL No. 7602.00-00

Examination of books and witnesses

INTERNAL REVENUE SERVICE NATIONAL OFFICE FIELD SERVICE ADVICE

MEMORANDUM FOR ASSOCIATE AREA COUNSEL (SB/SE), NEWARK CC:SB:2:NEW:2

FROM: Deborah A. Butler, Associate Chief Counsel (Procedure and Administration), CC:PA

SUBJECT: Financial Status Audits

This Chief Counsel Advice responds to your request for advice. Chief Counsel Advice is not binding on Examination or Appeals and is not a final case determination. This document is not to be cited as precedent.

ISSUES:

1. Whether a revenue agent may drive by a taxpayer's house prior to having a reasonable indication that there is a likelihood of unreported income.

2. Whether a revenue agent may conduct a Lexis search to ascertain if the taxpayer purchased real estate during the year(s) at issue prior to having a reasonable indication that there is a likelihood of unreported income.

CONCLUSION:

1. A revenue agent may drive by a taxpayer's house prior to having a reasonable indication that there is a likelihood of unreported income.

2. A revenue agent may conduct a Lexis search to ascertain if the taxpayer purchased real estate during the year(s) at issue prior to having a reasonable indication that there is a likelihood of unreported income.

FACTS:

Revenue agents have inquired whether they are still permitted to drive by a taxpayer's house or conduct a Lexis search to ascertain if the taxpayer purchased real estate during the year(s) at issue prior to having a reasonable indication that there is a likelihood of unreported income in light of the enactment of section 7602(e), which restricts the use of financial status audit techniques.

LAW AND ANALYSIS

The Internal Revenue Service Restructuring and Reform Act of 1998 (RRA' 98), Pub. L. No. 105-206, section 3412, 112 Stat. 685 (July 22, 1998), added new I.R.C. §7602(e), titled "Limitation on Financial Status Audit Techniques." Section 7602(e) provides that "[t]he Secretary shall not use financial status or economic reality examination techniques to determine the existence of unreported income of any taxpayer unless the Secretary has a reasonable indication that there is a likelihood of such unreported income."

¶1942

The legislative history concerning RRA'98 section 3412 reflects that prior to its enactment, the Internal Revenue Service (Service) could use financial status or economic reality audit techniques to determine the existence of unreported income.

The legislative history states that RRA'98 section 3412 merely prohibits the use of such audit techniques to determine the existence of unreported income until the Service has a reasonable indication that there is a likelihood of such unreported income. H.R. Conf. Rep. No. 105-599, at 270 (1998).

Prior to enacting section 7602(e), the Chairman of the House Committee on Ways and Means requested the General Accounting Office to report on the frequency and results of the use of financial status audit techniques to identify unreported income due to concerns over the treatment of and the burdens placed upon taxpayers. General Accounting Office Report GAO/T-GGD-97-186 (September 26, 1997), Tax Administration, Taxpayer Rights and Burdens During Audits of Their Tax Returns, at 3 and 9 (GAO Report). The term "Financial Status Audit Techniques" is not defined in the Code. As used in the GAO Report, financial status or economic reality audit techniques consist of indirect methods of examination such as the bank deposits method, the cash transaction method, the net worth method, the percentage of mark-up method, and the unit and volume method. GAO Report at 9; Examination of Returns Handbook, IRM 4.2.4.6. The General Accounting Office concluded that these techniques were never used alone and that they were used with other techniques that were used to explore issues other than unreported income, such as overstated deductions. GAO Report at 9.

There are two distinct types of methods of proof in tax cases, direct or specific item methods and indirect methods (financial status or economic reality examination techniques). In the direct or specific item methods, specific items are demonstrated as the source of unreported income. *United States v. Hart*, 70 F.3d 854, 860 n.8 (6th Cir. 1995); *United States v. Black*, 843 F.2d 1456 (D.C. Cir. 1988) [88-1 USTC ¶ 9270]. With the specific item method of proof, the government uses "evidence of the receipt of specific items of reportable income . . . that do not appear on his income tax return." *United States v. Marabelles*, 724 F.2d 1374, 1377 n.1 (9th Cir. 1984) [84-1 USTC ¶ 9189]. For example, the Service tracks funds from known sources to deposits made to a taxpayer's bank accounts rather than analyzing bank deposits to identify unreported income from unknown sources. *See United States v. Hart*, 70 F.3d 854, 860 (6th Cir. 1995) (tracing of unreported income from covert police fund is a direct method); *United States v. Black*, 843 F.2d 1456 (D.C. Cir. 1988) [88-1 USTC ¶ 9270](monies traceable from dummy corporations to the taxpayer was evidence of specific items of income and not the use of the bank deposits or cash expenditures indirect method of proof). *See also Pollak v. United States*, 1998 U.S. Dist. LEXIS 16224 (N.D. Ill. 1998) (recognizing, in dicta, that directly tracing money transfers from an entity would not be a financial status or economic reality technique).

The Service does not use specific items to support an inference of unreported income from unidentified sources. The use of direct methods simply does not implicate the provisions of section 7602(e). Thus, there is no prohibition requiring the Service to have a reasonable indication that there is a likelihood of unreported income before resorting to such methods.

When using an indirect method, a taxpayer's finances are reconstructed through circumstantial evidence. *United States v. Hart,* 70 F.3d 854, 860 n.8 (6th Cir. 1995). For example, the government shows either through increases in net worth, increases in bank deposits, or the presence of cash expenditures, that the taxpayer's wealth grew during a tax year beyond what could be attributed to the taxpayer's reported income, thereby raising the inference of unreported income. *United States v. Black,* 843 F.2d 1456, 1458 (D.C. Cir. 1988) [88-1 USTC ¶9270]. Indirect methods are used to support an inference of unreported income from unidentified sources.

The bank deposits indirect method is an analysis of bank deposits to prove unreported income from unidentified sources. This method, which computes income by showing what happened to the taxpayer's funds, may be considered to be a financial status technique when it is used without specific knowledge of a possible traceable source. As such, it is used to supply leads to possible unreported income from sources of such deposits. Examination of Returns Handbook, IRM 4.2.4.6.3.

With the cash transaction indirect method, the Service calculates the unreported income as the amount that the taxpayer's cash expenditures exceeded the taxpayer's sources of cash, including cash on hand at the beginning of the tax period in question, for the particular year. *United States v. Hogan,* 886 F.2d 1497, 1509 (7th Cir. 1989). The Service uses the taxpayer's tax return and other sources to ensure that adequate income has been reported to cover expenses. GAO Report at 9.

The net worth method requires establishing the taxpayer's net worth at the start of the taxable year by listing all assets, including cash on hand, and all liabilities, with the balance being the taxpayer's net worth. A similar analysis is made for the first day of the next taxable year. To any change in the net worth, the Service adds nondeductible expenditures for living expenses, then deducts receipts from sources that are not taxable income and the amounts represented by applicable tax deductions and exemptions. If the increase in net worth, as adjusted, exceeds the reported taxable income, the inference is drawn that there is unreported income. *United States v. Conway,* 11 F.3d 40, 43 (5th Cir. 1993) [94-1 USTC ¶50,009]; *United States v. Boulet,* 577 F.2d 1165, 1167 n.3 (5th Cir. 1978) [78-2 USTC ¶9628].

With the percentage of mark-up method, the Service reconstructs income derived from the use of percentages or ratios considered typical for the business or item under examination. This method consists of an analysis of either sales or cost of sales and the appropriate application of a percentage of markup to arrive at the taxpayer's gross profit. By reference to similar businesses or situations, percentage computations are secured to determine sales, cost of sales, gross profit or even net profit. Likewise, by the use of some known base and the typical percentage applicable, individual items of income or expenses may be deter-

¶1942

mined. These percentages can be obtained from analysis of Bureau of Labor Statistics data, commercial publications, or the taxpayer's records for other periods. IRM 4.2.4.6.6.

With the unit and volume method, gross receipts are determined or verified by applying price and profit figures to the volume of business done by the taxpayer. The number of units or volume of business may be determined from the taxpayer's books and records if they adequately reflect cost of goods sold or expenses. This method is recommended when the Service can determine the number of units handled by the taxpayer and knows the price or profit charged per unit. IRM 4.2.4.6.7 and IRM 4.2.4.6.7.1.

We have not been provided with any specific factual circumstances under which a revenue agent would drive by a taxpayer's house. Nonetheless, this activity would not be prohibited if used in determining whether there is a reasonable indication that there is a likelihood of unreported income so that the Service could resort to setting up unreported income under an indirect method. It should be noted that driving by a taxpayer's house would not be an intrusion on that taxpayer. It should also be noted that the Internal Revenue Manual cautions that due to privacy issues and the intrusiveness of inspecting a taxpayer's residence, such inspections should be limited. The purpose of inspecting the taxpayer's residence includes, but is not limited to, determining the validity of deductions for an office or business located in the residence and determining the taxpayer's financial status. IRM 4.2.3.3.5.

Conducting a Lexis search to ascertain if the taxpayer purchased real estate would be useful when using the net worth method. Such a search would not be prohibited if used in determining whether there is a reasonable indication that there is a likelihood of unreported income so that the Service could resort to setting up unreported income under the net worth method or any other indirect method. It should be noted that a search of property records that are available to the public is not an intrusion on a taxpayer.

If you have any further questions, please call Administrative Provisions and Judicial Practice, Branch 3, at (202) 622-7940.

Deborah A. Butler, Associate Chief Counsel (Procedure and Administration), Henry S. Schneiderman, Special Counsel to the Associate Chief Counsel (Procedure and Administration).

¶1943 Exhibit 19-3

CASH TRANSACTION (T) ACCOUNT

Debits		Credits	
Cash on hand 1/1:		Cash on hand 12/31:	
Business	$_____		$_____
Personal	_____		_____
Checking accounts 1/1:		Checking accounts 12/31:	
_____	_____		_____
_____	_____		_____
Savings/Investments 1/1:		Savings/Investments 12/31:	
_____	_____		_____
_____	_____		_____
Schedule D—gross sales	_____	Sch D—expense of sales	_____
Loan proceeds OR	_____	Loan repayments OR	_____
Increase in loans payable	_____	Decrease in loans payable	_____
Wages	_____	Schedule C:	
		Purchases	_____
Interest	_____	Expenses (less depr.)	_____
		Schedule F:	
Gross rental income	_____	Expenses (less depr.)	_____
		Rental Schedule:	
Tax refunds	_____	Expenses (less depr.)	_____
Other sources:		Expenses as employee (less depr.)	_____
_____	_____	Capital assets acquired:	
_____	_____	_____	_____
_____	_____	_____	_____
		Other capital expenditures:	
Schedule C receipts	_____	_____	_____
Schedule F receipts	_____	_____	_____
		Personal expenses Form 4822	_____
TOTAL	$_____	Other outlays:	
		_____	_____
Understatement	_____	_____	_____
TOTAL	$	TOTAL	$

ACCRUAL METHOD OF ACCOUNTING

Understatement above		$_____
Add: Increase in Accounts Receivable	$_____	
Decrease in Accounts Payable	_____	
Less: Decrease in Accounts Receivable	(_____)	
Increase in Accounts Payable	(_____)	_____
Increase—Understatement		$

¶1951 DISCUSSION QUESTIONS

1. You are an agent of the IRS and you have been assigned the audit of Clyde Conniver. Your examination of 2007 and 2008 shows a substantial understatement of income on the basis of specific items. Your group manager now asks you to audit the years 2005 and 2006. Unfortunately, most of Clyde's records were destroyed in a basement flood, so you are required to do a net worth analysis. Pursuant to your request, Clyde has submitted the following information to you:

Schedule A:	Assets
Schedule B:	Liabilities
Schedule C:	Furniture and Fixtures
Schedule D:	Real Estate
Schedule E:	Miscellaneous Information

Based on the information contained in these schedules, you have been asked to prepare a net worth statement and determine whether Clyde Conniver has understated, overstated or correctly stated his taxable income for the years 2005 and 2006.

For your further information, Clyde Conniver reports his business income on the accrual basis. He was married and had two dependent children during the years 2004, 2005 and 2006. On a Form 1040 for each of the years, the following information appears:

2004	Adjusted Gross Income	$33,000
	Taxable Income	15,760
2005	Adjusted Gross Income	$40,710
	Taxable Income	21,909
2006	Adjusted Gross Income	$18,000
	Taxable Income	-0-

SCHEDULE A
Assets

Description	12/31/2004 Cost	12/31/2004 FMV	12/31/2005 Cost	12/31/2005 FMV	12/31/2006 Cost	12/31/2006 FMV
Cash on Hand	$2,100	$2,100	$1,000	$1,000	$100	$100
Cash in Bank	4,500	4,500	6,000	6,000	7,500	7,500
Accounts Receivable	3,200	2,800	4,600	4,000	5,200	5,000
Loans Receivable	3,000	3,000	6,000	6,000	9,000	9,000
Merchandise Inventory	9,000	9,000	12,000	13,000	15,000	17,000
Stocks and Bonds	20,000	42,000	25,000	50,000	40,000	65,000
Personal Automobile*	15,500	14,000	17,500	17,200	17,500	15,000
Furniture and Fixtures	2,500	3,000	3,600	3,200	4,700	4,100
Real Estate	125,000	130,000	175,000	215,000	250,000	400,000
Misc. Personal Property	10,000	12,000	10,000	14,000	10,000	15,000
Total:	$184,800	$212,400	$250,700	$319,400	$349,000	$527,700

* The personal auto originally purchased in 2003 at a cost of $15,500 was sold by Clyde individually on May 15, 2005, for $13,500. A new car was purchased from a car dealer on the same date (May 15, 2005) for a total cost of $17,500.

¶1951

SCHEDULE B
Liabilities

	12/31/2004	12/31/2005	12/31/2006
Accounts Payable	$1,600	$2,400	$1,900
Notes Payable	-0-	2,100	3,200
Real Estate Mortgages	100,000	125,000	200,000
Accrued Payroll	800	1,200	1,600
Total:	$102,400	$130,700	$206,700

SCHEDULE C
Furniture and Fixtures

Date Acquired	12/31/2004	12/31/2005	12/31/2006
7/1/94	$2,000	$2,000	$2,000
10/1/96	500	500	500
4/1/03	-0-	-0-	1,100
9/1/03	-0-	-0-	600
11/1/03	-0-	-0-	500
Original Cost	$2,500	$3,600	$4,700
Reserve for Depreciation	(1,900)	(2,200)	(2,400)

SCHEDULE D
Real Estate

Description	Acquired	12/31/2004	12/31/2005	12/31/2006
Personal Residence*	6/1/90	$40,000	$40,000	$40,000
Rental Property				
K Street	1/2/98	25,000	25,000	25,000
L Street**	4/2/99	60,000	-0-	-0-
M Street	12/1/2002	-0-	110,000	110,000
Raw Land				
Hwy WZ	2/1/2001	-0-	-0-	75,000
Total		$125,000	$175,000	$250,000
Reserve for Depreciation		(6,625)	(4,500)	(7,875)

* Purchase price is shown. A $15,000 gain on sale of a prior home was deferred under prior Code Sec. 1034.
** Sold 11/30/2003 for $75,000. The reserve for depreciation on this property at the time of sale was $4,875.

SCHEDULE E
Miscellaneous

	2004	2005	2006
Food—Groceries	$3,500	$3,700	$3,900
Home Repairs	120	-0-	200
Domestic Help	520	550	575
Department Store	250	1,000	650
Recreation—Travel	-0-	799	-0-
Real Estate Taxes—Home	2,500	2,100	2,600
Other Miscellaneous Expenses	100	100	100

Outside Meals	400	600	500
Utilities—Home	350	350	400
Personal Auto	650	700	800
Life Insurance	425	425	425
Contributions	1,000	1,300	1,600
State Income Tax Withheld from Wages . . .	4,000	4,200	4,400
State Income Taxes Paid with Return	850	601	700
Tax-Exempt Interest	100	-0-	-0-
Gifts to Children	3,000	3,000	3,000
Inheritance Received	-0-	10,000	-0-

2. On the basis of the information set forth in the preceding problem, prepare a source and application of funds statement and determine the difference, if any, between the reconstructed and reported taxable income of Clyde Conniver.

3. Sean Shortcount owns and operates the Shortcount Sales Company, a sole proprietorship. His business employs the accrual method of accounting. Prepare a deposits and expenditures analysis and determine correct adjusted gross income for 2008.

Shortcount Sales Company
SCHEDULE C

Income		
Gross Sales	$250,000	
Cost of Goods Sold (Schedule C-1)	100,000	
Gross Profit		$150,000
Deductions		
Advertising	2,000	
Car and Truck Expense	4,000	
Commissions	3,000	
Depreciation	10,000	
Insurance	2,000	
Legal and Professional Services	3,000	
Profit-Sharing Plan	6,000	
Office Supplies	1,000	
Postage	500	
Rent	5,000	
Repairs	2,500	
Taxes	3,000	
Telephone	2,000	
Travel and Entertainment	8,000	
Utilities	3,000	
Wages	20,000	
Other	5,000	
Total Deductions		80,000
Net Profit		$70,000

¶1951

SCHEDULE C-1

Inventory at 1/1/08	$20,000	
Purchases	130,000	
Total		$150,000
Inventory at 12/31/08		50,000
Cost of Goods Sold		$100,000

SELECTED BALANCE SHEET ITEMS

	12/31/2007	*12/31/2008*
Trade Accounts Receivable	$60,000	$90,000
Trade Accounts Payable	60,000	40,000
Accrued Expenses—Business	15,000	10,000

OTHER ITEMS REPORTED IN 2008

Gross Receipts from Rents	$20,000
Less: Cash Expenses	(5,000)
Depreciation	(10,000)
Net Rental Income	$5,000
Dividends Received	25,000
Interest on Savings	3,000
Director's Fees	18,000

PERSONAL LIVING EXPENSES BY CHECK OR CASH

Groceries	$7,000
Meals Away from Home	5,000
Clothing	5,000
State and Federal Taxes	20,000
Contributions	3,000
Life Insurance	8,000
Medical Expenses	4,000
Auto	5,000
Vacations	4,000
Other	3,000
Total:	$64,000

BANK ACCOUNT TRANSACTIONS

Shortcount Sales Company Checking Account

Total deposits per bank statement*	$230,000
Checks for business purchases and expenses	200,000
Checks to Mr. Shortcount's personal checking account	30,000
Checks to cash	10,000
Checks to Shortcount's savings account	7,500

* $7,500 of customer checks deposited were returned due to insufficient funds in the customers' accounts; a customer's check for $5,000 received on December 30, 2008, was deposited on January 2, 2009.

Shortcount's Personal Checking Account

Total deposits per bank statement	$65,000
Checks for personal living expenses	30,000
Checks to cash	5,000
Checks to personal savings account	25,000

Shortcount's Personal Savings Account

Total deposits (including earned interest)	$50,000
Withdrawals	10,000

In 2008, Mr. Shortcount made cash gifts to his favorite nephew in the amount of $2,500. The estate of Mr. Shortcount's grandmother was settled in 2008, and he received a check from the estate in the amount of $8,000. For personal reasons, he held the check for several months and did not deposit it in his personal checking account until February 3, 2009.

CASE TABLE

Note: *This table includes only those cases substantively discussed or reprinted. Cases are listed by the taxpayer's name.*

HOM

FINDING LISTS

IRS Forms

IRS News Releases

IRS Notices

Letter Rulings, Technical Advice, Field Service Advice

Revenue Rulings

Regulations—5 CFR

Regulations—26 CFR

Index

All references are to paragraph (¶) numbers.

All references are to paragraph (¶) numbers.

All references are to paragraph (¶) numbers.

All references are to paragraph (¶) numbers.

All references are to paragraph (¶) numbers.

All references are to paragraph (¶) numbers.

All references are to paragraph (¶) numbers.

All references are to paragraph (¶) numbers.

All references are to paragraph (¶) numbers.

All references are to paragraph (¶) numbers.

All references are to paragraph (¶) numbers.

All references are to paragraph (¶) numbers.

All references are to paragraph (¶) numbers.

All references are to paragraph (¶) numbers.

PEN

All references are to paragraph (¶) numbers.

All references are to paragraph (¶) numbers.

All references are to paragraph (¶) numbers.

All references are to paragraph (¶) numbers.

All references are to paragraph (¶) numbers.

All references are to paragraph (¶) numbers.